Under the Editorship of

Joseph W. Towle

Washington University

St. Louis, Missouri

Managing the

HOUGHTON MIFFLIN COMPANY

Industrial Concern

HENRY G. HODGES, *Ph.D.*

University of Miami

With the Collaboration of

RAYMOND J. ZIEGLER, *Ph.D.*

University of Illinois

BOSTON

NEW YORK · ATLANTA · GENEVA, ILL. · DALLAS · PALO ALTO

TO MARGARET

Editor's Introduction

The complete revision of a college textbook offers many opportunities to the authors and the publisher. New topics can be added, material that is no longer relevant can be deleted, the subject matter can be brought up to date throughout, and experience with the text in the classroom can be drawn upon to improve the effectiveness of the presentation. Those familiar with the earlier edition of this text will see that in MANAGING THE INDUSTRIAL CONCERN, best advantage has been taken of all these opportunities. No resources have been spared in the effort to present a scholarly, balanced, modern treatment of the subject and, at the same time, a treatment suited to the special needs of the reader making his first acquaintance with the field.

This book is recommended as a basic text for the undergraduate course in industrial management, which endeavors to present management principles and organization theory along with the common practices and techniques employed in the management of an enterprise. Materials are included which represent current management philosophy and thought, as well as modern industrial practice. In addition to its use as a textbook for the general management course in colleges of business administration, we are confident that teachers in liberal arts colleges, junior colleges and extension programs, who are seeking a textbook for a general course in management, will find this text entirely appropriate. The operating and control techniques as well as the management principles described in the text have general application in business institutions of all kinds.

Professor Hodges is an eminently well qualified author. His writing reflects on every page his wide experience with industrial leaders as practitioner, consultant, and teacher in the management field. He speaks with "the authority of experience" when he describes the management function and the responsibilities of administrator, executive and supervisor in filling their special roles in the operation of the industrial concern. During his varied career, Professor Hodges has served as an officer or director of nine corporations, as a director of labor relations, and as a management consultant with his own firm, Hodges Associates. This rich business experience and his extensive teaching background both here and abroad have provided the author with insights — and an understanding of how to communicate them — which are most unusual. His book is a generous sharing of authoritative and penetrating analyses of management problems, and it takes a prominent place in the Houghton Mifflin series of textbooks in the field of management.

JOSEPH W. TOWLE

Washington University

Preface

MANAGING THE INDUSTRIAL CONCERN, as its title suggests, is occupied primarily with the problems faced by the *industrial* manager and with the principles and techniques he follows in solving them. Throughout the book, however, the emphasis is always on *general management,* not production management. Industry grapples with an exceptionally wide range of problems, and as a result many of its principles and practices carry over into wholesale, retail, and service concerns, as well as into many other organized activities. This text emphasizes these interrelationships and points out how techniques developed by industry are continually being borrowed by other branches of business. For this reason, the text will serve the introductory student well whether his later interests in management prove to lie in the industrial field or in the general business area.

Those familiar with this book's predecessor written in 1955 will see at once that the present version is a major revision. In addition to the fresh points of view and extensive rewriting throughout, the book presents a basic reorganization of the material. It is now broadly divided into six Parts, opening with general principles and moving through operations controls, problems of human resources, compensation, and the supporting industrial functions to a discussion of the management team. There are new chapters in Part One on Quantitative Analysis and Data Processing as aids to managerial decision making. A new chapter on the Board of Directors and another on the Executive have been added to the expanded treatment of the Management Team in Part Six.

There have been important improvements in the field of management since 1955. One of the most significant has been the gradually increasing application of quantitative methods to management problems in support of human judgment and experience. No general treatment of management today, even at the introductory level, can ignore entirely the techniques of Quantitative Analysis. The discussion of these techniques in this book, however, does not pretend to be either comprehensive or exhaustive. After a brief outline of the background of Quantitative Analysis and its current place in management, the student is introduced to the terms certainty, risk, and uncertainty. Elementary illustrations of the use of linear programming, waiting line theory, and simulation round out the discussion. No depth of mathematical background is assumed. Throughout the book the student's attention is drawn to applications of the techniques whenever a particularly illustrative situation is under discussion.

The new chapter on the Board of Directors is in sympathetic response to the growing public concern over the failure of too many Boards to recognize their obligations to their stockholder-owners, to their enterprises, and to society in general. The insights gained through my service on nine Boards in three states, sharpened by critical questions from students, will, it is hoped, lend credibility to my analysis of this problem and add weight to my suggested solutions. The chapter is not recommended as a tranquilizer for delinquent Board members.

New problems of the modern Executive faced with growing competition, increased technological complexity and widening social responsibilities demanded a fuller treatment of that subject in Chapter 35. The vital importance of careful executive training and selection programs is emphasized. The chapter also provides a thorough analysis of the steps involved in sound decision making, that crucial and ever-present test of the executive in action.

The case problems following each chapter in the book (with the exception of Chapters 1, 4, and 5) present interesting situations drawn from actual business experience though the names given to individuals and companies are fictitious. The problems force the student to recognize and choose among alternative solutions, thus engaging him directly in the decision-making process. All of the questions at the end of the chapters are new or rephrased and serve to focus individual student attention or class discussion on the most salient points in the text.

Naturally, no book covering this subject range is the product of one person: the number of footnote references is one evidence of this. There are other sources to whom I should like to give special credit. A former student, Daniel Brier, Director of Marketing for Werner Management Consultants, contributed considerably to the Marketing chapter. Berl C. Winters, Research Technician with Sperry Rand Corporation, made valuable suggestions for the chapter on Research. Professor Joseph W. Towle of Washington University, Houghton Mifflin's Editorial Adviser in the field of Management, made valuable suggestions that improved the effectiveness of the text. Many others contributed ideas that have made the book more timely and thought-provoking.

Finally, both my wife and the editors of Houghton Mifflin have been helpful in making the manuscript more readable in many places. It is scarcely necessary to add that the author assumes responsibility for errors and shortcomings since he will be credited with them anyway.

HENRY G. HODGES

Gainesville, Florida
January, 1963

Contents

PART FOUR
Compensating Employees

PART FIVE
The Supporting Industrial Functions

PART SIX
The Management Team

Managing the

Industrial Concern

Management of an

Industrial Enterprise

The triumphs of society are due to the substitution of observation and inference for authority. Every attempt to revive authority in intellectual matters is a retrograde step. And it is part of the scientific attitude that the pronouncements of science do not claim to be certain, but only to be the most probable on present evidence. One of the greatest benefits that science confers upon those who understand its spirit is that it enables them to live without the delusive support of subjective certainty.

BERTRAND RUSSELL

1

Background of Scientific Management

Men, materials, machines, money, markets — the effective coordination of these five elements is the job of modern management. Ever since the Industrial Revolution, which opened unlimited possibilities of expansion in production and distribution, the problem of coordinating these five elements has grown so enormously complicated that management has had to become a science as well as an art. If management is thought of as the problem of directing human efforts for productivity, then it can be said that there have always been "managers." But at no time in the past has the harmonious coordination of the five elements been so difficult as in the modern era. To understand the reasons for the present industrial situation, it will be well to consider its background.

There have been periods prior to the Industrial Era when all five elements did not have to be taken into consideration by the "manager." The task of coordination was much easier in the feudal period than it was during the Roman Empire, or at any time since, simply because two of the elements — money and markets — were irrelevant to the medieval economy. Since trade had virtually disappeared from Western Europe, and almost everything that was produced on the manor was consumed there, marketing did not present a problem. A few shillings were all the money anyone required.

When all five management factors had to be considered in the past, each of them was simple enough to make the problem of coordination relatively easy. The master weaver of the later Middle Ages took care of his own marketing, but he required no advertising or sales department to dispose of his goods.

4

Slave production

Probably the most significant development for management has been in the first of the five elements — men. The gang boss in ancient Egypt did not have to worry about psychological techniques for keeping the slaves happy. There was no shop steward and no grievance committee to present complaints to management. Slave labor formed the human and economic base of Egypt's pyramids and the civilization they represented. It was the economic surplus from slave labor that enabled a relatively small group of masters to make large contributions to temples and centers of learning such as Athens and Alexandria. During the slave period, the focused weight of mass labor compensated for primitive machines, hand tools, and crude management techniques.

Serf production

Whereas slavery bound human beings as chattels to other human beings, serfdom, or the "manorial system," bound the worker to the land he culti-vated. This pattern of production in Europe of the twelfth century divided the country into manors, held in theory by a king or prince, but in practice by his vassals, the lords. The serfs who worked the soil for their livelihood were permitted to do so only in return for dues and labor services paid to their lord. In spite of his lot, the serf was better off than the slave because it was his services that belonged to the lord, and not his person.

Artisan production

After the manorial system started to decline in the latter part of the twelfth century, free labor gradually arose in its place. Serfs began to buy their freedom with "quit rents," based on the value of their services rather than their land, and set up small independent farms. Many of the newly freed peasants turned from the soil to handicrafts, which were becoming especially important in the English economy.

Craft Guilds. As production skills and professional trading became more widespread, the craftsmen naturally formed organizations for their mutual protection and benefit. These craft guilds spread into the new indus-trial towns of Italy, Germany, France, and England. The guilds regulated wages, hours of work, the number of apprentices, the sales territory, and the selling prices of their products. They became so strong politically in many towns that they virtually controlled the local governments.

One of the reasons for the eventual downfall of the guilds was the use of their economic and political monopolies for selfish purposes. But it was the advent of the machine which hastened the disintegration of the guilds' power. They could not maintain their position against the onslaught of the machine's bid for cheap semi-skilled labor. They began to split internally as the masters set more and more restrictions on entrance into the group. Economic changes resulted in a social cleavage, with the masters on one side and the journeymen and apprentices on the other. The latter group soon formed a permanent wage class.

The Rise of Trade. The great discoveries of the sixteenth century opened new markets all over the world as well as new sources of raw materials, both of which the merchants were quick to exploit. The existence of this new class of independently wealthy merchants, with ever larger sums to invest, was a financial prerequisite to the industrial Revolution.

The Industrial Revolution

The Industrial Revolution ushered in the change from an agricultural society with local trade areas to an industrial society with world-wide markets.[1] The rise of the machine-factory system was nurtured by several interrelated factors, the most important of which were: (1) the expanding use of machines, (2) new basic inventions, and (3) the growth of world markets. These factors, together with available water power and access to raw materials made England the natural incubator of the Industrial Revolution in the eighteenth century. Within a single generation, a series of inventions revolutionized England's textile industry. Parliament had passed a law in the previous century which protected property rights in patents, thus assuring the inventor the rewards of his labor. Inventions spurred investment, and the expansion created by new capital brought new demands for technical innovations.

Machine production offered potential investors a new means for overcoming the increasing shortage of consumer goods, and for satisfying growing consumer demand for new products; as well as for circumventing growing craft arrogance. The textile revolution did not start in the woolen industry where guild controls were so tight, but in the relatively new cotton industry. Production of the new textile machines added further unlimited possibilities for investment.

Basic inventions

Textile production involves two main processes, spinning and weaving. It was the constant struggle to keep these two processes in equilibrium that demanded new machines. A series of five outstanding inventions met these demands. (1) The *spinning jenny* (1770), invented by James Har-

---

[1] The term "Industrial Revolution" was probably first used by Arnold Toynbee in a series of lectures delivered about 1880, and published as *Lectures on the Industrial Revolution in England.*

greaves, with eight spindles operating simultaneously, produced yarn eight times faster than the old spinning wheel. (2) About 1772, Richard Arkwright developed the *roller spinning frame* which improved the twisting phase of the spinning process. (3) Samuel Crompton (1779) combined the operations of the frame and the jenny to produce the *mule,* which eliminated hand-spinning. (4) When these aids to spinning put pressure on the weavers to keep abreast of the yarn supply, Edmund Cartwright invented the *power loom* in 1785. (5) The master stroke of the Industrial Revolution was the *steam engine* of James Watt, a Scottish engineer. Urged originally by the need for pumping water from England's industrial coal mines, the engine's revolutionary possibilities soon made themselves known. The new abundance of coal relieved the infant industry of its reliance on running water which went dry in summer and froze in winter. The new steam engine with its transported supply of coal could now be located in centers strategic to textile production.

The American contributions to the Industrial Revolution include the cotton gin, invented by Eli Whitney in 1792. This gin was a boon to England's new textile industry as it increased the possible per capita output of seeded cotton three hundred times. But Whitney's chief contribution to industrial development was the idea of *interchangeability of parts.* By making parts similar enough to be interchangeable, he made feasible the division of labor, and the assembly method of manufacture; thus he paved the way for mass production.

Results of the industrial revolution

Briefly, the Revolution accounted for outstanding consequences in three fields: economics, social welfare, and politics. *Economically,* it left many skilled workers jobless. They were compelled to accept inferior jobs as machine operators or learn the new machinist trade. Unskilled labor benefitted by learning to operate the new machines. It was the suddenness of these changes which stamped their revolutionary character. Another economic change was the prohibitive cost of the new machines. It became increasingly difficult for the old masters to establish themselves in the new textile industries. The foundation for the conflict between capital and labor was built on this situation.

The *social* consequences were plainly visible in urban areas. Workers moved in waves to cities where the sanitary conditions did not keep pace with the rapid growth and influx of population. Working hours were long under the new factory system, and the overcrowded factories and inadequacy of municipal sanitation facilitated the spread of contagious diseases. The crime rate increased due to the crowded living conditions and the increase of idle time.

The days of the so-called self-made, massproducing pioneers followed.

Unhampered by restraining legislation, these masters of production accumulated vast business empires. Their excesses in this industrial jungle period, however, solidified a growing rancor among the exploited workers.

The *political* consequences of the Industrial Revolution are still evolving. Organized labor has used an expanding franchise to build its political power to a point where some of its abuses parallel those which produced the downfall of the guilds. The Industrial Revolution produced the political climate which fostered this powerful pressure group.

Awakening of the Modern Period

The Industrial Revolution started in this country about 1800 and was well developed in mass production by 1900. The new production processes demanded a new kind of management. Not only did mass production draw large masses of workers into factories, but it also expanded commerce and trading. The resulting high cost of unskilled management drawn into these newly created jobs was absorbed in the new low cost of machine production. Growing consumer demand for cheap machine-made products, high rewards for the new machine entrepreneurs, and expanding markets combined to make the failure to apply scientific management principles by 1900 relatively unimportant.

Three methods of modern management

As production began to catch up with its markets, competition among producers and distributors started to restrict the profit prizes to those whose improved management produced superior results. It is customary to speak of three fundamental phases in the development of modern management. The transition from one phase to another is not clear, as two or more often blend in practice. The three methods, known as *rule-of-thumb, systematic,* and *scientific* represent an upward progression. The prevalence of the rule-of-thumb method is still frequently attested to in credit and bankruptcy reports.

Rule-of-thumb is the method used by managers who operate on a more or less inspired level. Their decisions are based largely on hunches. Our early business leaders employed this method simply because nothing better had been developed. These pioneers were essentially a product of their time and conditions. Today they would be publicly condemned for their methods and would be in frustrated rebellion against state and national business controls. Many rule-of-thumb managers are still with us, but they are no longer business leaders; they are more frequently business failures.

Shortly after the middle of the last century there developed a *systematic* approach to business management. It introduced planned procedures, chiefly in production and record-keeping. In a technical sense, methods, procedures, and systems are important today and worthy of a brief explanation.[2]

A *method* may be defined as an established way of doing something. Methods may become established through sheer habit or custom, or they may be set up after careful planning.

A *procedure* is an established sequence of methods and operations, usually involving several people in one or more departments of a concern. Whereas methods specify only *how* the single operation is to be performed, procedures lay down rules for the order in which operations are to be performed and tell who will perform them, at what time, and in what place. Like methods, procedures result from either custom or deliberate planning.

A *system*, in the present context, is a network of related procedures. The establishment of systems, with their standardized methods and procedures, was a necessary step in the development of the third, or *scientific*, phase of management. The notion of a system is essential to all scientific analysis. To summarize the last two stages of management: The systematic approach asks *What* practices have worked in the past? The scientific approach asks *Why* is it that certain practices have worked out in the past and why others have failed? Systematic management is essentially a mechanism; scientific management is a method.

Scientific management is equipped to deal with phenomena that are essentially dynamic. Its problem-solving is based on objective and scientific foundations. The scientific method is demanded in business where procedures have become so complex that they separate the line (directing) function from the staff (problem analysis and planning) function. Under scientific management, answers to problems requiring new methods and procedures are no longer based on the leader's positional authority or his inspired decisions, but rather come from established principles and the analyses of specialists in the various fields into which modern management has evolved.[3]

Management literature

The comparatively recent growth of literature in the field of management is an unmistakable indication of its newness in a professional sense. One writer made a list of the various books on organization and management

[2] Richard F. Neuschel has pointed out that there is no consensus today in defining "methods," "procedures," and "systems." Sometimes the words are used interchangeably. See *Streamlining Business Procedures* (New York: McGraw-Hill Book Company, Inc., 1950), pp. 9–10. The definitions offered here are similar to Neuschel's. However, the reader should realize that all authorities on management do not use the terms in just this way.

[3] The formulation of principles has been one of the major concerns of scientific management. A full discussion of this aspect of management, together with a presentation of some of the most important general principles, is found in Chapter 3.

referred to in a 1948 text. There were 82 such books. Of these, none was published prior to 1911; only two were published before 1921.[4] After 1930, published literature in this field grew apace. The 1947 edition of the *Bibliography of Industrial Engineering and Management Literature* included references to twelve hundred books and articles in the field of management, besides an index to over three thousand articles on motion and time study, and related subjects. The amount of recent literature on management techniques has far outstripped the time and ability of management to take advantage of them.

Fundamental Definitions

In the rapid development of the machine age, words seem to have developed in the same arbitrary way as the methods of rule-of-thumb managers. Consider the word "manufacture." Prior to the advent of the machine, handmade goods were referred to as custom-made. They were made on order. When it became necessary to distinguish between custom-made and machine-made, the English started to use the word "manufactured" for machine-made merchandise. This anglicized Latin derivative was patently born in the confusion of the Industrial Revolution. It is compounded from the Latin *manu,* meaning "by hand," and *factus,* which means "made." Thus we have the contradiction of describing machine-made goods as being "made by hand."

Definitions are necessary for common understanding in any scientific field. In management they are more than commonly important because of the lack of general agreement about the meaning of some of our fundamental terms. The field of management would be well served if there were some recognized authority who could establish official definitions.

The distinction, or lack of it, between "management" and "administration" is an example. Among some writers in the field of management, there is a tendency to blend (if not to make synonymous) the concepts of administration and management. Majority opinion holds that administration determines general policies, while management sees that they are carried out. The confusion evidently arises from the fact that various levels of management often *influence* policy-making. It is on this basis that management is occasionally credited with *making* policies, a conclusion which unnecessarily blurs the distinction between the two ideas.

Management

Some authorities justifiably seek to describe management rather than define it. The objection to this practice is that several pages of description

[4] Thomas H. Nelson, "The Credit Executive's Place in Management," *Credit and Financial Management* (July, 1949), Vol. 51, p. 7.

tend to throw a haze about a word which can be defined satisfactorily. Let us take a few definitions at random and see what they have in common.

The ASME (American Society of Mechanical Engineers) calls management "the art and science of preparing, organizing, and directing human effort applied to control the forces and utilize the materials of nature for the benefit of man." Oliver Sheldon's definition is frequently quoted: "Management proper is the function in industry concerned in the execution of policy, within the limits set up by the administration, and the employment of the organization for the particular objects before it."[5] A more recent definition is Thomas H. Nelson's: "Management in business is the science and art of combining ideas, facilities, processes, materials, and people to produce and market a worthy product or service profitably."[6] Petersen and Plowman define management in general as "a technique by means of which the purposes and objectives of a particular human group are determined, clarified, and effectuated."[7]

These are only four of a large number of definitions, but there is no reason to believe that they are not typical of the literature as a whole. Superficially, there appears to be a lot of disagreement among them. For example, Nelson and the ASME agree on calling management "a science and an art," whereas Sheldon refers to it as a "function" and Petersen and Plowman as a "technique." Perhaps a more important disagreement is the question of *what* it is that is *being managed*. The ASME says "human efforts"; Sheldon says "the organization"; Petersen and Plowman say "a particular human group"; and Nelson says "ideas, facilities, processes, materials, and people." Henri Fayol confines management to human relations[8] but includes material factors as an essential part of his definition of organization.

Finally, the goals of the managerial process are all stated differently: "To control the forces and utilize the materials of nature for the benefit of man"; "the employment of the organization for the particular objects set before it"; "to produce and market a worthy product or service profitably"; "to determine, clarify, and effectuate the objectives of a particular human group." Despite this diversity in the statement of goals, it is important to point out that all of these writers agree that orientation to goals, whatever they may be, is an integral part of the definition of management.

For the purpose of this book, let us say that *"management is the accomplishment of objectives through the use of men, materials, and machines."* This definition seems to us to have the virtues of simplicity and generality.

[5] Oliver Sheldon, *The Philosophy of Management* (New York: Prentice-Hall, Inc., 1923), p. 32.

[6] Nelson, *op. cit.*, p. 4.

[7] Elmore Petersen and E. Grosvenor Plowman, *Business Organization and Management,* 3rd ed. (Homewood, Ill.: Richard D. Irwin, Inc., 1953), p. 33.

[8] Henri Fayol, *General and Industrial Management,* trans. Constance Storrs (London: Sir Isaac Pitman & Sons, 1949), p. 19.

It might be argued that the inclusion of machines seriously narrows the applicability of the definition. And yet, it is difficult in our day to think of any enterprise, economic or otherwise, where the use of machines — from the office typewriter to the fully automatic plant — is not a factor to be taken into consideration by the manager.

It was pointed out that Nelson and the ASME both refer to management as "a science and an art." The distinction is useful. It may well be that the techniques involved in the managerial process make up the *science* of management, whereas the task of obtaining the cooperation of employees in accepting any activity using these techniques is the *art* of management.

Management as defined by specific functions

It may be remembered that in the beginning of this chapter management was defined as the coordination of men, materials, machines, money, and markets. This definition has much to recommend it, but the difficulty with calling management the *coordinator* of activities is that coordination is merely one of the important functions of management. Besides coordinating, management must plan, organize, direct, and control. Indeed, this is the way in which the most famous of French authorities on the subject, Henri Fayol, defined management: "To manage is to forecast and plan, to organize, to command, to coordinate, and to control."[9] This way of breaking down the management process into five distinct functions, or phases in a cycle, has come into wide use by writers on management. The scheme will be used in this book as a convenient operational definition of management.

Administration

Overall-all policy-making is the chief concern of the administrative function, and in the corporate form it is the prerogative of the board of directors. General control of management is another prime duty of administration. The chief purpose of general control is to coordinate such activities as finance, production, and sales, so that they tie in with the general policies of the organization.

Organization

Although organization has been listed above as one of the five functions of management, in one sense it is a more basic concept than management. "Organization is the form of every human association for the attainment of a common purpose."[10] We shall use the word in a more restricted sense to

[9] *Ibid.*, pp. 5–6.
[10] James D. Mooney, *The Principles of Organization*, rev. ed. (New York: Harper & Brothers, 1947), p. 1.

refer to the process of building the structure of an enterprise which will provide for the separation of activities in a framework which indicates their hierarchical importance and functional association. This definition will be elaborated in Chapter 7 under Principles of Organization.

The operating relationship among organization, administration, and management may be expressed briefly as follows: *Management carries out the policies of administration through the framework of the organization.* There are many other terms in the field of management which must be used in a technical sense, but the three considered here are fundamental.

Pioneers in Scientific Management

Frederick W. Taylor (1856–1915) is universally referred to as the "Father of Scientific Management."[11] Because of eye trouble, Taylor was compelled to leave Phillips Exeter Academy without graduating. Some years later, after serving an apprenticeship as machinist and between jobs in industry, he graduated from Stevens Institute of Technology in 1883.

Taylor's functional foremanship attracted considerable attention in those industries interested in the new science of management. He came to the conclusion that the machine shop foreman must, besides being a good machinist, perform eight other functions. He also decided that only a few foremen possessed the ability to perform even three or four of these functions properly. It was natural, therefore, that the foreman's work should be broken down into its component skills and that specialists should be assigned to each of them. Taylor's analysis of the foreman's job divided it into the following activities:

Office	Shop
Time and cost clerk	Gang boss
Instruction card clerk	Speed boss
Work order and route clerk	Repair boss
Disciplinarian	Inspector

He explained that "functional management consists in so dividing the work of management that each man from the superintendent down shall have as few functions as possible to perform."[12]

Although the new plan did not show up well in practice and was generally abandoned by 1920, nevertheless his idea led to wide acceptance of

[11] To some extent the famous French industrialist, Henri Fayol, to whom we have already referred, is recognized as sharing honors in the original analyses of scientific management. His chief work, cited previously in translation, is *Administration Industrielle et Générale,* published originally in France as a bulletin of the Société de l'Industrie Minérale (1916).

[12] Frederic W. Taylor, *Shop Management, Transactions* of the ASME (1903), Vol. 14, p. 99. A bibliography of Taylor's most important writings is given in the following footnote.

the functional principle of management. It supported the line-and-staff type of organization, discussed in Chapter 6. It also resulted in the foreman being unburdened of some of his excessive duties. The inspection function of the foreman, for example, has been taken over by the inspection department. The time-and-cost-clerk functions have been transferred to the payroll and costing departments. The instruction-card activity is now performed by industrial engineering. The work of the repair boss has been shifted to the maintenance department. And the job of the work-order and route clerk has been taken over by production control. All of these activities are now operated as functional aids (staff) to the (line) foreman.

Not long after his employment by the Bethlehem Steel and Cramps' Shipbuilding companies, Taylor was engaging in general management consulting. The chief task he set for himself was to increase worker productivity by improving and standardizing machines, tools, methods, and work-places. His writings are not so voluminous as one might expect from the time he devoted to a wide range of management subjects. Two of his early papers were presented at meetings of the ASME. The first, in 1895, was entitled "A Piece-Rate System"; the second, on "Shop Management," was read to the Society in 1903. In 1905, he collaborated with Sanford Thompson and Edward Smulski in publishing *Concrete, Plain and Reinforced*. His presidential address to the ASME the same year was "On the Art of Cutting Metals." *Shop Management* was published as a book in 1911, followed in the same year by *The Principles of Scientific Management*.[13]

During the latter part of his life, Taylor was the subject of many criticisms by organized labor, who complained that his methods led to speed-up of the worker. Labor's negative attitude was reinforced by the rise of a management cult whose members dubbed themselves "efficiency experts." Without training, experience, or a professional approach, these charlatans were responsible for a temporary eclipse of the scientific management movement. In explaining his attitude toward labor, Taylor declared that he was not opposed to its separate organizations, but he contended that if the principles of scientific management were adopted, there would be no need for labor to organize to obtain adequate wages, reasonable hours, or improved working conditions.

[13] Testimony to the vitality of Taylor's writings is the frequency with which they have been reprinted. The following bibliography includes the more recent editions:

"A Piece-Rate System" first appeared in the *Transactions* of the ASME, Vol. 16 (1895), pp. 856–903. It is reprinted in Thompson, *op. cit.*, pp. 636–683.

Concrete, Plain and Reinforced, 4th ed. (New York: John Wiley and Sons, Inc., 1925).

On the Art of Cutting Metals (New York: The American Society of Mechanical Engineers, 1907).

Shop Management, which appeared originally in the *Transactions* of the ASME, Vol. 14 (1903), pp. 1337–1456, and *The Principles of Scientific Management*, originally published by Harper & Brothers (1911), are both reprinted, together with excerpts from the testimony before the House Committee, in F. W. Taylor, *Scientific Management* (New York: Harper & Brothers, 1947).

In conclusion, these are the fundamentals that Taylor stood for and urged on both workers and management:

1. *Research* and experimentation with machines, tools, materials, workplaces, operators, and all other phases of production and management for continued improvement and better productivity.
2. *Planning* of all the operations of management and production, including routing and order of work, specifications, written instructions, and availability of materials.
3. *Training* of workers in the skills for which they were fitted and the improvement of those skills by competent supervision.
4. *Standards* for operations including methods, times and wages; for workplaces, tools, materials; and for the plans and procedures of management.
5. *Controls* for checking results against established standards.
6. *Cooperation* between workers and management.

Henry L. Gantt was directly associated with Taylor at the Bethlehem Steel Company, and it was natural that his philosophy of management should follow the Taylor pattern. His writings emphasize substitution of scientific methods for the habit of basing industrial decisions and procedures on what had been done or what someone thought could be done.[14]

The *Gantt Charts* have probably done more than anything else to establish the fame of their author. They are used extensively for control, planning, machine and department loading, machine and man idleness, and for recording progress trends. Gantt is also known for the "human touch" he added to Taylor's differential wage plan. Taylor's wage plan paid much higher over-all piece rates to those who met the scientifically determined time standards. This idea worked a financial hardship on those who just missed the mark. Gantt felt that more consideration should be given to mediocre workers, to whom Taylor's plan assigned an over-all low piece rate.

Harrington Emerson popularized "efficiency" both as a technical standard and as a philosophy. In fact, he called his philosophy the "gospel" of efficiency. In the introduction to Emerson's *The Twelve Principles of Efficiency*, Charles B. Going wrote: "The doctrines of efficiency therefore define something infinitely greater than a system of management. They set forth a morality, and provide practical measures of attainment."[15] He also

---

[14] The principles which Gantt espoused are contained in his three books: *Work, Wages and Profits* (New York: The Engineering Magazine Company, 1913); *Industrial Leadership* (New Haven, Conn.: Yale University Press, 1916); and *Organizing for Work* (New York: Harcourt, Brace and Howe, 1919).

[15] 5th ed.; New York: The Engineering Magazine Company, 1919, p. ii. The twelve principles are:

1. Clearly defined ideals
2. Common sense
3. Competent counsel
4. Discipline
5. Fair deal
6. Reliable records
7. Dispatching
8. Standards and schedules
9. Standardized conditions
10. Standard operations
11. Written standard instructions
12. Efficiency control

emphasized the importance of the line-and-staff type of organization as a tool for carrying out his principles of management, suggesting that "the industrial hook-worm disease is defective organization."[16]

Frank B. Gilbreth is best known for his contribution to the field of motion and time study through utilization of motion pictures. In connection with the analyses and improvements of workplaces, methods, and worker motions, he continually sought the "one best way" known at the time. Gilbreth was assisted in his micromotion studies by his wife, Dr. Lillian Gilbreth, who made important contributions of her own in the psychology of management. Because of the large volume of their published work, the Gilbreths are probably the most widely discussed of the pioneers in the field of management.

Morris L. Cooke was active as a consulting management engineer for many years. Also associated with Taylor in his experiments in and around Philadelphia, Cooke is notable for going beyond the industrial field in applying the principles of scientific management. When Director of Public Works of the City of Philadelphia, he consistently applied scientific methods for solving problems of city management.[17]

One of the early studies of the Carnegie Foundation on the management of universities was made by Cooke. He applied the accepted principles of industrial management to the situations found in a number of our universities.[18] A fourth area for Cooke's application of the principles of management was in the field of labor-management relations. After considerable study and work in this field, he collaborated with Philip Murray, President of the CIO, in writing *Organized Labor and Production.*[19]

These five names do not by any means exhaust the list of pioneer leaders in the field of scientific management, but they do form its core.[20] Fayol, in France, was inspired to his *General and Industrial Management* by the so-called "Taylorism." Later other countries, including Russia under Lenin, gave consideration to the new science. The first International Management Congress was held in Prague in 1924.

[16] *Ibid.,* p. 29.

[17] Many of these new methods in city management are discussed in Morris L. Cooke, *Our Cities Awake* (Garden City, N.Y.: Doubleday, Page and Co., 1918). The author was associated with Mr. Cooke during his last year as Director of Public Works.

[18] Morris L. Cooke, *Academic and Industrial Efficiency* (New York: Carnegie Foundation for the Advancement of Teaching, 1910), Bulletin No. 5.

[19] Philip Murray and Morris L. Cooke, *Organized Labor and Production* (New York: Harper and Brothers, 1940).

[20] Others who made outstanding contributions to the field of management, all of whom are now deceased:

Robert Owen	Alex H. Church
Charles Babbage	Oliver Sheldon
Henry Metcalfe	Mary P. Follett
Henry R. Towne	Harry A. Hopf
Russell Robb	George H. Mayo

Recent Trends in Industry and Management

Objectives of modern management

Certainly until 1900, and probably for some time after that, the objective of management was definitely expressed as the "profit motive." With the development of a more social outlook, the thinking of management gradually changed, and the social motive was added. One may conclude that the social idea is now so firmly entrenched as one of the objectives of modern management as to be called management's social imperative. One important aspect of this social obligation is concerned with *productivity*. Modern management must assume the obligation of producing a reasonable minimum of all kinds of goods for all people, at a price they can afford to pay. Failure to attain this world-wide objective will eventually leave a gap for the infiltration of ideologies that will promise something better.

Schools of modern management

Maturing scientific management attracted the attention of various scientists, some of whom had not been previously interested in the subject. Their studies of the purposes, processes, and systems of management have led to the recognition of certain "schools," which are not clearly defined, mutually exclusive, nor officially recognized.[21]

The *Process School* considers management as a process of accomplishing objectives through the efforts of others, in organized groups. It analyzes processes to suggest principles of general management for improving its techniques. It encourages research to improve procedures and systems, and their testing in practice. Its exponents are mainly practitioners and teachers of management.

The *Human Relations School,* also known as the Behavioral Science School, holds that since management consists of getting things done through others, it must emphasize interpersonal relations. This school, led chiefly by psychologists and social scientists, feels that group dynamics offers the chief tool for successful management.

The *Empirical School* approaches the improvement of management procedures chiefly from the experiences of managers, as a basis for selecting those experiences which have had successful results. This emphasis naturally turns to the study of actual cases for the benefit of managers, and the preferred method for teaching the subject.

The *Quantitative Analysis School* emphasizes managerial decisionmaking by the methods discussed in Chapters 4 and 5. Its chief proponents are

[21] For a more extended discussion of these and other "schools," see Harold Koontz, "The Management Theory Jungle," *Journal of the Academy of Management* (December 1961), pp. 174–188.

economists and mathematicians. It reduces problems to various types of "models" for analysis of the problem and of its alternative solutions.

Growth of modern industry

The expansion in all lines of business, including industry, has been continuous and often spectacular in this country since the establishment of the first cotton mills in New England prior to 1800. New processes and inventions have exerted stimulating influences throughout our entire economy. Interchangeable parts and the production-line method are outstanding examples. Inventions in the radio, television, and electronic fields have contributed the most recent stimulus to business growth, which is observable in one or more of the following:

Capital investments	Floor space in use
Number of employees	Power consumption
Volume of production	Volume of sales

Expansion has been both vertical and horizontal. *Horizontal* growth adds units similar to the original concern. *Vertical* expansion extends the business of the original company into different levels of the basic production function.

Accompanying the phenomenal growth of modern industry in this country has been the rise in the living standards of all classes. The resulting increased consumer demand has required higher production quotas, thus leading to an ever-expanding circle of supply and demand. The remarkable results of a hundred and fifty years of virile industrial growth is a record which no other country has equaled. Mass production and mass consumption have been the two outstanding factors of this period. Along with these two, we have experienced high productivity, high employment, increasing time for leisure, and increased stability in all phases of business. Growing pains have been the natural result of our rapid growth.

Unfortunately, the records show that war's demands have been the greatest stimulus to increased productivity. In two years of World War II, for example, assembly-line techniques and the substitution of welding for riveting cut in half the number of man-hours required to build a Liberty ship. Instead of eight hundred rivets per day per man, the new machine made one hundred welds per minute.[22] Rising productivity in the future will depend on improved organization techniques, better management methods, more multi-operation and fully automatic machines, improved production methods, horizontal as well as two-way vertical communication, and a large flow of new ideas from the man-at-the-bench, who himself will benefit from the increased productivity.

[22] See Charles R. Walker, "American Productivity: I," *Fortune* (January, 1946), Vol. 33, pp. 150–156, 174–184.

Ownership and management

During the first hundred years of the Industrial Revolution, the rule-of-thumb operators of business were largely individual owners. Many adopted the corporate form,[23] but continued to control their companies. Henry Ford is an outstanding example. Under the corporate form we have reached a situation where many large concerns are ruled by a group of self-perpetuating professional managers. The democratic organization often becomes a dictatorial operation. Most stockholders do not realize this change, and those who do are usually satisfied as long as they receive satisfactory dividends. Whether or not this practice of business management should come closer to its theory of owner determination is one of our current business problems.

Conclusions

It is not only helpful, but necessary to know some of the details of production and the relations between workers and management as they existed prior to the Industrial Revolution and as they have developed since that time. It is against this background that we must consider our industrial situation today. The advent of free labor and the extension of the franchise account for the present economic and political changes which the machine has made possible. Many of the vicissitudes of today's labor-management relations are unconsciously conditioned by events which took place during that earlier period.

In spite of the huge contributions from America's workshop, there is a continuous cry for more and better tools and equipment. Our progressively increasing production of goods has had several economic results:

1. National wealth and buying power have increased.
2. Productivity has risen about 3 per cent annually.
3. The number of jobs has steadily increased.
4. Working hours have sharply decreased.

Scientific management must give serious consideration to three factors in continuing to improve our standard of living: *first*, improving the productivity of the worker through still higher investment in machines; *second*, minimizing wastes of all kinds, including the inefficiencies of industry and government; and *third*, finding better ways of doing things. It is also reasonable to expect that management will exert more effort and contribute better results to organization and its techniques, fields which have been relatively neglected in the emphasis on production.

It is obvious that an abundance of natural resources, inventive genius, the profit motive, and a free political society are in a large sense responsible for our industrial productivity and general business progress; nevertheless, the

[23] The various forms of ownership are explained in Chapter 11.

successful coordination of these factors has been dependent on the resource-fulness of scientific management.

QUESTIONS

1. Which of the five elements of management did not have to be considered prior to the Industrial Revolution? Why?
2. Some authorities contend that management is a science, while others believe it is an art. How would you support the text's contention that it is both a science and an art?
3. How did slaves compensate for the ineffectiveness of crude tools and rule-of-thumb management existing in ancient times?
4. What was the outstanding difference between the relationship of slaves and serfs to their masters?
5. Name two reasons for the eventual downfall of the medieval guilds.
6. Arnold Toynbee coined the phrase "Industrial Revolution." What was the outstanding characteristic of that period that justified the word "revolution" rather than "evolution"?
7. What were the two production processes that mothered the series of inventions during the 1700's in the textile industry?
8. Why was Eli Whitney's idea of the inter-changeability of parts more important to society than his invention of the cotton gin?
9. What were the chief economic consequences of the Industrial Revolution?
10. Explain the reasons for the pressing social consequences of the Industrial Revolution. How were they eventually ameliorated?
11. What outstanding political change in the status of workers resulted from the large transfer of skills to the machine?
12. How have systematic procedures aided in the development of scientific management?
13. What is the relationship among methods, procedures, and systems?
14. What change developed in the relationship between management principles and management literature before and after 1920?
15. If "manufacturing" is derived from the Latin *manus* (hand) and *facere* (to make), why was the word used to denote machine-made?
16. What is the difference, if any, between "management" and "administration"?
17. How does "organization" define the relationship between administration and management?
18. Since Taylor's functional foremanship failed of adoption in shop practice, how did the idea contribute to the subsequent development of scientific management outside the shop?
19. How many of Emerson's "Twelve Principles of Efficiency" can you recall?
20. Describe briefly four of the generally recognized "schools" of Modern Management.

2 : Management Problems

All businesses have problems; their solution is one of the chief tests of management's ability. In the unfortunate cases, the nature of the problem is often not recognized until it is too late to apply the remedy. In all cases, the prevention of disaster by the application of tested principles in the ordinary course of business is, of course, the best plan. Taylor said that the solution of management problems requires about 25 per cent technical or scientific treatment and 75 per cent common sense. But it must be obvious that a knowledge of the techniques of good management is of great assistance in applying common sense to a particular situation.

Managers often insist that the problems of their businesses are so different that they defy the application of general principles. Lack of knowledge of the problems of other concerns and the principles applied to their solution is usally father to such thoughts. It was the universality of the problems of management that gave birth to the international conferences for their consideration.

In what fields do most of management's problems fall? The list is a long one, even when one considers them merely as categories. Financial, purchasing, mechanical, production, and sales problems are all placed in the lap of management for decision. Social changes affect demands for products and the prices consumers will pay. Economic changes have both short- and long-term effects, the most striking being the business cycles. Politics confronts management with problems of taxation and regulation. Finally, labor poses problems of supply, training, wages, grievances, and productivity, to mention but a few.

The "pulls" on management

Management's problems are intensified because many of them are influenced by a number of "pulls," each of which is antagonistic to the others in certain respects. Those major pulls have their origins in the interests of

employees, stockholders, customers, competitors, various levels of government, and the general public. Figure 2.1 illustrates this situation. In theory,
these pulls represent a composite picture of sharply defined groups, with the
desire of each being represented as urging management's attention in opposition to the interests of the other groups. For example, while the employees
of a particular concern may want higher wages, the stockholders will
generally be interested in holding wages as low as possible. Similarly, the
stockholders may want higher prices for their products while the customers
insist upon lower prices.

However, complete opposition will seldom, if ever, hold true. Frequently,
two or more of the groups will be in at least partial accord on certain issues.
There should be little opposition on the degree of quality necessary for a
company making high explosives. Both employees and customers will
demand high quality in the finished product to insure safety in production
and use. The general public and the various levels of government will also
demand high quality from the standpoint of the company's moral obligations to those who use its products. In this example, at least five of the
groups will be in accord in their respective demands. The concern's competitors, however much they may desire freedom from keen competition,
will certainly want to see the opposition's products in this example free
from public dangers on purely moral grounds. By going down the line
from complete accord to sharp opposition, it will be seen that the possible
combinations of opposition and agreement of the six pulls on various issues
are innumerable.

In actual practice, members of one group may also be members of one
or more of the other five groups. For instance, a customer or employee may
also be a stockholder, and a stockholder will also be a member of the general public. While in one situation a person may be demanding low prices
as a customer, he might also demand high prices to increase his dividends
as a stockholder.

Figure 2.1

Six Pulls on Management

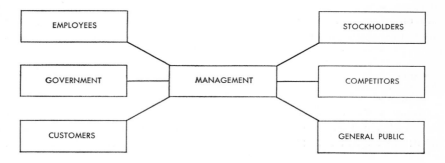

As these examples illustrate, the picture of the six major pulls loses its sharp focus and tends to become a jumbled mass of overlapping demands and groups. It is management's job to recognize these pulls and attempt to achieve some sort of balance among them. It is also management's job to reconcile the various pulls while maintaining the concern in a sound and progressive position. If management goes too far in satisfying the demands of one group, it will soon incur the wrath of one or more of the other groups.

In certain situations, management must consider more seriously the demands of one group than those of the others. This is obvious when the employees are represented by a strong aggressive union. The stockholders' interests must often yield when in conflict with the demands of the workers. The success of the company may hinge more strongly on good labor relations than on any other factor. A different situation affects a concern operating in a highly competitive field where the consumer market must receive prime consideration. Another example of the necessity for special attention is a government law or regulation which must be accepted and acted on to save management from certain trouble. Thus it may be seen that specific conditions and circumstances often temper the actions of management in achieving balance among the six pulls. Finally, we repeat that the effect of these opposing pulls often intensify management's chief problems.

The constant effort on the part of management to maintain all groups or pulls in comparative harmony is frequently reflected in attempts to identify the interests of two or more groups. The post-war effort to sell stock to employees and to the general public has such a purpose. Management makes other efforts to identify the stockholders with the employees, and the general public with the stockholders. The purpose of these activities is to lessen the distinctiveness and opposition of the various pulls — to blend them for a greater degree of harmony.

No matter what specific plan management may adopt, it is important that a point of balance be reached where all groups are at a maximum level of satisfaction in relation to the other groups. It is not enough for management merely to recognize the existence of the pulls. It must also recognize the significance of each group's demands, actively seek to maximize satisfaction for each group, and finally recognize the possible disastrous effects if one group becomes the exclusive concern of management to the serious detriment of the others. At best, the pulls present a delicate situation which must be handled with full cognizance of the effects of misguided activity.

Finances

Finances and labor are too often unrecognized by management as the sources of its chief problems. Records of the credit agencies show that the majority of business failures are caused by the lack of managerial training, skill, and experience. The management of finances is often the early stumbling block that leads to the final fall. Although figuring initial capital requirements is about as elusive for the amateur as determining the cost of altering a home, nevertheless there are certain basic considerations. Credit terms allowed to customers, the product price field, the time that raw materials and finished products must be held before processing and distribution, the length of the production cycle, the channels of distribution, and the necessity for research are all important factors influencing capital demands.

The nature of the product often determines the relative amount of required capital investment. A crushed stone business has relatively low cash requirements for raw materials and processing equipment. It may keep its investment low by selling at the pit, thus avoiding the purchase of trucks. On the other hand, many manufacturing concerns make large outlays for machinery, equipment, and tools. If some machines are of the special purpose type, obsolescence will increase capital requirements. The national average for machinery investment per employee has now reached about $10,000. In steel production it is now reported as nearly double that figure. Since productivity is dependent largely on investments in machines and equipment, their cost per worker will rise as the pressure for increased productivity continues.

Another financial problem of management is the balance among its common and preferred stocks, bonds, and commercial borrowings. If relatively steady profits are assured, the business may be financed by a majority of bonds at low carrying charge, thus providing higher returns for the risk capital. If annual profits are not reasonably assured, then common stock will be a protection against the annual interest charges of bonds. The question of stock control is also important. In some cases it suggests two classes of common stock — voting and nonvoting. In many states, failure to pay dividends on preferred stock for a certain number of years permits a representative stockholder committee to take over management of the company. When commercial borrowing is depended on for a portion of the operating expenses, it must be of such a temporary and recurring nature as to permit periodic liquidation. Otherwise, such financing is looked on as a "capital loan," suggesting that the business has not been adequately financed.

The purpose and amount of reserve funds is another financial concern of management. Even when such decisions are made by the policy-determining board of directors, management customarily furnishes the data and recommendations on which the the conclusions are based. With the increasing financial demands and contingent liabilities faced by all business concerns, there has been developing a marked tendency in the better managed companies to "play safe." Such protective foresight, in the form of various reserve funds, has been nurtured by the income tax laws which allow them as deductions under approved circumstances. Against which eventualities the concern should protect itself and to what extent are problems which must be re-examined from time to time as economic, social, and political changes require.

Labor

With the rise of organized labor and its political contacts with governmental agencies, management's problems in this field have grown apace. The expansion of business concerns into units so large as to minimize the personal touch with the worker or his organization is another cause of friction.[1] The preachments of many labor leaders have strengthened the centrifugal forces that separate management and the workers. Management's lack of appreciation of the main causes of the breach and the obvious desire of certain elements to hide their heads in the sands of time hoping that the storm will spend itself are equally indefensible.

Occasionally labor strife, but more often management's desire to increase productivity, leads to such improvement in machine techniques that even skilled workers are thrown on the labor market. Whereas the investor's interest and that of the general public favor technical improvements in production, the public as well as the labor organizations look to management to take care of the workers who suffer because of technological improvements. Technological unemployment is now recognized as one of the problems for which management must find a solution by providing other jobs through expansion or retraining, or in setting up protective reserve funds on a company or industry-wide basis.[2]

Against management's efforts to increase productivity, organized labor often interposes an unofficial and artificial restriction of output. Foundry core-makers are able to cut drastically their normal bench production without observable conscious effort. Many journeymen and other workers are apparently able to adjust their work pace so as to "come out even" on any preconceived production schedule. For those concerns which do not plan production on a scientific basis, restricted output is a major management headache. This problem applies largely to hourly rated workers where the guilty either enter a categorical denial that they are restricting output or plead management's demands for quality production as a defense.

"Feather-bedding" increases unit costs and selling prices. It is a polite form of dishonesty which no one seriously denies, which management has

---

[1] The National Labor Relations Act (1936) and the Taft-Hartley Act (1947) have greatly restricted the opportunities for employer and employee to associate or deal on a man-to-man basis.

[2] This was one of the principal assignments given Secretary of Labor, Arthur Goldberg, by President Kennedy in 1961.

ranted about for years, but which no one has had the courage to stop.[3] Whereas one might expect the government to take measures against such economic waste, it has actually encouraged the practice in notable instances through mandatory legislation such as the railroad Full-Crew Law.

"Fringe-benefits" should have been considered long ago by management as a part of wages. Some benefits are justifiably an obligation of management; others are in a questionable category; still others find their justification purely in economic pressure. Increasingly these "benefits" have become problems for management. They will be discussed more fully in Chapter 21.

Labor-management negotiations, irrespective of the subjects considered, involve problems which are predominantly human. A large section of management increases its labor problems by putting them in the legal category and employing only those learned in the law to assist in their settlement. Experience shows definitely that the use of legal assistance in direct negotiation of heated disputes with organized labor is usually detrimental to both sides. What is needed is negotiation and arbitration, neither of which is advanced by legal pleading.

Marketing

Price fields and sales outlets are important management problems. Should the concern make or deal in low-, medium-, or high-priced merchandise? The low-price field requires less capital investment in materials and often in mechanical equipment; its production cycle is shorter; and, consequently, turnover is faster. Profits are smaller on a unit basis, but production volume is greater; hence total net profits are usually commensurate on equal sales volumes. The high-price field is customarily more difficult to break into, but the low-price field always has greater competition, partly because more beginners start on that level in order to avoid high capital requirements. The medium-price field has a combination of the advantages and disadvantages of the upper and lower price fields.

The scientific method for appraising the comparative opportunities at the various price levels involves primarily a survey of the supply and demand for the commodity at different levels of quality. If the concern is new, such a survey may find a solution to the problem, assuming that financial backing is available for any price field. If the concern is not new, other factors will be involved. To what extent will it have to invest in new machinery for

---

[3] On a large underwater construction job in Atlantic City, the union insisted that the contractor employ a "pressure inspector" for the benefit of the workers, at an attractive daily stipend. After the contractor discovered that the inspector was doing his caisson inspection on the surface, he insisted that the function be performed in the air chamber. The pressure inspector resigned; he had never been in a caisson and did not care to share such a risk with his labor brothers. On a hotel construction job in the same city, the union insisted that a steel rigger ride along with the driver from the railroad yards to the construction job "in case a beam falls off the truck."

production in a new price field? What are the comparative demands for production floor space? What are the territorial limits within which the various quality levels can be distributed? This question involves a comparison of values and bulk with transportation costs. Will the new equipment be of a special or general type? If special, then the extent and continuity of the market are essential considerations.

After a price level has been established, the sales channel must be determined. Manufacturers' sales agents, wholesalers, jobbers, retailers, and direct selling to consumers are some of the possibilities. A combination of two or more such outlets may be the solution. Even if it is decided that direct sales to consumers will result in the largest net profit, there are still at least two further possibilities — solicitation by catalogue and mail order, and door-to-door sales.[4]

If the manufacturer, jobber, or retailer is successful in attaining a wide distribution, a protecting trade-mark may become a valuable asset. The use of a trade name may also influence the sales channel to be used.[5] If a trade-mark is used, should all orders be solicited from jobbers and retailers under that label, or should some of the merchandise be sold under the trade-mark of the purchaser? These are merely a few of the outstanding problems of marketing.

Purchasing

The first problem in purchasing is whether buying should be centralized in a separate department on a functional basis or be done by the individual departments of the concern. In department stores, it is customary for the sales-department heads to do their own buying. The purpose is to fix responsibility for sales. The same practice holds in wholesale establishments. On the other hand, it is customary for some concerns to concentrate buying in a special department. This method often obtains better prices and quality, more prompt delivery, and better service from vendors, besides keeping total inventories at a reasonable minimum.

Whether buying is done on a functional or a departmental plan, there is always the question of controls. Shall purchases above a fixed amount be subject to the scrutiny of superiors? If so, what is the maximum amount which shall be allowed buyers on their own initiative? Above that maximum, shall purchases be reviewed by a vice-president or by a committee? Shall purchases be made on a monthly basis or by annual contracts? Shall prices be on a contractual basis or at the market level? What arrangements

---

[4] Fashion Frocks, Inc., of Cincinnati, uses the door-to-door sales plan for dresses in the low-price field. Florida Fashions, Inc., of Orlando, operating in the same price field, sells through mail orders solicited by seven catalogues mailed throughout the year. Both plans are successful.

[5] Because of its widespread sales, Sears Roebuck uses several trade names for items produced for it by other concerns on a contractual basis.

shall be made for inspection and possible adjustment if items are unsatisfactory?

There is also the question of whether the purchase of certain large
quantities, especially raw materials, shall be made by some specialist or a
committee rather than by the director of centralized purchasing. To what
extent should company policy permit speculation in the purchase of raw
materials? How should purchasing quotas be established — on a production-
cycle basis or otherwise for industrial concerns, on a seasonal or some other
basis for retailers and jobbers?

Should purchasing be made by sealed bids or by personal negotiation
with the vendors? For obvious reasons, public institutions lean toward the
sealed-bid plan, while private concerns feel that they can get better prices
by negotiation.

Buy or produce?

Most jobbers and retailers buy their merchandise, although there are
outstanding exceptions among large concerns which manufacture at least a
part of the goods they offer for sale. The problem is more difficult for
manufacturers, where it applies mainly to parts (components). Should
certain parts be bought or made, and what circumstances should be considered in arriving at a decision?

Quality being equal, price would be a primary consideration unless
special circumstances dictate otherwise. For example, it might be thought
inadvisable to have some work done outside the plant because of the desire
to have its composition or nature remain confidential. Or quality may be so
important that the concern does not care to take the risk of having the job
done on the outside. Assurance of delivery is always important, especially
in assembly work where time is of the essence. Failure to deliver on time
not only may increase unit costs but also will result in delayed delivery to
customers.

When general business conditions are dull, outside contractors will be
likely to give a favorable price, prompt deliveries, and a product that meets
rigid specifications. What will happen during boom periods when a manufacturer depends on contracting out a large share of his components? Price,
quality, and delivery may all suffer to the detriment of the buyer.

Another consideration is the cost of the equipment necessary to make the
desired parts or components. If production involves expensive machinery,
possibly of a specialized nature, the capital expenditure may be inadvisable
or even impossible. Here the question of volume would have some weight
in the decision. If, on the other hand, idle general-purpose equipment is
available for making the part, the decision is simple.

Besides the necessary machinery and equipment, there is the problem of
getting employees capable of doing the work. If production of parts neces-

sitates extensive training of present employees, or the hiring of capable workers, the advisability of contracting on the outside is suggested.

Again it may be that the part in question is so highly specialized that it is difficult for the buyer to know whether he is getting a fair price. If the machinery investment is not too great and the problem of finding qualified workers not too difficult, it may be well to make some of the desired components. This solution will give the concern some first-hand data on costs. It will also be in position to improve the production processes and pass on such ideas to the supplier of the other parts. In addition, the user will not be in a complete dilemma when boom conditions cause the outside contractor to raise his price, slow up on his deliveries, or cut the quantities. The user will have an opportunity to increase his production of the item by expanding facilities, especially since he already has experience with its manufacture.

From the foregoing suggestions, it is clear that management's decision whether to buy or produce parts or components is not an easy one. Before reaching a decision, all of the elements must be weighed in accordance with the special situation.

Specialization versus diversity

This problem asks the question: Should a concern concentrate in making and/or selling one or a few products, or diversify its line into a larger number of items? There are the further questions of how extended the diversity should be and to what extent the products considered should be of similar or different natures.

Some years ago, the canny Scotsman, Andrew Carnegie, announced the business principle of "put all your eggs in one basket, and then watch the basket." It is obvious that specialization leads to improved production "know-how" and lower unit costs. Since marketing has also become a highly technical function, specialization in production would appear to promote sales. On the other hand, it is contended that a "full line" of a given commodity or a wide variety of items in related fields increases the salesman's opportunity to interest his prospect. Should the brush manufacturer add floor wax and furniture polish to his product line?

Diversification is prompted by three sets of circumstances. One is to meet the competitor's offerings, another is to invest free funds, and the third is to erect a protective economic covering for those periods when sales fall off generally, or when one or two lines are adversely affected by changing public habits or styles.

Wholesalers promoted a vertical expansion of their lines before retailers in specialty lines caught the idea. During World War II, when it was difficult for retailers to buy many kinds of consumer goods, they turned to diversification. They bought anything that was avaliable and added it to their stock in trade. Gasoline stations became small shops for gadgets of all kinds. Drugstores expanded into small department stores.[6]

General Motors is an outstanding example of production diversification. It started as a producer of motor cars and trucks and first diversified by buying the production facilities and trade rights of other automobile manufacturers. Then it expanded into the production of goods in allied lines, either starting from scratch or absorbing established producers. Production of brake linings is an example of its expansion into an allied line. Subsequently, it went out of its original field altogether and added plants for making such things as powdered metal parts, electric motors, and refrigerators. Currently it has more than 100 plants in this and other countries producing an almost countless number of items. So spread out is its empire that organization is an important management problem.

One of the chief pitfalls of diversification of dissimilar lines flows from the corporate desire to invest large cash balances in a relatively short time. Expansion involves the human frailty of prestige. Too often the urgency of this craving for prestige leads to rash decisions which more thorough investigation would have dubbed unwise. This is particularly true when new plants, new machinery, and new managerial skills are bought on the open market in contrast to absorbing plants already in operation. Additional operating funds, access to needed raw materials, and the necessity for steady distribution are a few of the added problems, whether the expansion is an addition to the existing plant or an additional plant manufacturing a dissimilar product. Effective management becomes more difficult as diversity is extended into multiple-plant operations involving the production of dissimilar products.

In conclusion, it is suggested that before a company decides to add a new type of product, it should consider such questions as the following:

1. Will the new product make use of some of the existing machines and equipment?
2. Does the company have enough of the management and worker know-how to avoid an extended period of experimentation?
3. Is there a sufficient and available market, subject to penetration, in which to dispose of the new product profitably?

Machine replacement

The replacement of machinery and equipment is a continually recurring problem for management. Its solution depends on two groups of factors. One group is subject to more or less exact financial measurement, while the

---

[6] An outstanding example of diversification in the drug business is the "Webb City" concern at St. Petersburg, Florida, advertised as "the largest drug store in the world." It is spread over several contiguous stores with two or three floors in various sections, offering everything from ladies' wear of all kinds to tonsorial services. It also sells drugs!

other must depend largely on management's judgment. An example will best explain this problem.

The production superintendent wants to replace an old machine with a new model because he believes the old machine has become obsolete. Management has two problems in the direct financial category. One is the comparative annual operating costs of the old and the new machines; the other is liquidation of investment in the new machine. The cost price of the new machine is $12,000, and its life expectancy is ten years. Its salvage value is estimated at $2000. The annual depreciation is, therefore, $1000 — $10,000 spread over a ten-year period.

The company is also entitled to interest on its investment in the new machine. One idea is that interest on the annual investment should be at the same rate the company has to pay for borrowed money. The other contention is that the company should charge interest at the same rate it is earning on its total investment. The company's bank borrowing rate may be 5 per cent, while its earning rate may be 10 per cent. Naturally, the 10 per cent rate is more conservative from the machine-purchase standpoint, so it is used in the subsequent calculations.

The other annual charges against the new machine include such items as labor, supplies, power, repairs, space used, and apportioned factory overhead. Calculation of the estimated annual cost of the new machine is shown in Table 2.1.

The original cost of the old machine was $10,000, and its life expectancy is estimated at ten years. It has already been in operation for seven years. Its salvage value at the end of its three more years of life is $1000, and its present worth is $4000. Since it has three more years of useful life, its annual depreciation charge will be $1000 after allowance for a salvage value of $1000. The total annual costs of operating the old machine are also shown in Table 2.1.[7]

Table 2.1 tells us that if our method of estimating the operating costs of

---

[7] The method of calculating the average annual interest for these two machines may need a word of explanation. This figure ($750 for the new machine, $300 for the old) is obtained by adding the interest on the present value of the machine to the interest on the value of the machine during its final year of operation, and then dividing this sum by two. (For a new machine, the "present value" is, of course, the same as the cost of the machine — in our example, $12,000.) The value for the final year is the salvage value *plus* the figure for annual depreciation (since the salvage value applies only *after* the final year of operation, not during it). Thus, if:

$$V = \text{current value of machine,}$$
$$D = \text{annual depreciation,}$$
$$S = \text{salvage values, and,}$$
$$r = \text{rate of interest,}$$

then the formula for the average annual interest (i) is seen to be:

$$i = \frac{rV + r(D + S)}{2}$$

Table 2.1

Comparison of Annual Costs for New and Old Machines

COSTS OF NEW MACHINE

---

1. Depreciation		$1000
2. Average interest at 10%		750
3. Operating Costs		
a. Labor	$2000	
b. Supplies	100	
c. Power	200	
d. Repairs	100	
e. Space rental	50	
f. Allocated overhead	100	
Total Operating Costs		2550
Total Annual Costs		$4300

COSTS OF OLD MACHINE

---

1. Depreciation		$1000
2. Average interest at 10%		300
3. Operating Costs		
a. Labor	$2650	
b. Supplies	150	
c. Power	250	
d. Repairs	200	
e. Space rental	50	
f. Allocated overhead	200	
Total Operating Costs		3500
Total Annual Costs		$4800

---

the two machines is accurate, the company's total annual costs will be $500 less for the new machine, and its annual operating costs will be $950 less. Since both annual and operating costs are lower for the new machine, it is obviously a good buy for the company.

Those factors influencing machine replacement which do not lend themselves readily to such measurement include:

1. Available funds
2. Comparative quality of product
3. Demand for the product involved
4. Obsolescence period of the new machine
5. Flexibility in the use of the two machines
6. Degree of operating safety of both machines
7. Relative repair downtimes

The final management decision to buy or not to buy may rest on an evaluation of such relatively indeterminate factors as these, especially if the annual operating costs of the two machines are nearly equal.

Another accepted approach to the purchase decision is based on the time required for the new machine to pay for itself. Some concerns have a definite policy about the length of time allowed. For special-purpose machinery, the period may be as short as two or three years. For general-purpose machinery, where obsolescence is not so important, the standard repayment period may be as long as ten years. The annual operating savings of $950 for the new machine in our example are only a part of its profit-making potential. Assuming that both machines can make an annual operating profit of $1000, then the $950 annual operating savings on the new machine should be added to its annual profitability, making a total of $1950. On this basis, it would take about five years for the new machine to pay off its $10,000 net investment.

Break-even point

Management must always be concerned with the break-even point — the point at which expenses or costs are equal to income or sales. It can be plotted on a chart (the break-even chart) which shows the relations of sales to both volume of production and unit costs. (In nonmanufacturing businesses, "expense" is substituted for cost of production.)

The break-even point is not an ultimate goal toward which management strives; it is more in the nature of a mark beyond which management can call itself successful, and below which danger signals are raised. The businessman wants to know what volume of sales he must have at given unit costs of production in order to make a profit, which starts just above the break-even point. This is one of his pressing and often mystifying problems. The break-even chart does not give the whole story. When, for example, the break-even point is not reached, the chart does not tell whether the problem is primarily in the area of sales or expenses. But if it does not tell *what* is wrong, it very definitely says that *something* is wrong, and in this respect it is a valuable guide to be supplemented by management judgment in planning action for increased sales, or decreased expenses, or both.

The profit-and-loss statement has for many years been the conventional method of measuring management's effectiveness. Its chief defect is that it tells the story only at the end of the fiscal or operating period. The break-even chart shows the results in advance, based on varying conditions of sales and costs. The president of the National Association of Cost Accountants has called it "one of the most valuable tools in the management kit."

Since the chart's break-even point and the amount of profit or loss are dependent primarily on the unit cost of production, these costs must be computed as accurately as possible. There are three types of costs which relate to sales volume:

1. *Fixed costs* are those which usually do not vary so long as the company is operating. Interest, taxes, insurance, and depreciation are examples. To a large extent, such costs are beyond the control of management.

2. *Semi-fixed or controllable costs* do not vary directly with sales, but they can be regulated or controlled to a certain extent by management in relation to sales volume. Advertising, research, and salaries are examples of items which can be increased or decreased at the discretion of management or administration.

3. *Variable costs* are those which vary directly, to a large extent, with sales volume. Direct labor and materials, overhead, and the cost of sales are examples.

Since fixed and controllable (semifixed) costs are relatively stationary in their relation to sales at a given time, they are considered as constant in a simple form of the break-even chart. Variable costs are composed of groups of similar expense items which may be broken down for refined control purposes. Fixed and variable costs may be computed separately, or variable costs may be subtracted from total costs to determine fixed costs, which are sometimes considered as a lump sum because they have fewer components. Fixed costs are more difficult to allocate if the chart is being prepared on a departmental basis. To make further comments more tangible, a typical simple form of break-even chart is illustrated in Figure 2.2.

The horizontal axis (GF) represents units of production, and the vertical axis (GN) represents cost in dollars. The line GM indicates volume of sales, running from zero at the lower left-hand corner of the chart to full production at the upper right-hand. Fixed costs are indicated by the perpendicular distance between the parallel lines GF and BE. These lines are parallel because fixed costs are regarded as the same amount irrespective of the volume of sales. Controllable (semifixed) costs are also considered as the same regardless of sales, so they are indicated as the perpendicular distance between the parallel lines AD and BE. As has been stated, fixed and controllable costs are not considered as variable in the ordinary sense.

The angle CAD represents the rate of increase in variable costs, which rises as production increases. The line AC shows the rise in variable costs with increases in production. The perpendicular distance from the horizontal axis GF to line AC represents total costs for the amount of production at any point selected on the base line GF. The point O, where the "total cost" line AC crosses the sales line GM is the break-even point.

At the break-even point, sales (or income) equal the total cost of production (or outgo). The Angle AOG, referred to as the "loss wedge," shows

Figure 2.2

Break-Even Chart

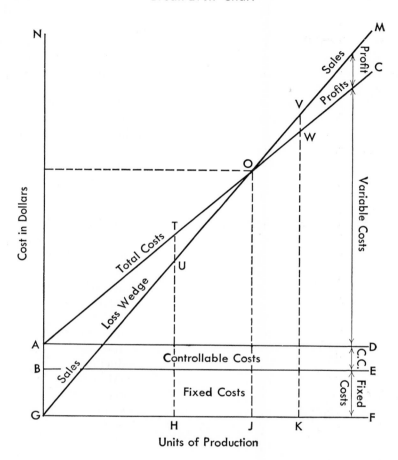

Units of Production

increasing loss from operations as sales decrease. In other words, it indicates the ratio of loss to decreasing sales. Likewise, the angle MOC, referred to as the "profit wedge," indicates increasing profits from operations as sales increase. It shows the ratio of profits to increasing sales. The loss resulting from the volume of production at point H is represented by the line TU, and the profit resulting from the volume of production at point K is VW. The volume of production required to break even is represented by the point J on the horizontal (or "Units of Production") axis.

The usual ways for turning a loss to a profit are by decreasing variable costs, or increasing sales, or both. It is assumed that some help can be had from controllable costs, but none from fixed costs. The managerial problem amounts to finding ways to decrease costs and/or increase sales. Obviously, any reduction in the unit selling price will require an increase in production sufficient to stabilize the dollar volume of sales; otherwise there would be a decrease in profits or an increased loss.

It may happen that severe competition compels lowering the selling price, or a growing demand makes it possible to raise the selling price. Figure 2.3 is a graphic representation of what happens to the break-even point under these two conditions.

Normally, the volume of production and, consequently, the variable costs will be increased by lowering the selling price. On the other hand, when the selling price is raised, normally the volume of production and, consequently, variable costs will be decreased. In Figure 2.3, line AC

Figure 2.3

Break-Even Chart Reflecting Changes in Selling Price

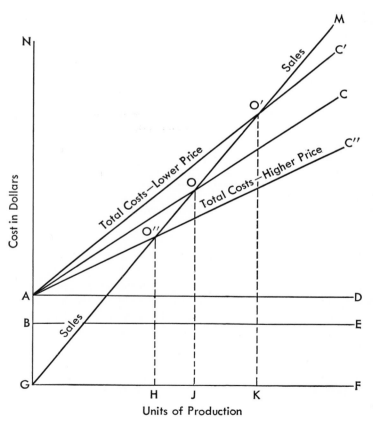

represents total costs at various production levels before either of the price changes. The break-even point is at O, where the cost line AC crosses the sales line GM. Line AC′ shows the rising variable costs as production increases at the lower price. The point where this line crosses the sales line at O′ is the new break-even point. Line AC″ shows the variable cost trend of different production volumes at the higher price, which would customarily reduce sales. Point O″ is the break-even point for this situation.

It is obvious, therefore, that a decrease in the selling price, with unit costs remaining the same, will require a higher volume of production to break even. Decreased variable unit costs may accomplish the same purpose as increased sales. An increase in the selling price will lower the break-even point if the volume of sales and variable costs are maintained.

The break-even chart may be used for still another type of problem.

Figure 2.4

Break-Even Chart Showing Results of Machinery Modernization

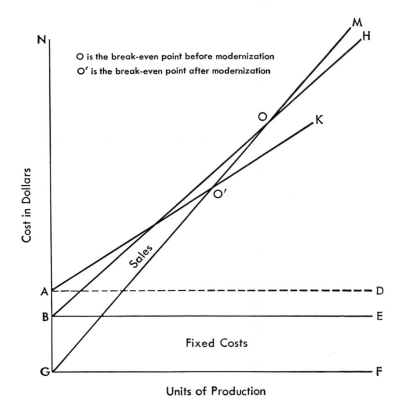

Units of Production

Instead of a single machine replacement as already discussed in this chapter, it is proposed to spend a large amount of money for machinery and equipment modernization, involving increased fixed costs for such items as interest and maintenance but decreased variable costs because of improved productivity. A chart such as Figure 2.4 estimates the profit or loss which will result and, hence, the desirability of the proposed change.

The chart shown is a simplified form but sufficient to illustrate the principles involved. In actual practice, there are other cost variables which may affect the result. For example, if a plant is operating on two or three shifts, the ratio of cost to volume of production might well vary among the shifts, making it necessary to draw the cost lines as curves or even as a wavy line. However, it is possible to determine the break-even point for each shift. Although most of the cost factors will be more difficult to determine with acceptable accuracy, comparative profitability of the different shifts can be shown graphically.

In Figure 2.4, GF represents units of production, GN the cost in dollars, and GM the sales. The perpendicular distance between lines GF and BE measures the sum of fixed and controllable costs before the expenditures for machine modernization. The distance between lines GF and AD represents the sum of fixed and controllable costs after the increase in capital expenditures. Line BH shows the increases in variable costs as production increases — before the modernization. The point O, where line BH crosses the sales line GM, is the break-even point.

The purpose of the modernization is to increase productivity and thus reduce variable costs. Line AK is the new variable cost line after modernization, and point O', where AK crosses the sales line GM, is the new break-even point, which should naturally be lower than point O if the modernization is well planned. When the costs are accurately plotted, the location of O' will determine whether the modernization should be carried through as planned.

Decentralization of operations

Most large concerns and many medium-sized ones give serious consideration to the problems of centralized operations. For many years it has been normal to increase plant size with each increase in production capacity. Recently, however, the advantages of decentralization through geographically scattered plants have become more obvious. Normally it should be easier for management to operate and control a centralized operation, but normality changes with the times.

Labor and markets have both been important considerations in the new emphasis on scattered plants. Living conditions for employees are often better in small communities, whereas large centralized operations tend to make over-sized communities. Labor relations have been found more congenial where small-unit plants have taken the place of a single large one. Also, community relations, a factor of growing importance in all lines of business, can be handled more effectively by relatively small units.

If a system of management combining decentralized command of operations with home-office centralization of policy-making and operations control can be made to work effectively, many of the objectionable features of multiple-plant operations are overcome. In justifying the decentralization of his company's operations into a number of small plants, Don C. Mitchell, president of Sylvania Electric Products, Inc., explained that the physical changes were part of a "policy of decentralization of manufacturing wherein line authority is out in the field and functional authority stays at headquarters."

The Sylvania company decentralized production in a number of small scattered plants, all but five of which have fewer than one thousand employees. The smallest plant employs 230, and the largest about 2900. The improvements reported are more flexibility in operations, better employee morale and community relations, and superior executive development because of more independence of action. In the labor field, managers of the small plants are closer to the workers than was possible under the former centralized operations and management.

Operating standards

Many concerns have only a limited confidence in their operating standards, and many more have no standards. In most cases, the various operating standards are based on company experience rather than on scientific analysis. Standards based on experience can be just as unreal as the experience itself can be out of line. In other cases, no recognition is given to the fact that standards change with the conditions that create them. Improved machines, equipment and worker training in improved methods call for new standards. The same is often true when materials or working conditions are improved.

An equally important problem with operating standards is worker acceptance. Unless the workers are convinced that company standards are honest and scientifically correct, they may do more harm than good in lowered morale. So there are two important phases to this problem of operating standards: they should be correct, and the employees must believe that they are correct. The first phase is a problem for scientific analysis, while the second is a problem of psychological persuasion.

Research and development

As yet, there are no laws or rules to determine whether the company should spend any money, and if so, how much, for research and development of products, methods, distribution, and many other activities of management. These problems still have to be left largely to the judgment of administration and management. The same is true with the distribution of research and development funds among the different categories considered.

It is now a well-established fact that most large concerns, and many medium-sized ones, attribute a large share of their success to product research and development. Many of these companies set aside a percentage of sales for research. Often research expenditures extend over a period of years before tangible results are obtained. Sometimes no usable results materialize.

For large and medium-sized companies, the problem is how much to spend on research and development and how to distribute those funds. For the small concerns, the problem is whether to budget any money at all for research and development. Occasionally they feel that if the large companies have profits from research, they themselves ought to institute research programs. But it may well be that those large competitors spend more on research annually than the total capital investment of the small imitator. In spite of the allure of large-company successes in the research field and of the special cases of small-company success, common sense suggests a distinctly conservative policy for the small companies.

Government regulation

It is almost impossible to listen to management men discussing their problems without hearing something about government regulation of business. Not only is the required reporting on a multiplicity of forms disturbing, but many official regulations, with their changing administrative interpretations, are worse. To the small company, the regulations are vexatious, confusing, and sometimes a source of actual fear. Many large companies have expensive special sections devoted exclusively to municipal, state, and federal reporting; reports to the federal agencies are the most exacting and time-consuming.

Business cycles

Finally, recurring business cycles, which have increased in intensity with the years, are a management problem which always threatens future planning. Why is it, for example, that the big steel companies have expanded their productive capacities with great reluctance in spite of the fact that the demands for their wares have increased periodically for a number of years? From bitter experience, they fear that a recession will find them with plant capacity far beyond their ability to sell. These cyclical economic storms are weathered by the large companies; for the little fellows, they are often disastrous. Smallness alone is accountable for some of the business failures in an economic crisis, but another cause is failure to consider the cycles in their planning, if indeed they plan beyond the demanding present. Large concerns — unlike small ones — can afford to employ economic analysts to advise them of the time and nature of future business cycles, with their possible effects on company operations, with respect to both volume and types of products. They can even afford to contribute to the leveling of certain types of recessions in their particular fields.

Conclusions

There are several broad considerations affecting management decisions about any of the problems discussed. In the first place, profits still measure, in a general way, the success of business operations. Directors and management feel bound by this criterion. Business losses may be temporary or chronic. It is the latter type which demands management's scientific analysis and best judgment. The welfare of employees, stockholders and the buying public are important considerations in making management decisions; so also is the prestige of the company. New office buildings are often constructed to satisfy management's desire for prestige, in spite of the fact that they may involve expenses not offset by commensurate savings.

Finally, public and employee welfare receive attention after an acceptable profit base has been established. Likewise, the prospect of losses has often interfered with the prosecution of such plans. The policies and actions of competitors are an important influence on employee welfare plans. While they are often adopted in the hope that they will result in increased productivity, the desire to reduce labor turnover appears to be a more compelling motive.

The mere mention of these considerations which demand management's most critical judgment suggests the involved problems posed by the "six pulls" discussed at the beginning of this chapter. The ramifications and interrelations of those basic interests are involved in many of the other problems which have been treated. The adjustments necessary for balancing the respective interests of these six groups underlie, in large part, the degree of success in establishing and maintaining profitable operations and expanding socio-economic interests.

QUESTIONS

1. How and why is problem-solving a measure of managerial ability?
2. To what extent, and in what way, do social, economic and political changes affect the solution of management problems?
3. What are the chief "pulls" on management, and what is the correct plan for satisfying the various group "pulls"?
4. Which are probably the two outstanding problems of modern management?

5. What is the relationship between the product processes and the required capital investment? How does the price level of the product affect the company's capital investment?

6. How can management determine the correct relative amounts of company debt as reflected in common and preferred stocks, bonds and bank loans?

7. What suggestion did President Kennedy make for the protection of labor against the pressures of technological unemployment?

8. What are the chief social and economic arguments used in opposing "featherbedding"? What is your reaction to the railroads' proposal to terminate the employment of approximately 140,000 workers?

9. Why is it that more concerns do not adopt door-to-door selling of consumer goods and thus save several middle-men's profits?

10. Several Latin American countries pay their purchasing agent a percentage of the cost of the purchases he makes for his company. What do you think of this plan, and why?

11. Which purchasing plan do you favor, and why — sealed bids or negotiation? Why do public agencies usually require sealed bids?

12. Under what circumstances is it usually desirable for a concern to make the components used in its manufacturing processes?

13. Since specialization in production usually leads to lower unit costs, what is the advantage in wide diversity such as practiced by General Motors?

14. What is the difference between diversity of production and vertical expansion?

15. What are the three questions that any concern should ask itself before deciding to add a new product to its line?

16. What factors should be considered before deciding on a machine replacement?

17. What is the purpose of the break-even chart?

18. How can the break-even chart be used to determine the advisability of machinery modernization?

19. What are some of the advantages accruing to large concerns through decentralizing their operations? How would you answer this question in reference to manufacturing companies: How big is too big?

20. How should a relatively small concern determine the amount it should spend on research and development?

CASE PROBLEM

THE MUNFORD MANUFACTURING COMPANY

The Munford Manufacturing Company is considering the purchase of an improved machine to replace one that may soon become obsolete. In addition, the superintendent feels that the new machine may reduce operating costs for the processes under consideration.

The present machine cost $6000 when it was new. It is now five years old, with a life expectancy of five more years. Its present value is estimated at $3500, and its scrap value at the end of five more years is fixed at $1200. Its annual operating cost is: labor, $2400; supplies, $200; power, $600; repairs, $120; space rental, $100; and allocated overhead, $150. In addition, annual depreciation and interest on the investment must be considered, the latter at 4 per cent, the rate at which the concern borrows from its bank.

The new machine will cost $15,000 and have a life expectancy of ten years, after which its salvage value will be $2500. Interest on the investment should be figured at 4 per cent, as with the old machine. The machine-tool supplier has estimated the cost of annual operations as follows: Labor, $2000; supplies, $50; power, $350; repairs, $50; space rental, $50; and allocated overhead, $38.20.

PROBLEM: From the facts given, what advice would you give the committee that makes decisions regarding the purchase of capital equipment? Would your decision be different if it were established that the new machine will have 60 per cent higher productivity than the present one? Support your conclusions.

3

Management Principles

It seems appropriate to discuss the generally accepted principles of management before elaborating on the various subjects they cover. This chapter brings together the major principles in preparation for their application throughout the book. Consideration of these principles as a group will help clarify the interrelations among them and show how they contribute to the general success of management.

Management, as we have seen, is the accomplishment of objectives through the use of men, money, materials, machines, and markets. Scientific management, in its practical applications, is the planning and organizing of activities for attaining goals; directing these activities for smooth and balanced functioning, or coordination; and finally checking them against established standards and plans, or control.

Modern management, however, is not an entirely materialistic institution, operating for profit alone. On the contrary, with each passing decade, business becomes more and more a social institution, sharing the results of its efforts with its owners (the stockholders), management, its employees, and the general public.

The stockholders must have a reasonable return on their investment, otherwise it will be difficult to raise funds from the public for corporate expansion. Management must be rewarded in some relation to its financial success in operating the business. The employees rightly expect a wage scale that provides an acceptable living standard with enough left over for eventual retirement. The general public looks for superior products at reasonable prices — usually cost plus a fair profit where cost is determined by reasonably adequate criteria. Taken together, these goals may be referred to as management's social imperative.

Laws and principles

Ever since management started to formulate guides for operating its various activities, there has been controversy among mature students of the field as to whether these guides are "laws," "principles," or "rules" and how many of each should be included in a given category. As a matter of fact, the controversy is often fed by a lack of common understanding as to the meanings of these terms. The dictionary defines a *law* as *a statement of an order or relation of phenomena which, so far as is known, is invariable under the given conditions.*[1] Well-known examples would be any of Newton's Laws of Motion which are invariably true under given conditions. The "law" is static as far as its application is concerned, but management is a dynamic concept. The principles which guide it must be related to changing conditions. Many who did not realize that fact have fallen by the wayside. It would not be reasonable, therefore, to expect to find a long lists of "laws" for management guidance. However, the late L. P. Alford, a recognized authority in the field of management, published a book entitled *Laws of Management Applied to Manufacturing* in which more than fifty such laws are discussed.[2] Alford undoubtedly had in mind ideas or concepts which we now generally recognize as principles.

A *principle* may be defined as *a rule of action, of general application, which exercises a directing influence on decision-making.* This is an adaptation of the dictionary's definition as applied to the field of management. A "rule of action" connotes flexibility, which is one of the outstanding features of management. The principle as a rule of action must be suited to the circumstances to which it is applied at any given time. In fact, circumstances may so change over a period of time that the principle covering them must be altered for general application. This then is the chief difference between laws and principles. Laws are fundamentally static, that is, they are always true under given conditions. Principles are essentially dynamic in their application to changing circumstances. Naturally, the latter are much more useful as guides to successful management. In fact, laws of management are decidedly limited. If it were not so, then managing would be placed, to its detriment, in a strait jacket. Such a condition would minimize the flexibility for guiding actions in many fields of management where changing conditions are the rule. For example, Taylor's *laws* of metal-cutting are as true today as when he formulated them, but there have been so many inventions of new and better tools, that his laws are now useless for practical purposes.

What has this to do with management which deals not simply with relations among material things, but also with human beings? Taylor's laws of metal-cutting were almost exclusively concerned with material processes, and it was for this reason that he was able to reduce metal-cutting to exact laws. When one introduces men and their motives as important variables, the problems take on quite different proportions. To say that a situation is

[1] *Webster's Third New International Dictionary* (Springfield: G. & C. Merriam Company, Publishers, 1961), p. 1279.
[2] New York: the Ronald Press Company, 1928.

affected by "intangibles" — as we will have to do many times throughout this book — is not an admission that the conditions are beyond the power of management to analyze and control. It is more in the nature of a warning that there is an area where we have not yet identified all the variables that may be operating, or that we are not able to specify all the underlying conditions and are, therefore, not able to formulate hard-and-fast laws to govern the situation.

One writer on this subject contends that there are "few laws of management, and there are relatively few principles of management, but there are many *fundamentals* of management."[3] The author of this objection contends that what most writers regard as principles are merely "fundamentals or truisms." There could be no objection to that statement, especially if "merely" is omitted as extraneous. Then he goes on to say that "to be a true principle of management, there must exist a general guide to thought or action; that is, there must be a statement of probability of cause and effect to guide a person's judgment in the process of decision-making, which is the essence of the managerial functions." Most specialists in the field of management would accept a statement of that kind as a definition of a management "principle" and still include the accepted principles listed in most texts as satisfying the definition. After all, a principle is supposed to be a fundamental truism. All of which merely supports what has already been contended — that the categorizing of laws and principles is a matter of definition.

A *rule,* as far as management is concerned, is *an instruction for action or behavior.* Every medium-sized or large company issues "Rules and Regulations" to govern the conduct of its employees. These rules are frequently found in the back of the labor-management agreement covering the relations between the union and the company. They have no uniformity as among companies nor within a given company at different times. Here are two examples: "Work shall continue until the fifteen-minute bell for clean-up." "No intoxicating liquor nor weapons of any kind are permitted in workers' lockers."

Science or art?

Management is a science to the extent that its accepted principles represent classified knowledge that can be used in making sound decisions that result in successful actions. It would be stretching the imagination to contend that management is a science to the degree that this is true of some of the older fields of knowledge such as economics. Some successful managers contend that management is simply an art, but it may be that they are only rationalizing their lack of training in its principles.

The author holds that management is both a semiscience and an art. It

[3] Leon C. Megginson, "The Pressure for Principles," in the *Journal of the Academy of Management,* Vol. 1, No. 2, August 1958, p. 7.

is a semiscience chiefly because it has not yet matured sufficiently to be accepted as a distinct field of classified knowledge. However, its group of accepted principles comprise a semiscientific tool for the manager. In his application of those tools, he calls on his art as a manager. Principles combined with art produce superior results. It may seem that the management exercised by an "inspired" leader is devoid of a conscious use of the accepted principles. But this successful leader is actually using many of the recognized principles without being conscious of it. Such a leader would be generally more successful if he were able to use the recorded principles more objectively and less as if they were personal discoveries.

On the other hand, it cannot be presumed that one who is familiar with all the principles of management will necessarily make a good manager. A professor may make it his business to learn something about management from the textbooks, and yet not be able to comprehend the art of managing. The successful manager understands both the science and the art of management. He is therefore able to get his subordinates to *want to do the things he wants them to do.* This is truly an art. Without the general consent of the managed, the manager won't get very far no matter how much he knows about the principles of management. The greater his authority and the more he relies on it for results, the longer he will be able to hold on, but eventually he will go the way of all unsuccessful managers.

An actual example known to the author was the president of a corporation with about 700 employees who knew neither the principles nor the art of managing. In fact, his lack of schooling combined with his personality make-up made it impossible for him to realize that there might be some fundamental principles behind successful management. Any opportunity for his display of the art of management was nullified by an unconscious feeling of inferiority which led to bursts of anger. He was dismissed because the stockholders resented his inability to show a profit, and because they had no fear of his resentment. He was too old and too sure of himself to learn what he should have known before he accepted a top-management job. The board of directors of this concern was largely culpable for selecting such an "unprincipled" manager in the first place. We will take a closer look at the responsibilities of the board in Chapter 34.

A final word on the "art of applying principles." It will be remembered from Chapter 1 that Taylor's principle of functional foremanship was found to be at odds with the principle of unity of command. Such conflicts among principles are not hard to find. This only serves to underline the importance of *flexibility* in the application of principles. "The fact is," says Henri Fayol, "that the light of principles, like that of lighthouses, guides only those who already know the way into port, and a principle bereft of the means of putting it into practice is of no avail."[4]

---

[4] *General and Industrial Management,* trans. Constance Storrs (London: Sir Isaac Pitman & Sons, Ltd., 1949), p. 15.

Evolution of principles

In the next section of this chapter, we shall present some of the most important principles of management. They did not come into being as a group with the scientific management movement. Some of them were recognized centuries ago. Alford and Beatty point out that the Chinese used the division of labor principle as early as 1644 B.C., and that the principle of the minimum wage rate was known to the Babylonians by 1958 B.C.[5] The history of the formulation of management principles has had a long evolution, but it was not until the inception of the scientific management movement that those principles began to be formulated and classified on a large scale. There are about one hundred principles of industrial management, many of them overlapping, in the writings of Taylor, Gantt, and Emerson. It should be noted that most principles of industrial management have valid application in other fields of management.

Management Principles

Presented below are the most important of the general management principles. They may be thought of as "operating" principles of management. In addition to this category, the first three — Unity of Command, Span of Control, and Homogeneity — may also be classified as "organizational" principles of management. These (and others) will appear again in Chapter 6 where they will be pictured on an organization chart. However, these three organizational principles are too crucial to the general-management process not to be included in the present list.

1. Unity of Command

Each member of an organization should receive instructions about a particular task from only one superior. In an organization built on the unity-of-command principle, each member knows to whom he reports and who reports to him. The chain of command applies to all layers of the line, staff, and service functions of the organization. For the purpose of exercising authority and responsibility, each person reports to one superior or supervisor. Unity of command makes both control and planning more effective. It aids in fixing responsibility for errors in judgment or action. It is based on the lessons of experience which point to the virtue, if not the necessity, of having a recognized chief for effective management and control.

If this rule is broken, says Fayol, "authority is undermined, discipline is in jeopardy, order disturbed, and stability threatened."[6] Someone has aptly said that a two-headed organization is a freak of management. Even

---

[5] L. P. Alford and H. R. Beatty, *Principles of Industrial Management* (Rev. ed.; New York: Ronald Press Company, 1951), p. 30.

[6] *Ibid.*, p. 24.

when two or three appear to have equal authority, there must be a *primus inter pares* to avoid confusion. This principle applies to the management of all types of organization and has been recognized for centuries in the church, the military, government, and business.

2. Span of Control

There is a limit to the number of subordinates whom a superior can direct effectively. The span of control[7] is variously fixed at from three to seven, depending on the nature of the responsibilities involved, the capacities of the superior, and his subordinates, and the distance between them. If this number seems small, it must be realized that the supervisor's contacts cover more than *direct* relationships with his subordinates. In addition, his *cross-*and *direct-group* relationships must be taken into consideration. That is, if a manager has three subordinates — Jones, Smith, and Brown — then he must pay attention to the relationship between Jones and Smith, between Jones and Brown, and between Smith and Brown; these are called the "cross" relationships. It may be that there are antagonisms between any two of these men which the supervisor should realize in assigning responsibilities. Furthermore, the supervisor will often relate himself to these three men as groups, rather than as individuals. At different times and for different problems, there are four different groups that can be recognized: Jones-Smith, Jones-Brown, Smith-Brown, and, of course, all three men together. These are known as "direct-group" relationships. Now it will be seen that the manager with three subordinates has ten relationships to consider: three direct, three cross, and four direct group.

The number of such relationships expands rapidly with the addition of each subordinate.[8] One authority summarizes the span-of-control principle in the following manner:

The ideal number of subordinates for all superior authorities appears to be four. At the lowest level of organization, where what is delegated is responsibility for the performance of specific tasks and not for the supervision of others, the number may be eight or twelve. The number of levels in any organization

---

[7] The span of control is occasionally confused with the span of management. Obviously "control" is a more involved task than primary management. While the latter refers to directives or orders based on authority, the former goes further by checking on performance and taking the required action to assure return to control when it is lacking. The span of management will be, therefore, much greater than the span of control.

[8] The Theory of Graicunas establishes the relationships of the chief to his executive subordinates. The formula for the number of relationships is the sum of the three types already mentioned. If A represents the number of direct relationships, then the cross relationships, or B, would be $\frac{A}{2}(A-1)$, and the direct group relationships, or C, would be $2^A - (A+1)$. The total relationships would be $A+B+C$. Using this formula, the total relationships for two subordinates is 4; for five subordinates, 41; and for ten subordinates, 1068. See V. A. Graicunas, "Relationships in Organization," in Luther Gulick and L. Urwick, eds., *Papers in the Science of Administration* (New York: Columbia University, Institute of Public Administration, 1937), pp. 181–187.

should be a minimum sufficient to permit of this distribution of subordinates. . . . The subdivision of activities into too few levels encounters far more dangers than their subdivision into too many. Centralization of authority should always be regarded as a necessary evil to be kept at a minimum. It is a passport to bureaucracy.[9]

3. Homogeneity

An efficient organization should group only those duties which are similar or closely related. It follows from the division of labor, which is really a law of nature, that every person or unit in an organization should be assigned a single major task as far as possible. The object is to get better results with less effort. Homogeneous assignments should be specific, should not overlap other assignments, and should be within the capabilities of the assigned worker or unit.

4. Delegation

Management is facilitated when all possible matters are reduced to procedural standards and plans, and assigned to subordinates for action. Exercise of the delegation principle relieves the executive of standardized operations, enabling him to give more attention to organizing, planning, and controlling. This improvement can be accomplished by delegation of managerial authority on all levels, including the foreman. The principle of delegation derives from the Exception Principle, which provides for executive attention to only those matters which are of an exceptional nature and cannot, therefore, be reduced to standard operating practices. The exception principle implies delegation.[10]

Furthermore, an unlimited span of control may easily lead to autocratic authority. Delegation is essential to the hierarchical form of organization, which assigns responsibility for entire functions to subordinate levels.

5. Planning

To secure satisfactory results, action should be planned. The development of a plan brings possible difficulties to the attention of the planner, making it possible to avoid pitfalls that might not otherwise be foreseen. Adequate planning visualizes the results before operations are started. Preliminary investigations may even lead to abandonment of a plan because of predictable obstacles. If it develops that the contemplated actions or procedures are feasible, then the plan points out not only what should be

[9] L. Urwick, "Axioms of Organization," *Public Administration Magazine* (London: October, 1935), pp. 348–349. Quoted in Elmore Peterson and E. Grosvenor Plowman, *Business Organization and Management* (3rd ed.; Homewood, Ill.; Richard D. Irwin, Inc., 1953), p. 117.

[10] To illustrate our earlier contention that many of the fundamental principles of modern management are of ancient lineage, see Moses' application of the exception principle (Exodus 19: 25–26): "And Moses chose able men out of all Israel and made them heads over the people . . . And they judged the people at all seasons: the hard causes they brought unto Moses, but every small matter they judged themselves."

done, but how, where, when, and, occasionally, by whom it should be done. A good plan promotes the confidence that helps lead to success. The importance of having a complete plan prior to action is so well recognized that some concerns have separate planning departments.

Taylor demonstrated that in industrial concerns prior planning of the day's assignment for each worker, even though it means paying money for full-time planning personnel, actually reduces the total cost of operations by eliminating the wastefulness that results when planning is left to the individual worker. This follows from Taylor's more general principle that management should assume at least as much responsibility for producing a day's work as the workman himself. When planning is left to the worker, the result is often no planning at all.

6. Policy-Making

Effective management requires policies that are definite, complete, and understandable. Policies are the precepts which guide administrative and executive decisions. They are based on the objectives of the organization for which they are established, and they are formulated by its administrative group.

Because policies are intended primarily as instructions for making managerial decisions, they should be capable of use in actual practice. Policies, like principles, are fundamental guides to action, and they should be accorded that degree of stability which makes possible the accomplishment of planned objectives. At the same time, policies should have whatever flexibility is necessary to meet changing conditions. They should deal largely with fundamentals and only sparingly with details of procedure. Finally, they should be based on factual analyses rather than personal opinions.

If the organization is of considerable size, its policies should be contained in a manual for the guidance and instruction of those whom it affects. Policy manuals may be issued in sections for top management and for individual departments such as production and personnel.[11] Whether issued departmentally or as a whole, such a manual prevents many misunderstandings, fixes responsibility for errors of judgment, and aids in the indoctrination of members of the management team with company objectives.

7. Leadership

Wise leadership is essential to successful operations. Leadership is the ability to get things done by enlisting the efforts of other people. It is

---

[11] An example of top-management or basic policy would be: "Competitive prices shall be effective in all lines, quality and quantity considered." An example of policy for the Personnel Department would be: "(a) Every effort shall be made to operate the cafeteria at cost. (b) The company's athletic program shall be planned to include maximum participation of employees." Many large concerns also issue foremen's manuals, but these deal more with specific instructions than with company policies.

primarily a psychological attribute. The good leader is able to have his subordinates *want* to do the things he wants them to do. He can also maintain discipline and instill a spirit of cooperation at the same time. He finds ways to develop an *esprit de corps* that will allow the group to work together toward its common objectives in harmony and unity. Leadership, whether it is formal (official) or informal, is the personal quality which moves the organization on to the attainment of goals.

8. Staff Function

Management is facilitated in its directing function when there exists a staff whose responsibility is limited to the development of plans, ideas, and standards for use by the line (directing) personnel. Because of the increasing complexity of business problems in general and industrial problems in particular, top executives are making increasing use of staff advice. Complete investigation prior to decision takes much of the guesswork and subsequent failure out of executive decisions. Proof that staff services are desirable is found in the increasing variety of problems submitted to staff agencies.

The staff agencies have no authority over actions within the organization except under extraordinary and temporary circumstances, as assigned by the line superior. The only authority which the staff has is the authority of ideas. It may operate on its own intiative or on a referral basis, depending on the authority assigned to it.

9. Balance

The effective management of an organization requires that its various subdivisions be assigned the authority merited by their importance to the accomplishment of over-all objectives. Balance should be sought in both the internal and external activities of the concern, but balancing the internal subdivisions will generally be found more difficult. Lack of balance is more prevalent than generally believed. It arises from the fact that many top executives reach their positions from continued and successful leadership in one of the company's main spheres of activity, such as sales, personnel, production, or the controller's office. Long experience in any one of these may give them an exaggerated idea of the importance of the activity which they previously managed.

It is for this reason that over-all top managers are difficult to find. The top executive should play no functional favorites, lest the management of the organization be thrown out of balance. This lack of balance often happens, for example, when the director of sales is promoted to president. His lack of experience in other fields is likely to lead to an undue emphasis on the importance of sales for company success. As a result, the sales portion of the budget becomes lopsided.

10. Coordination

The greater the specialization, the greater is management's need for coordination of men, materials, and machines. It follows from the organizational principles of management already presented above that as an organization is broken down into more and more subdivisions, with each unit performing a single task and each subordinate reporting to a single superior, the possibilities of chaos are enormous unless management is constantly attentive to the synchronization of these subdivided activities. Coordination, which provides for the timed dovetailing of all operations, is one of the most important of management's functions.

Coordinative problems are present at every level of management. The supervisor must see that the proper tools, materials, and supplies are available to his men at the right place at the right time. On higher levels, management must see to it that the operations of whole divisions and subdivisions of the organization are dovetailed. Not only must management provide for synchronized operations, it must also assure harmonious working relations among the personnel both within and between departments. In addition to this horizontal coordination, there is always the problem of synchronizing operations vertically among the various levels of management.

11. Responsibility and Authority

Assignment of responsibility must be accompanied by authority sufficient for its accomplishment. Conversely, responsibility is a natural consequence of authority and should exist to the extent that authority has been granted. Since authority is not only the right to command, but also the right to obtain obedience to commands, it is most unwise for authority to exist without correlative responsibility.[12]

12. Decision

Decisions should be made at the lowest competent level. Making decisions on the lower echelons of competency saves the time of superiors and is valuable training for those making the decisions. Furthermore, decisions can be made more quickly at the action levels because they do not have to go up through the chain of command for answers. It is understood, of course, that having the responsibility for making decisions does not preclude the right — and the wisdom — of conferring occasionally with superiors about these decisions. The right to make decisions usually includes the

---

[12] Some writers object to the word "responsibility" as representing the obligation of a subordinate to perform the task assigned by his superior. They prefer the word "accountability" as more truly expressing the subordinate's obligation. Their reasoning is based on the contention that the superior is always "responsible" to *his* superior, a responsibility which he cannot escape by delegation. This is perfectly true, but it does not prevent the subordinate's chief from holding him personally responsible for accomplishing the assigned task, which is, of course, only a part of the chief's over-all responsibility to his superiors.

right to standardize these decisions (when they are of the recurring type) in the form of regulations.

13. Standardization

Predetermined standards for measuring operations, procedures, and controls are outstanding aids in management. As the statement implies, standards may be used in most types of engineering, in production, purchasing, safety, inspection, procedures, and other management activities including management itself. The main purpose of standardization is assurance of desired results through control. To be effective, standards should consist of the kinds of measurements that are readily applicable to the situations they are intended to control. Management effectiveness is measured in relation to standards established for its performance. The information applied to such measurements is often obtained by means of an activity survey. One of the chief uses of standards in connection with production of any kind is the application of methods and time measurements required for proper performance. This type of measurement is applicable to activities in many lines of business.

14. Control

Management's authority is not completely exercised until it has checked compliance with its orders through the use of controls. Control is the process of assuring that performance corresponds with plans. Standards are the measurements used for control. When orders are accompanied by instructions, performance is being guided by the standards contained in, or suggested by, the instructions. These stated or implied standards can be used to measure or control performance. Control provides the means for determining whether or not, and to what extent, all the subdivisions of the organization are performing the functions assigned to them, and in the manner provided. It is a form of management inspection which measures performance against established standards. Effective control is practically unworkable under any system of divided responsibility. Centralized management control of properly grouped and delegated functions is the directing principle, while integrated responsibility for the application of standards is the tool by which control is effected. Standards are neecssary for control, and controls are necessary for balanced and coordinated management.

15. Flexibility

Ability to adjust to changing conditions is a measure of successful management. The ability to adapt policies, functions, and activities to changing conditions is part of the rational approach to management. Institutions are never static; they are moving continually in some direction. When management adopts a static attitude toward its own operations and their relationships, dry rot has started at the core and is spreading, whether or not it is visible on the surface.

Business is essentially dynamic and must be managed with that axiom in mind. No business will run itself. Progressive management continually seeks to anticipate changing conditions and adjust its policies and operations accordingly. The ability to adjust is the power to survive.

16. Facts

Action based on opinion will lose in competition with action based on facts.[13] This is simply a statement of the relation between rule-of-thumb and scientific management, including predictable success for the latter. The analytical approach, based on facts, is the accepted scientific method of all disciplines. Facts are, therefore, the basis for management's decision-making processes. Decisions must always be tempered by managerial judgment, but decision based on judgment alone is only rule-of-thumb management. All management problems must be approached by this fact-and-analysis method if consistency in decisions is to be maintained.

17. Human Relations

People perform better when they are recognized and treated as human beings. Fifty years ago, the significance of human relations to business was given little more than lip service. Today there are probably more pages being published on this subject than on any other phase of management. Increase in union power is only one of the reasons. A new recognition of the human element is noticeable all through society. This new awareness has given rise to so much social-welfare legislation that it is estimated that one out of every six persons now receives a government check for one reason or another. It is the reason for the establishment and support of the United Nations and such group interventions as the war in Korea. In this country, there has developed a strong "feeling for our fellow man," even when he lives far away and speaks a different language. Business became imbued with this feeling after it was demonstrated that the principle really pays dividends.

Practical experiments show that on the average, happy workers are the best producers. It took management a long time to learn that workers have similar motivational patterns. One often wonders why so many professionally unqualified managers will drive themselves long hours, subjected to intense mental and physical strain, only to enjoy expensive funerals long before their appointed times. Such behavior might well be motivated by the love of power, which is merely one phase of the desire for recognition.

All workers desire recognition. Although financial reward is a powerful urge for both workers and management, both are sometimes influenced by

[13] Henry L. Gantt, *Industrial Leadership* (New Haven: Yale University Press, 1916), p. 89.

tokens of merit awarded at ceremonies attended by their peers. Special privileges for long years of service and other signs of personal recognition are highly valued by most human beings. In many instances, management is more susceptible to the appeal of such symbols than the employees. Why is it that some members of top management, whose chief claim to fame is the accumulation of a fortune, are so pleased at the offer of an honorary university degree? One reason is its evidence that their merits are recognized in a field for which they have never felt qualified — a type of recognition all the more gratifying because it is unexpected.

We have already suggested that scientific management has become convinced that maximum productivity is achieved by workers who are relatively happy on their jobs. This sort of incentive is a far cry from the "this-or-else" method used by the now defunct bull in the production shop. It is also different from the paternalistic pattern of incentives, which traded a no-longer-wanted suit of clothes for extra hours at regular pay. The scientific approach, which is always the best at any given time, realizes that people perform better when they are recognized as human beings. The problem of management now is to find out what things appeal to workers while at their benches, not after the workday is over.

The five remaining principles to be presented here are primarily applicable to industrial management. However, it will be seen that they are relevant to other types of management as well.

18. Specialization

Specialization improves the quality of the product (or service) and increases output or productivity. Production specialization applies to the product, to the machines and tools used to produce it, to the job of producing it, and to the skill of the worker who is responsible for its production. The principle of specialization was consciously employed in ancient Greece. It was developed on a town basis in Europe during the medieval period, and it exists in this country on a spectacular level in Detroit's automobile industry.

Division of work is necessary to mass production. The greater the number of subdivisions, the more pronounced becomes the skill of the worker on any unit operation. Special-purpose machines and tools improve the quality of products and decrease unit costs through increased productivity. The skill required of the operator varies inversely with the amount of skill which has been transferred to the machine. Product specialization, which is the reduction of the number of kinds and sizes of goods to be produced, improves quality and lowers unit costs. The same result is obtained where businesses or plants specialize. Finally, management specialization at the middle and lower levels means narrowed responsibility and increased efficiency.

19. Simplification

Elimination of unnecessary procedures, and the utmost simplification of those required, reduces human effort and improves managerial effectiveness and control. Simplification is achieved through the breakdown and analysis of activities, methods, procedures, functions, and systems. It seeks to find the "one best way" by combining, eliminating, substituting, and changing the sequence of elements or factors in a given method, procedure, or operation. The simplest way is usually the best. Large concerns use unnecessarily elaborate methods and procedures more often than the smaller; hence, large operations often offer the most fertile field for simplification analyses.

In small concerns, necessity alone makes for simplicity. That is one of the reasons why they can compete against large-scale operations. Simplicity of methods and procedures, the ability to make quick decisions, and the superior service born of direct customer contacts all contribute to the efficiency of small concerns. The antithesis of managerial simplicity is red tape, which is usually found in most abundance in large institutions.

20. Individual Productivity

A worker attains his best productivity when assigned to the work of his highest skill, either natural or acquired. This statement appears to approach the universality of a law. Everyone is less discontented when engaged in the type of work he can do best. His positive attitude toward the job induces a high degree of skill in performance, resulting in the best quality and quantity of which he is capable. Most natural skills can be improved through adequate training. They can be further improved through good working conditions and relative freedom from economic pressures. These attributes for promoting individual productivity with acceptable quality apply to all employee levels from the unskilled worker to the top executive.

21. Task and Accomplishment

The average worker accomplishes most when assigned a definite amount of work to be done in a given time. This principle comes directly from Frederick W. Taylor. Examples of its application are found everywhere. It is the exceptional person who can arrange his day-to-day activities efficiently when he has only a long-range target to shoot at. In the majority of cases, better results are obtained when long-range objectives are broken down ino a series of short-range goals. Many students are lost without definite daily assignments. Examination grades in specific courses are far more likely to provide a student with an incentive for performing assigned tasks than the more general goal of success in college. In the same way, the daily task assignment in industry has been found to produce the best results.

The quality set for the assigned task is just as decisive as the quantity. If the type of assignment is beyond the ability of the worker, his discontent will make average performance impossible. If the task is beneath his ability, he will lose interest, and the lack of motivation is likely to show up in poor results. To provide the proper stimulus, the work assignment should be of the quality and quantity that will bring the employee's highest ability into play while working at his normal speed.

22. Incentives

Incentive wages must be based on standards of accomplishment. Workers should be financially rewarded when they accomplish the standard task. The standards should be such that the average worker can meet them while working at a pace which he can maintain without unnatural fatigue. Taylor's incentive philosophy made it costly for the worker who did not meet the standard production times. The present incentive-wage philosophy guarantees the worker the hourly rate for his wage classification even when he fails to meet standard production times.

Experience has shown that the average worker produces more under the stimulus of financial incentives if he is convinced that the production-time standards are fairly set. To take advantage of this principle, management should set time standards only after working conditions and methods as well as machines, tools, and materials have been geared to continuous production with favorable results. Equally important is the continuity of assigned time standards, unless some important factor such as materials, methods, machines, or working conditions has changed considerably. There is no general agreement as to the extent of change necessary for retiming. It can be assumed that both the workers and management should be reasonably satisfied that a change in the standard is advisable.

There are financial incentives other than those based on standard production times, and there are also employee incentives that have no direct relation to financial considerations. All types of incentives improve productivity if they are adaptable to the type of work and worker involved. This is one field where ready-made plans will be unsatisfactory in most cases; they must be tailor-made to fit the circumstances they are meant to serve.

Conclusions

It is important to recognize the distinction between a principle and a law. The latter is a fixed truth, while the former is a fundamental guide for making policies and carrying on operations. Principles must not be inflexible to the extent of stifling progress. They should be adjusted periodically to long-term and important changes. In practice, principles are the working tools of scientific management. As Gantt suggested, management based on scientific methods is as valuable as the plant or its equipment. Principles make up the core of scientific management, which develops systems to assure the execution of its purposes.

Some of management's principles can be applied in any endeavor where two or more persons are trying to effect a common purpose. Unity of command is a principle of universal application. So is the principle of span of control in large group efforts. The person who does not know how to delegate responsibility with adequate authority is no manager. His effectiveness is curtailed to the extent that he tries to do the entire job himself. The principles of human relations and planning are important factors of most operations and vital parts of one that extends over a long period of time.

Well-defined and properly communicated policies aid the coordination of mutual effort, which is one of the outstanding principles of management. Wise leadership not only values highly the coordinative principle, but it leans heavily on staff assistance for important decisions. It soon learns that decisions based on factual analysis are superior to those based on the authority of position.

Individual initiative, which is usually one of the assurances of success, is stimulated by various incentives, one of which is the practice of having decisions made at competent action levels. Initiative must be checked by effective managerial controls for measuring compliance with policies and instructions. By isolating exceptional cases for the attention of superiors, managerial time is saved for planning and organizing.

There are other management principles in the making based largely on a growing new relation between applied economics and management, a trend which is evidenced by an expanding literature cutting across the two fields. The growth of cooperative plans in both buying and selling is one influence of economics on management. The separation of ownership and management in medium-sized and large concerns is an almost completed shift which requires new principles for its control. Cumulative voting at annual stockholders' meetings is one attempt to obtain some limitation on the power of the proxy. The mutual rights and obligations created when financial interests other than risk capital dominate both owners and management are not currently guided by any principle of management. Finally, to what extent are new principles of management required for controlling the new business bureaucracies for the mutual interests of the employees, the owners, the general public, and management?

QUESTIONS

1. What is the difference between a management theory and a management principle?
2. Give some examples to indicate that industrial management is becoming less materialistic and more social as an institution.
3. Why are principles rather than laws preferable for managing a business?
4. What is the relationship between the science and the art of managing?

5. How did the principles of management become formulated?

6. How did Taylor's functional foremanship violate the Unity-of-Command principle?

7. The Roman Empire had a tripartite ruling groups, with the understanding that one of the three was *primus inter pares* — first among equals. Though this plan violated the Unity-of-Command principle, what contributed to its success?

8. Which rationalization of the Span of Control do you favor? Or are you unwilling to accept any plan as an over-all guide, and if so, why?

9. If you accept the principle of Homogeneity, what would you do in a situation where the concern's treasurer dies and no replacement can be found either within or outside of the company?

10. What, if any, duties should the general manager of a corporation NOT delegate?

11. Should company policies be made by the management team? If not, then what would you advise in a situation where the company has an inside board — entirely composed of members of management?

12. How would you define "leadership"?

13. Under what circumstances, if any, should a staff officer assume line functions?

14. What is the relationship between specialization and coordination?

15. What is the relationship between authority and responsibility?

16. What is the purpose of managerial control over activities?

17. How would you prepare a plan for making workers happy *on the job,* thus leading to increased productivity and lower unit costs?

18. What is the relationship between simplification and unit costs?

19. What is the purpose of definite task assignments in spite of the risk that they may lead to pegged production?

20. Do you believe that financial incentives are the most influential in determining the quantity and quality of worker production? Why, or why not?

CASE PROBLEM

Henderson Products, Inc.

Henderson Products, starting as a small proprietorship in 1898, was reasonably profitable from its beginning chiefly because of Mr. Henderson's long hours of application to details. A natural mechanic, he organized his inventive proclivities for making various components for the electrical trade. Although he had no formal engineering training other than that gained from a correspondence course and trade journals, confidence in his technical ability assured him that his business ability would carry him through to success as prospective customers experienced the quality of his products.

After some thirty years, Henderson Products, with 300 workers and sales approaching five million dollars, was incorporated. In the meantime, Mr. Henderson continued to hold all the reins of his maturing organization. He felt that the simple fact of incorporation presented no reason for any radical change in his organization or management of the business. The purpose of the incorporation, as he saw it, was to put his financial affairs in better shape for his estate, with the added possibility of saving something in taxes.

By 1930, the business included a well-developed engineering department, pattern shop, and foundry. Mr. Henderson continued to insist on surrounding himself with what he was pleased to call "practical" supervisors, probably as a defense mechanism. It was quite natural for him to feel that his financial success put the stamp of approval on the methods he used. In line with his intuitive decisions, he hired a helper for the foundry superintendent as soon as Joe Davis made it clear that the load was getting too heavy for one man. To promote close cooperation between Davis and the new man, Mr. Henderson gave the latter the title of co-superintendent with authority equal to that of Davis. The new plan for supervision of the foundry was on a "share-the-load basis" between the two co-superintendents, rather than any functional division of the work.

The foundry organization included five foremen, all of whom reported to which-ever co-superintendent was available at the time. One of the foremen had a particularly heavy load compared to his fellow workers. His exacting duties of melting metals, sand mixing, and service to coremakers were more than a match for his mental ability, a situation which occasionally resulted in loss of materials.

The supervisor of the engineering department, Norman Baker, was a trade-school graduate. Mr. Henderson respected Baker's training background because he felt that it had not interfered with his practical approach to engineering problems. In fact, Baker was so sure of his position that he tended to make it somewhat of a sinecure by delegating most of the work of the department to his eight subordinates in whom he had such complete confidence that controls were largely eliminated.

Philip Best, superintendent of the pattern shop, was unhappy with his job because of Mr. Henderson's habit of changing the instructions and work assignments of several of the pattern-makers. Best made clear his resentment of Mr. Henderson's interference by telling his men that he would fire anyone who failed to follow his, Best's, instructions in the future. When he complained to Mr. Henderson about the matter, he was told that he should be more appreciative of help offered in a friendly spirit.

Whatever the organizational arrangement, Mr. Henderson continued to hold all the reins. The corporate board of directors was made up entirely of management supervisors, with Mr. Henderson as president. All the members of this "inside" board owed their jobs to the Boss. As a result, Mr. Henderson never failed to get majority support for the suggestions he made at board meetings.

After two years under the corporation, several supervisors who always went along with the Boss at board meetings began to discuss grievances among themselves in private. This group gradually developed into a sort of kitchen-cabinet which fostered general discontent to such an extent that it finally came to the attention of President Henderson. The following board meeting resulted in an open break with top management, led by the pattern-shop superintendent. A motion was passed appointing a committee of three board members to discuss with Mr. Henderson the grievances that were now in the open.

PROBLEM: What were the chief causes of the trouble between the president and the unofficial group within the board? What suggestions would you make to correct the situation?

4

Quantitative Analysis
For Management

Every manager is a decision maker. In no other area of his business life
is he tested so frequently and with such obvious consequences. Short-run
decisions, long-run decisions; minor decisions, major decisions; simple decisions, complex decisions: the pressure to make them is great and constant.
In each case, a number of problems must be identified and solved before
decisions can be reached.

The wise executive supports in many ways whatever native capacity he
may have for good judgment. One is that he always follows sound principles of decision making. Another is that in solving his problems he calls
on the help of staff and specialists whenever they are needed. We will
discuss the general principles behind sound decision making in Chapter 35
when we take a closer look at the duties and qualifications of the Executive.
In the present chapter and the chapter that follows, we will examine briefly
some of the techniques used by a group of specialists whose skills are being
used with increasing frequency in solving some of the important problems
of modern management. These are the operations-research specialists with
their "tools" of Quantitative Analysis.

Quantitative Analysis for Management

Background

The manager's role as a problem solver is, of course, not unique to him.
Many other professionals fill the same role. A scientist busy at his desk or
in the laboratory is also a problem solver using his ingenuity to probe the
secrets of nature. The engineer, too, in his work on a new design is a problem solver applying the methods of science to the technical problems of an
industry. The similarity of the problem-situation processes of the manager

to those of the scientist led many to ask whether the methods of science might not also be applicable to the problems of management. The idea was not new. It has already been pointed out and will be emphasized frequently throughout this book that Taylor and his associates were trained in and used the well-known scientific method.

However, in recent years there has been a more pronounced movement in this direction partly as a result of World War II experience in applying science to warfare. It was the intricate problems of the military that gave impetus to the idea. Decisions had to be made quickly and accurately, yet the problems were so vastly complicated that only teams of specialists working together could provide solutions in time. Typical military problems involved the optimum size of a convoy under given conditions, artillery firing problems, and the best location for anti-aircraft defenses. Other problems facing the military cut across different disciplines, and as a result, economists, physicists, astronomers, biologists, and many other combinations of specialists could be found working together successfully as a team. The nature of the problem determined the make-up of the team. The technique was so successful that after the war some of the specialists who had been involved felt that the team approach might be applicable to solving problems of industry and government, and so, in fact, the transition was made.

Definition

Today, however, the Operations Research activity in industry rarely involves the use of these costly interdisciplinary teams. OR has come to mean primarily the application of quantitative, mathematical approaches to industrial problems. Probably no one definition of OR as it applies to industry is completely satisfactory, but the following definition offered by the Operations Research Conference of the Society for the Advancement of Management, at New York in 1954 is adequate:

> Operations Research is the exacting and critical application of the scientific method by *scientists and subject specialists* to the study of the basic laws governing a given operation. Its purpose is to give administrators a basis for predicting quantitatively the most effective results of an operation under given sets of variable conditions, and thereby to provide a sound basis for decision making.

When the "scientists and subject specialists" referred to above were asked to look at business problems far removed from their normal technical fields, it was natural that they should try the same reasoning and techniques that they had used with such success in their laboratories. The scientific method was closely followed. Many branches of mathematics and probability statistics were applied, and electronic computors were put to use. The results in many cases were highly rewarding. The similarity of many of the problem situations studied led to the evolution of specialized techniques, and these in turn brought a host of new words into the business vocabulary. Terms like "linear programming," "waiting-line theory," "simulation" and "mathematical model" were commonly used by the specialists — often to the bewilderment of management.

Quantitative analysis today

Quantitative Analysis has its supporters and its detractors. There are those who claim more for it than it is capable of providing, and those on the other hand who refuse to admit that it has any appreciable value. Each of these attitudes is a refusal to face facts. Quantitative Analysis is not a panacea, but it is a technique of great value to managers in making decisions. There are many strong evidences of its acceptance. While as recently as 1954 the average business school curriculum included no course work in OR techniques, today's curricula offer many such courses; and the majority of young Business School and Industrial Engineering graduate students are acquainted with the tools of Quantitative Analysis in greater or less degree. Virtually all consulting firms now offer assistance in the area, and some industrial firms have OR departments or their equivalent.

It has been said that not every firm will make optimum use of Quantitative Analysis, as is true of motion study, budgets, and similar innovations that have been in use for some time. But a failure to acquaint himself with new developments is not characteristic of the ideal executive, a point we will stress in our discussion of executive development in Chapter 35.

Everyone interested in the higher levels of management should be able to recognize the terms of Quantitative Analysis and to have at least a general idea of their nature and of how they can be useful to the manager. It should be remembered, however, that these techniques are specialized — sometimes highly so, sometimes less so. For that reason, our discussion of them in this chapter and the next must be simplified. But it will also be illustrative, and the reader who studies the examples carefully and tries to answer the questions at the end of each chapter will find that he has developed a rudimentary grasp of what these techniques are designed to accomplish. At the end of Part One, the interested student who wants to read further in the subject will find listed in the bibliography books devoted exclusively to the study of Quantitative Analysis and its methods.

Decision Making under Certainty

To give some order to our discussion of the techniques of Quantitative Analysis in this chapter and the next, we will divide them quite arbitrarily into two groups. In the first group we will include those techniques which are usually applied to problems where the result of a decision can be predicted with great certainty. The second group has been developed specifically for situations where the outcome of a particular decision is entirely uncertain or where it can, at best, be predicted with only limited certainty.

The Series E Bond provides an example in which both the cost of taking action (buying) and the results of the action (principle plus interest) are known with great certainty. This pattern is in sharp contrast to problems in which the consequences of the action taken are not certain. For example, in a purchase of stock, the cost is known approximately but the eventual dividend or sales price is subject to considerable variation. This distinction — between certainty and uncertainty or limited certainty — is a natural one for classification of the specialized techniques of Quantitative Analysis. In general, these techniques call for different analytical approaches. When the results of alternative actions are certain, the methods of algebra and possibly those of calculus will be adequate to the solution of the problem. When no one result can be predicted with certainty, the mathematics of probability and statistics will also be necessary in dealing with the problem. The problems involving limited certainty and uncertainty are more common. The techniques for dealing with them will be discussed in Chapter 5. In the remainder of this chapter, we will look briefly at the techniques usually related to problems involving certainty. (It should be pointed out in passing that some of these techniques could well be applied to either type of problem.)

The scientific method

Through many years of trial and error, the scientific method has developed as a system for problem solving. The method has many applications, and it will be referred to in other parts of this book. One possible statement of it as it is applied by the Quantitative Analyst is as follows:

1. Identify the problem
2. Construct a model
3. Derive a solution from the model
4. Test the model and the solution

Let us take a look at each of these steps in relation to management problems.

Identifying the problem. Identification of the problem would seem to be an easy starting point, but its simplicity hides the difficulty of achieving a fully acceptable statement of a problem. Whenever more than one person is involved in the discussion of a problem, it can be expected that each person will have his own view of the "real problem." Clearly the management scientist first must identify *the* decision maker. Next, a measure of effectiveness must be chosen. This measure must then be applied to the system under study to determine the success of the existing facilities, methods, etc., in achieving partial or complete effectiveness.

Most systems leave much to be desired in this respect, and regardless of how effective a particular system may be, an active imagination is always necessary in isolating the elements that constitute *the* problem of importance. Consider, for example, the difficulties in problems of inventory control. A firm may have a very liberal limit on total inventory and yet have trouble with stock outs. An extensive search may be necessary to locate *the* cause and to maintain an adequate level of service.

Constructing the model. Model construction can be considered as the identifying feature of management science. Models may take many forms. The most obvious form is the model which *looks like* the system. The three-dimensional models mentioned in Chapter 13 in connection with plant layout are an example. However, models need not look like the system to be useful. Many valuable two-dimensional models give little idea of physical appearance. An organization chart like that shown in Chapter 6 (Figure 6.1) and the flow process chart in Chapter 13 (Figure 13.4) are examples of two-dimensional models.

The models we have mentioned up to this point have great descriptive value, but it is not always convenient to construct them. An attempt to improve models in this respect leads to *less descriptive* but *more convenient representations.* Several graphical techniques such as the break-even diagram (see Chapter 2, Fig. 2.2), the quality control chart (see Chapter 17, Figure 17.1), and the Gantt chart (see Chapter 10) are examples of less descriptive but more convenient models. These models have descriptive value only to those who have become familiar with their method of conveying information. The data is represented on them by points and lines. The advantage of these graphical models lies in the ease with which they can be made to represent variations in the system and to allow simultaneous evaluation of each change. Thus a break-even diagram quickly predicts the profit or loss for a given sales volume, a control chart easily identifies significant changes in quality, and a Gantt chart can rapidly indicate an expected delivery time. In many cases, these conveniences more than offset the advantages of the more descriptive models.

A further level of abstraction is achieved through the use of mathematical models. In a mathematical model, all the variables in a system are represented by alphabetic or numeric symbols, and their relationships are shown by equations. Such models are a very efficient way of describing a system. However, the description is meaningful only to those who have learned the symbols and the operations that can be performed with them. Symbolic models are extremely easy to manipulate, either by hand or by computor.

We will take a closer look at examples of such models in this chapter and the following one.

Deriving a solution.   Once the system containing the problem has been represented in a model, the problem may be attacked. Deriving the best solution involves the invention and testing of a host of alternative solutions. The search for such alternatives is an important function of management. The testing of alternatives is the function of the *model,* but it is up to the *manager* to discover and define the alternatives in the first place. A good model permits the decision maker to test each possible decision without the expense of actually trying it on the firm.

Testing the model and solution.   Step one of the scientific method was to examine and isolate the real problem in a particular situation. Steps two and three involved representing that real problem in terms of an abstract model. At this point it is important to emphasize that *the solution is only as good as the model.* It is essential that every model and every solution derived from it be tested against the actual problem. Many methods exist for conducting such tests. Experiments can be designed using statistics to take full advantage of information generated by the trial run of a model. But such techniques are still costly. One ingenious solution is to test the model by imposing its solution on the firm's past history. That is, the performance of the firm is contrasted to the way the firm would have performed if the solution had been available in the past. Tests like these have proved of great value in demonstrating defects in models and their solutions. We will discuss this further when we take up simulation in Chapter 5.

Recurring problems and models

The quantitative analysis of management problems properly begins with the application of the scientific method. However, the repeated use of this procedure has often led the analyst to some already existing model or to a minor variation of a model for which a solution exists. A problem of production, or finance, or distribution might very well present the same mathematical form. Such similarities have led to specialized techniques for the solution of these common problems. We will now discuss some of these techniques along with some representative applications of them. It is apparent that if a given problem situation can be identified as fitting one of these techniques, an appreciable savings can result in the time necessary to formulate and solve the problem.

An inventory analysis

One of the oldest applications of quantitative methods to management problems is found in inventory control. A common problem is to decide on the order quantity and the order frequency which will minimize the annual costs. Certain inventory costs tend to increase with the size of the order. These are the costs associated with carrying a large quantity in stock. They include taxes and insurance on goods as well as interest charges on the investment in the goods. Other costs tend to decrease with order size. These include the costs of ordering and receiving a purchased lot or the machine setup costs for lots to be produced within the firm.

Figure 4.1 shows how these costs may be represented by a simple graphic model. The curves permit a rapid visualization of the effects of the two cost components. The sum of the two costs has been drawn and labeled as the total cost. If this drawing were available for every item used by the firm, it would be an easy task to select the most economical order quantity. This is the order quantity with the minimum total cost.

While the figure above permits ease of understanding, it has a common failing of graphical models in that it is not easily modified. To gain this advantage, the lines may be replaced by their mathematical equivalents. Notice that here we are raising a descriptive model to a level of greater abstraction. The line representing the carrying (holding) costs may be replaced by the formula $\frac{IQ}{2R}$ where I is the inventory carrying cost for one year, Q is the order quantity, and R is the annual requirements. The number 2 in the denominator comes from the fact that average inventory will be one half the maximum inventory. Note that by dividing by the annual require-

Figure 4.1

COSTS ASSOCIATED WITH ORDERING AND CARRYING INVENTORY

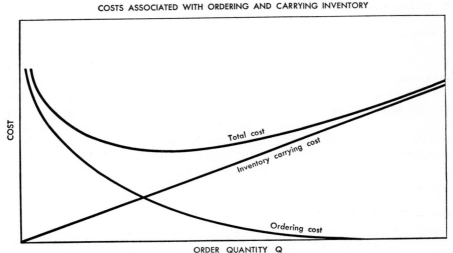

ORDER QUANTITY Q

ments the costs become unit costs. This is true where an equal amount of stock is used every day. Note that this is an assumption which must be justified before the formula can be applied. Such assumptions are common in mathematical analysis and they must always be justified in practice if the model is to provide reliable solutions.

The line representing inventory ordering costs can be replaced by the formula $\frac{S}{Q}$ where S is the setup cost for each order. With these equivalents

for the cost components, the total cost becomes $\frac{IQ}{2R} + \frac{S}{Q}$.

In order to see how to minimize the costs, it is necessary to find the minimum of cost curve. Ordinarily this would require the use of calculus. For this simple case, however, it happens that the minimizing order quantity coincides with the intersection between the curve representing the cost of ordering and the curve representing the cost of holding. Setting the two

cost components equal to each other, we find that the value of Q is $Q = \sqrt{\dfrac{2SR}{I}}$

Example: A store sells facial tissues at an approximately uniform rate of 10 boxes per day throughout the year. Ordering each lot costs about $2.00 for clerical work and stock handling. As the item is bulky, it requires substantial storage space which is estimated to cost $0.10 per box per year. The store is open 200 days throughout the year. How many boxes should be ordered? Noting that $R = 200 \times 10 = 2000$ and applying the formula $Q = \sqrt{\dfrac{2 \times 2 \times 2000}{0.10}}$, we find that our answer is 283 boxes.

This analysis of the inventory problem of order size is an uncomplicated application of quantitative analysis. No manager would have any difficulty in applying this formula to his problem. But the application is deceptively easy. For instance, what if the demand were seasonal instead of uniform? How good would the results be if this formula were applied? Consider the costs. Are they really variable with extra inventory, or is excess capacity always available? It is imperative in any application of an existing analysis that every assumption be verified.

Linear programming

Many management problems arise when more than one use exists for a given resource (e.g. time, money, or space). When these demands exceed the available supply, the manager must choose between the various possible uses. This problem is called "allocation." There are many extremely important allocation problems. A refinery manager must decide which oil products will be made from the incoming crude. A manufacturer must decide which customers are to be supplied from a particular factory. A feed manufacturer must choose among the various feed components which can go into his product. In each of these problems, the decision maker is limited in his action since he must live within the restrictions of his plant size, and his available finances or manpower.

Mathematical solutions to problems such as these fall under the general heading of what is called mathematical programming. One highly developed area of mathematical programming is linear programming. Linear programming is nothing more than a systematic or programmed way of comparing the results of alternative management actions. This system is applicable only when the problem restrictions and results can be plotted as straight lines (hence the term, *linear*). An example of a straight-line result is that plotted by the sale of a product when each additional unit sold brings one dollar of profit.

Let us look now at an illustration of a linear programming application.

Example: A firm manufactures two products requiring the use of three machines. The first operation is weighing and grinding, the second is blending and the third is packaging. The products require machine time as listed below for each 100 pound bag.

Table 4.1

	Minutes on Machine 1	Minutes on Machine 2	Minutes on Machine 3	Profit
Product A	1.2	3	2.4	$0.40
Product B	2	1	1.6	$0.30

These machines may run up to 480 minutes per day. The total profit for these products would be the number of bags of product A times $0.4 plus the number of bags of product B times $0.3. In mathematical form, letting A and B represent the number of bags of each product, one would write,

Total Profit $= 0.4A + 0.3B$

This is a linear relation. From it can be seen that total profit may be made as large as desired by increasing either A or B. However, in this problem situation, such an increase is limited because only 480 minutes are available on each machine. This restriction means that for machine 1 the number of bags of product A times 1.2 plus the number of bags of product B times 2 must be less than or equal to 480 minutes, the time available on machine 1. In the mathematical form, we would express this as $1.2A + 2B < 480$. Again this is a linear relation. Reasoning similarly for machine 2, $3A + 1B < 480$, and for machine 3, $2.4A + 1.6B < 480$. A graphical presentation like the one in Figure 4.2 will help clarify these restrictions. On the graph, the capacity line corresponds to reducing output of one product in favor of the other. In the extreme case, the intersection of each machine-capacity line with the product A axis represents the maximum

Figure 4.2

GRAPHICAL PRESENTATION
OF A PROBLEM IN LINEAR PROGRAMMING

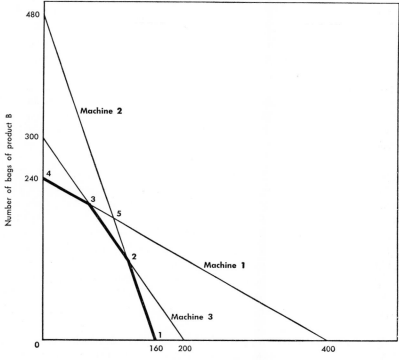

amount of A that can be produced within the limitation of the capacity restriction on each machine. In practice, all machine requirements will be met so that only points on the heavy line are feasible. The problem is to determine which of these points will represent the highest profit.

For a problem as uncomplicated as this, the potential profit at each of the breakpoints can easily be computed simply by solving for the points of intersection between each pair of lines and evaluating the profit for that point. For example, the student might begin by determining the maximum number of units produced on machine 1: $480 \div 1.2 = 400$ Units of A, $480 \div 2 = 240$ Units of B, etc. These results rounded to the nearest whole bag are given in Table 4.2.

To give some idea of the side benefits that can be realized from linear programming, let us look at a variation of this example. Consider the increase in profit which would be realized if the restriction on machine 3 were removed. This might be done simply by scheduling overtime on this

Table 4.2

Point	Number of Bags of A	Number of Bags of B	Profit
1	160	0	$64.00
2	121	118	$83.80
3	67	200	$86.80
4	0	240	$72.00

The tabulation indicates that the most profitable product mix would be 67 bags of product A and 200 bags of product B. This is point 3 on the graph. Such a solution is correct as long as all assumptions about prices and methods remain the same.

machine. If sufficient overtime were scheduled, point 5 would become the most profitable point. Point 5 represents production of 100 bags of product A and 180 bags of product B resulting in a profit of $94.00, an increase of $7.20 over the profit at point 3. This increase in production would require 48 [i.e. $(2.4)100 + (1.6)180 - 480$] minutes of overtime on machine 3. Such overtime is justified if its cost amounts to less than the resulting increase in profit. Linear programming can be of great value in obtaining solutions to problems like the one in this example. It can be of further value in analyzing the effect of changes in profits or methods. This flexibility of the linear-programming technique adds greatly to its value as an aid to business decision making.

For the problem above, no complicated method of solution was required. Consider, however, the difficulty we would have met in solving this problem if instead of two products there had been ten and instead of three machines there had been twenty. A problem of these proportions is beyond the range of feasible hand calculation. Fortunately, computors can be programmed to solve such problems. With the added help of the computor, linear programming becomes a convenient tool for the solution of a wide range of complicated management problems.

The following are examples of management problems in which linear programming has been successfully used:

1. Arriving at make-or-buy decisions
2. Deciding on the most profitable product-mix with the existing facilities
3. Scheduling operations to production centers to meet delivery commitments at the lowest cost
4. Determining equipment investments that will maximize profits
5. Locating warehouses for lowest transportation costs
6. Determining orders to be assigned to various plants in consideration of production and distribution costs

7. Arriving at equitable salary determinations
8. Maximizing profits in consideration of cost of plant facilities, cash, and inventory[1]

Linear programming has been called Purchasing's newest cost reduction tool. As a management-planning technique, it offers many advantages. In many instances, it will provide management with plans or solutions which will be superior to those determined by the older and more usual methods.

Transportation method of linear programming

Of the special cases involving quantitative procedures where there can be reasonable certainty about the outcome of a decision, one which is of particular interest is the transportation method of linear programming. It should be pointed out that the word transportation is suggestive of the use of this technique but in no way a limitation on it. The transportation method has been used with great success in many areas of manufacturing and distribution management.

In Figure 4.3 we see the elements of a typical problem which lends itself to solution by this technique. In the figure, the problem is presented as a choice between alternative programs for supplying the three warehouses from the two plants.

In a problem as limited as this, it is possible to guess the solution which will give the lowest cost of manufacturing and shipping. If plant 1 supplies 100 units to warehouse B and plant 2 supplies 75 units to warehouse A, 100 units to warehouse C and the remaining 25 units to warehouse B, the total cost of manufacturing and shipping will be $13.00. For example, the student might begin by determining that it costs $3.00 to ship 100 units from plant 1 to warehouse B ($3¢$/unit $\times$ 100 units), $6.00 to ship 100 units from plant 2 to warehouse C ($6¢$/unit $\times$ 100 units), and so on. Other alternatives can be costed out in this manner, but none will give a lower cost. Guessing, however, has its limitations. For instance, some of the can-manufacturing firms in this country have as many as 50 plants, which supply hundreds of food processers and other users. It is inconceivable that a guessed-at solution could be optimal or even a reasonable approximation of the lowest cost solution.

To simplify the solution for large problems, various computing procedures have been developed. One such procedure is the simplex method of linear programming. This is a very general procedure which may be used to solve problems such as the one given in the example under linear pro-

---

[1] Robert O. Ferguson and Lauren F. Sargent, *Linear Programming* (McGraw-Hill Book Co., 1958), pp. 10–11.

gramming. The simplex method is often the one used in computer programs. It may also be used to solve transportation problems.

Example: Let us add a third plant and a fourth warehouse to the conditions of the problem we have just described above. These additions complicate the graphical presentation, so the data is presented in tabular form (in Figure 4.4). Along the outer edges of the table are shown the availabilities at each plant and the requirements of each warehouse. Each rectangle represents a route from plant to warehouse. In the upper right corner of each rectangle is given the total cost of producing and shipping each unit for the particular plant and warehouse represented by the row and column. For example, it costs four cents to produce one unit at plant 3 and ship it to warehouse C.

In this problem, the measure of effectiveness is the total cost of producing and shipping 450 pieces, and the goal is to minimize costs according to the limitations of plant capacity and warehouse demand.

The cost function and limitations can be formulated as linear equations. Therefore, the general method of linear programming *could* be used, but

Figure 4.3

A Problem Involving
The Transportation Method of Linear Programming

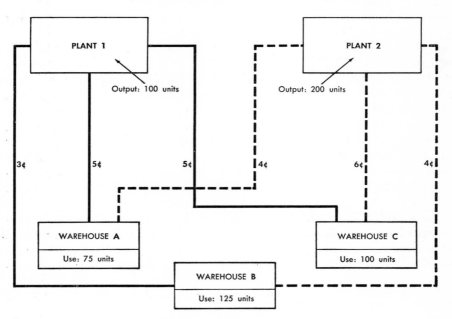

Lines,━━ and ━ ━━, indicate Production and shipping charge per unit

the method is unnecessary for this problem. The limitations equations would all have coefficients of either zero or one. However, a much simpler solution is possible, as we will see from what follows below.

In Figure 4.4 a trial solution based solely on intuition has been indicated by the circled values. The 75 in rectangle two of column one means that if this program were to be used, plant two would supply 75 units to warehouse A. Notice that all capacities have been used and requirements satisfied. To cost out this program, the quantity to be shipped by each route is multiplied by the cost of using this route. To perform this calculation we multiply and add as follows:

$(75 \times 4) + (25 \times 4) + (100 \times 6) + (100 \times 3) + (50 \times 2) + (100 \times 2).$

Our total is \$16.00, *possibly* the lowest cost solution.

The next step is to test this solution to see whether any change could result in a lower cost. Even if a better solution does not exist, it is possible that an alternative solution may be revealed that will show the way to some flexibility in planning. The testing of the proposed solution calls for the evaluation of each unused route (represented in Figure 4.4 by the empty rectangles) in terms of the net effect on total cost of shifting one unit to that route. This evaluation can be accomplished in several ways, the simplest being presented here. As an example, consider the route 3C. This route has not been used in the solution up to this point. However, if one unit were shipped along this route, the cost would be increased by four cents. To

Figure 4.4

The Transportation Problem with the Addition of
A Third Plant and a Fourth Warehouse

WAREHOUSE

	A	B	C	D	Output
PLANT 1	5	3	5	2 (100)	100
PLANT 2	4 (75)	4 (25)	6 (100)	3	200
PLANT 3	5	3 (100)	4	2 (50)	150
Use	75	125	100	150	

add one unit to this route would force one unit less to be shipped along 2C in order that the warehouse requirements remain satisfied. If this is done, a savings of six cents will result. This, in turn, requires an adjustment in other routes to stay within the plant capacities. The simplest adjustment would be to move one unit from 3B to 3C and one unit from 2C to 2B. Checking the costs of each of these shifts, it appears that the net effect of the shifts is $4 - 3 - 6 + 4 = -1$ or a savings of one cent per unit. In effect, our exploration of this alternative shows that it costs one cent *not* to use route 3C.

Each of the remaining routes can be evaluated in this way, assuming that one unit is added to the empty route and that the three other routes now figuring in our solution are adjusted so that the requirements remain satisfied. When this has been done, all unused routes will have numbers assigned to them representing the net effect on total cost of shifting one unit to that route. These numbers will be either above, below, or equal to zero. Each route having a value above zero will indicate that no improvement would come from using that route; on the contrary, the cost would be increased. Each route having a value below zero (negative) will indicate a route that should be used in order to reduce the costs. The program should now be modified by placing one unit in the route showing the highest reduction (greatest negative value). But since one unit can be moved with a cost savings, then as many units as possible should be moved. In the case of route 3C, up to 100 units can be moved. If this is done, the net reduction will be $100(\$.01) = \$1.00$. Each route having a value of zero indicates that that route may be used with no change in the total cost.

This process of solution and testing must be repeated until all unused routes are zero or positive. The change made above satisfies this condition, so no further improvement is possible. The $1.00 saving involved represents a 6.25% reduction in the production and distribution costs, a reduction that would result in significant savings for any firm.

This process may not sound particularly convenient. However, it should be remembered that a manager is not expected to perform these calculations. They have been simplified to the point where a clerk can be taught to carry them out in a relatively short time. Better yet, the process can be programmed for a computer. Thus, the effect is not to place an additional burden on the manager, but rather to make it possible for him to make important decisions in less time. In addition, the manager knows that the solution is as good or better than any he could have arrived at without the model and after far greater expenditure of his valuable time.

Conclusions for Decisions under Certainty

Unlike the physical sciences, there are relatively few management problems where the future is certain, and this would seem to reduce the usefulness of methods such as linear programming. Fortunately, however, there

5

Further Aids
in Decision Making

The outcomes of management's actions seldom match perfectly the predictions made before the actions are taken. This is an inescapable problem of management since all decisions affect the future, and the future is never perfectly predictable. But even though perfect knowledge of the future is not available, there are techniques of quantitative analysis that can help managers to select the best course of action. In this chapter, we will look at some of these techniques and will treat them under two headings. The first deals with problems involving limited certainty or risk. By this is meant situations where it is possible to predict many possible future outcomes each having assigned to it a *probability* that it will occur. The second deals with complete uncertainty where probabilities cannot be assigned in any *rationally* acceptable manner.

Decision Making Involving Risk

The majority of management decisions must be made to influence situations involving a large amount of risk. A production schedule must be set though sales for the given period are merely predicted. A machine must be selected when the period of use can be at best only crudely estimated. In such situations, solutions must be based on (1) the visualized possible future conditions, (2) the possible decisions that can be made affecting these conditions, and (3) the visualized rewards or losses associated with each of these conditions and with the probabilities that one rather than another of these conditions will come about.

A simple example will help to clarify this general statement of the task of managers in making a good decision in situations involving risk.

Example: A weekly news magazine goes on the stands on Friday. Most sales take place on that day while a lesser number are sold on each day following up to the next Friday. Any magazines left over are a total loss. It is not feasible for the news company to restock during the week. Therefore, it is necessary each Friday to estimate the best number of magazines to place on each stand. Each magazine sells for twenty cents of which one cent is profit. This must be viewed as a loss if a would-be customer finds the supply exhausted. Likewise, if a magazine goes unsold, the variable manufacturing costs of three cents must be taken as a loss.

Table 5.1 presents a simplified view of this problem.

Table 5.1

The Losses to the Company Related to Number Stocked

Number Stocked

		1	2	3	4	5
Potential Sales	1	0	3	6	9	12
	2	1	0	3	6	9
	3	2	1	0	3	6
	4	3	2	1	0	3
	5	4	3	2	1	0

The numbers in the body of the table give the losses for each visualized number of sales opportunities (possible futures) and for each number stocked (possible decisions). For instance, if four magazines are stocked and only two are sold, a loss of six cents is suffered on the two unsold magazines.

An analysis of past sales for an extended period, when a surplus number of magazines were stocked, leads to the following estimates of the probable sales.

Table 5.2

Estimated Potential Sales Distribution

Sales	Probability
1	.1
2	.2
3	.3
4	.3
5	.1

The expected loss for each decision can now be evaluated. For a decision to stock one magazine, the expected loss would be

$$0(.1) + 1(.2) + 2(.3) + 3(.3) + 4(.1) = 2.1$$

This is just the sum of the product of each loss times its probability of occurring. The expected losses for the other decisions is given in Table 5.3.

Table 5.3

Number Stocked	Expected Loss
1	2.1
2	1.5
3	1.7
4	3.1
5	5.7

A cost-conscious manager faced with this list would stock two magazines.

The analysis given in the example above is much simplified but, nevertheless, representative of the application of probability theory to inventory problems. Several points should be noted. The solution did not result in stocking the average number demanded. The average would be 3.1 so that three would be the nearest number to stock. But this would lead to a higher loss. What is more important is that the lowest cost solution implies that on the average, 0.7 (i.e., .3 + .3 + .1) of the potential customers would not find a magazine available. Clearly, this solution is contrary to intuition. It is entirely unreasonable that this company would try to satisfy less than one-third of its potential market.

The lesson to be learned from this last observation is that a technically correct solution may not have solved the right problem. It is possible that the problem statement is not complete. Omission of some factors might be justified if their effect is small, but omission of a significant factor may render a solution worthless or even damaging. The effect is somewhat like judging the cost of an evening out on the basis of the price of the entree on an à la carte menu.

In the example, several factors have been omitted. The behavior of the potential customer who does not find a copy available is certainly of importance. If he can be trusted to go to a different store, the publisher may still be satisfied with the solution. If he simply does not buy or switches to another magazine, some permanent damage may be done.

In this highly competitive area, most publishers are greatly concerned about circulation. This is a factor affecting the value of advertising space, a big source of revenue to the firm. If the manager were to follow the solution obtained on all stands, circulation would certainly be reduced. The resulting loss in advertising revenue could more than offset the direct-cost savings.

It is of utmost importance that mathematical models correctly represent the true problems of management. This constitutes the greatest problem in application. All too often, models are taken as *proven* in general when, in fact, they are true only under highly restrictive assumptions. *The manager is well advised to insist on a full understanding of all assumptions before a solution is applied.*

The search for alternative actions and the evaluation of profits or losses was discussed in the last chapter. Two new requirements enter in problems of risk: *multiple futures* and *probabilities*. Instead of viewing the future as a single possible set of conditions, the future is viewed as consisting of many possible sets of conditions. Conceptually, this is a more involved problem than the idea of a single future. In practice, it is more difficult only in that each envisioned future adds one more condition to be evaluated. The calculations to be made for each possible future are the same as those made for the single future when making decisions under certainty.

It is the second of the new concepts, the evaluation of the *probabilities* of these future conditions coming to pass, which causes difficulty. While probabilities can be introduced as a convenience in a mathematical solution, it is another matter to work with them in making an actual management decision. Many managers would balk at a request that they assign a probability to a sales volume for the following year. This is the result of the struggle over the years to reduce all possible sales volumes to a single estimate. Managers have learned to resolve the conflicts in data and produce a single expected value, realizing that sales may be either larger or smaller than this value. What must now be asked of them is that they provide the *full probability distribution* for the potential sales volume. Such estimates are a common requirement in the solution of business problems.

Probabilities arrived at without benefit of past history or simple conceptual experiment are called *subjective probabilities*. They have been criticized as being too personal. No two managers would be expected to view the future in the same way. However, a moment's reflection shows that this is the very nature of the management problem. Quantitative analysis cannot be expected to eliminate the need for judgment. It can, however, limit the exercise of judgment to those factors which truly require that a judgment be made.

Waiting line theory

The importance of studying the behavior of waiting lines or queues may not be immediately evident to the student of management. Admittedly, the presence of a line at a tool crib or cafeteria may suggest the need for studying the service activity. However, these obvious problems are a trivial study when compared to other "waiting lines." For "lines" actually exist in many areas. There are orders waiting to be filled, machines waiting for repair, trucks waiting to be loaded or unloaded, and even problems waiting for a manager's attention. These lines are every bit as real and possibly more pressing than lines of men.

Waiting-line theory starts with the discussion of the *average number in line,* or the *average waiting time* for the service facility. Eventually, the theory is concerned with what the capacity of the service facility must be to assure economic service of the *calling population.* The italicized words require rigorous definition before the theory can be developed. However, it will not be possible for us in this brief discussion to explore this topic in depth. Therefore, consider the intuitive meaning of these words as they appear in the following example.

Example: A fuel-oil delivery firm offers as sales incentive a heating-system service contract. Prompt service is the key to satisfied customers. To provide this service, the oil firm employs several servicemen, and this move costs the firm not only the servicemen's salaries, but also the fixed costs of the fully equipped trucks. The customers (i.e., *the calling population*) call for service at random, each call taking a random length of time averaging two hours. With the present complement of three servicemen per shift, the *system waiting time* is as shown in Figure 5.1. For comparison, the system behavior is also given for two and four servicemen.[1]

Figure 5.1

PERCENTAGE OF THE DAY DURING WHICH n CUSTOMERS
ARE WAITING OR BEING SERVED

Customers Waiting n	TWO Servicemen per Shift	THREE Servicemen per Shift	FOUR Servicemen per Shift
0	1	.7	17
1	1	16	26
2	3	25	23
3*	9	22	16
4	17	14	9
5	27	9	5
6	23	4	3
7	12	2	1
8	7	1	0

[1] For *three* servicemen, up to three customers may be served simultaneously so that "waiting" begins with the fourth customer. The broken line relates to a similar statement for two and four servicemen.

Ordinarily the development of line characteristics requires the application of probability theory and either mathematical analysis or simulation. An understanding of this manipulation is not required in order to understand the problem or its solution.

In effect, in this problem there are two waiting lines, the customers and the servicemen. As servicemen are added, the customer waiting time is reduced. The customer waiting time can be reduced to zero only by adding a huge number of servicemen. Clearly, this would not be economical.

It may be observed that for three servicemen, the percentage of the day with n customers waiting can be used to assign cost. These percentages indicate that one per cent of the time, a customer will join the line as the eighth member. He must then wait until five (i.e., 8–3) customers have been served before a serviceman will get to him. Since the case of three servicemen is being considered, a customer moves up one place each 40 minutes

$$\left(\text{i.e., } \frac{2 \times 60}{3} = \frac{\text{average time per call}}{\text{number of servicemen}} \right)$$

Therefore, this customer will wait 200 minutes on the average for service. Extending this anlysis over the other line possibilities with three servicemen, we find:

n	Time for Service
4	(.14) 40 = 5.6
5	(.09) 80 = 7.2
6	(.04) 120 = 4.8
7	(.02) 160 = 3.2
8	(.01) 200 = 2.0
	22.8 minutes
	average waiting time

This is hardly a long waiting period.

Continuing our calculations for the case of two servicemen, we find the average waiting time would be 3 hours and 11 minutes, while for four servicemen the average waiting time would be only 4.2 minutes. A common-sense comparison might now lead to deciding to employ three servicemen. A more sophisticated analysis would call for computing the cost of employing additional servicemen and comparing it to the cost of customer dissatisfaction with fewer servicemen. The evaluation of the last cost is based largely on the competitor's level of performance.

Waiting-line (or queuing) theory has provided an important aid in designing telephone exchanges and in studying airport and dock facilities. As yet, however, its application by middle management has not been great.

Learning theory

Another area of limited certainty is the study of *learning* in an organization. Out of this study has come the now widely-accepted learning curve.

This curve simply states that the time necessary to complete the one-hundredth unit will show *about* the same improvement over the time necessary to complete the tenth unit as the tenth unit improved over the first. Thus, it may be possible to predict the time necessary to complete the one-hundreth unit.

It is not known when this theory was first used as a technical innovation in the field of management. The author used this device thirty-five years ago to analyze problems of two manufacturing establishments. Such applications are now common in industry.

An example of application comes from the aircraft industry. Prior to World War II, the production of airplanes was on quite a small scale. Orders of only a few airplanes of one design were commonplace. But during the war, the Air Force negotiated contracts calling for hundreds and even thousands of planes.

Since the companies had had no experience with such large orders, they had no real basis for calculating the times necessary to produce a given plane in a production sequence. An estimate based on experience with the first plane often showed an embarrassingly large error when applied to later production of the same model after learning was well advanced.[2] The result was that contracts frequently had to be renegotiated. The writer renegotiated such contracts for the Air Force. He found the companies genuinely surprised with the improvement brought about through learning. Most companies were cooperative in agreeing to accept reduced prices so that excess profits did not occur.

The learning curve may be applied to negotiation, make or buy decisions, pricing, or the forecasting of direct-labor hours. The first two applications are especially useful in procurement. In purchasing negotiations, changes in labor time may be applied to successive orders of materials or components, and thus form a rational basis for the buyer's asking for lower prices on successive orders for the same items from vendors.

The learning curve can also be used to advantage in:

1. Estimating labor loads on the factory
2. Determining the effect of increased lot size on labor costs
3. Evaluating the effectiveness of training programs for groups.

However, as with all quantitative aids to management, the learning curve should be used with caution. No prediction from it will be perfect. Some error must always be expected, but this error diminishes with the size of the group being evaluated. If only one person is involved, the variability may well be so large that prediction based on it will be worthless.

[2] As a specific example, it is estimated that the 1000th B–29 took only 3 per cent of the time required to produce the first plane. See Victor H. Pooler, Jr., "How to Use the Learning Curve," *Purchasing* magazine, July 17, 1961, p. 70.

Decision Making under Uncertainty

Many decisions involve a more difficult evaluation of probabilities. Consider a motel owner who finds that he is regularly turning away customers because all his units are filled. He wonders whether additional units should be built. With any reasonable experience, he will not find it difficult to develop estimates of the probable level of occupancy for these new units. So far, he has been facing a problem involving risk. If it should happen that a new route is under consideration for the highway on which he is located, his problem becomes decidedly different. Only the smallest change in routing, or exits, or speed limit may serve to double or halve the motel-owner's trade. Probabilities in such a situation are exceptionally difficult to assess.

Such difficulties have led to the development of special theories to help in making decisions under uncertainty. Of these, perhaps the oldest and intuitively most appealing is to assume all possible future events to be equally likely to occur. Thus, in the case of the magazine-sales distribution in the last section, the probabilities would be assigned as 0.2 for all levels from one to five magazines. Once probabilities had been assigned in this manner, the approach to the solution would be the same as the method outlined in that section.

A radically different assumption is that nature is antagonistic, so that the best decision would be the one that would be best *under the worst possible future*. Stated rigorously, this is known as the minimax criterion of choice. It finds application in "game" situations (such as war) where the decision makers are clearly antagonistic. A great deal has been written about its application under the title of *game theory*.

Several other principles of choice have been proposed. None of these gives solutions which are entirely acceptable to management. Nevertheless, the study of such theories is of immense value to management. Out of it has come a better understanding of competitive behavior.

Simulation

Earlier in Chapter 4 when we talked about testing the model, we mentioned simulation. Although this does not constitute a *model* under any one classification, simulation *is* a method of problem solution. However, it is a method in a sense entirely different from the sense in which calculus or linear programming are methods. Both of the latter techniques under suitable conditions guarantee to maximize or minimize the chosen measure of effectiveness. Simulation provides no such guarantee. Simulation is simply experimentation applied to a system in a way that is enough like the real problem to aid in its solution. As such, it is limited to the *testing of decision rules*.

As an example, consider a production-control system for which two rules have been proposed. The first rule states that the next order to be processed should be the first order to arrive at the machine. An alternative rule calls for selecting the next order on the basis of the total investment in the order up to this point. Simulation can certainly be used to evaluate these two rules in terms of the minimum average delay time.

What simulation does not do is invent new rules. It remains for management to decide which rule shall be applied once the simulations have been carried out. For this example, dozens of reasonable rules can be proposed and tested. However, with such a procedure there can be no guarantee that the best rule has been tried.

Example: Simulation can be used in a problem situation such as that given earlier involving the magazines. In this problem, the most important feature of the method is its generated sales distribution. This distribution implies a sequence of weekly sales which when accumulated over, let us say, 100 weeks would show approximately 10 weeks with sales of 1 magazine, 20 weeks with sales of 2 magazines, 30 weeks with 3, 30 weeks with 4, and 10 weeks with sales of 5 magazines. To generate this distribution, a simple spinner such as that used in parlor games may be put to work.[3] The path traced out by the pointer will be divided into 100 divisions. Since it is desired that 10 percent of the weeks have sales of one magazine, the interval from 0 to 10 will be taken to represent a week in which one magazine is sold. The interval from 10 to 30 (i.e., 20% of the perimeter) will represent a week in which two magazines are sold. The remainder of the perimeter is assigned in the same way. To represent each week's sales, the pointer is spun, and the interval in which it stops determines the sales for that week.

Now simulation can commence. First, a decision rule is chosen, such as: "stock 3 magazines." Next, the pointer is spun for each week. Referring to the loss table, the resulting loss can be determined for each number stocked and each number sold. Ten spins of the pointer (i.e. ten weeks) might produce the sequences of sales 4, 4, 4, 3, 4, 1, 5, 5, 3, 4. Under the decision rule, "stock 3," this sequence gives the losses, 1, 1, 1, 0, 1, 6, 2, 2, 0, 1, involving a loss of 15 cents over ten weeks. Under the decision rule, "stock 4," following this sales sequence, the loss would be 17 cents. This simulation of magazine losses under two decision rules indicates that following the rule, "stock 3," results in smaller loss than following the rule, "stock 4."

The simulation of a large-scale system may require hundreds of equations containing both deterministic or probabilistic variables. Solution of a large complicated system by means other than simulation is often extremely difficult or impossible. In the example above, the events of only 10 weeks were simulated. Ordinarily many years would be used.

Because of the tremendous number of calculations required, most simulations are programmed for a computer. To make programming of system

---

[3] A table of random numbers could also be used.

simulation more convenient, several compilers have been developed. These specialized programs make it possible to submit a problem to the computor in a standard form much like the usual algebraic equation. Through their use, many hours of programming time can be saved.

Two notable compilers or programming aids are the Dynamo compiler of Industrial Dynamics,[4] and the I.B.M. Job Shop Simulator.[5] The first of these provides a method of simulating a large system in considerable detail although some grouping of subsystems, e.g., men and machines or departments, is necessary. The second is a much more detailed scheme for simulating a small portion of the firm, usually the manufacturing department.

Simulators make it possible to test decision rules developed for individual departments. Since decisions in one department may ultimately affect the whole firm, the desirability of testing a specific rule in a general model becomes obvious.

Business games

Simulation techniques offer an additional benefit to management and to management education. They do this by providing the equivalent of a management laboratory in the form of a business game. So far, most of our discussion has centered around *rational* decision rules. These rules were evaluated on the basis of the extent to which they minimized or maximized some measure of effectiveness. But as we have emphasized before, not all management problems are solvable by quantitative methods. Management judgment will always be an immensely important ingredient of successful business. Through the years, industrial and educational institutions have sought effective ways of developing management judgment. One problem has been that an effective laboratory did not exist which would permit the student to try out his judgment. Through simulation, this problem has been partially overcome.

There are a substantial number of business games. One of the most widely used is the I.B.M. game which permits individuals or groups to make several decisions each period throughout the playing of the game. These decisions set the level of investment in research and marketing as well as market price and the amount to be produced. Sales volume, manufacturing, cost, etc., are generated by the program. The program gives back to each individual or team a balance sheet, profit or loss statement and a statement of marketing effectiveness. Through such games, a student can be exposed to a variety of managerial problems. In the course of solving them, he is

[4] Forrester, Jay, "Industrial Dynamics," M.I.T. Press and Wiley, 1961.
[5] "Improved Job Shop Management Through Data Processing," International Business Machines Corporation, 1960.

free to experiment with new and aggressive policies without risking the penalties which such action might evoke on the job.

Data Processing

It has been apparent throughout our discussion of the techniques of Quantitative Analysis that massive amounts of data can be accumulated in the course of using these techniques. These data must be summarized in records and reports before they are available for control purposes. Large organizations make their control procedures more accessible and accurate by the use of data-processing systems.

The U.S. Bureau of the Census reports that one out of every twenty employed in 1910 were engaged in clerical or allied occupations; in 1940, that ratio had risen to one in ten; and in 1958, it took another jump to one in seven. This situation was brought about by the enormous increases in paperwork, and the Census Bureau reports that the trend is still continuing. As organized workers have continued to demand shorter hours and higher pay, the resulting increased unit costs have urged management to adopt more labor-saving equipment. Electronic data-processing (EDP) is the latest device for coping with this fast-developing dilemma. This new processing technique for overcoming the time element required to digest piles of paperwork and for aiding in the solution of management problems, reduces the time element of the workload, decreases total clerical employment, and creates new labor demands for a still shorter workday.

Data-processing systems include groups of machine units for accumulating, computing, storing, comparing, recording, and transcribing all kinds of information. These machine systems have the ability to compare results with predetermined answers, and if deviations occur, they are able to choose the proper course of action. The outstanding feature of machine data-processing is the speed made possible by the new computers. Many operations can take place simultaneously, and information can be fed into the system from various sources at the same time. The result is that procedures not previously attempted because of the prohibitive cost in time and money have become fast and routine operations at low cost. This is the background of the current so-called office revolution.

Deciding to use DP systems

Several factors must be given serious consideration when deciding whether to use a data-processing system. First, how will its cost compare with the existing manual method? Second, can the present manual system be adapted to mechanical processing? Third, are the source data continuous or are they intermittent and dissimilar programs? Fourth, can the new system take care of a combination of similar operations with increased effectiveness and less cost?

Cost factors of importance must be considered before accepting any data-processing system. Properly trained processing personnel are relatively expensive. It is often necessary to provide special training for these operators. All of these costs must be compared to the existing manual methods of processing paperwork.

Another question involves buying or leasing the DP equipment. Although some concerns buy their equipment, it seems more reasonable to lease because of periodic technological improvements in this field. If a company is going to use DP on a large scale for many different operations, it is usually more reasonable to lease so as to avoid losses on the original investment in several machines. Another desirable factor in leasing is the savings in maintenance costs which are frequently absorbed by the lessor.

Data-processing equipment

There are three types of modern data-processing equipment: (1) electronic data processing (EDP) which stores data magnetically or electrically; (2) integrated data processing (IDP) which stores data mechanically in punched cards and tapes; and (3) automatic data processing (ADP) which is a combination of EDP and IDP. The ADP machine can serve as an aid to the cost accounting and production departments, to controllers and engineers, and for expediting procedures.

The reorganization of our current procedures and systems by integrated data processing influences the data from their point of origin through to their final use. Its rapid processing provides management with current information on which to base decisions and take corrective action on procedures and tasks subject to managerial control.

An excellent example of the savings in time and inventory investment is the electronic data-processing system set up at the Army Transport Materiel Command at its St. Louis headquarters in 1959. It has become the center of a global military supply network. It is estimated that the system will save a half-million dollars a month, besides processing requisitions for aircraft, marine, and railway equipment five times faster than the previous method. Through wire and radio circuits, it will serve military installations all over this country and on four other continents. "More than 1000 requisitions are sent through the Transport Materiel Command computer daily for parts and equipment out of a $780 million inventory, ranging from penny washers to quarter of a million dollar helicopters. This cycle used to take about fifteen days. Now the computer gets the material on the road in less than seventy-two hours.[6]

Another recent outstanding application of the use of computers is in the Internal Revenue Service audits. The first change is from alphabetical lists of taxpayers to numbered accounts. When the new installation is completed,

[6] *Army Times,* December 19, 1959.

there will be two master files. Individuals will be filed by their social security numbers, while business will be given new numbers. The plan is already
gradually being put into effect at the Martinsburg, West Virginia Computer
Center. It is generally conceded that the new system, with its cross index,
will build a better system, and probably increase the federal government's
tax intake.[7]

The application of DP to statistical studies produces some startling results. A nuclear energy problem required coefficients of a multiple equation based on 500 observations and 39 variables. Such problems can be
solved without a computer, but they require many man-hours of intensive
calculations. A large computer, however, requires only a few seconds to
bring the data into its memory, about twenty minutes to manipulate the
data internally, and a few seconds to record the answer.

Insurance companies and banks, in addition to many industrial concerns,
are making constant use of computers. Since 1956, the Bank of America has
used a special-purpose computer which pre-codes each check with magnetic ink. "When a check is presented with withdrawal, the teller inserts it in
a machine, and punches the amount. The machines 'reads' the magnetic
code, tapes a magnetic memory at the central computer, subtracts the
amount of the check from the customer's account, or flashes a stop order
to the teller, and strikes a new balance. At day's end, the computer sorts
the day's transactions, and enters them on a tape in the account serial order.
From this tape, monthly statements and other information for management
are prepared."[8]

Computer centers

Ever since large concerns began to use computers, students of the subject have been concerned about the disadvantages in which the small
companies are placed. It did not take too long, however, to develop a plan
which enables the small firm to meet the challenge. The so-called "industrial park" which leases space to small concerns has been installing data-
processing equipment for the use of small lessees. This plan enables them
to adopt the latest improvements in office equipment without large and
often impossible investments. Now these tenants have the advantage of
high-speed computers which enable them to take advantage of operations
research and faster planning.

A faster growing aid to computer use by concerns which cannot afford
a large investment is the "computer center," used by groups of companies,
usually in the same line of work. One such center, known as "Tamcor," is
located in the heart of the financial district of New York. It keeps the books
for four brokerage firms. A larger installation ("Span"), starting in 1958

[7] "Computers Take Over Tax Audits," *Business Week,* October 28, 1961, p. 30.
[8] *Business Week,* April 7, 1956, p. 56.

with an investment of a million dollars, is used jointly by four insurance companies. These associations are springing up all over the country as joint operations, saving their owners vast installations of filing cabinets through the use of magnetic tapes. Manufacturers of computers are also establishing centers for small companies. Service Bureau Corporation, a subsidiary of I.B.M., had seventy such centers in 1961, and Remington Rand Univac, a division of Sperry Rand, had thirty-seven centers performing calculations for 5000 accounts.[9]

A big objection to computer centers is the fear of their users that competitors may obtain information the users want kept confidential. This objection is also shared by many group owner-users. The managers of the computer centers claim, however, that safeguards are being set up to overcome this objection.

A word of warning

Computers have become virtually a status symbol for progressive management. A survey of 631 companies by the American Management Association in 1958 concluded that the modern technique of applying mathematical computer methods to the solution of business problems has been firmly established and is growing fast.[10]

It is true that the "computer revolution," as it has been called, brings new opportunities to management in the form of more available data with no increase or even a decrease in clerical expense. In turn, however, the feasibility of more and more elaborate reports poses new problems for management. Each control group, wishing to take full advantage of the new machines, has developed a wide variety of new tabluations and graphic displays. Just how can a manager hope to analyze this immense collection of "indisputable" facts?

The computer must be recognized for what it is. It is a robot capable of doing only what it has been told to do. It will function with speed and accuracy, but there its function ends. The information fed into it must be correct, otherwise the answers are worthless. The trade has a name for this phenomenon known as G.I.G.O., which means "garbage in, garbage out."[11]

[9] Other centers are maintained by National Cash Register, General Electric, and Radio Corporation. See also "Computers for Everybody," Dun's Review, December 1961, pp. 42–46.

[10] Clifford J. Craft, Manager of Manufacturing Division of American Management Association, in Systems Magazine, for July-August, 1958, p. 22.

[11] A joint committee of the American Bar Association and the American Law Institute held a three-day seminar in Washington in March 1961 on this problem: "A Chicago bank, accepting for deposit a check drawn on a New York bank, makes a mistake in magnetically encoding the amount of the check, overstating the amount by $1,000. The rest of the check processing is handled by the computer. The New York customer's account is over-debted by $1,000. The next check he writes, to pay his life insurance premium, is returned for insufficient funds. The policy lapses and

To be used to full advantage, the computer must be instructed to do more of the manager's work. The machine must be given decision rules such as those which have been described in this chapter and in Chapter 4. The output must lead to the solution of problems, not to more work for the manager. The computer can be a real asset to management. Whether it will be depends on the inventiveness of the manager and his supporting staff in putting the computer to the best use.

Conclusions

It seems reasonable to warn that the business millennium has not been attained by the various techniques discussed in this and the previous chapter. Some of the inability of the new techniques to meet expectations is due to management's failure to understand their methods and purposes. Too susceptible to the blandishments of exact answers presented by operations researchers from mathematical models, management is often not capable of questioning their recommendations. As a matter of fact, any shifting of the final decision-making responsibility from the line executive to the operations researchers was never intended. Such malfunctioning of a scientific process is probably due more to the lack of understanding of the executive than to the enthusiasm of the researchers.

The number of quantitative techniques available to management is steadily growing. Every management publication presents new and often untried techniques. While it is reasonable that a manager acquire a familiarity with these, it is not necessary that he understand their mathematical complexities. The manager's role in the use of quantitative techniques will usually be the recognition of problem areas. Other members of the firm may possess the specialties needed to study the problem area and construct and solve the model. If not, specialists in management science and operations research may be hired or retained as consultants.

The manager should be always aware that quantitative analysis does not eliminate management judgment. The manager's effectiveness will be enhanced and increased by the new management techniques of Quantitative Analysis, but the manager will continue to assume full responsibility for making decisions. Quantitative Analysis, however, often forces the manager to reevaluate his reasoning in decision making. His judgment becomes a part of the solution. Ultimately, the results of the application are his responsibility alone.

---

the New Yorker dies before the mistake is discovered. Can a widow sue for the amount of the insurance? Which bank is responsible? What if the error occurred not because of a wrong encoding but because there was a fault in the check or in the magnetic tape to which the information was transferred, or because the computer itself did something wrong? With human beings handling visible records, there has been a good chance that errors would be caught somewhere along the line." "Computers Tangle with the Law," *Business Week*, April 8, 1961.)

QUESTIONS

1. Who could more reasonably treat his problems as involving *certain* futures: the sales manager or the plant engineer? Why?

2. What is the basic difference between decision making under risk and under uncertainty?

3. Suggest an alternative criterion (other than cost) for the magazine example. Would the same solution still apply?

4. Define a subjective probability.

5. In the queuing example, verify the cost with four repairmen.

6. For what proportion of the day is a serviceman idle when only two servicemen are employed?

7. Would it be reasonable to make minimum serviceman waiting time the objective? Why not?

8. Would it be reasonable to make both minimum serviceman and customer waiting time the objective? Why not?

9. Could a learning curve be applied to classroom performance? Whom would it evaluate? (Hint: Not the student)

10. What reasons might be given for an *individual* deviating from the established learning curve?

11. How would you define simulation? What is a decision rule?

12. Evaluate the loss for the decision rule, "stock 2 magazines," for the simulated ten-week sales period as given in the example.

13. Simulation could also use past sales history as a sequence on which to try different decision rules. Do you see any danger in this method? How might the danger be minimized?

14. What do you think is the most significant value of business games?

15. How did electronic data-processing aid in expediting requisitions sent by military users to the Army Transport Materiel Command?

16. How is the Internal Revenue Service making use of data-processing?

17. To what extent are computer centers aiding businesses that are too small to afford such expensive equipment?

18. Do you think it is fair to refer to computers as "robots?"

19. Why will Quantitative Analysis never eliminate the need for management judgment?

20. Why should executives make it their business to learn more about the methods and purposes of Quantitative Analysis and data processing?

6

Organization Principles

Organization is a structural design for grouping a number of activities with respect to their responsibility and authority for accomplishing an objective. Any group of two or more persons requires a mutuality of effort for accomplishing a common purpose. Unless organization is provided for prior to engaging in an enterprise, the objective will likely fail. Organization is, therefore, born of the necessity for accomplishing objectives. In other words, organization provides for a division of labor so that a group will be able to accomplish more than the sum of its members' efforts acting as individuals.[1]

If two men are trying to push a car out of a snow bank, they must first agree on the direction in which to push, and for best results, they must time their action so that they are both pushing together. Without such elementary organization, they would be working at cross-purposes. This is perhaps the simplest form of the division of labor, where the participants are all performing the same action at the same time to attain a goal that no one of them could reach alone.

An equally common and more important form of division of labor is the situation in which two or more persons must perform different operations — and often at different times and in different places — to accomplish a common purpose. This way of organizing human effort is universal. For example, anthropologists have found that in all nonliterate societies, the division of labor between men and women is always clearly defined. The particular tasks that each is expected to do differ from one tribe to another, but there is always a general agreement that if a sufficient food supply and adequate protection against the elements are to be maintained, the work must be subdivided in some way so that different people can be performing different and necessary tasks at the same time.

[1] Three excellent sources for detailed study of the philosophy of organization and its principles are: Alvin Brown, *Organization of Industry* (New York: Prentice-Hall, Inc., 1947); James D. Mooney, *The Principles of Organization,* rev. ed. (New York: Harper & Brothers, 1947); and L. Urwick, *The Elements of Administration* (New York: Harper & Brothers, 1944).

In one respect, the primitive communities enjoy an advantage over modern industrial societies because in the former, the assignment of tasks is largely a matter of tradition. Primitive economic organization, when it remains uninfluenced by industrial civilization, is conservative. The same processes repeat themselves year in and year out, and the division of labor changes very little. A child will grow up with a fairly clear idea of just what operations he is going to be performing throughout his adult life.

The modern business or industrial entrepreneur can count on no such culturally preordained arrangements of activities and no such fixed expectations on the part of the workers. He must organize his enterprise from the ground up. But the modern manager — or at least the scientific manager — does not have to start his job of organizing completely "from scratch." He has at his disposal a growing body of organizational principles to serve as fundamental guides to action. By applying these principles through established methods, procedures, and systems, modern management has raised organization to a science and banished the untrustworthiness of knowledge gained from tradition and experience alone, knowledge which may, but just as often may not, apply in the rapidly developing and ever changing economic world of today.

For the purposes of this chapter, we can return to the more specific definition of organization as set forth in Chapter 1, where it was defined as *the process of building, for any enterprise, a structure that will provide for the separation of activities to be performed and for the arrangement of these activities in a framework which indicates their hierarchical importance and functional association.* Like the broader definition, this more specific statement views organization as an association of persons for accomplishing a common purpose. In addition, it introduces the notions of hierarchy and functional associations among the activities to be performed. It should also be emphasized that organization includes not only persons, but also things and ideas. It is obvious that without organization, formal or informal, management would be a composite of floundering and confusion.

The Structural Elements of Organization

There are five fundamental elements which must be considered in building the organizational framework of a business.[2]

1. *Determination of the scope and purpose of the enterprise.* Before an organization structure can be built, the nature of the enterprise must be clearly specified, as well as the territory in which it proposes to produce and sell, and the channels through which it will distribute.

2. *Demarcation of distinct and dissimilar functions and activities.* Closely

---

[2] Parts of this discussion are based on the suggestions of Dr. H. A. Hopf, in an address entitled "Organization, Executive Capacity and Progress," delivered at the annual conference of the Life Office Management Association in Boston in September, 1944, and published in *Advanced Management* (June 1946), Vol. 11, pp. 34–47.

related activities should be grouped and, conversely, dissimilar activities should be kept apart in drawing up an organization. When the organizational structure does not follow function, there arises a further disruptive tendency for the jurisdictions of many executives to overlap with one another.

3. *Definition of levels of authority and responsibility.* Authority and responsibility should be clearly defined for each of the various executive levels. The degree of authority and responsibility should be commensurate with the importance of the activities assigned at any given level. This fundamental will be discussed in more detail later under Principle 12.

4. *Establishment of means of communication and interaction.* It is essential to build into the structure means of communication and interaction that will pervade the organization and bind together the activities that had to be broken down. This necessary interaction of the separate parts will not be spontaneously generated but must be established by techniques of communication, coordination and control.

5. *Provision for adaptation and growth.* Any structure must be flexible enough to allow for adaptation to change and growth. Once the organizational design has been transformed from a lifeless structure into a living and growing organism, it is in a state of perpetual movement and change. It must respond as a whole to changes in the external environment, and it must undergo internal transformations to facilitate the interaction of its component parts. If the structural design is not constantly re-examined and adjusted to fit the needs of the organization in action, the structure may become an instrument of constraint, eventually choking the life out of the living organism.

Executive capacity

An important factor in the translation of executive skill to organizational design has to do with the differences in the *nature of the skills*. These differences may be accentuated to advantage by dividing the structure into major administrative, managerial, and operating divisions or levels. This breakdown is illustrated in Figure 6.1. Different kinds of skills are required at each of these three levels.

The administrative level requires conceptual skills. The conceptual skill emphasizes the ability to comprehend the organization as a whole. It understands all departments of the business and their mutual effect on each other. It goes further in its comprehension of the relations of the business to the industry of which it is a part, and to the social, political, and economic conditions in the community. It is on the basis of this conceptual skill that the administrator is in a position to establish basic company policies.

The managerial level requires coordinative skills. This level gives effect to the basic policies developed by the administration. Its essential ability

Figure 6.1

Primary Organization Levels

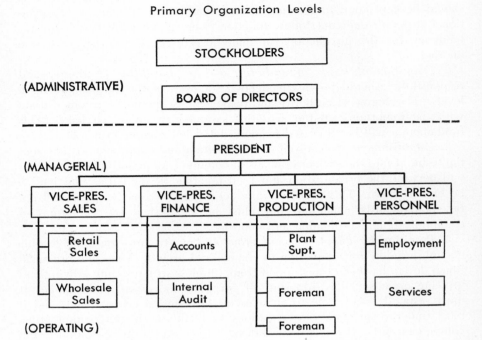

is to coordinate the activities of the various departments. Like the administrator, the manager must see the enterprises as a whole. He must also be able to see the significant details, the signals that something is getting out of control, without allowing himself to be bogged down by matters that can be handled by others. Unlike the administrator, the manager is continually called upon to make decisions quickly. This requires a stable and resolute personality and makes human-relations skills particularly important at this level. The manager must know how to work effectively with his subordinates, and he must know his men well enough to be able to delegate assignments with the assurance that they will be carried out.

The operating level requires technical skills. This is true in any line of business, but especially in industrial concerns. It should be stressed that a man with the education and intellectual ability to be a brilliant engineer may often lack the combination of conceptual and human-relations skills which make a successful executive.

To achieve balance between executive capacity and executive responsibility, the organizational structure should be divided into the smallest number of levels that will permit rational distribution of functions. If there are more levels than necessary, there is a tendency toward over-organization, with consequent confusion. On the other hand, if the levels are too few, they cannot be set up on a strictly functional basis, so will tend to produce overlapping of activities.

To relieve superiors of unnecessary workloads and to obtain action based on personal knowledge of the factors involved, decisions should be made as far down the line as competency exists. Furthermore, decisions should originate, as far as possible, at the place where the action is taking place. This rule is based on the assumption that, admitting competency, those responsible for taking the action will have the best information on which to base a decision.

Executive levels

To prevent over-organization or overwork of executives, it is important that attention be given to the number of executive levels in any organization. The maximum number has been generally agreed on as six, with recommendation for five. In a five-step executive organization, the levels are usually known as top, senior, intermediate, and junior executives, and the supervisory group. Figure 6.2 shows the types of executives ordinarily included on the various levels. Management levels are important because they determine to a large extent the range of responsibilities and authority, and the salary scale.

Communication

Communication is essential for effective coordination, and coordination is the prime necessity for successful management. The channels of communication should be definitely established and thoroughly explained to all those concerned. In general, descending lines show authority which is responsible for policies, orders, and instructions. Ascending lines supply information and reports to aid in executive control of activities, including their coordination. However, with the recent attempts on the part of management to make the supervisors feel that they also "belong," descending lines should also carry all types of information that enable the lower echelons to make decisions based on pertinent facts and proposed plans. Supervisors should not be humiliated by getting information from their subordinates who obtained it from their union officers.

The directness and speed of communication are both crucial. Orders going down the line are usually timed and their flow uninterrupted. Speed of upward communication is equally important because information and reports which are to be the basis of decisions are valuable to the extent that the loss of time between source and destination is reduced to a minimum. Horizontal or cross-communication among executive members on the various levels is also important for promoting cooperation and coordination. Communication downward is the easiest to maintain, upward is more diffi-

Figure 6.2

Management Levels

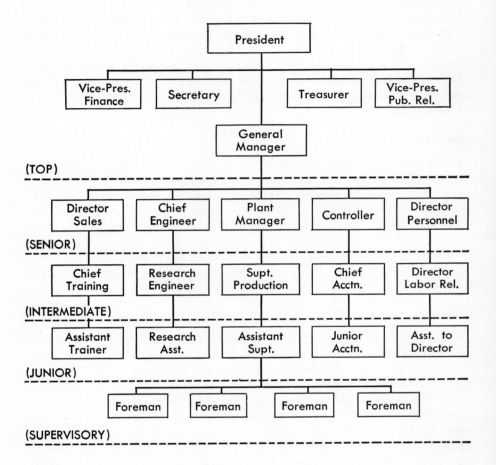

cult, and laterally is the most difficult. It is only in recent years that serious attention has been given to stimulating communication techniques, particularly the horizontal type.[3]

Principles of Organization

The purpose of organization is to work out a plan which will provide the most effective operation of a concern; the purpose of management is to carry

[3] Horizontal communication has been given scientific attention by Henri Fayol, who illustrates the situation with his "bridge" or "ladder." See Fayol, *General and Industrial Management*, trans. Constance Storrs (London: Sir Isaac Pitman & Sons, Ltd., 1949), pp. 34–36; and L. P. Alford and J. R. Bangs, *Production Handbook* (New York: The Ronald Press Company, 1948), pp. 28–29.

out the plan profitably. It is obvious, therefore, that the two purposes are complementary. Because of this dovetailing, certain principles or guides for action in the two fields are necessarily similar, as will be observed by turning back to Chapter 3.

The scientific analysis of organization and the formulation of guiding principles in this area are more recent developments than scientific attention to the principles of management. As a consequence, the principles of organization still lack refinement and recognition. The future is promising, but much remains to be done. Business has too often failed to see the practical relationship between scientifically planned organization and effective management. In presenting the principles of organization, we make no pretense of covering the subject completely. The following principles are offered as the most important.

1. Objective

A clear and complete statement of the objective is a necessary preliminary to all activity. Statements of policy, the development of plans, and even the approach to the organization structure are dependent on the objective to be attained. Since organization is a means to concerted effort, the objective of the effort must be clearly formulated before the organization begins to operate. A change in the organization's over-all objective will require alteration in its structure.

2. Functionalism

The organization structure must be built around distinct and dissimilar activities, and not around individuals. Functionalism distinguishes between kinds of duties. It is essential that activities be divided according to their nature to obtain control of related parts by a common source. Any other basis for the structure will lead to organized confusion. It is only by the observance of functionalism that the power of organization as a whole is greater than the sum of the powers of its parts.

3. Homogeneity

An effective organization must be designed so that only duties and activities of a similar nature are assigned to an individual or group for accomplishment. Homogeneity should be understood to include, as far as possible, all related elements in a managerial assignment and to exclude all duties unrelated to the assignment. The reason is simple from a managerial standpoint. The object is to promote the efficiency which results from specialization. It is equally obvious that the farther down the hierarchy, the easier becomes the homogeneity of duty assignments.

4. Coordination

The proper arrangement of a group effort is absolutely essential to unity of action in pursuit of a common purpose. Means of coordination must be built into structure; the spark motivating it is the leadership of authority, which is the exercised right of command. Authority is the supreme coordinating power. The purpose of many of the other principles is to obtain coordination within the structure. Coordination of operations and effort is the foundation of smooth performance.

5. Communication

Adequate communication is essential to effective coordination. The longer the chain of command, the more essential is the establishment of adequate channels of communication for speeding the flow of policies and orders downward, and suggestions and reports upward. Unless the channels of communication are sufficiently short and direct, there is a tendency to "jump" or avoid them by members of the executive groups, particularly by those who want to "get things done." Jumping channels does more harm than good in the long run, but the tendency is always present where the channels are indirect and unnecessarily long.

6. Scalar Process

It is necessary that there be a formal gradation of steps from top to bottom of the organization through which the coordinating authority can operate. The result of this process of providing graded steps of responsibility and authority within the organization is called the scalar chain or hierarchy. The word "scale" means an ascending or descending series. The scalar process refers to the ranking relationship of duties, as distinct from their functional classification.

7. Control

Organization should provide for the control of functions, activities, operations, and personnel within structurally defined areas of jurisdiction. Control means checking to see that everything is done according to the plans, rules, procedures, and orders that have been issued. They must establish standards against which accomplishments can be measured for the purpose of control. Control is the basis of what used to be known as "trouble-shooting." The difference is that controlled trouble-shooting provides the means for reporting results and comparing them with established standards. It enables the person doing the controlling to distinguish between those things which require attention and those which do not.

Since control is based on records or reports and the recommendations compiled from them, certain guides have been set up for reporting so that control can be made as effective as possible. These guides require that control reports should contain only matter useful for the control contemplated (utility), that the data represented should be expressed in uniform terminology or standards (uniformity) and present information comparable with prior reports (comparison).

8. Span of Control

The number of executive or technical subordinates whom a superior can directly supervise and control is definitely limited. Various writers on the span of control suggest definite numbers of subordinates who can be controlled by a single superior. On the executive level, the number ranges from three to six or seven. The span depends, of course, on the vigor and intelligence of the superior and the effective capacity of his subordinates. It also depends on the intricacy and differences of the subject matter handled by the subordinates. The physical distance between the supervisor and those he controls is another factor which must be considered.

The fixing of definite numbers of subordinates for control purposes is based on the theory of Graicunus, which was discussed in Chapter 3. Graicunus contends that a superior with 5 direct single relationships has 10 cross-relationships and 26 direct group relationships, a total of 41. This, he feels, represents the limit of control for the average executive. On the other hand, a National Industrial Conference Board survey shows that the executives of successful industrial concerns control 9 subordinates on the average.[4] Although the practice here is clearly out of line with theory, there is nothing on either side to point to a definite conclusion.

9. Exception Principle

The effectiveness of management is improved when executives devote their attention to exceptional matters such as questions of policy and changes in plans, procedures, and standards. The "top man in a one-man show" is no executive; his approach to management may be that of a high-grade supervisor. Those top managers who know how to select capable sub-executives and then stimulate their initiative by delegating all but the high-level problems, can relieve themselves of the necessity for carrying home brief cases bulging with "homework." If the chief reserves for individual attention the exceptionally difficult and over-all company problems, his part of the total job will be done better and his working contacts will be improved.

10. Delegation

One of the principal purposes of the organization structure is to obtain superior management through delegation of duties to subordinates by their superiors. When the organization grows to the point where face-to-face leadership is no longer possible, then the chief executive delegates not only the authority to perform specific responsibilities, but occasionally he may also delegate the right to delegate, a process known as subdelegation.

Delegation is a method of getting things done through other people. The

[4] *Organization Standards and Practices* (New York: National Industrial Conference Board, Inc., Studies in Business Policy No. 18, 1946), p. 15.

performance of delegated duties is, of course, improved through the structure of a balanced and coordinated organization. Delegation of duties has two facets of responsibility, that of the delegatee to perform the assigned duty, and that of the delegator to see to it that the assignment is carried out. Delegation is often a test of leadership in that the good leader knows what, when, and to whom to delegate. When the organization is properly set up, with a limited span of control, authority should be delegated as far down the chain of command as competency can be obtained. Such delegation not only spreads the managerial load, but it promotes initiative and leadership.

11. Staff

An efficient organization should provide for personnel whose principal functions are to gather and analyze data and make recommendations to line officers. Occasionally, and for brief periods, the staff may supervise when so ordered by the line, usually in connection with installation of a staff-recommended plan. The staff type of leadership support is continuous, personal, and positive, in contrast to delegation which aids the leader by reducing the number of his directing activities.

12. Authority and Responsibility

The responsibility for accomplishing an assigned task must be accompanied by authority over the means necessary for its accomplishment. A new relationship between authority and responsibility has been developed with the growth of business concerns. When the organization was so small that the boss could maintain direct contact with at least all of his supervisors, he did not necessarily grant authority commensurate with the responsibility of the assigned task. Because he was able to keep a watchful eye over all activities, he could retain considerable authority over delegated tasks and even over entire departments.

But when the organization grows so large that it must be broken down into functional divisions and departments, then correspondence between authority and responsibility must be built into the organizational structure. Not only should authority be commensurate with responsibility, but the converse is equally true. The responsibility of everyone who exercises authority should be absolute within the confines of that authority. This one-to-one correspondence between authority and responsibility is sometimes referred to as the "principle of correspondence."

Subsidiary Principles

The following statements have to do with improving the adequacy of the organization and its structure. Some writers regard them as principles. Whether or not they are entitled to that dignity, they are at least important.

13. Simplicity

Unnecessary elements should be eliminated from all activities as well as from the processes and procedures established for carrying them out. This principle may seem to be axiomatic, yet it is frequently violated in practice. Method analysis should be the primary technique for isolating unnecessary procedures in organization, just as it is for simplifying processes. Violation of the principle of simplicity is more prevalent in old organizations than in those newly established. The older ones have had too much time to accumulate barnacles of pride and empire.

14. Standardization

Organization designs and processes, as well as such factors as materials, quality, and effort, should be expressed in the best current standards. Since form follows function in building an organization, its structure cannot be effectively standardized until quality of products, methods of manufacture or procurement, and other primary factors have been determined. To a considerable extent in an industrial concern, the design and processes of the organization structure are built on the simplified and standardized products, or objectives, of the company.

15. Specialization

"If practicable, the work of each man in the management should be confined to the performance of a single leading function."[5] This is a corollary of functionalism, which distinguishes among the kinds of duties. Specialization has to do with assignment of duties. It is merely a technical statement of the long-accepted belief that the cobbler should stick to his last. Breach of this principle arises from the human weakness that tempts some men to enlarge their sphere of responsibility so they may cater to their self-esteem. Like many principles, specialization has its limitations. When carried too far, it becomes a case of rationalizing absurdities.

16. Continuity

The organizer should provide a structure for future continuity in pursuit of the organization's objective. Most concerns are corporations with continuing legal existence after they have grown to any size. It is the purpose of this subsidiary principle to point out the relation that should exist between such legal continuity and pursuit of the concern's main purpose. Since it is individuals who give effect to the structure, its future will depend, among other things, on a continuing supply of competent personnel.

17. Flexibility

The structure must be flexible enough to provide for organizational adaptation to changing conditions for meeting company objectives. Flexibility

[5] Taylor, *op. cit.*, p. 90.

may be thought of as the golden mean between rigidity and aimlessness. It bows to the demands of real change, while holding the organization to its established objective. Examples of flexibility in practice are expansion and contraction of an organization to meet increasing or decreasing demands for its product, or changing of product styles. Organizations must be flexible because they must be dynamic for survival.

18. Balance

"Each portion and function of an enterprise should operate with equal effectiveness in making its allotted contribution to the total purpose."[6] Balance among functions naturally leads to more effective results. Too often, organizational balance is sought by increasing the number of activities and departments, a plan which is more likely to produce checks rather than balances. The principle of balance warns organizers against expanding organizational minutiae to a point where the costs are greater than the gain. Organization resulting from insignificant subdivisions may actually impair control.

19. Direct Contact

Slowness of action through the chain of command can be reconciled with the speed requisite for results by establishing special channels for the direct contact of persons responsible for the same type of action process. Direct contacts can be developed into a recognized procedure when authorized by the superiors of those involved who report back their conclusions to those same superiors. It is a technique of management which can be built into the organization, as a substitute for unauthorized "jumping of channels." Its results are usually more effective because the method employed is operated in the open by the general consent of those concerned.

Measuring the Organization

One of the outstanding problems of management is to devise plans for increasing the speed of correct decisions. Speed is an element second in importance only to correctness. With increases in the size of business, the layers of supervision increase, slowly leading to the technical question of *how big is too big*. One answer is that the concern is unwieldy when its controls start to lose their effectiveness. To correct this problem, top management should check the following:

1. *Is the type of organization suited to its purposes?*[7] The type of organization should be determined on the basis of its main purpose. A military organization, for example, requires a different structure from that of a business concern. A department organization usually requires a distinct

[6] Urwick, *op. cit.*, p. 121.
[7] A discussion of the several *types* of organization is postponed until Chapter 7.

setup. Church and governmental organizations have evolved from different historical backgrounds and patterns. An industrial concern with scattered plants needs organizational treatment suited to its peculiar problems of operation and control.

2. *Is the division of work on a sound functional basis?* Unless the functional divisions are mutually exclusive, there is bound to be overlapping of jurisdictions with consequent confusion. It is also imperative to include all related activities within each main division.

3. *Is there a proper ratio between supervisors and subordinates?* If there are too few supervisors, expensive delays are the result. If there are too many supervisors, some of them are not fully occupied, and unnecessary expense and poor employee morale result. Secondly, subordinates are more likely to cross supervisory channels, seeking authoritative answers they desire. In the third place, such a situation breeds rivalry among supervisors, with consequent friction and lowered supervisory morale. Finally, too many supervisors with too little work to occupy their time are prone to spend some of their efforts trying to corral more activities in order to justify their existence and enlarge their own sections of the organization, an activity known as "empire building."

4. *Are department objectives clearly defined?* Unless the functional definitions of departments are unmistakably clear, jurisdictional disputes are sure to arise. Departmental objectives are the basis for defining their activities. Both cooperation and coordination are hindered when departmental activity boundaries are blurred.

5. *Are authority and responsibility clearly defined and properly delegated?* In general, authority should be commensurate with the delegated responsibility. It should be of sufficient scope to enable effective discharge of the assigned task. To establish the desired amount and kind of authority, the delegatee's range of responsibility must be definitely and clearly set forth and properly delegated. Proper delegation includes several factors, chief of which is the right of the superior to delegate the activity concerned.

6. *Are policies clear and properly communicated?* The best way to ensure the clarity of policies is to write them in the form of a manual so that all concerned will have an opportunity to criticize. Clarity is more likely to result when policy statements are checked during preparation by a group of executives in consultation. Policies not communicated have little use.

7. *Are decisions made at the lowest competent level?* This is really a test of the exception principle. Decision-making at the lowest competent level, which means as close as possible to the action level, encourages the exercise of initiative by subordinates and helps prepare them for greater responsibilities. It also reduces the workload of superiors.

8. *Are expenditures subject to adequate budgetary controls?* This organizational factor can be taken care of in the functional definition of the activities included in the organization manual. Adequate budgetary procedures

must also be provided for in a policy manual or standard operating procedure to make such controls applicable and effective.

9. *Does the flow of work represent proper functional sequence?* The over-all organizational pattern will furnish an indication of the adequacy of functional sequence. A smooth flow of work and communications without back-tracking is a measure of good organization.

10. *Are adequate controls installed and operating?* Organization is a tool whose effectiveness is dependent on its proper use. Without technical controls, it is impossible to be sure about what is going on or what may be expected in the future.

Conclusions

In all phases of work, good organization is prerequisite to good management. As has been stated before, organization is a primary tool of management. The final test of an organization is its smooth operation in action. If the executive with a pile of papers on his desk can place most of them in outgoing baskets for attention with real confidence in the results, he is functioning in a well-planned organization. The following terse observations for practical guidance add life and interest to the more or less dry bones of the principles:

1. To adhere to the substance of organization rather than to worship the form in which it is cast.
2. To view organization as a means to an end, rather than an end in itself.
3. To recognize the values inherent in improvisation, rather than to rely exclusively on the virtues attaching to organization.
4. To insure liberation of human energies rather than their suppression or regimentation.
5. To respect the authority of knowledge rather than the authority of position.
6. To strive for the maintenance of loyalty on the part of executives to their subordinates, rather than stress the essentiality of the reverse process.
7. To develop well-rounded and intellectually well-balanced executives, rather than one-sided and narrow specialists.
8. To imbue executives with a spirit of tolerance toward one another, rather than permit the existence of conditions productive of intolerance.
9. To inculcate in the minds of executives the wisdom of rendering themselves dispensable, rather than of cherishing the illusion that they are indispensable.
10. To sacrifice almost any other value rather than cause injury to the foundations upon which inspiring leadership rests.[8]

[8] Harry A. Hopf, "Evolution in Organization During the Past Decade," *Advanced Management* (September 1947), Vol. 12, p. 109.

QUESTIONS

1. How does the organization structure affect the efficiency of management?
2. What organizational advantage did primitive societies enjoy as compared to our modern industrial complexity?
3. How would you define the modern organizational process?
4. What are the five fundamental elements usually considered in building the modern industrial organization?
5. How important is the concept of communication in any organization?
6. Are conceptual skills improved or hindered when the board of directors is composed entirely of members of management — known as the "inside board"?
7. Is coordination more important on the administrative or managerial level? Why?
8. What are the respective disadvantages of over-organization and under-organization?
9. Why is it important to secure balance between executive capacity and executive responsibility?
10. What is the advantage of functionalism as a principle of organization?
11. What is the relation between communication and coordination?
12. Why does Sears Roebuck prefer a wide span of control for the organization of its retail stores?
13. What is meant by the exception principle of control for executives?
14. How far down the organizational line should management activities be delegated to subordinates?
15. What is the proper relationship between authority over and responsibility for the accomplishment of any assigned task?
16. How does standardization of designs and processes aid management, and how should standards be expressed?
17. Why is flexibility necessary for effective management since many of its guides are expressed in accepted principles?
18. What are some of the criteria for measuring the effectiveness of an organization?
19. To what extent does delegation depend on the exception principle?
20. Which principle of organization do you consider most important, and why?

CASE PROBLEM

NORTHERN UNIVERSITY

Northern University's Athletic Association is receiving an unusual amount of adverse criticism, with the result that Northern is losing prestige among its student body and losing the support of the alumni. The festive spirit of the university's recent centennial celebration was considerably subdued when the football team lost its major annual game. The general reaction among those interested is to fire the coaches and get a new Athletic Committee. There is even some talk of shortening the tenure of the president unless he performs a major operation to cure the malady.

Organized sports are advised and managed at Northern by a series of committees. Chief among these is the Athletic Committee which coordinates the work of the others. The decisions of the Athletic Committee are carried out by its chairman, who is a member of the faculty.

Among the other committees, the following are outstanding:

The Scouting Committee pays the expenses of a coach to visit the major high school games in the eastern section of the country and report likely candidates to the Athletic Committee's Subcommittee on New Players. This subcommittee is authorized to offer scholarships with free room and board to prospects whom it approves.

The Coaching Committee makes recommendations to the Athletic Committee for renewing contracts or hiring replacements for those who it feels should be dropped from the staff. It is the policy of this committee to solicit recommendations from the head coach, members of all the teams, and the presidents of the campus fraternities. Selection of coaches is made by the Athletic Committee, with salaries subject to approval by the university's Budget Committee.

The Training Committee issues instructions to the head coach on matters of policy, for which purpose it has prepared a manual. It also polices coaching practices to see that its policies are carried out.

Care of the athletic fields is supervised by the university's Department of Grounds & Buildings, which receives recommendations from the Subcommittee on Athletic Fields. However, Grounds & Buildings can use its own discretion whether or not to comply with the recommendations, so that the function of the Subcommittee on Athletic Fields is purely advisory.

Publicity for games is handled by the Advertising Department of the College of Business Administration. Arrangements for the sale of tickets for all games are taken care of by the Purchasing Department of the Business Manager's Office, which also buys all uniforms and other equipment and supplies for the Athletic Association. The reason for combining these two activities in the Purchasing Department is to allow for the possibility of business persuasion in the purchase of blocks of tickets for minor contests by the university's vendors.

Concessions for the games are in charge of the Bureau of Student Self-Help, which reports to the Dean of Men. The director of the Bureau has final authority for the distribution of concessions, the income from which goes to the social fund of the Student Council.

By order of the Board of Trustees, half of the receipts from football and baseball games are budgeted for the support of the minor athletic teams. These funds are allocated to the individual sports by the university's Budget Committee on the basis of estimates submitted by several subcommittees (one for each of the minor sports) of the Athletic Committee. In general, the requests for funds are about double the amount available for the purpose.

The Athletic Committee of eight members was selected originally, for two-year terms on a staggered basis, by the president of the university. One-half of the committee retires each year, and their successors are chosen by the remaining members. Since retiring members are allowed to succeed themselves, the committee has become self-perpetuating. The Athletic Committee membership has been the same for years because the holdover members have continued to re-elect the retiring members to succeed themselves. Further inbreeding has been brought about by the chairman's practice of appointing his fellow committee members to the several subcommittees which the Athletic Committee supervises. He has explained this policy as an attempt to achieve coordination through the top committee.

The low ebb of the athletic program from the standpoint of losing intercollegiate games has disgusted both the student body and the alumni. The Alumni Association has served what amounts to an ultimatum on the president of the university: either he correct the situation, or a face-to-face appeal will be made to the Board of Trustees at its next meeting.

PROBLEM: The president of Northern received his doctorate in education thirty years ago and finds nothing in his training to assist him in this dilemma. What do you recommend? Draw an organization chart of the Athletic Association as it now operates and another containing your suggestions of revisions. Explain why you have made the detailed changes.

7

Organization

Techniques

Organization is fundamentally a study of structural design. It is a process of grouping related activities into separate compartments for ensuring the benefits of specialization. Coordination of the operation of these separate specialized activities draws them into an effective unit for promoting the accomplishment of the organization's objectives. System, which has been referred to as a group of sequential procedures, guides the organizational process to its desired purpose. Finally, control measures the results of the separate activities against accepted standards or norms for their special functions.

Practical planning and operation of a new organization, or the revision of an existing one, include the following fundamental steps:

1. Determine its objective or objectives
2. Study the means for obtaining the objective
3. Prepare plans for accomplishing the objective
4. Carry out the plans in actual operation
5. Observe and control the results
6. Make improvements suggested by observation

New Trends in Organization

In the previous chapter, we observed that organizational techniques have lagged behind those of management. Organization has, however, made progress in some distinct innovations since the first edition of this text was published six years ago. This is particularly true with respect to softening the rigid lines of authority, as exemplified in the tendency toward group decision-making in place of one-man rule. It is only one sign of the new awareness that people are at least as important as the functions they perform.

Another new organization concept is increased decentralization of authority, although this may be observed more in theory than in practice. The change is reflected in a more or less general increase in responsibility left to the middle-management group. This tendency is only slowly emerging, for many concerns still keep their control guards well poised. Liberal advances in this phase of organized relationships often make it necessary, or advisable, to increase the number of policies handed down from the top echelon as guides to action for middle management.

The Organization Chart

In the sequence of steps required for building a successful organization, drawing up a chart is of primary importance. The chart is the structural design of the organization. But it is merely a static picture of a group of dynamic activities which must be coordinated to function successfully. A static picture cannot properly represent the pulsating operations of an organization in action. As a guide and standard, however, such a picture is important. It is often said that a harmonious group of qualified executives can achieve success without a planned organization. But a group of harmonious executives has an organizational plan even if it has never been expressed in graphic form. Furthermore, an uncharted organization is headed for trouble when one or more of its leaders fades out of the picture. Organizations must be charted to give directives in the event of possible changes so that shifts in personnel do not leave the organism gasping. They must also chart plans for progress, otherwise they may take the unchartered course of atrophic demise.

When the organization is "tacitly understood" but not charted, results cannot help being unsatisfactory unless the concern is very small. A survey[1] of eighty-five universities revealed that 51 per cent did not have organization charts. The reasons were given as "too small," "unnecessary," and "makes operations too formal," which means that the ultimate in management flexibility was considered the prime requisite. But like most desirable attributes, flexibility can be carried too far.

Another important consideration is the age of an organization chart. The average chart has nearly reached, or just passed, its fifth birthday. Some are framed, which endows them with nothing but historical interest. Since successful concerns are dynamic, their organization plans are truly representative only after the necessary corrections have been made on their charts. One commentator has aptly suggested that the only thing more out-of-date than last year's organization chart is yesterday's newspaper. The most effective plan for keeping charts as well as organizations up-to-date is the periodic organization audit or survey.

Charts do not necessarily signify good or poor organizations. Many

[1] Henry G. Hodges, "Management of Universities," *The Southern Economic Journal* (July 1952), Vol. 19, pp. 79–89.

charts do not correctly picture their organizations. Only an organizational survey can determine whether or not the chart is correct. Charts may be purposely dishonest; those who made them may not have understood the principles of organization or the techniques of chart drafting; or the charts may be merely fuzzy representations of what they purport to picture.

Chart-making

The mere process of charting an organization has beneficial results for the management group that takes part in its consideration because:

1. It requires all executives to give thought to the responsibilities and authority assigned to their positions.
2. It also requires each executive to become familiar with the roles of the other members of the management group. This information leads to improvements in the relations with his supervisors, peers, and subordinates.
3. It occasionally leads the members of management directly to a study of the principles of organization, and indirectly to a consideration of the principles of management.
4. It promotes management morale because the members of the team acquire a clearer understanding of their duties and relationships as members of a chartered organization.

Chart forms

The organization chart form to be used will depend largely on the personal preferences of the chart-makers. The methods for showing subordinate and functional relationships, however, are more nearly standardized. The following pages will illustrate and explain the typical chart forms.

First is the *pyramidal chart*, illustrated in Figure 7.1. This form has the advantage of being simple, clear, and easy to understand. In emphasizing the single and direct line of responsibility between the superior and his subordinates, it minimizes the tendency to get lost in a maze of relationships. This form is commonly used in the simple line form of organization, with or without functional divisions or staff agencies, as will be discussed later in this chapter.

The *vertical chart*, also illustrated in Figure 7.1, is used to advantage where space-saving is important. Whether it is more or less clear than the pyramidal form depends on the individual reaction.

The *horizontal chart* also appears in Figure 7.1. It is believed by some members of management to be more easily understandable than some of the other forms.

The *circular chart*, illustrated in Figure 7.2, is enjoying a recent vogue. It is claimed that showing the functional relationship in concentric circles, which represent levels of authority, minimizes the psychological frictions

Figure 7.1

Organization Chart Forms

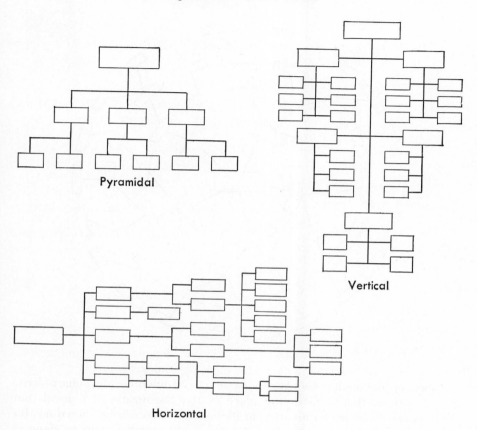

Pyramidal

Vertical

Horizontal

among executives on different organizational levels, thus tending to eliminate the "emotional aspect" of the pyramidal form. The circular chart
depicts the flow of authority outward in all directions. Another version of
this chart form is semi-circular, with the president's position located at the
center of the diameter.

The *linear chart,* illustrated in Figure 7.3, is relatively new. It was designed by a Dutch consultant, Ernst Hijmans, early in 1957. Its purpose is
to show quickly "who's who" and "what's what" in an over-all company
chart, or to give similar information on a divisional or departmental level.
Its proponents contend that it is superior to the older charts which require supporting explanations. Eighteen functions are listed down the left-
hand side of the chart. Along the top are twelve executive positions.
Either side of the chart can be expanded to suit a specific situation. A

Figure 7.2

Circular Chart Form

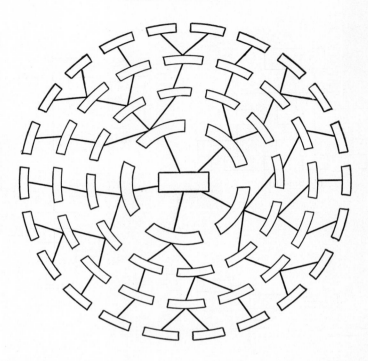

number of nationally known companies have adopted this chart form. Some contend that it takes the place of the organizational manual, but there is usually more information in the manual than can be shown on this chart form. One critic insists that it is impossible for the chart to show in "black and white" the various executives' functions and relationships. In spite of adverse criticisms, this chart form gives concrete evidence of the expanding study going on in the field of organization.

Defects discovered through charting

Some organization defects can be detected by observation, especially if a good job of charting has been done; but many defects must be discovered by surveying the organization and matching findings against the relationships shown on the chart. Outstanding organization defects include the following:

1. The span of control may be violated, throwing impossible work loads on certain executives.

Figure 7.3

Linear Responsibility Chart

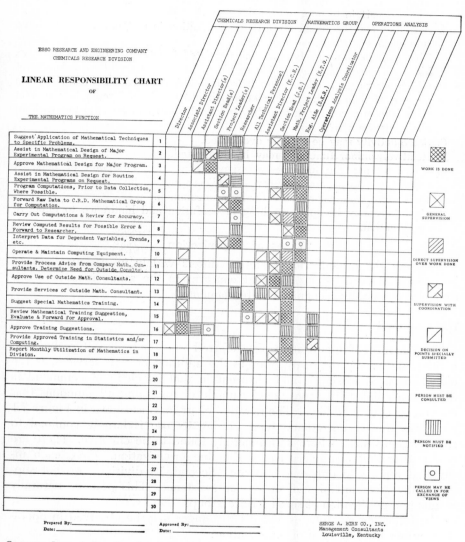

Courtesy: Serge A. Birn Co., Inc.

117

2. Functions may be improperly divided when the plotted activities are not mutually exclusive, leading to overlapping of functions.
3. There may be an improper stressing of the relative importance of functions which is certain to be a morale destroyer.
4. Activities may be illogically arranged, resulting in assignment of unrelated subdivisions to the same authority.
5. The same person may be handling unrelated functions. Situations do arise, however, where one person is capable of handling two different functions, which are so assigned because it is impossible to obtain a capable person for one of them. The two functions should be charted separately so that when the opportunity arises, the personnel setup can be adjusted without changing the chart.
6. Some activity may be entirely overlooked.
7. Relatively minor functions may be duplicated.
8. Functions may be improperly assigned from the standpoint of personal capabilities. Inspection may reveal mediocre men in important positions, or the reverse, a defect which is far from uncommon.
9. Functions may be split, resulting in confusion and hindrance to effective coordination.

Types of Organization

Although the organization structure differs widely in various lines of business, and even among different concerns in the same line, there are four plans generally recognized as fundamental.

The line type

The line form of organization, also referred to as the military type because of its wide use by the army prior to the addition of staff services, is the oldest form. It is simple and clear-cut in that its chain of command is direct, each link being considered capable of managing all functions that support its command level. The pyramid chart form as shown in Figure 7.1 illustrates this organizational type. Today its use is largely confined to small organizations, where it is generally found to be effective. There are two outstanding characteristics of the line organization. First, each individual reports to only one superior. Second, its divisions are not supported by any kind of staff or service assistance. This practice naturally results in a duplication of small service groups.

The following advantages and disadvantages may be observed in operations under the line type of organization:

Advantages
1. It is simple and easily understood.
2. It is adaptable to quick decisions and action.
3. Authority and responsibility are clear.
4. Discipline is easily maintained.
5. Its simplicity encourages stability.

Disadvantages

1. It is relatively inflexible.
2. It often leads to one-man autocratic rule.
3. An impractical span of control is developed.
4. Cooperation and coordination tend to be minimized.
5. Lack of specialization produces inferior operation.
6. It forces too much planning on the work level.
7. It tends to resist improvement.
8. It often delegates responsibilities with inadequate authority.

Line-and-staff type

The primary purpose of staff service in a line-and-staff organization is to aid the line with information, plans, and advice. The staff idea probably developed as a technical service in the military, where a growing multiplicity of weapons and services expanded beyond the capacity of line officers to give adequate attention to them. Aides, or staff officers, took over problems assigned to them by line officers to whom they were subordinate.

The simple distinction between the line and staff is that the former commands and the latter advises. Fundamentally, the line has total authority, while the staff has its tasks assigned to it by the line. There are occasions, however, when the staff exercises authority temporarily, or to a restricted degree. In an emergency, the staff may exercise special and temporary responsibility under authority delegated by the line. The line may also command the staff officer to carry through some plan he has recommended, thereby establishing his contact with subordinate line levels. This is referred to as the supervisory phase of staff service. When any staff activity is carried on by more than one person, its chief exercises line authority over his own organization. Individual or group staffs may be attached to line activities at any number of organizational levels.

Staff services may act independently in the interests of the function to which they are attached, or the various staff services may be organized in a hierarchy of their own, always subordinate to the line service to which they are assigned. This form of staff organization is particularly useful when one of its services is to infiltrate company doctrine throughout the organization.

The complexities of modern business, especially of industry, have caused a recent expansion of the staff-service idea, resulting in some confused relationships between line and staff officers. Confusion may develop because of the many kinds of leaders. Some look with such favor on the staff function that they are inclined to lean on it to the point where it becomes a crutch. At the opposite extreme is the executive who is distrustful of an organizational technique to which he was opposed from the beginning. He is likely to make a few staff assignments and then not use the advice which they offer. Somewhere in between is the correct balanced use of staff services. For example, the director of sales in a wholesale concern may consider it important to check his prices against the trend in the market. The desired information may be collected, analyzed, and submitted by a staff employee, based on competitors' selling prices. Gathering the data may be more difficult than analyzing it; it is a time-consuming task which any busy line officer can well afford to shift to a staff member experienced with such problems.

The line-and-staff plan is adaptable to medium-sized and large organizations. It would be cumbersome and expensive for a small concern. Reference to Figure 7.4 will aid in understanding some of the advantages and disadvantages of the line-and-staff type of organization.

Advantages
1. It provides for the advice of specialists.
2. It eliminates the confusion of multiple bosses.
3. It provides additional supervision in emergencies.
4. It relieves executive burdens.

Figure 7.4

Line-and-Staff Organization

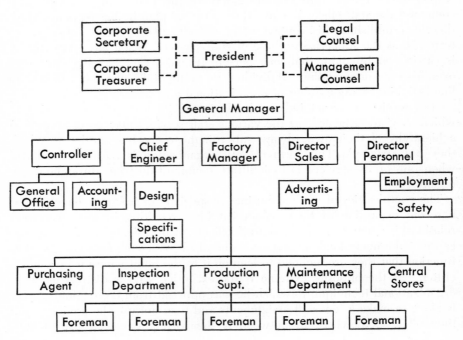

Disadvantages

1. It can cause jealousies between line and staff.
2. Its undue centralization promotes staff "authority."
3. It decreases initiative in some line activities.
4. It requires a high degree of executive cooperation.

Most of the disadvantages of this form of organization can be overcome by complete written descriptions of the respective duties of line and staff officers. When the various executive activities are set up on a functional basis, and the personnel employed are qualified and properly assigned, the line-and-staff type of organization is the best that we know about at this time.

Functional type

The functional type of organization is derived from Frederick W. Taylor's functional foremanship. Taylor categorized the foreman's duties into eight distinct activities. Because he reasoned that no foreman could handle all of these adequately, he devised the plan of functional foremanship, by which individual supervisors were assigned to each of the eight activities so that the worker would have the advantage of specialized supervision. Under this system, each worker reported to the eight specialists for the various phases of his work. Figure 7.5 indicates the operation of Taylor's functional foremanship plan.

Taylor's purpose was to divide the total supervisory task so that each

Figure 7.5

Taylor's Functional Foremanship Plan

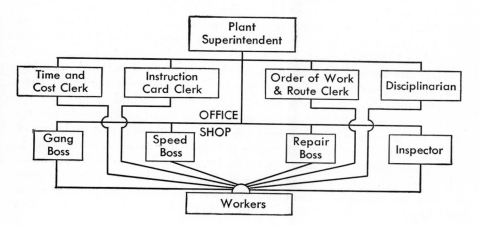

foreman would have a single activity, to ensure the superior results that follow specialization. It can be seen from the functional diagram that the worker is most concerned with the lower group of "bosses," the gang, speed, and repair bosses and the inspector. His contacts were less frequent with the other four — the time-and-cost clerk, instruction-card clerk, order-of-work and route clerks, and the disciplinarian. The advantages and disadvantages of Taylor's plan follow:

Advantages
1. Division of function is based on specialization.
2. Planning is separated from manual work.
3. Subordinates are assured better supervision.
4. Functional foremen are easier to train.

Disadvantages
1. Lines of authority over workers are divided.
2. "Buck-passing" is encouraged among foremen.
3. Personal frictions develop among the specialists.

Chiefly because of the confusion produced among the workers by multiple bosses, Taylor's plan is seldom found in use today. He felt that eventually his idea would be applied to all levels of management below the top executive. The higher up the command ladder the plan is extended, the greater is the resulting confusion and resistance because of the nature of the work and the greater articulateness of the subexecutives.

In spite of its weaknesses, Taylor's philosophy of functionalism made a distinct contribution to the field of organization. It led to the development and successful use of various types of functional staff services on an advisory level. Also, the application of functionalism to the line-and-staff form of organization has greatly improved its effectiveness. The functional operator performs the same tasks as the staff operator, but he also issues the orders in his own name. His decisions, however, are based largely on standard practices and procedures, rather than on personal or group opinions related to individual cases.

There are two advantages in the application of the functional organization to the upper layers of management. First, it reserves the chief's time for over-all planning, organizing and controlling. Second, it provides for rational decisions and standard practices. Functional operators do not require the questionable aid of committees to help them in the problems of management, because each operator performs the duties for which he is best fitted, rather than a group of duties assigned on a workload basis. This approach relieves subexecutives of duties for which they have neither training nor successful experience. Whereas functional management means individual decisions based on written standard procedures or technical knowledge, committee management means compromises reached by discussion. Under functional management, the upper layers of supervision are more hemmed in by standards, but in those less routine matters not covered by accepted standards, they have more real authority. What is more important, they have more time to perform leadership functions demanding their highest skills.

The committee type

The committee can only marginally be termed a type of organization since it is usually attached to one of the other other three plans. It is conceivable that an institution could be managed by a group of functional committees, coordinated by an executive committee, but the plan is unusual in its pure form. However, committees are used so extensively in connection with the other organizational forms that they must be considered here.

There are several kinds of committees, variously referred to as executive, policy, management, and advisory. The functions of the *executive committee* are, or should be, set forth in the organizational manual. In general, its duty is to assist or guide the chief executive in the over-all coordination of the enterprise. It is customarily made up of those members of top management who are capable of guiding the concern's activities in accord with its established policies and toward the accomplishment of its objectives.

The *policy committee* formulates top policies for the guidance of executive officers in performing their functions. It is usually composed of two or three executives and an equal number of directors. Where either executive or policy committees are found below the top level of administration or management, their decisions are circumscribed by policies, rules, and regulations from above.

Executive and policy committees arrive at those useful decisions which invariably flow from the consultation of individuals who are skilled in particular subjects and interested in common objectives. It should be observed that although executive and policy committees do not directly manage any function or activity, their decisions are "law" for those whom they affect. Many concerns could improve their management by adding executive and policy committees to their organization. It is also probable that many companies use the executive and policy committee plan without having established it as a formal part of their organization.

In addition to the useful executive and policy types, it is evident that many institutions, especially the larger ones, are plagued with committees.[2]

[2] One state university with 8000 students has 37 "administrative committees." Normally, administrative committees would determine policies, which the organization manual shows is not true in this case. They are management committees. The prevalence of so-called management committees in large business concerns and governmental agencies is only of lesser degree.

It is advisable from several standpoints to have a reasonable number of advisory committees, provided that their fields do not overlap and that the committee members are qualified to discuss the subjects they consider.

For purely managerial purposes, the committee recognized as most effective is the committee of one. One defense offered for committee management is that it is "democratic." It is debatable whether the concern is efficiently served by the actions of groups whose members are often bureaucratically selected and are not qualified to consider intelligently the subjects they discuss.

Gwilym A. Price, chairman of the board of Westinghouse Electric, in discussing the company's Policy and Finance Committee at the annual stockholders' meeting of 1958, said that "three men with different points of view, different backgrounds, and different problems could reach better balanced and more effective basic policy decisions than could one man." Then he noted that "no company can be run soundly by a committee — it must have a boss." William H. Newman suggests that "there is probably no administrative device more commonly abused than this one," referring to the committee. He feels that "it is an opiate taken in lieu of effective administrative action."[3]

Counting committee noses is neither a democratic nor a scientific process. It frequently enables the numerical majority to serve selfish interests, even to the extent of perpetuating its dictatorial status. The old aphorism that two heads are better than one can be a mathematical fraud. It may or may not be true, depending on what is in the heads. The validity of committee decisions is not enhanced by any number of unintelligent opinions. If the subject is of a general nature, opinions based on general knowledge may be fruitful; if the problem is specific in nature, fruitful opinions can come only from those with specific or scientific training and experience.

There is another undesirable facet of advisory committees — there are too many of them. If the concern is overorganized, or if there is an accepted technique of establishing committees to check the decisions of other committees, the committee chain may be come so long as to weaken even a good committee plan. Figure 7.6 shows the application of committees to a line-and-staff organization.

For effective committee operations, the following rules should be observed:

1. Committee membership should be limited to not more than five to operate effectively.
2. An agenda for committee meetings, listing items in the order of their importance, should be prepared by the chairman well in advance of the meetings and distributed to its members before meeting time.

[3] *Administrative Action* (New York: Prentice-Hall, Inc., 1951), pp. 217, 218.

Figure 7.6

Committee Plan of Organization

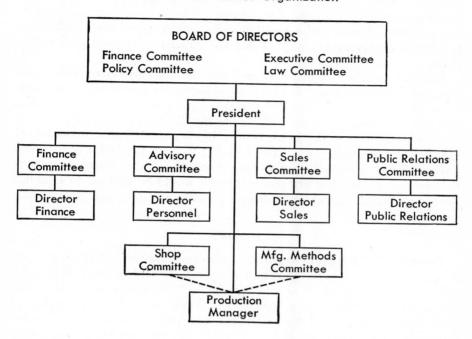

3. Committee meetings should have definite beginning and closing times so that important matters will be decided, and dalliance reduced to a minimum.
4. The chairman should hold the reins and use them to keep discussion on the track and aiming toward conclusions.

Multiple Management

Although the word "management" is loosely used in this title, the techniques which it introduces are important because they have been found eminently successful by many concerns. It is really a superior application of the advisory committee technique. "Multiple management" was first introduced in 1932 by the McCormick Spice Company of Baltimore, where it has proved to be effective. The plan provides for a Junior Board of Directors whose members are selected on a merit basis. Semiannually, the Junior Board retires those three members who receive the lowest merit ratings by their fellow members, making way for three new board members. After successful experience with the original Junior Board, the McCormick Company added a Junior Factory Board and finally a Junior Sales Board.

The function of these three boards is to make recommendations to the senior or corporate board of the company. There is no obligation on the part of the corporate board to accept their suggestions. However, experience has shown that the junior boards are careful and conservative in sending up suggestions, and the majority of these have been adopted by the corporate board. The multiple-management plan has promoted a number of supervisory employees into the upper management of the company.

Although members of these junior boards do not participate in the management of the company, the program is superior to most other advisory-committee plans because of the psychology involved. Not only does multiple management benefit the company from the standpoint of the employee members of the junior boards, but it also improves the morale of the rank-and-file employees. They feel that through the junior boards they have a direct approach to top management and the corporate policy-determining group. For obvious reasons, it would be difficult to establish the junior-board system in a company with a strong and antagonistic union.[4]

Manuals

Because it is impossible to tell the entire organizational story on a chart, it is advisable to fill in the gaps by more complete explanations. This is the purpose of the manual. It aids in bringing a static picture to life. Because the interests of the various management levels are focused according to their responsibilities and authority, it is advisable to prepare manuals accordingly. The *policy manual* is primarily intended for top management, although its contents should have some interest for the entire supervisory group.

The *organization manual* explains in detail the duties, responsibilities and authority on a functional, divisional, or departmental basis. It also defines the duties of individual positions within the management hierarchy. The *department manual* does the same thing for the departments, in addition to showing relationships among the departments and with the upper levels of management. Many large companies also issue *supervisor manuals*. Besides general organization matters with which the supervisor should be acquainted, they sometimes explain the legal relations between the workers and the company, and often include the agreement with the union.

Charts and manuals are merely explanations of the entire framework, making it easier for the personnel to cooperate by knowing what is expected of them, how it can be accomplished, to whom they must look for guidance,

---

[4] The author organized and helped operate a junior-board installation during the first year of its existence for the Dayton (Ohio) division of the National Tag Company. From that experience, it was concluded that this keen tool must be used with great discretion during its initial period. If it gets past the first year as an accepted improvement by the lower supervisory group and the rank-and-file employees, it will probably become an established institution of great merit.

and over whom they exercise supervision. The preparation of these manuals requires the effort of many employees. It is a laborious but interesting job because the manuals must dovetail with the organization charts. Preparation of manuals, which normally follows completion of the charts, may lead to corrections and changes.

What are some of the auxiliary advantages which flow from the use of the chart-and-manual guide?

1. It definitely fixes responsibilities and authority.
2. It specifically defines functions and duties.
3. It substitutes written for oral instructions.
4. It minimizes "buck-passing."
5. It paints a complete picture of the organization.
6. It improves management classifications and salaries.
7. It aids in budget planning and cost determinations.
8. It is a solid basis for rational organization changes.

Standard Practice

Standard practice instructions, also referred to as "standard operating procedures (SOP)" and "standard practice procedures," are written guides for carrying out the activities included on the organization chart and explained in the manuals. They are also issued for guidance in performing work or operations. Charts, manuals, and standard practice instructions encompass organizational and procedural operations. The omission of any one of these three weakens the organization and the operation which it prescribes.

It is readily seen that the organization chart tells "where" in a company a function is placed, the organization manual tells "what" the detailed nature of the function or position is and indicates its relationships to other functions and positions, while the standard practice instruction tells "how" the functions are to be carried on and the duties and responsibilities are to be discharged.[5]

Standard practices (Figure 7.7) represent the best known methods at the time they are compiled. They must, like the chart and the manual, be subjected to periodic examination to meet changed conditions. Current issues of standard practice instructions should be handy for ready reference, and even when they are outmoded, they should be kept for possible future reference; they may save duplication of mental effort.

[5] L. P. Alford and John R. Bangs, *Production Handbook* (New York: The Ronald Press Company, 1948), p. 58.

Figure 7.7

STANDARD PRACTICE INSTRUCTIONS

(For Purchase Orders)

I. Purchase Order shall be issued on National Standard Purchase Order form of the National Association of Purchasing Agents.

II. The Purchase Order form shall be made up in ten copies, and distributed as follows:

1. Original shall be sent to the Vendor;

2. Acknowledgement copy shall be sent to the Vendor, for acceptance of the order, and signifying of delivery date;

3. Copy for the Procurement Department file;

4. Copy for the Receiving Department as notice to expect the order (purchase);

5. Copy to the Accounting Department as notice to charge commitment to proper budget account, and for subsequent reconciling with invoice;

6. Copy to the department making the requisition as notice of compliance with request:

7. Copy for Procurement's expediter for use as follow-up;

8. Copy to the Inspection Department for use when notified to inspect by the Receiving Department;

9. Copy to the Costing Department;

10. Copy to Materials Control for Central Stores' records.

What are some of the advantages of standard practices?

1. They give the worker a detailed picture of how to proceed with his job. They not only save the worker's time but also frequently provide answers beyond his own ability to analyze and plan.
2. They provide a means for employees on similar work in scattered branches to do their jobs according to a uniform pattern and in the one best way known at the time.
3. They save analysis and planning time of supervisors all down the organizational line.
4. They fix responsibility for procedural and operational errors.
5. They aid in determining costs and analyses.
6. They stimulate the thinking of everyone who takes part in compiling them, thus leading to further possibilities of improved methods and procedures.
7. They increase productivity and reduce unit costs.
8. They conserve supervisory time for planning improvements and controlling operations.

Conclusions

The organization structure is the framework through which management activities circulate. Ascending information and descending orders are outstanding examples of the necessity for free circulation throughout the organization. It is important that communications move expeditiously in all directions through the entire framework to obtain intelligent cooperation and effective effort. In spite of the flow of decision-making through main channels, it has been found beneficial for corresponding subordinates on the same level in different vertical channels to deal directly with each other, provided they maintain the established relationships with their superiors. Here again we see the fundamental organizational relationships being maintained while providing for faster horizontal decisions.

Without organization, no plan requiring the participation of two or more people could attain success except by mere chance. Without techniques for setting the organization in motion, its effectiveness falls short of its possibilities. Organization is one of the primary tools of management. Its effectiveness is a distinct aid to leadership. The combination of good organization and capable leadership is one of the deciding factors for attaining any objective.

QUESTIONS

1. What are the six fundamental steps for planning a new organization or revising an existing one?
2. Why have the techniques of organization lagged behind the development of management principles?
3. Can you name two of the more recent new concepts in the techniques of organization?
4. It has been said that the organization chart is a static picture of an organiza-

tion. Is this the reason why many top executives have their chart framed for office wall display?

5. How dependable are organization charts for predicting the success of a business? What is the explanation when a poorly drafted organization is financially successful?

6. To what extent is chart *making* helpful in obtaining coordination of activities among a group of executives?

7. What advantages over the older chart forms are offered by the new linear chart of the Dutch consultant, Ernst Hijmans?

8. Name some of the organizational defects that may be discovered through charting.

9. What is the chief defect of the line type of organization?

10. How does staff service aid management even though it ordinarily has no line functions?

11. Why was Taylor's functional type of organization for foremen discarded so generally since it was based primarily on the effectiveness of specialized skills for supervisors? What later contribution did Taylor's plan make to the general field of organization?

12. What are some of the disadvantages of the committee type of organization for management activities?

13. To what extent, in your opinion, is committee management democratic?

14. Is Multiple Management actually managerial in function, or is it merely advisory? If the latter, what contribution has it made to progressive management techniques?

15. What is the purpose of the organizational manual? Under what circumstances does it best accomplish its main purpose?

16. What other manuals are used to advantage by management?

17. How would you explain the contention that "charts, manuals, and standard practice instructions encompass organizational and procedural operations"?

18. The text lists eight advantages of standard practices. How many of them can you recall?

19. What do you think will be the effect of the new idea of raising the responsibility of the middle management group?

20. How does the "splitting of function" affect coordination?

CASE PROBLEM

SIMPSON PLASTICS CORPORATION

Simpson has had a phenomenal growth during the ten years of its existence. Incorporated in 1952 with $100,000 common stock capital, the rapid expansion of its business, and profit growth, led to two $100,000 increases in its outstanding capital during the first five years. The three incorporators were well balanced in their backgrounds for the plastics business. One had ten years' experience in the production end of the business with a successful company in the same line. Another had worked as general sales manager for a large furniture manufacturing company for eight years, and the third member of the organization group received his Master of Business Administration degree about ten years before the incorporation.

The business-trained member of the trio became president and general manager, while the other two were designated vice presidents in charge of sales and production. All three had accumulated some savings for investment in the new company. In addition, the family of one of the incorporators subscribed generously to the original capital stock issue. Based on substantial accomplishments, the two subsequent stock issues sold themselves among a fairly large group of friends and business contacts.

The business was started in Cleveland, and as the result of a well-planned advertising program conceived by the sales manager, the company's customers were soon spread through a large portion of the Lakes region. The original specialty was plastic sheets for the furniture trade. Each year some new specialty was added to the line. The first was translucent building panels, followed by fiberglass for boat building, and later plastic rods and tubing.

Sales to boat builders covered a large section of the east coast before they finally reached Florida, where a year-round market was opened for small boat materials and components. The Florida boat and building expositions led to the establishment of sales agencies in Central America, especially for the plastic sheet business. A line of kitchen and bathroom specialties opened up new business among home builders in many fast-growing communities on both sides of the border.

Expansion into the various lines of plastics required constant additions to machinery and equipment. Finally, the establishment of warehouse facilities along the Atlantic coast and in several Central American countries made it necessary to increase the company's capital to half a million, partly for the purpose of reducing its over-extended bank loans. By 1958, Simpson's sales volume had reached the seven million mark.

In that same year, Simpson's president felt that a two-for-one stock split would hasten the sale of a new $200,000 stock issue by reducing the price of its over-the-counter offering. The idea of the stock split was favored by both the sales and production managers. The sales manager argued that a wider distribution of the stock would naturally make it possible to interest more boosters for the company's products. The production manager, who soon laid claim to a sizeable portion of the proposed "new money" for purchasing improved machinery, felt that he could reduce his unit costs and thus increase the profit margin or lower the selling prices to obtain a more favorable competitive position.

By 1962 sales had increased to ten million, and company employment had grown to about 500. Sales branches and warehouses were set up in ten locations, four of which were located in Latin America. The profit and surplus account amounted to $200,000, with inventories valued at practically the same amount. Bank loans were up again — past the $300,000 level.

PROBLEM: Draft a detailed organization chart aimed at securing the continuing success of the Simpson Corporation.

Part One • Suggestions For Further Reading

Anderson, E. H. and Schwenning, G. T., *The Science of Production Organization*, New York: John Wiley and Sons, Inc., 1938.

Argyris, Chris, *Understanding Organizational Behavior*, Homewood, Illinois: The Dorsey Press, Inc., 1960.

Baum, Bernard H., *Decentralization of Authority in a Bureaucracy*, Englewood Cliffs, New Jersey: Prentice-Hall, Inc., 1961.

Bethel, Lawrence L., Atwater, Franklin S., Smith, George H. E., Stackman, Harvey A., Jr., *Industrial Organization and Management, 4th Edition*, New York: McGraw-Hill Book Company, Inc., 1962.

Bowman, E. H., and Fetter, R. B., *Analysis for Production Management*, Rev. Ed., Homewood, Illinois: Richard D Irwin, Inc., 1961.

Buffa, Elwood S., *Modern Production Management*, New York: John Wiley and Sons, Inc., 1961. Parts I and II.

Churchman, C. W., Ackoff, R. L., and Arnoff, E. L., *Introduction to Operations Research*, New York: John Wiley and Sons, Inc., 1957.

Cornell, William B. and Madeheim, Huxley, *Organization and Management in Industry and Business, 4th Edition*, New York: The Ronald Press Company, 1958.

Cruickshank, Henry M. and Davis, Keith, *Cases in Management, 3rd Edition*, Homewood, Illinois: Richard D. Irwin, Inc., 1962.

Dale, Ernest, *The Great Organizers*, New York, McGraw-Hill Book Company, Inc., 1960.

————, *Planning and Developing the Company Organization Structure*, New York: American Management Association, Research Project No. 20, 1952.

Dauten, Paul M., Jr., Editor, *Current Issues and Emerging Concepts in Management*, Boston: Houghton Mifflin Company, 1962.

Davis, Ralph C., *Fundamentals of Top Management*, New York: Harper & Brothers, 1951.

Drucker, Peter F., *The Practice of Management*, New York: Harper & Brothers, 1954.

Fayol, Henri, *General and Industrial Management* (originally published in French in 1916), London: Sir Isaac Pitman and Sons, Ltd., 1949.

Ferguson, Robert O. and Sargent, Lauren F., *Linear Programming*, New York: McGraw-Hill Book Co., 1958.

Gregory, Robert H., and Van Horn, Richard L., *Automatic Data-Processing Systems*, Belmont, California: Wardsworth Publishing Company, Inc., 1960.

Haimann, Theo, *Professional Management: Theory and Practice*, Boston: Houghton Mifflin Company, 1962.

Haire, Mason, Editor, *Modern Organization Theory,* New York: John Wiley and Sons, Inc., 1959.

Haynes, W. Warren and Massie, Joseph L., *Management: Analysis, Concepts and Cases,* Englewood Cliffs, New Jersey: Prentice-Hall Inc., 1961.

Ireson, W. Grant, and Grant, Eugene L., *Handbook of Industrial Engineering and Management,* Englewood Cliffs, New Jersey: Prentice-Hall, Inc., 1955, Sections 1, 2, 3, 13, and 15.

Jamison, Charles L., *Business Policy,* New York: Prentice-Hall, Inc., 1953.

Jones, Manley Howe, *Executive Decision Making, Revised Edition,* Homewood, Illinois: Richard D. Irwin, Inc., 1962.

Karlin, Samuel, *Mathematical Methods and Theory in Games, Programming and Economics,* Reading, Massachuestts: Addison-Wesley Publishing Co., 1959, Vol. I.

Koontz, Harold and O'Donnell, Cyril, *Principles of Management, 2nd Edition,* New York: McGraw-Hill Book Company, Inc., New York, 1959.

Lansburgh, Richard H. and Spriegel, William R., *Industrial Management, 5th Edition,* New York: John Wiley and Sons, Inc., 1955.

Learned, Edmund P., Christenson, C. Roland and Andrews, Kenneth R., *Problems of General Management,* Homewood, Illinois: Richard D. Irwin, Inc., 1961.

Likert, Rensis, *New Patterns of Management,* New York: McGraw-Hill Book Company, Inc., 1961.

Luce, R. Duncan, and Raiffa, Howard, *Games and Decision: Introduction and Critical Survey,* New York: John Wiley and Sons, Inc., 1957.

March, James G. and Simon, H. A., *Organizations,* New York: John Wiley & Sons, 1958.

Martin, E. W., Jr., *Electronic Data Processing,* Homewood, Illinois: Richard D. Irwin, Inc., 1961.

Merrill, Harwood F., Editor, *Classics in Management,* New York: American Management Association, 1960.

Mooney, James D. and Reiley, Alan C., *The Principles of Organization,* New York: Harper & Brothers Publishers, 1939.

Moore, Franklin G., *Manufacturing Management,* 3rd Edition, Homewood Illinois: Richard D. Irwin, Inc., 1961.

Newman, William H. and Summer, Charles E., Jr., *The Process of Management,* Englewood Cliffs, New Jersey: Prentice-Hall, Inc., 1961.

O'Donnell, Cyril, *Cases in General Management,* Homewood, Illinois: Richard D. Irwin, Inc., 1961.

Parkinson, C. Northcote, *Parkinson's Law,* Boston: Houghton Mifflin Company, 1962.

Petersen, Elmore and Plowman, E. Grosvenor, *Business Organization and Management, 4th Edition,* Homewood, Illinois: Richard D. Irwin, Inc., 1958.

Pfiffner, L. M. and Sherwood, Frank P., *Administrative Organization*, Englewood Cliffs, New Jersey: Prentice-Hall, Inc., 1960.

Richards, Max D. and Nielander, William A., *Readings in Management*, Cincinnati: South-Western Publishing Company, 1958.

Rubenstein, Albert H. and Haberstroh, Chadwick J., *Some Theories of Organization*, Homewood, Illinois: Richard D. Irwin, Inc., and The Dorsey Press, Inc., 1960.

Schell, Erwin Haskell, *Administrative Proficiency in Business*, New York: McGraw-Hill Book Company, 1936.

Schlaifer, Robert, *Probability and Statistics for Business Decisions*, New York: McGraw-Hill Book Company, Inc., 1959.

Shull, Fremont A., Jr., Editor, *Selected Readings in Management*, Homewood, Illinois: Richard D. Irwin, Inc., Second Series, 1962.

————, *Selected Readings in Management*, Homewood, Illinois: Richard D. Irwin, Inc., 1958.

Simon, Herbert A., *The New Science of Management Decision*, New York: Harper and Brothers Publishers, 1960.

Spriegel, William R., *Principles of Business Organization and Operation, 3rd Edition*, Englewood Cliffs, New Jersey: Prentice-Hall, Inc., 1960.

Spriegel, William R., and Myers, Clark E., *The Writings of the Gilbreths*, Homewood, Illinois: Richard D. Irwin, Inc., 1953.

Summer, Charles E., Jr., *Factors in Effective Administration*, New York: Graduate School of Business, Columbia University, 1956.

Taylor, Frederick Winston, *Scientific Management*, New York: Harper and Brothers Publishers, 1947.

————, *Principles of Scientific Management*, New York: Harper and Brothers Publishers, 1911.

Urwick, L., *The Elements of Administration*, New York: Harper and Brothers Publishers, 1943.

————, *The Golden Book of Management*, London: Newman Neame, Ltd., 1956.

Vance, Stanley, *Industrial Management*, New York: McGraw-Hill Book Company, Inc., 1959.

Ziegler, Raymond J., *Principles of Industrial Management Case Book*, New York: The Macmillan Co., 1961.

•

The quotation at the beginning of Part One is from: Bertrand Russell, *The Impact of Science on Society*, New York: Simon and Schuster, 1953, p. 89.

Controls for

ndustrial Operations

It may be stated as a general principle that while Art seeks to produce certain effects, Science is primarily concerned with investigating the causes of these effects.

Thus, independently of the intrinsic importance of the art selected for illustration, there always seems room for a corresponding science, collecting and classifying the records of the past so that the future operations of the art may be more effective.

CAPTAIN HENRY METCALFE

8

Managerial Control

Control arises from the possibility of error in carrying out plans or standards. It assures that performance corresponds with the plans or standards set up for guidance. Managerial control starts with a guide for action, which is referred to as the control standard. Its purpose is to accomplish some management objective. The standard may be quantitative or qualitative, or it may consist of a plan of action. Its purpose, we repeat, is to serve as the instruction for accomplishing a desired objective.

Comparison of a partial or completed performance with the standard is the beginning of control. If the standard or plan has been followed, the action is said to be "under control." If there is a significant deviation, the action is "out of control." The part of this procedure which compares the standard to the performance is the *first* phase of managerial control. The *second* phase is concerned with getting the action or performance "back under control" if the standard has not been followed.

The *third* phase of managerial control involves the revision of a standard or plan when it is decided that the original cannot accomplish the desired objective or is impossible of attainment in action. This is simply an acknowledgment that the original standard was not adequately devised. Although the performance may have been under control as far as it related to the standard, an analysis of its results and their causes shows that the standard requires revision. Because the more important phases of planning are referred to as administrative rather than managerial, this revision phase is sometimes spoken of as administrative control. The comparison of a performance with its standard would be designated as managerial control.[1]

Techniques and Processes of Control

Controls consist of techniques and processes. Budgets and other financial statements are techniques. The process of control operates when some

[1] For an interesting discussion of this subject see Raymond J. Ziegler, "The Application of Managerial Controls in Selected Business Firms," *Advanced Management* (August 1958), Vol. 23, No. 8, pp. 10–12.

comparison furnishes a possible basis for decision, and the control authority is responsible for bringing about an adjustment for accomplishing the desired objective. We are here chiefly concerned with the processes of control.

The standard in a control process may, for example, consist of a specified number of machine-made pieces that an operator is expected to produce in an eight-hour day. If he does not meet that goal, the operation is out of control. It is the responsibility of the controlling agency to discover the trouble and get the operation back under control. The difficulty may be with the operator, who is either unqualified, undertrained, or suffering from some temporary physical or mental stress. The machine may be at fault, owing to excessive wear on some part, a loose set-screw, or any one of a number of reasons. Poor materials can result in failure to meet the quantitative or qualitative standard, or both.

If the machine is defective, the situation will probably be referred to Maintenance. If the materials have caused the trouble, their specifications must be corrected or the vendor dealt with for not following the specifications. If any materials or supplies are entirely depleted, the responsibility lies with procurement for not ordering on time or with the vendor for not meeting the scheduled delivery date. Faults of the operator, the purchasing agent, or the vendor may lead to sanctions. If the operator is at fault, he may be transferred to some less exacting work, given an opportunity to overcome any temporary difficulty, assigned for further training, or dismissed. Punishment for the purchasing agent will depend on the financial seriousness of his dereliction. If the fault lies with the vendor, he may be notified that another delay in delivering materials without prior warning will result in his being dropped by the purchasing department.

If, as the result of management's analysis of the situation, it is decided that the quantitative standard is not reasonable, it is the responsibility of the controlling agency to make necessary changes in the standard, including reduction in quantity if that appears reasonable. On the other hand, it may be decided that the standard would be well within the capacity of the average operator if the speed of the machine is increased or some improved parts installed.

The discussion so far has not touched on a situation where the quantitative standard is too low. Decisions in such cases must be approached with all the facts at hand. If the quantitative standard is too low, the average worker can beat it with ease. Will he keep his pace down to the point where it just meets the standard? What will be the reaction of the fast worker who can surpass a standard which is presumably correct for the average worker? In this type of quantitative control, it becomes evident that some kind of an incentive reward should be developed for superior workers. Since it is generally agreed that quantitative standards should not be changed unless there has been some significant change in methods, machines, or materials, the important of correct standards becomes crystal clear.

Purpose of control

The purpose of control is to serve management so that it may be better able to make correct decisions and take considered action faster than it has been done in the past, and on time. Since control has a distinctly scientific approach, it is a keener management tool than the rule-of-thumb method which it replaces.

Controls are the guiding factors of business; they are the warning signals for management; they are one of the most important bases for scientific management. Properly worked out and used, controls are the indicators, or acceptable standards, for production, finance, sales, and numerous other activities. Over a period of time, they mark out the path by which the present situation was reached in any activity subjected to restraints. They supply experienced human judgment with an opportunity for charting the path ahead by indicating the means and methods for following that path.

Furthermore, since controls are based on standards of some kind, they relieve management of making decisions which are essentially repetitive. The result should be better planning, organizing, and co-ordinating. Controls also provide for uniformity of operations and plans where they are essential, thus leading to more effective coordination. By the use of established and communicated standards, plans and operations going on in widely scattered areas or in adjoining departments can be dovetailed for superior accomplishment of the desired objective.

Control as a cycle

Management has been described as a cycle of planning, organizing, directing, coordinating, and controlling. It is obvious that control would be impossible without attention to all four of the earlier phases of the cycle. Seen as the process of assuring that performance corresponds with plans and standards, control can be broken down into *four basic steps:* (1) setting standards, (2) checking on performance, (3) evaluating results, (4) taking corrective action. One of the chief ways that corrective action can be taken is in the formulation of new plans or standards, so the fourth step of the process becomes the first step in a new cycle of the control process. This cycle can be diagrammed as in Figure 8.1.

It may be assumed that a list of the types of control should be arranged according to some classification plan. For example, the owner of an installment furniture store would likely be most interested in control of accounts receivable. The manager of a hospital might prefer controls for

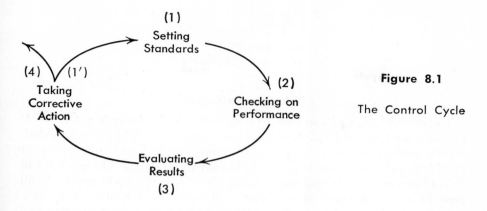

Figure 8.1

The Control Cycle

salaries and wages because they account for more than 60 per cent of his total costs. The classifications used in our listing include five general types:

I. Company-wide Controls
 1. Profits
 2. Position in industry
 3. Policies
 4. Organization structure
 5. Sales
 6. Procurement
 7. Finance
 8. Research

II. Divisional Controls
 1. Profits
 2. Percentage of market

III. Department Controls
 1. Output
 2. Costs — materials & labor
 3. Quality of product

IV. Operational Controls
 1. Labor standards
 2. Material standards
 3. Variable overhead
 4. Scrap

V. Functional Controls
 1. Sales
   a. Products & territories
   b. Advertising
   c. Credits
   d. Salesmen
   e. Product mixture

 2. Procurement
   a. Quality
   b. Costs
   c. Inventory

 3. Finance
   a. Cash
   b. Receivables & payables
   c. Capital expenditures
   d. Capital structure

 4. Research & Development
   a. Pure and applied
   b. New products
   c. Cost reduction
   d. Individual projects

5. Personnel
   a. Selection and training
   b. Incentives
   c. Wages and salaries

Objections to Control

The general idea of controlled performance in business is not new. It predates the Industrial Revolution, and as we go back in history, its sanctions for nonconformance were increasingly severe. Aside from the influence of this historical pespective, it is simply human to be opposed to any kind of compulsory control. Questionable applications of control still appear in all types of autocratic management. Prior to the turn of the century, it is probably true that controlled performance in many businesses was expressed as "Do this or else." Worker reaction to this former technique still lingers.

Furthermore, controls are usually exercised after the job is completed, when the corrective factor may include some form of punitive action for results that do not meet the established standard. Many of those responsible for setting the standards are so convinced of the virtue of their universal application that they establish far too many unjustified controls. Someone has said that when a cannon is shot off incessantly, it attracts no more attention than the hum of machinery. Even sanctions do not always have the desired effect.

Too often neither the purpose of specific standards nor the basis for their determination is explained to those subject to their control. Another cause for complaint is the juggling of time-control figures established by professional stop-watch measurements — usually to the detriment of the workers. Added to all these objections has been an inexcusable neglect of communication between many managements and their workers.

Overcoming the objections

1. *Too many controls* tend to diminish their importance and acceptance by those being controlled. Managerial control is a very important tool; its opportunities should not be minimized by indiscriminate applications.

2. *The manner of approach* by the control agency should promote a cooperative atmosphere. If the approach suggests punishment, the idea involved will be resisted. With most workers, the approach is often just as important as the problem involved. Voluntary explanations of the standard and how it was obtained should be the keynote in promoting acceptance of its control. Since it is normal for employees to want to know when they have done an acceptable job, a reasonable standard should boost worker morale.

3. *The control feature should be decentralized* at the point where the

performance takes place, even when the establishment of the standard is centralized.

4. *Flexibility of the standard is important.* It serves the concern's best interests, lessens worker discontent, and may promote worker initiative if he is invited to make suggestions.

5. *Communication* is an absolute in promoting the most effective use of managerial control. There are still too many executives who believe that the workers (and even the stockholders) "will not understand." There is usually a suspicion that the reluctant teacher does not know enough about his subject. It is natural to be suspicious of the unknown. It behooves the control contact to allay natural suspicion and to start with communication.

Control Standards

The chief tools of control can be listed as: methods, procedures, systems, statistics, records, reports, and standards.

The first three of these tools were considered in Chapter 1 as part of the discussion of systematic management. To recapitulate briefly, *methods* describe the ways for performing operations — mental, manual, or mechanical. Although they are standardized, methods are not fixed for all time. On the contrary, they should be improved constantly as the search goes on for the "one best way" at any given time. A *procedure* is a standardized sequence of operations specifying the methods to be used, who will use them, and when and where they will be used. A *system* is a network of procedures combined in such a way that all the repetitive operations for any major activity of an enterprise can be specified in advance.

Statistics, which are often found in records and reports, are important aids to control in comparing past achievements with current conditions and suggesting the future path to be followed with respect to the activity or procedure involved.

Reports are often compiled from *records.* Recorded items are summarized, with conclusions and recommendations for management's consideration, in the form of reports. From reports and the records on which they are based, those responsible for control have a valuable source of information.

The *standard* is by far the most important tool of managerial control. A standard, or standard practice, may be defined as a *method, means, or procedure to be used as a guide or model for carrying on a specific type of task.* So defined, it is a set of instructions or specifications for the performance of a given task. It is by relating subsequent performance to the standard adopted that control is achieved. If the performance is not under control, responsibility is fixed so that the individual or section in charge of that control can place the blame and advise the appropriate line officer about the corrective action necessary to bring the task back under control. Control media and agencies are illustrated in Figure 8.2.

Figure 8.2

Control Tools and Agencies

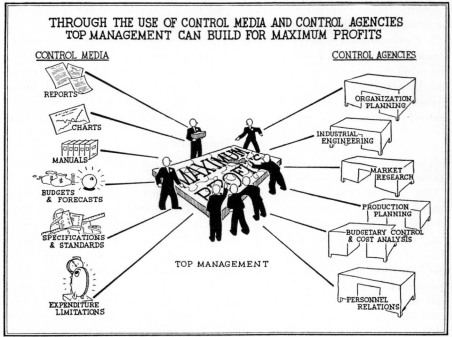

THROUGH THE USE OF CONTROL MEDIA AND CONTROL AGENCIES
TOP MANAGEMENT CAN BUILD FOR MAXIMUM PROFITS

CONTROL MEDIA

CONTROL AGENCIES

REPORTS

CHARTS

MANUALS

BUDGETS & FORECASTS

SPECIFICATIONS & STANDARDS

EXPENDITURE LIMITATIONS

ORGANIZATION PLANNING

INDUSTRIAL ENGINEERING

MARKET RESEARCH

PRODUCTION PLANNING

BUDGETARY CONTROL & COST ANALYSIS

PERSONNEL RELATIONS

TOP MANAGEMENT

Courtesy: A. E. Werolin, Associate, McKinsey & Company

The generality of standards

A standard is a specific tool of management arrived at by careful deliberation and then made definite, usually in writing, so that there will be no excuse for misinterpretation by persons whose performance will be evaluated in terms of that standard. It is in this very specific sense that the word "standard" is used by many authorities on management. Thus, for example, in Figure 8.2, standards are listed as one of the "control media" along with specifications, manuals, charts, budgets, forecasts, and so on. Again in Figure 8.3, another authority lists standards as one of the five "planning tools" in his scheme for management control. We have broken down the control process into different categories, but the general similarity among the three schemes will be apparent.

Standards are always necessary in any act of evaluation or control. Judgments are always made and corrective action is always taken in terms of some standard or norm. It is in this more general sense that we can say that standards are based on the other tools of control. Thus, statistics and records are valuable because they supply the data on which standards are based. Viewed from this perspective, methods *are* standards, and procedures and systems are sets of standards. Although in the following discussion we shall be talking about standards in the sense of definite instructions for specific operations, the fact that standards are necessary in all mechanisms of control should be borne constantly in mind.

No standard is perfect; it must, therefore, be flexible. It may be the one best way known at the time of its adoption, but subsequent knowledge may devise a better way which should replace the existing standard. *Flexibility*, therefore, may be considered as one of the generalities of standards. A reasonable objection to the overemphasis on standards is rooted in the fear that their importance may tend to freeze the method or procedure which they regulate. The answer to this objection is that standards should always be thought of as subject to improvement. The way to insure flexibility of standards is to provide for their periodic review by a

Figure 8.3

Relation between Planning and Control

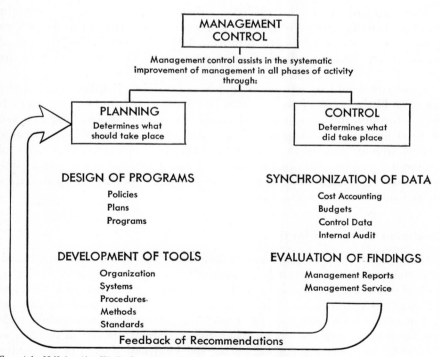

level of management that will have the authority to coordinate any new standard with those already existing.

Some typical standards

To give an idea of the variety of standards, the following list presents examples in each of several different business and industrial activities:

Activity	Types of Standard
Financial management	Fiscal ratios
Budgetary control	Experience records
Maintenance	Standard times
Production control	Scheduling
Inspection	Specifications
Inventory control	Ordering quantities
Job evaluation	Training times
Service rating	Absences
Procurement	Production cycles

Communication of standards

The standard should be officially issued and *in writing*. Unless the standard is written, there is always the danger of its being lost to the process because of labor or executive turnover. Oral instructions for the use of standards are liable to individual interpretations by those to whom they are given.

Standards should be written as *simply* as possible. Simplicity and clarity are more likely to ensure that the standards will be adhered to, thus promoting uniformity and a minimum of errors. Whenever simple language can be used in place of technical verbiage, the advantage is obvious. Because control should provide the means for effectively operating a number of scattered, complex business operations from a central headquarters, the standards on which such control is based should be so drawn up that they are not subject to misinterpretation.

Conclusion as to standards

Controls are just as good as the standards on which they are based. Important criteria of standards are simplicity, comprehensiveness, flexibility, and attainability. A standard may be set so high that it becomes valueless for practical purposes in addition to lowering worker or executive morale. Just as controls are necessary for appraising accomplishments against goals and for taking corrective action when the operations are out of control, so standards are necessary for suggesting the kind and degree of corrective action. In many cases, the setting of workable standards is more difficult than actually using them as tools of control.

The establishment of standards for intangible achievements is more difficult than for tangible accomplishments. For example, production standards may be developed by time-study, a relatively scientific procedure. Morale standards, on the other hand, must necessarily be based on more subjective criteria. The same is true of training programs and the standards for gauging the effectiveness of communications. Also, it is easier to control line than staff activities, most of which have highly intangible elements.

Who Does the Controlling?

A problem that recurs in management is the fact that whereas functions tend to remain constant, organizational responsibility for their performance varies with the size and complexity of the organization. Who controls, therefore, has no simple answer. The control process goes through much the same kind of four-step cycle whatever the size of the organization, but a program for control becomes more complicated as the concern grows and subdivides into separate functional units.

Small versus large concerns

In the small company, line and staff activities tend to be performed by a single person. Here one-man management can exercise effective control without the elaborate fact-finding and analysis required in large and complex organizations. In fact, the small business enjoys a competitive advantage in matters of control because of the boss's intimate knowledge of his workers, materials, finances, and customers. His directing and restraining actions are often made in terms of standards that are based on long experience and dependable facts.

As businesses increase in size and their activities, products or services become more complex, a high degree of technical planning becomes necessary for establishing adequate records. Line and staff responsibilities can no longer be combined in the same personnel. Widely scattered business units further complicate planning and the exercise of controls.

Preliminary considerations

Before turning to the problem of allocating responsibility for control in a large company, there are a few general considerations to be mentioned.

Essentials for Control. In order to draw up a comprehensive program for control, attention to the following items is essential:

1. Definite objectives
2. Suitable organization
3. Prepared programs
4. Established policies
5. Adequate procedures

6. Budgeted funds
7. Trained personnel
8. Progress inspections
9. Measuring standards
10. Regular and special reports

Too much or Too Little. The typical executive is interested in controlling a wide variety of operations, procedures, plans, departments, persons, and things. The "inspired" manager usually feels that he is capable of muddling through. At the other extreme is the one who is oversold on scientific controls. He may have his control staff working on such a variety of subjects and problems that their efforts are dissipated and their results questionable. The costs of a far-flung control program may exceed its value, even though the program is nominally successful.

Importance of Communication. Through the dissemination of information contained in control media, management aids the important function of communication. Reports based on dependable records, manuals, budgets, specifications, and standards all contribute to effective managerial action. Part of such superior results is due to the comparative care with which control media are compiled. Another part results from the nature of the media which generally cross activity lines.

Controls for Research. One of the most difficult phases of management control is the field of research. Here the intangibles appear in their purest form. Applied research has a definite objective but highly variable factors. The control of applied research is generally expressed in terms of time and costs. Periodic progress reports advise the control agency about the likelihood of meeting these standards. Progress already made determines whether the allowed time and costs shall be extended. Pure research is almost beyond the realm of control, except for the power to have it stopped when the reports on which decisions must be based indicate that impassable hurdles have been reached.

The exception principle of control

The over-all responsibility for control rests with top management. In a complex organization, that individual or group does not have the time to attend to every aspect of the control program. The inspired manager, as Taylor wrote some fifty years ago, "feels that by having this mass of detail pass over his desk, he is keeping in close touch with the entire business. The exception principle is just the reverse of this. Under it, the manager should receive only condensed, summarized, and *invariably* comparative reports . . . and have all the exceptions to the past averages or to the standards pointed out, thus giving him in a few minutes a full view of progress which is being made."[2] This is the exception principle of control; Taylor's first outstanding contribution to industrial engineering.

Delegation. This was discussed in Chapter 6 as one of the fundamental principles of organization. Delegation is the technique of getting a job done by the assignment of tasks to others. If all the assigned tasks result in success, coordination has been given a great boost. But this represents the ideal. If it were not for the possibilities of stabilized management through controls, the results of delegation would be precarious. Managerial controls make it possible to extend delegation and thus permit the executive to accomplish more tasks with reasonable confidence that they will be done well.

The central control section

When the concern is so large that it is practically impossible for one person to collect and analyze information necessary for adequate controls, the work may have to be done by a group of specialists. For this purpose, the central control section has evolved in recent years.

Centralized control provides for the smooth flow of pertinent information from its source through to the point where it becomes the basis for managerial corrective action. This central control section has only staff functions; the line retains complete authority.

Testing the Need for Central Control. If a large organization with diversified operations scattered over wide areas is considering the establishment of a central control section, the decision should be aided by surveying existing control units, the number of personnel employed in them, the cost and the results achieved. Effectiveness can be measured in part by the number of statistical studies and reports that are being duplicated under the present system; by the kinds and nature of the manuals now in use; by the accuracy, dependability, quality, and timeliness of the current organization charts; by the existing methods for introducing and controlling new procedures; and by the procedure for compiling and controlling the budget.

Purpose of Central Control. The purpose of central control is to collect facts and recommend action to management based on these facts. It aids management through its analysis of its findings and its subsequent suggested remedies for deficiencies. It aids communication, when executive members of the line so order, by issuing directives in management's name. Planning, fore-

---

[2] *Shop Management,* reprinted in F. W. Taylor, *Scientific Management* (New York: Harper & Brothers, 1947), pp. 126–127.

casting, methods-enginnering and internal audits may all be considered phases of the central control section's duties.

Duties of central control

There are some control duties that the chief executive can and must attend to personally; for others he must have the assistance of staff specialists. The latter's duties include: (1) programs and plans, without which the executive's personal duties could not be performed effectively; (2) the coordination of departmental duties; (3) appraisal of individual and departmental performance, or "internal auditing"; and (4) the formulation of measures for correcting unsatisfactory performances. These responsibilities of central control can be allocated under five general functions as shown by Figure 8.4.

The improvement and coordination of reports is a fit subject for centralized control. Many large concerns go along year after year with overlapping and useless reports. The situation regarding forms is probably worse. Poorly designed, unstandardized in size and distribution, they are continued simply because no one authorized their discontinuance.

Internal Audits. The word "audit" has traditionally referred to an operation primarily fiscal in nature and performed by the company's finance department. The purpose of this kind of audit is to prepare financial reports for the guidance of top management. They are usually statistical compilations about operations, expressed in terms of dollars.

Figure 8.4

Central Control Organization

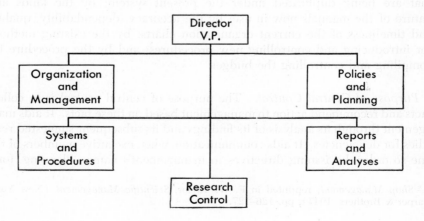

The *managerial internal audit* under discussion here, however, is a relatively new phenomenon. It is an analysis of company activities based on accepted standards or norms. This type of audit has been made at fairly long intervals by outside management-consulting firms. The internal audit of the central control section, on the other hand, is going on continually. Besides this advantage of survey continuity, the control section has an ever-expanding knowledge of company conditions, practices, and personnel. The central control personnel have a sort of protective coloring which enables them to move about inconspicuously as they make their surveys of both line and staff operations.

It is customary for the control section to include survey information, together with an analysis of general business and economic conditions, in a monthly report. Schooled in the art of preparing control information in charts and tables, as well as in words, the control section can make its findings more accessible and useful for busy policy-determiners. Besides the regular periodic reports, it is common practice for the section to prepare many kinds of special reports at the request of directors and management.

Corrective Action. Line officers have the sole responsibility for taking corrective action when reports of the central control section indicate unsatisfactory findings. An important point about corrective action under centralized control is that the section may often correct troublesome conditions by making direct suggestions to the departments concerned. If one assumes that the section's suggestions are reasonable, it is easy to understand why they would be followed in most cases, rather than be allowed to appear in a report to top management.

Conclusions

Because of the constantly increasing tempo of competition in most lines of business, it seems reasonable to conclude that the control factor will become correspondingly important as its techniques are refined. It is also apparent that as the territorial spread is expanded and operating complexity intensified, large business enterprises will depend more and more on centralized sections for the solutions to their control problems.

Planning and control are closely related. Planning determines what should take place; controlling compares it with what actually happened. If these two — planning and performance — are not in harmony, then the performance is said to be out of control, and something must be done about it. Follow-up with corrective action is essential if control is to be worthwhile. Checking actual results with plans is a necessary preliminary action to enforcing compliance.

Control is facilitated when everyone concerned is conversant with the desired objectives. This suggests that communication cannot be left to chance. In some cases, it is unfair to allocate responsibility for control unless positive plans are provided for the communication of objectives and other pertinent data to all those who are participating in the task.

It has been found in practice that when control techniques are carried too far or too fast, they may leave an irrevocably bad impression before any positive results appear. When faith in the control principle has been undermined in this way, it may be that even a rational substitute will not be acceptable. Controls should first be applied to those outstanding phases of operations which are important enough to attract general attention. Besides being damaging to the progress and acceptance of the control idea, *overcontrol* is likely to cost more than it is worth.

A good control program should not only establish standards and enforce them, but it should be constantly alert for improving them. It should specify organizational responsibilities and then check them in action. It should furnish basic information for the formulation and revision of important policies, procedures, and directives. Checking, evaluating, and improving are of the very essence of good control.

Finally, centralized control represents the keystone of coordinated controls for those situations where it is applicable. Unless the company or agency using centralized control has several thousand employees scattered over wide territories with complex operations, this highly refined tool of management may turn out to be a millstone. However, the future of centralized control for large-scale operations will probably represent one of the fascinating evolutions of modern management.

QUESTIONS

1. What is the purpose of the control technique?
2. Where do we look for faulty results in the production processes in an effort to get the situation back under control?
3. How would you defend the allegation that controls "are one of the most important bases for scientific management"?
4. What is the absolute essential for exercising the control function?
5. Name the four basic steps of the control cycle.
6. What are the four operational controls?
7. What are some of the objections to the use of control techniques?
8. Why is the flexibility of standards important for maintaining effective controls?
9. How do methods, procedures, and systems aid in the control process?
10. What is the most important tool of managerial control?
11. How are statistics and records related to managerial control?
12. Name five types of standards.
13. Who should do the controlling in a small company?
14. Which is worse for management — too many or too few controls?

15. What are the two known controls for research? How valuable are they?

16. What is the relation between managerial controls and delegation?

17. What criteria should be used in determining whether or not to centralize the control processes?

18. What is the purpose of the managerial internal audit?

19. Who has the responsibility for corrective action when activities are out of control?

20. What is the chief objection to over-control?

CASE PROBLEM

Dixon Distributors, Inc.

Dixon Distributors, Inc., was started about twenty-five years ago in Michigan and has always maintained its headquarters in Detroit. Its management has been progressive, resulting in average sales of about $25,000,000 for the past three years. It has five warehouses in the eastern and southern parts of the country, and one in Toronto. Sales offices are located in each of these six warehouses. All branch sales offices are under a local manager who also has charge of the warehouse, which is relatively simple as a bookkeeping operation. The branch sales managers are controlled from Detroit, their manuals leaving them little opportunity for initiative.

Merchandise distributed by the Dixon firm is obtained in various ways. Some of it is bought outright from manufacturers. For most of the merchandise, the company has exclusive territorial franchises from producers, and it has bought controlling interests in three small industries. Finally, the Detroit headquarters is located in an industrial building where the company assembles some of its items.

Accounting, purchasing, and sales are all centered in the home office. The company is a closed corporation in which two majority stockholders serve as president and treasurer. They exercise tight supervision and control. Thus from an organizational standpoint, the business is highly centralized.

During the past two years, the two men who control the business have begun to feel the pressure which has resulted from rapid expansion. They are further conscious of the fact that some of their real control is being lost in the increasing volume of detail with which they must keep abreast. They have been considering the advisability of drawing the purchasing agent, sales manager, and chief accountant closer to top management. In the past, these three have been receiving instructions from their two chiefs, who have never set up a clear division of responsibilitiy between themselves.

It has been decided to have an internal managerial audit for the purpose of getting a clearer picture of operations from the standpoint of managerial efficiency and to work out plans for reorganization.

PROBLEM: Should the Dixon concern call in an outside consultant or should they do the auditing job themselves? Or should they follow some combination plan? How can this initial job be made the basis for a more or less continuous internal audit of the company's affairs?

9

Managerial and Production Planning

Management planning

As the first of the five functions of management, planning naturally precedes organizing, directing, coordinating, and controlling. Without planning, the concern's organization would be useless for all practical purposes. Since it leads the other management functions, planning is intensely thought-consuming. Furthermore, it must choose among alternative objectives, policies, and programs, as well as methods, procedures, and techniques for making the plan effective. In choosing among these alternatives, the planners must constantly fix their sights on the company's main objectives and basic supporting policies. In fact, the formulation of most plans employs the typical scientific methodology, including:

1. Determination of the objective
2. Selection of data pertinent to the problem
3. Analyzing the possible courses of action
4. Synthesizing the results in a conclusion
5. Evolving a plan to obtain the solution
6. Trying out the plan in action
7. Making changes suggested by the trial

When it is done well, planning influences the other four functions toward a unified goal — the chief objective. Not only is the organizing built around a master plan, but the main purpose of directing or managing is to make that plan materialize. Coordination is the function of balancing and synthesizing human efforts, to accomplish unified operations in furtherance of specific plans. Finally, the purpose of controlling is to insure that established plans and procedures are carried out, that standards are met, and that situations "get back under control" when they go astray. Although all management levels must share to some extent in the planning process, the top level has to assume the principal decision-making role.

Production planning

Production planning guides the conversion of raw materials and components into more valuable forms for use. Production planning is concerned with controlling these conversion processes, called manufacturing. Planning of the production activities consists of routing, scheduling, and dispatching of work orders, all of which will be discussed at some length in the next chapter. Routing of the work order refers to its path through the production processes; scheduling has to do with timing the sequence of the various operations; and dispatching sees that the planning details are carried out. Then comes control of the total activity for the purpose of comparing the plans with their results. The objective of production planning is to aid in the profitable operation of the business. That objective is attained, in part, by using the best-known methods for balancing output with the existing demand for the product. The objective is materially aided by making products of the right quality in amounts to meet customer orders or to go into storage for future sales.

Production Responsibility. Production planning is the direct responsibility of the production department, subject to the policies laid down by top management. To meet its responsibility, the department makes use of three main factors: (1) machines and equipment, (2) raw materials and component parts, and (3) labor. Labor converts the raws materials and components into finished, marketable products by using the necessary machines and other facilities.

It is also the responsibility of production planning to manufacture products at a total cost which is less than their selling price. The difference between these two figures is profit. Top management policies guiding production planning must be formulated and constantly reviewed to minimize the ever-present risks in the manufacturing and marketing fields.

Product Risks. The chief risks of loss from the production processes result from the changing costs of materials and labor, and the inefficient use of machines and equipment. When machines are poorly adapted to their uses, unit costs of production are unnecessarily high. Another risk springs from idle machines and labor. Machines create expense even when they are not operating. When labor is unproductive because of machine downtime, due to improper production planning or poor maintenance, labor must still be paid. Production costs are also materially increased by machines which are idle due to lack of demand for their products. The costs of idle machines include rent for the floor space they occupy, interest and insurance, lubrication and other care, depreciation and the possibility of obsolescence. All of these expenses reduce the company's profits.

The question of whether, and when, to dispose of idle machines is highly problematical. As a result, they may stand idle for extended periods until market conditions improve. Careful planning of production is the only reliable way to minimize idle machine time. One method for maintaining a balance between machines required and machines available is to plan a program of "time and facilities," even if some of the product must be made for stock. Proper routing, scheduling, and dispatching of materials and men will surely aid in reducing machine downtime.

The life of productive machines is divided between setup and production. Setup time is required to put the machine in condition for production. It includes machine adjustment of feeds and speeds, and inspection of the first short run of its operation. Machine production time is self-explanatory. Other things being equal, the profitableness of a machine increases as its setup time is decreased.

Importance of planning

Denial of the necessity for planning ignores the fact that a business is usually facing a choice among alternatives. When the need for planning is denied, action is based on chance. If the factors that influence business were static it might be possible to stumble onto a line of action that would yield a profit. But business is so highly dynamic that occasionally some of the alternatives are ignored. Depression and war are two drastic examples of factors that affect business. There are many lesser shifts in the dynamic field of business that can be warded off or minimized by planning. With change as an accepted certainty, it is clear that planning can blunt the sharp edge of style changes, for example, thereby reducing their cutting economic effects.

Planning is also necessary in adjusting the parts to the service of the whole. A large department store discontinued paying bonuses, based on volume of business, to its departmental buyers after at least twenty years of this common practice. It was decided that the new straight-salary plan would increase the interest of the firm's buyers in the store as a whole, without jeopardizing their individual deperament interest.

The Economics of Planning

Management literature indicates a new consciousness of the principles of economics on the part of business leaders.[1] They are paying more atten-

[1] Two examples: Joel Dean, *Managerial Economics* (New York: Prentice-Hall, Inc., 1951) and Walter Rautenstrauch and Raymond Villers, *The Economics of Industrial Management* (New York: Funk & Wagnalls Company in association with Modern Industry Magazine, 1949).

tion to "economic studies" as the basis for planning. In other words, planning is one of the functions which is stimulating management's attention to economics.

The planning period

One phase of planning economics is determination of the planning period for various business programs. For what period of time should the operating *budget* run? Some budgets are planned for two years, but the common practice is for one year. Realizing the possibility of sudden economic changes, a small percentage of budget-makers plan their estimates on a semiannual or quarterly basis. Further protection against rapid changes can be provided by monthly reviews of the budget.

The improvement budget, on the other hand, may be planned over a long term, usually five to ten years. Some managers feel, however, that the recent rapid changes in many of the fundamentals of business operations make even the five-year improvement budget unsound. The operating period of any kind of budget must be based on economic conditions and their susceptibility to change.

Machinery replacement is frequently a problem, especially when the present machines are still profitable and not obsolete. The solution is difficult when an improved model has distinct advantages. Since it is impossible to predict when further improvements in design may be on the market, an important economic question is: how long will it take the new machine to pay for itself? A predictable period, based on an economic study, often decides the question.[2]

Enlargement of buildings, such as an office building, plant, or warehouse, presents the same type of problem, including a choice of alternatives. *Corporate investments* must also be made on the basis of broad economic planning. *Industrial research* presents an unusual risk, but essentially the problem it poses is based on the probable recovery of the capital investment. The difficulty of comprehensive planning in connection with capital investments is again illustrated in the necessity for keeping in mind the master plan while ensuring a reasonable return on the investment. It should also be recognized that there is often a relation between short- and long-term investment plans. For superior results, the two must be coordinated as fully as possible.

The national economy

The close relation between the national economy and managerial planning is emphasized in the divergent policies toward company expansion adopted

[2] The method of determining whether to replace a machine is described in Chapter 2, page 31.

after World War II by Montgomery Ward and Sears, Roebuck. Montgomery Ward adopted a strict policy of inventory and store retrenchment, based on the historical decline of prices that followed our wars. Sears, Roebuck & Company, because of the pent-up civilian demand for goods after wars, followed the opposite policy of extending inventories and opening more stores. Both concerns had available the same facts; they emphsized different data affecting the national economic situation.

Marginal analysis is another economic planning tool of management. Any concern is operating at the margin when its revenues equal its costs. More and more companies are making use of the break-even chart to determine the marginal point in their operations, for economic planning.

Forecasts

Planning is based on forecasts. Forecasts, in turn, are based on both internal and external data; the latter are more involved and less predictable. They include general business conditions, which may be affected by political and social changes. The labor, materials, and capital markets are external conditions affecting planning for the individual enterprise. Internal company data used for planning include present and anticipated sales, nature of equipment, managerial personnel, credit facilities, and others of similar nature.

As with budgeting, forecasting is valuable training for management. Both processes require intelligent thought on subjects that support decisions and actions. Both promote consideration and discussion of business problems in their entirety, based on essential data. Forecasting leads to planning on a rational rather than on an emotional basis. To that extent, it promotes controls for the support of desirable change and coordination for effective group efforts.

The *business cycle* must be given serious consideration in forecasting. Study of past cycles has revealed certain key factors that must be watched for as indicators of general movements in the economy as a whole. Some of the most important of these factors are wholesale price trends, size of inventories, and the total amount of credit spending and speculation.

When forecasting suggests that a decline in sales is probable, management can swing into action. If the forecast indicates that the decline will be general in the industry, management may plan to curtail production. On the other hand, if the predicted decline is expected to be more limited, the proper corrective measures may be additional advertising and more intensive sales methods.

Some events that will have a marked repercussion on business cannot be forecast with any degree of accuracy. Strikes, new government regulations, new inventions, wars — all of these are only more or less foreseeable. Nevertheless, management which is sensitive to the value of looking ahead will develop alternative emergency plans to deal with such contingencies.

Levels of Planning

Frederick W. Taylor often emphasized management's dereliction in leaving too much of the planning function to the workers. He rightly held that the duties of the workers should be guided by the orders of their superiors. The supervisors' orders should, in turn, be based on plans formulated by middle management for the purpose of carrying out company policies and objectives. In any type of business, the actual working plans specify the "what," "where," "how," and often "by whom" of any given job. It is the supervisor's duty to translate the managerial plans into worker action.

If the concern is small enough to be managed by a single individual, the entire planning burden is centralized in that person. Not only must he make plans for accomplishing the objectives, but he has the further problem of seeing that the plans are successfully carried out. In large enterprises, which usually adopt the corporate form of organization, the board of directors determine long-range plans for accomplishing objectives. On this first level (Fig. 9.1), the fundamental plans for attaining objectives are often known as policies. The board of directors, as trustee for the stockholders, exercises over-all management responsibility for making the policies or plans which they feel will result in success for the enterprise. This top policy-making level is known as the administration, and its policy-making powers are called administrative, in distinction to the second level, whose powers are managerial.

The top managerial level is responsible for carrying out the policies formulated and announced by the board of directors. Top management makes the underlying and long-range plans for giving effect to the board's policies. This does not mean that lower levels of management cannot also make shorter-range plans for this same purpose. As a matter of fact, that is one of their functions, but the planning undertaken on the third level is more concerned with details, many of which will be sent down the line of command in the form of orders.

Just as the management group on the third level contributes to the concern's general planning, so does top management often contribute to the policy-making of the board of directors. Although top management has no authority to formulate high-level policies, it is in close touch with the board, and often influences top policies by the advice it offers at board meetings. In actual practice, the president of the concern usually acts as chairman of the board, as well as general manager of company affairs. In this dual capacity, he naturally influences top policies and coordinates board policies with management action, for which he is directly responsible.

Middle management, listed on the chart as Level 3, is responsible to the president (top management) for planning on this lower level. The planning details on this level are designed to support and give effect to top management's planning. It should be observed that this third level is oversimplified on the chart. It often comprises three or more levels in a large organization.

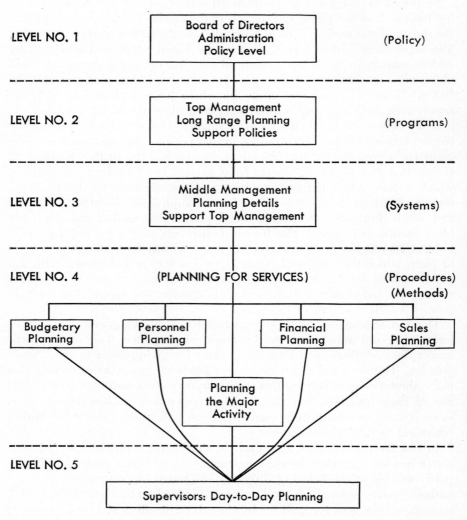

Figure 9.1

Levels of Planning

The executives on this third level also make recommendations for plans and minor policies to top management. On all levels, management planning recommendations go up the line of authority, while management orders based on plans originating at the various levels are sent down the line.

It should also be noted that any of the managerial levels may be assisted in their planning by one or more staff members. This phase of managerial planning is not shown on the chart because the line, or management, officers must assume the responsibility for whatever planning ideas they receive from their staffs, if those plans are put into practice. In other words, the line or managerial officers are responsible for the success or failure of plans formulated by their staffs.

The fourth level of the chart is composed of service functions. These services, especially engineering when it is included, often do more planning than any of the upper levels, but their plans are cast on a lower and operating level. At the same time, their plans are circumscribed by policies of the board, of top management, and by the plans of all the higher levels. This group issues most of the orders going directly to supervisors. On this level, the emphasis is on "Planning the Major Activity" which will be discussed in the following section.

The supervisors comprise the fifth level. It is their job to translate all plans and orders from above into detailed instructions for the guidance of the worker level, which is not accounted for on the chart for the simple reason that it does no managerial planning. By the time management's plans have reached the worker level, they should be laid out in all details necessary for deciding "what," "where," "when," "how," and "by whom."

There is one other important detail concerning planning levels. The chief of each level and functional service, and each supervisor, is responsible for planning the coordination of his subordinates' activities. When planning defines, as it should, the authority, responsibility, and relationships of the various jobs in the management group, the difficulty of coordination is considerably reduced.

Finally, some qualifying explanations should be made regarding Figure 9.1 and the managerial planning levels to which it refers.

1. For small enterprises, many of the managerial levels will be combined. Some businesses may be so small that all of the planning responsibility must be carried on by one person.

2. The chart is oversimplified, especially on the third and fourth levels. Important services such as maintenance, central stores, and engineering could be included on the fourth level.

3. Besides the possibility of staff planning, there might be both permanent and *ad hoc* planning groups on the third level.

Planning the major activity

Planning the major activity refers to the more detailed and special planning necessary for guiding and operating the principal work of an enterprise. Storage, for example, is the major activity of a warehousing concern, construction is the major activity of a building firm, and production is the major activity of a manufacturing company.

We shall refer, in this section, to five instances of planning the major activity in as many different kinds of business, largely to exemplify the need for mapping out in advance the path for obtaining company objectives. Four of the following business examples will be discussed briefly due to the similarity of their planning fundamentals. Production planning, however, will be treated at length as a major topic because of the widespread application of its principles to other lines of business, and because of the planning techniques which industry has developed.

Construction of large buildings intrigues sidewalk observers by the seemingly haphazard manner in which the various mechanics and laborers are intent on independent jobs. Actually, every foreseeable detail of the largest construction job can be planned in advance of operations. The architect's drawings, blueprints, and specifications are the physical evidence of synchronized planning, including instructions about what materials, workers, and equipment are to be where and when, and how the work is to be done. If the detailed operation times were not known in advance, the contractor could not be sure of his costs, nor could the owner depend on the promised completion date. The subcontracting plumbers and electricians would not know when to start their part of the work.

To eliminate these doubts and the resulting confusion, the path or sequence of the operations (routing) is planned in advance. Detailed and sequential timing (scheduling) is necessary for coordination of operations and the prevention of construction bottlenecks. And finally, someone must be charged with the responsibility (dispatching) for seeing that the routing and scheduling of materials, equipment, and manpower are carried out according to plans. Planning takes care of bottlenecks before they occur. Construction planning is the reason for the sidewalk observer's interest in watching apparent confusion develop into planned harmony.

Department stores also make use of the planning techniques of routing, scheduling, and dispatching. To increase sales, the layout of departments is carefully planned with attractive items near the entrances. The routing of merchandise to sales centers is planned to avoid interference with customers and the crossing of other lines of traffic. Introduction of new styles, special sales, and incoming and outgoing deliveries are all carefully scheduled. The directing or dispatching of the store's numerous operations is a carefully planned procedure for harmonizing relations among employees and coordinating their activities.

Wholesale and mail-order businesses use standard times for scheduling operations, for costing, and for developing incentive-pay plans for some of their employees. Standard times are not set until the operations for which they serve as norms have been broken down into the best possible sequence. The layout of wholesale warehouses is planned for the most effective handling of goods from the standpoints of cost and maneuverability.

Service enterprises, such as laundries, must do careful planning for profitable results. Routing and scheduling of their work is vitally important to secure the most effective sequence and speed in operations. Many insurance companies use routing and scheduling techniques at their home offices to improve and control "production."

Transportation agencies, such as railroads, steamship and air lines, are outstanding users of planned routing, scheduling, and dispatching. In fact, these terms are in everyday use by such concerns.

Production Planning

As has been suggested, production planning, as the fifth and last example of major-activity planning, will be considered at length because of the contributions it has made to planning in many other lines of business.

What is production planning?

Production planning may be defined as *the technique of foreseeing and plotting in advance all the steps in a series of operations in a manner that assures their accomplishment.*

To attain its goal, production planning predetermines *what* the work shall consist of, *how* it shall be accomplished, *where* it shall be performed, *who* shall do it, and *when* it shall be completed. The answers to these questions involve an analysis of the task (what), definite and complete instructions (how), the path of operations required to perform the task (where), the time sequence of operations, including breakdown into standard operation times (when), and, frequently, the operator (who), as the basis for determining the completion date.

To make production planning the accurate instrument that it is today, three important techniques had to be developed: (1) *routing,* (2) *scheduling,* and (3) *dispatching,* all three of which will be treated in detail in the next chapter. Closely related to the technique of scheduling are *methods and time study,* which will be discussed in Chapter 16. Because control is, by definition, the process of assuring that performance corresponds with plans, it is difficult to separate planning and control in different chapters. However, there have to be plans before there can be controls, and this chapter emphasizes the planning phase.

The need for production planning

The need for production planning as a separate activity and often as a separate department of any large manufacturing concern is more than anything else a result of the division of labor. The more a total production process is broken down into separate operations, all of which are mutually interdependent in making the finished product, the greater the need for bringing together the planning of these operations in one central place and the greater the need for the kind of charting techniques that have been developed by production planners.

Under mass production, with its highly specialized breakdown of skills, the operator may be cutting steel stripbars on motor-driven shears with fixed guides and according to the instructions of a job ticket handed to him by his foreman. He has no idea what the pieces will be used for, nor does he know where the steel strips came from. They are delivered to his machine with a "move ticket," and the pieces he cuts are taken away by a trucker to another operation about which he knows nothing. If chaos is not to result when this process is multiplied in many operations throughout the plant, there must be some plan underlying all these movements.

Factors affecting production planning

There are four principal factors which make the adoption of scientific production-planning techniques necessary:

1. The complexity of modern production
2. The need to determine definite completion times
3. The need for coordination of all elements affecting costs
4. The need for flexibility because of process changes

The intensification of the problems of coordination because of the highly developed specialization of labor has already been discussed. The pre-determination of the time required for the production cycle is important because it frequently has a direct relation to customer demand; if demand is miscalculated, inventory may pile up and equipment stand idle. The greater the coordination that can be effected among men, materials, and machines, the lower the costs. Finally, the need for flexibility is an important reason for systematic planning; the planning personnel must prepare for cyclical and seasonal fluctuations in demand for both production and consumer goods.[3]

Types of manufacturing

Planning techniques in the field of production depend to a large extent on the type of manufacturing involved. Two of the outstanding classifications will be discussed. One has to do with the "stock or order" distinction, and the other with "continuous or intermittent" processes.

Stock versus order production. Manufacturing for *stock* offers many advantages from the standpoint of planning, especially in the production of automobiles, typewriters, cameras, and similar lines. While these planning processes involves a large amount of data-gathering, research, and details

---

[3] Certain phases of production planning naturally depend on the volume of future orders. This factor may be determined, subject to management judgment, by the Probability Theory, as discussed in Chapter 5.

in setting up assemblies and subassemblies, the subsequent control of operations is relatively simple. Planning for stock prouction does not involve scheduling to meet delivery dates of customer orders, and thereby elminates one of the persistent problems in other kinds of planning. Also, material handling is reduced, as is the cost of direct labor and some services. One disadvantage of producing for stock is the possibility of making goods which may be difficult or impossible to sell because of changes in style and habit among buyers.

Production for customer orders has the distinct advantage of following the market in both demand and price. Even though the cost may be higher than on items produced for stock, nevertheless excessive inventories and storage facilities for finished goods are obviated. Ship building and the production of power plants and machine tools are examples of this type of manufacturing. Production planning for customer orders is naturally more complicated than production for stock. To avoid some of these complications, customer-order production is often planned on a "lot" basis, as is always the case in producing for stock.

The chief disadvantage of producing for customer orders is their susceptibility to "peak-and-valley" workloads. They not only increase unit costs, but make steady employment difficult. Because of this disadvantage, it is becoming more usual to combine stock and customer orders. While this combination involves higher inventory investment, it has the advantage of holding together the working organization and facilitating production planning.

Continuous versus intermittent production. Continuous production is simply what the title implies. It is followed in making shoes, cameras, and cement where the process is continuous from the raw materials to the finished product. Manufacturing of this type simplifies the planning process. Actually, planning for continuous production may well start with plant construction and layout. Because of its continuous nature, the "how" and "where" of planning are fixed by the layout of equipment. Only the "what" and the "when" are left for detailed consideration, and the "when" is made relatively simple if the equipment is properly arranged in balanced sequence.

The advantages of continuous production are the relatively few changes in equipment, high specialization of labor, minimized handling, and reduction of the special services of indirect labor. The outstanding disadvantage is the possibility of obsolescence due to market changes.

Intermittent production means that the plant is used to produce different parts or components, frequently from different materials. It may even cause the same department to produce different items on the same machine, necessitating changes in machine setup. The typical machine or tool shop represents this type of production. Advanced planning for intermittent production often uses conveyors which can usually be rearranged to take care of new operations for different items. It should be realized that production in a single plant is not necessarily either all continuous or all intermittent. Various departments may operate on one or the other plan. However, intermittent production requires more complicated planning than the continuous method. Under any production plan, any increase in the number of assemblies and subassemblies, and in the number of parts and operations, complicates production planning.

Coordination of facilities

By facilities are meant machines and equipment, including those for material handling and storage. The planning agency must have detailed information about all facilities in order to coordinate their functioning in production. For example, the speeds and feeds of all machines must be known, as well as their numbers, sizes, and locations. This information is necessary to determine the sequence of operations and the use of the material-handling equipment for coordinated internal transportation. Machine capacity will determine scheduling, and existing machine loads are always a consideration in determining the routing of orders. The degree to which products, operations, and equipment are standardized also has a paramount influence on production planning.

Production planning requirements summary

The fundamental data required for efficient production planning are:

1. *Production design:* blueprints showing the dimensions, tolerances, material specifications, assembly and subassembly layouts; parts lists.

2. *Machine data:* locations, type of work, speeds, feeds, and availability.

3. *Tool data:* location and condition of all tools, dies, jigs, and fixtures.

4. *Raw-material data:* material available for commitment in stores; purchase orders for materials not yet received; possible material substitutes on hand or available for purchase.

5. *Employee data:* breakdown into worker skills by shift and by department.

6. *Time standard data:* schedules and cost determinations; time is also a factor to be considered in maintenance and the correction of rejects.

Planning Boards and Process Charts

The usual purpose of planning boards and process charts is to provide a picture of the plan for scheduling men, services, machines, and equipment, and to show to what extent actual operations are proceeding according to plan. They are also adapted to the planning and controlling of such activities as sales, procurement, personnel management, and inventory control. Some of the elements which may be charted in production are machine loadings, the distribution of partial orders by operations, and main and subassemblies.

Planning boards are simply improved examples of planning methods made famous by Henry L. Gantt. As progress records, they are particularly valuable in comparing actual situations with planned schedules. Their information does not supplant records, but rather makes them visual in such a way that the information is available at a glance, making them particularly valuable for the responsible members of management. They are graphical interpretations of the records.[4] Figure 9.2 shows a typical visual control board.

Process charts are used for improving office and other procedures. There are several types of process charts, each fitted to the purpose it is to serve. Figure 9.3 illustrates the various kinds of these charts and the uses to which they can be put. Process charting is a method which has been used successfully in simplifying all kinds of office and management procedures. It can be used to save expense and man-hours in planning work for better and faster results. It has proved effective in eliminating bottlenecks and duplication of effort. The process chart is a picture of procedures as they exist; it can be used to develop a parallel picture of proposed improvements. It is much easier to analyze procedures from static pictures than to study the dynamic operations. This accounts for the value of planning with the aid of the process charts in which standard symbols represent various items suited to the situation to be improved. Some of the savings resulting from the use of process-chart analyses in many businesses are actually startling.

Organizational Relationships of Planning[5]

The organization of the planning function of any business depends on the amount of planning necessary for the smooth operation of dissimilar departments. Production planning is chiefly concerned with the coordination of all its departments in order to maximize productivity of a quality product at minimum cost. In all lines of business, planning is also interested in the improvement of methods and procedures.

In nonmanufacturing concerns, planning has the same objective of producing "results" (whatever they may be) in the shortest time, with the least worker fatigue, at minimum cost. In either a wholesale or a retail business,

---

[4] One plant superintendent, referring to the use of planning boards by his foreman, states: "Foremen now have the complete picture as they plan their work. They are better managers because they understand better what is to be done. We no longer use hot-lists to put pressure on them, yet we are getting better output per machine-hour and better deliveries." Quoted from a customer in Remington Rand literature.

[5] When we speak of the process of planning, we shall simply use the word "planning." But when the reference is primarily to those responsible for planning, whether they constitute a department or group, we shall capitalize "Planning."

Figure 9.2

A Typical Visual Control Board

Courtesy: Martin Company

results are measured by the ability of the organization to get the right merchandise to the right customer on time and at the right price.

The size of the concern, the nature of its product or service, and the attitude of top management are all important considerations. In small companies, planning is necessarily a function of the manager or owner. In the large concern, the organization of planning depends largely on top management's opinion of its planning leaders.

How much of the planning function is concentrated at or near the top of the management group may be measured by that group's confidence in the planning ability of the lower levels of the hierarchy. The importance of managerial planning may depend on the number and kind of other departments of the company. For example, Planning might have charge of methods and time study, the results of which are used in production. If adequate cooperation is lacking, it is possible that the planning agency within Purchasing might extend its influence to Central Stores. Since all the elements of any business must dovetail for efficient operation, it is not uncommon for a department like Planning to achieve such good results through close association with other departments that the latter are eventually absorbed into the sphere of influence of the former.

The planning function is relatively simple in continuous industries, and its place in the organization is correspondingly unimportant. In a job or order shop, the opposite situation will prevail. In large assembly industries like automobile production where planning becomes extremely complex, its organizational position is correspondingly important; and there is a consequent natural tendency to have its planning closely scrutinized far up the organization line.

It might be assumed from its title, for example, that Production Planning would report to the superintendent of Production. There are valid arguments for and against such a relationship. It is felt that if a manufacturing concern is large and its products diverse, its planning function will get better results if it reports to a member of top management rather than to the Production chief. It is also pointed out that the Production chief will tend to resent the implication included in any method or procedural changes suggested by Planning.

The Planning Department's organizational relationships will also be guided to some extent by the attitudes of those departments with which it must exercise closest cooperation in effecting its purposes. These associations may include any one or more of such departments as Sales, Stores, Purchasing, Standards, Maintenance, Inspection, Tools and Equipment, Shop Transportation, and Plant Layout. Figure 9.4 shows the position of Planning in a large department where the function is considered important. Under this arrangement, the Department of Planning & Controls will sometimes have a general supervisory check on plans made by other service departments located on Level 4 of the chart on page 160.

As a final note on the organizational relationships of Planning, it may be observed that top management may take a major interest in planning, assisted by a staff agency specializing in the subject. On the other hand, top management may have a penchant for dispersing planning for the

OBJECTIVE	CHART TO USE	ILLUSTRATION OF CHART
To study the sequence of major operating steps in an activity and the organization units performing them.	WORK FLOW CHARTS give a general description of the steps in one column; other columns represent organization units. The connecting lines show the flow of work.	**A B C D DESCRIPTION** — Application prepared for examination; Examined, certified and approved; License prepared, validated and issued; Distributed and recorded
To analyze the detailed steps in a flow of work that is quite complex or involves several organization units.	MULTI-COLUMN PROCESS CHARTS show steps in greater detail than on a work flow chart — symbols are used to describe steps.	MAIL CLERK / CLERK / TYPIST / ANALYST / CHIEF
To study the detailed steps in a relatively simple procedure such as one within a single organization unit.	SINGLE-COLUMN PROCESS CHARTS are often drawn on printed forms; work flow is shown by connecting the appropriate symbols	1 Case on desk; 2 Enter in register; 3 Out basket; 4 To file clerk

		A	B	C	D	E
Application Form 1036		1 2 3	① ② ③	② ③	② ③	①

FORM DISTRIBUTION CHARTS show the number of copies in the first column. The flow of each copy of the form is traced from unit to unit.

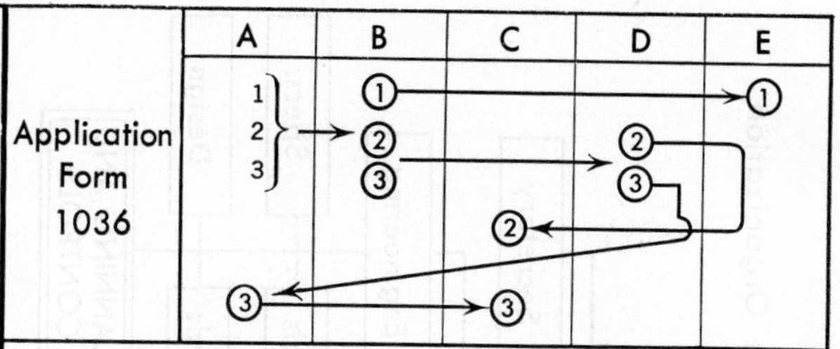

To study the flow of copies of a multicopy form.

LAYOUT FLOW CHARTS involve a diagram of the office made to scale — the flow from desk to desks is shown by arrows.

To improve the layout of the office so that unnecessary steps can be avoided.

CHIEF STENO CHIEF CLERK CLERK

LEFT HAND		RIGHT HAND	
1.	Move to drawer	1.	Move to paper
2.	Pick up clip	2.	Pick up paper
3.	Move clip to paper	3.	Idle
4.	Attach clip to paper	4.	Idle

OPERATION CHARTS are of several types; the one shown in the next column is commonly used to study the motions of each hand.

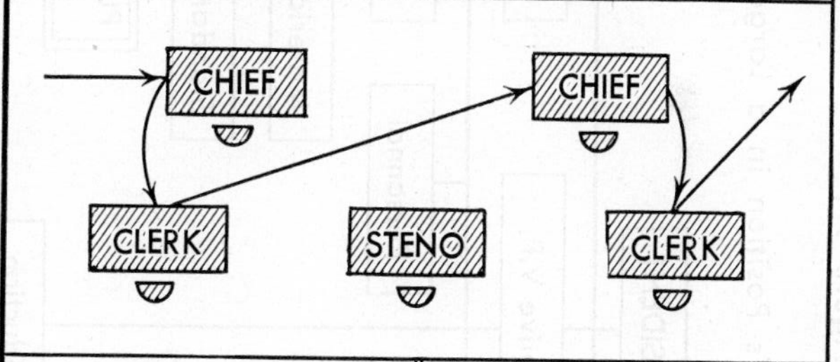

To simplify the steps in an operation performed by one employee.

Figure 9.3

Process-Chart Selector

Courtesy: U.S. Government Printing Office

Figure 9.4

The Planning Department's Position in a Large Organization

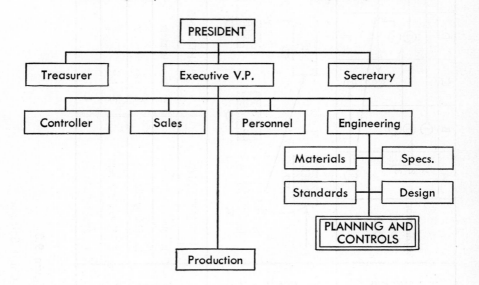

purpose of promoting initiative down the managerial line. In such a solution, a centralized over-all staff agency may be set up for checking on the plans of the various departments to see that they are coordinated with each other and with top plans and policies, which are presumably geared to company objectives.

Centralization of Planning

Planning is customarily centralized in proportion to the number of departments involved and the degree of their interdependence. At least this is the theory. In practice, the procedure depends largely on the attitude of management toward centralization in an Engineering or Planning Department. Where a number of different and important functions are included in an organization, there must be a reasonable degree of centralized planning in order to coordinate the departmental plans and to minimize confusion and costs. In any large business involving different departments, it is clear that there must be careful coordination of plans for all such functions as purchasing, selling, financing, personnel management, and the scheduling of operations. Coordination of planning under such conditions is possible only under centralized supervision.

When planning is checked and coordinated at some central point, supervisors are relieved of details which they are not always competent to handle in a large concern. This is especially true when departmental plans must be synchronized with the broader plans and policies of top and middle management. Under such an arrangement, the supervisor's time is released for maintaining coordinated operations within the department. Planning should be centralized in direct proportion to the number and intricacy of the activities to be planned, and to a certain extent in inverse proportion to the desirable capacities of the supervisors affected.

This generalization points to one of the *disadvantages* of centralized planning. It minimizes the responsibilities of supervisors. Whether this is serious depends on the circumstances and the men involved. Because carrying responsibility helps to build good leaders, it is highly desirable for their own personal growth that supervisors should have to meet challenges.

Another serious disadvantage of highly centralized planning is its tendency to be unwieldy and inflexible. The higher up the source of planning, the less information is available about lower-level problems. Especially in emergency cases, such as the absence of a highly skilled person who figures prominently in the central planning agency, the advantages of having some dispersion of planning responsibility can be seen. Furthermore, the centralized agency can plan only for the foreseeable matters; supervisors with some degree of planning authority on the lower levels are in a position to handle unforeseen occurences more expeditiously than can be done by an over-all staff agency.

Decentralized Planning. Planning at lower levels is particularly desirable in establishments with unrelated departments. The extent to which coordination among departments is unnecessary largely measures the opportunities for delegating considerable planning authority down to the supervisory level. The use of a machine for simple operations facilitates decentralized production planning. However, this opportunity is not so great as might be expected because of the typical requirement for two or more machines to complete a single operation.

Combination Planning. In actual practice, some combination of centralized and decentralized planning is the rule. Plans which involve precise routing and scheduling among business or production departments will be drawn up by a central agency, while those planning details which can be cared for on the supervisory level, without interfering with the over-all plan will be determined there. It is fair to conclude that the current tendency is to decentralize as much as possible, for reasons already suggested: decentralized planning promotes supervisor initiative and permits flexible and prompt decisions at the bottom of the organization ladder where the unexpected is most likely to happen.

Coordinating plans

All planning requires coordinating when it involves dissimilar functions. In such cases, it must consider much more than knowledge of procedures and processes, however important they are to the whole picture. The planning agency must work closely with Sales, Engineering, Purchasing, Personnel, and Internal Transportation. Sales estimates supply the basic information for many forms of planning. When Engineering supplies designs, the designs often form the basis for planning. Since materials are frequently necessary, planners must know that they will be available when needed. This means that materials and supplies must either be on hand or on order. In either case, Purchasing must cooperate with Engineering Design to learn the kinds of materials or items desired and, in cooperation with Sales and Planning, find out the amounts to be purchased and when they will be needed.

Since manpower is necessary in all lines of business, those responsible for planning must find out from the Personnel Department what skills are available, and in what numbers. Based on this information, arrangements must be made with Personnel to fill gaps in the work force.

Internal transportation, or material handling, is another element of planning. It comprises such a large percentage of costs in some lines of business that it should be given consideration in plant layout. Production must, of course, cooperate closely with the Planning Department.

Finally, there is always the question of finance. It is not always possible to plan in the most practical manner because of the expense involved. Planning compromises are sometimes dictated by available cash or credit. This is the point where top management enters into over-all planning.

The Cost of Planning

The excessive cost of scientific planning techniques is frequently cited as an argument against using them. The same argument is advanced in opposition to motion study and many other of the newer techniques of management. Of course any costs may be excessive when compared with the results obtained. When the costs of planning are greater than the benefits derived, they are certainly excessive, and something should be done about them.

The success of any type of planning can be measured to some extent. Some of the measures are customer satisfaction, adherence to delivery dates, unit costs, quality of product and services, and worker morale. Morale can scarcely be measured in dollars, but improvement in morale may be indicated by a decrease in official grievances, absences, layoffs for infractions of company rules, and work stoppages. In addition to these statistical criteria, there is an atmosphere which can be gauged by those in daily contact with the workers. It is axiomatic that if the planning activity seems to be causing deterioration in morale, or in any of the other factors just mentioned, then it should be reviewed and revised.

Experience proves that scientific planning is always profitable in medium-sized and large concerns. The record is full of examples where most of the benefits to be expected from scientific planning have materialized in fruitful measure. It may well be, however, that some companies are too small to support the style of planning which they have been influenced to install. There are no positive criteria by which the size of an enterprise can be matched with the proper degree of planning. In the last analysis, common sense dictates the obvious benefits of proper planning in any type of endeavor.

Conclusions

Planning provides for the prearranged coordination of activities. The factors of production planning are primarily men, materials, and machines. The aim of planning in any business is smooth operation and economical costs. The opposite of planning is the "hot-list" system which closes loopholes and bottlenecks by using on-the-spot expediters. The hot-list system is remedial; planning is preventive.

There is no patent system for planning or control in any type of business. Like any aid to the main effort, scientific planning must be patterned to serve the departments involved. When patented planning and control systems are not related to the conditions which they are supposed to serve, they can hurt both their buyer and their seller.[6]

Because of the possibilities for constructing mechanical puzzles from the many techniques in the planning field, there is a tendency to confuse intricacy with profundity. Simplicity and profundity are more closely related. The purpose of planning and controlling is to reduce confusion and save money. When savings are not realized, the fault is with the planner.

Overelaborate systems waste money in the cost of their maintenance and in increased unit costs. The latter waste arises largely from delays due to lack of coordination. The best plan is the simplest system that effects its purpose for the circumstances at hand, and is at the same time subject to control. To copy a system used successfully elsewhere is about as fallacious as buying a friend's shoes because he found them comfortable.

QUESTIONS

1. What are the typical steps of scientific methodology as they are applied to managerial planning?
2. What is the purpose of production planning?

[6] This comment does not apply to planning and control boards which are adaptable to varied circumstances.

3. What are the chief risks of loss in the production processes?

4. How can routing, scheduling, and dispatching of materials and manpower aid in reducing machine downtime?

5. In what fields can economic studies be instrumental in effective planning?

6. Following World War II, Sears Roebuck and Montgomery Ward adopted diametrically opposite policies regarding accumulation of inventories and the opening of additional stores. How could these two retail leaders come to opposite conclusions working with the same basic economic facts?

7. What is the primary basis of all business planning?

8. How would you synchronize or coordinate the various planning "levels"?

9. Why is it advantageous for management personnel to use staff services?

10. Why do the service functions often do more planning than the upper levels of the industrial hierarchy?

11. To what extent is the planning for "major activities" often more detailed than typical production planning? Why is this situation factual, and what are some of the major activities to which it applies?

12. How would you define production planning? What factors does it predetermine?

13. What are the three primary steps in production planning?

14. Which production problems are resolved or ameliorated by effective planning?

15. What are the disadvantages of production for stock as compared to producing for orders?

16. Where should planning start in industries devoted to continuous production?

17. Is production planning more complicated in the continuous or the intermittent plan of manufacturing? On what do you base your conclusions?

18. How can production planning be pictured for the effective scheduling of men, services and equipment

19. What are the basic criteria for determining the organization of inter-related planning activities for different types of industries?

20. To what extent and under what circumstances should the planning function be centralized in industry?

CASE PROBLEM

THE GRENNELL CORPORATION

The Grennell Corporation manufactures sheet steel products to customers' orders. It makes a serious effort to use scientific procedures in all of its departments, and is constantly seeking to improve the planning methods in its central office, in its executive relationships, and in production. The company is well established, has 650 employees, and about 400 customers, half of whom send it repeat orders. Its ability to secure repeat orders is advantageous because of the drawings, patterns, and jigs involved in most of its processing. This advantage is especially true for such products as blades and casings, machine guards, and similar items.

The trend of the business has been toward a multiplicity of relatively small orders. For some of its older customers, production runs of a thousand are still possible, but its expansion efforts of the past five years have greatly increased the number of new customers ordering an average of one hundred of a single item. When the order represents something new, detailed drawings are required, and often patterns as well, so that the selling price necessary to get the business on a competitive basis allows less than the normal profit. In such cases, the orders are solicited with the expectation that they will lead to repeats at the same price, with better profit margins. These expectations have not been realized to the extent anticipated.

About five years ago, Grennell had a firm of industrial engineers lay out its production processing. During the past two years, its net profits have decreased while its sales were increasing. The president of the company, who is a business college graduate with twenty-five years' experience, is not satisfied with the explanation given by the concern's controller that the decrease in profits results from increased labor and material costs. The president has figures to show that the percentage increase of these items is about balanced by higher selling prices.

After conferring separately with the heads of his various departments, the president suspects that their production planning may be overorganized. The records show that the percentage of overhead to sales increased faster than the ratio of direct labor to sales after the process planning was completed by the industrial engineers. They told him to expect a cost increase due to the new controls and accompanying paper work, but assured him that the increase would be more than offset by the improved coordination of production activities and the reduced cost of trouble-shooting. In spite of these assurances, the president feels that their current record-keeping, including detailed machine, tool, material, and manpower data, is top-heavy. The present production procedures have been summarized by the Engineering Department as follows:

1. *General Office.* Sends mail and phone orders to the Sales Department.

2. *Sales Department.* Interprets and prepares orders in skeleton form for the Order Department.

3. *Order Department.* Writes up the orders for the Production Department on the basis of information from Sales, assigns the proper company order number, posts the order in the Register, attaches memos and correspondence to the order, and sends it to the General Engineering Department.

4. *General Engineering Department.* Analyzes orders, and if they are repeats, obtains drawings from the files. Advises the Factory Engineering Department about costs if the order is from a new customer, or if it is a different order from an old customer. Prepares working drawings as well as jigs, etc., after consultation with the Standards Department. Issues and sends orders to the Tool-Making Department for jigs and patterns, when necessary. Prepares the production order; returns the original order and accompanying papers to the Order Department. Sends the production order and drawings to Material Control.

5. *Material Control.* Determines the availability of materials in Central Stores. Prepares and sends an Obligation-of-Stock Order to the Purchasing Department if the materials are not available. Notes available stock on the Production Order, which is sent, along with the drawings, to the Standards Department.

6. *Standards Department.* Secures specifications from the files if the order is

a repeat; prepares new specifications if it is not. Makes up an Order Card to be put into the Order Envelope with the specifications, drawings, and any other processing instructions, and sends it to Production Control.

7. *Production Control.* Enters the Production Order on the Production Schedule, with recorded times for the various operations, and the final date for shipping. Determines the time for release of order to Production, based on availability of materials, machines, manpower, and the promised delivery date, and sends it in the Order Envelope to the foreman of the first operation.

8. *Foreman.* Draws the necessary stock from Central Stores on authorization which Material Control has placed in the Order Envelope. Draws jigs and patterns from the Tool Room, also on authorization in the Envelope. Checks the operation setup, and assigns an operator to the job. Inspects the completed operation unless instructions in the Envelope call for checking by the Inspection Department. In the latter case, sends for the inspector and holds the job until it is released by him as satisfactory. Signs the Production Card and prepares the Move Ticket to the foreman of the next operation. Sends the order, the materials, etc., to the next production department. Prepares Spoilage Report for Production Control and a Move Ticket to the Salvage Department.

9. *Inspection Department.* From the last production operation, sends the order to Inspection for checking against the drawings and specifications. Notes acceptance or rejection, with reasons, on the Order Card. Sends Order Envelope to the Standards Department, and the product, together with the Order Card, to Shipping.

10. *Shipping.* Checks quantities against the Production Order, and returns it to the General Office, marked for billing. Returns the Order Card to Production Control, and ships the order.

PROBLEM: Would you advise the president of the Grennell Corporation to simplify his production-planning procedures? If so, how would you revise them so as to reduce the cost of the production records and various procedural steps, and still be in a position to maintain adequate controls over processes, machines, materials, and manpower?

10

Production Controls

The previous chapter considered the subject of production planning and management. This chapter will discuss the controls for assuring the accomplishment of the production planning, a staff service function which bases some of its decisions on market research and analysis. One of the objectives of this research and analysis is to estimate the country's capacity for absorbing a given product. This estimate then poses the problem of deciding what percentage of the total consumption can be captured by the company's sales organization, and that decision, in turn, must be matched with the concern's capacity for producing the proposed percentage.

The sales department naturally assumes a role in both phases of this problem. However, Sales is characteristically not only optimistic about its own ability, but rather fanciful in its idea of the company's production capability. Production planning aims to inject realism into these optimistic attitudes on the part of Sales, and usually gains the support of top management in the final compromise decision. In this sense, Production Planning coordinates sales volume with manufacturing capacity.

Meaning of production control

The function of production control is not always understood even in the industrial field. Occasionally it is conceived of as synonymous with material control, which is usually the function of Procurement, aided by Production Engineering. In other cases, production control is explained as a scheduling of the production processes, but this is only one of its phases. Actually, production control properly refers to the effective synchronizing of men, materials, and machines for accomplishing the results determined by production planning for a given situation.

Naturally, Planning's objectives presuppose adequate materials and manpower if Production Control is to meet the sequential timing of operations. It is the responsibility of the purchasing department to secure the materials and components necessary for Production to meet the planned schedules.

In this case, the duty of Control is to effect a working cooperation between the procurement and the production departments. As we shall see later, scheduling also involves the number of machines and operators as determined by time studies.

Production control is, therefore, the task of synchronizing the factors of production through the use of tested procedures for achieving the production plans. The use of these procedures aids in obtaining the desired results; their enforcement is one of the action phases of production control. Other considerations besides sales forecasts and estimates of plant capacity are necessary for assuring the success of the over-all production plans. For example, adequate inventories of materials and parts must be controlled for the purpose of guaranteeing continuous plant operations. This is usually a function of Procurement, assisted by the using departments and Central Stores. Inspection, or quality control, of raw materials and the processing operations is another important controlling activity. Control of tools is also necessary for effective plant operations.

Finally, there are the manufacturing controls known as routing, scheduling, and dispatching, which will be subjects for detailed discussion late in this chapter. It is sufficient here to state that if these three controls were to be expressed by single words, routing would be the "path" of operations through the factory, scheduling would be the "timing" of these operations, and dispatching would represent the "action" or release of planned orders in the manufacturing procedure.

Factors of production control

1. *Production Planning.* Starting with design of the various products, production planning proceeds to a break-down of the quantities necessary in each case, as well as the dates for their completion. Machine capacities are involved in figuring the processing times.

2. *Inventory Control.* Inventory Control keeps Procurement advised as to the quantities and times for arrival of the materials and parts required for maintaining continuous production. Central Stores is also an important link in inventory control.

3. *Tools Control.* This is obviously a necessary factor in maintaining continuous production.

4. *Routing.* To maintain a continuous flow of operations without backtracking, the most effective path for progress of the various production processes through the plant must be determined. These routes must not only be planned, but they must be maintained, which is a function of control.

5. *Scheduling.* This is the production timetable for controlling the progressive steps of the different operations. It is based largely on production times.

Figure 10.1

Is information processed efficiently?

This information   **... Is processed by this method (%)**

This information	Manually	Control boards	Edge-notched cards	Punched card tab. equipment	Computer	No method
Customer delivery schedules and order backlog	58	7	2	27	10	4
Production order: Quantity and timing	66	8	1	15	11	1
Preparation	67	3	2	15	8	2
Detail schedules for production department	69	11	1	11	5	7
Follow-up reporting of progress and schedules	68	7	1	14	5	4
Inventory records: Finished goods	56	1	1	34	15	1
Work in process	59	3	3	24	9	5
Raw materials	67	1	1	23	10	1

Figure 10.2

How much are you using Operations Research techniques?

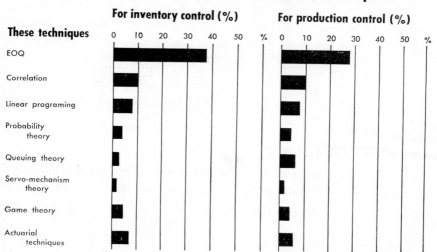

For inventory control (%)   **For production control (%)**

These techniques

EOQ

Correlation

Linear programing

Probability theory

Queuing theory

Servo-mechanism theory

Game theory

Actuarial techniques

6. *Dispatching.* This is the action phase of production control. It starts the chain of operations when so advised by Production Control and follows through to the finished product. This activity may appear to be purely clerical, but later elaboration of the duties of the dispatcher will thoroughly dispel such an impression.

7. *Inspection.* Inspection is also referred to as quality control. It checks the production processes periodically to see that the various operations are meeting the specification requirements assigned to them. Inspections are often made at the beginning of important operations to prevent additional expense on an item that may be already defective. It is the duty of the inspector to stop further processing of defective items. The dispatcher may aid in determining whether such partially completed products shall be reworked or treated as salvage or scrap. Usually the engineering department makes the final decision in doubtful cases. Inspection of the completed product is also necessary.

Recent changes in production controls

In discussing the factors of production control, it should be made clear that processing the data of production and inventory control is still largely a manual operation despite the implications about computers made by new literature in the field. According to an April 1961 survey of 387 plants by *Factory Magazine,* fewer than 10 per cent of all plants are using computers for controlling production orders and schedules. Only 5 per cent use them for follow-up reporting on the progress of production schedules. In processing information on inventories, computers are used 10–15 per cent of the time. Reasons given for the reluctance of the surveyed concerns to use the new methods of production and inventory control stems partly from lack of management support, while others feel that the new mathematical techniques surrender judgment to figures. (See Figures 10.1 and 10.2.) We have already taken a closer look at the tools of Quantitative Analysis for management in Chapters 4 and 5. The stress in this chapter is placed upon the fundamentals of production controls operative under all systems — manual, control boards, edge-notched cards, punched-card tabulating equipment, and computer.[1]

Scope of production control

Because the operation of any production control system depends on the nature of the business and on the relations of the control system with other

[1] Figure 10.3 illustrates the steel industry's first automatic reversing roughing mill in operation at Jones and Laughlin's Aliquippa Works at Pittsburgh, Pennsylvania. With Prodac control (programmed digital automatic control), the operator pushes but two buttons. The schedule-advance button stores card data in the Prodac memory; the pass-advance button turns the data over to Prodac decision-making equipment. This operation contrasts sharply with manual control.

Figure 10.3

Prodac Control in The Steel Industry

Courtesy: Westinghouse Electric Corporation

departments and with top management, there can be no stock plan for its procedures. The techniques for control must fit definitely into the formal and informal phases of the organization in which they are used. Production Control, for example, bridges the gap between Sales and Manufacturing. In that capacity, it is charged with setting up systems that ensure the production of the right products in the right quantities and of the right qualities within the time limits allowed, and in the most efficient manner. At the same time, Control is obliged to perform its service in an expeditious manner so that its work is harmonious with over-all operations. It must also avoid unnecessary expense resulting from a mass of paper work or from conflicts with other departments.

Production Control must have authority to set up schedules, economic lot sizes, inventory quantities, and routing of work. To effect a proper coordination of these duties, the control manager must have considerable authority over operations after everyone concerned has agreed to the applicable procedures. Obviously, all the functions undertaken by a Production Control Department would be performed by someone even if such a department did not exist. The purpose of centralizing some or all of the control activities is to relieve scattered personnel of that work, and to do a better job under a single supervisor. A central control organization has an opportunity to coordinate group activities, and is continually studying related operations for the purpose of simplification by combining, eliminating, or changing the sequence.

Three primary controls

Routing plots the "production" path to be followed through the plant, office, warehouse, or store. "Stores-issue forms" are prepared from route sheets, which show the original station and subsequent moves, the various operations and their sequence, and the places where inspections are to be made. The actual ordering of moves indicated on the route sheet is the function of the dispatching section of Planning.

Scheduling is the procedure of plotting the time sequence of the work to be done, including instructions as to which one of a group of operations, customer orders, or production lots is to be undertaken first, and all subsequent moves until the job is completed. Scheduling fixes the beginning and ending times of each operation. In production, the order of work and the time required for the various operations depend on what machines, tools, jigs, fixtures, materials, and personnel are available. Needed materials are checked by the balance-of-stores clerks. When the items required from Stores are ready for issue, the dispatching section sends the releases, along with the order identification tag.

Dispatching, as suggested earlier, is occasionally referred to as a clerical job, but it must be handled with a proper understanding of the entire planning system, operations, and equipment. The dispatching section carries out the orders of the routing and scheduling sections of the Planning Department. For industry, it starts operations by sending instructions to the production centers. It procures the stores-issues and identification tags, and sends them to Stores, which attaches them to the materials so that they follow through all production operations intact. Dispatching sends the move tickets to plant transportation, with instructions to move materials from Stores to production centers. It sees that orders are carried out with respect to drawings, tools, and the instruction cards needed for the various operators. It notifies Inspection of the completion of jobs. It sends the time and inspection ticket to the Accounting Department for bonus and payroll purposes and for costing. Dispatching has the important additional job of deciding on deviations from routed or scheduled instructions in cases where unforeseen circumstances, such as machine breakdown, lack of materials, or absence of manpower, require changes. Since cursory explanations cannot measure the significance, or even the content of these three controls, we must look to their use in operations for a clearer understanding of their purposes. Whatever the type of business concerned, it is conclusive that routing, scheduling, and dispatching are necessary for controlled planning.

Routing

The elements of routing in their natural sequence, as applied primarily to industry and in a more restricted sense to other businesses, can be summarized as follows:[2]

1. Analysis of the product to determine possible methods of making it.
2. Assembling of complete data on available machines, equipment and tools useful for the job to determine their capacity and plan for requirements to establish balanced production.
3. Study of the various methods to determine the "one best way" under existing circumstances.
4. Determining, on the basis of methods adopted, what type or kind of special equipment or machines can be used to advantage, and whether the advantage justifies their construction or purchase.
5. Deciding on machine speeds and feeds for the purpose of establishing maximum productivity and operation times.
6. Figuring operation times for the purpose of balancing production, or other activities, through proper routing. Over-all production time includes machine setup, average machine downtime, inspection, and material handling.
7. Determining the sequence or route of operations.
8. Route sheets must be broken down into subassemblies so that all components will be available for synchronizing with the main assembly. This process is applied in department-store and warehouse operation, and in production.
9. Preparing work sheets for carrying out the routing details.
10. Working out plans so that routing fits into the operations of centralized or decentralized planning procedures already established.

The one best way

The method of performing an operation in any business will determine its routing. But since there is usually more than one way of performing an operation, the person responsible for planning has to decide which is the best routing plan under the circumstances. Besides making a complete analysis of the operation to be accomplished, or product to be manufactured, he must know all the facts, including the completion date. The degree of accuracy called for in the specifications will help to decide the type of

---

[2] These elements are adapted in part from G. B. Carson, *Production Handbook*, 2nd ed. (New York: The Ronald Press Company, 1958), Section 3.

machine and degree of worker skill to be used. Availability of equipment for first choice and substitute uses must be figured and planned. The effect of using auxiliary equipment for quality work or to increase productivity must be considered. Whatever the type of business, there is always the question of availability of materials and equipment, as well as the justification of added expense for completion of the work. Finally, there is the important question of comparative costs under the various plans which are considered feasible.

Routing forms

The *route sheet* is used whenever an operation must be handled by two or more departments. If an operation can be completed by a single department, it is customary for the supervisor to plan and route the job within his department. Centralized routing offers a simple technique for obtaining coordination among a group of departments, a cooperative effort that involes more complicated instructions. The route to be followed in each department is outlined on the route or operation sheet, illustrated by Figure 10.4. From this master record are prepared the individual work orders, time cards, material requisitions, tool orders, inspection tickets, material identification cards, and move orders.

The *work order* gives detailed instructions for the employee who is to perform an operation. The worker's operation times are shown on his work order for costing purposes. In large industries producing on the intermittent plan, work orders are made out for each operation listed on the route sheet. Figure 10.5 is typical of the simple work order. Sometimes the operation is indicated by title only, with the assumption that the worker can get more detailed information from his supervisor. The order indicates the type and make of the machine to be used, as well as part and assembly numbers.

Material requisitions authorize Stores to issue specified materials for the work concerned. In a large operation, material requisitions must originate in the Central Planning Department. In connection with routing, requisitions are timed for delivery so that the materials will be where and when needed. Whether or not the exact quantity needed is requisitioned for production jobs depends on the nature of the work. For example, companies making special products to specifications often requisition extra raw materials because of a possible spoilage in processing. The relation between any kind of planning agency and Central Stores is also important. Not only does Central Stores get a list of needed materials well in advance, but the Planning Department must see that the materials are available or on order.

Tool orders are requisitions on the tool crib. Some concerns allow workers to draw and retain the tools required for their jobs as long as they are

Figure 10.4

Interdepartmental Route Sheet

ROUTING SHEET							

Part Name _____ Material _____

Part No. _____ Quantity _____

Order No. _____ Issue Date _____

Route No. _____ Complete By _____

Operation Number	Dept. Number	Operation	Machine Number	Tools	Standard Time	Price

Figure 10.5

WORK ORDER

Order No._____ Employee's Name Clock No._____

Quantity_____ _____ Dept. No._____

Type Machine	Machine Number	Part Number	Assembly Number

OPERATION:

	Operator's Time								
Date									
Time									

employed and have use for them. In large companies where an effort is made to get maximum use from tools, they are requisitioned by the Production Planning Department for use on particular jobs and to designated workers. When special tools are expensive, their issue and control are correspondingly detailed. Before a job can be routed, the Control Department must find out from the Central Crib whether the desired tools are available. On large orders, it may pay to have special tools made for the job. Planning may well discuss such matters with an experienced tool-crib man, especially since he has some knowledge of the possible future use for special tools.

Inspection orders ordinarily go to a centralized Inspection Department when the components of various products follow different routes through the concern. In some operations, inspection is a routine affair, performed at fixed stations. However, where work orders are necessary, inspection may be anything but routine. In such cases, the Control Department must notify Inspection what, where, and when to inspect.

Move tickets are just what their name implies. They notify department heads that the operations will follow the path indicated on the route sheets in timed succession.

Identification tags are used in wholesale and retail establishments for assembling a group order from two or more departments by reference to the customer's order number. In some production plants, the identification tag accompanies materials through all the various processes. It contains varied information, but always carries the order number and the operations to be performed. The tag helps in directing the materials from one operation to another, and sometimes replaces move tickets.

Instruction cards are common in a well-rounded control system. They give detailed information to the operator about methods to be followed, and frequently contain a detailed analysis of the operation, including the standard time required for its completion. In production shops, the cards show the machine tools to be used, together with their speeds and feeds, and the amount of materials required.

Other routing criteria

There are many other tickets and orders used to control various kinds of operations. Their number depends on the amount of control desired. In some cases, the multiplicity of tickets seems to serve the whims of the person in charge of the system. Simplicity should be the keynote of control.

The capacity of different machines and individual operators helps determine routing as well as scheduling. With these data and the others already mentioned, the routing chart is a graphic display of the steps through which the operation must pass. In a straight-line manufacturing setup, routing is comparatively simple after the production line is established. Many types of concerns are able to process some of their subassemblies on a straight-line basis, which is naturally the most expeditious plan. The limited capacity of some machines requires detailed consideration to accomplish planned operations and prevent bottlenecks. Conveyors are a prominent factor in line assembly work; intensive study is often required to find the special type most suitable to a given situation.

Many concerns engaging in repetitive operations maintain routing specialists who are continuously employed in refining the flow process for the purpose of increasing productivity. This job is concerned chiefly with work simplification or methods engineering. The use of flow charts in this connection was referred to in the preceding chapter. From the seemingly unnecessary number of technical terms used in this line of work, one might conclude that a deliberate conspiracy to confuse is afoot. But actually, this specialized vocabularly gives a very accurate picture of the common-sense measures dictated by the nature of the planning process.

In conclusion, routing is a very important part of the general problem of control. Its planners require a thorough knowledge of the concern for which they work, as well as its equipment and operations, and the personnel available. Routing is the basis for scheduling control, which will now be considered.

Scheduling

The schedule controls timing from the first operation to delivery. Its ultimate aim is to minimize equipment and worker times, and provide for deliveries as promised. Scheduling is charged with seeing that materials, machines and tool equipment, components and patterns are available when and where needed. It was in the area of scheduling that Gantt laid out the first charts showing work planned and done in proximate relations.

Improved forms of scheduling charts compare work done with work planned, as well as the allotment of various materials with the amounts used during an hour or a work-day. The chief aids to scheduling are the work-load and the machine-load charts, which indicate the days and times that workers or machines are allotted for use. The blank spaces show personnel or machine availability. This simple system makes accurate scheduling possible and can lead to a full utilization of personnel and facilities if sufficient orders are available.[3]

It must not be supposed that scheduling is as simple as the load charts indicate. In every concern of any size, there are interruptions and delays due to facility breakdowns, absent personnel, and other causes. Even scheduling of materials is not absolutely accurate because the supplier may be having similar machine and worker troubles, including strikes.

Figure 10.6 is a graphic composite chart of automobile production, scheduling, and routing. It starts in the upper left-hand corner and proceeds to the finished car, in the lower right-hand corner. Feeder or subassembly lines are indicated on both sides of the main assembly line. A brief study of this chart shows the enormous amount of work involved in planning automobile production. Each feeder line must proceed along the proper path (routing) to the point where it meets the main assembly line, and it must reach that point on time (scheduling). It is also easy to comprehend how one mistake in planning or some unforeseen happening may throw this intricately timed mechanism out of joint. The one word that best expresses the operation of such planning is rhythm.

Simulation

The ultimate in scheduling is arranging a number of operations so that they are all being performed at the same time. This type of scheduling is called "simulation." Alford, in his "Laws of Management," refers to simulation as the third principle in production progress (division of labor and transfer of skills to the machine are the other two).[4]

Considerable use of simulation developed during World War II, especially in automatic machining operations, where bar stock on a rotating frame is fed simultaneously to each of the operating slots on the drum. If the operations were numbered one to seven, naturally there would not be a full simultaneous working of the seven operations until the rotating stockholder

---

[3] Determining the proper number of available machines is important, especially in a job shop. The Waiting Line Theory, discussed in Chapter 5 will aid in this determination.

[4] Simulation is the subject of Chapter 17 in John Younger and Joseph Geschelin, *Work Routing, Scheduling and Dispatching in Production*, 3rd ed. (New York: The Ronald Press Company, 1947). This reference is recommended to anyone desiring the operational details of simulation.

Figure 10.6

Composite Production Scheduling and Route Chart

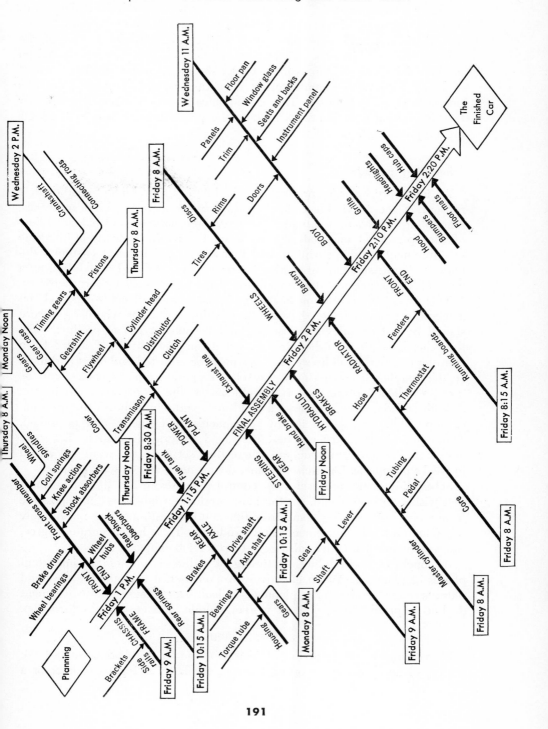

made a complete circuit of the operation heads. After the first complete circuit has been made, all operations are performed simultaneously with each station move of the rotating frame holding the raw material.

A significant feature of simultation is that the pace set is that of the average worker. Since the conveyor or machine sets the pace, pay based on individual incentive is impossible. Under the conveyor-paced plan in effect in many automobile-manufacturing concerns, individual wage incentives give way to group bonuses. The psychological question arises as to whether the simulation plan improves morale; the production economies it effects are unquestioned.

Scheduling periods

An inventory, sales, or production schedule is a time budget. Although it recognizes the inevitable difficulties with men, materials, and machines, scheduling is a scientific attempt to bring about an even and balanced flow of sales, personnel, materials, and equipment to minimize waste in idle time of equipment, working capital, and man-hours, and to meet customer deliveries. Top management is also interested in controlled scheduling as a means for bringing about an even flow of business on a long-term basis.

This aspect of scheduling leads to a consideration of control periods on a monthly or even longer basis. The schedule indicates whether pressure should be put on sales for business, and for what types of products. On the other hand, if the schedule shows that the concern is sold ahead for a considerable period, delivery promises must be adjusted and sales curtailed. In the merchandising business, the schedule-period type of control can be used to indicate future financing problems. If the term considered is long enough and the schedule shows a "sold-up" condition, it poses the question of a possible increase in inventory capacity, investment, and personnel. These period schedules are best portrayed by graphic charts. They are more complicated in production, where they set forth the workload ahead in weeks or months for each machine, department, and type of product.

Scheduling charts are useful for control purposes in any line of business that wishes to plan ahead. In the mass-production industries, it is possible from records of experience and from time study to estimate quite accurately the schedules for departments and products. To a less accurate degree, future schedule loads may also be set up for job shops.

In conclusion, scheduling, or timing of orders, is one of the important phases of planning. When effectively worked out, it smooths the flow and reduces costs. Improperly planned, it leads to delays with consequent decline in productivity, general worker morale, and customer satisfaction.

Dispatching

Dispatching gets into action as soon as authority is released to start the routing of an operation or order, whether the latter is for a customer or a

machine in the shop, those with long experience often ignore instructions and find pleasure in proving, when operation times are recorded, that they know better ways for doing the work. This human factor makes a naturally trying job of control little less than exasperating for the dispatcher.

Job-shop dispatching demands a much higher than average skill. Those working in the dispatcher's office must have a complete knowledge of shop and equipment conditions and all the methods which can be used for performing a given job. For a given volume of business, job-shop dispatching requires more and better clerks than for any other kind of dispatching.

Departmental Relations

Production control and procurement

The problems concerning material quantities to be bought and their delivery dates bring Production Control into its most important relationship with Procurement. The quantities requisitioned do not always represent economic lots from the purchasing standpoint. Some of these disagreements can be avoided if Procurement provides Production Control with a schedule of economical purchase quantities of important materials and parts. Delivery dates should be based on mutual agreement and specifically set forth in the purchase order. If Production Control gives Procurement reasonable notice of requirements, there will be little difficulty in securing vendor delivery promises, especially if past dealings have been satisfactory and profitable to the vendor.

Another problem affecting the relations of these two departments is the question of follow-up with vendors after the purchase orders have been issued. Procurement contends that it represents the company with all vendors and can, therefore, deal with them about deliveries with less effort and paper work and with more satisfactory results than is possible for Production Control. Procurement feels that Production Control will be unnecessarily aggressive in "demanding" deliveries and that this will impair relations between the concern and its vendors.

Production control, on the other hand, contends that Procurement is simply an unnecessary intermediary, and that as such it delays negotiations with vendors. A further contention of Production Control is that it has more intimate knowledge of the concern's manufacturing problems and so is in a better position to force compliance from the vendor, which is exactly what Procurement fears. This problem would be minimized if Production Control were able, as it should be, to specify deliveries in terms of months or weeks instead of days. Other things being equal, a company will usually favor Procurement for carrying on follow-up negotiations with the vendor.

Dispute about specifications should not exist between Procurement and Production Control, since specifications are drawn by Engineering in most cases. Problems arise chiefly because of Procurement's acknowledged right to question specifications even though Engineering has drawn them in accordance with the expressed wishes of the using departments. When disputes of this kind arise, it is recognized that Engineering must be the final arbiter, and there should be little reason for any outstanding conflict on specifications between Production Control and Procurement.

Production control and engineering

Here disputes concern Production Control's contention that specifications as drawn up by Engineering are not clear. Worse than that, Production Control is disturbed by "Change Notices" from Engineering which occasionally cause alterations in the routing process, not to mention rearrangement of inventory schedules and machine loads. Production Control's suspicions might be allayed if Engineering made an effort to justify its specification changes. Such changes become so irritating in some cases that group decisions are necessary in which Production Control and Procurement demand to be represented.

Production control and sales

The sales department often causes troubles for Production Control by promising delivery dates that are difficult to coordinate with the manufacturing processes. Changes in delivery schedules may also affect maximum utilization of plant capacity. Friction between these two departments could be materially lessened if Sales were kept informed about plant loads. The main trouble is that Sales makes delivery promises without any consideration of manufacturing schedules, of which they usually have a profound ignorance. Their motto is that the customer must be satisfied. Sales should have some appreciation of the necessary lead times involved in both Procurement and Manufacturing, but such an appreciation must be based on information which Sales rarely receives. Under-utilization of plant capacities may be almost as expensive as the loss of customers because of failure to meet Sales' delivery promises. The answer to this problem is that Sales must be kept informed of plant loads for the concern's various products, while Production Control must develop a willing but pragmatic flexibility in meeting Sales' requests.

Production control and manufacturing

There is a vigorously debated question as to the advisability of complete centralization of Production Control in the concern's over-all interest. When Production Control is located at a distance from some operations, however, its supervision of these operations may decrease flexibility, while increasing paper work. Furthermore, the unavoidable channels demanded by centralization, with their weight of detailed instructions, may require more expensive personnel. Decentralized departmental control, on the other hand, leads to faster decisions by supervisors, and to more satisfactory handling of problems of machine breakdowns and absentee operators. Departmental difficulties, so the proponents of decentralization claim, must be handled by the supervisors.

One answer to this debate is that only a central activity with an over-all knowledge of the total situation can cope with isolated problems with any reasonable hope of success. Another solution may be to allow the department supervisor to assign the operators and machines within his department, while Production Control retains coordinating responsibility among all departments. This plan requires that supervisors be advised in advance of the demands they will be called upon to meet.

Production control and personnel

Since machine operators are equally as important as machines in completing the production processes, coordination will be improved to the extent that Production Control advises Personnel well in advance of the number of employees who will be required to meet the different job classifications. This is particularly true in times of tight labor markets.

Conclusions concerning interdepartmental relations

An understanding of the working relationships among the departments cannot be over-emphasized if Production Control is to be responsible for their successful coordination. The techniques employed must necessarily be workable and fitted to the particular situation involved, but equally important is Production Control's ability to promote a cooperative spirit among the department supervisors and their operators. The extent to which the intangible human aspect of this problem is understood will largely determine Production Control's degree of success.

Conclusions

Success in any line of business is largely dependent on planning. In most cases, the extent of proper planning forecasts the probable degree of success. To the extent that this observation is true of the general planning functions, it is also true of routing, scheduling, and dispatching. In most lines of business, these three controls are vital to success. In continuous and repetitive industries, the conveyor does the routing and scheduling, as well as the pace-setting, but it must be realized that the closest kind of routing and scheduling was necessary to set up the conveyor-operated process in the first place. In fact, it was the routing and scheduling concepts that led to the conveyor method.

Planning in any business will lead to smooth operations if the control techniques are enforced. Smooth operations usually bring about maximum utilization of materials, men, and machines and account for minimum costs. The more complicated the business, the greater the need for adequate plans and their controlled operation. Increasing competition practically ensures the failure of any business that neglects proper planning and controls. When the mechanical processes were simpler, and the chief difficulty was in satisfying an ever-increasing demand, rule-of-thumb operations often produced satisfactory profits. These conditions do not exist in today's market place. Another current consideration demanding detailed planning is the growth of government regulations on the national, state, and local levels.

These factors all add to the necessity for business being ever on the watch for better ways of doing things and better ways for controlling the new methods. At the same time, there is an occasional tendency, especially in large-scale operations, to develop control systems to the point of diminishing returns. One definite measure by which we can evaluate controls is that they should not cost more to operate than they save. Any control system should show a wide margin of savings over costs. At the same time, it must be realized that controls can effect more benefits than appear directly in dollar savings. Smooth operations, for example, are valuable from an over-all organizational standpoint. To the extent that they reduce managerial friction and operational confusion, they have real values, of which morale is not the least.

Planning of the controls discussed here involves both mental and mechanical or physical preparation. The mental preparation includes decisions about what, when, how, where, and by whom. The mechanical preparations include the procuring of equipment, materials, and manpower needed for carrying out the plan. The two working together bring quality performance on time at minimum costs.

QUESTIONS

1. What is the relation between market analysis and production planning?
2. What two aspects of the salesmen's optimism affect the planning and control of production?
3. What are the three chief factors which production control has the responsibility for synchronizing?
4. How do we express the three primary factors of production control?
5. To what extent are computers being used for controlling production orders and schedules? Justify the percentage you name.
6. It is customary to say that production control bridges the gap between two important functions of industry. What are the two functions?

7. What single word can be used to describe each of the three primary production control activities?

8. To what extent is dispatching of production clerical rather than a matter of judgment? What are the reasons for your answer?

9. Who is responsible for production routing within individual departments?

10. For whose benefit is the work order prepared?

11. Can you mention five or six routing forms and their purposes?

12. What procedure is known as the "ultimate" in scheduling operations?

13. The text enumerates nine items, besides "tickets," which the dispatcher must account for before he can start a production order on its route. What are some of those items?

14. What two courses of action must the dispatcher take when he finds that a production order is stymied in process?

15. What is the relation between communication and control in the dispatcher's function?

16. There are occasional disagreements between production control and the procurement department. What is the cause of such unfortunate situations, and how can they be avoided?

17. Should production control, in your opinion, be permitted to deal directly with vendors for the purpose of expediting material deliveries? Why?

18. What is the cause for disagreement between production control and engineering, and how can it be minimized if not eliminated?

19. How can production control remedy its disagreements over delivery times with the sales organization?

20. What is your solution for the ever-continuing disagreement about the overall company effectiveness of centralized production control? Would decentralization be better in some cases, and if so, when?

CASE PROBLEM

Precision Instruments Corporation

The Precision company was founded by Norman Griffith and Walter Cole about twenty years ago. Griffith is a graduate electrical engineer whose background of experience was chiefly making estimates on installations for two large contracting firms. Cole is the "junior Steinmetz" type, but he has not made any outstanding contribution in his chosen field. He formerly operated as a lone wolf in his small laboratory, peddling minor inventions wherever he could find sufficient capital to finance a trial balloon. He sold himself to Griffith over the years through his requests for technical advice on prospective inventions.

Both men were in their middle fifties when they launched Precision, so they had well-set patterns of behavior when the concern started business. Such a management combination could scarcely augur well for the future prosperity of the new concern, although Griffith's previous contacts enabled him to sell most of the original stock issue of $200,000.

The company makes various types of meters including those for taxis, for measuring water and electrical consumption, and for a general line of coin-operated machines. The business has been able to enjoy a conservative growth chiefly because both men agreed to take only living expenses as salaries. Their machine and equipment investment was considerable, but they leased their factory building for a long term at a nominal base rent and a percentage of sales. By 1961 they were employing 150 workers, about half of whom were women on assembly jobs. Their annual sales were just above one million dollars.

In the production of several varieties of five different types of meters, the parts required numbered more than three hundred, most of which were made in the company's own plant. About 25 per cent of the parts inventory was bought from outside suppliers. Labor accounted for approximately 75 per cent of the costs of the business. Most of the balance of operating expenses was used for raw materials and accounts receivable.

Precision had no technical materials or production control procedures. Foremen sent estimates of purchased parts requirements to Purchasing at intervals of about two weeks, based on customer order information given them by the plant manager, who received his advice from Sales. Inventory requirements of parts made in the plant were estimated by the various foremen concerned — also based on the plant superintendent's information concerning customer orders. Made and bought parts were stored in two large separate rooms in the center of the one-story plant where they were readily accessible to all department foremen. Withdrawals of parts from the storerooms were made by foremen, who served themselves and left withdrawal slips for the parts. This plan was adopted to minimize production delays. Since there was little cooperation between the foremen and Engineering, occasional changes in specifications, without prior notice to the foremen, left unused portions of parts withdrawals stored in the departments. No provision was made for returning unused parts to plant inventory.

Parts bought on the outside were kept in a separate storage room so the purchasing department could decide by observation when they were getting near the reorder point. If a foreman found that a customer order required 70 or 80 parts of the same kind, he took a box, usually containing 100 parts, from inventory. Any parts left over were retained in the department for future use. The interval between uses for some parts was so long that they were often not presentable for use, so a new box was taken from inventory. The result of these loose inventory withdrawals made it impossible to reconcile end-of-the-year records of book inventories with the physical counts. In turn, this situation made the company's profit and loss statement questionable.

Since Mr. Griffith, as president, took general charge of co-ordinating the concern's activities, the personnel and financial functions were managed by Mr. Cole as vice-president. Scarcely qualified for either of these activities, Cole concealed his lack of ability by maintaining an aloof attitude toward the foremen. Since sales estimates were erratic over the years, Mr. Cole played safe by not retaining any pool of prospective employee applicants. The resulting delay in satisfying foremen's applications for additional help had its predictably adverse effect on meeting production schedules.

Lack of any general or specific understanding between the factory manager and Sales created a situation where salesmen were promising impossible delivery dates to customers. Because of the ups and downs of production volume, it was next to impossible for the plant superintendent to predict production schedules on more than a daily basis. In addition, the sales department also had no dependable idea of the plant's production capacity.

The final difficulty arose when Precision failed to meet a number of promised delivery dates to two outstanding customers. One dropped Precision altogether, and the other gave notice that its volume would be cut 50 per cent until Precision demonstrated the ability to meet its promised deliveries. Both Griffith and Cole were understandably upset. The plant manager urged a survey of production methods for his department. Cole went along with the suggestion, but Griffith's attitude was that as a graduate engineer he felt his opinions regarding production management were practical and correct. He blamed the plant manager for the new turn in events.

PROBLEM: What are your recommendations for correcting the production situation at Precision?

11

Financial Management

The most comprehensive business plans are practically worthless if the proper amount of money is not available at the right time. Failure is almost assured when a business program is prepared without making certain that the required funds are available from the start. This fact has not always been realized, but the past five years have witnessed a renewed interest among businessmen, consultants, and schools of business in the subject of financial management. The prosperity that followed World War II led all levels of business managers to feel that the money markets would welcome them with open arms. However, with the stiffening of credits by national regulation, it became even more important to know the sources of capital and the requirements for tapping them.

Determining financial policies and plans and controlling them in practice are vital to the progress, and often the existence, of any enterprise. Planning and controlling are parts of the same procedure, and both are necessary for success. These twins of finance cover determination of policies, or administration, and the execution of those policies, or management.

Financing is the process of raising and using various kinds of funds for establishing and operating an enterprise. It is one of the fundamental activities of modern management. The outstanding cause of failure among business concerns, especially the smaller ones, is the general lack of training and experience of their leaders in the general techniques of management, and especially financial management. Included in management inexperience are four causes which fall in the category of financial management. They are: heavy operating expenses, receivable difficulties, inventory calculations, and excessive fixed assets.[1] The Studebaker-Packard financial difficulties emphasize that even professional managers of large corporations would do

[1] For a summary of the underlying causes of business failures as compiled by the U.S. Department of Commerce, see Louis P. Starkweather, Erich A. Otto and H. Randall Kreger, *Policies and Practices in Corporate Finance* (New York: New York University Bookstore, 1951), pp. 261–264.

well to understand the relationship between available money and profitable business.

Many failures could be avoided if financial requirements were well planned in advance. Starting a business with inadequate assets is courting disaster. Too much money, on the other hand, may lead to poor investment of surplus funds. Furthermore, the company's credit and the market value of its common stock are both depressed when earnings do not bear a reasonable relation to its total assets. The average earnings of successful concerns amount to approximately 10 per cent of their sales. The relation between assets and volume of earnings depends on the turnover of assets as related to sales volume. It is practically impossible to decide whether under- or over-capitalization is worse because of the many factors involved and their application to varying conditions.

Operating a company with insufficient funds during its early stages, on the assumption that additional financing can be taken care of as the need arises, is often fatal. Even when investment capital is seeking opportunities, it may have a suspicious nature. It wants to know all the facts, and if interested it starts to bargain. Any concern in "urgent need" of funds, be it newly organized or with some maturity, is suspect. There is always the fair assumption that it does not know how it stands or where it is headed, simply because its management has no financial plan. The lack of a plan may be due to the absence of data and records useful for control purposes. The failure to control invariably springs from the lack of established standards. A company in this predicament is a poor credit risk, a condition which prevents normal dealings with the recognized sources of funds.

After the concern is established and operating with a reasonable amount of funds at its disposal, problems involving finances are continually presenting themselves for solution and decision. Business is essentially dynamic if it is successful. It is either expanding because of increased demands for its products or contracting because of a general decline in economic conditions or a lessened customer demand. In either case, financial adjustments are required. The farther ahead market analysis can foresee these changes, the more effective is the financial planning to cope with them.

The chief financial problem of management is to maintain a constant flow of funds into circulating assets such as raw materials, work-in-process, and finished products. These working assets represent the blood stream of business. Cash must be used to buy raw materials which are converted into finished-product inventories to be sold to customers. Inventories must be turned into receivables due from customers to whom the products have been sold. When customer receivables have been collected, they are converted into cash, ready to make a new start in the process or flow over which financial management must exercise a controlling hand. The excess of collected receivables over the total cost of products is profit.

Financial management must supply the correct amount of funds at reasonable cost and at the right time to maintain this flow from cash to cash. Excess of inventories or frozen receivables will slow the circulating process of current assets and reduce profits. If the circulating process is impeded over a long period of time, the entire organism may be stifled and the business fail.

Assets, Liabilities and Working Capital

The assets, or resources, of a company are of two general kinds — fixed and current. Liabilities are likewise divided into fixed, or long term, and current.

Current assets, or circulating capital, are also referred to as "quick" or "liquid." They include cash and marketable securities, accounts and notes reecivable, inventories, and any advances made by customers. They are called "liquid," because they are cash or they can be converted into cash with reasonable dispatch, and "circulating," because they move through the various stages of production and receivables, and back to cash.

Current or circulating assets must be large enough and sufficiently liquid to meet currently maturing liabilities, including such items as payroll, materials, interest, and dividends. Sometimes a portion of current assets may be used to buy fixed assets, such as machinery and equipment, which are slow in circulating if indeed they may be considered to "circulate" at all. When an excess of such conversions occurs, serious financial difficulties may result. Conversion may also operate in the opposite direction, when reserves that are set aside for depreciation of fixed assets are used for current operations. In this way, cash can emerge from fixed assets and become a part of current funds.

Fixed assets are permanent in nature and not easily converted into cash, except at considerable loss. They include land, buildings, machinery, equipment, furniture and fixtures, and good will when this item appears on the financial statement. Investment in subsidiaries is another form of fixed assets.

Current liabilities represent company debts which will be payable within a relatively short time, in no case longer than a year. They cover accounts and notes payable to trade customers and others. In some cases, bonds payable within the year are classed as current liabilities. They also include accrued expenses such as taxes, interest, and salaries. Declared dividends are current liabilities until paid. Finally, this category includes reserves set up to meet various future obligations payable within the year, such as income taxes.

Long-term or *fixed* liabilities include bonds, notes with a maturity of longer than a year, and mortgages.

Working capital, which is defined as the excess of current assets over current liabilities, is the prime fund for financing the circulation of raw materials to finished products and back again to cash.[2] When a concern's liabilities exceed its assets, it is insolvent, which means that it cannot pay all of its creditors. Whether the creditors allow it to continue operations in the hope that the situation will improve is often a question of business judgment.

Long-term funds are naturally required to finance fixed assets. Because fixed assets consist of such items as buildings and machinery, it is relatively easy to determine the financial requirements for them. On the other hand, figuring the needs for current assets and working capital involves a number of elastic factors.

1. *The cost of material, labor, and overhead* naturally influences the amount of circulating funds needed to finance a given volume of production for a manufacturer, or sales for a merchandising concern. Producing for the high-quality market demands relatively expensive materials and high-priced labor.

2. The *volume of production* (or volume of sales in merchandising companies) is another important consideration influencing working capital requirements. Stepped-up production increases the need for cash by a fairly proportionate amount for all costs except overhead. It means, among other things, large inventories and more accounts and notes receivable.

3. The *length-of-production cycle* refers to the time it takes to transform raw materials into the finished product. The number of components, especially if they are made rather than bought, may influence the production cycle. When material and labor costs must be financed during prolonged production cycles, the working-capital needs are increased.

4. The *ratio of sales to investment* indicates the turnover of the funds used in the business. Such concerns as public utilities have large capital investments compared to their volume of business. Therefore their turnover is low. Some companies may turn over their capital ten times a year. Retail concerns should have a higher turnover. Chain grocery companies may turn over from thirty to fifty times a year. When the ratio of sales to investment is high, the working-capital funds required to operate the business are relatively low.

5. When the *credit terms granted by vendors,* or suppliers, are extended, the amount of working capital requirements is reduced. In other words, vendors are contributing to working capital in proportion to the length of credit terms they allow buyers. If the production cycle is also of long duration, working-capital requirements may be high in spite of favorable vendor credits.

[2] Some writers in the field of finance use the term "working capital" to cover both fixed and current assets, on the theory that the plant and equipment are also part of the concern's working tools. In such cases, the term "net working capital" is applied to the difference between this figure and current liabilities. See Starkweather, Otto Kreger, *op. cit.,* p. 138.

6. The extension of *credit terms granted to customers* has the reverse effect on the amout of working capital requirements. Chain groceries selling for cash may operate with comparatively small working capital, particularly if they can secure long-term credits from vendors.

Assets may be obtained for short, intermediate, and long-term purposes. The *short-term* source is usually a commercial bank, on notes running thirty to ninety days. With renewals, the notes may be extended for as long as a year. These funds are used to pay for materials, labor, and other items that lead to quick turnover of the investment. *Intermediate funds* are payable in from one to five years and are customarily used to purchase machinery and equipment. *Long-term* funds, usually invested in land and buildings, may be liquidated over a period of ten to fifty years. Short and intermediate

Figure 11.1

Hansford Manufacturing Company
Condensed Balance Sheet
December 31, 196–
Assets

Current Assets		
Cash (On hand and in bank)		$ 85,000
Accounts Receivable (Owed by customers) .. $ 95,000		
Less reserve for doubtful accounts 5,000		90,000
Notes Receivable (Customers and others)		8,000
Inventories		
Raw Materials	$125,000	
Work-in-process	60,000	
Finished Goods	150,000	335,000
TOTAL CURRENT ASSETS		$518,000
Fixed Assets		
Land (owned by the company)		$ 30,000
Buildings (Owned by the company)	$150,000	
Less reserve for depreciation	60,000	90,000
Machinery & Equipment	240,000	
Less reserve for depreciation	50,000	190,000
TOTAL FIXED ASSETS		$310,000
Other Assets		
Unexpired Insurance (Paid in advance)		$ 3,000
TOTAL ASSETS		$831,000

loans are sometimes shifted to the long-term category by renewals or by refinancing as part of a long-term loan.

The task of financial management

A successful business requires both fixed and working capital. The amounts and the relations between these and other financial factors help determine the success of the enterprise. To produce its livelihood of profits, proper financial management must pay attention to the following:

1. Acquiring the proper amounts of fixed and working capital
2. Having the required capital available at the right time

Condensed Balance Sheet

Liabilities & Net Worth

Current Liabilities

Accounts Payable (Owed to vendors and others)			$ 75,000
Notes Payable			
To banks		$ 75,000	
To vendors		15,000	90,000
Accruals (Owed but not yet due)			
Federal Income Tax		$ 60,000	
Other Taxes		15,000	
Other Accruals		10,000	85,000
TOTAL CURRENT LIABILITIES			$250,000

Funded Debt

4½% Mortgage Bonds (Due to bondholders)		$ 60,000

Net Worth

Capital Stock (Due to stockholders)	$400,000	
Surplus (Earned)	121,000	$521,000
TOTAL LIABILITIES & NET WORTH		$831,000

Net Worth		$521,000
Working Capital	$518,000	
	250,000	$268,000
Cash Sales		$75,000
Credit Sales		$2,500,000
Total Sales		$2,575,000
Net Profit		200,000

3. Securing borrowed funds as cheaply as possible
4. Arranging repayments that will not strain company finances
5. Investing in uses that will promote the business
6. Controlling expenditure for profitable objectives
7. Controlling the use of profits from operations

The Financial Statement

To point up the discussion thus far and to indicate the significance of the financial ratio analyses to follow, a condensed financial statement, or balance sheet, is set forth in Figure 11.1. Most of the items on the balance sheet are self-explanatory; however, some of them are explained in the brackets following the item title. The chief purpose of the statement is to present figures for analysis so that those interested can get an accurate idea of the condition of the company from the operating and financial standpoints. Much of this analysis is based on the use of *ratios*. Ratios are not dependable as an over-all picture of company affairs unless several of them are considered simultaneously. Taken as a group, they may give a fairly clear idea of the current financial and operating situation. It is usually advisable, also, to consider the *trends* of the various ratios. For this purpose, the ratios of previous years should be compared with current ratios. Only the more important ratios will be considered here.

Ratio Analyses

Current Assets to Current Liabilities. Various relationships between fixed and current assets and liabilities are used to show the purported financial strength of the enterprise. One such comparison, called the *current ratio,* is found by dividing current assets by current liabilities. Until recent years, the current ratio was given great weight by bankers and vendors in determining their willingness to extend credit and in fixing the amount and terms. A ratio of two dollars of current assets to one of current liabilities, known as a "2-to-1," or more simply as a "2" ratio, is still considered acceptable for credit purposes. On our sample balance sheet in Figure 11.1, the current ratio is found by dividing 250,000 into 518,000, which gives us the ratio of 2.07, or slightly better than 2 to 1.

In recent years, progressive bankers have recognized that the nature of the business, the quality of its management, and other nonfiscal matters must be recognized, thus minimizing the influence of the current ratio as a lending norm. A concern with a poor current ratio may be an acceptable credit risk if it has lately acquired new management with a history of successful operations.

Another asset and liability ratio, known as the *acid test or quick ratio,* relates cash, receivables, and marketable securities to current liabilities. It is found by dividing the sum of the first three by the last. From the sample balance sheet (Figure 11.1), the acid test or quick ratio is calculated by dividing the total current liabilities (250,000) into the sum of cash (85,000), accounts receivable (90,000), notes receivable (8,000), and marketable securities (none), or a total of 183,000, showing .73 as the quick ratio.

As with the current ratio, this measure of credit acceptability may lead to questionable conclusions. For example, a high current or quick ratio may result from withholding reasonable dividend payments. When these ratios are high, they hold out a temptation to non-owning professional management to cater to its pride by investing company surpluses in speculative ventures such as grand office buildings or plant expansions which fail to stand the strain of industrial cycles.

Total Assets to Total Debt. This ratio shows in another way the coverage which the owners give to the company's creditors. From our sample balance sheet, the ratio of total assets to total debt is found by dividing the sum of the total current liabilities (250,000) and the funded debt (60,000) into total assets (831,000), making 2.7 the ratio. The relation between net worth and total debt also indicates the relative value of creditor protection. This ratio is found from the balance sheet by dividing the total debt, consisting of total current liabilities (250,000) and funded debt (60,000), into net worth (521,000), resulting in a 1.7 ratio.

Fixed Assets to Net Worth. This ratio will indicate whether too large a proportion of the net worth has been invested in land, buildings, and machines. From the sample balance sheet, this ratio is determined by dividing the fixed assets (310,000) by the net worth (521,000), which fixes the ratio as .6. In other words, the company has about 60 per cent of its net worth invested in fixed assets. When investments in fixed assets are too large, not enough of the current assets and working capital will be available for current operations. This situation is common among companies which seem to be prosperous but cannot pay their current bills.

Turnover of Inventory. Inventory-turnover ratio is found by dividing either year-end or average inventory costs into annual sales. Because the rate of inventory turnover is subject to fluctuation, the figure for year-end inventory could be artificially high or low. Therefore, the *average* annual inventory cost is a more dependable base line for computing this ratio. A defect of this ratio — whichever way it is computed — is the fact that inventories are taken at cost, whereas sales ordinarily include a profit. For showing periodic trends, however, the ratio is valuable. It is important because an excess of inventory is a frequent cause of financial difficulties, especially if a considerable portion of it is slow moving. When this ratio is not representative of the industry as a whole, it means that either the inventory should be reduced or sales increased. The inventory-turnover ratio for our sample balance sheet is obtained by dividing total year-end inventories (335,000), consisting of raw materials (125,000), work-in-process (60,000), and finished goods (150,000), into total sales (2,575,000), including cash sales (75,000) and credit sales (2,500,000). The result shows that inventories were turned about 7.7 times during the year covered by the statement.

Credit Sales to Accounts Receivable. The ratio of credit sales to receivables indicates the condition of collection of customer accounts. If thirty days' credit is allowed, then collections are poor to the extent that the total of accounts receivable amounts to more than the average credit sales for thirty days. The sample balance sheet shows credit sales for the year as $2,500,000 and accounts receivable as $95,000.[3] Using 360 days for the year, the average daily credit sales amount to $6,944. When this amount is divided into the outstanding receivables, it shows that fewer than fourteen days' average sales are outstanding, which is an unusually good record. As with excessive inventories, poor collections tie up working capital and lead to financial trouble.

Although the ratios explained are fewer than half the number used by careful financial analysts, nevertheless, if these few are computed from any adequate financial statement, a fairly clear picture will emerge of the concern's financial condition, as well as the likely defects in its financial management.

Forms of Business Ownership

The form of ownership of a business organization often makes a difference in the sources available for acquiring its capital funds. A sketch of the outstanding forms of ownership will help clarify the reasons for this.

Individual proprietorship

Ownership by an individual is the oldest form of business enterprise. It has several distinct *advantages:*

1. Ease of establishment
2. Simplicity of coordination through one-man control
3. No organization or franchise taxes
4. Limited governmental regulation and control

Its *disadvantages* become more pronounced with the increasing capital needs for the operation of modern business:

1. Its growth is limited by the owner's credit.
2. Its existence expires with the owner's death, insanity or bankruptcy.
3. If it extends beyond one-man ability to manage, it often becomes inefficient because of the owner's reluctance to relinquish controls.

[3] Credit sales become accounts receivable until they are paid.

General partnership

A partnership is the association of two or more co-owners in the operation of an enterprise. A general partnership is based on a contractual relationship by which the partners may act individually as agents for the concern, sharing in its management, its profits, and its losses. Any partner may, by his single act, obligate the group individually and severally. Each partner is responsible for the concern's liabilities to the extent of his private fortune.

Partnerships evolve from the inability of an individual to finance a business. As with the individual proprietorship, the partnership organization is simple, and involves no franchise taxes. Because experience shows that the partnership form is fraught with possibilities for disagreements, and because of its extinction by the withdrawal of a partner by court order or mutual consent, the contract which establishes it should be given serious consideration.[4]

The advantages and disadvantages of the general partnership may be summarized as follows:

Advantages

1. Easily and inexpensively organized
2. Has no organization taxes
3. Relatively free of government control
4. Its owner operates the business
5. Unlimited liability promotes its credit

Disadvantages

1. Susceptible to sudden termination
2. Partner relations potentially complicated
3. Individual liability deters investment
4. Unlimited responsibility with divided authority
5. Effective action depends on continuing harmony

The corporation

The corporation is the outstanding form of American business enterprise. Its exact origin is unknown, but usually attributed to the Romans. In a broad sense, the corporation is an association of persons enfranchised by sovereign authority to pool a part of their resources and act as a legal entity in carrying out a common purpose or enterprise.[5] The public franchise changes the group of associated persons into a single corporate entity, or

---

[4] The codification of decisions resulting from a large volume of partnership litigation has produced the Uniform Partnership Law, which has been adopted by a number of states.

[5] The most quoted definition is that of Chief Justice Marshall, which can be found in the case of the Trustees of Dartmouth College *vs.* Woodward, 4 Wheaton 636 (1819).

artificial person, in which capacity it has most of the privileges and obligations of a natural person, with continuity of existence in addition.

The importance of the corporation on the American business scene is of relatively recent origin. In 1800, there were 335 charters in the entire country. Of these, only 8 were issued for manufacturing purposes, the others being for banking, insurance, navigation, turnpikes, water supply, and docks.[6] It was not until after the Civil War that the rapid expansion of industry stimulated growth of the corporate form. Its real impetus came with the turn of the century, when increasing demands for large-scale industry made incorporation almost imperative for raising the large amounts of capital required. By 1939, although few in number compared with the other forms of business, corporations employed about 90 per cent of our industrial workers and contributed approximately 90 per cent of the value of our production.[7] These percentages are even greater today.

As with other business forms, the corporation has both advantages and disadvantages.

Advantages

1. *Autonomy.* It has rights as an artificial person, among which are the privilege of suing and being sued, owning and controlling property, and entering into binding contracts.

2. *Continuity.* In about half the states, charters run in perpetuity unless dissolved by the stockholders or the courts. In the other states, perpetuity is practically guaranteed by charter renewals.

3. *Limited Liability.* In general, the liability of stockholders is limited to the amount of their investments. This is a distinct risk advantage over the partnership and proprietorship forms, and makes it possible for corporations to attract large sums of private funds.

4. *Ownership Transfer.* The divisibility of owner interests into stock certificates (shares) makes it easy for the individual investor to buy into the corporation or dispose of his shares when he wants cash.

5. *Representative Management.* This attribute allows the owner to separate himself from the management of the concern. As a stockholder, he elects the board of directors who, in turn, select managers to operate the company, permitting the hiring of specialists. It also permits expansions in the concern's capital investment without disturbing the management personnel.

---

[6] Joseph S. Davis, *Essays in the Earlier History of American Corporations* (Cambridge, Mass.: Harvard University Press, 1917) treats the development of American corporations through 1800. George H. Evans, Jr., *Business Incorporations in the United States: 1800–1943* (New York: National Bureau of Economic Research, Inc., 1948), covers the last century and a half.

[7] Harry G. Guthmann and Herbert E. Dougall, *Corporate Financial Policy*, 2nd ed. (New York: Prentice-Hall, Inc., 1948), p. 9. Many other comparative details on the same subject may be found in the U.S. Census of Manufacturers.

6. *Flexibility of Management.* With general management a responsibility of the board of directors, the individuals engaged in the direct management of the concern can be changed from time to time without affecting, or being affected by, the stockholders.

7. *Blanket-Purpose Charters.* The development of charter purposes has been broadened so that today's corporation is no longer restricted in its activities. Before blanket-purpose charters were granted by state statutes, it was customary to allow only a single purpose to the incorporating concern. Under this plan, any new or additional purpose had to be applied for under the statutes.

8. *Transfer of Control.* The share method of evidencing ownership makes it easy, technically, to transfer controlling ownership in the concern.

9. *Expansion without Loss of Control.* Successful concerns, by selling nonvoting common and preferred stocks and bonds, can ordinarily expand their capital without loss of control by the original group of investors.

Disadvantages

1. *Cost of Formation.* The corporate form can be both complicated and expensive in the initial stages. Money must be spent for legal, engineering, and entrepreneurial talent; and taxes must be paid for the act of incorporation.

2. *Taxes and Regulation.* The corporation is usually subject to heavier general as well as special taxes. Corporate earnings are subjected to double taxation, first on the profits of the company, and then on dividends paid to the stockholders from corporate profits.[8] The corporation is also subjected to many regulations by the federal and state governments.

3. *Differences in State Corporation Laws.* Every state has a voluminous section in its statutes concerning the formation and regulation of corporations. Furthermore, corporate regulations differ widely among the states. Since they are the creatures of statutory regulations, corporations encounter more difficulties in operation than do the nonstatutory forms of organization.

4. *Lack of Stockholder Control.* Although the corporation appears to be an industrial democracy, in reality the stockholders have relinquished real control through a device known as the proxy, which periodically transfers owner rights for making corporate decisions to an inside group of the board of directors, or the professional management.

Forms of Corporate Interest

The forms of corporate interest are important as representing debts of the corporation. Outstanding common stock is a debt owed by the corporation to those who are taking the primary financial risk in its future. Various

---

[8] The Internal Revenue Code of 1954 allows some relief in this double taxation feature by granting a partial credit, but the savings to the taxpayer are not so great as has been popularly believed.

other corporation debtors are represented by groups assuming lesser risks, with proportionately reduced opportunities for gain. These differences, together with the privileges and obligations incurred, should be known to all security owners.

Stocks

Stocks are of two kinds — common and preferred. *Common stock* represents that class of ownership which assumes primary risk in the enterprise. Where other security forms exist, common stockholders come last in receiving profits in the form of dividends, or any funds in event of dissolution.[9] Common stockholders control company affairs through voting rights. However, this right has been considerably diluted and dissipated through use of the proxy. The interest of the stockholders is evidenced by certificates which indicate the class of stock, the number of shares held, and their par value, unless the stock is without par value.

Par values are delusive since the market value usually differs from par. Furthermore, all shares have several values, such as *par, book,* and *market.* Common stock has no maturity date, so the owner can retrieve his investment only by selling and transferring ownership.

The privileges and obligations conferred upon the owner of *preferred stock* vary from issue to issue; they are always specified on the stock certificate. In the past, preferred stock has normally been nonvoting, but more recently many preferred issues may obtain voting power after the lapse of dividends for a specified period. Preferred stocks usually receive preferential treatment in the matter of dividends; in the event of dissolution, they have precedence over the common. Ordinarily the preferred has a fixed dividend return, which is usually cumulative and must be paid before the common participates in earnings.

Some preferred stock is convertible into common at a predetermined price. The conversion privilege is not ordinarily exercised unless the market price of the common rises above that of the convertible preferred. It is also customary for the issuing company to have the privilege of paying off, or retiring, its preferred issues after a stipulated date, and at a price usually in excess of its par value. There are many other stipulations regarding the privileges and obligations of preferred stocks, all of which appear on the certificates of ownership.

Bonds

Bonds are long-term negotiable debts of the issuing company, customarily running for ten years or longer. They represent claims fixed in amount,

[9] The interest of common and preferred stockholders is called "equity capital."

maturity date, and interest rate. Bondholders' claims to interest and principal take precedence over any payments to the corporation owners — the stockholders. Bondholders have no voice in the management unless the debtor defaults on the terms of payment or some other stipulation contained in the trust agreement, which specifies the conditions on which the bonds are issued. Because bonds are more secure than stocks, bond buyers accept smaller returns than would attract prospective stockholders, who are willing to take a greater risk for a potentially larger return.

Bonds enlarge the sources of a company's funds, especially long-term funds. Since they are a prospective source of large funds at comparatively low rates of interest, they offer the stockholder-owners an opportunity to earn profits amounting to the difference between this debt and interest costs cf the bond funds and the earnings of the business. This profitable use of borrowed funds derived from senior corporate obligations is called *trading on the equity*. With the idea of making bonds more attractive, some issues provide for their conversion into common stock at a predetermined price.

There are three general classes of bonds — mortgage, collateral trust, and debenture. *Mortgage bonds* are secured by definite real property of the debtor. If the issuing company defaults on these bonds, the bondholders, under the trust agreement, may take possession of the pledged property. *Collateral trust bonds* are secured by the deposit of stocks or bonds by the debtor with the trustee for the bondholders. *Debenture bonds* are secured by all debtor assets not otherwise pledged. The word debenture signifies a debt, so that originally all bonds were debentures. However, as practice in this country tended to differentiate among the various classes of security supporting bond issues, the debenture bond lost caste as compared to the more definitely secured mortgage and collateral trust bonds, which can usually be sold at a more favorable interest rate.

Asset Requirements

Estimating asset requirements

The amounts of capital required by a company are never constant. The requirements will be different at the time of starting a business from what they will be later on; and after the company is in operation, capital needs will vary during periods of expansion and contraction and during normal seasonal fluctuations. This variation holds true for both fixed- and current-asset requirements. To estimate what the specific needs will be, we have to take a different set of facts into consideration according to whether the focus of our interest is on fixed or current assets, but in either case the general approach will be the same. A further differentiation in treatment is necessary as between large and small concerns.

It might be assumed that fixed assets require a constant amount of investment, but because they wear out or become obsolete, capital requirements for them are only relatively fixed. Replacements may amount to more or less than the original costs, but usually more. Current assets, on the other hand, are considered essentially variable or fluctuating. They represent a fixed investment only to the extent that a minimum investment in inventory is maintained. With all capital requirements, the fixed portion is the minimum total on which the concern can get along; the variable portion is the difference between assets at their maximum and minimum. This variable portion, including cash and inventories, is the most difficult to estimate.

It is easy to understand that most incorrect estimates of capital requirements fall in the working-capital category. This is because of the elastic nature of three important factors of financial management: (1) the length of time of the production cycle, (2) the terms of credit to be extended to customers, and (3) the amount of expense accruing until the concern "hits its production stride." This "until" period tends to be longer than most organizers figure.

Estimating the financial requirements of a business is the first problem of financial management and a difficult task under the best of circumstances. Many inexperienced organizers fail to prepare for it, and many writers gloss over this phase of the subject by failing to point out its pitfalls. The initial capital needs of a company, including a plant built to its specifications, will include most of the following items:

1. Preliminaries to organization
   a. Inquiry as to social and economic factors
   b. Survey of the competitive situation
   c. Legal and engineering counsel
   d. Survey of the raw-materials market
   e. Survey of machinery and equipment market
   f. Market survey of sales opportunities
   g. Meetings of prospective investors
   h. Estimating costs of fixed investment
   i. Estimating amount of working capital
   j. Survey of security markets
2. Obtaining the charter and other franchises
3. Fees for the sale of securities
4. Purchase of the factory site
5. Architect's fees for plans and supervision
6. Engineering fees
7. Cost of the factory building
8. General contractor's charges
9. Taxes, interest, and insurance during construction
10. Organization expense during construction
11. Setting up for operations
    a. Recruiting executive and supervisory personnel
    b. Recruiting the sales force
    c. Recruiting office and production personnel

    d. Machinery, equipment, and tools
    e. Office furniture, fixtures, and supplies
    f. Raw materials, components, and production supplies
    g. Setting up accounting systems and controls
    h. Operating until the break-even point is reached
    i. Advertising
12. Legal fees and promoters' charges

It is obivous that because of their different nature, fixed and working asset requirements should be figured separately. At the same time, it must be recognized that they have a direct relationship. The fixed-asset investment will be determined by the volume of production, and production is important when estimating working-capital requirements. After careful planning and accurate estimates have determined the amount of assets required, the next problem is the source of funds.

Sources of capital assets

Capital is either owned or borrowed. Owned capital is contributed by those who have a proprietary interest in the business, while borrowed capital is contributed by those who have a creditor interest.

The nature of the business seeking capital influences the source to be used and the amount and kind of capital to be secured. Many sources cater to particular kinds of business, as evidenced by the establishment of "Farmers" and "Drovers" banks. The amount of capital required will, of course, vary greatly from small businesses to large, but some of the problems involved can be illustrated by the case of small businesses, which may find long-term loans for amounts under half a million dollars not only relatively expensive to obtain but difficult to negotiate in the regular long-term channels. The kind of capital required — long-term or short-term — will vary according to the purpose for which it will be used. Long- and short-term capital must be sought in different markets.

The financial market is generally recognized as "free" or "tight," or something in between. Whether it is only temperamental or bases its moods on justifiable business conditions is beyond the power of the borrower to adjust. Companies which plan their finances in advance, to avoid emergencies, can afford to wait for a favorable climate of the money market. Large concerns are usually in this position, which may account for their ability to become large. When a company with unplanned finances finds itself in an emergency during a tight money market, it is in real difficulty.

Internal Financing. Financing from earnings has several advantages and disadvantages. The use of surpluses permits expansion free from dictation of external sources. Successful expansion from profits indicates financial stability and strengthens the company's credit position. On the other hand, it decreases the investors' purchasing power through the diminution or absence of dividend payments, thus possibly contributing to recessions. It also promotes involuntary savings in that stockholders are forced, by decision of the board of directors, to contribute a considerable portion of company earnings to expansion. Decreased demand on the money market, as a result of internal financing, also tends to lessen the number of investment outlets for individual savings.[10]

External Financing. The financial requirements of modern enterprises are so large that management must often look beyond plowed-in profits for normal expansion outlays. Until the thirties, companies paid a large share of profits to stockholders as dividends. This policy made external financing a more important source of funds than it has been since that time because of a larger retention of profits for growth.

Demands for outside capital include funds for both initial financing and expansion. Either because equity owners (stockholders) do not care to lose or dilute their control, or because their companies need more new funds than earnings after dividends can provide, the so-called capital market must be used for the sale of long-term securities and the money market for short-term funds.

The *capital market* for long-term securities is a nation-wide financial network which attracts and distributes investment funds. The firms, individuals, and institutions which comprise this network filter so many requests for capital funds that their sensitive reactions to the investment supply and demand act as a barometer of the capital market.

Investment banks of various types are one of the chief sources of capital funds from the sale of common and preferred stocks. They originate security issues, and underwrite or guarantee their sale. Occasionally they buy the whole or part of issues for resale. They also promote corporate combinations and handle the security transactions of new concerns.

Commercial banks are still the chief source, directly or indirectly, for short-term and intermediate loans. Their commercial loan volume declined after World War I, and the resulting gap has been partly filled by the *commercial paper houses* which buy the notes of business concerns and sell them to commercial banks or other investors desiring short-term maturities. One reason for the rise of the commercial paper houses was the depression policy of the commercial banks of increasing their investments in government securities. This new trend promoted the stability and liquidity of the banks' investments, whereas customer notes were often subject to more or less forced renewals.

---

[10] For an excellent discussion of the economic effects of financing from internal sources, see Hiram L. Jome, *Corporate Finance* (New York: Henry Holt & Company, 1948), pp. 250–265.

Finance companies are often referred to as a general group specializing in different kinds of installment loans. Usually they lend on accounts receivable or installment leases given to retailers by their customers. Automobile finance companies take a large volume of these installment leases. This whole group of lenders has flourished chiefly because of the commercial banks' reluctance to accept accounts receivable as collateral. The *factor* buys accounts receivagle outright after approving the credit of the debtors. All of these external credit sources are used chiefly because the borrower does not have access to regular commercial bank loans.

One advantage of dealing with finance companies and factors is the quick expansion and contraction of loans which their system offers. They do not require annual liquidation of loans as is often the case with commercial banks. When receivables are purchased by factors, the seller has less concern about credit risks and collection costs than with most other sources.

The independent *small loans company* is a relatively new source of credit for small business concerns. Sparked by the chain of Morris Plan companies, whose announced purpose was to supplant the "sharks" in the small loans field, these independents spread rapidly after 1920. By offering lower rates of interest, they have attempted to displace the "42 per cent companies" recommended in the Russell Sage Foundation report of 1916, on the basis of which many legislatures established 42 per cent as the legal maximum rate for loans of three hundred dollars or less.[11]

There are two special groups which business concerns frequently turn to for long-term funds: employees and customers. In both cases, the company's desire for additional funds is frequently intermingled with other motives. *Employee ownership of company securities* became popular during the twenties as a means for encouraging employee interest in company affairs, with the hope of increasing productivity and improving labor relations. *Customer participation in company financial affairs,* which came somewhat later than the sale of securities to the rank-and-file employees, attempted to tie an outside interest to company success. Local utility companies have been leaders in this movement, pointing out to customers that the returns on a specified amount of preferred stock or bonds would pay their light and gas bills. It is presumed that customer interest in the investment will also help decrease public antagonism to the utilities' requests for increased service rates.

Financing the Small Concern

The financial problems of the small enterprise, both at the time of organization and during the first few years of operations, are so distinct that if space permitted, and extended discussion of the subject would be worth-

---

[11] For a detailed discussion of this subject, see Henry G. Hodges, *Cyclopedia on Pawnbroking* (Cincinnati: J. W. Taylor Publishing Co., 1943), pp. 25–43.

while for the student of management. The relative position of the small concern in the economy of the nation is not generally appreciated. Figures from the U.S. Department of Commerce show that the small companies account for 40 per cent of our industrial personnel and contribute a little more than 35 per cent of the value of our manufactured products. Another important economic consideration is that the smaller concerns feed the larger with materials, components, and services. It may be presumed that the large companies look to the smaller for these contributions because they can buy from them to advantage. Finally, but by no means least important, small concerns represent the backbone of free enterprise in this country. Practically all large companies had small beginnings. They became large either by plowing back profits, by raising expansion capital through public subscriptions, by mergers or consolidations, or by some other form of combination.

Access to initial and expansion capital has been conspicuously denied the small enterprise. In former times, when capital requirements were not large, the problem was not so important as it is today. The cost per dollar of raising the modest funds required by small companies is far in excess of the rates for the substantial amounts used by large concerns. The sources for short-term loans for small enterprises are few and far between, and often undesirable because of the high interest and service charges involved.

Conclusions

All management functions are important to the general success of any enterprise, and financial management ranks high in determining that success. The outstanding problem in financing a business is adequate planning, which is vital during the organizing stages. It is difficult, at best, to determine financial requirements, and these will not be dependable in any sense unless they are guided by a comprehensive check-list of the factors involved. The necessary provisions for borrowed funds in the early operating stages should be prepared for during the organizing period. Left until the concern is in operation, when results may not measure up to expectations, borrowing will be extremely difficult in the regular channels of finance.

Akin to the principles of financial management, and almost a part thereof, is an understanding of all the other principles of management. Even a plentiful money supply may turn out to be a millstone unless the other factors of scientific management are appreciated and acted upon. The sources of both short- and long-term credits must be recognized and approaches made to them in language which those in charge will understand. That language should include the ratios discussed in this chapter, plus evidence of adequate controls based on acceptable standards. The relation of ratio analyses to inside control and outside credit sources is particularly significant to successful financial management.

QUESTIONS

1. What techniques are known as the "twins of finance"?
2. How would you define the financing of an enterprise?
3. On what does the relation between assets and volume of earnings depend?
4. What do we mean by the "flow from cash to cash," and why is it vitally important to maintain its constancy?
5. How can fixed assets become a part of current funds?
6. How would you define working capital?
7. What effect does the length of the production cycle have on the amount of working capital required?
8. How do credit terms given by vendors affect the amount of required working capital?
9. What procedure is necessary for using ratios as a dependable criterion for an evaluation of over-all company affairs?
10. To what factor or factors has the current ratio largely surrendered as a lending norm by bankers?
11. What is the disadvantage of using turnover of inventory as a measure of business success?
12. Which ratio is used for determining the condition of collection of customer accounts?
13. What are the disadvantages of the individual proprietor form of business ownership?
14. What is the credit advantage of the partnership form of ownership?
15. How is ownership of a corporation effected?
16. To what extent is the corporate form actually democratic in practice?
17. What are the determining factors in establishing the proper ratios among common and preferred stocks and bonds in the financial structure of a corporation?
18. What is the disadvantage to common stockholders of internal financing of a corporate expansion program?
19. What plan would you suggest to alleviate the present difficulties encountered in financing small concerns?
20. Why have debenture bonds lost the interest of the investing public?

CASE PROBLEM

HANSFORD MANUFACTURING COMPANY

The Condensed Balance Sheet of the Hansford Manufacturing Company is presented on pp. 206–207. It is a medium-sized concern, which has been making a line of steel products for the past thirty years, and is considered reliable by its customers and credit-worthy by its bank and vendors.

Because of a contemplated expansion involving additional manufacturing space and machinery, the company is seeking a new banking connection. Hansford started doing business with its present bank when both were small and relatively new. Their dealings have been mutually satisfactory through the years, and the bank has lent its legal limit of $125,000 to the company on several occasions. Hansford financial needs will soon reach a figure beyond the bank's ability to service its account.

The factory addition will cost $50,000 and the new machinery will cost twice that amount. The directors feel that the contemplated increase in the volume of business will require additional working capital of approximately $75,000. Since that amount is already owed the bank, the new bank accommodation will have to be $150,000. This is exclusive of the $150,000 which will be needed to pay for the plant addition and its machinery.

The present land and buildings are valued conservatively at $175,000 although they stand on the books at $120,000, due to liberal depreciation for tax-saving purposes. If the new buildings and machinery costs of $150,000 are added to the present mortgage of $60,000, it would certainly be considered an unsatisfactory risk for industrial property — a $210,000 mortgage against a probable going-concern real estate value of $175,000 plus $50,000 cost of the addition, or a total equity of $225,000

Adequate mortgage financing would be relatively easy if Hansford agreed to include its present and new machinery as security. However, the company's treasurer fears that such a lien might have an adverse effect on their subsequent open credit line. He may not have considered the possibility of inventories security for open bank credit.

PROBLEM: How would you advise the Hansford concern to do its new financing? After you have worked out your financing plan, prepare a justification for the bankers, based on the current ratio, ratio of total assets to total liabilities, and fixed assets to net worth, as taken from your statement as it will appear after the new financing has been completed (usually referred to as a *proforma statement*). To encourage further the bankers' acceptance of your proposition, show the company's inventory turnover and ratio of credit sales to accounts receivable as reflected by its current Condensed Balance Sheet.

12

Budgetary Control

In the chapter on Managerial Control (Chapter 8), the budget was mentioned as one of the chief tools of control. It is because the budget is considered a tool or form of control that it is subject to considerable controversy. (In fact, it is occasionally observed that any controller who is generally esteemed among his peers and subordinates is probably not very effective in the role assigned to him.) It has also been suggested previously that controls are just as good as the standards on which they are based. Since the budget is a group of standards affecting all departments of a concern under normal conditions, it is extremely important that the facts or predictions on which its plans are based should be as valid as possible.[1] It happens occasionally that the facts, records, and reports which underlie the budget estimates are not trustworthy. This is one of the outstanding causes for discontent with budgetary procedures among subexecutives and supervisors.

The budget is a written plan for future operations, expressed in monetary terms. It determines in advance, for specified periods of time, the company's over-all operating goals. The budget's estimates of income and expenditures frequently cover all activities of the organization. The various budgetary goals for sales, production, procurement, personnel, and other activities are, as has been noted, expressed in dollars. Even when the estimates fix the number of personnel to be employed and the quantities of materials to be used, they are eventually expressed in financial terms. Since expenditures of all kinds are ultimately dependent on the volume of sales, the budget is built upon that estimate. Sales provide the income against which expenditures must be balanced after allowance has been made for the necessary reserves and profits.

As a master plan, the budget provides for over-all coordination of the con-

[1] For a comprehensive exposition of the budget as an executive control device, see Walter Rautenstrauch and Raymond Villers, *Budgetary Control* (New York: Funk & Wagnalls Co., in association with *Modern Industry*, 1950).

cern's activities. From the top-management level, coordination is obtained by breaking down the master plan into a number of departmental goals or objectives. It is through coordination that the success of the parts contribute to the success of the whole. The budgetary goals are standards for the guidance of subexecutives and supervisors. As standards, they also serve as bases for control over the personnel to whom their money allocations are assigned. It is this personal application of controls that promotes, in part, individual antagonism to the budgetary process.

As a control device, the budget goes through the four basic steps of the control process: setting standards, checking on performance, evaluating the results, and taking corrective action. Checking on the performance and taking corrective action invariably affect some individuals, and the action is not always pleasant. Even more, it is easy to understand that these control aspects of the process are often distasteful, irrespective of the results. Allocation of responsibility, however, is a valuable aid to top management, even when it has detrimental effects on occasional individual cooperation — a conflict that we will discuss later.

Budgeting versus Cost Accounting. The purposes of budgeting and cost accounting are often confused. The primary purpose of budgeting is to plan and control the *future* activities of management. The primary purpose of cost accounting is to determine costs *after* production has been completed. Cost accounting has its value in guiding prices and recommending where expansion and contraction should take place. Budgetary control fixes responsibility for deviations from a plan; cost accounting is not concerned with who is responsible. Budgeting is based on foresight, cost accounting on hindsight. Both techniques are important but in different ways.

History of the budgetary idea

The word budget is evidently derived from the French *bougette*, which is a leather bag or briefcase. Starting about 1870, the English Chancellor of the Exchequer, in reporting the estimated tax needs for the coming year, was in the habit of opening his *bougette* before the House of Commons. The association of the Chancellor's briefcase with its use on this occasion accounts for the word budget as applied to the income required to balance estimated expenditures.

Although the word budget is of relatively recent origin, some writers claim an ancient lineage for the budgetary procedure. It may be reasonably assumed that the budget was first used in public affairs. An ancient custom was for the state to auction off the taxing rights to the highest bidder. Thus, the state knew beforehand how much money it would have for expenses for the coming period. If the budget is considered only as an estimate or plan for governmental expenditure of an income already received, then the ancient-lineage theory has some support.

In this country, the budget first appeared about 1912 in some of our cities in response to their financial plight. American business recognized the budget as a tool of management about 1922, the same year that the national Bureau of the Budget was established to control federal expenses and tie them in with estimated tax revenue. Budgetary procedures were accepted rapidly by business, owing largely to the influence of a book entitled *Budgetary Control* by James O. McKinsey, published in 1922.

If the annual budget is a relatively new idea, thinking in terms of budgeting for long-term future planning of capital expenditures is even more recent. Today the budget techniques are also used to plan capital expenditures for improvement and expansions of equipment and buildings over a period of years. It was only natural that financial planning should receive secondary consideration prior to 1920, during an era when the most pressing problem of business was that of increasing production to meet growing public demands.

Budgetary Essentials

There are several essentials which must be given preliminary consideration in establishing budgetary procedure.

1. The budget plan must be geared to the organizational setup. Overlapping or gaps in the organizational plan will largely defeat prospects for control through the budget.

2. Divisions of the budget should correspond with the accounting classifications, or vice versa, so as to present accounting details useful in controlling items of the budget.

3. The budget should conform to the business for which it purports to be a mechanism of planning and control. Such considerations as the nature and size of the business and the characteristics of its management are determining factors.

4. The make-up of the budget should be as simple as possible. At the same time, its separate classifications must be drawn so as to identify the associated major executives for the purpose of measuring their effectiveness and controlling their management.

5. Flexibility is a prime consideration of good budgeting. It should be possible to adjust to changed conditions without unnecessary strains on the budget allocations.

6. The independent or departmental budgets must become parts of the unified whole in order to establish an effective master plan.

Compiling the budget

There are two methods used for making up the budget. One method starts the planning at the top of the management hierarchy. A small group of top executives maps out company objectives for the coming fiscal year. Sales is the pivotal figure for estimating company income, so the sales manager is included in the top-planning group. The conclusion concerning his estimate of sales will determine the total production required. The production figure will form the basis for estimating the types and quantities of parts and products to be made, materials and supplies to be bought, employees to be hired, and so on, during the budgetary period. All of these estimates are passed on to those responsible for carrying on the activities necessary to fulfill the master plan as expressed in the budget. These individuals, including subexecutives, managers of departments, and possibly supervisors, are given an opportunity to discuss those items which affect their activities.

The sales group may feel that it cannot sell the planned volume in one or more product categories. Personnel may be concerned as to whether it can find the workers required to carry out the new program, and they may argue that even if they can recruit the necessary workers, more money will be required under the new wage contracts. Procurement may claim that anticipated price advances will demand a larger allotment of funds than those allowed by the executive group. Such discussions will be prolonged, supported by all possible evidence, until the budget document is finally completed. Then, and only then, is it issued as a group of standards which will be necessary to carry out the new master plan for the company.

The second approach to budget compilation starts at the bottom of the hierarchy. Production is furnished with a breakdown of projected sales. It informs all supervisors as to what will be expected of them. From these figures, the supervisors estimate the required number of workers of various skills, additional machines to meet the new production goal, services for maintenance on old machines, and their other needs. In the same way, all the other related departments will prepare their estimates, which will be passed up to the next higher level of management for discussion and correction. At the various levels, subordinates are called in to defend their figures against the suggested cuts made by their superiors. Finally, there is a mutual agreement or a unilateral decision by top management.

In the last analysis, total costs of operation (including overhead), must show a margin of profit when compared to total sales. If there is a failure at this point, then selling prices are too low or costs are too high. In either case, the break-even point will be elusive unless some total change can be made in costs or sales figures. Since sales totals are probably based on competition, the expense side of the budget will likely go through another combing process. After the document is in final shape, there is one more hopeful thing to look forward to: the next budget — may it be easier to compile and more dependable in its promises!

Problems in compiling the budget

Budgetary Honesty. There is a persistent problem that springs up during the planning stage of the budget which may be termed "budgetary honesty."

This form of honesty, which almost invariably appears in the first few years of budgeting, differs materially from what we commonly think of by the word. The person making detailed estimates reasons from experience that the budget officer or committee will "clip" his final figure, maybe by as much as 50 per cent. Convinced that this is going to happen whatever he does, he doubles his true estimate. In an organization where this practice is habitual, the budget authority reasons, in turn, that many of the detailed estimates have been "padded" and proceeds accordingly to revise the estimates downward — again, as much as 50 per cent. Such practices are merely making a game out of the budget principle. Only a skilled budget officer, with experience in the concern he is serving, can handle such a situation.

Another form of "budgetary honesty" is the determination of operating managers to exhaust their allowances during the budget term "no matter how." This nefarious practice stems from the fear that the amount of any surplus stemming from their "effective management" will be cut from their future budgets. Proper control would do just that, with suitable rewards for beating the budget allowances. The "spending-all-of-it" theory is peculiarly prevalent in large concerns and government agencies where effective budgetary control runs counter to empire-building. This warning directive is an example:

> May 16, 1949. To reach the $—— commitment goal of 1950 funds by July 1, Mr. —— requested that the initiation of Purchase Requests be accelerated since at present only $—— of the Purchase Requests have been initiated by this Division. All Division activities concerned have been given proportional target figures to shoot at.

Those making the recommendation to shoot at such a target cannot have much respect for budgeting.

Centralization versus Decentralization. A good budget should correspond with the company's organization chart. In this connection, the question of centralization or decentralization of budgetary procedures often arises. During the past fifty years, there has been a shift from one operating method to the other. At the turn of the century, the emphasis lay on the centralization of operations; since that time, because the rapid expansion of business has produced operating units so large that they defy adequate control, the stress has come to be placed more and more on decentralization. When the question is asked, "Which plan should the budget follow?" the answer is obvious. Budgeting emphasizes the thought processes, whereas operations emphasize action. The thought processes involved in adapting budgetary controls to over-all company policies require that such controls be centralized. Proper budgeting, in fact, aids the decentralizing process of operations through its control features. Centralized budgeting is as necessary as centralized policy-making.

Scope and Length of the Budget.   Determination of the scope and duration of the budget are decisions for top management. The *scope* of the
budget refers to the extent of its application to the enterprises concerned.
Should it be applied to one or more functions or to the entire organization?
This decision can be important in influencing the ultimate success of the
budgetary procedure in companies where it is being installed for the first
time. It is often contended that when the budget plan is being newly
adopted, its application should be limited to a single department on a sort
of trial run. If the trial is to be limited to a single department, sales would
be the normal selection because it is the starting point for an over-all budget.
If the trial is successful, so it is contended, managerial acceptance will be
based on a solid foundation of experience rather than mere lip service. It is
universally agreed that management's wholehearted support of the budgetary idea is essential to its success.

On the other hand, there is a well-considered opinion that budgets cannot be used as adequate instruments of control unless they are adopted on
an over-all company basis. If the company is long established and profitable,
with a progressive and confident management team, the budget idea may be
applied simultaneously to all departments with fair chances of success after
careful planning and comprehensive consultation among all levels of
management. Participation of subordinates from the beginning usually
improves their cooperation in the execution of the plan.

The *length* of the budget period depends on such factors as the production
cycle, the accounting period, and the general nature of the company's
market. Stable market conditions permit more extended budgetary estimates
and require fewer revisions. Most budgets run for one year, but many are
for shorter terms where fluctuating economic conditions are the rule. The
so-called long-term budget, running for five or even ten years, is concerned
with capital improvements and expansions. It must be tied in with bond and
mortgage retirements to provide an even keel for fixed capital expenditures.
It is common practice to add a year's estimate to such long-term budgets at
the beginning of each new budget period.

Responsibility for the Budget

Over-all responsibility

The question of who should have over-all responsibility for budgeting and
budgetary control always produces differences of opinion. In actual practice, the prime responsibility for the budget is assigned to individuals who
range in status from the company president all the way down to the cost
manager. The National Industrial Conference Board, in a survey made of
93 companies, found that chief responsibility for the budget was assigned
to individuals with 21 different titles. The controller and the treasurer accounted for 51 per cent of the assignments, the controller having a slight

edge on the treasurer. This wide range of assignments points vividly to the immaturity of budgeting.

Large companies frequently have a director of the budget, while the smaller ones use their treasurer, president, or proprietor if they do any serious budgeting. As experience with budgeting accumulates, it becomes clear that the chief budgetary responsibility cannot be assigned at random; certain principles are emerging to guide the decisions in making this assignment. For example, whenever the person in charge of the budget has other executive responsibilities, the opportunity is wide open for jealousy and misunderstanding on the supposition that he is favoring his own section of the organization. When this is true, objective control is difficult.

Those who consider the budgeting responsibility from a scientific point of view are coming to choose between the controller and the treasurer. It would seem that the decision should be based on the individual's qualifications for the prime duty of budgeting, which is control. If the treasurer who is custodian of receipts, disbursements, and accounts is accustomed to controlling his activity only through auditing, then he must learn to approach budgetary control from a much wider point of view.

Whenever possible, the controller or budget officer should have no other responsibilities. Where the concern is too small to afford such an officer, the treasurer is the likely person for the assignment. However, an independent controller is well worth his salary in any concern large enough to employ a qualified full-time person for the execution of this function. Irrespective of the budget-duty assignment, final responsibility rests with the chief executive officer of the concern. It is equally true that the person handling the budget should report directly to that chief executive.

The Budget Committee. Another consideration in connection with budgetary responsibility concerns the budget committee. Should it be used and, if so, in what capacity? The prevailing opinion is that the committee's role should be an advisory one; it should not be used as the budget-operating agency. For budgetary control, it is usually felt that a committee is clumsy, slow, and it tends to compromise — to split differences. To get a decision may require days on many questions. It seldom sees any one problem decisively enough to take aggressive action.

However, the budget committee can have important auxiliary duties. It can be useful in helping the budget officer criticize and coordinate the estimates. As a group of representative executives, it can also stand between the budget officer and those whom he controls. Since it understands the budgetary process from the inside, the committee can act as an invaluable aid in "selling" the budget to all those concerned. It can also gather criticisms of a constructive nature and report them to the budget officer for his consideration.

Lower-level responsibility

When it has settled the question of where the over-all responsibility for the budget should be assigned, management must further decide how responsibility will be allocated at the next lower levels of authority.

Viewed as an executive's control mechanism, the budget must be set up so that it can be applied to individual executive responsibilities. That is, its estimates of income and expenses must be tied to those members of the management team who are responsible for the concern's various activities. As a control device, the budget is used to plan, coordinate, and stimulate the management group in two ways. First, it controls the accomplishments of members of the executive group by establishing norms or standards against which to measure the total results of their efforts. Second, it compares the actual cost or expense of their activities with their advance estimates of what those expenses should be.

Stated in another way, functional estimates control functional operations, while personal estimates control the activities of individual executives or supervisors. This distinction is important to the extent that functional divisions do not always coincide with the activities of individual members of the management group, a situation which is frequently found in small or medium-sized companies, and only to a lesser extent in large corporations. When two or more functions are managed by the same individual in a small concern, it is relatively easy to hold him responsible for the operation of his multiple phases of the budget. His responsibilities cover entire activities or even entire functions, and they are the criteria for setting up the budget.

When, on the other hand, coterminous responsibility for a single functional phase of the budget is assigned to two persons, there is an evident conflict in the personal and functional ideas for budgetary control. Since the functional basis of budgetary control is determining, both managers involved have responsibility, individually and together, for meeting budgetary requirements. The way out of this apparent dilemma is to separate the function concerned according to the most rational plan available, and then to make the budget setup correspond to the new managerial situation.

Types of budgets

There are various types of budgets to meet different needs. The *fixed budget* requires that details be adhered to; a common measure of its adequacy is the number of deviations which management must accept. The *semifixed budget* permits transfer of funds from one budget item to another with greater freedom. The *variable* or *step budget* provides for two or more complete budgets based on different prospective sales volumes. This type is frequently used in wholesale, retail, and production concerns. Budgets based on different sales volumes are prepared simultaneously because of top-management skepticism as to estimated sales.

The *flexible* budget takes care of different sales levels by working out ratios between sales volume and costs for individual budgetary items. These ratios are used to adjust the fixed, proportional, and variable costs of the adopted budget to actual production. The fixed-cost items are relatively few and simple in their application to various production volumes. Interest, rent, and taxes are illustrations of items which rarely fluctuate with production. Proportionate relationships are also few in number and easy to compute because they vary directly with volume. Direct labor and materials, discounts, and some supply items fall in this category. Because variable costs do not move in any direct relation to changes in the volume of production, they are the most difficult for which to determine expense ratios. An example of this third category would be the ratio of indirect labor costs to production volume.

While ratio determinations for variable budget items require considerable work, they can save time in the long run. The time spent in computing expense items for these budgets depends on the number of budgets to be set up. Both the variable and flexible budgets recognize the effect of volume on unit costs and are predicated on the desirability of periodic budget revisions based on different production levels.

The *lump sum budget* assigns allowable expenses in lump figures to departments or activities, while the *detailed budget* breaks down the expense assignments for more refined control. *Scheduled budgeting* assigns time periods for the use of expense items. These budgets may be divided into monthly or other time-limiting installments for the guidance of designated activities. The purpose is to prevent abnormal or total use of the budget allowance before the end of the budgetary period.

Overhead Control. Of all the expenditures related to production volume, overhead is probably the most difficult to determine. Its allocation to various activities on the basis of any total budget is difficult in itself. If really scientific control of expenses on an activity or unit-production basis is desired, allocation of overhead should be established on an exact basis, and this is practically impossible. The real problem is assignment of overhead expenditures under constantly changing conditions, which represents the actual situation. It is unusually difficult to relate a given amount or the rate of overhead to units of output because the solution is ordinarily complicated by many related problems. However, predetermined budget amounts, or rates, are the only effective tool which management now has for controlling overhead expenditures.

Functional budgets

The over-all operational budget is customarily divided into a number of functional budgets for the control of such activities as sales, purchasing, production, materials, labor, manufacturing expense, plant and equipment, and financial management. Each will be discussed briefly to show the application of estimating and controlling to these activities.

The Sales Budget. Budgeting starts with sales. The sales budget comes first because of its importance to both production and finance. To assist production and finance, the total sales budget should be expressed both in units of goods and dollars of sales. The first acts as a guide to production, and the second is one basis for the distribution of expenses. Since sales always represent the bulk of the concern's income, they are obviously the determining factor in many of top management's budget decisions.

Compilation of the sales budget may start with the top budgeting authority or with the salesmen in the field. If top management has decided to expand or restrict sales for the coming year, the figures they set will be forwarded to the director of sales. He will determine the need for more or fewer salesmen, depending on the new goal set by management.

The other plan for making up the sales budget starts with the men in the field. In spite of the exaggeration that might seem to be a concomitant of the average salesman's prevailing optimism, it is presumed that he has a better knowledge of the sales potential in his territory than anyone else in the organization. However, the salesmen's estimates are reviewed up the management line, just as are those of the individual foremen in the production department. If the company has a national distribution, salesmen's estimates are first reviewed by the district sales managers. Unusual alterations should be made only after conferences with the salesman concerned. After review by the district sales manager, a more objective criticism is made by the general sales manager, and finally the estimates are reviewed by the budget committee — if there is one — and the chief executive.

What are some of the criteria which enter into revisions of the field estimates? One is the general condition of the market. This guide should be established by a market analysis. Buyer markets for both production and consumption goods are dynamic and subject to changing emphasis. In addition, shifting populations may have a marked effect on prospective sales in specific territories. A change in the nature of the population is another important consideration. Whether sales involve the wholesale or retail trade, it is desirable to know the purchasing power of various sections of the country. Changes in consumer demand, bank deposits and the scale of earnings all have an effect on sales. The standard of living of the local population is another factor. All of these are taken into account when reviewing the estimates of salesmen in the field.

Sales budgeting helps guide company affairs in many other ways. The likelihood of a future sales slump in items produced by industry or sold by retail concerns serves as a signal to look around for other items to take up the slack. A slump in the regular line may be due to changes in buyer habits, or to a change in general business conditions. To meet these conditions, a decrease in selling prices may be in order or some new item may be added even without profit, to keep the organization intact while waiting for better markets. On the other hand, a large expected increase in sales may have a serious effect on the manufacturing company's production facilities or its financial standing. If the volume of sales is greater than productive capacity, then plant expansion is considered — if finances permit and if the market gives promise of holding up to the new estimates. Plant expansion and increased sales both require more capital. The first demands greater investment capital, and the latter requires more working capital for the purchase of raw materials, cost of labor, and carrying of customer accounts.

The *sales estimate* is the amount of prospective sales as determined by the various levels of the sales department. The *sales quota* is the prospective amount of sales assigned to each salesman or territory. The *sales budget* is the figure finally determined after the several reviews of sales estimates. All three of these figures are only relatively correct. They represent the best judgment based on experience and an analysis of the general market and its territorial divisions. Because of the close connection between sales on the one hand and expenses and general finances on the other, it is clear that the concern's stability is dependent largely on the accuracy of the sales budget.

The cost of sales, or *sales expense,* is the other half of the sales budget. Cost of selling is based, to a large extent, on previous sales volumes. The average cost of unit sales is the fundamental guide. Deviations from this norm result from decisions as to whether the sales effort in particular territories should be intensive or extensive. If certain sections appear to have increased sales potentials, additional expense may be allocated for intensive development. If, on the other hand, experience shows that specific territories have been canvassed at a loss, it may be decided to reduce the funds allotted to these territories and continue sales only on an extensive basis, getting whatever business is available on a low unit cost of sales.

Advertising Budget. The advertising budget may or may not be a part of the sales budget. More often, its total is determined by top management as a given percentage of expected sales. Distribution to the various media of advertising should be decided by top management in consultation with the general sales manager. It is obvious that the amounts assigned to different advertising outlets will vary considerably with the type of business.

Production Budget. The importance of the production budget ranks second to sales, on which it is dependent. When the sales budget is divided into time periods, the scheduling of production is materially aided. If anticipated sales are not estimated on a monthly basis, for example, production is likely to lay off workers when business drops off for a while;

whereas a month-by-month estimate may show that the slack in sales is likely to be only temporary and, consequently, there need be no interruption in the level of production. The accuracy of sales prognostications also helps in placing large orders for materials at advantageous prices. When plant operations are maintained at an even rate, many savings result. For example, overtime work at premium wage rates may be avoided. Employment of a steady work force reduces training costs and maintains productivity on a higher level. Furthermore, the regular use of machinery reduces maintenance costs and improves productivity.

Materials Budget. Materials are divided into *direct*, which become components of the production process, and *indirect* or auxiliary items, consisting mostly of supplies. Indirect materials are often included in a manufacturing expense budget. In either case, the budget will depend largely on the materials called for in the production budget. Besides being of direct service to production, the materials budget is used by purchasing and finance. When the materials budget is set up on a scheduled basis, with weekly or monthly delivery dates, purchasing can have better control over price, quality, and deliveries. Since purchases may total from 30 to as much as 90 per cent of total costs, the materials budget is important to the person responsible for having cash available to meet purchases.

Purchase Budget. Estimates of required materials, supplies, tools, and equipment come mainly from the production department. However, most departments report items which must be purchased, and all such estimates are working guides for the purchasing department. If the required items are scheduled on a time basis, purchasing can do a much better job. Some purchases must be made well in advance to meet sales or production schedules. Other items have fluctuating market prices, in which case a time schedule of requirements aids in placing orders under advantageous market conditions. The problem in scheduled buying is to match deliveries with requirements so that work will not be interrupted. Obviously, purchasing will have its own operating-expense budget.

Labor Budget. Labor is also classified as direct and indirect. Indirect labor serves the workers who are engaged directly in the production processes. As with indirect materials, indirect labor is commonly included in the production-expense budget. The amount of direct labor for the various classifications is estimated, in the first instance, by supervisors. Labor requirements are expressed both in dollars and numbers, since labor estimates are used by the personnel department for recruiting.

Experience with labor turnover aids in estimating the requirements for additional workers. The sales budget supplies the information which indicates the number of workers who will be needed in the various job classifications. From the number on hand at the beginning of the budget period is subtracted the estimated number of separations that will occur. When this result is subtracted from the average number required for operations during the budget period, the difference represents those whom personnel must recruit during the year.

Production-Expense Budget. Production or manufacturing expense, formerly referred to as "factory overhead," but currently called "burden," encompasses a number of items which do not vary proportionately with the volume of production. Indirect labor and indirect materials have already been referred to as such items. Others include superintendent and foremen salaries, supplies, maintenance, material handling, and clerical help. It is important to know the relationships between the cost of these items and the volume of production. Cost accounting is very much interested in such ratios. Personnel and purchasing are also interested. In large concerns, engineering or planning is responsible for figuring these ratios, which is not a simple matter.

Relationships between overhead costs and production or sales volume are sometimes important in connection with incentives. Many industrial concerns figure the supervisor's bonus not simply on the basis of his department's productivity, but also on the amount by which he is able to beat overhead or burden targets set for him in the budget.

This leads to another consideration of expense items. Some of them are relatively fixed, irrespective of volume of business. Salaries are an example. The same is true of "rent" when charged to manufacturing expense. The cost of clerical help varies only within narrow ranges. Because all of these are items over which the supervisor has no control, they should not be included among the variables which are considered in rewarding or punishing his management.

Plant and Equipment Budget. This budget, as has been suggested, covers a longer period than other budgets, although that portion which applies to the current period may be included. Expenditures for expanded plant and equipment are capital items for which budgetary planning is just as important as for current items. Capital budgets may be estimated for from five to ten years, with a new year added at every annual budget period.

When this type of budgetary planning is not used, poor execution of expansion programs will result, as well as unnecessarily high costs. It frequently happens, especially when greatly increased sales result from war production, that management will go into an expansion program without adequately studying its postwar market. Owners and management frequently lose control of the business because of such foolhardiness.

Common sense suggests budgetary planning of capital expenditures. If management looks ahead, it can draw on reserves taken out of profits to finance a planned building program carried out at a time of low construction costs.

Finance Budget. The financial budget summarizes the results of all the other budgets, its purpose being to show the financial condition of the concern at the beginning and end of the budget period. If the individual budgets are set up on a scheduled basis, the financial condition may be shown for each month of the budget term.

It includes a summary of all estimated receipts and expenditures. It furnishes the over-all control for top-management guidance in all operations of the company. It provides the picture which can be used as a guide in borrowing, in payment of dividends, and in determining the transfer of profits to the various reserve funds.

Budget Acceptance

The budget is often looked on by subexecutives, supervisors, and workers as a management pressure device for attaining ever higher goals in sales, production, and purchasing without additional expense. The budget authority must face the fact that most people resent being pressured and then controlled to determine whether the pressure has been successful. Many people also resent being judged. In this sense, they feel that budgetary control is a sort of report card. The situation is worse whenever the workers are suspicious that those who report on the controlling do not understand the factors involved in meeting specific standards. In some companies, the budget is fixed for the duration of the budget period, irrespective of changing market conditions for materials and labor, and the many other factors that affect both supervisors and workers.

Some companies make up two budgets, an "external" one for the directors and stockholders and another for the "internal" use of top management. When the two-budget plan is adopted, the so-called internal budget is scaled on a more optimistic level than the one for directors and stockholders. The idea, of course, is to make sure that the more conservative "external" budget will be met. The worker grapevine usually finds out when this two-budget plan is used. They don't understand it; they are suspicious; and they don't like it.

What is the effect of this budgetary pressure? What is its basic purpose? In answer to the second, it can be said that the employees believe, not without some justification, that management feels they are inherently lazy. In fact, many members of management have expressed that opinion in no uncertain terms. Management's suspicions also have justification in many cases, but some executives are too prone to exaggerate the situation. One executive summarized the situation vividly, if not scientifically, in this way: "I'll tell you my honest opinion. About 5 per cent of the people work,

10 per cent of the people think they work, and the other 85 per cent would rather die than work."

The answer to the first question concerning the effect of this budgetary pressure is that management pressure aimed at increasing production is often met with an equal worker pressure against the idea. Those individuals who have been putting forth their best efforts are the first to feel resentment. As the idea is discussed throughout the plant, a widespread tension may develop. It is not too long before groups are formed and the situation is discussed in the open. This group reaction helps relieve the tension of the individual who begins to see that he is not alone. In some cases, there is a gradual development of ways "to beat the budget" by reverting to the former work speed. So the unfortunate reaction may be an unwritten agreement among the workers to defeat the new pressure from management.

With such colorful but honest feelings on both sides, it is little wonder that the budget, which is the most widely used control instrument of management, is looked on with suspicion by many workers, and with skepticism by some members of management. How can this situation be improved, even if not eliminated?

It must be remembered that the budget is a comparatively new control device. Many managements have not learned how to use it in general, nor how to apply it to their companies in particular. Our previous illustration of 'budgetary honesty" makes that clear. If management as a whole is deficient in its use of budgetary procedures, it is easy to understand why the employees can be honestly antagonistic to it. Some large concerns and governmental institutions use the budget idea to get more than standard results from their workers, and some department heads use it to obtain larger allotments than they honestly require.

The first step in promoting acceptance of the budget idea is to build understanding of its proper use. The second step is to demand honesty from the budget makers. The third step is to see that management actually knows what estimates from below are padded, so that the budget items concerned may be cut to satisfy legitimate needs. Fourth, if a supervisor or subexecutive has operated so capably as to keep his expenditures below a scientific estimate of his requirements, he should be rewarded in some way for his exceptional ability. Rewards should also be given workers who beat reasonable standards. Incentives for superior performances will promote honest estimates.

Finally, all members of the management team should not only be allowed, but urged to participate in budget discussions. The budget is certainly important enough to justify the time required for such a plan. If this plan is followed the lower echelons as well as the workers can be led to believe that budgeting is a cooperative endeavor. When that point is reached, all concerned may be more willing to cooperate in carrying out the budget's provisions. Along with this procedure, effective communication is absolutely necessary. To say that employees do not understand, solves nothing and only clouds the issue. They can be taught and indoctrinated in budgetary procedures so that they *will* understand. The development of such "understanding" is one of the prime responsibilities of management.

Conclusions

Purpose of Budgeting. Budgets are the financial results of planning. Plans include standards which are used for control. However, budgets are not automatic controls. They must be used by management to compare results with estimates. Control is the technique used by both administration and management to keep themselves informed about the results of their plans and directives. The emphasis of control must be to obtain current figures soon enough to use them for planning changes when necessary. Controls will be relatively ineffective unless the subordinates in the hierarchy have been indoctrinated with the budgetary idea. Effective control, therefore, requires more than bare figures. From forecasting to planning, to organization, to direction, and finally to control, logical steps must be followed if effective management is to result.

Advantages of Budgeting. Because budgeting is planning and because planning requires thoughtful analysis, the process is stimulating to those who participate. The entire management team sees the business as a new and complete picture. Cognizance of relationships is a helpful stimulant to managers.

Control is the purpose for which budget planning furnishes the means. Since control requires standards, responsible members of the management team fix goals for accomplishment. Meeting goals produces satisfaction from a job well done. Exceeding goals is an added stimulant which produces initiative and should lead to incentive rewards.

Planning, coordinating, stimulating, controlling, and fixing of responsibility are the five outstanding advantages of good budgeting.

Budget Acceptance. Acceptance by the entire management team and employees is necessary for successful budgeting. Because there is a natural antipathy to the controls which the budget includes, management must make definite plans to develop budget understanding on the part of the worker. This is especially true of supervisors who have direct contact with the workers, but indoctrination in this field starts with top management.

Dangers in Budgeting. When sharp tools are used for the wrong purpose or when their use is not understood, they can become dangerous weapons. This is true of the budget tool. One trouble is that too much is expected of it too soon. Another is that too many of the management team pay only lip service to it. This attitude may result from two causes, one of which is misunderstanding, and the other, aversion to new and untried processes. The latter often results in the kind of subtle sabotage previously described as "budgetary honesty." Such dangers must be avoided if the budget is to function to best advantage.

QUESTIONS

1. Why is the budget one of the chief tools of control?
2. What is the difference between the purpose of budgeting and that of cost accounting?
3. Why did our budgeting procedures first appear in cities?
4. What is the primary reason that the budget plan be geared to the organizational setup?
5. Do you favor starting the proposed budget figures at the top of the organization hierarchy, or at the foremen level? Why?
6. Why are sales estimates the primary guide in budgeting, in spite of the prevalent feeling that salesmen's opinions are untrustworthy?
7. If you were president of a company, how would you go about eliminating budgetary honesty as it is explained in the text?
8. How does decentralized budgeting aid coordination of activities?
9. Why are industrial budgets tending to cover short time periods?
10. What qualifications would you demand of a candidate in selecting a Controller of the Budget?
11. How can budget estimates be applied to individual executive responsibilities?
12. How did the step or variable budget evolve from top-management's opinion of the judgment of sales managers?
13. Which of the expenditures related to production is probably the most difficult to estimate and control?
14. Why is it necessary for the procurement department to make up two estimated budgets?
15. What is the financial advantage of making a long-term capital equipment budget?
16. Why do some concerns make separate and different budgets for stockholders and directors on the one hand, and members of the management team on the other?
17. What caused the delay in acceptance of industrial budgeting in this country, in your opinion, before the early 1920's?
18. What purpose can best be served by a budget committee?
19. For what different purposes are functional and personal estimates used in budgeting?
20. What is meant by a functional budget?

CASE PROBLEM

THE CONCORD COMPANY

The Concord Company, located on the west coast, makes and sells small internal combustion engines. The concern has enjoyed a steady growth and good profits since its incorporation about twenty years ago. The boundless energy of Norman Petro, its president, makes up for his lack of management skill. About three years ago, two important changes resulted in increased sales, but sharp drops in company profits. The first change added power lawn mowers to the concern's line. Its small gas engines offered an excellent foundation for the power-mower production. In a short time, sales increased by 30 per cent.

Spurred on by his new enthusiasm, Mr. Petro secured agreement from the board of directors to make the second change: expansion of the sales department to cover additional territory in three neighboring states. Sales jumped again by 60 per cent within eighteen months. When new successes seemed just around the corner, the financial statement started to show sharp declines in profits. Mr. Petro was not satisfied with the explanation that increased labor costs was the sole reason. It was true that they had maintained their selling prices in the face of two across-the-board wage increases, but he felt sure that due to increased sales, decreased unit overhead costs had more than offset increased labor costs.

Mr. Petro's nephew, George Petro, came to the company five years ago after completing a course in business administration at the University of California. During those five years, his uncle had shifted him from one department to another with the idea of using him as a personal assistant after he had garnered some "practical experience." "Here is his opportunity to show what he has learned," figured Uncle Norman. So George was delegated to find out why profits were on the downgrade.

With the background of his departmental experiences and his college training, George investigated every angle of the business. His only instructions were: "No hurry — find out the trouble and figure out the answer."

The company had established clear-cut objectives and formulated policies aimed at their accomplishment. George praised these two accomplishments, but he contended that the objectives would have to be broken down on a departmental basis before any appreciable coordination could be established among the various members of the management group. Before the company doubled its sales, the president was able to coordinate these activities; now different methods were necessary. Standards for carrying out the objectives were limited, and in some departments they were nonexistent, so administrative expense was costing 12 per cent of sales.

Sales estimates were based solely on the sales manager's findings which were far from scientific. There was very little coordination between sales and production. The production manager had no confidence in the sales estimates, so he delayed many purchase requisitions until orders were received from customers. The controller fixed cost standards on the basis of his lowest historical costs. The sales manager had charge of advertising allotments, which always favored those groups with the best sales records. Because of the production manager's attitude, purchasing operated largely on a hand-to-mouth basis, and the personnel depart-ment was compelled to act on a hunch-and-rush schedule because of the gyrations in production.

George made a complete report, on the basis of which he recommended a system of budgetary control based on carefully established standards. The uncle approved his plan and instructed George to put it into effect at once. Most of the management group were opposed to the idea as unnecessarily restrictive of their activities. At the end of the first budget year, there was a small company loss. Uncle Norman made an immediate decision as soon as he saw the profit-and-loss statement. He ordered the budget idea abolished forthwith.

PROBLEM: What control techniques would you have introduced along with the budget, and how would you have gone about the budget's installation to avoid the general management antagonism?

13

Plant Location

Generalizing is the outstanding danger in selecting a state or region in which to locate a new plant or relocate an existing plant. One of the well-known plant-locating services states that differences of as much as 40 per cent for operating costs may result from regional factors. A two-page spread in Dun's Review for March, 1960, evaluates twelve important plant location factors for the forty-eight continental states. But such a survey does not show the marked differences in some of the factors for various areas within the states.[1]

Nothing shows the necessity for comparative technical information regarding comparative locations more than the numerous advertisements appearing in newspapers and magazines. Certainly all the states (and numerous regions within the states), cities, railroad companies, chambers of commerce, and industrial realtors literally bewilder the seekers of suitable business locations with their advertiseemnts. Anyone who spends a few hours reading these enticing offerings in industrial magazines must conclude that some of the copy is patterned after patent-medicine advertisements.

Sources of evaluation

The average concern is well advised to employ an agency specializing in the appraisal of business sites. Their information is certainly more objective and is focused on the business or industry of their client. Second to such an evaluation is probably the one submitted by a railroad company. All the large railroads keep detailed records on available industrial property along their lines from which they are able to furnish unbiased reports to location seekers, fitted to the purpose of the prospect. Local chambers of commerce

[1] The survey appears on pages 78–89 of a "Special Report" issue on industrial plants. Some of the factors considered are: Average hourly earnings, percentage of earnings rise 1950–1959, right-to-work law, percentage of AFL-CIO workers, corporate income tax, per capita tax burden, and six others.

or state industrial commissions are most likely to "puff" the location opportunities they have to offer. They frequently suggest free locations or relief from local taxes for a period of years. An industrial magazine warns that "deluged with offers of heaven, earth and sewerage systems, companies are eyeing bids from communities with delight or suspicion." The final gauge in selecting a plant or business location should be its effect on profits.

Scientific analysis is the new approach to plant location. The older rule-of-thumb criteria attached weighty consideration to such factors as cheap labor and lax labor laws, tax exemptions, and free land offers. Experience has shown that, though these varieties of bait are highly palatable, they often serve to cover up a most indigestible hook. Cheap labor, for example, may mean impoverished communities with inadequate local services and shifting populations. The workers who remain in such localities do not represent a group which can be depended on for steady work or low-cost production. Modern labor demands and receives favorable living conditions.

Low taxes point to poor community services. Tax-free offers suggest that someone else is carrying the community tax burden for the business newcomer, who will shoulder the same burdens for other newcomers in the future. Adequate public services are necessary to attract capable workers, and they must be paid for from public revenues. When one group escapes these legitimate levies, some other group makes up the difference.[2]

Cheap labor is often considered synonymous with the absence of labor unions. For some years this condition has led new industries to the South. Recent events demonstrate that the national labor organizations will continue their efforts to organize the so-called cheap-labor markets until their wage standards compare favorably with the rest of the country. Unions are forced to this program to satisfy their membership located in the higher wage sections of the country. Furthermore, regional cost-of-living differentials are fast disappearing. Wages and standards of living go hand in hand, and living standards frequently determine the quality of the labor group. Business advantages cannot be based on labor exploitation, freedom from local taxes, or free land.

Relocation

Possibly a scientifically prepared comparative analysis of the present and the proposed locations may show no long-range advantage in the move. Industrial relocations are both expensive and disrupting. While the official representatives of many towns and cities are clamoring for new industries, others are antagonistic to their invasion. Also, the local desire for new

[2] For an excellent discussion of this aspect of the tax problem, see Joseph S. Floyd, Jr., "The Effects of State and Local Taxes upon the Selection of Industrial Locations," *Proceedings,* Forty-fourth Annual Conference on Taxation (National Tax Association, 1951).

industries can be anything but rational when there is a tight labor market or lack of community facilities such as sewerage, housing, and recreation.

When General Motors was considering the establishment of a new gray iron foundry in either Defiance or Tiffin, Ohio, it inserted help-wanted advertisements in the local papers to measure the available labor supply in both places. The first two days brought 833 applications from Defiance and only 536 from Tiffin. Numbers alone did not settle the question, because General Motors was also interested in the quality of the applicants.

If a new plant is involved in the contemplated move, it may be that building costs are so high, compared to the cost of the present plant, that a new and continuing overhead will be added out of proportion to the advantages gained. If the new location is in another section of the country, moving costs must be taken into account for both the company and its workers. Time required for the move may mean a considerable loss of profits and occasionally of customers who are forced to seek new sources of supply. When skilled workers are prejudiced against the new location, they may not move, even when the employer pays the bills. Human associations and home investments will influence employee feeling against the new location.

A poorly planned relocation is shown in the following case.

An industrialist who decided to make a move told how he located twelve acres in a rural district and was highly pleased with his purchase. When he considered future expansion, he decided more room was required, so he bought eighteen contiguous acres which involved sixty separate real-estate transactions. That was only his first headache. Although his company had a prosperous record, he had difficulty in raising funds for the new plant, with consequent heavy financing charges. While construction was going on, a heavy snow and sleet storm caved in the new roof. Moving day finally came. Holes had to be knocked in the walls of both the old and the new plant in moving some of the heavy machinery. When the company move was completed, the old factory was put up for sale. Misfortunes mounted: the industrial-building market collapsed; the general contractor on the new building suffered financial reverses, so a number of his subcontractors filed mechanics' liens against the new factory.

"Next," said the owner, "we had inventory troubles because we allowed our raw materials to dwindle too near the vanishing point in order to save moving expenses." Re-orders and back-orders followed in rapid succession. While administrative changes were being made at the new location, his competitors started to make inroads on his customers, chiefly because of delayed shipments. Finally, because he built the plant for future expansion, the unused space interfered with internal communication. As a result, costs went up instead of down for almost a year after the move.

Some workers who are involved in an enforced change may regret it, with detrimental effects on their health, happiness, and productivity. If one of the reasons for the change is low-cost labor, the anticipated bonanza may not materialize either in quantity, quality, or price. All of these factors, and many others, may influence a decision against the move after an objective analysis has been made.

Location fundamentals

What factors are fundamental in analyzing a new plant site? The following list is a minimum guide:

1. Objectives sought
   a. Production advantages
   b. Financial advantages
   c. Raw-material sources
   d. Finished-product markets
   e. Required labor supply
2. Land requirements
   a. Room for expansion
   b. Parking space
   c. Recreation area
3. Type of plant required
4. Areas considered favorable
5. Data summaries of cities and towns
   a. Facts from consultants
   b. Community attitudes
6. Data summaries of sites
   a. With and without buildings
   b. Aerial photographs
   c. Detailed field notes
7. Final summary
   a. Comparative site costs
   b. Comparative operation costs
   c. Comparative labor supply
   d. Comparative transportation facilities
   e. Comparative living conditions
   f. Weighted rank of sites considered

General Area. In determining the area of location or relocation, the first step is to list the requirements considered vital. Then the search starts for a general area in which these needs can be satisfied. For reasons which have already been outlined, it is important that the change shall be an improvement if a relocation is involved. Locations are important for the simple reason that any site decided on should be considered permanent. A change may involve the sale of the old location, which represents only one of the possible expenses of the move. It must be understood, also, that the main factors governing selection apply to small as well as large enterprises.

Since the purpose of business is to make a profit, that is the acid test in any final decision. In the main, profits are based on the costs of delivered goods and competitive selling prices. If the trading area is small, selling prices are important. If the product is sold nation-wide, the location assumes importance as a national distributing center from the standpoints of transportation facilities and costs.

The Markets. The choice often has to be made whether to locate the firm close to the sources of raw materials or near to the markets for finished goods. When the product is bulky and heavy in relation to its value, the finished-goods market may receive prior consideration because of transportation costs. On the other hand, the location of raw materials may be a factor of great weight, irrespective of distribution costs of the finished product. The location that favors both of these considerations is always a wise choice, other factors being equal. When the question of product sales is paramount, distribution costs may be kept within reasonable bounds by establishing scattered warehouses. The automobile industry uses this plan in setting up assembly plants strategically located with respect to the customer market. The establishment of branch manufacturing plants reduces distribution costs and improves customer services. Finally, small concerns depending on local customers find it desirable to give more weight to the finished-goods market rather than the source of raw materials.

Transportation. Most advertisers of plant sites mention the transportation facilities they have to offer. Different kinds of businesses will have varying preferences for transportation by rail, water, road, or air. Immediate accessibility, connecting facilities, and rates must all be considered in a site-location study. The relative importance of the different kinds of transportation depends on the type of business to be served. However, with the recent developments in air transportation, planes are able to carry heavier commodities each year — apparently at justifiable rates. In any case, a nearby airfield serves potential emergency needs for many concerns, not excepting the machine-tool industry.

Labor Supply and Wage Rates. An adequate labor supply means the availability of those types of workers necessary for the purpose intended. The extent to which supply is at hand lessens the training problem in the new location. The Puerto Rico Trade Commission advertises training facilities because its population is largely unskilled. Since manufacturing industries use a major proportion of machine operators, the training problem is not always serious. Other things being equal, a business may locate where the available supply of workers can be trained quickly by those key employees who move with the establishment.

Wage rates are important from the standpoint of competitive costs. If the available labor supply consists of highly skilled workers, they will not be interested in machine-operation jobs except at wage rates the concern cannot afford. If the shifting concerns feel that they can use local labor at rates prevailing in an unorganized field, they may be due for a disappointment after the worker demand they create leads to union organization.

A steady, home-owning employee is clearly the most desirable. Since labor turnover adds to costs, contented workers with families and home roots in the community are to be preferred. The percentage of home owners is a valuable figure to know in gauging the labor market.

Power Supply. Most manufacturing concerns, and many other types, require adequate power at competitive prices. It is more advantageous that the power supply be dependable than that it be located near the new site. For this reason, access to a large electric-power supply is often favored. But the sources of the power are not always decisive, especially when they are located far from raw materials and sales markets. TVA power has not attracted large plants for this reason. The same is true of the large power potentials in some parts of the West. Niagara Falls, on the other hand, has other features besides cheap power to offer industry and has experienced a commensurate industrial development.

Business Neighbors. There are many advantages accruing from a site surrounded by businesses in the same line. Most distributors of cotton piece goods in New York City are located within a few blocks on Canal Street. It makes both buying and selling easier. Every merchant picks up discontended customers from his competitors when they are in the immediate neighborhood. Members of the "trade" can keep in closer touch with changing markets, thus helping to stabilize their line of business.

Manufacturing, wholesaling, or retailing enterprises experience some of the following advantages or disadvantages by being near their competitors.

1. *Financing is easier* because local banks understand the special trade with which they do a general banking business.

2. *Sources of supply* are more numerous and better able to serve grouped concerns in the same line. Yarn salesmen visit oftener those localities where hosiery or other textile mills are concentrated. It is to the companies in a textile community that the salesmen offer odd lots and other advantageous buys. It is also in these communities that the yarn houses establish warehouses for better and quicker service to customers.

3. *A ready and advantageous labor supply* is available to a group of similar businesses located in the same territory. Labor relations may be strained in these communities, but training costs are reduced. If the type of industry involved is highly organized, it may be that labor trouble in one industry will affect the entire group. This is an outstanding disadvantage.

4. *Waste and by-products* may be more easily disposed of, and at higher

prices, because complementary concerns will be set up in such areas to utilize these offerings.

5. *Power and transportation facilities* are likely to give better service to a group of business customers.

Taxes. Taxes are part of the operating expense of every business unless the community has exempted newcomers for a specified period. Even then, as has been suggested, the new company may find itself paying higher levies at the end of the grace period. The amount of tax is not so important as the services that are suppied for a given rate. However, the popular clamor to "soak the corporations" lends credence to the observation that "the power to tax is the power to destroy." With this in mind, it is prudent for the business analyst to find out something about the attitude of the local populace and its taxing authorities.

Climate. Climatic conditions may influence the manufacturing processes involved, or the contentment of the workers, or both. Textile plants were located in New England because of its moist climate. Today we can often create the desired production atmosphere within the plant. It appears that many of the moves to the southern part of the country are due partly to the favorable outdoor living climate. In any case, care should be exercised to avoid climates that are too dry, wet, cold, or warm for comfortable living.

Housing Facilities. This is naturally a weighty consideration in making a business move. In some cases where other factors make the move appear advantageous but houses are lacking, the company may decide to provide its own facilities. This is the kind of investment that only large and well-established concerns can afford. Occasionally, the plant-hungry community may agree to provide proper housing for the new workers.

Education and Recreation. The site-seeker neglects to consider educational and recreational facilities at his peril. With the human side of business attracting more attention, these former luxuries have become everyday necessities. Labor unions are setting the pace in this field by demanding that employees see to it that they or the community provide these essentials in the always rising American living standards. Recreational opportunities may be supplied naturally in some regions. Educational opportunities have become so important with organized labor that it is fostering educational programs of its own, often focused to a special purpose. Adult education courses are always an attractive inducement for the average-worker group.

Local Government Activities. This is a worthwhile consideration for the long pull. A small community in Pennsylvania lost its only large industry because the city council would not allow the purchaser to build a bridge across a side street to connect its two buildings. The plant equipment was moved to a distant city, offering the not particularly attractive opportunity for many of its employees to follow their jobs. Local capital bought the dismantled plant and established two businesses in the separate buildings, and both proved unsuccessful. In this case, the small town and its council felt that it should not be ruled by "foreign" capital. Similar cases, varying only in details, are not difficult to find. Local communities whose officials are likely to be antagonistic to newcomers should be avoided.

Plant Size and Location. The continued expansion of some business organizations lead to physical units so large that eventually coordination and control become difficult. The advantages of large-scale individual operations finally reach a point of diminishing returns. For this reason, expanded businesses sometimes decide to decentralize their operations with centralized control in the home office. These decentralizing tendencies naturally lead to plant-location problems.

In addition to the general over-all management problem, decentralization may be influenced by one or more advantages suggested by economic studies of areas some distance from the home office. Since the world situation is so fraught with rumors of war, decentralization has been given a new stimulus for security reasons. Several European countries have been systematically scattering their industries ever since World War I to obtain better security from enemy mass destruction of their production facilities.

There is also a growing relation between the size of the business and the type of area for optimum operations. For example, it is customary for small companies to locate in large cities. With a minimum of capital for investment, they can rent space in loft buildings. The city usually offers better opportunities for employing trained workers. It also affords easier banking credit. Supervisors and machine operators in the various trades are available in large numbers. There are other advantages for small concerns in large cities.

Large industries, and even large office buildings of insurance companies, are moving to rural areas in increasing numbers. When they are well-financed, they can establish desirable housing and stores and places for amusement, education and recreation. The Hershey Chocolate Company built its own community around the plant at Hershey, Pennsylvania. The latest trend is for such companies to locate where they can buy large tracts of land at reasonable prices. Their subsequent community developments often enable them to reduce their permanent investment by selling the surplus land holdings at a substantial profit.

The medium-sized concern customarily finds its best area in the suburbs of some town which has the desired facilities that the medium-sized company cannot afford to provide. The small and the large companies find distinct advantages in large cities and rural areas respectively, while medium-sized companies are seeking the suburbs of average-sized towns.

Conclusions

The outstanding feature of plant location through 1960 has been the selection of the outer fringes of the suburbs or the more open country. The prediction of the specialists in this field is that the present trend will increase, leaving large obsolete industrial areas in many of our cities. Even now, many large cities are trying to combat this loss of tax revenue in a number of ways.

The past decade has witnessed the increasing use of scientific procedures in selecting plant locations. Proof of this trend is the number of new agencies devoted to locating and appraising plant sites for clients. Small companies which cannot afford this service are still finding industrial homes in the loft buildings of our large cities. Medium-sized concerns tend to gravitate to suburban locations. All but the small companies are definitely interested in enough ground to provide for expansion, parking, and recreational areas for their employees. Because of the increasing demand by workers for comforts and satisfaction on the job, the surroundings of many new plants resemble college campuses. Worker satisfaction means increased productivity, and that means profits which are the prime purpose of every business.

Layout

Planning the layout for today's business operation involves general principles and technical tools scarcely heard of forty years ago. It was once the custom to build a strong, imposing factory building, office, store, or warehouse, and then fill it up with the equipment or furnishings. Currently, the placement of machines, departments, work centers, and storage spaces, personnel offices, washrooms, and material-handling equipment are all planned in advance; the building is then "wrapped around" the complete layout. This is the functional approach to architectural planning.

The layout planning of production processes and other business operations has, as its basic tools, the flow chart and the layout diagram. The layout employs some form of the template for the floor plan and three-dimensional scale models for the completed job. The final planning development for a multiple-story structure includes models of the various floors laid out in transparent plastic drawers which are slid into the three-dimensional framework. The flow chart, which will be referred to in more detail later, pictures in graphic form the sequence of operations.

To meet modern competition, planning the floor layout must involve more than placement of machines and equipment. Two important considerations are: *material handling*, and *processing* or *production methods*. With material handling representing as much as 25 per cent of labor costs in many industries, the machines and equipment used in modern material handling must be given major consideration in planning the layout of many operations. Aisles, elevators, and the utilization of overhead space must be planned in advance as must the placement of such internal transportation equipment as moving aprons, chutes, cranes, and monorails.[3]

Floor and other plans must conform to *methods* used in the manual and mechanical processing operations. Methods affect the placement of both the operator and his workplace and the storage of parts for assembly, to mention only a few of the relations between methods and layout. The problem will be dealt with more fully in the discussion of product and process layouts further on in this chapter.

Flexibility. New attention is being given to flexibility of layout by planning engineers. One reason for this emphasis on flexibility is the increasing problem of machine obsolescence, leading to the need for new machines and a rearrangament of equipment to maintain balanced operations and to prevent bottlenecks. Another reason, and probably more important, is the constant possibility of a shift in products, materials, and processes. An important change in any one of these three may seriously affect the current layout. The purpose is to accomplish necessary layout changes with the least cost in time and expense. The newest consideration demanding flexibility is the growing use of automated departments or plants. Industrial design engineers are now planning for this possibility in laying out new plants.

Basic considerations

The *nature of the business or industry* has a direct effect on layout. If the business is classified as heavy production or warehousing, a single-story structure with firm foundations will naturally be preferred. This would apply to steel production or steel warehousing. If it is a comparatively light industry, such as knitting of seamless hosiery or office work, the building can be of light construction.

Fire and other hazards will also control both the type of structure and the layout. The building may be fireproof or fire-resistant either in its entirety or for certain departments. Numerous hazards such as fire, fumes, and acids may even demand separate buildings for the affected operations.

Multiple buildings may be demanded either because of specific hazards or because of the nature of the business. If some operations require heavier building construction than others, it may be both convenient and cheaper to plan for separate structures.

Single- or multiple-story buildings must also be fitted to the nature of the

[3] The relation between layout and material handling is considered in detail in the next chapter.

business. For heavy industry, the decision is easy: one story. For those concerns whose operations and materials are relatively light in weight, material-handling needs may guide decisions about the number of stories. Since material handling is always expensive, whether by machines or by hand, any possible handling that utilizes gravity should lead to reduced costs. The major operations of a mattress factory, for example, may be divided into five or six departments, each of which may be located on a separate floor, with material handling largely dependent on gravity. The top floor may be used for raw cotton, where bales are opened and the contents run through pickers from which they fall to felting machines on the floor below. The rolls of felt are dropped or lowered by chute to the next lower floor for filling the mattresses, which again are dropped to the next floor for finishing. The final gravity handling takes the finished product to the ground floor for baling or boxing, and shipping.

There are many lines of business and industry where multistory operations provide cheap material handling through the use of gravity. Few can drop their materials and finished products from one floor to another through holes made for the purpose, but many can use various kinds of chutes or gravity-fed handling. In some cases where there is a tendency to high-speed gravity handling, spiral chutes or baffles can be used to reduce speeds. Occasionally, the handling of materials can be accomplished to advantage by building on a grade. When such a site is available, direct entrance can be obtained on two or three ground levels.

Location of the plant site may determine the number of operating floors. Expensive locations within large cities necessarily lead to multistory buildings. The added investment under such circumstances is not so vital if the type of business lends itself to multistory operation.

Special building types have a direct effect on plant layout. Most common is the windowless plant or office building which is independent of natural light and outside temperature conditions. With artificial lighting and controlled temperatures, layout is less restricted. Due to the hazardous nature of the business and to minimize damage in event of enemy air attack, an industrial plant at Corpus Christi, Texas (Figure 13.1), was built in part without walls. Climate is naturally a factor in such construction and a plant of this type sets up certain restrictions on layout.

A third type of plant or warehouse goes underground in a natural or artificial cave. This idea started in Germany several years prior to World War II for protection against enemy bomb attack. Some of Sweden's basic industries went underground during the war, for the same purpose, and have remained there. Sweden reports that her underground plants are not only safer in time of war, but have the advantage of being impervious to weather conditions as well as not requiring outside maintenance. Temperatures are relatively stable, and the absence of drafts has reduced illness among the workers. It is reported also that although original underground

Figure 13.1

Plant Constructed without Walls

Courtesy: Corn Products Refining Company

construction costs are about 15 per cent higher than surface building, underground operation over a thirty-year period will be about 10 per cent cheaper. Our Army Corps of Engineers started studying the advantages of underground operations at the end of World War II, conducting surveys in England, Japan, Germany, and Sweden.

Product and process layouts

The two chief *methods of manufacturing* also have a marked effect on plant layout. The better known *product method* places the various machines in their proper sequence, connecting them in different ways for handling materials and parts between operations until a complete production line is established. The *process method,* on the other hand, groups similar machines in departments or operation centers. These two methods are basically different, involve different plans for control, and are consequently decisive in the fundamental layout. Which system to use depends on the circumstances. The same plant often employs both methods in different departments. The advantages and disadvantages determine which plan shall be used in a given operation. The advantages of one plan often become the disadvantages of the other.

Advantages of product layout:

1. Material-handling costs are lower because of production-line operation.
2. Unit costs of production are lower where large quantities are manufactured.

253

3. Minimum inspection is easier than under the process method.
4. There is a smaller amount of work-in-process, thus reducing the investment.
5. Unit-production times are lower.
6. Less floor space is required per unit of production.
7. Closer and simpler production control is permitted, thus lowering costs.
8. Better opportunities are provided for group incentive-wage plans.

Advantages of process layout:
1. Greater flexibility in production is permitted.
2. Lower investment in equipment is required.
3. Better supervision by specialists is obtained.
4. Better control of inspection is possible.
5. Incentive wage rates can be put on an individual basis.
6. Machine breakdowns are easier to handle because of duplicate equipment.
7. Absentee problems are easier to handle because of similar skills.

Product layout is adapted to the manufacture of large volumes of one or a few products. It also permits closer time studies, and therefore better standard times can be obtained. It is easier to maintain a balance of machines and personnel if the system is properly set up. Machines and personnel are in proper balance when production proceeds with a smooth flow. When a minimum of inspection is required, it is performed more easily on a product layout. The product plan is most efficient when a minimum number of changes in machine setups are necessary. Finally, the product plan reduces material handling to a minimum.

On the other hand, *process layout* is necessary to take care of special orders and style products where frequent changes are necessary. The process plan often requires more inspections than the product plan. Balance of machines and personnel is more difficult to achieve under this method, and hence utilization of both is lower — the natural consequence of specialty or job work. For the same reason, standard times are more difficult to establish. Flexibility of operations is one of the virtues of the process layout. The machines used under this plan are always available for more than one kind of operation. Finally, a machine breakdown, or employee absence, does not necessarily hold up the flow of production, as is the case under the product layout.

Preliminaries to planning the layout

A certain amount of detailed information, which can be broken down under six categories, is needed before the actual job of laying out a plant can begin. In large part, this preliminary information is also needed in laying out a large warehouse, office building, or store. We are primarily interested in plant layout because it includes all the factors influencing layout in other types of business. Fundamental to any planning is a knowledge of physical inventories of building, equipment, and transportation facilities. The details obtained from these inventories are used in conjunction with a complete operation analysis to make the flow process chart and the flow diagram.

Building inventory starts with the blueprints, which show floor sizes, locations of partitions, columns, doors, aisles, ramps, elevators, and all other fixed limitations to operational layouts. Many other details, such as floor- and elevator-load limits, ceiling and clearance heights, and the location of service facilities are vital to a workable finished plan. Service facilities include such items as electric and gas lines, heating, lighting, and ventilating equipment.

Equipment inventory covers all relevant information concerning machines and equipment, including their location, size, weight, and a brief description of how they will be used.

Transportation inventory includes items used for internal transportation or material handling. Everything from tote boxes to traveling cranes should be on this list, not only by descriptive names, but also by capacity, weight, use or uses, type of power required, and, finally, according to whether the item is fixed or movable.

Operation analysis is the heart of the problem to be solved. How the product is to be made or the service performed is the guiding factor in layout. For balancing production-line operations, it is vital to know the total time for an operational cycle. The cycle is also basic for building the flow process chart. This analysis must refer to any special considerations in the process, such as lighting, power, floor strength required, types and sources of power, and special installations to minimize vibration and noise.

Process charts are used in the planning stage to represent graphically the movement of materials and the sequence of operations. Symbols for the construction of these charts have been standardized by the American Society of Mechanical Engineers. Figure 13.2 shows the conventional symbols for operations, transportations, inspections, delays, and storages. The ASME distinguishes two types of process chart. The *operation* process chart is a graphic representation of the points at which materials are introduced into the process and of the sequence of inspections and all operations except those involved in material handling. This is illustrated in Figure 13.3. The *flow* process chart focuses on sequence. It differs from the operation process chart by depicting transportations, delays, and storages as well as inspections and operations. A typical flow process chart is shown in Figure 13.4. The great virtue of process charts is that in reducing a process to a set of static symbols, ways are suggested in which operations can be combined, or rearranged, or altogether eliminated in the interests of saving time or space.

The *flow diagram* is similar in purpose to the process chart. However, instead of representing operations symbolically, it is more in the nature of a map or a partial floor plan of operations. The flow diagram lays special

Figure 13.2

Symbols for Process Charts

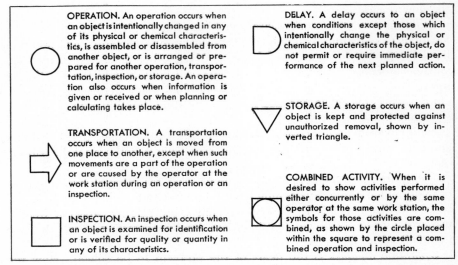

OPERATION. An operation occurs when an object is intentionally changed in any of its physical or chemical characteristics, is assembled or disassembled from another object, or is arranged or prepared for another operation, transportation, inspection, or storage. An operation also occurs when information is given or received or when planning or calculating takes place.

TRANSPORTATION. A transportation occurs when an object is moved from one place to another, except when such movements are a part of the operation or are caused by the operator at the work station during an operation or an inspection.

INSPECTION. An inspection occurs when an object is examined for identification or is verified for quality or quantity in any of its characteristics.

DELAY. A delay occurs to an object when conditions except those which intentionally change the physical or chemical characteristics of the object, do not permit or require immediate performance of the next planned action.

STORAGE. A storage occurs when an object is kept and protected against unauthorized removal, shown by inverted triangle.

COMBINED ACTIVITY. When it is desired to show activities performed either concurrently or by the same operator at the same work station, the symbols for those activities are combined, as shown by the circle placed within the square to represent a combined operation and inspection.

Figures 13.2–4 extracted from ASME Standard Operation and Flow Process Charts, 1947, with the permission of the publisher, the American Society of Mechanical Engineers, 29 West 39th Street, New York 18, N. Y.

emphasis on the amount of back-tracking that occurs in any given sequence of operations. It is relatively simple to construct a flow diagram for a single-floor operation; in multistory buildings, isometric drawings are required to show such items as elevators, chutes, and service facilities.

The layout plan

Having secured his preliminary information, the engineer is ready to start his layout. Machine templates, based on information from the equipment inventory, are moved about within the floor-plan drawings, based on the process or product plan, to obtain the desired layout. Templates must be made to the same scale as the floor plans. Within either manufacturing plan, the purpose is to obtain balance among the machines with smooth production flow. Under any plan, "flow" will prevent backtracking of the production processes.

When multistory operations with coordinating services are involved, two-dimensional templates should be replaced with three-dimensional models. For good visual presentation, it is customary to mount models of production and material-handling equipment, service lines, elevators, and the like on transparent floors drawn to scale. These "floors" should be inserted in a

Figure 13.3

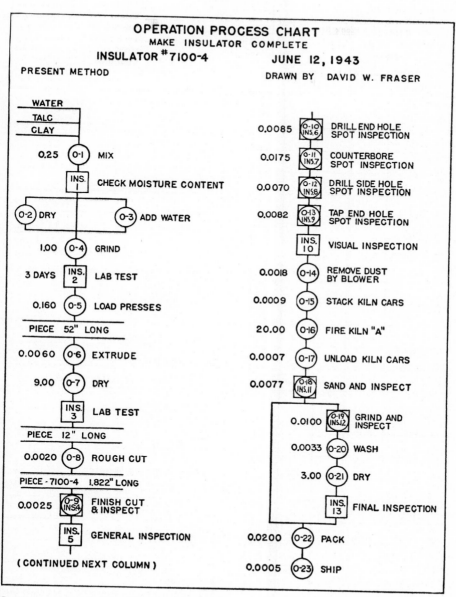

OPERATION PROCESS CHART
MAKE INSULATOR COMPLETE
INSULATOR #7100-4   JUNE 12, 1943

PRESENT METHOD   DRAWN BY   DAVID W. FRASER

WATER
TALC
CLAY

0.25   (O-1)   MIX

INS. 1   CHECK MOISTURE CONTENT

(O-2) DRY   (O-3) ADD WATER

1.00   (O-4)   GRIND

3 DAYS   INS. 2   LAB TEST

0.160   (O-5)   LOAD PRESSES

PIECE   52" LONG

0.0060   (O-6)   EXTRUDE

9.00   (O-7)   DRY

INS. 3   LAB TEST

PIECE   12" LONG

0.0020   (O-8)   ROUGH CUT

PIECE - 7100-4   1.822" LONG

0.0025   (O-9)(INS.4)   FINISH CUT & INSPECT

INS. 5   GENERAL INSPECTION

(CONTINUED NEXT COLUMN)

0.0085   (O-10)(INS.6)   DRILL END HOLE SPOT INSPECTION

0.0175   (O-11)(INS.7)   COUNTERBORE SPOT INSPECTION

0.0070   (O-12)(INS.8)   DRILL SIDE HOLE SPOT INSPECTION

0.0082   (O-13)(INS.9)   TAP END HOLE SPOT INSPECTION

INS. 10   VISUAL INSPECTION

0.0018   (O-14)   REMOVE DUST BY BLOWER

0.0009   (O-15)   STACK KILN CARS

20.00   (O-16)   FIRE KILN "A"

0.0007   (O-17)   UNLOAD KILN CARS

0.0077   (O-18)(INS.11)   SAND AND INSPECT

0.0100   (O-19)(INS.12)   GRIND AND INSPECT

0.0033   (O-20)   WASH

3.00   (O-21)   DRY

INS. 13   FINAL INSPECTION

0.0200   (O-22)   PACK

0.0005   (O-23)   SHIP

Courtesy: American Society of Mechanical Engineers

Figure 13.4

FLOW PROCESS CHART

SUBJECT CHARTED RELIEF VALVE BODY						CHART NO. 1021	
DRAWING NO. A-520612 PART NO. 16150						CHART TYPE	
CHART BEGINS Barstock Storage						CHARTED BY J. Smith	
CHART ENDS Assembly Department Storeroom						DATE 9-9-43	

SHEET NO. 1 OF 1 SHEETS
COST UNIT 1 Valve Body

◯ OPERATION   ⇨ TRANSPORTATION

▢ INSPECTION   D DELAY   ▽ STORAGE

DIST. MOVED FT.	UNIT OPER. TIME Hr.	UNIT TRANSP. TIME Hr.	UNIT INSPEC. TIME Hr.	DELAY TIME Hr.	STOR-AGE TIME Hr.	CHART SYM-BOLS	PROCESS DESCRIPTION OF *Proposed* METHOD
						▽1	Stored in bar stock storage until requisitioned
10	.0002					◯1	Bars loaded on truck upon receipt of requisition from machine shop (2 men)
210		.0002				⇨1	Moved to #301 machine
10	.0002					◯2	Bars unloaded to bar stock rack near #301 machine
				4.00		D1	Delayed awaiting for operation to begin
8	.0550					◯3	Drill, bore, tap, seat, file, cut off
				2.00		D2	Delayed awaiting drill press operator
20		.00002				⇨2	Moved to drill press by operator
8	.0350					◯4	Drill 8 holes
				2.00		D3	Delayed awaiting moveman
300		.0011				⇨3	Moved to burring department
				1.50		D4	Delayed awaiting burring operation
6	.0100					◯5	Burr
				2.00		D5	Delayed awaiting moveman
550		.0005				⇨4	Moved to seat lapping machine in detail department
				6.00		◯6	Delayed awaiting operator
6	.1700					◯ 0-6 INS	Lap seat, test, and inspect
				2.00		◯7	Delayed awaiting moveman
400		.0004				⇨5	Moved to paint booth
				6.00		◯8	Delayed awaiting painter
15	.0380					◯7	Mask, prime, paint, dry, unmask, and pack in box
425						⇨6	Sent by conveyor to assembly department storeroom
					60.0	▽2	Stored until requisitioned

Courtesy: American Society of Mechanical Engineers

frame, representing the multiple floors of the structure. With professional scale models supplied by a number of specialty concerns, one can construct a realistic multistory three-dimensional plan which will enlist the cooperation of all levels of management during the progress of the planning operation.

It is through the enthusiasm of top management and supervisors that the best floor and plant plans are worked out. Plan after plan may be made and improved by the suggestion of employees. It is customary to make photographs of the completed plans so that the changes and improvements may be preserved.

Color codes are used to indicate various types of service facilities, such as steam and gas lines, and for many other purposes. When photography is used extensively in reproducing multistory plans which include color codes, color photography is advisable. Colors are also useful in picturing process and product methods of manufacturing.

Contributing Facilities

Some of the facilities associated with many types of business include research and development, engineering, pilot plants, warehouses, cafeterias, and recreation centers. There is a strong tendency to locate research and development away from the production processes. Some concerns feel that

Figure 13.5

Consolidated Electrodynamics Corporation Technical Center, South Charleston, West Virginia

Courtesy: Consolidated Electrodynamics Corporation

they should be at least a hundred miles apart. There are several reasons for this attitude: (1) to provide room for expansion in a suburban or rural area; (2) to prevent production from using research time for non-scheduled projects; (3) to protect confidential projects; (4) to secure more pleasant surroundings; (5) to escape plant and labor difficulties. Other companies prefer to have research, development, and engineering in the main plant to make them more cost and production conscious. However, the tendency is to favor their separation. One advantage of these technical groupings is that they bring together the company's physicists, chemists, metallurgists, and engineers for teamwork in what has become known as "operations research."

From a construction planning standpoint, flexibility is one of the prime considerations behind these professional centers. Rapid technological changes, especially in the field of automation, suggest the need for laboratory additions to take care of new research opportunities.

New uses in plant construction for plastics, ceramics, and porcelain are now finding expression in architects' specifications. Current controversies include "all glass" or "no glass" construction. Plants must be functional inside, with a pleasant appearance outside. Some of the new laboratories have been set in parks. This outside layout requires more land than industrial buildings have used in the past. With city land costing twenty times as much as suburban acreage, it is little wonder that industry is moving with population centers — beyond city limits. It is predicted that by 1975 the suburban industrial population will exceed by more than half that of the cities.

The old warehouse facility has not only changed its purpose, but also its name. It will be a "distribution center" or "customer service center." These centers of the future will be more or less mobile, to the extent that they are prefabricated. In changing from solidly constructed warehouses to a more mobile type, management hopes to promote market penetration by fast delivery and customer servicing. The new "distribution center" is being used to boost sales.

Conclusions

Scientific layout of the production processes is continually improving. Today the physical facilities for research and engineering are highly fluid. Layout is not nearly so simple as it appears from this discussion. Many skills and professions are used in making an involved plan for a large installation. Although intricate layouts are expensive when planned properly, most companies report that the results are worth many times the original cost.

The maximum utilization of vertical space is receiving more attention. It is necessary that the plans of one floor not interfere with between-floors facilities. As a safeguard in this phase of planning, models indicating storage required for work-in-process should be included.

Although this discussion has hit only the high points of the many factors involved in plant and warehouse planning, it indicates some of the problems involved in a well-planned layout. Because of the many modern improvements in machines, facilities, and service centers, and the number of dangers which must be guarded against in advance, it is clear that we can no longer make satisfactory floor plans for our factories and other structures by waiting until a building is completed and then arranging the inside requirements on the basis of production know-how.

QUESTIONS

1. What are some of the important plant location factors to consider as determined by *Dun's Review* for 1960?
2. To what extent are plant site evaluations issued by the major railroads dependable for prospective industrial locations?
3. What should be the final gauge in selecting a plant or business location?
4. To what extent should tax-free offers of local communities be given consideration by companies seeking new plant locations?
5. Why is an industrial relocation decision more difficult than deciding on an original location?
6. What are some of the factors that are fundamental in analyzing a new plant site?
7. Under what circumstances are raw material markets given greater weight than finished goods markets in determining plant locations?
8. To what extent should comparatively low wage rates determine industrial plant locations?
9. Are business neighbors in the same type of business an asset or a detriment, and to what extent?
10. How important is it to see that the local government in an otherwise desirable location will be cooperative in its relations with the industrial newcomer? Can you cite an example of the importance of this contingency?
11. Why is it usually preferable for a small concern to locate in a relatively large city?
12. What are the basic tools for layout of production processes?
13. How important is within-plant material handling to total plant layout?
14. Why is it that some new industrial plants are so constructed that they can be easily converted to bonded warehouses?
15. Why are multistory buildings constructed when the type of materials used in the industry are lightweight or capable of withstanding reasonably rough handling?
16. What are some of the advantages of windowless industrial plants? What are the advantages of plants without walls?
17. What is the difference between product and process industrial layouts?
18. What are some of the preliminary data required for layout planning?

19. What is the difference between the process chart and the flow diagram?

20. How are prefabricated warehouses adaptable for use as customer service centers?

CASE PROBLEM

THE LOGUE-WEAVER PAPER COMPANY

The Logue-Weaver Paper Company, located in Holyoke, Massachusetts, is a combination of two old manufacturers of high-grade rag papers. Both concerns started, in a small way, in the late seventies, always operating as keen rivals until their consolidation in 1910. The two mills are located within a quarter mile of each other and both obtain their power from the same stream. The earlier generations of this two-family concern were decidedly conservative. A few years after the consolidation, one of the plants was enlarged by about 50 per cent, which was the only change in seventy-five years. It was at that time the company divided production of their paper varieties with the idea of reducing costs through specialization.

The present officers include two representatives of the Logues, who are cousins, and the three Weaver brothers. For about six months, the group has been discussing the advisability of moving the concern south, or at least starting a southern branch plant, preferably in Florida. The idea originated with the Weaver brothers and is opposed by the two Logues, who are of a somewhat earlier vintage than the Weavers. Cyrus Logue, the oldest of the group, feels that the Weavers have developed their interest in Florida chiefly because of their winter vacations in that state. The Weaver brothers, on the other hand, contend that volume and profits would be better if they expanded their line into the craft and specialty lines in the South. They also argue in favor of the possibilities offered by the large Florida supply of slash pine and its rapidly expanding electric-power facilities. Movement of the paper industry as a whole to that state was also offered as a factor which must have some significance for them.

To soften the shock of the move, the Weavers have suggested that the company establish the Florida plant as a branch whose product would not conflict with their present line while the new business was being built to a point where it might be feasible to sell the Massachusetts plants. Due to the age of the concern and its conservative financial management, there would be no considerable problem in obtaining the necessary cash and credit for the move, even if the old plants were retained.

Finally, it was decided to employ an industrial engineer to make a survey of a west Florida coast site proposed by the Weavers. The engineer summarized the following data:

1. *Land.* Five acres of the proposed site can be purchased for $2500. This compares with the suggested market value of $5000 for the two acres of land occupied by the present mill sites.

2. *Building.* To construct a paper mill according to the plans submitted, with double the capacity of the two small mills, will cost approximately $120,000. The market value of the two Holyoke mills, including land and buildings, is about $65,000. This figure does not include machinery and equipment.

3. *Machinery.* This item should scarcely be considered since the equipment necessary for the new location would cost about the same in Massachusetts or Florida. However, the paper-machinery house estimates the cost of machinery listed by the company's officers at approximately $25,000. The same agency estimates the value of the present machines and equipment in the Holyoke mills at $60,000.

4. *Transportation.* Railroad, truck, and air transportation are about the same in both places. Truck transportation is likely to be somewhat cheaper per mile in Florida, but the distances are greater to both raw materials and finished-goods markets. The Florida location has a decided advantage for water transportation, since the site has a fair harbor on the Gulf.

5. *Taxes.* Commercial property and business taxes are about 10 per cent higher for the same valuation in the Florida location. Because of the $5000 homestead exemption, taxes on employees' homes will average about 10 per cent of the Holyoke charges, assuming that the market value of their homes will approximate $9500. Assessments are about 60 per cent of the market value.

6. *Raw Materials.* For the paper products contemplated, the Florida location offers excellent possibilities. If the company wishes to start a program of raising its own pulpwood, large tracts can be bought for the purpose at about $25 per acre. Such available timber land is about twenty-five miles inland.

7. *Finished-Products Market.* These markets are not so favorably located as in the New England territory, but the southeastern section, and Florida in particular, is growing rapidly. Certain paper specialty items can be shipped at rates which will permit reasonable competition within five hundred miles.

8. *Living Conditions.* This factor will be a more or less personal matter with the present employees. Some may consider the move desirable. This should be true of a nucleus necessary to start operations. The Florida climate offers possibilities not found in New England, and vice verse.

9. *Labor.* There is a sufficient supply of both semiskilled and unskilled labor in the vicinity of the proposed site. Skilled papermill workers are available in reasonable supply, owing to the proximity of established mills in the state, especially on the west coast at Panama City.

10. *Wages.* On the average, wages are slightly lower, but this differential will gradually disappear as organized labor becomes stronger in the South. The local unions covering this type of business are reported to be reasonable in their dealings with management at the present time. This industry is fairly well organized.

PROBLEM: Would you advise the Logue-Weaver Paper Company to establish a new mill on the west coast of Florida at the proposed site? If so, should the company retain its present holdings, or make a clean change of location? To what extent have you considered the difficulty of building sales in its new line in the southern territory? It is reported that there is already fairly stiff competition producing craft papers in that region. Would you advise a canvass of the employees of the Logue-Weaver Company as to the contemplated change before making a decision, and why? If you are undecided about any change, what additional information would you require before making up your mind?

14

Material Handling

Transportation of materials is the original and still the primary purpose of material handling. But progress in this field during the past twenty years has reached the point where the real success of material handling depends on its integration with production, packaging, and storing activities. Integrated material handling has been aptly defined as the "design and scientific utilization of equipment and methods for the production, transportation, packaging, storage, and handling of all materials."[1] The rapid evolution of material handling into a process integrated with production, packaging, and storage has been dictated by the pressure to reduce handling expenses which amount to from 20 to 50 per cent of the cost for conversion from raw materials to the finished product. Integration has been hastened by the conviction that only by this close relationship can management hope to minimize its over-all handling costs. One must not infer, however, that most concerns, or even a majority, have integrated their material handling with its associated activities.

While the labor shortage and rising wages incident to World War I aroused management's interest in material handling, the following recession progressively dampened that interest as the labor supply started to exceed the demand. World War II, with its longer span, forced the government to speed the movement of personnel and the piles of materials at the ports of embarkation. The scientific studies undertaken to relieve these bottlenecks brought about such unexpected results that industry became interested in both the speed and the savings. The lead that production techniques achieved over the progress of material handling began to shorten. Farsighted executives pioneered studies for better and cheaper methods of material handling until that activity became a recognized phase of engineering in many lines of business and industry. The large amount of published

[1] Charles L. Hanchett, "Integrated Material Handling at the Ford Division of the Ford Motor Company," in Report No. 21 of the American Management Association (1958), p. 35.

material on this subject since 1940 is evidence of its current importance. A surprising interest centered around new types of material handling equipment which soon developed an expanding market. The annual materials-handling exposition displays more than ten million dollars' worth of new machines and gadgets to over 25,000 business executives and material-handling specialists from more than 200 concerns.

Since this subject is particularly interesting to industry, its techniques and progress will be discussed chiefly from the industrial standpoint. However, handling is a considerable factor of total costs in many lines of business, and the principles considered here are applicable to numerous activities involving the movement of light and heavy objects of all kinds. In department and other retail stores, wholesale and warehouse establishments, and in many service businesses, material handling is being constantly improved by the application of procedures discussed in this chapter.

Cost of handling materials

When considering economies in the use of indirect labor (sometimes referred to as unproductive labor), management becomes impressed with the opportunities for saving in material handling. Obviously, the final responsibility for analyzing the values and costs of material handling should not rest with the supervisor who is in direct charge of the handling operations, but should be assumed by the highest levels of management. A pertinent observation concerning the handling of materials is that *it adds nothing to the value of the product* as far as the producer is concerned. In spite of this fact, material handling remained for a long time outside the active interest of upper management. It is still the practice in some job shops, for example, for machinists to charge direct-labor time for bringing materials to their benches. Such practices not only overload direct labor costs, but they make it practically impossible to determine true material-handling costs.

Because the techniques of material handling have fallen behind those of production, they offer a fertile field for material-handling engineers. Case studies indicate that on the average, about fifty tons of materials are handled for every ton of finished products. It is estimated that material handling averages almost 25 per cent of total production costs, and well over 50 per cent of overhead costs. In a steel mill with one thousand or more workers, up to 80 per cent are assigned to handling materials. Figure 14.1 shows a breakdown of production costs, including the percentage required for handling materials.

The significance of material handling is made clear when one realizes that it begins with the raw materials and does not end until the finished goods are in the hands of the consumer. But any handling program to justify itself must contribute to the effectiveness of production operations without increasing costs to the consumer. One company, with a remarkable lack of

Figure 14.1

Break-down of Material-Handling Costs

Breakdown of a Typical Product Cost

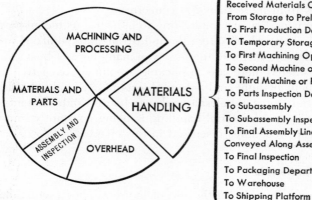

Received Materials Conveyed to Storage
From Storage to Preliminary Fabrication
To First Production Dept.
To Temporary Storage
To First Machining Operation
To Second Machine or Process Operation
To Third Machine or Process Operation
To Parts Inspection Department
To Subassembly
To Subassembly Inspection
To Final Assembly Line
Conveyed Along Assembly Line
To Final Inspection
To Packaging Department
To Warehouse
To Shipping Platform

Redrawn from Mill and Factory *with permission of the publishers*

study or planning, installed an expensive and elaborate conveyor system only to find that it not only did not improve production efficiency, but that it required six semiskilled operators, whereas the previous method required only two unskilled laborers. Since material handling equipment is sometimes an intricate and costly tool of management, it is obvious that a complete economic and operations study should be made prior to its purchase.

Objectives of material handling

The purpose of integrated material handling is to obtain better utilization of plant, equipment, and personnel, the outstanding cost-savers. These objectives are accomplished to the extent that handling is faster and safer. Modern mechanical equipment makes it possible to pile higher, safer, and faster in warehousing, which is very important to companies which emphasize forward buying of their raw materials and components. Safer handling also maintains the quality of materials. Improvements in packaging to expedite handling enables faster loading and unloading of trucks and railroad cars. The time element practically eliminates the expense of demurrage, and full-car loading reduces freight and trucking costs. All of these objectives reduce unit costs in material handling, plant operation, operation of machines, and the wages of workers.

Return on the labor investment depends on the workers' opportunity for effective accomplishment, not on the number employed. In practically all work situations, mechanical handling systems require fewer man-hours than manual methods. When workers are able to direct and control mechanical power instead of "making" it, the labor investment pays much greater dividends. Mechanical control of the worker's "power" results in reduced unit times, greater safety, decreased fatigue, and less damage to materials. It is such factors as these that enable mechanical handling to pay its original cost faster than most other types of machine investment.

The objective of the material-handling engineer in reducing these costs is to select the most suitable production machines, so arranged as to minimize the needs for material handling equipment. It is his job to provide the optimum in systemizing both production and material-handling equipment. On an over-all basis, this means proper selection of machines for production and material handling, together with their integrated arrangement. From a still broader point of view, successful plant planning requires simultaneous consideration of material handling problems, the proper selection of production machines, and the best possible integrated arrangement of all plant facilities.

Classification of material handling

The classification of material handling is an aid to the engineer in applying the proper equipment to the existing problems. Classification into five groups is generally accepted.[2]

1. Types of apparatus — conveyors, cranes, hoists, and trucks
2. Service performed — lifting and transporting
3. Materials handled — loose, pieces, packages, boxes, and barrels
4. Industry served — mining, transporting, producing, and building
5. Mobility of equipment — fixed path, wide or limited area

This classification by type and use will be discussed later in considering the details of material-handling equipment.

Advantages of proper material handling

A properly integrated material-handling system usually includes the following advantages:

1. Lowers unit handling costs
2. Reduces inventories
3. Speeds and improves inventory-taking
4. Shortens production cycles
5. Makes indirect labor more efficient

[2] Amrine, Ritchey, Hulley, *Manufacturing Organization & Management* (Prentice-Hall, Inc., 1957), p. 211.

6. Lowers accident records
7. Reduces damage to materials
8. Promotes utilization of floor space
9. Levels the flow of production
10. Improves customer deliveries
11. Reduces demurrage charges
12. Reduces worker fatigue

Elaboration of these advantages will be made in subequent discussions. It is pertinent to point out, however, that many possible improvements will be lost to production processes unless the accepted techniques of material handling are fully utilized. Maximum utilization of machines dovetails production with material-handling schedules to produce minimum internal transportation costs.

A quotation from an economics text, published before material handling was given any scientific attention, illustrates the point. "If the annual expenses for interest and replacement of fixed capital are $300,000 in any business, and the product value is $1,000,000, then the cost of the fixed capital will be thirty cents for each dollar of product. Now if the output of the business be increased to $1,500,000 by merely utilizing the machinery to the greatest degree possible, then the cost of the fixed capital will be only twenty cents."[3] This is exactly what properly engineered material handling should accomplish — the maximum utilization of productive facilities. But this will not come about until the principles and techniques of material handling have been worked out as thoroughly as have been the principles and techniques for direct production processes.

Trucks

In general, there are two elementary types of material-handling equipment — hand operated and machine powered. The *hand truck* is the most universally used and under certain circumstances, it is often the most economical to operate. The stevedore hand truck has two wheels, whereas the hand-platform type has four to six wheels.

The *machine truck* is powered by gasoline, electric storage batteries, or gasoline-electric units. Of the machine-powered units, the fork truck is most used, customarily for moving pallet loads, as will be explained later. Figure 14.2 illustrates two simple types of truck. The power fork truck in the illustration is moving merchandise on a pallet. The choice of trucks to be used on any given operation is judged by the same criteria influencing the use of any material-handling equipment, namely, that which gives the lowest cost per unit of materials handled or that which handles the materials

[3] Charles J. Bullock, *Introduction to the Study of Economics* (New York: Silver Burdett Co., 1900), pp. 173–174.

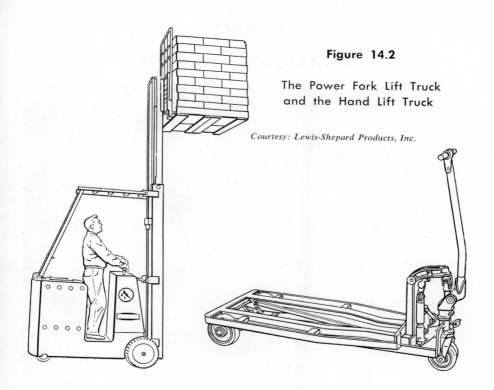

Courtesy: Lewis-Shepard Products, Inc.

Figure 14.2

The Power Fork Lift Truck
and the Hand Lift Truck

in the fastest time. The decision must be based on the facts in the case under consideration.

The Lift Truck. The earliest progenitor of today's powerful lift truck came into use in 1887. It was manually operated, its small platform lifting relatively light weights about three feet by means of a winch. By 1904, hand-operated portable elevators with revolving bases were used to pile material loads of three hundred pounds about six feet high, chiefly in warehouse storing. Two years later, the Pennsylvania Railroad added power drives to its four-wheel baggage trucks. The first lifting device capable of raising substantial loads came in 1915, and the next step was a truck capable of both vertical and horizontal movements. The first machine-powered fork truck, built in 1919, used a winch arrangement to pull and hold its load in place. It lifted its load straight up, but not high. A real improvement in design came in 1924 when the battery was placed in the rear to balance the front load. It permitted safer center operation and a shorter wheel base. The 1933 truck combined hydraulic lifting, center control, front-wheel drive, and rear-wheel steering.

This fifty-year development of the primary material-handling tool is insignificant compared to that of the past ten years. Figure 14.3 illustrates the

Figure 14.3

World's Largest Lift Truck in 1962

Courtesy: Yale & Towne Mfg. Co.

world's highest capacity lift truck of 1962 which can handle up to 200,000 pounds. It is reported that this truck carries more than twice the average load formerly carried. What the future holds for carrying capacities of fork trucks can be estimated from the enormous strides forward of the past decade. Yet not all fork trucks are out for heavyweight championships. The increasing number of uses for them in various phases of production and hauling is actually their chief bid for adoption. For example, the fork truck is rapidly acquiring an important place in foundry operations. By pouring molten metal into a series of flasks, it has cut the time by 50 per cent, with the truck driver as the only operator. Previously, mechanical pouring was done from a much slower monorail ladle which required two operators. The fork-lift dumper is also being used for many similar operations. The box container is left at the place where its load is to be received. Later, the fork lift picks up the loaded container and takes it to its destination where it is dumped automatically by special equipment attached to the lift. The hydraulic-bellows type of lift is one answer for situations requiring low clearance or close quarters when the truck is not in use. The bellows lift rises directly from the body of the truck to which it can be completely collapsed when not in use. This device allows the truck to be operated inside freight cars and other places with low clearance.

Pallets and unit loads

The pallet is illustrated in Figure 14.4. As can be seen from the illustration, the space between the top and bottom sides of the pallet provides an entrance for the truck's forks, on which the pallet is lifted and carried to its destination. When the pallet's crosspieces are properly spaced, the truck's forks can also enter the front and rear of the pallet. The pallet saves the time of the truck and its operator, who avoids having to pile the load directly on the truck's forks. This time-saving feature was the original purpose of the pallet.

Subsequent development of the pallet has greatly enlarged its usefulness. In the first place, it is now almost universally related to *unit loads*. A unit load is one that has proved most convenient from the standpoint of size and weight for hauling, storing, and shipping purposes. The palletizing of unit loads has led to such secondary advantages as easier inventory-taking, improved worker safety, and reduced damage to materials. Although many products still pass around plants and commercial establishments in small packages, increasing attention is being given to transportation economies resulting from moving large unit loads on pallets.

If the pallet is to be used effectively, consideration must be given to its size, construction, and strength. Skids were used for transporting and storage long before the development of pallets and fork trucks. There were several disadvantages to skids. For one thing, the legs of the skids damage many materials. Furthermore, skids tend to be more costly than pallets. Because they are higher than pallets, a certain amount of space is inevitably lost. A final drawback to the increased use of skids was the failure to standardize their sizes. Those professionally interested are determined that this mistake shall not be repeated with pallets. The dimensions most often suggested for pallet bases are 48 inches by 40 inches, because bases of this size will fit into freight cars and trailer trucks without need for expensive bracing during transit. However, there is a large demand for other sizes, so that the final suggestion is for three or four standard sizes capable of taking care of

Figure 14.4

The Pallet

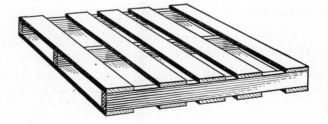

most uses. If such standardization could find general acceptance, it would be possible to establish pallet pools in various parts of the country from which local concerns could borrow pallets as needed.

If pallet bases can be standardized in a small number of sizes, the height is relatively unimportant. Many concerns require pallet heights fitted to the size and weight of the objects making up the palletized unit loads. These requirements can be numerous when applied to external and internal plant transportation and storage. Some pallets are made with collapsible sides of various heights; in other cases, the material on the pallet forms the pallet sides.

Because high-cost pallets have to be returned to their owners, continuous experimentation has been going on to find ways to construct cheaper pallets with adequate strength for many uses. The latest result is the so-called "paper" pallet which several large concerns report having used successfully. The standard-sized pallet made of compressed paper weighs about six pounds, which is only 10 per cent of the weight of a wooden pallet of the same size. One objection to the paper pallet is that it cannot be hoisted on board ships by ordinary slings without damage to its sides. Another objection is that it is weakened by moisture, a feature which is being overcome by the use of moisture-resistant chemicals.

The possibilities of palletized unit loads are almost unlimited, and certainly they are not being utilized to anything like their capacity. Semifinished products of irregular shape but requiring no protective packing may be developed into palletized loads with the aid of steel straps or pallet sides. Certain types of goods may be formed into unit loads with steel strappings without the use of pallets. Modern packaging, material handling, and shipping practices must all three improve together in order to bring about reduced costs in production and distribution.[4]

The combination tractor-trailer-pallet-fork-truck is well worth mentioning. Because the tractor is more economical than the fork truck for distance hauling, it is often a good practice to have the fork-truck load pallets on a number of trailers to be hauled by tractors for long inside hauls, between plants, or to storage. Another fork truck can be used to unload the trailers at their destination. This feature is explained to show the effective use of fork trucks for short hauls as compared to the effective long hauls by tractor-trailers.

Conveyors

Conveyors represent an outstanding phase of material handling because of the infinite number of operations they can accomplish. One manufacturer

[4] The Brooklyn Naval Depot reports that cars formerly requiring fifty-six man-hours to load are now being loaded with fork truck and pallet system in less than one man-hour.

of conveyors advertises twenty-two different kinds. Half that number will illustrate the versatility of conveyors:

Apron	Coal and ash	Live roller
Belt	Elevators	Overhead trolley
Carrousel	Gravity roller	Oven
Chain	Gravity-roller spiral	Portable
Chutes	Hoists	Vertical

A few representative conveyor types are shown in Figure 14.5.

The coal industry furnishes an outstanding example of the use of the *belt conveyor*, which is hauling heavier loads of bulk materials over longer distances almost every year. The conveyor has so many uses in production, handling, and storing that it has led to the expression "Belt-Conveyor-Era." Thomas A. Edison was probably responsible for the first adaptation of the conveyor belt to coal mining when (1890) he worked out several improvements for reviving a New Jersey coal mine. He designed a troughed rubber belt five hundred feet in length which was used successfully for two years.

The world's longest belt conveyor links the Ideal Cement Company's plant at Ada, Oklahoma, with its quarry at Lawrence, Oklahoma, a distance of five and one-half miles. Figure 14.6 is an air view of this conveyor. It carries 1000 tons an hour from the quarry to the plant with push-button control. The designer and constructor of this conveyor (Link-Belt Company) states that it operates at lower cost than any other form of transporation.

Another outstanding example of material handling equipment is the German LMB bucket-wheel excavator. Figure 14.7 pictures its excavating wheel, which is 52 feet in diameter. It will dig 13,000 cubic yards an hour, the equivalent of about 300 sixty-ton coal cars. The discharge from its boom belts is a relatively uniform flow.

The results of using belt conveyors in coal mining are indicative of their possibilities in other fields. The coal industry reported that with the use of 240,000 fewer men than in 1920, nearly 51,000,000 more tons of coal were mined in 1947. Outstanding production achievements are possible only when the conveyor's continuous flow can be maintained. Mechanization of coal mining requires conveyor handling of the coal in order to provide steady production. Without the conveyor system to keep pace with continuous cutting and loading machines, the advantage of mechanized operations would be quickly lost.

The *trolley (overhead) conveyor* has a wide use in business and industry because of the range of its capacity, flexibility, and length. This type of conveyor is an endless chain with joints operating in vertical position, suspended by trolleys from an overhead track. Conveyed products are hung from the trolley joints or, if they are light in weight, may be suspended from

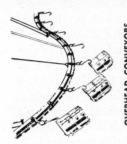

APRON FEEDERS AND CONVEYORS

Apron Feeders and Conveyors are suitable for handling fine or lumpy materials. Sprockets, chains, rollers and overlapping pans are made of manganese, steel or other metals. Chains on loaded run are supported on rugged rollers. Made in a range of sizes and types for numerous applications.

OVERHEAD CONVEYORS

Put ceilings to work—take traffic off the floor and turn aisles and storerooms into production areas. Relieve manpower by moving materials efficiently with Overhead Trolley Conveyors. Combine movement with processing such as cooling, heating, drying, pickling, etc.

SCREW CONVEYOR

For handling bulk materials horizontally, on an incline or vertically. A self-contained unit which may be dust-proof or weather-proof if necessary. Simple—few moving parts—easily accessible. Drives are compact and may be self-contained.

BELT CONVEYORS

Belt Conveyors are the efficient and low-cost method for mass handling or inclined transfer of bulk materials. High capacity, extreme flexibility for loading and discharging. Precision anti-friction bearing equipped idler rolls. If you handle bulk materials manually—investigate this economy.

BULK-FLO ELEVATOR, FEEDER, CONVEYOR

For efficient mechanical handling of bulk, flowable, granular, crushed, ground and pulverized materials that are non-corrosive and non-abrasive. Self-feeding, self-discharging, self-clearing. Handles material gently with minimum breakage, degradation or dusting. Travels horizontally, vertically or on an incline.

BUCKET ELEVATORS

Investigate the economies of Bucket Elevators, Conveyors and Carriers. Made for all capacities. Line includes the Centrifugal, Internal, Perfect Discharge, Continuous, Gravity Discharge types and Pivoted-Bucket type.

CHAIN CONVEYORS

Chain conveyors are made in two broad classifications. The drag chain type which operates in a trough and conveys bulk materials such as saw dust, cement, coal, ashes, etc. The single or multiple strand chain type, with a flat surface or attachment to support the product being handled, for conveying crates, coils, bottles, logs, packages, etc.

OSCILLATING FEEDER CONVEYORS

If you handle sharp, abrasive or hot materials, the "PA" and Hydra-Flo oscillating and vibrating feeder-conveyors may reduce handling costs. Can be installed in "tight spots" where clearance is minimum. Material may be fed or discharged at several locations. Any length. Trough widths 12" to 48".

Courtesy: Link-Belt Company

Figure 14.5

Representative Conveyor Types

Figure 14.6

World's Longest Belt Conveyor Links

Courtesy: Link-Belt Company

any portion of the chain. The path of the trolley conveyor may run along a horizontal plane, turn up or down, go around corners, or take any other direction necessary to perform its function or avoid other operations in its path. The trolley conveyor can be used for transportation, storage, processing, and assembly. Details of some of these uses include:

1. Moving incoming parts and materials from platforms to storage, and outgoing materials and parts from storage to shipping platforms
2. Moving materials and parts from storage to production centers, and between production centers
3. Moving between buildings
4. Providing temporary storage between operations or in the warehouse
5. Moving work-in-process through inspection to packing
6. Towing industrial trucks in warehouses and other places
7. Handling parts from spraying, sanding, washing, drying, sandblasting, enameling, heat treating, and many others
8. Pouring and oven baking in foundry operations

The conveyor cuts the cost of performing many operations such as spraying, dipping, and heating; it speeds production by moving parts as soon as an operation is completed; it reduces trucking expense; and it releases floor space for more valuable purposes.

Figure 14.7

The German LMB Bucket-wheel Excavator

Courtesy: Link-Belt Company

Figure 14.8

Subfloor Tow-Line Conveyor

Courtesy: Mechanical Handling Systems, Inc.

More than four miles of Chevrolet conveyor lines at Flint are suspended from monorails at bench height rather than rolled along the floor. Better accessibility of parts to the worker is credited with stepping up production to a car a minute. Nonstop production via conveyors has been the watchword at the Zenith Radio plant since it was entirely "conveyorized" in 1947. Standardization of conveyors was expanded to include jigs, fixtures, workbenches and assembly sequence. The results were reported as follows: "All production schedules reached or exceeded, unit costs cut, product quality improved, employee morale raised, and labor turnover lowered."

Conveyors may be operated by power or gravity. Many uses are being developed for gravity conveyors, especially in multistory buildings. Roller spirals and gravity rollers are equipped with free-running rollers in metal frame. They have numerous designs such as curves, Y-Shapes, switches, portables, and many others adapted to special uses. Spiral chutes or slides are used when the pull of gravity is sufficient without the use of rollers.

Miscellaneous aids to handling

Improvements in the operation of material-handling equipment are almost without end as long as the system is under the supervision of mechanically-inclined and imaginative men. Indeed, some of the latest devices are electronically operated. *Automatic loaders and unloaders* can unify the operations of a group of automatic machines, and when transfers are made electronically, the elementary use of automated control is being practiced. The tying together of machines in this fashion not only reduces production costs, but permits later rearrangements for different combined operations. This type of loader is also used for transferring loads to standard-sized pallets. In this same field, one of the newest material-handling devices is the electronic control for selecting items from storage. Punched tapes guide the collecting truck to the proper aisle and position for selecting order items and placting them on the waiting truck. It is reported that one man can handle two or three such trucks simultaneously from a single position.

Subfloor tow-line conveyors represent another aid to material handling. This equipment moves tow-pinned dollies and hand trucks over predetermined paths to stockroom or production-storage centers without overhead equipment or floor-obstructing devices. The conveyor chain runs just below the floor level and is protected by floor-level cover plates. Figure 14.8 illustrates this operation. If a relatively complete system is installed, it will be flexible enough to meet most changes in operating conditions.

A *new manually operated truck* which will handle lift-truck pallet loads of all types of building materials has just been put on the market. Known as the "Ezy-Load Straddle Truck," it is ideal for use on multiple-story construction job involving loads up to 1200 pounds. Figure 14.9 demonstrates its use.

Specially equipped *freight shuttle cars* are being used to move materials and parts from the supplier's plant to the buyer's factory. *Rail spurs* running into one end of the plant and out the other speed loading and unloading, and provide maximum comfort for handlers during all kinds of weather. The *tote box* is probably the oldest of the aids to material handling. Although of homely origin, it has had as much technical study as many other pieces of handling equipment. From the original square box for "toting" tools and materials, its shape has been changed so that it can be either nested or tiered, with its contents visible from either end when tiered. Its end handles, which facilitate tiering, are also used to transport it by monorail conveyors.

A unique use of material-handling equipment is that of *moving machines to the job,* rather than moving work to the machines. In a rather common operation where large and small presses are used in sequence, the American Seating Company claims that it saves 35 per cent in handling costs and 40 per cent in floor space by mounting its small presses on heavy steel pallets and moving them to the large presses as needed. The plant engineer reports

Figure 14.9

A Typical Wheeled Pallet Mover

Courtesy: Valley Craft Products

that "large, counterweighted fork trucks pick up the small presses and move them from job to job. No change in layout was required in the straight-line positioning of the large presses. However, almost all of the floor space formerly required for the small presses has been saved." This idea of "moving the mountain to Mohammed" is receiving increased attention as industry reports cases where it has been applied successfully.

Operating aids for most types of material-handling equipment include common-sense rules for keeping down operating costs and injuries. Aisles should be plainly marked in white or orange floor paint and be kept clear of overhead obstructions. Mirrors should be placed at blind corners to reduce safety hazards. Cooperation of production workers expedites handling and reduces accidents. Handling costs are reduced when drivers are regularly assigned to the same trucks. Another operating aid is the assignment of single responsibility for lubrication and upkeep of all material-handling equipment. Often this responsibility is divided between two or more activities such as electrical and mechanical maintenance.

Material Handling and Plant Layout

Most layout engineers attest to the valuable aid contributed to their work by men skilled in the methods of material handling. When such aid and advice is not sought, the planning job done by the layout engineers is likely to be less satisfactory. Modern business layout of any kind requires facilities designed to do specific tasks effectively and at lowest possible cost. To meet the required work and cost objectives, facilities of many types must be considered and coordinated, not the least of which is material handling. Layout planning is aimed at lower handling costs, reducing safety hazards, and improving housekeeping. Obviously, therefore, the person responsible for material handling can make a real contribution to any layout.

The mere listing of some of the major considerations involved in good layout for production plants, warehouses, or even large offices illustrates the part played by facilities for material and personnel handling — facilities

Figure 14.10

Modern Material Handling Methods in the Publishing Industry

Rapistan of Chicago, Inc.

Pictured above is part of a 7000-foot system of conveyor and gravity-flow racks in the new distribution center at Houghton Mifflin Company's Geneva, Illinois, office. The system facilitates the handling of as many as 100,000 books per day during peak seasons.

which cost much more to install when they are not included in the original plans. All of the following areas involve material-handling plans and equipment.[5]

Receiving   Warehousing
Shipping   Overhead Equipment
Rail Traffic   Yard Storage
Plant Transportation   Movement of Personnel
Floors — Aisles — Doors — Elevators

Material Handling and Warehousing

Warehousing is another activity that profits from careful planning of material handling. For example, new warehouses are now frequently designed for maximum utilization of vertical storage space and the type of equipment best suited for that purpose. There is a distinct trend toward increasing automatic controls for large warehouse spaces. Another type of control is the use of the walkie-talkie. Standard-sized packages also facilitate efficient storage in warehouses. So-called "live storage" is in use in highly efficient warehouses. It may consist of a rolling floor or roller conveyors with spurs.

One engineer has suggested that pallets be stacked at an oblique angle to the aisle to cut labor costs. Flexibility has been improved by classifying goods into large and small lots, or fast and slow-moving items. This practice has the advantage of tending to increase material turnover. Its objective may also be aided by integrating the material-handling system with inventory control. The unit load, especially when it is palletized, is a distinct advantage in maximizing storage space.

The Material-Handling Analysis

A congestion of materials between departments and around machines is a fair indication that the handling system has not kept pace with increased productivity. It is also reasonable to assume that such a material-handling situation is actually impeding output and creating a dangerous work area. Poor utilization of valuable floor space usually indicates poor material handling. No productive system can be more efficient than the material-handling plan which accompanies it.

Thoroughgoing analysis may reveal that what has appeared to be intense and highly productive activity on the part of the workers is really more a matter of energy expended in trying to keep out of one another's way in a congestion directly attributable to poor handling of materials. Again, what appears as cramped floor space may actually turn into surplus space under

[5] These items are paragraph headings of an article on "How the Materials Handling Man Can Contribute to Better Plant Layout," by R. W. Mallick, Staff Engineer of Westinghouse Electric Company, appearing in *Modern Materials Handling*, Vol. 8 (May 1953), pp. 150–155.

modern handling operations. Matching handling opportunities with the best-known techniques suited to the situation has frequently postponed the supposed need for plant expansion.

Many questions must be answered in making an analysis of any material-handling situation. Such questions concern space, persons, machines, materials, and methods. A complete survey may indicate a need for several types of handling equipment. It may even indicate the need for several types of conveyors. The data required for an analysis of "space" may lead to hundreds of questions. There are so many ramifications of the subject that an adequate job can be done only by a person who has had training and experience with all phases of the subject.

There are, however, a few rough indicators of the general types of equipment required for given situations. For example, a continuous flow of small units over the same route suggests some type of conveyor system. Of all the various systems, the conveyor type is most likely to require special adaptation to the job under consideration. It may well be that the conveyor-handling problem can be solved best with a combination of several conveyor types.

If relatively heavy objects are to be moved into any and every spot within a small area, the overhead crane is a possibility. But there are also many types of cranes, and the one selected must not only be adaptable to the work at hand, but also one that does not interfere with production machines or other floor equipment. "Other equipment" introduces many possibilities of interference that may influence the type of crane to be used. The mobility of truck-mounted cranes makes them more desirable in many situations than those which operate on fixed rails. In spite of the advantages of handling with cranes, the demand for overhead space for storage or utility services may eliminate them from consideration.

Long-distance moving of materials from a central point, such as a receiving platform, to a number of use stations suggests the selection of a tractor and trailers. But even after this decision has been made, there still remains the question of which type of tractor will be most useful. Since the trailer-and-tractor system will generally be used in combination with a lift truck, these three types of equipment would have to be considered together.

When it is necessary to move materials higher than the capacity of the lift truck, some type of movable or stationary elevator is required. Lifts from ground to truck or boxcar level may suggest both the elevator and fork truck if the job is large enough.

When the movement of materials — whether intermittent or regular — involves a number of routes, the lift truck probably offers the best solution. The flexibility of the lift truck makes it the first line of offense for many handling jobs. It can fit into a large variety of loading and unloading jobs, as well as stacking, moving and storage assignments. In addition to these daily chores, the use of various attachments such as scoops and crane arms in place of the standard fork equipment, enables the lift truck to perform another long list of routine material-handling jobs. One manufacturer of all types of material-handling equipment states that "because it combines features of all other materials-handling systems, the lift truck will be found adaptable to almost any problem, especially those not easily solved by the use of conveyors, cranes, or tractor-trailer combinations."

Breaking down the analysis

Material-handling analysis may be set up under five general headings: Production, Receiving and Storage, Packing and Shipping, Costs, and Handling Systems. Under each of these general headings, there are a number of subtopics for investigation. In selecting the industrial truck system to be used, for example, basic information is required about distances traveled, tons per trip, trips per shift, and the number and height of the tiering operations in store and stock rooms.

It is not always obvious, but true nevertheless, that those charged with the production processes must be interested not only in the handling of materials while in their possession, but with the entire handling process from raw materials to the ultimate consumer. It would not be feasible to set up a new handling system in one department that increases handling costs in other departments. The same conclusion is valid in material-handling relations with outside firms. The way in which a company receives its supplies may decidedly affect its handling costs, and cooperation with the supplier is one way to reduce such costs. But the unilateral adoption of a new receiving and handling plan by a buyer may so increase his supplier's costs as to make the new prices outweigh his handling savings. Likewise, a change in the method of delivering to customers may so increase the customers' handling costs as to price the seller out of the market until he reduces his internal handling costs.

Cutting handling costs

Determination of handling costs and the installation of new handling equipment are closely related. Improved handling methods are often disregarded simply because there is no plan for determining their costs. When manual handling costs are known, the change-over to mechanical methods usually results. It frequently happens that production motion-and-time study involves material-handling operations, with consequent suggestions for handling improvements. This is especially true when part of the operator's activity involves the handling of materials. The establishment of standard-operation times dictates the elimination of those operator motions which can be done by machines. It should also be noted that to the extent that the accident rate of manual operations can be reduced by the use of mechanical equipment, the cost of handling is also reduced.

There are two principal methods for determining material-handling costs. One plan uses formulas developed by the Materials Handling Division of the American Society of Mechanical Engineers to fix the time required for amortizing the investment from savings. The other plan is based on cost per unit moved. Both methods are employed in making economic surveys to determine what advantages will accrue from suggested installations. The ASME allowances cover investment, insurance, taxes, maintenance, depreciation, power, and supplies. Savings in fixed charges and direct labor, credit for increased production, rate of equipment utilization, and original cost are also considered in the formula. Whether or not the time required for amortizing the investment fits company policy determines whether the contemplated change is economically feasible.

The other plan uses a cost-per-unit basis with equipment investment spread over the life expectancy of the items involved. The proponents of this plan contend that "how long it will take to pay for itself" does not give a true picture because it fails to take into account the difference between long- and short-life equipment. It is to circumvent this alleged deficiency in the economic calculation that the unit costs are based, in part, on life expectancy of the equipment.

Organization

As with most other activities, the organizational setup for material handling depends on the size of the concern and the nature of its product. Naturally, handling activities assume more importance in the total functioning of a company as the number of uses for them increases. When, for example, not only transportation of materials but some of the operations performed on them (such as dipping and drying) can be handled mechanically, the activity becomes more important and may well occupy the full time of a manager. Under such circumstances, material handling requires constant attention for smooth operation and possible improvements. When considering situations involving both the transportation and production functions of a maze of constantly moving conveyors of various kinds, one can easily conclude that such responsibility might challenge a trained and experienced person of executive rank.

In many plants and other business establishments, the material-handling problem is relatively simple. The person in charge of the system may well combine these duties with such activities as motion-and-time study, work analysis and planning, or some similar function. Irrespective of the size of the installation, its maximum value will accrue only when it has the attention of some member of management and is a definitely assigned responsibility of some one person. A material-handling system is usually automatic, but it cannot think itself into coordinated operating relationships and improved layouts; it must be under the control of a single guiding mind capable of comprehending the system as an entity.

Objectives and Principles

The chief objectives of handling techniques are to reduce costs and increase safety by improving controls. To accomplish these objectives, all handling should be reduced to an absolute minimum, and then done by machines as far as possible. If the "don't touch it" idea is applied assiduously, costs will be reduced automatically. The most fruitful fields for the application of handling principles are those production processes where the flow of materials should be automatic between machines and assemblies and such production operations as dipping, spraying, and drying. Proper handling reduces costs through increasing productivity, saving space, and relieving fatigue. Many improvements in the production processes have been initiated by applications of material-handling principles.

Continuous study by specialists has produced a group of handling principles which have supplied effective rules of action. The following list is suggestive:

Reducing Handling Costs
1. Elimination of unnecessary handling is the first step in saving costs.
2. Combining operations minimizes internal transportation.
3. Gravity is the cheapest form of handling.

Planned Layouts
4. Planned layout should provide continuous flow through proper coordination of processes and assemblies.
5. Layout should be set up on a unified plan to accomplish overall handling economies.

Handling Equipment
6. Existing equipment should be used most effectively before considering substitutes or replacements.
7. The simplest equipment applicable to a given situation is most desirable.
8. Other things being equal, standard equipment is preferable to special.
9. Handling equipment adapted to special circumstances may not be readily applicable to other situations.

Costs
10. Equipment cost should be figured on a service basis rather than on purchase price.

Operations
11. Handling operations should be coordinated whenever possible to reduce machine idleness.
12. Handling operators should likewise synchronize their work, whenever possible, to reduce operator idleness.
13. Largest units practicable should be used in loading and unloading operations.

14. To minimize sorting of materials, avoid mixing them in the first place.
15. Maximum vertical storage saves floor space and reduces costs.
16. Effective handling requires related packaging.
17. Operator training, equipment maintenance, and the elimination of operating hazards definitely improve handling operations.[6]

Conclusions

The three outstanding trends in handling announced as the result of a survey made by *Factory Management and Maintenance* magazine at the Material-Handling Institute's exposition in Cleveland in 1959 are:

1. *Narrower aisles,* made possible by more maneuverable equipment
2. *Fewer pallets* because of the possibilities of bound unit loads
3. *Less handling labor,* largely resulting from the "use of a Radox transistorized radio transmitter the size of a cigarette case by which one man can start, stop, and steer as many as three tractor-trailer trains from up to 200 ft. away."

The very novelty of such changes in contrast to what were considered top methods, especially in the first two cases, vividly indicates the striving for improvements in the material-handling field.

If material handling is to reach its maximum potentialities, it must have the active interest of top management. If the concern is large enough to warrant it, a material-handling engineer should be employed and given authority sufficient to set up and maintain an efficient system. The handling engineer must be able to work cooperatively with the packaging and sales departments so that there will be no conflict between the size of the units to which the handling system is geared and the size of the units intended for distribution to the customers.

Material handling goes beyond mere transportation to include various controls and several phases of the storage operation. Floor plans should always give weighty consideration to facilitating material handling. Comparison of machine and hand costs of handling is only a part of the advantage of a coordinated system. The quality and quantity of production, reduction of damage and waste, relief from congestion and the improved housekeeping it makes possible, better utilization of floor space, relief of physical strain, and safe working conditions all must be considered in designing a good material-handling system.

One of the major factors preventing medium-sized companies from adopting more modern handling operations and methods more rapidly is the technical inability of these companies to analyze either current manual handling or a mechanical substitute for it from the standpoint of costs and

[6] These rules are summarized from L. P. Alford and John R. Bangs, *Production Handbook* (New York: The Ronald Press Company, 1948), pp. 937–938.

savings. With the present lack of general knowledge of this subject, it will be up to those concerns which sell material-handling equipment to make the advantages of their products more generally known.

QUESTIONS

1. About what percentage of total production costs is spent for material handling inside and beyond plant walls?
2. What factors led to the intensified scientific interest in material handling during and after World War II?
3. If, as alleged, material handling costs are so high, what value do they add to the producer's products?
4. What are the fundamental purposes of integrated material handling?
5. Can you list ten advantages of a properly integrated material handling system?
6. Which piece of material handling equipment is most universally used?
7. How has the use of pallets improved warehousing and the time and cost of taking physical inventories?
8. The text lists fifteen different types of conveyors. In light of this, how would you rate the conveyor as an average contributor to the effectiveness of material handling?
9. For what production process is the overhead trolley conveyor used?
10. What is the oldest piece of material handling equipment?
11. How do standardized pallets increase the storage capacity of warehouses?
12. What is the relation between material handling and plant layout?
13. What is the advantage of stacking loaded pallets at an oblique angle to the aisle?
14. How would you proceed in making an analysis to show what types of material handling equipment are best for a given situation?
15. What type of material handling equipment is probably best for moving materials from a central point to a number of use stations?
16. Comment on this observation by a manufacturer of material handling equipment: "Because it combines features of all other material handling system, the lift truck will be found adaptable to almost any problem."
17. What are the two principal methods for determining material handling costs?
18. How would you proceed in determining the organizational setup for material handling in a large concern making various products and their components?
19. What is the cheapest form of material handling?
20. What is the significance of this observation: "Other things being equal, standard equipment is preferable to special."

CASE PROBLEM

THE ENTERPRISE IRON FOUNDRY

The Enterprise Iron Foundry has been in operation since 1910 making castings for industry. It was started by three foundrymen friends in a garage and moved to its present quarters in 1912, financed by endorsed bank loans. Because of tight financing, it was not able to install the best-known equipment when the new foundry was built. However, reasonable success over the years provided the capital for up-to-date equipment. The outstanding need, as the owners realize the chief cause of their high competitive costs, is a complete overhaul of their handling equipment.

The sketch shows a ground floor 165' x 240' with a small offset at the end of the building where new sand is stored and prepared for the molders and core-makers, and waste sand is dumped after the castings are shaken out of the molds. The scale of the drawing is 30 feet to the inch.

Internal transportation is all done by carts, wheeled ladles, and racks. The racks are used to take the finished sand cores to the bake ovens, and from the ovens to the floor molders or the pouring room. Small ladles of molten iron are carried from the "cooking" room to the nearby molds in the pouring section. Large pots of molten iron are wheeled to the pouring room, where the pouring is done by dipping with hand ladles. The large pots are also wheeled to the floor-molding department. Hand carts carry castings to the sand-blasting and burring departments. From this section, the castings are later wheeled to the packing and shipping rooms.

Hand carts are also used to haul treated sand to the core-making and floor-molding departments. The same type of cart hauls the poured molds to the shakeout machines, and the waste sand from shakeout to the sand dump. Pig iron is unloaded by gravity conveyors from freight cars to the cooking room. A similar type of conveyor unloads sand from freight cars to the sand-mixing sheds. Heavy hand trucks are used to carry the large castings from the floor-molding department to the packing and shipping room.

The metal racks that carry the sand cores are large and heavy. They are equipped with wheels for hand pushing. Loaded, they probably weigh 500 pounds, but the cores they carry do not weigh over 10 pounds on the average. The small hand ladles weigh about 10 pounds empty and twice as much when loaded with the molten metal. The large pots for carrying molten metal weigh about 500 pounds loaded. They are equipped with wheels of the carriage variety. The general-purpose hand carts are similar in size to the large pot carts, but equipped with deep steel bodies which can be dumped. Their weight depends on their contents, but in any case can be regulated by the amount of material loaded into them.

The second floor covers a portion of the ground floor at the office end of the building. About half of this floor is occupied by the pattern shop, while the other half is divided between the laboratory for examining test bars taken from each of the "heats" and a storage room for patterns. All transportation between the second and ground floors is carried by hand on a stairway located in the packing room. Both test bars and wood patterns are light in weight so that an elevator is not actually necessary.

Enterprise now employs 625 men, of whom 46 are giving full time to internal transportation.

PROBLEM: Redraft, if necessary, the floor plans so as to provide for the installation of modern equipment necessary to reduce handling costs. Designate the kind of material-handling equipment you would recommend for the transportation problems involved. How many of the 46 transportation laborers will your new plan eliminate? What advantage to the foundry's productivity will result from your plan?

Figure 14.11

Floor Plan of the Enterprise Iron Foundry

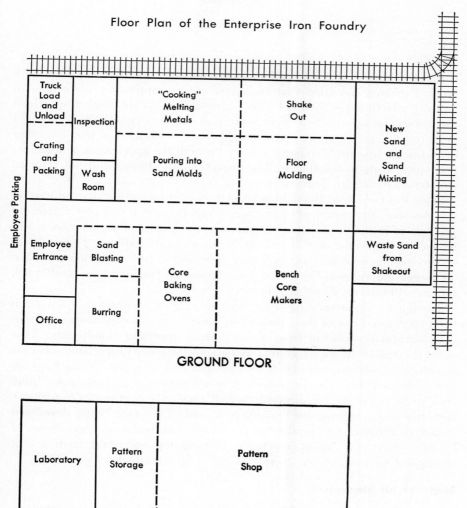

GROUND FLOOR

SECOND FLOOR

15 Maintenance

A recent survey of 687 manufacturing companies listed on the New York Stock Exchange revealed that their collective maintenance costs amount to about two-thirds of their net profits. Irrespective of the angle from which the subject is approached, maintenance is big business today. As with procurement, maintenance has changed from a service function for other departments to a profit-making activity through the application of scientific principles to its management. Accountants of the future will not refer to maintenance costs as "burden."

Since the Industrial Revolution placed an ever-increasing dependence on the machine, that phase of maintenance has become a constantly growing problem of business. As we go further into the period of automation, maintenance will become one of industry's major considerations. The problem of keeping the new intricate machines operating at full utilization will have an increasing relationship to profits. Preventive maintenance and quick repairs will take on a new significance.

Though its importance has long been recognized, maintenance has often been considered one of the "blind spots" over which management could not exert satisfactory control from either cost or operating standpoints. That opinion is gradually losing ground as some of the more progressive concerns establish maintenance standards for time and cost of materials as a basis for incentive pay. Perhaps the notion of maintenance as an inevitable "blind spot" arose because it has always had such a wide range of duties to perform. Nevertheless, standards for maintenance control are now being developed under conditions considerably more varied and technical than those of twenty years ago. Maintenance has become too important from a cost standpoint for management to rely on hit-or-miss methods.

Scope of maintenance

Maintenance is responsible for the upkeep of buildings, machinery, equipment, and numerous miscellaneous items and activities. It has charge of the broad functions of "housekeeping," including janitorial and cleaning work of all kinds. Periodic inspections for detecting in advance the need for repairs and replacements should be one of its primary responsibilities. Progressive maintenance makes suggestions for the improvement of machinery and equipment designs so that operating costs will be reduced, and the life and efficiency of machines increased. Occasionally, even operating activities such as the power plant are assigned to the maintenance department. On top of all these duties is the task of keeping detailed records of all maintenance activities and their costs. No wonder that the maintenance function has been receiving constant attention from the technical magazines and a group of progressive engineers.

There is no standard list of maintenance activities, but those covered should be noted in the company's policy manual and spelled out definitely in a departmental handbook. Unless this procedure is followed, there are bound to be conflicts between production and maintenance. The nature of the company's business and the policy of its management are the basic determinants of the scope of its maintenance services.

Cost of maintenance

The *direct cost* of maintenance was referred to in our opening sentence. The *indirect costs* under a poorly managed maintenance department will be much higher than the direct costs. When machines are not kept at high efficiency, operating costs are increased, production schedules must be revised, and delivery promises become problematical. In addition, machine downtime (loss of machine time for adjusting, repairing, etc.) may result in wage payments for idleness which is beyond the operator's control. Such costs are impossible to calculate. On the other hand, a scientific approach to maintenance reduces machine downtime, prolongs their productive life, and minimizes the cost of repairs and replacements.

The proper amount to spend on maintenance varies with the problems of individual concerns and must be based on judgment and experience. It is simply impossible to determine accurately the savings resulting from superior maintenance operations. In many cases, proper maintenance is still considered something to wish for but do little about. Under such conditions, management can only try to keep down maintenance costs, as a necessary evil. Such treatment frequently appears to give satisfactory results only because delayed maintenance means renewals rather than repairs to machines and buildings, with frequent charges to the capital account rather than to upkeep.[1]

Some cost formulas have been used with benefit by individual companies. They are generally based on ratio relationships between maintenance and

[1] Maintenance servicing of machines can be estimated by applying the Waiting Line Theory, discussed in Chapter 5.

other costs. An example is the ratio of maintenance expense to the value of equipment. Another is the ratio of maintenance expense to operating costs or net sales. The numerical ratio of the maintenance force to the total plant force is a favorite measure. Any one of these ratios may be excellent for individual cases, but their value for comparisons among companies is extremely doubtful. There are too many variables such as age of the plant and its equipment, types of operation, and the number of working hours in a day for dependable comparisons.

Property records

The prerequisite to any kind of orderly machine maintenance is an equipment inventory. Properly compiled and used, it will save its cost many times over. A simple record can be kept on a 5″ x 8″ card for each piece of equipment, identified by the serial number of the machine. Equipment numbering should be by department, allowing for additions and changes. On its face, the record card should show all relevant data about the piece of equipment, such as the date of purchase, cost, weight, and other details. When advisable, drawings, specifications, and parts lists should be attached. This record can be helpful on many maintenance jobs, and should be referred to on all jobs for the purpose of showing (on the reverse side) the nature of the fault, the cost of correcting it, and suggestions of the inspector.

Because of the scope of its coverage, the maintenance department should maintain an over-all property map, detailed plans and specifications of all buildings and the service lines between them, departmental floor plans with machine layout, and maps showing underground piping and service. It is surprising to learn how many concerns grow large, with active maintenance departments, but without some of these records. The costly evidence of past dereliction is frequently seen in the form of narrow trenches dug near locations suspected of harboring uncharted pipes and other servicing equipment. Similarly, walls and floors are opened to look for unmarked wires and pipes inside of buildings. Someone knew all the answers once, but he died before the elementary principles of management secured a foothold with his company.

Organization of Maintenance

How maintenance should best be organized depends on its importance within a business and the nature of the business itself. Even when maintenance is important in the production processes, management often relegates its supervision to some minor executives. A worse tendency is to select third-rate supervisors for maintenance while hiring first-rate supervisors for production. The cost of maintenance is always greater with a poorly organized and poorly staffed crew.

The organization must be streamlined for superior results. Many concerns are reorganizing the maintenance department to provide for new planning responsibilities. Reporting to managers higher in the company hierarchy is another innovation of today's organization. One change is to have the chief of maintenance report to the general manager instead of the plant manager. Under this plan, maintenance is given more responsibility and greater spending authority without requiring consent of higher authority. While the proverbial limit has been about $100, except for emergencies, in the smaller concerns, many companies with sales of ten million or more are allowing maintenance responsibility for single expenditures as high as $2,500.

An organization chart for maintenance is necessary for fixing authority and responsibility, but it is only an aid in getting the work done well and at low cost. A diagram of functions to be performed will not guarantee an efficient organization. Organization principles have general validity, but they always have to be applied to specific situations.

Line and Staff. A good maintenance organization will provide for line-and-staff management. The chief should report to some member of top management in a large production concern. In some companies where maintenance is intricate, the department should have equal standing with the production organization. Engineers and draftsmen acting in a staff capacity can well serve in building, electrical, and other special maintenance functions, some of which have become so complex that they are handled by outside specialists. This practice may be followed to advantage by small companies.

Clerical Work. There are maintenance auxiliary services which deserve better treatment than they are now receiving. One is clerical help and another is the stockroom for parts, tools, and supplies. It is an inexcusable mistake to have clerical work done by maintenance operators in the average-sized organization. Trained clerks will do better work at less cost, besides relieving operators for their specialties. This also applies to such routine matters as cost and equipment records, work orders, dispatching, and reports for executive control.

The Stockroom. The maintenance stockroom has a direct effect on the department's efficiency. Its purposes are maintaining an adequate stock, good records, and quick service. Adequacy of stock means having on hand what is needed; substitutes are unsatisfactory. Good records keep inventory at a workable level without unnecessary costs, minimize waste, and aid in accurate costing. Quick service saves the wages of idle workers — both production and maintenance — by speeding maintenance jobs. Good storeroom methods, facilities, and a sufficient number of service employees are necessary to accomplish maximum results.

It is desirable that the maintenance dispatcher plan to have storeroom tools, parts, materials, and supplies delivered directly to maintenance jobs. This practice saves the time of skilled workers who could move from one scheduled job to another without the necessity of wasting time on trips to the stockroom. Another time-saving stockroom idea is to provide projecting rotary bins of small items so that workers can help themselves to parts and supplies of insignificant value. In some places, craftsmen are allowed to withdraw from the stockroom on their own signature and have their requisitions reviewed at the end of the day or job.

The Dispatcher. The dispatcher's work in a large maintenance organization is similar to that of the production dispatcher, but occasionally more important with respect to the number of operations he is responsible for initiating. He receives orders for repairs from the operating departments and from maintenance. He sees that the accounting requirements and necessary approvals are in proper shape. He checks the completion dates and, in some cases, does the scheduling. He keeps a complete record of the maintenance load on the department's control chart. Finally, he assigns the maintenance jobs, receives time tickets from which he prepares reports for the payroll department, and closes out the completed jobs by filling out the proper forms and removing the job from the control board. With these duties, the dispatcher becomes the key work-horse for the control of maintenance operations.

Communication. It is just as necessary to have the organization chart displayed as it is to draft it. Besides promoting coordination, it is good psychology. Members of the entire organization can see that they "belong," where they fit in, and the extent of their duties and responibilities. Without the planned coordination which comes from posted charts, the will for cooperation does not carry far in the right direction. One maintenance engineer cites the case where an oiler was fired because he was overdoing his job. Later it developed that he was having the unsolicited help of two machine operators who were really causing machine trouble by their gratuitous lubricating acivities.

Centralization versus Decentralization. The question of centralized or decentralized maintenance is another controversial organization problem. Both plans have sturdy supporters. The group favoring centralization contends that it reduces operating costs — particularly in spread-out plants, makes possible better inventory control of parts and supplies, and improves coordination and inspection. The other side contends that departments have special problems which can be solved better by locally assigned operators, and at less expense. Another plan, a compromise of these two, is to provide decentralized-area shops for routine maintenance jobs while assigning special and emergency jobs to a centralized section.

A final observation regarding maintenance organization is the advisability of separating planning and performance. In an organization large enough to warrant this treatment, better work will be done at lower cost.

Maintenance Policies

The purpose of policies is to guide management in the accomplishment of company objectives. Maintenance policies should be written and submitted to top management before they are issued in final form, so that they may be made to conform to the company's over-all policies. Policies should never be merely "understood"; in that form they soon become misunderstandings. The best plan for formulating policies so that company objectives will be completely covered is to make a check list of objectives. This plan guides the policy-makers to tailor-made results. Above all, maintenance policies should not be copied from those of some other concern.

Maintenance policies may be divided into two classes: (1) those important enough to receive top management attention from the start, and (2) those which are formulated on the departmental level and then submitted to upper management for approval or change. The kind of policies which should originate with top management can best be expressed by a series of questions. When should repairs be charged to the capital account? How should the cost of replacement parts be treated from a financial standpoint? Should repairs be kept down so that replacements will be more frequent? When should replacements be charged to operating costs? What should be the basis for estimating machine and construction depreciation? Should there be one plan for company bookkeeping and another for tax purposes? How should maintenance approach the problem of standardization of machines and equipment for reducing parts inventories?

Some concerns require that the department managers should be consulted regarding maintenance plans and actions. Others go further and require that maintenance must have the affected department's consent before planning or action. It is not unusual to stipulate that inspections shall be made by department operators except where special skills are necessary. This idea aims at reducing maintenance man-hours. Also, it accepts the notion that the machine operator has the "feel" of his machine. Finally, maintenance may be required to make certain inspections on a scheduled basis, and in important cases, top management may specify the intervals.

On the other hand, maintenance's policies may provide for the types and times of preventive inspections. Another policy often left to the maintenance department covers the priorities assigned to its various types of work. Some maintenance departments have established the policy that they shall take care of the overhaul of all machines which they have designed. Another policy may cover the standard for determining the number of clerks for each maintenance department where there are multiple plants. There is frequently a policy stating that completed jobs must be inspected by both production and maintenance.

Preventive Maintenance

There are two general plans for approaching maintenance work. One is *remedial,* which makes repairs or replacements after a breakdown of some kind. This is the older approach and scarcely requires comment. Progressive concerns are getting away from remedial maintenance as much as possible. It has high direct costs and still higher indirect costs. The other approach to maintenance is known as *preventive,* and it too is self-explanatory. Preventive maintenance depends absolutely on scheduled inspections. It is maintenance's prime cost-cutting tool. It is usually estimated that preventive maintenance will cut costs by about 15 per cent. Its savings in the category of emergency breakdowns usually average 25 per cent. Whereas remedial maintenance takes care of trouble after it has developed, preventive maintenance prevents the trouble from happening.[2]

Preventive maintenance practically eliminates major breakdowns, prolongs the productive life of buildings and equipment, cuts maintenance costs when properly scheduled, and is an aid in meeting customer deliveries. An effective preventive program demands the cooperation of all machine operators and supervisors throughout the organization, as well as watchmen and even routine workers who may well suggest conditions requiring attention.

Inspections

The first step in preventive maintenance is to make a property list of all items that have to be inspected. The next step is to determine how often these items must be inspected.

Frequency of inspection will depend on two considerations. The *first* is the relative difficulty of repairing or replacing a given piece of machinery or equipment. It stands to reason that items which are not likely to break down suddenly or which are easy to repair when they do break down do not have to be inspected so often as more delicate machinery. The *second* consideration determining frequency of inspection is the importance of a given item to the productive process. If the breakdown of a particular machine will cause a serious disruption in the over-all flow of production, it will have to be inspected more frequently. An analysis of the property list will show that the care of many small production and auxiliary units can be left to departmental mechanics because the disruptive effects of improper

---

[2] In those few cases where the cost of preventive maintenance exceeds the remedial costs, and the latter does not unduly interfere with production, it is naturally to be preferred.

maintenance of these units are relatively insignificant. If these criteria are followed, serviceable schedules for preventive maintenance will gradually be compiled.

The following is a list of the types and frequencies of fifty general plant inspections made at the Kearney Works of the Western Electric Company:[3]

Not Scheduled Regularly
Boiler accidents
Elevator accidents
Sprinkler leakage
Good housekeeping
Turbine inspection
Sprinkler shutoff

Daily Schedule
Watchmen's reports

Quarterly Schedule
Emergency stretcher stations
Carbon dioxide systems
Hoisting chains & slings
Electric trucks
Film storage
Fire insurance inspection
Gas and oil equipment
Gas masks
Ladders and scaffolds
Machine guards
Poisonous substances
Portable electric cranes
Safety belts
Scales
Temporary wiring
Double-check water valves
Sewage effluent
Sprinkler alarms

Monthly Schedule
Boiler and powerhouse
Underground flammable tanks

Six Weeks' Schedule
Elevators
Exhaust systems
Fire & patrol boxes
Fire hydrants, etc.
Flammable tanks
Locomotives
Cranes

Four Months' Schedule
Compressed gas cylinders
Portable furnaces & torches

Semiannual Schedule
Cotton fire hose
Electric temperature alarms
Underground sprinkler leaks
Machinery & equipment
Safety & waste containers
Steam containers

Annual Schedule
Fire equipment
Grounds & bulkheads
Powerhouse electric equipment
House & sprinkler tanks
Low-voltage electric systems
Sprinkler system pressure
Pressure test on coffee urns
Linen fire hose

This illustration shows the comprehensive scope of inspection, but it gives only a single listing to machinery and equipment under the semiannual schedule. In most concerns, machinery and equipment are the outstanding

[3] Harry L. Husson, "Elaborate Maintenance Surveys Key to Plant Fitness," *Factory Management and Maintenance*, Vol. 105 (May 1947), p. 82.

items for an inspection schedule. The machines can be set up in groups for purposes of inspection, or each may be listed by number for individual inspection. In either case, inspections should be made on a fixed time schedule. Figure 15.1 illustrates the machine-inspection record.

As has been suggested, there is some tendency to inspect unnecessarily for preventive maintenance — "just to make sure." Half of the value of a preventive program lies in determining realistic inspection schedules. The other half lies in scheduling arrangements as a continuous job. A new machine, for example, does not necessarily require the same inspection schedule as the one it replaced. Furthermore, schedules should be adjusted to operations, which also require changes. If a certain item is found satisfactory for six monthly inspections in succession, thought should be given to lengthening the inspection interval.

One company has injected flexibility into its inspection schedule by having

Figure 15.1

Machine Inspection Record

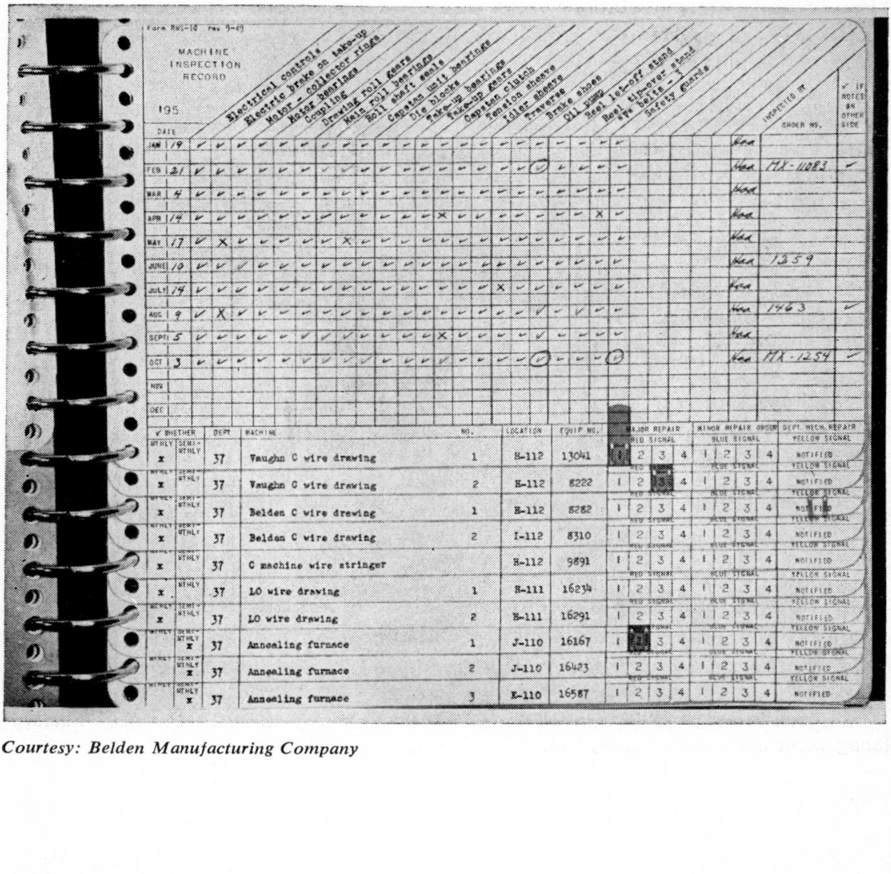

Courtesy: Belden Manufacturing Company

the plant engineer set up a few common-sense guides to give the maintenance planners some leeway in making and changing the schedules. To promote the use of this initiative, the plant engineer agrees to assume responsibility for consequent trouble. The inspectors feel free to exercise their judgment and report results and causes as they find them, without fear of the consequences. With accurate reports from the inspectors, the plant engineer has a realistic basis for changing some of the schedules, with effective inspection at reduced costs.

For inspections to be effective, records should be made of the findings, including the cause of the trouble and recommendations for correcting it. The cumulative inspection record tells a definite story about the machine, and sometimes about its operator. It may also suggest a change in the frequency of inspections. This record procedure is the most practical scheme for correcting inspection intervals which were originally determined by engineering skill.

The work order

Preventive inspection determines the condition of the equipment, suggests how an adverse condition should be remedied, reports the probable cost and the relative importance of a possible breakdown. The inspector's recommendations are reviewed by the plant manager if the costs run over a fixed amount — from $50 to $150 as a rule. Below the maximum, the inspection engineer is allowed to order the work done on his own initiative. In some plants, work costing less than $50 may be requested by the foreman and performed by the plant or department mechanic. Work orders costing more than the maximum allowed the inspection engineer must have the approval of the plant manager. Relatively large expenditures, such as machine renewals, invariably go to top management for approval. Figure 15.2 is a typical maintenance engineer's report. It records the faults of the machine, makes recommendations for correcting them, states whether safety or an emergency is involved, and gives the estimated cost of the repairs.

Besides the periodic inspection procedure and the resulting report with recommendations for corrective action, maintenance must include a system of control to see that the approved action has been carried out, and how its actual cost compares with the engineer's estimate. When inspection check-lists are used, they are actually the primary control for inspection details. Inspectors' reports employ various symbols of colored check-marks and crosses to indicate such conditions as "satisfactory," "adjustment needed," "poor condition but no immediate repairs," "emergency," and the like.

Lubrication

Proper machine lubrication is naturally an important part of preventive maintenance, since many machine failures are due to faulty oiling. The

Figure 15.2

Maintenance Engineer's Report

MAINTENANCE ENGINEER'S REPORT TO DEPT. HEAD OF MACHINE CONDITION & RECOMMENDATION FOR REPAIR

To department head | Dept.

Machine name & No. | Equip. No.

Signed, maintenance engineer | Date

Item No. | Machine condition report | Correction | ✓ Item classification (Safety / Emergency repair / Engr. recommend'n)

ESTIMATED REPAIR COSTS

Cost distribution | Total item costs (All listed / Recommended)
- Material
- Labor
- Overhead
- Total

Engineer's remarks

DEPARTMENT HEAD DISPOSITION

✓ Approved item repairs | Remarks
- All
- Safety
- Emergency repair
- Engineer's recommendation
- Other (see remarks)
- None (see remarks)
- Repair order issued

Signature | Date

INSTRUCTIONS: MAINTENANCE ENGINEER send copies 1 & 2 to head of dept where machine is located. Retain copy 3 for follow-up file. Refer to Ind Eng Procedure, filed under Machine Shop, number 7, for instructions. DEPT HEAD indicate approved repairs in check boxes. Use Remarks box to request additional information, instructions, etc. Return original copy to Maintenance Engineer, with repair order, if issued.

Courtesy: Belden Manufacturing Company

problem is threefold — what lubricant to use, where to use it, and how often. The large oil companies try to find scientific answers to these three questions, and they use their findings to aid their present customers and to attract new ones. The plan is a salesmanship device, but at the same time, to be successful it has to come up with the right answers.

For small concerns, the oil companies are ready to make lubrication surveys of machinery and equipment for the purpose of recommending the proper oils and greases for machine parts and for setting up lubrication schedules. The simple plan provides a sticker for the machine, noting the kind of lubricant or grease to be used, where it is to be applied, and how often, with parallel columns for "when" and "done" and the operator's initials. When the concern is large enough to employ lubrication specialists, it prefers to make its own analyses and thus feel freer in the choice of lubricants. Whether the lubrication is done by a group of maintenance workers or by the machine operators, an initialed record fixes responsibility for failures.

Contract Maintenance

Maintenance by some outside agency or company is not infrequently provided for on an annual contract basis. A large foundry in Dayton, Ohio, for example, contracted for its electrical maintenance work. Its heating of metals to a liquid state, as well as other processes, required complicated electrical installations under dangerous conditions. The practice is similar to the renting of machines and automotive equipment from concerns specializing in the business. For maintenance work, specialists in particular fields are "rented" under contract to do a special line of work for the maintenance department. Although the savings are greater in large concerns, smaller companies can also use such services to advantage. Occasionally, all of a company's maintenance work is let out under contract.

Maintenance contract work may also include periodic overhaul of the equipment covered by the contract. Such services are particularly advantageous in those cases where the overhaul loads occur at regular intervals. Contract maintenance is also advisable in cases where the maintenance department suffers from poor management. If the company interested in contracting its maintenance services has reasonable cost records for maintenance, it is easy to compare them with contracting estimates. The question of quality and service is more important, especially for companies which have suffered from delays in production because of inferior maintenance.

Maintenance Controls

The maintenance department should compile monthly and semiannual control reports for top management. Such reports are, of course, valuable for the chief of the department as a basis for his planning and corrective action. They should include the following:

1. Schedule of inspections, showing the times scheduled and times when the inspections were completed, as well as those not completed, with the reasons
2. Cost estimates of scheduled jobs, and the actual cost
3. Breakdowns, with their causes, results, and recommendations
4. Detailed report of production hours lost

These reports should be sent to the engineering department, the executive responsible for maintenance control, and the controller if there is such an officer.

The semi-annual report should be in the nature of a review of the maintenance job.[4] It should include suggestions for altering processes and designs, improved plans for overhauls and periodic replacements of machines and equipment, and shifts to different makes or types of equipment, all for the purpose of reducing maintenance costs.

These control reports must be based on departmental paper work and a comprehensive control board similar to those used in production. The control board shows what is going on in the shop, and furnishes a primary check for seeing that assignments are completed on schedule. The chief of maintenance should have summary progress reports on all jobs at stated intervals, preferably weekly. Investigations of holdups may show that the crews need prodding or that the workload is too heavy for the number of employees.

In approving a completed job, it is suggested that the following questions be asked to stimulate progressive maintenance:

Have you replaced all safety guards?
What was the cause of the repair?
What do you suggest to prevent recurrence?
What changes in methods, tools, or materials would you make if you were doing this job all over again?[5]

Work authorization, cost estimates, and job specifications form the primary controls. The maintenance budget is an over-all control that can be effective in provoking thoughtful consideration of important jobs that must be done and in pointing up their relation to company policies. The budget is a natural check on the department's total operations and a test of its knowledge of maintenance work.

---

[4] "The Preventive Maintenance Program," by Kenneth H. McBrady, in *Factory Management & Maintenance* for January, 1959, p. 63.
[5] Carl G. Wyder, "Keep Your Plant Up, Keep Your Costs Down," *Factory Management and Maintenance*, Vol. 108 (January 1950), p. 62.

Training for Maintenance Work

Training for maintenance work is not only largely neglected, but where it is done, it is done poorly. Even craftsmen need special training for applications of their skills to maintenance. Done properly, training always shows distinct benefits by improving employee morale and reducing employee turnover. Both results save money for the employer.

The three important factors in training maintenance workers are the training locale, the equipment used, and the trainers. It is very seldom that all three are satisfactorily provided for in maintenance training programs. Since maintenance is called for all through the plant, that is one of the important areas where training should take place. Certain types of work must be done in the maintenance shop, and that is the other place where training should take place. Maintenance equipment is not rated so important as production machines in most industries, so maintenance equipment is often of poor quality and out of date. And yet first-class maintenance jobs require the best available equipment. Such equipment saves time and money, and encourages the workers. Since maintenance includes a number of skills, an over-all trainer is unsatisfactory. The answer is particular training assignments filled by qualified shop-men skilled in the various trades covered by maintenance. Such men are not easy to find, but it is the responsibility of the chief to find them and prepare them for training new recruits. It has been suggested that the World-War-II technique known as "Job Instruction Training" is probably the best plan for such maintenance trainer training. It is also suggested that considerable assistance can be obtained from company vendors for certain jobs. One thing seems certain — maintenance training cannot be assigned to the personnel department.

Maintenance Management

The first step in the management of maintenance is the planning, scheduling, and dispatching of the workload. The schedule adopted for preventive maintenance is the first step in this direction. All maintenance work cannot be planned, but when most of it is, the difficulty in taking care of emergencies is proportionately decreased. Preventive maintenance can be planned on a long-term schedule. All except emergency maintenance can be planned on a weekly or daily basis, and most of the maintenance crew should know their assignments the day before, at the latest. Emergency problems can be taken care of by drawing crew members from routine jobs where they can be spared.

As far as possible, maintenance work should be done without interfering with regular operations or production. When this is not possible, some workers are being paid for idle time. It is often possible to do preventive work on machines when they are normally idle. Some maintenance work can be done at night in plants having a one-shift operation. When plants shut down for vacation periods, over-all maintenance jobs have a clear field.

Another production-saving idea is to have duplicates of important equipment for installation while regular pieces are being serviced. The faulty machine can be taken to the maintenance shop where a better, faster, and cheaper job can often be done. One company has its glass furnaces on rails so that they can be transferred to a central relining station and another towed into operating position over the same rail.

Standard-practice instructions should be provided for the installation and maintenance of all major pieces of equipment. The maintenance department should always be on the lookout for possible improvements in methods, both in its own work and for production in general. In repairing a machine, the maintenance worker can often see ways in which improvements in design or operation will reduce both maintenance and production costs. Such suggestions can then be incorporated in the standard-practice instructions.

Cost estimates for maintenance aid in controlling the work. When the estimates show a wide variance from the actual costs, management has a right to question the reason. This procedure spurs maintenance to improve its methods and make a closer study of its operations and expenses. Careful cost estimates are indispensable to a satisfactory crew job, and furthermore, the crew will have a sense of personal satisfaction when it meets or beats the estimate. Time estimates are an important phase of costs; for control purposes, they should be broken down for all crafts working on a job.

Approval of the maintenance chief should be obtained for scheduling rush jobs. In this way, he will be responsible for investigating every call upon maintenance, and those departments demanding unnecessary preferential treatment can be kept in line. It is also good practice to schedule in advance only those jobs which have fixed completion dates. Under this procedure, other jobs of non-emergency character can be performed during dull periods, thus promoting a more even workload. No maintenance job should be scheduled until the dispatcher is assured that the special tools and materials are available. A final suggestion for maintenance planning is the daily conference of maintenance supervisors for the purpose of revising schedules and discussing new problems.

Conclusions

As new techniques are applied in the maintenance field, the "blind spot" idea will disappear. How soon it will happen is the challenging question. Because maintenance is closely related to productivity, safety, and profits, it should be receiving more attention from top management and will as its true significance is realized.

Important items for future attention in the maintenance field are time and process standards, better planning and scheduling for its long-term activities, and improved controls. The maintenance budget tends to furnish poorer controls than those for most other departments. When maintenance wants to make a "favorable" budgetary impression, it cuts expenditure estimates below a practical minimum. The result is that while maintenance costs go down, production costs go up. A proper system of accounting will show realistic maintenance costs before budgets are finally adopted, and those costs should be used to guard against maintenance's predilection to submit budgetary boasts to management. Another way to inject realism into the maintenance budget is to require that it show estimates for each operating department separately.

A few simple rules will help management improve the maintenance function:

1. Establish a record of all items that require maintenance, and note their condition periodically.
2. Maintain a work-order system that permits adequate control.
3. Schedule lubrication on a standard-time basis, and then make spot inspections.
4. Plan a full days' work for each mechanic, and postpone the less essential work in favor of emergency jobs.
5. Record all costs by job order and each piece of equipment worked on.
6. Plan stockroom inventory on the basis of experience, and make changes dictated by new experiences.
7. Pay wages and salaries that will attract the most competent workers; cheap workers are expensive on the maintenance crew.
8. Arouse and maintain top-management interest through reports which give facts and which interpret them, especially from the standpoint of costs and potential savings.
9. Provide maintenance with better tools and equipment.

QUESTIONS

1. What is the relation of maintenance costs to net profits?
2. How will increased automation affect maintenance costs?
3. To what extent can pay incentives be applied to maintenance work for the purpose of reducing costs?
4. What types of work are included in the typical maintenance schedule?
5. What criteria would you use for determining the reasonableness of maintenance costs?
6. If, as alleged, records are essential to effective maintenance, what types of records would you compile for that purpose?
7. To what extent, if any, can staff service be made advantageous to maintenance work? Cite some examples.
8. In what ways can a dispatcher's contribution to maintenance affect profits?

9. Under what circumstances should the maintenance function be decentralized?

10. What is considered the absolute essential for profitable preventive maintenance?

11. How can the best inspection timing be determined for preventive maintenance? How is flexibility of inspection timing determined?

12. What rules would you establish for determining responsibility for maintenance work orders?

13. If proper lubrication of machines and equipment is so important to proper maintenance, what plan would you use for determining the kinds and timing of lubrications, and the responsibility for their application?

14. Under what circumstances and in what types of maintenance should maintenance work be contracted out to specialists?

15. What plans would you outline for establishing effective control of maintenance?

16. How can a typical control board be used to expedite and balance maintenance activities?

17. Where would you recruit the various types of mechanics for maintenance work, and what supplementary training, if any, would you require?

18. How can planning, scheduling and dispatching be used in the management of the maintenance function?

19. Under what circumstances do you feel that duplicate machines and equipment would be profitable in aiding the maintenance activity? How would such duplicate machines be used to accomplish the intended purpose?

20. When should repairs to equipment and machines be charged to capital accounts? Such charges naturally reduce the maintenance budget.

CASE PROBLEM
Lucas Boat Builders

The Lucas Boat Builders produce various types of pleasure craft, some of the smaller sizes being made for stock during the slow production periods. Boats costing over $1000 are all custom-made to individual orders. The company also builds a standard marine engine in three small sizes. Engines for the larger craft are bought ready to install. The company employs 760, the majority of whom are skilled mechanics.

Lucas has been catering to the southeastern pleasure-boat demands for twenty-five years and making excellent profits, especially on its custom-built boats. The business started in the small-boat line, which it still sells through wholesale sporting-goods channels. During the first ten years of its history, the company was compelled to specialize on this type of craft because of the large capital requirements demanded by the longer construction periods of the more expensive boats.

With its machine tools for making engines, a complete line of woodworking machinery, and the expensive special equipment used in boatbuilding, the company has about one million dollars invested in its machinery-and-equipment account.

There is no fixed policy governing the replacement or addition of machinery. Standard equipment is replaced when the engineering department agrees with a foreman or shop superintendent that the costs of maintaining and operating it are becoming prohibitive. New types of machines are purchased as additions and substitutes whenever engineering's written analysis demonstrates the need for them or the savings to be effected. The company does not have a specific allowance for machines and equipment in its budget, but charges the cost of such items to the several depreciation reserves provided for that purpose.

The maintenance department reports to engineering, which sets up the paper records for its guidance. Foreman can request maintenance to make repairs to machines when the cost is estimated to be less than $25. Actual costs are checked against the foremen's estimates by the engineering department. Repairs costing from $25 to $250 are requested by one of the superintendents of the twelve "shops" and ordered done by engineering after a substantiating survey. Amounts over $250, which usually involve replacements, are submitted to the vice-president in charge of production.

Repair and maintenance costs are kept on a "shop" basis and reported to the accounting department in separate amounts for labor and materials. Maintenance is accounted for on a "shop" basis because the shop superintendents work on an incentive system which considers standard operating costs as part of the formula.

During the past year, the vice-president of production has been complaining about maintenance costs. The chief engineer blames the superintendent of maintenance, who contends that his authority is so curtailed by engineering that he cannot install the procedures which he has repeatedly recommended to his chief. The latter claims that the maintenance superintendent is not cooperative and makes no effort to improve his work or reduce its costs.

The maintenance superintendent prepared a written report of complaints and recommendations for his superior, the chief of engineering, and sent a copy to the vice-president in charge of production. It summarizes the situation as follows:

1. Ninety per cent of the engineering department's orders for repairs are marked "rush," making it practically impossible for maintenance to schedule its own work.

2. Engineering does not cooperate in allowing maintenance to keep on hand a reasonable supply of stock parts.

3. Engineering maintains supervision of machine lubrication, but does not exercise proper controls, thereby creating unnecessary maintenance costs.

4. Most of the machine downtime could be avoided by having one each of six different standard machines for replacements while repairs are being made.

5. Foremen should have authority to order repairs up to $50, thereby saving downtime and repair costs.

6. Individual records should be kept on most of the machines as an aid in deciding what makes to buy for replacements.

7. Foremen should be given monthly records showing the exact cost of keeping their various machines in repair.

8. Maintenance should have a budget allowance for labor and material expense so that it has an official target to work toward.

9. Maintenance should report to the vice-president in charge of production and be given an opportunity to work out the procedures for its operations without daily interference in details.

PROBLEM: If you were vice-president of the Lucas concern, what would you do to solve the maintenance problem? Would it make any difference to you that the maintenance superintendent did not send his report to the vice-president through the channel of the engineering department? If you were assuming control of the maintenance department as vice-president of production, what instructions would you give the maintenance superintendent in view of his recommendations?

16

Methods and

Time Study

Stop-watch time study was first developed by F. W. Taylor in 1881. Although many refinements have been made in the past fifteen years, even in the early days Taylor analyzed and improved operation methods before attempting to establish standard times by stop watch. For many years after 1881, both organized labor and management opposed the new standard times techniques and their findings. Today, however, although a few labor leaders still condemn the practice, it is generally accepted as beneficial and far superior to the former rule-of-thumb methods for fixing workers' production capacities and their wages. Ralph M. Barnes, a recognized specialist in this field, estimates that currently about 70 per cent of manufacturers are using time standards.

Methods and time study are the foundation for effective business operations and industrial productivity, as well as the basis for sound wage policies. They can also be used to improve employee relations and cost controls. The study and improvement of methods as a background for making standard-time measurements involve an examination of the operator's motions, the condition and operation of his machine, the suitability of the materials being used, and the workplace. The workplace layout is particularly important for assembly operations. The general environmental situation must also be considered for establishing standard working conditions with respect to sanitation, lighting, ventilation, temperature, and other conditions. Standard times are not possible with nonstandard methods and working conditions. Since standard times are the basis for scheduled production and most incentive plans, the conditions requisite for proper timing are essential.

After determining the best methods for accomplishing the work as well as the proper quality of materials, the proper machine adjustment, and the workplace layout most helpful to the worker, the improved situation should

309

be standardized under those conditions. Only after the worker has been instructed and is reasonably experienced under the improved conditions should the timing of actual operations start.

Advantages of methods and time study

Methods and time study are the fundamental tools of management for the following purposes:

1. Analyzing manual motions and machine operations for the purpose of increasing productivity and decreasing costs
2. Fixing standard operation times for incentive wages
3. Establishing production quotas for hourly rated employees
4. Balancing the work force with the volume of work
5. Determining plant and machine capacities
6. Aiding in the purchase of new equipment
7. Improving tools, dies, jigs, fixtures, and equipment
8. Improving the quality of the work
9. Reducing worker fatigue

Improving Operations. Operations can be improved by analysis and study of the motions of the machine operator or assembly worker for the purpose of eliminating false or fatiguing motions by balancing and re-arranging the sequence of his movements so that he accomplishes better work faster and with less fatigue. The improvement of the machine's operation is often accomplished by changing its speed. Any improvement in method reduces production costs.

Standard Times. Standard times are necessary for setting reasonable piece rates or any type of incentive wage. They may be determined purely on the basis of experience, but that method is in no sense scientific, since it may be based on erroneous data. Standard times are also used to determine production quotas for hourly-rated employees. For this use, they are frequently slowed somewhat to insure the quality production which hourly rates emphasize.

Balanced Work Force. It is only through the establishment of standard operating times that management can determine the number of workers necessary to accomplish a given workload. The number of workers sets the standard for the number of machines and equipment required, as well as the quantity of materials and supplies. Balance in operators and equipment is essential for planning a balanced operation or production program. Finally, plant capacity as determined through the use of standard operating times is essential in fixing sales quotas for which delivery promises can be maintained.

Buying New Equipment. Skilled method and time-study engineers, by cooperating with the maintenance department, are in a position to offer valuable suggestions for the purchase of new machines and equipment. In their study of present machines, they obtain ideas about what changes will increase productivity and reduce unit costs.

Quality Production. Methods engineers also appreciates the relation between proper materials and the production of quality work — an important form of insurance against the inroads of competition. Quality results from proper materials, adequate machines, and skilled workers. The methods engineer is conversant with all three of these essentials, and is in position to pass on his findings to top management and the production department, thus assuring the turnout of quality merchandise.

Worker Fatigue. There are two kinds of fatigue. One is the healthy variety which results from pleasant and effective work. In this case, energy is recouped through rest and sleep. The other kind of fatigue comes from lack of harmony in body and mind at the workplace. Here, energy is not entirely recouped by rest: fatigue can accumulate to the detriment of both the worker and his production. Proper body motions on the job aid the worker in changing from the unhealthy to the healthy fatigue. Standard times and well-distributed workloads, together with proper environmental conditions, improve the worker's mental reactions on the job and stimulate healthy fatigue.

Development of methods and time study

The first book on time study in the United States was written in 1920 by Dwight V. Merrick, a time-study man who worked with F. W. Taylor. The techniques for determining standard operating times have made substantial progress during the past forty years. First known simply as "time study," the plan later added the dimension of "motion study." The title then became "time and motion study," showing the historical development of the subject, but probably used in this sequence for euphony.

Later, because motion study preceded the taking of times, the title was changed to "motion and time study." And finally, as the study of operator motions was expanded to include the machine, materials, workplace, and the general working environment, the subject came to be known as "methods and time study." These changes indicate how the field has developed.

Although time studies were made in England and France prior to 1920, Taylor's work in this field (starting at the Midvale Steel Company in 1881) developed more detail by breaking down operations into motions and elements. An *element* is the smallest number of motions than can be practically isolated and for which dependable elapsed times can be recorded.

Frank B. Gilbreth and his wife subsequently developed many of the improved techniques now in general use in the study of machine- and assembly-operator motions. They classified hand motions under seventeen fundamental types, now known as "therbligs," a word coined from spelling Gilbreth backwards. Figure 16.1 shows the hand-motion symbols developed by the Gilbreths.

Many changes and improvements in methods and time study have developed from discussions and papers read before the Society for the

Figure 16.1

Standard Symbols and Colors for Fundamental Hand Motions

Name of Symbol	Therblig Symbol		Explanation-suggested by	Color	Color Symbol	Dixon Pencil Number	Eagle Pencil Number
Search	Sh	⟂	Eye turned as if searching	Black		331	747
Select	St	→	Reaching for object	Gray, light		399	734½
Grasp	G	∩	Hand open for grasping object	Lake red		369	744
Transport empty	T E	⌣	Empty hand	Olive green		391	739½
Transport loaded	T L	⌣	A hand with something in it	Green		375	738
Hold	H	⌂	Magnet holding iron bar	Gold ochre		388	736½
Release load	RL	⌒	Dropping content out of hand	Carmine red		370	745
Position	P	9	Object being placed by hand	Blue		376	741
Pre-position	P P	8	A nine-pin which is set up in a bowling alley	Sky-blue		394	740½
Inspect	I	○	Magnifying lens	Burnt ochre		398	745½
Assemble	A	#	Several things put together	Violet, heavy		377	742
Disassemble	D A	⧺	One part of an assembly removed	Violet, light		377	742
Use	U	U	Word "Use"	Purple		396	742½
Unavoidable delay	U D	⌒o	Man bumping his nose, unintentionally	Yellow ochre		373	736
Avoidable delay	A D	⌞o	Man lying down on job voluntarily	Lemon yellow		374	735
Plan	Pn	⌐	Man with his fingers at his brow thinking	Brown		378	746
Rest for overcoming fatigue	R	⌐	Man seated as if resting	Orange		372	737

Reprinted from Ralph M. Barnes, Motion and Time Study *(New York: John Wiley & Sons, Inc., 1953) with permission of author and publisher.*

Figure 16.2

Normal and Maximum Working Areas for the Two Hands

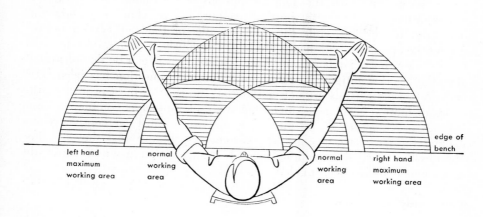

Advancement of Management (successor to the Taylor Society), the American Management Association, and others.

Methods analysis

The time-study engineer does not make his analysis of methods and motions haphazardly. He is concerned with the performance of the human body, arrangements and conditions of the workplace, design of tools and equipment, and correct procedures for analysis. Many principles and corollaries of motion economy have evolved for finding the best methods of gaining rhythm, maximum performance, automaticity, minimum fatigue, and proper motion sequence. Even the location of tools and materials is important for promoting proper sequence of worker motions. A semi-circular workbench is usually provided for assembly operations where the prepositioned tools and materials are arranged in an arc within the normal reach of both hands. Figure 16.2 shows the normal and maximum working areas for the hands.

Charting the study

Since it is important to study the operation from an over-all point of view, a process chart is used to plot or picture the progress of the worker, the materials, and the paper forms through the office or plant. The purpose of analyzing the chart is to reduce the distance and travel time of the worker and materials by establishing improved and systematic procedures through study of existing methods. (See Figures 31.1 and 31.2 in Chapter 31).

A further analysis of operations can be obtained by an operation chart, also known as the "right-and-left-hand" or "simo" chart. The simo chart registers simultaneously the detailed motions of both hands at all stages of an operation, together with the times required. The chart may show that one hand is working while the other is idle, or that for certain periods during the operation both hands are idle. Obviously, maximum productivity results when both hands are employed constantly. It can be demonstrated, also, that worker fatigue is minimized when this condition has been satisfied. When both hands are not working all the time or most of it, the principles of motion economy — including such alterations as combining, eliminating, or changing the sequence of motions — must be considered for making the necessary changes and corrections. Figure 16.3 shows a simo chart with recorded operations for a bolt-and-washer assembly after the improvements have been made.

Time study equipment

The essential tools for time-study work include a stop watch, time-study observations sheets, and a clip-board to hold the watch and sheets. Holding the board on his left arm, with left hand at the watch control, the time-study man has his right hand free for recording the observations. Most time studies are made with the decimal minute watch on which the large dial is divided into hundredth parts of a minute, with its hand making one revolution per minute. The small dial shows runs up to thirty minutes.

Either the snap-back or continuous method may be used in making stop-watch studies. The continuous method allows the watch to run throughout the study, making it necessary to subtract successive readings to get element times. However, this methods avoids numerous watch manipulations. The snap-back method permits the entry of element times directly on the observation sheet without the subtractions. All information relating to the time study is recorded on the observation sheet, including such items as the date, department, operator, timer, the element being timed, and remarks by the timer. Observation-sheet information is not only vital to the answer sought for the element involved, but it can be very important at a later time in defending the answer with union representatives. Figure 16.4 shows the timing board with stop watch and typical time-study sheet attached.

When it is necessary to time elements of short duration, the stop watch may not be so reliable as some other timing device. If the element runs for .01 of a minute or less, it can be timed more accurately by the Marsto-Chron machine. Another device, the wink counter, makes accurate readings to .005 of a minute.

Preliminary steps in time siudy

Methods or time study should not be undertaken except with the com-

Figure 16.3 315

Simo Chart for Bolt and Washer Assembly
After Improvements Have Been Made

MICROMOTION STUDY

SIMO CHART

PART Bolt and Washer Assembly—Improved Method   DEPARTMENT AY16 FILM NO. X75
OPERATION Assemble 3 washers on bolt   OP. NO. A32
OPERATOR M.S. Bowen   1C4327   DATE 2-11-37   MADE BY S.R.M.   SHEET NO. 1   OF 1

DESCRIPTION LEFT HAND	THERBLIG SYMBOL	TIME	TIME IN 2000THS OF A MIN.	TIME	THERB. G SYMBOL	DESCRIPTION RIGHT HAND
Reaches for rubber washer	TE	10		10	TE	Reaches for rubber washer
Selects and grasps washer	St G	1		1	St G	Selects and grasps washer
Slides washer to fixture	TL	13		13	TL	Slides washer to fixture
Positions washer in fixture and releases	P RL	14		14	P RL	Positions washer in fixture and releases
Reaches for steel washer	TE	12		12	TE	Reaches for steel washer
Selects and grasps washer	St G	1		1	St G	Selects and grasps washer
Slides washer to fixture	TL	17		17	TL	Slides washer to fixture
Positions washer in fixture and releases	P RL	13		13	P RL	Positions washer in fixture and releases
Reaches for lock washer	TE	12		12	TE	Reaches for lock washer
Selects and grasps washer	St G	1		1	St G	Selects and grasps washer
Slides washer to fixture	TL	14		14	TL	Slides washer to fixture
Positions washer in fixture and releases	P RL	8		8	P RL	Positions washer in fixture and releases
Reaches for bolt	TE	10		10	TE	Reaches for bolt
Selects and grasps bolt	St G	10		10	St G	Selects and grasps bolt
Carries bolt to fixture	TL	12		12	TL	Carries bolt to fixture
Positions bolt	P	8		8	P	Positions bolt
Inserts bolt through washer	A	48		48	A	Inserts bolt through washer
Withdraws assembly	DA	3		3	DA	Withdraws assembly
Carries assembly to top of chute	TL	10		10	TL	Carries assembly to top of chute
Releases assembly	RL	1		1	RL	Releases assembly

Reprinted from Ralph M. Barnes, Motion and Time Study *(New York: John Wiley & Sons, Inc., 1953) with permission of author and publisher.*

plete understanding and cooperation of top management. As a technical device, it should be accepted throughout the organization by foremen, union leaders, and workers before operations are begun. Standard times are not always accurate, otherwise time-study engineers could not find different answers to the same problem. This weakness of the technique should be frankly conceded. But it should also be emphasized that the timers have professional reputations at stakes and are honestly interested in being as objective as possible.

Figure 16.4

Timing Board with Stop Watch and Time-Study Sheet Attached

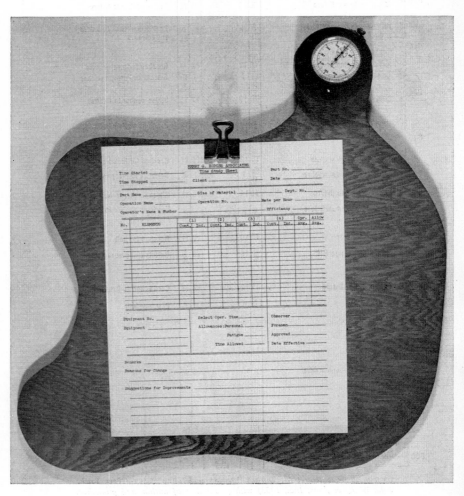

The initial study in a plant or office should be made where there has been trouble about the pay or amount of work expected. Under such conditions, both sides are receptive for an outsider's opinion. When the operation has been selected, the work should not start until the foreman and the worker to be studied are both cooperative and, if possible, also interested. At the start of the timing, an effort should be made to put the operator at ease. He should be told to work at his normal pace and forget that he is being timed. An uncooperative operator may try to make slow times for the benefit of his "brothers." On the other hand, another operator may try to see how fast he can work. It is possible to correct both of these abnormal times, but better results are obtained from the worker who can and does maintain his normal pace.

Since operators vary in skill, effort, consistency, speed, and other factors, the one to be used for the study should be chosen from a group having more than one worker on the same operation. Management may want one of the fastest workers timed, hoping thereby to influence other workers to use his methods. Labor may object, feeling that all workers will be expected to maintain the pace of the "fireball." Many engineers favor timing the above-average worker because his speed is usually more consistent and his motions are better coordinated. The person most often selected for the study approximates a normally skilled operator, working at a normal pace under approved and standardize working conditions.

The human factor in the time study is naturally important. After the foreman has selected the employee whom he considers a normal worker, the question of that employee's willingness to cooperate must be considered. If the first few minutes of operation show that he is consciously slowing down, it is customary for the time-study man to suggest that he is "probably not up to snuff today," and to excuse him until "some other day" which may never come.

As already noted, all necessary information such as the names of the operator, the operation, department, machine, parts, fixtures, and other items is recorded on the observation sheet. Occasionally, a drawing of some piece of equipment and of the work performed on it is included. It is also well to sketch the workplace, with significant dimensions indicated.

Steps in time study

1. *Methods improvement.* The first task of the time study engineer is to make an analysis of the operation for the purpose of improving the methods by which it is performed. There may be suggestions for changes in equipment or the layout of the workplace. Such changes should be discussed with the worker's supervisor and, after mutual agreement, the worker's cooperation should be solicited by asking for further suggestions. When

the feasible changes have been made, the time-study man may then determine the operating elements to be timed.

2. *Operation data.* Detailed information concerning working conditions and the methods of operation, including the equipment, tools, gauges, machine speeds, and workplace, should be recorded on the observation sheet. Comments about the working environment are also helpful. This information is particularly useful for developing standard-time data. It is also important if retiming is requested by the union because of changes in any of the essential conditions under which the original timing was made.

3. *Element determination.* The operation is broken down into "elements" which consist of two or more motions. The more care used in determining the elements, the more useful the time study. We have already considered the operator's motions as analyzed by the Gilbreths. An element is the smallest division of an operation that can be timed with reasonable precision. The beginning and end of an element are readily determined by an experienced timer, whose reflex observations are vital to the timing process. A description of the start and finish of each element is helpful in analyzing these basic divisions of accomplishment. The element terminals serve as a tool for over-all motion study since each element is a combination of motions which are definitely recognizable.

Each element must be measured often enough to provide a truly representative time figure. There is also the question about which, if any, timings are to be disregarded. It must not be thought that all abnormal times should be eliminated. The nature of the job may be responsible for occasional longer times. For example, drilling on a hard casting may require more time, and this should be recorded, possibly with an explanation. On the other hand, abnormal timings resultings from an error in reading the stopwatch or from a piece sticking in a die would be eliminated.

4. *Operating observations.* This step refers to the recorded observations of the time-study engineer regarding items that may be helpful in determining final times, or that may be useful in making suggestions for improvements to upper management or the supervisor. They may include personal observations regarding the operator and various delays observed (avoidable or unavoidable) with explanations.

5. *Analysis of the record.* Exceptional time readings, with explanations as to why they have been retained or eliminated, are made a part of the record. It is from an analysis of this record that the standard times are fixed. The method of their computation will be explained presently.

6. *Development of allowances.* Time allowances are added to the stopwatch times for such factors as personal needs, fatigue, and unavoidable delays due to faulty equipment or materials. Allowance for personal need is usually an arbitrary amount such as 3 or 5 per cent of the recorded time. Fatigue allowance depends on the nature of the operation, usually figured as a percentage of the calculated time value. If machine downtime allow-

ances are used, they are figured on the basis of experience. Material shortages or defective portions are usually cared for as they occur by allowing an hourly rate for the time lost by the operator.

7. *Computing the time.* Once sufficient timings of an element have been recorded, there are several methods for determining the value to be assigned to the element. The *average time value* (arithmetic mean or, simply, mean) for an element is computed by adding the readings which have been retained and dividing the total time by the number of readings. Since average time is based on all acceptable readings, its value can be substantially influenced up or down by the high or low readings. This fact may lead to some subjective eliminations of the extreme readings.

The influence of extreme readings is automatically eliminated when the *median value* is used as the computed answer. Since the median is the middle value of an array of numbers, it is a positional measure on which the high and low readings have no effect. Table 16.1 illustrates the median for Element X, where the middlemost value lies between 5 and 6. Since both 5 and 6 have a value of .12, the reading 5.5 will also have the value of .12.

The *modal value* (mode), or the most frequent reading, can also be determined for Element X from Table 16.1. Since .12 appears four times, and no other reading appears more than twice, it is by definition the mode.[1] High and low readings influence the mode only when the addition or deletion of such a reading causes a change in the most frequently recorded time.

8. *Rating and leveling.* Workers classified as good, excellent, and supreme take less time to perform a given element since they work with greater skill

Table 16.1

Computation of the Median for Element X

Readings		Values
1		.09
2		.10
3		.11
4		.12
5	MEDIAN	.12
6		.12
7		.12
8		.14
9		.14
10		.15

[1] The values of the average, median, and mode may be different, but it is possible for any two, or all of them, to be the same.

and speed, and perhaps with better-directed effort than the average worker. The workers who are classified as fair, poor, and failing spend more time on the same element because of less skill, and perhaps less effort, than the average worker. It has already been pointed out that in establishing a standard time, the attempt is made to study the "average" man while he is working at his "normal" speed. However, this is an ideal which can only be approximated in practice. Even if the time-study man could select the "average" worker with complete precision, the problem would still remain whether he was giving his "normal" performance at the time of the study.

For this reason, every time study involves a subjective judgment on the part of the time-study man; he must form an opinion as to how nearly average the worker and the performance under consideration may be. This judgment is known as *rating* the worker. The time-study man must then make a correction in his recorded times in terms of this rating in order to arrive at the standard time. This process of correction is known as *leveling*.

Human Variability

It can be seen from the normal or bell-shaped curve of worker variability in Figure 16.5 that the spread is in terms of standard deviations around the arithmetic mean M. Since standard operation times are used in setting up incentive wage plans, a knowledge of the distribution of work productivity is useful in adjusting such wage plans to management wage policies. In adjusting the technical standard to management policy, it may be decided that a "tight" (fast time) standard, with a high premium for attainment, will urge the workers with mediocre ability to meet the standard.

The opposite view holds that unless the technical time standard is adjusted upward (slow time) with relatively low premium pay so that more than the majority of workers can meet it, discouragement will soon prevent their trying. These two time plans, faster and slower than the technical standard, usually result in similar unit labor costs. The difference is mostly one of psychology in deciding which plan will result in greater effort on the part of the largest number of workers. The answer may well differ under various sets of circumstances.

Although the highest point (M) on the normal curve fixes average worker performance (around which the greatest number of workers will be found) it is important to note that worker performance will vary within the approximate range of six standard deviations, three above and three below the average M, or when looking at the normal curve figure, three to the right of M and three to the left of it. The standard deviation is the statistician's method of showing the spread of the number of items (in this case, workers) above or below the arithmetic mean, which refers to those between selected points on the horizontal axis. For example, if productivity is plotted on the horizontal axis, and the number of workers on the vertical axis, the

Figure 16.5

Worker Variability

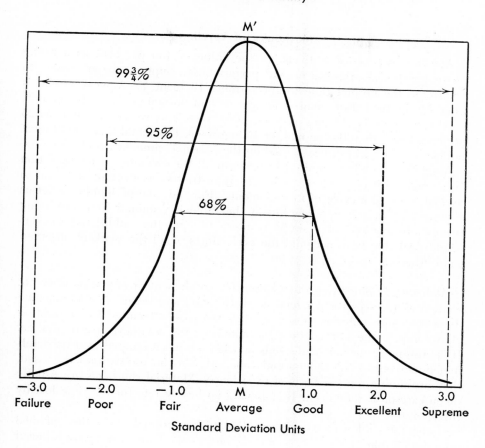

study of a large number of workers performing a given operation would probably show that half of them were above average in performance and the other half below average.

Most of the workers would be close to the average, with slightly more than two-thirds found within one standard deviation above or below M. The area between the arrowheads in the figure is approximately two-thirds of the total area under the curve and, hence, represents two-thirds of the workers. This group will vary from "fair" through "average" to "good," while those workers who fall between one and two standard deviations from the mean will be classified as either "poor" or "excellent." This entire group, from "poor" through "excellent," will include 95 per cent of the workers under normal conditions. The area from three standard deviations below the mean to three above will include practically all the workers from "failure" to "supreme" classifications.[2]

Mechanics of Leveling

A common practice is to assign the value of 100 per cent as a *rating factor* for the hypothetical normal performance. Suppose we are trying to determine the normal time for performing Element Y. A worker who is rated by the time-study man at 125 per cent of normal performs Element Y, on the average, in .12 of a minute. Now since this worker is rated as 25 per cent faster than the normal, or 100 per cent, the actual time of .12 must be increased by 25 per cent to obtain the "normal" time, or .15 of a minute.

A *cycle* is the time required to perform all the elements of an operation on a single unit of product. Table 16.2 illustrates the leveling of actual to normal times in a cycle of four elements. For the sake of simplicity, let us assume that each watch reading in the table is obtained from averaging twenty observations of a single worker. (In practice, additional workers would probably be timed and the cycle times of all the workers observed would then be averaged.)

Allowances. Since the normal time for an element or operation does not contain allowances for personal needs, fatigue, and delays due to machine downtime and material shortages, they must be accounted for by adding allowances to the normal time for obtaining the standard operation time. It is customary for personal needs and fatigue to be lumped as a predetermined percentage of the normal time. If machine downtimes are used, they are figured on the basis of experience. Material shortages are usually taken care of as they occur by allowing an hourly rate for the time lost by the operator.

If the total allowance to be applied to the normal cycle time of 4.63 minutes (Table 16.2) is 10 per cent, one method for calculating allowed time is to multiply the normal cycle time by 1.10 to determine the total standard time. Multiplying the production-cycle time of 4.63 minutes by 1.10 gives the standard time in this case as 5.09 minutes.

Before the time-study man leaves his job, he should go over his work with the foreman to make certain that they are in agreement, and the foreman should be given a copy of the observation sheet. It is not satisfactory to make a time study one day and leave it the next. The study should follow through, possibly for several weeks, to make sure that the work has been done adequately.

[2] There is only a slight possibility that a worker will fall above or below the range of six standard deviations, but this does sometimes happen. Notice that the tails of the normal curve shown in Figure 16.5 never quite touch the base line.

Table 16.2

Leveling for a Cycle of Four Elements

Element	Watch Reading (Minutes)	Rating of Time-Study man (per cent)	Allowed Normal Time (100%)[3]
A	.98	150	1.47
B	.32	125	.40
C	1.88	75	1.41
D	1.00	135	1.35
		Cycle Time	4.63

[3] *The time that an average operator would require to do the job if he worked at normal speed.*

Standard Element Times

If all the different elements that have been studied for a given work classification were correctly recorded, standard time data could be developed for use on the same elements appearing in subsequent operations. Such a possibility has encouraged several groups to work toward such an objective. Time study cannot be really scientific until it develops measurement standards capable of serving as controls. But standardizing the methods used in a given work classification is necessary before standard-element-time data can be accepted for practical use in various operations including the same element. To the extent that this goal can be attained, it will be possible to use standard elements synthetically. Such standardized elements are referred to as *synthetic times* when used in an operation different from the one for which they were originally timed.

In using synthetic times, it is necessary to analyze the motions involved in the supposedly same motion of the new operation. If some additional or new motion appears in the element contemplated for use as a synthetic time, it is really a different element, and the new or different motion must be timed to prevent the use of an elemental time that is either too tight or too loose. Standard data derived from numerous observations and adjusted to normal times are necessarily costly. To the extent that such standard times are correct, however, they can be used over and over in many different operations, making the initial cost well worthwhile in the long run.

The best-known attempt to develop standard data, known as "Methods-Time-Measurement" and referred to as MTM, was started about 1948 by the Methods Engineering Council in Pittsburgh. By 1960, it was reported to have over one hundred users, among them some well-known national concerns. At the same time, some specialists in the field of time study have referred to MTM as merely wishful thinking as far as its attempt to make any general application of synthetic times is concerned. The purpose of MTM is to get rid of the subjective element in time study and, through the use of predetermined elemental times, to eliminate criticism of the timer. The approach, as its title signifies, is to establish standardized element times in the field of motions through intensive research. It is necessary, therefore, to be sure that the elemental time being used synthetically is characterized by identical methods throughout the industry before it can be accepted as the established MTM standard. The motions used in the studied element are highly significant. If one or more of the motions used differ in an operation including a supposedly identical element, the standard is not applicable. But, say the critics of MTM, it is unusual that where two plants perform the same or smilar operations, these operations should contain elements composed of methods and motions exactly the same as those of the standard. Theoretically, therefore, the "same" element in the operation of a different company would have to be stop-watch timed.

Because of its emphasis on methods and motions, MTM does promote improvement in these areas. In this respect, there is a distinct contribution to the use of standard times. The MTM standards are established only after many months of research, yet the proponents of MTM are not smugly satisfied with their results. They openly admit that considerable research will be necessary before universally satisfactory results are attained.

Conclusions

Time study has been condemned, and questioned, and eventually praised by both management and labor. Combined with methods study, it has amply proved its effectiveness in operation. Qualified methods-and-time-study engineers have demonstrated to business and industry how an analysis of methods and proper element times will more than pay for their costs. Labor's desire for better working conditions and properly determined incentive plans rests upon techniques that have been proved by experience.

To provide ever-increasing confidence in standard times, the engineer should go over his work with the operator's supervisor before he leaves the job. They should reach an agreement before the results are finally compiled, and the supervisor should be given a copy of the observation sheet. Great advances have been made in objectivity, but the problem will not be solved until improved data make it possible for two or more time-study men to arrive at equal time values under a given set of circumstances.

Methods and time study are not completely scientific, but the trained and experienced judgment of qualified observers is fairly reliable. Their analyses have given both management and labor an opportunity for improving their respective expectations. It will help in the future if the approach taken with the worker is to explain methods and time studies as a way of lessening his fatigue by planning easier ways to do his job.

Much of the earlier opposition to time study can be traced to the manner in which the studies were formerly conducted. It was not only a question of what was done, but also how it was done. Stories of a man of mystery suddenly appearing in the plant without explanations to the workers are all too true. Management wondered how an outsider could improve production times and methods when the foremen with years of experience had not been able to do so. Labor was justifiably suspicious of a technical device which it did not understand. In addition, management occasionally tightened times which had been technically determined, in collusion with the timers, to reduce unit labor costs unfairly.

General acceptance of methods and time study by organized labor is achieved today through frank discussions with management. In addition, trained labor representatives are now frequently participating in the determination of standard times. Current acceptance is based on management's feeling that standard times reduce costs and increase productivity and labor's belief that through methods improvement the job is made easier, and that honest standard times permit the worker to increase his earnings. We shall return to this subject in Chapter 22 when we come to discuss labor's attitudes toward various wage plans.

QUESTIONS

1. To what extent have management and organized labor agreed in their reactions to methods and time study?
2. What steps should be taken in the improvement of methods before taking standard time measurements?
3. The text lists nine advantages of methods and time study; how many of them can you recall?
4. What is the relation between measured time study and the establishment of a balanced work force?
5. How can time studies establish reasonable piece rates?
6. Define the word "element" as used in time studies.
7. How is the process chart used in methods-and-time-study work? What is the purpose of the simo chart in these studies?
8. Why is it advisable to time elements of comparatively short duration?
9. What justification would you give for studying the operations of a "fireball" in arriving at standard times?
10. What relation does the selection of elements have to the quality of the resulting time study?
11. Would you recommend fatigue allowance in time-study work if you knew that the employer provided for rest periods twice a day? Why?
12. How does the median value influence the high and low stop-watch values in time-study work?
13. Why must "rating" precede "leveling" for obtaining standard times?

14. Do you prefer tight times and high premium pay or loose times with more liberal premium payments? Support your opinion.

15. How is the rating of an operator obtained in relation to the standard?

16. What is the relation between a cycle and an operation?

17. How are synthetic times used in time study?

18. How can skilled methods-and-time-study engineers aid in buying better equipment in cooperation with the maintenance department?

19. What is the meaning of a "therblig," and how are they used in determining the proper elements to be used in time study?

20. For what purpose is the Marsto-Chron machine used in time-study work?

CASE PROBLEM

FRANKLIN TOY COMPANY

Most large and medium-sized plants rely on methods and time-study engineers to analyze repetitive jobs and set standards of production. In smaller plants, however, although the work may be less repetitive, the need for setting operation-time standards remains and must be taken care of by some member of management, or the owner if a specialist is considered too expensive. Such was the case with the Franklin Toy Company, where the responsibility was undertaken by the owner and manager, Robert Franklin.

Mr. Franklin was an interested student of business conditions, and felt that unless he was able either to increase sales or lower unit costs, he would be forced to lay off some of his men. The firm employed five production operators who did the identical work of cutting out, assembling, and painting wooden toys. Although the quantity and quality of the materials, as well as the working conditions, were fairly well standardized, Mr. Franklin noticed that some of the toys were better assembled and painted than others, and that while some of the operators worked at an apparently normal speed, others seemed to be unnecessarily slow. He realized that if a worker turned out fifty of a given toy in a week, for $100, the unit labor cost was $2.00. If another turned out forty of these same toys in a week, for $100, then the unit cost was $2.50. In order to determine how many toys each of the five men was making, he kept a record of their production on the two types (A and B) of toys being manufactured that week, with the following results:

Number of Toys of Either Type Produced per Day

Day	Bruton A	Bruton B	O'Connell A	O'Connell B	Mathews A	Mathews B	Pafko A	Pafko B	Logan A	Logan B
Monday	4	4	3	3	4	4	2	3	2	2
Tuesday	4	5	2	3	5	4	2	3	2	2
Wednesday	6	6	6	5	5	4	4	3	3	2
Thursday	7	6	5	4	5	5	4	3	4	3
Friday	4	4	6	6	3	4	4	4	3	2

The data show that Bruton produced the most and Logan the least, but Mr. Franklin wanted to know the number which should be produced in a week by a normal worker. To get more information on the subject, he decided to work for a week in the shop under the same conditions as his five workers and on the same toys. The results were as follows:

	Franklin	
	A	B
Monday	5	5
Tuesday	6	5
Wednesday	6	6
Thursday	6	5
Friday	5	5

Mr. Franklin was a skilled worker in this trade before starting his own business, and he realized that few employees would produce with the same interest as the owner-manager. He also realized that if the standard were set too high, his men would become discouraged, and that if it were set too low, the chance of improving performance would be very slim.

PROBLEM: Should the weekly production standards for Toys A and B be set at 28 and 26 respectively? If not, should the standard weekly production rate be set at 19.8 for Toy A, and 18.8 for Toy B, representing the simple average produced by the five operators for the week's work recorded by Mr. Franklin? If the standards for the production of Toys A and B should be some figure different from those mentioned above, what should they be, and why?

17
Quality Control

Quality control is the term used to express the enlarged scope of the inspection department. The function of inspection has always been to pass on the acceptance of materials and parts; the new idea encompasses taking positive action to assure product quality. The causes for rejects are now analyzed so that a system can be established for warning of unacceptable items as they are being processed. American business has been conscious of the value of assured quality for a long time, but modern conditions of production and consumption demand new ideas in the quality field. When small producers depended on skilled artisans, pride in workmanship assured quality products. As production demands mounted and an ever-increasing division of labor took place, the quality of the finished product required different kinds of controls.

The problem of matching the control of quality with expanding production and the fragmentizing of skills finally led to the formation of the American Society for Quality Control. It is industry's incessant demand for high productivity, proper quality, and minimum costs that acts as a constant stimulant to finding greater assurances of quality control.

Some of the causes behind a more scientific approach to quality control include the following:[1]

1. The rise of specialization
2. Mass machine production of goods and services
3. Means for measuring physical and chemical properties
4. The concept of interchangeable parts
5. Development of new precision industries
6. The flow of goods among industries, with ever-widening separation of designers, process engineers, operators, and inspectors

[1] J. M. Juran, "The Economics of Quality," *Quality Control Handbook* (McGraw-Hill Book Company, Inc., 1951), p. 5.

Objectives of quality control

There are at least three primary objectives of quality control. The *first* is to separate the satisfactory items or tasks from those which are unsatisfactory. This elementary purpose stems from the realization that no machine or individual ever produces two pieces or accomplishes two tasks that are alike. It is necessary, therefore, to have a control process important enough to give rise to scientific inspection as a separate function in industry. Industrial inspection must maintain the quality of the outgoing product at the standard fixed by the specifications, however simple they may be. As we shall see, it is not necessary that all pieces shall be identical. The necessity for "exactness" is usually a practical matter depending on the intended use of the parts or product. Whatever variations are allowable without destroying the intended use are expressed as plus or minus quantities of some measurement or quality standard. In other words, quality control must maintain the allowed quality variations that are set forth in the specifications.

The *second* objective of quality control, after defective items have been separated, is to determine which defectives can be reworked or salvaged at reasonable cost, and which must be disposed of as scrap.

The *third* and most important objective is to evaluate the processes of production. If too many defectives are being made, Inspection notifies the person authorized to find out why and to remedy the cause. There are many causes for defective items. Some of the most obvious are a run of poor materials, a machine which has lost its adjustment, or a careless operator.

Another plan for classifying the objectives of quality control is in terms of the things to be inspected. In industry, they may include anything from the raw materials to machines and tools, chemical and heat-treating processes, packaging, gauges of all kinds, and salvage operations. Quality control is by no means restricted, however, to manufacturing establishments, although it was here that scientific inspection techniques were first developed. In the nonproduction businesses, inspection has also become a significant aid in evaluating and controlling the quality of services rendered. In all lines of business and industry, quality control is continually used to ensure customer satisfaction.

Quality standards

For purposes of inspection, the "quality" of a product refers to that quality or degree of accuracy, within prescribed limits of allowable variation, required by a set of specifications or instructions. The variation works both ways. For example, to use materials of a higher quality than is specified for a particular job is an unnecessary expense, and, of course, materials falling below the quality standard are equally unacceptable. If quality standards are properly set, compliance with them will turn out a product or service acceptable for the prescribed purpose — no better and no worse.

There is the further problem of who should be responsible for setting the quality standards. It is customary for production standards to be set by conference among the sales, design, and manufacturing departments. Under this plan, the role of inspection is to see that the standards are met. If, as occasionally happens, the inspection department sets the standards, it is in the position of passing judgment on its own work, which is not a healthy control situation.

It must be realized that quality is always relative to some norm. Specifications of quality represent the ideal, usually with allowable variations. How close quality control should adhere to the ideal is well expressed as that amount of variation in the desired characteristics which is as narrow as possible within practical and economical limits.

Specifications

Standards are set forth in specifications. Specifications for products or instructions for services define the quality for the purpose intended. The purpose of inspection is to determine whether or not the product or service is satisfactory according to the specifications set or for the purpose intended.

In this connection, it is pertinent to observe that occasionally those responsible for determining the specifications "play safe" by making the requirements more rigorous than necessary. For example, postwar investigations showed that many items rejected because of "tight" specifications were actually usable. Unnecessarily tight specifications always lead to higher prices both in wartime and in peacetime, but the fault is doubly serious during a war when useless rejections leave the fighting forces in short supply. Most specifications are made by engineers, and it has been their professional habit to demand tight tolerances. Engineers should follow the physicians' practice of consulting with other members of their profession when accurate diagnoses and prescriptions are needed, so that critical and costly items will not be made inordinately expensive and "acceptable rejects" will be given proper consideration.

Specifications present several important inspection questions:

1. Do they set up proper inspection requirements?
2. Which operations are important for inspection?
3. Are specified tolerances and other requirements necessary?
4. Will greater tolerances be satisfactory and less costly?
5. Will new processes improve quality?
6. Do inspectors understand the specifications?

Quality control is made less effective when the specifications are so drawn as to make inspection difficult. Some types of inspection depend of necessity on personal judgment. Taste, odor, and color are examples of difficult qualities to inspect with objective precision. When products can be specified by standard grades, inspection is easier and more objective. Cocoa, for example, is specified by country of origin, and some metals are specified on the basis of their alloys. The engineering test for performance is sometimes specified. When this is possible, quality control is more likely to be satisfactory. Unnecessary precision carries a high price when performance is satisfactory without it.

Inspection

The inspection process

Inspection involves two important considerations: one is planning, and the other is cooperation. Irrespective of when, how, or where the inspection is made, it should be planned so as not to interefere with production. It should act as an auxiliary to maximum productivity. Planning provides for the expeditious transfer of inspected items from one operation to another. Plans for handling defective items must also provide for their prompt removal to the place where they are either salvaged for reworking or consigned to the scrap section for disposal.

Every effort should be made for close cooperation between those engaged in inspection and production. Although it may not always be within the power of Inspection to guarantee the cooperation of its personnel with machine operators, nevertheless inspectors should be instructed to take the initiative in achieving harmonious relations.

Extent of inspection

The extent of inspection depends on the circumstances and should be determined by common sense. Expensive or crucial items should have carefully supervised inspection during the production processes. The same is true when the product concerned is being made by skilled labor. If, on the other hand, the item is being made on automatic machines, inspection may be reduced once the item is coming off the machines in a satisfactory condition. Under such circumstances, the inspections may be made at continually greater intervals in the process as long as quality standards are maintained.

There can be too many inspections as well as too few. Unnecessary inspections may slow production, and too few may result in too many rejects. In either case, the cost of production is higher than it should be. A continuous process of perfect production is impossible, so the decision must be to do whatever is necessary to maintain the required quality standards.

Types of inspection

The two chief types of inspection are remedial and preventive. The purpose of *remedial inspection* is to sort the acceptable items or services from the defective. The purposes of *preventive inspection* are to determine the causes of the defective results and to correct them.

These two types are not mutually exclusive. It is true that a repetitive kind of remedial inspection, performed by semiskilled operators, is not likely to result in suggestions for product or service improvements. Or, again, it would scarcely be economical to have top-flight inspectors slipping bolts into a gauge for eight hours a day in a routine process of sorting out acceptable items from rejects when their time might be better spent in a preventive inspection program seeking the causes of rejects. But as we shall see in the next section, preventive inspection can be remedial, and a good remedial inspection program should be alert to sources of defects which might be eliminated in the operating departments.

How to Inspect

There are several standard methods of inspection, some of which include both the remedial and preventive approaches. The four most important methods are known as sorting, sampling, statistical quality control, and engineering. Each of these will be considered in detail.

Sorting Inspection. Sorting, or 100-per cent inspection is the separation of all defective items from any lot. It was used originally to detect defects in handmade products. Even now, expensive or vitally important machine-made items may be inspected on a 100-per cent basis. The tendency, however, is definitely away from this method of inspection. It is unnecessarily expensive in many cases, is naturally slow, and not always reliable. It is the type of job that customarily requires close attention more than skill because of the many adequate tools used in the inspection processes. Because the inspector's job is not found in the high wage brackets, mediocre personnel tend to be recruited for the job. Finally, because the job is monotonous, fatigue tends to lower dependability of results. Routine sorting inspection gives reasonable assurance of high outgoing quality only at excessive costs.

Sampling Inspection. To understand why the cost of 100-per cent inspection is frequently excessive, consider the case of a manufactured product which is produced quickly and cheaply to be sold in bulk. Let us take, for example, two-inch finished nails which have a retail value of twenty cents a pound, with roughly one hundred nails to the pound. Obviously, if every one of these nails is to be individually inspected for such characteristics as proper length and absence of burrs, it is going to cost the manufacturer more to inspect the nails than to produce them. Such a situation is intolerable because inspection does not create quality; it merely aids in controlling it.

This kind of situation arises frequently in industry not only in the manufacture of cheap finished goods for bulk sale, but just as often in the production of component parts. The manufacturer wants some way to guarantee reasonably high quality in his product without resorting to 100-per cent inspection. He wants some method by which he can decide either to accept or reject a lot of a given product by inspecting only a *sample* from each lot.

In earlier times, the typical manager probably based his sampling inspection on a rule of thumb: "Try out a few items from each lot. If the items you select look pretty good, accept the whole lot. If there seem to be quite a few defective items in the sample, reject the lot." Such a system might work out very well in practice, or it might not. The inspector, for example, might not be using a large enough sample to give a reliable picture of the lot. Or again, he might be getting just as good results by using a sample one-half or one-quarter as large. The weakness of this approach lies in the fact that when a sampling system is not derived from mathematical laws of statistical inference, there is no way of knowing how large or how small a sample can tell you about the mass of items from which it is drawn.

As soon as a quality-control program turns from sorting to sampling, a number of questions arise and demand to be answered if the sampling system is going to be of any use at all. How large should the lots of items be? Given the lot size, how large a sample from each lot should be inspected? Finally, once the lot and sample sizes are determined, what is the criterion for accepting or rejecting a given lot? For example, if there are one hundred items in a lot and a sample of ten is inspected, how many defectives can be allowed in that sample? If one item out of the ten is defective, should the whole lot be rejected? Or should the lot be rejected only if two or more, or three or more, items are defective?

It was to provide reliable answers to questions such as these that the scientific method of acceptance sampling was worked out by Dodge and Romig at the Bell Telephone Laboratories over thirty years ago.[2] Other plans, such as the Military Standard 105–A and "Sampling Inspection" as

---

[2] Harold F. Dodge and Harry G. Romig, "A Method of Sampling Inspection," *The Bell System Technical Journal* (October, 1929) p. 628. An elaboration of this article by the same authors is *Sampling Inspection Tables* (New York: John Wiley & Sons, Inc., 1944). No attempt will be made here and in the following section on statistical quality control to give a mathematical presentation of the statistics involved. The discussion focuses instead on the applications of statistical method and on the kind of inferences which statistics permits. The student who is interested in the underlying mathematics will find a simple and excellent presentation in Norbert L. Enrick, *Quality Control* (2nd ed.; New York: The Industrial Press, 1954).

developed by the Statistical Research Group at Columbia University, have subsequently been devised and put into practice. The present discussion centers around the Dodge-Romig system, which is in widespread use today among all kinds of industries where sampling inspection is needed.

Acceptance sampling is based on the laws of probability. Ideally, we should like to know everything there is to know about the quality of a lot of items from the evidence of a sample. But the only way to do this with certainty is to inspect each item in the lot. If there is only one defective bolt in a lot of 1000 bolts, there is always that one chance in a thousand that we should not discover it until after we had inspected the other 999. Probability sampling represents a compromise. It does not tell us how many defectives there will be in any given lot of items. It does tell us, however, that if we inspect a great many lots, with a fixed sampling plan and with a specified criterion of acceptability (for example, a manufacturer may decide to call a keg of 10,000 nails acceptable if not more than 3 per cent of them are defective), then x per cent of the time (let us say 95 times out of 100) a lot that passes the sampling test will be "acceptable" by the definition agreed on, and only 5 per cent of the time will unacceptable lots be getting by.

Notice that this process of acceptance sampling leaves two important decisions up to the manufacturer or whoever is responsible for setting standards of acceptability. He must decide (1) what proportion of a lot of items can be defective and still be considered acceptable, and (2) what proportion of the time he can allow an "unacceptable" lot to get by the inspection station. Obviously, the answer to these two questions will vary with the value of the item itself or with its importance in a production process. There are many instances in which the savings to be gained in the inspectors' time make it more economical to allow a relatively high proportion of defectives to get by. But the important point to be made here — what distinguishes scientific sampling from rule-of-thumb methods — is that once the standards of quality have been decided upon, the manufacturer can read from the Dodge-Romig tables the proper lot and sample size, and the number of defectives allowable within the sample to be reasonably sure that for x per cent of the time, only acceptable lots will pass inspection and unacceptable ones will be rejected.

As soon as a sampling plan has been adopted, quality control must see that it is adhered to. The plan may be to reject a lot if three or more of a sample of fifteen items are defective. If an inspector finds three defectives but decides that the whole lot "looks pretty good," draws a new sample in which there are only one or two defectives, and thus accepts the lot, eventually a much larger proportion of unacceptable lots is going to get through, and, furthermore, there will no longer be any way of estimating how many bad lots are slipping by.

Another important caution is that acceptance sampling demands that the sample be a random one. If an inspector always picks up the first ten items of a lot, he may be consistently rejecting lots that are really acceptable. Perhaps in this case the machine-operator who makes the items takes a few minutes to "warm up" each morning and, after turning out four or five defectives at the start, goes on to produce hundreds of perfect items for the rest of the day.[3]

Acceptance sampling, as we have just described it, is a form of remedial inspection. If the program is well supervised, then roughly the same proportion of unacceptable lots is always going to get *by* the inspector. However, the ratio of acceptable to unacceptable lots turned up at the inspection station may vary a great deal. When the sources of defects in the items are not random, one should expect a rise in the number of lots being rejected, and this — as in any inspection program — is the warning signal for quality control to seek out these sources of error and suggest remedies to eliminate them.

Statistical Quality Control. Statistical quality control is a form of preventive inspection. Its purpose is to observe and record all variations from fixed standards of quality in the hope of discovering the causes of undesirable variations and eliminating them. In statistical control, "quality" refers to those characteristics of an item which can be measured in accordance with a set of specifications. The specifications will include not only the ideal, but the range of allowable variations about the ideal. In production, quality may refer to a number of characteristics such as kind of material used, size, color, strength, weight, and a great many others. The degree of quality necessary varies with the nature of the product. An automobile-engine piston, for example, requires more exact adherence to the specified norms than a lawn sprinkler. The allowable tolerance will be greater for the sprinkler.

A simple form of *control chart* is shown in Figure 17.1. For concreteness, let us say that this is a chart illustrating successive inspections of brass joints coming off the same machine. The specified diameter of these joints is one inch. In Figure 17.1, a *solid* line is drawn across the chart at 1.00, representing the specification line (SL). Let us say further that the specifications have set .06 of an inch as the amount of allowable variation. Thus, counting off six hundredth-inch units from either side of the SL, we draw a *dotted* line across the chart at 1.06 to show the upper specification limit (USL) and another one at .94 for the lower specification limit (LSL). The circles represent the diameters of joints selected for inspection at half-hour

---

[3] At the same time, in dealing with machine-made items, it is important to inspect an initial short run to be sure that the machine is properly adjusted. If machine-made items are inspected during operations, at relatively short intervals in the beginning, and found satisfactory, then the length of the interval may be gradually increased as long as the product continues to be satisfactory.

Figure 17.1

Statistical Control Chart

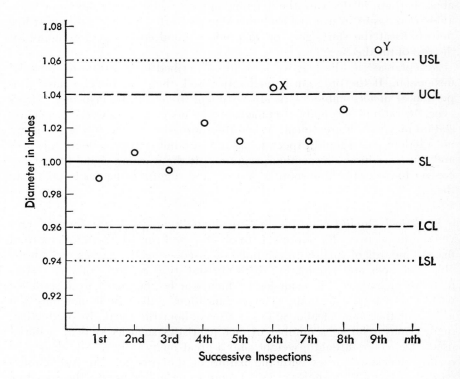

Successive Inspections

intervals.[4] In this case, of the nine joints inspected, only one (Y) falls outside the specification limits, its diameter being slightly over 1.06 inches.

Falling between the specification line and the upper and lower specification limits are two *dashed* lines, called the upper control limit (UCL) and lower control limit (LCL). It will be noticed that these are only .04 of an inch away from the SL. In other words, for control purposes the diameters must fall within a narrower range than that set by the specification limits. Whenever a measurement falls beyond the control limits — even if it is acceptable as measured by the specification limits — the control man is warned that here is a situation that must be investigated.

The variation that occurs between the UCL and the LCL is generally of the type referred to as *chance* or *random* variation. For each deviation from the norm (in this case, the SL of 1.00 inch), there is always some reason; but when these deviations all cluster about the norm and, hence, all the

[4] More typically in practice, each circle would represent the *average* diameter of an inspection sample of from three to five joints.

336

items are acceptable, it is not worth the time and effort to seek out those reasons. On the other hand, measurements falling beyond the control limits are thought of as variation due to *assignable causes.* They indicate that the situation is very close to getting out of control and serve as a signal for the control specialist to halt the production process and find out what is causing the deviation.

It will be seen that this is a form of *preventive* quality control, because the warning signals go up while the variation is still contained within the specification limits. Thus, the situation illustrated in Figure 17.1 is one that should almost never occur in practice. For when the control man finds that the sixth measurement (X) has passed the control limits, he will stop the machinist then and there and find out what is causing such a large upward deviation from the norm. If the source of the trouble is discovered and the situation remedied, then we should not expect to find measurement Y — three inspections later — not only falling outside the specification limits, but deviating also in the same direction as measurement X.

There is still another kind of information which a control chart can provide at a glance. This can best be shown by an illustration. Imagine that in Figure 17.1 the measurements X and Y are not out of control, but that both of them fall just below the UCL at 1.04. Now we have a picture in which all the variation lies between the control limits. There is no single measurement that will make the control man sit up and take notice. And yet of all the nine measurements, seven lie above the specification line and only two of them below. If the variation about the SL were perfectly random, we should always expect to find nearly the same number of measurements falling on either side of the SL. But the mathematical laws of probability tell us that there is only about one chance in ten that such a distribution as the one just illustrated is attributable to random factors alone. It looks more as if there were some consistent source of deviation. In this instance, it might be that the machine is slightly out of line so that the average joint coming off the machine is 1.02 inches.[5] Once again the control man is alerted, from the evidence of the control chart, to take remedial action before the situation is actually out of control.

The Statistical Tool. In the two examples just presented, the story is told by a mere glance at the chart: a measurement either lies within or without the control limits; the variation either is distributed evenly about the specification line or it is not. Simple as they may seem, both kinds of analysis are grounded in mathematical laws of statistical inference.

Nothing has been said as yet about how the upper and lower control limits are set. There is more than one accepted method of fixing these

[5] Strictly speaking, the variation about this new mean average may still be *random;* the important point for the control specialist here is that the *mean* measurement has shifted.

limits. One of the most common of these employs the standard deviation, a numerical measure of the average range of variation in any set of measurements. This statistic tells us that when all variation is random, approximately two-thirds of the measurements will lie between the area from one standard-deviation unit above to one unit below the average. Another 30 per cent of the cases will fall in the area between one and two standard-deviation units away from the average.[6] With this information at hand, the control man can fix control limits for a given process with a reasonable assurance of how often a measurement will fall outside the limits, if the variation is truly random. Let us say that the standard deviation of the distribution of measurements shown in Figure 17.1 is .02 of an inch. Then there are only about five chances in a hundred that a measurement will "normally" fall outside the UCL and the LCL, which are placed two standard-deviation units to either side of the average of 1.00 inch. Such a measurement as X in Figure 17.1 then would surely be warning enough that something should be looked into quickly before the process gets out of control.

A knowledge of the standard deviation is useful to the control specialist in other ways. For example, it might be found that the standard deviation for joint diameters coming from a machine supposedly identical with the one illustrated in Figure 17.1 was .04. This would mean that one-third of the joints could be expected to fall outside the control limits and would give ample indication that something was wrong — either with the machine, or the operator, or the materials used. Again, it might be found that the standard deviation of products from all the machines was so great that the specification limits were not likely to be met more than two-thirds of the time. Such a finding would suggest either a relaxing of the specifications or a complete revision of the production process.

The above examples give some idea of the use of the statistical method in quality control. Statistical analysis of the variations indicates whether or not they are large enough to be subjected to control by removal of the causes. In the absence of statistical control, this decision is made by the specialist in the production processes concerned. Statistical control substitutes an objective decision for the production specialist's subjective opinion. With the aid of statistical control, the person in charge of quality control should be able to reach his conclusions without specialized knowledge of the processes concerned. His objective conclusions are superior to the experienced judgments of the production specialist.

Control of quality by statistical methods is not only more dependable than the opinion of the production specialist, but it is also less expensive. After a manufacturing process has been brought under statistical control, there is less need for inspection, thus reducing costs and improving quality.

---

[6] This will be recognized as the "normal distribution," already described and illustrated in Chapter 16.

Furthermore, statistical quality control is frequently used as the basis for improving processes which the production specialist has accepted as satisfactory. It is also important to realize that the application of statistical controls to many processes can be handled by capable foremen after a reasonable amount of instruction.

Statistical Control in Nonproduction Businesses. Statistical quality control was first applied to the production of machine-made articles and is still used predominantly in that field. However, there is an expanding use of this method for controlling the quality of *methods* or *practices.* Statistical quality control has, for example, been applied with success to improving the quality of service in merchandising. A statistical analysis may be made of past merchandising errors in kinds, quality, color, and size. Customer-contact errors include such items as pricing, billing, and delivery, including delivery time. Statistical analysis points out the types of prevalent errors and the frequency of their occurrence; in some cases, even the cost of such errors may be calculated. Analysis leads to inquiry about the probable causes of errors and plans for their correction. Approached in this manner, the field for quality service control has wide application in wholesale and retail business management.

Statistical quality-control techniques have been applied with dispatch and profit to the operation of the mail-order section of a large store's dress department. In this case, the ratio of the section's overhead to sales led to a statistical analysis. The report showed the probable cause. Because the section manager was paid a base salary and a bonus figured on volume of sales, mail orders were not filled accurately. If the customer's color, size, or price was not available, the section manager used his judgment in filling the order, thus adding to his bonus volume. The method and extent of this practice were exposed by the analysis. The excessive overhead was caused by the large number of "merchandise returns." The remedy might be found in a new section manager or a new plan for figuring his bonus.

Use of Statistical Control. Adoption of statistical quality control has been slow among producers. The word "statistical" has set up a fearful hurdle which prevents many firms from even trying this technique. The statistical part of the method is overemphasized. Once the statistical design for analysis has been worked out, the analysis can be applied without a technical knowledge of the statistics that underlie the design. During the war, the federal government set up ten-day courses covering the subject.

Engineering Inspection. The term "engineering inspection" refers to the observation and testing of a product (or one of its components) in action to determine whether or not it will perform in accordance with the specifications for its operation. This is sometimes called the "use test." For example, the engineering inspection of an airplane ready for delivery to the military is made by representatives of the manufacturing company and the branch of service concerned in actual flight. The plane's general performance will be observed and all its equipment will be tried out before acceptance by the purchaser. Delco Products, a subsidiary of General Motors, makes the final or engineering test of its small motors in action. As each motor is finished on the assembly line, ready to move to the shipping department for packing, it is connected electrically and continues its journey in actual operation. If it fails to function properly, it is put to one side when it reaches the packing department.

Another phase of engineering inspection — a special case of the use test — is the "destruction test." An automobile tire may be run under simulated road conditions until it blows out. Load factors and simulated distance traveled are noted on dials and transferred automatically to charts. This type of inspection is a form of sampling. It would be unreasonable to destroy an entire lot to determine its qualifications in operation. On large items, this form of inspection becomes very expensive. For example, the Air Force, in its laboratory at the Wright-Patterson Air Force Base in Dayton, Ohio, performed a destruction test on many different aspects of a B–36. The purpose was to determine the capacity limits of the plane and its components under various conditions. It was assumed that the results obtained would apply to other planes of the same quality made by the same manufacturer.

Where and When to Inspect. Inspections can be made at inspection cribs away from the production floor or at designated stations on the production floor. Crib inspections are effective and quick because they can make use of superior equipment and a high degree of specialization, which makes it possible to use cheaper help. When it is necessary to have a controlled inspection atmosphere, crib inspections are best. Finally, inspection is easier to control in the cribs.

There are, however, disadvantages to crib inspections. Products must be taken from and returned to production centers, requiring larger inventories and added expense for material handling. When crib inspections are not made promptly, products pile up there with the possibility of creating production bottlenecks.

Floor inspections are of two types: at fixed stations or by roving inspectors. Fixed stations are located where important processes are going on, thereby reducing production costs by eliminating defectives before they accumulate. The inspector becomes efficient on highly repetitive operations. The disadvantage of the fixed station method is the possibility of favoritism developing toward some operators, especially if they are on a piecework basis. The roving inspector, on the other hand, must have a wide knowledge of the production processes and their quality requirements. Both fixed station and roving inspections permit uninterrupted production and require no material handling.

Inspection may also be done on a departmental basis by either the crib or floor plan. Departmental inspection is usually satisfactory, with the added advantage of allowing the work to be put on a competitive basis, with defectives serving as the evaluation criterion.

The chief factors that determine when to inspect are at the beginning of the production process, at points where failures would be costly, and when work is transferred from one department to another.

Tools for Quality Control

Early quality control was doubtless visual, a method still practiced by some businesses. In certain phases of sheet-steel production, it is the practiced eye that determines which sheets shall be marked with the stamp of approval. However, visual control of quality is rapidly giving way to inspection tools which have hastened and improved the process. A mere enumeration of some of the outstanding tools will serve to indicate the rapid progress being made in this field:

Go and no-go gauges	Photoelectric cell
Working gauge	Industrial X-ray
Master gauge	Thermocouple
Snap gauge	Stroboscope
Plug gauge	Induction gauge
Profile gauge	Photoelasticity
Electric eye	Reflectoscope
Micrometers	Multigauges

There is a growing group of automatic quality-control devices. The electric eye, for example, is used in production lines for rapid detection of defects. "The photoelectric cell has . . . been used to grade such products as beans, to sort raisins at the rate of 1,000 per minute, to select electric resistances, to control enamel thicknesses on wires, to check the level of the contents of a tank, to control the filling of bottles, and to locate fine cracks in metallic surfaces."[7]

The industrial X-ray has a wide range of testing uses. It is used in foundries to examine the quality of "test bars" drawn from a heat as well as for testing completed castings. These subsurface tests detect flaws which might not be known otherwise until the casting failed in use. Such testing is carried to great lengths on many kinds of airplane-engine castings. The thermocouple is another electrical device used to measure high temperatures. The stroboscope measures the deflections of rapidly moving particles.

[7] Lawrence L. Bethel and others, *Production Control* (New York: McGraw-Hill Book Co. Inc., 1942), p. 159.

Figure 17.2

Spectrographic Analysis of Metals

Courtesy: Electric Storage Battery Company

The supersonic reflectoscope tests metals and other materials by means of high-frequency vibrations. The advantage of this equipment is that it frequently eliminates the need for testing to destruction. The reflectoscope is reported to have located defects in forgings and castings up to ten feet in depth.

A recent development is the mechanically controlled multi-inspection gauge for testing a number of qualities almost simultaneously. Of one of these machines, the manufacturer writes: "At a speed of 3,000 plus per hour, this conveyor-fed multi-inspection gauge measures and sorts piston pins for hardness, triangular out-of-round, taper, and diameter along the full length of the work piece. The pins are automatically sorted into ten disposal units: out-of-round tolerance, .00005"; taper tolerance, .0001"; hardness, O.K. and bad; diameter, five groups of .0001" difference, plus over and under."[8]

Automated Quality Control. Recent developments in the automation of production processes will naturally lead to devices for the automatic control of quality. Faster production demands faster and more dependable quality control. Industry has been using automated tape control of the production processes for several years, so it is not unreasonable to look for a similar

[8] Federal Products Corporation, Providence, R.I.

approach to the quality process. It is also reasonable to expect that new forms of inspection and quality control will develop improved controls for maintaining quality standards. The new approach will simply follow further development in the field of tape control. When automated inspections are applied to sorting and sampling, costs will be reduced and dependability improved. The new processes will open the way for determining tolerances suitable to product uses. The new emphasis will lead to building quality control into automatic machines.[9]

Louis Polk, in "New Horizons in Inspection Techniques," explains that "elaborate inspection devices are assuming more and more of the part played by human senses. Electronic feedback circuits take information from sensing devices and send messages that control the position, speed, and operation of the tool performing the work. These gauges, electronic circuits, and tools are far faster and less subject to fatigue than human eyes, brains, and hands. The reliable automated machines improve quality and further the aim of quality control. Under automation, quality control thus becomes inherent in, or built into, the machines."[10]

Under its sixth Five-Year Plan, the leaders of the U.S.S.R. set up a

Figure 17.3

Snap Gauge

Courtesy: Federal Products Corporation

---

[9] For more detailed information, see "Automating the Quality Control Function" by W. S. Tandler, in American Management Association's Report No. 9 on the subject of "Quality Control in Action," 1958, pp. 99–104.

[10] *Ibid.*, p. 113.

Ministry of Instrument Construction and Means of Automation. This official action on the presidium level not only points up the international interest in electronic controls, but gives some indication of the rivalry that will take place in future trends in feedback control of quality.

Cost of quality control

It is difficult to obtain useful cost estimates of inspection or the broader area of quality control. If management were sufficiently interested in developing cost figures in this field, accuracy would demand their breakdown into the various types of inspections and products. For comparative purposes, costs based on sorting, sampling, and statistical controls would be enlightening. Inspection costs are usually considered as a part of factory overhead, or they are charged to direct or indirect labor. When the costs of inspection are segregated, it is customary to express them as a ratio to the hours required for production. Another plan is to compare the inspection payroll costs to the total payroll.

When various products require wide variations in the number of man-hours for inspection and control, serious attempts to control their costs would have to be on a product basis. A multiplicity of products makes it very difficult to establish standards for the various categories, and it is obvious that the quality control costs of a product mix provide no usable standard. Wide cost variations exist among different companies producing the same product. Under such circumstances, cost trends are the most useful criteria, whether they are compared to production costs or to some other function.

The high cost of making defectives will furnish the incentive to management to establish quality control in many concerns. Such a cost analysis points to money wasted in producing inferior results. This situation usually stems from an emphasis on segregating the defectives rather than preventing their manufacture early in the production process. In other words, there is too much inspection and not enough quality control. Too often, unnecessarily high rejection costs lead to increased inspection instead of to improved quality control. The emphasis should be on prevention through better control of the production processes. The preventive approach to quality control may mean new investments in more modern machines, gauges, and automatic inspection tools with built-in controls, but such improvements will more than pay their way in reduced production costs. It must be understood that no concern can "inspect quality into" its product.

Conclusions

Quality control, like modern procurement, increases productivity and profits. Since quality control creates costs that ordinarily cannot be recouped in selling prices, it is important that it not only be dependable, but that its costs be held to the minimum. Quality control costs will be reduced as new tools are used to replace manual inspections. The possibilities of automated tape control will be the outstanding achievement in the future.

What does management expect from quality control? Most importantly, it expects a new emphasis on the *prevention* of defectives. This emphasis must lead to increased quality control of the production processes. Reduction of inspection costs is another expectation of management. With improvements in this field, a new quality consciousness should develop among those engaged in industry and the services, from operators through all levels of management. Furthermore, better quality control of products will lead to more satisfactory relations with vendors as well as with customers.

Future writers will probably have much more to say about the quality control of services. This subject was not even considered until a few years ago, and probably is not yet discussed in textbooks.

Finally, in the fields of production and distribution, an improved cooperation must be developed between those who make, distribute, and service, on the one hand, and those who protect the quality of goods and services on the other. The line and staff services of these two factions will have to overcome some of their jealousies while we are waiting for automatic controls of quality. When top management realizes the profit possibilities that result from quality control, it will demand an improved cooperative spirit among the human factors involved.

QUESTIONS

1. What is the relation between quality control and inspection?
2. Name some of the factors that increased the attention to quality control in modern industry.
3. What are the three outstanding objectives of quality control?
4. What is the meaning of "quality" of materials or components as the term is used in manufacturing processes?
5. How do tight specifications increase costs?
6. What is the timing rule for inspection of work being done on automatic machines?
7. Why is the sorting method of inspection relatively undesirable?
8. For what purpose is the Dodge-Romig formula used?
9. Why does sampling inspection of machine-made items start with an initial short run rather than a random lot of the item?
10. What is meant by "allowable variations" in connection with statistical quality control — variations from what?
11. What type of quality variation is thought of as due to assignable causes?
12. What is the most commonly used method for determining the upper and lower control limits on the statistical quality control chart?

13. Why is it that the statistical control method of quality determination is often less expensive than the production specialist's opinion?

14. How can statistical quality control be used in a merchandising business?

15. How would you explain, in two words, the application of engineering inspection?

16. What is the relation between engineering inspection and the "destruction test"?

17. What are the disadvantages of crib inspections?

18. On what basis are locations of fixed inspection stations determined?

19. If we are ultimately successful in developing automated quality control, what will most likely be the fundamental approach?

20. How would you determine the quality control costs of a product mix?

CASE PROBLEM

PUTNAM TOOLS

Putnam Tools is a medium-sized privately owned company, founded by its present owner thirty years ago. Until five years ago, Roger Putnam supervised and controlled all phases of the business, including finance, production, and sales. He always felt that it should be his responsibility to coordinate activities while the business was small. Mr. Putnam was originally a toolmaker by trade, with three years' experience selling machine tools immediately prior to establishing his present business, which produces hand tools for machinists.

The tool line grew gradually with the concern until five years ago. Since that time, the business has grown very rapidly, and the line of tools has kept pace with the general expansion. At the time of the owner's semi-retirement in the midst of the expansion program, the organization was put on a more functional basis, with delegated authority fairly commensurate with the assigned responsibilities. That is, the treasurer now has complete charge of finances, the director of sales operates and controls his activity, and the superintendent of production has control of the production side of the business, including the engineering department.

The various activities are coordinated by a general manager, acting as assistant to Mr. Putnam.

The company has built a reputation for quality tools which was relatively easy when the employees numbered fewer than 25. At present, operations are largely on a production basis with 175 workers, most of whom are semiskilled machine operators. The jigs and fixtures for operations on the cheaper grades of tools are made by machinists. The company's line of gauges is made by highly skilled workers to precision specifications.

With the more elaborate line and production ten times greater than it was five years ago, difficulties are developing with inspection of products. Customer complaints have led to some friction within the management group concerning control of inspection. The *chief of production* maintains that all inspection should be under his direction and control. The *head of engineering* contends that inspection is a natural function of his activity. The *director of sales,* who feels a keen responsibility in the matter, wants a separate department for inspection, with its chief reporting to the general manager. The general manager, who is trying to resolve the difficulty, has an open mind about the matter, but is somewhat confused by the seemingly logical arguments of the three contenders.

In analyzing the situation for the general manager, the head of engineering has pointed out that the total line of products can actually be divided into three categories as far as the difficulty and care of inspection are concerned. Such items as hammer heads, cold chisels, and iron clamps do not have exacting measurement specifications. Their metal must be free of flaws, but that kind of inspection has always been made on a sample basis by engineering as the raw materials are received. A second group of products, such as dividers and calipers, require closer inspection to secure their accuracy in use. The third category would include the entire line of gauges and similar items which must be made to very close specifications and accuracy.

The general manager is impressed with this engineering analysis which appears entirely objective. In addition, he would like to be relieved of direct responsibility for the inspection activity which, he feels, is technical and represents a field in which he has had neither training nor experience. The *general manager* is inclined to have all inspection done by engineering, holding them directly responsible for the control of quality, while he reserves authority over engineering's administration and management of the function.

All four of the proposals have been submitted by the general manager to the interested group, requesting their choices in writing, together with reasons for their decisions. He also asks specifically for the reasons against his own proposal, as well as against the other plans which one of the sponsors must necessarily oppose.

PROBLEM: If the general manager called you in as a consultant on this organizational problem of the inspection function at Putnam Tools, which of the four plans would you favor, and why? If you have a suggestion different from all four plans submitted by the group, what is it, and why do you think it is superior?

18

Management and Control of Inventories

Inventory problems increase with the volume and complexity of a company's products. The fact that inventories — consisting of raw materials, work-in-process, finished products and supplies — range from 50 to 80 per cent of a concern's investment in plant and equipment is sufficient for visualizing the importance of inventory management and control. In spite of this financial importance, many companies still manage their inventory investment on a rule-of-thumb basis. This attitude can be explained only on the assumption that these concerns fail to see the profit possibilities in a scientific approach to inventory management. The same observation is true with respect to the procurement function, as will be pointed out in Chapter 28. In fact, procurement and inventories are so closely related that inventory control is often assigned to the procurement department.

The frequent failure to formulate adequate procedures for controlling inventories demonstrates that inventory control must be preceded by inventory management on a top level. Top management must furnish the policies and rules for guidance of the inventory control activity. That capable management should carry this responsibility is axiomatic, not only in the field of inventory control, but in many other fields as well.

The easy plan for managing inventory is to purchase replenishments when the supply is low or exhausted. The trouble with this plan is that management often makes decisions too late to avoid the possibility of serious consequences in the form of an operating loss. One of the prime essentials of successful inventory management is reliable forecasting of general business conditions and the condition of particular commodity markets. This is a difficult assignment because in addition to the variables involved, certain internal forces work against rational solutions even when they are patently obvious.

Two of these forces are the sales and the production departments. Sales is not only proverbially optimistic, but it has a natural penchant for attempting to be all things to all customers. These inclinations may lead to non-standard products as well as promises of immediate deliveries, both of which may involve unnecessarily large inventories. Production, on its part, has an uncanny urge for uninterrupted processing of raw materials. It is happy only when it sees huge piles of raw materials and components awaiting processing. These two despoilers of scientifically determined inventories are difficult to hold in check.

The obvious counteracting influence is that management must state a philosophy of inventory control and assure its enactment by establishing written policies and procedures for the guidance of those in charge. Management's inventory policies must have broad bases, free from the detailed reports of daily purchases and usage. Unless such bases are clear and workable, inventory management becomes embroiled in details that lead to defeat in the midst of confusion. In too many cases where there are no fundamental regulations, top management becomes suddenly upset when the treasurer reports financial difficulties. The chief executive may then come to grips with the situation by ordering all purchase requisitions to cross his desk before going to Procurement. His idea of control is to blue-pencil requests until enough cash is squeezed out of inventory to relieve company finances. This remedy may simply trade a sorry financial condition for an impossible production muddle, with consequent loss of profits.

Purposes of Inventory Management

Although we have been explaining the necessity for basic management policies in controlling inventories, it seems best to postpone consideration of the details of such policies until we have discussed their broad purposes. The chief purpose of management's control of inventories is to maintain the minimum investment in materials, components, and supplies that will ensure a steady flow of production and assembly, based on current and prospective sales.

There are several benefits resulting from a steady flow of production. One is customer satisfaction; another is steady employment. The concern's suppliers are favorably impressed when their orders are predictable. Continuous production also results in lower unit costs and a more rational purchasing program. When Procurement deals with positive knowledge of future requirements, it can buy to better advantage, and this in turn has a salutary effect on profits.

Although the functions of the inventory control section will vary with the type and size of the enterprise, the nature of its product, and its organizational structure, it may be responsible for any or all of the following activities:

1. Planning for a future period, based on the production cycle, sales, and market conditions, in order to maintain an adequate production program to meet sales obligations.
2. Translating inventory planning into a feasible purchasing program.
3. Receiving goods for stores inventory or for immediate transfer to production centers.
4. Inspecting quantities and condition of materials, and checking them against nontechnical specifications.
5. Storing and issuing raw materials, components, parts, supplies, and finished products.
6. Record-keeping for store items.
7. Supplying information for materials costing and other data used for the financial accounting of inventories.
8. Salvaging or scrapping and disposing of defective products.
9. Recommending items for standardization and substitution.

Inventory Problems

For general consideration, the National Industrial Conference Board reports four leading aspects of the inventory problem:[1]

1. Management's general dissatisfaction with inventory control.
2. Absence of guiding principles for inventory control.
3. Failure of small concerns to visualize inventory profits.
4. Complex control in some concerns, and none in others.

Details of the "inventory problem" are actually continuous because of the number of contributing factors, such as:

1. Changes in sales, production, and purchasing programs.
2. Inability to forecast business conditions accurately.
3. Desire of Production to "play safe" by hoarding.
4. Lack of established management policies.
5. Failure to deal with dependable suppliers.
6. Lack of product standardization.
7. Seasonal accumulation of inventories.
8. Tendency to depend too much on experience.
9. Failure to make use of research analysis.

Excessive and inadequate inventories are both costly. Unnecessary investment in inventories reduces profits; inadequate inventories may halt production, and so lose customers as well as profits.

Inventory Policies

Management policies should fix standards for the operation of inventory control. Like all standards, those used to guide inventory personnel must

[1] Summarized from "Inventory Management in Industry" by Carl G. Baumes, as a section of *Studies in Business Policy*, No. 88 (1958), p. 6.

possess a certain flexibility, making them adaptable to specific situations. In fact, inventory policies must be even more flexible than the average. They should also be subjected to frequent general review as markets and company products change.

Establishing optimum inventory levels for individual types of materials, as well as the total inventory investment, presents a particularly interesting challenge to management when they attempt to determine standards. For items used repetitively, the problem is relatively simple except for the possibilities of changes due to style or product differences. For repetitive items, it is adequate for top management policy to stipulate standard maximum and minimum quantities. Similarly, plans can be formulated for fixing the number of days' supply to be carried for important commodities.

At the other end of the commodity scale, the "sensitive" items which are subject to rapid price changes rarely lend themselves to standard quantity purchases. The policy most frequently enacted in the case of this group provides for inventory decisions to be made by a committee representing Sales, Production, Engineering, and Finance. This committee may employ a market analyst on a full-time basis. An alternate plan is to place responsibility in the hands of a member of management or an outside specialist who is recognized as a leader in a particular commodity field.

Management may also require periodic reports on a total inventory basis, showing the ratio of inventory investment to sales. This approach involves consideration of the inventory turnover, which is a pertinent factor in making profits. Such reports may also cover turnover on an individual commodity basis, thus drawing attention to possibilities of obsolescence. As a general rule, management will allow liberal inventories on a low-value commodity. Quantity discounts allowed by suppliers also affect inventory decisions.

Work-in-process usually demands close attention by management, and this normally leads to consideration of the production cycle. Short-cycle production is less risky from the investment standpoint because of the rapid use of materials. Larger stocks are, therefore, carried under this production plan. Finally, management's chief guide for all stock levels must be based on realistic sales and commodity forecasting.

Inventory Control Factors

The elementary factors used for control of inventories are:

1. Classification of inventory items.
2. Proper arrangement of storage facilities.
3. Perpetual inventory records.
4. Adequate cost system geared to company policy.
5. Records of inactive, obsolete, and damaged items.

These five elements of material control can be summarized as: classification, planned storage, perpetual inventory, costing, and reporting of items requiring the attention of top management. The other functions of stores can be thought of as service rather than control activities.

The Aeroquip Corporation, with two plants in Jackson, Michigan, one in Van Wert, Ohio, and one in Burbank, California, centralizes its inventory records daily at the home office in Jackson by using electronic equipment. Reports compiled during the night at the four plants are available at the start of the following day in the inventory control section. The reports emphasize exceptional items that will require the attention of management. Aeroquip states that the new system enables it to reduce inventories, give better customer service, and effect interplant shipments of five million dollars' worth of components annually. Before installation of the new system, each plant posted manually about 30,000 stocked items. Interplant relations were formerly controlled by telephone, a process that was both slow and costly, while causing numerous stock-outs and overstocked items. Yet company management reports that the cost of the new system is less than that of the decentralized plan it formerly used.[2]

Inventory Control Forms

One authority lists twenty-eight forms used for inventory control; suggesting, however, that since different companies call the same form by different names, the long list probably contains duplications. Although no concern has so many forms, many have more than is necessary. Common sense suggests that the forms should be kept to the minimum required to exercise the desired controls. An explanation of some of the more important forms and records will aid in understanding the procedures of inventory control. The purpose of many of the forms is obvious from their titles.

The *purchase requisition* is a request to buy materials, directed to the purchasing department. Its purpose is to replenish stores or satisfy the needs of some using department. The production-order requisition is a request, also directed to the purchasing department, to buy materials or other items needed to fill a customer or stock order. These requisitions are written by the production planning or control department, where one exists.

The *receiving report* is made out by the receiving department, if there is a department for this activity, or by the receiving section of central stores. It records the details about materials received from vendors, from other departments as surplus from production orders, or as defective items. Materials received from vendors are checked against copies of the purchase orders received from the purchasing department. All needed and useful information is recorded on the receiving report including the source of delivery, the time, quantity, condition of materials, and any other data required by accounting or necessary for stores' own procedures.

The *inspection report* is made out by a section of central stores, if the

---

[2] "Overnight Inventory Control" (ed.), *Factory Management and Maintenance* (September 1960), p. 117.

inspection is not technical. When technical assistance is necessary, the findings are attached to the inspection report. As has been mentioned, a summary inspection is made for the receiving report, and this may be all that is needed for most concerns. From a functional standpoint, receiving and inspection normally precede acceptance into storage under any plan of inventory control.

The *identification tag* (Figure 18.1) associates a lot of requisitioned materials with the production order for which it is to be used. Identification tags serve other purposes, but this is the most common one. Bin tags (Figure 18.2) are hung on hooks or placed in containers where the related materials are stored. They are important running records of the time and amounts of materials going in and out of the storage bins, and the balance on hand. Bin tags are the primary record of merchandise in stores. Frequently, new bin tags are made out for each new lot received, so that the old tags can be sent to the control section for checking against the inventory records. Some accountants object to bin tags because they duplicate the inventory record, and because the untrained personnel using them are often likely to make clerical errors.

The *stock record,* or *perpetual inventory,* is the control record for inven-

Figure 18.1

Figure 18.2

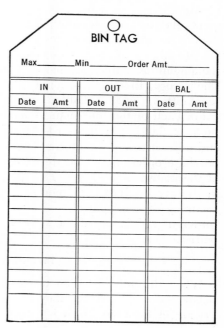

tories. It usually is kept on separate cards for each classification. The information contained on these stock-record cards is obtained from purchasing requisitions, purchase orders, bin tags, inventory adjustment reports, notices of materials received, inspected, and accepted or rejected, stores-issue forms, and receipts for materials issued. The stock record gathers together all information needed to control the inventories in stores.

The *balance-of-stores record* is important for the production-control department because its "balance available" shows how much of any stored item is available for production planning. Its original purpose was to maintain a perpetual inventory of materials, supplies, parts, and finished products. As control techniques developed, the balance-of-stores record was expanded to supply information to the accounting departments. This expanded record includes:

1. Classification of materials concerned
2. Unit prices to be charged on requisitions from stores
3. The value of inventory on hand
4. Periodic requirements based on production cycles for manufacturing concerns, or on sales for other businesses
5. The formula for replenishing stores on repetitive items, including ordering point and ordering quantity
6. A running record of the amount on order, on hand, committed to manufacturing orders or sales, and available for issue

Figure 18.3 shows a balance-of-stores record. From the production standpoint, the amount of materials *available* for requisition is the important item. This amount may be less than the amount *on hand* because of quantities already committed. Outstanding purchases not yet received also affect the amount available and make the amount on hand relatively unimportant. The record, therefore, accounts for "ordered," "on hand," "appointed" or "committed," and "available."

For each of the four main items on the balance-of-stores record, details such as dates, purchase-order numbers, work-order numbers, quantities, and unit costs supply information for control. To expedite storing control, purchase orders based on this inventory form should indicate the location of the materials in stores. This simple precaution makes for faster storing in the proper place and more accurate bin-tag records. To establish the accuracy of this control, the sum of the final quantities "on hand" and "ordered" should equal the sum of the "available" and "apportioned" final entries.

Inventory Valuation

When the financial data concerning inventories are not carried on the balance-of-stores record, they are kept in an *inventory* or *stores ledger.* Pricing of items in stores is important because material costs are often a

Figure 18.3

BALANCE OF STORES RECORD

Material   Code No.   Maximum   Minimum   Location

ON HAND		ON ORDER				COMMITTED				AVAILABLE		
Date	Amt	Date	Amt	P.O. No.	W.O. No.	Date	Amt	W.O. No.	Cost	Date	Amt	Cost

large proportion of total costs. When items are issued from stores, their costs are deducted from the total inventory value and are added to production orders as material costs by the cost-accounting department. Issues of supplies are also subtracted from inventory values and charged as an expense to the using department. Inventory values are also important in making up financial statements showing profits and losses.

When market prices are changing, several lots of a particular commodity will probably have been bought during the inventory period at different unit prices. For figuring the value of the commodity on hand at the end of the accounting period, several methods are used. Whichever plan is adopted for appraising the inventory, it must be used consistently for tax purposes as well as for comparison with the figures of former inventories.

Cost or Market. Cost or market, whichever is lower, is a common method for figuring inventory values and is relatively simple for appraising a single lot. But if a number of lots were bought at different unit prices during the year, a different method must be used.

Average Unit Cost. The average unit cost may be used when the inventory contains lots bought at different prices. It is found by dividing the number of units bought into their total cost. The unit price is then multiplied by the number of units on hand to find the inventory value.

First-in, First-out. This method of valuing inventory is based on the principle that lots bought first are used first. The method is best understood by an illustration.

Date Bought	No. of Units	Unit Price	Total Cost
2/1	500	$5.00	$ 2,500.00
5/1	500	5.50	2,750.00
8/1	500	6.00	3,000.00
11/1	500	6.50	3,250.00
	2000		$11,500.00

Of the 2000 units bought, let us say that 600 are still on hand at the end of the accounting period. The problem is to find their value under the FIFO plan. Since 1400 units were used during the period, they represent the 1000 units bought on 2/1 and 5/1, plus 400 of the 500 units bought on 8/1. The units left in the inventory (600) include 100 of those bought on 8/1 at $6.00 each, or $600, plus all (500) units bought on 11/1 at $6.50 each, or $3,250. The inventory value, therefore, by the FIFO method at the end of the period is $3,850.

Last-in, First-out. This method of valuing inventory is based on the principle that lots bought last are used first. Using the same illustration as in FIFO, the inventory value includes 100 units bought on 5/1 at $5.50, or $550, and the 500 units bought on 2/1 at $5.00, or $3,050. The inventory value at the end of the period is thus $3,600.

It is easily seen by comparing these two plans that the FIFO method results in a higher inventory value when prices are rising. When prices are falling, the two methods have the reverse effect. When the inventory is high, profits are high from an accounting standpoint. Because of this "appearance" feature, some of the favorable profit figure is referred to as "inventory profit."

Determining Quantity to Order

The so-called economical order depends on the purchase price, the rate of consumption, the cost of making the purchase, and the inventory carrying charges. The purchase price customarily depends on the amount of the order. Special quantity discounts are usually given for large orders, and sometimes this concession is a distinct advantage to the buyer. The cost of purchasing a large order is frequently the same as for a small one, which may also be a worthwhile consideration. The inventory carrying charges must be weighed against the savings just mentioned. It has been estimated that the average annual carrying charges amount to 20 per cent of the original cost. They include such items as the cost of storage facilities, insurance on the materials and the storage space, taxes on the storage space, cost of transportation and handling within the plant from storage to production, depreciation, obsolescence, and interest on the investment.

It is advantageous to make a comparative study of the over-all costs of buying various amounts, including the factors listed in the preceding paragraph. A summarized example of such a comparative study, based on a year's requirements of $60,000, is shown in Table 18.1.

Table 18.1

Average Annual Cost of Ordering Various Quantities

Item	Number of Orders per Year				
	1	3	5	10	20
Size of Order	$60,000	$20,000	$12,000	$6,000	$3,000
Average Inventory	$30,000	$10,000	$ 6,000	$3,000	$1,500
Discount Allowed on Total Annual Purchase	5%	4%	3%	2%	—
Net Cost	$57,000	$57,600	$58,200	$58,800	$60,000
Carrying Charge at 20% of Average Inventory	6,000	2,000	1,200	600	300
Cost of Buying	10	30	50	100	200
TOTAL COST	$63,010	$59,630	$59,450	$59,500	$60,500

In this example, the annual requirement is $60,000 worth of the materials concerned. The question is how many purchases are most economical. The carrying charges are figured at an over-all cost of 20 per cent of the average inventory in each of the five plans. The cost of making a single purchase is arbitrarily set at ten dollars. It is assumed that use of the item is about evenly distributed over the period considered. It is evident from the tabulation that the most economical buy is obtained by placing five orders of $12,000 each, spaced throughout the year at intervals of about two-and-one-half months.

Classification and Symbols

Inventory classification, or the listing of commodities in logical groups with respect to their nature or use, should be directly related to company production (or distribution in the case of non-manufacturing concerns) and to maintaining its accounting records. The established classifications of inventory items determine their location in central stores, as well as their assignment to costing and general accounting records.

Since there is no standard plan for inventory classification, the number of classes depends on the nature of the business and the details of its accounting procedures. Some classifications list as many as forty basic divisions. When the number is small, each group is customarily broken down into a number of subgroups.[3]

The most comprehensive classification is that of the federal government, which includes ninety-two general groups. In many cases, the classification of stores follows that used by the purchasing department, but the two patterns need not be identical. When they are not the same, that used for stores inventory is more detailed.

Besides aiding in the layout of stores, the classification of commodities expedites stores issues. It also has at least a suggestive influence on the elimination of needless varieties, and so encourages the standardization of materials. It has a direct relation to purchasing when buying is done in terms of the same commodity classifications.

Symbols are used to identify commodity classifications because they save time and reduce errors. Numbers, letters, combinations of numbers and letters, the Dewey Decimal system and mnemonic symbols are the chief methods for abbreviating commodity classifications. The Dewey Decimal system is not generally favored because of the difficulty store employees have in juggling the decimal points, thus leading to more errors than the other plans.

F. W. Taylor is credited with being the first to apply a system of mnemonic symbols to the classification of inventory items. A mnemonic symbol is usually a letter or group of letters which abbreviates the name of the item symbolized. Thus the single letter "P" might stand for "pipe" and the combination "Pb" stands for "brass pipe." Each company must make up its own set of symbols, reserving the single-letter classifications for the most important inventory items. The combination "Pb" might very well stand for "big potatoes" to the manufacturer of potato chips. Since each symbol is a direct memory cue, mnemonic systems are readily learned and retained by stores clerks and have proved to be a very successful method of inventory classification.

Simplification and Standardization

Simplification refers to the elimination of needless varieties in sizes, colors, types, and grades of supplies, materials or products. The word is used in production to denote the simplification of methods and processes. In the use considered here, it is presumed that when a product, part, or type of supply has been reduced to the smallest number of serviceable or salable varieties, it should be standardized at that number. Simplification

---

[3] Stuart F. Heinritz, *Purchasing* (2nd ed.; New York: Prentice-Hall, Inc., 1951), pp. 200–201, gives the example of a manufacturer of printing equipment who uses a four-way classification to cover 50,000 items. The basic groups in this case are: (1) factory materials and supplies, (2) raw materials, (3) commercial parts, and (4) investment items. These four classes are broken down into 42 subclasses.

precedes standardization, and standardization freezes the item officially at the number of varieties agreed on until some change is made by management. In other words, the final simplification should be made the working standard.

Lack of reasonable product standardization is proverbially blamed on customer desires. The sales department opposes simplification because it wants to make selling easy by supplying customers anything they ask for. It is often contended by the sales department that simplification will reduce sales. However, since a simplified standard line means lower production costs, customers should be sold on the idea of receiving better merchandise at the same price, or the same products at lower prices. Either lower costs or improved quality should promote customer acceptance.

It has already been pointed out that the greatest opportunities for simplification lie in the area of supplies. Although the cost of any one new variety is probably not important, the total expenditures for supplies may run into large figures, and the greater the number of varieties purchased, the larger the total expenditure will be. Besides running up inventory investment, needless varieties of parts and supplies promote waste. The material-control section should be cognizant of items of low use and remedy the situation by requiring standard-item substitutes.

Advantages of Inventory Control

1. *It promotes buying economies by determining requirements scientifically, modified by experience and market conditions.* Controlled inventory not only plans buying on time for use, but also guides the quantity of purchases by such factors as the production cycle, quantity prices, and market trends.

2. *It prevents duplications in ordering for stock by centralizing the source of requisitions for purchase.* By recording purchase orders, acquisition and stores issues, the perpetual inventory record poses an automatic stop signal against duplicate purchase orders. Such a signal should be effective in central stores as well as in the inventory-control section.

3. *It facilitates the interchange of materials among departments.* Inventory control can act as a clearing house for matching surplus items in one department with the needs of another.

4. *It minimizes, and should prevent, losses connected with incoming materials.* Such losses arise from wrong count, poor quality, and damage. Undetected or unreported damage to incoming materials may result in serious loss, whether the damage is the fault of the vendor or the common carrier. Time is often of the essence in damage claims. For example, since central stores was not qualified to inspect a costly piece of technical equipment for one company's laboratory, the apparatus was sent direct to the using department. The laboratory delayed opening the equipment until three months later, when it was required for use. It was clear that serious

damage was caused in transit, but the time interval before inspection freed the public transportation agency from liability.

5. *It reduces losses to stored materials resulting from mishandling and theft.* The simple plan for reducing this type of loss is to establish automatic responsibility, which is accomplished by the stores section of inventory control. Added to fixed responsibility goes training and experience in handling materials, parts, and products. The theft of unprotected small items was the initial reason for setting up supervised tool rooms and parts departments for repair shops. In addition to preventing such losses, proper control of any kind improves employee morale, if for no other reason than that it increases the workers' respect for management's operations.

6. *It shortens the time between receipt of raw materials and completion of the finished product.* The ultimate in shortening this interval occurs in continuous assembly industries, where an effort is made to have materials and components go directly to the assembly line.

7. *It aids cost accounting by allocating material costs to orders, departments, and operating accounts.*

8. *It aids management in making cost comparisons among operations and between time periods.*

9. *It provides data for perpetual inventory records which are used in preparing financial statements.*

10. *It minimizes the investment in inventories* by fixing the maximum amount of materials that should be on hand or available.[4] This is particularly true for items in repetitive use. It is also customary for inventory reports to call attention to slow-moving items. When demand ceases altogether, this fact also appears on the reports of inventory control.

11. *It reduces the number of varieties of a given material* by suggestions resulting from critical analyses of materials and parts, and their uses. The opportunity for savings through standardization is particularly marked in the area of supplies. Carbon paper, oils, cleaning materials, and a host of other items are frequently bought in unnecessary variety merely to satisfy the personal whims of their users. The standardization of low-cost items is often overlooked by the engineering department, but such items are constantly visible reminders to a competent stores-keeper.

12. *It eliminates the old-fashioned "inventory week"* once or twice a year. When the company's fiscal year follows the calendar year, at least one inventory-taking time arrives during the Christmas season. For holiday reasons, and because the longer the "taking" drags on the more boring it becomes, accuracy decreases as the job progresses. If the physical inventory is incorrect, the resulting profit position on the financial statment is false. The perpetual inventory records of central stores eliminate the necessity of rushed physical stocktaking. The regular practice under the improved system is to make a few physical checks daily against the perpetual records.

[4] For the distinction between "on hand" and "available," see page 354.

13. *It improves general employee morale,* which always goes along with the feeling that management knows what it is doing. Workers get materials and parts as they are needed, and they learn to count on that type of service. It improves their willingness to increase productivity. The fact that all inventory items must be accounted for according to a scientific plan eliminates those occasions when employees may be wondering "who did it."

Centralization of Stores-Keeping

The degree of stores centralization depends on the size of the concern and the purposes it is intended to accomplish. Obviously, small concerns should centralize stores operations. The question is not so easily answered with medium-sized and large companies. If a large company has a one-story plant in a single location, it may well consider decentralizing its stores activities.

The question of single or multiple stores has two phases. One concerns the physical layout and the other the control. If it is decided that decentralization will increase production by bringing stores closer to the production line, then the question of centralized control becomes more important. Certainly there must be central control, but the difficult question is how much.

If the company has more than one plant, there is even more reason for decentralization of stores. The approved plan is a generous degree of decentralized operation, subject to established stores policies and centralized controls.

Another argument in favor of multiple stores — an argument which applies to decentralization in general — is that more individuals are given an opportunity to show initiative in directing the separate operations than would be the case under centralization, and this situation always tends to improve both morale and productivity.

The number of storerooms and their location depends on the nature, value, and turnover of the commodities involved. The layout of the plant, the volume of materials needed for its various centers, and the available space are also pertinent considerations. Decentralized storage must also take into account items stored temporarily as well as heavy, light, spoilable, and dangerous materials.

The stores layout must ordinarily provide for:

1. Storage of all kinds of materials
2. Receipt and inspection of incoming items
3. Issuance of materials for use or shipping
4. Aisle space based on the circumstances
5. Flexibility of physical arrangements

Storeroom physical arrangements should follow the established classification plan, if possible. The other arrangement is based on the amount of use for the various items, or the most convenient use of the fixed physical conditions. Either of these arrangements will require an index to expedite the location of stored commodities.

How materials get into stores

The ordinary purchase of specific materials or parts is based on requisitions from one of three sources. One source is those individuals who are authorized to requisition. In those cases where foremen make purchase requisitions, they should have a general authorization from their superiors. Another common source of requisitions is from the inventory-control section of central stores, at regular intervals and in regular quantities. This plan applies particularly to repetitive items. The control section of stores requests purchases when its stock of a given item has reached the prescribed minimum or ordering quantity. The amount requisitioned is that necessary to bring the item back to its designated maximum. The quantity ordered is the difference between the maximum and the minimum.

The third common source of requisitions is the production-control department, which authorizes purchase of items not ordinarily carried in stores. Such requisitions are based on the production schedules for customer or stock orders.

When purchasing contracts are placed on a production-program basis, orders against the contract for inclusion in the stores inventory are often made on a so-called "float" basis. A "float" is the number of days' supply required on the production floor, in stores, or on orders. These time-supply floats are naturally based on the production cycle, but the volume of the float may represent materials needed for two or more cycles, often many more.

Materials bought on the basis of these several procurement plans go to the receiving department or the receiving section of central stores where they are checked against the purchase order for quantity, inspected for quality and condition, and sent to stores if satisfactory. If the material or parts are unsatisfactory, some type of report or ticket is sent to the person or department responsible for adjusting the discrepancy or disposing of the item. The initiation of this kind of action is a distinct function of inventory control.

Another source of stores inventory comes from materials, parts components, and finished products made in the company plant and consigned to stores until it is required by production or sales. It is common practice to send such items through the receiving department for inspection because central stores is held responsible for the number and condition of everything accepted by it, even though the transaction takes place entirely within the company.

Besides items manufactured within the plant, central stores also receives left-over or unused items returned by the production departments to which stores originally issued them. Left-over and unused items result from over-ordering or from discontinuance of a product line. All of the transactions discussed have forms for recording the facts. Without records, controls are impossible.

How materials get out of stores

One of the primary functions of inventory control is to keep an accurate record of incoming and outgoing materials of all kinds. All issues from stores are based on authorized requisitions which originate in the following manner:

1. *Where there is no central production-control procedure*, requisitions from stores are made by department heads or by foremen on authorization of their superiors.

2. *When there is a central-control procedure*, requisitions from stores are made by the production-planning section against specific job orders to which they are charged by stores. Under a production-control system, the requisition is sent to the central dispatching office after the materials have been earmarked for the job in question.

3. *In continuous-production industries*, regular daily schedules for materials are sent to central stores, which delivers to the using department.

4. *In mass production of repetitive lots, materials may go direct from the vendors to the assembly lines*, subject to control by central stores. To keep centralized storage space at a minimum, bulky materials are customarily delivered by vendors to assembly lines for one day's production, while small items may be so delivered to cover a week's or a month's supply. It is important to remember that even under such a plan, the control section maintains constant vigilance on material receipts from vendors and issuances to the production or using centers.

5. *In special cases* covering replacements for damaged or unsuitable materials, or for shortages in the original requests, requisitions may be made by the foremen, department head, or some higher executive, depending on the company's procedure. In any case, central stores makes out a record explaining the reason for the special requisition.

Recent trends in warehousing[5]

1. Increasing automation where applicable
2. Standardization of packages by size and markings
3. More management control — to make warehousing simpler and less costly. Produces gains in continuous flow, smaller inventory, shorter handling time, and fewer man-hours

[5] Summarized from "Today's Trends in Warehousing" (*Factory Management and Maintenance,* March 1960), p. 102.

4. Faster communication, especially with two-way radios
5. More flexibility to accommodate inventory surges and drop-offs
6. Single-story buildings, especially for heavy items
7. Higher stacking — today's limit is approximately 20 feet

Inventory Organization

The number of inventory-control's organizational relationships is evidence that it is a comparative newcomer to the fold of scientific management. Its newness is only one of the reasons for its unsettled place in the organization structure. Another is the shifting influence of other activities or functions, often considered more important, to which inventory control has become attached as a subordinate. A third, often based on rational considerations, arises from the nature of the association between inventory control and the organizational unit to which it is assigned.

Inventory control may be found reporting to purchasing, central stores, or the superintendent of production. A large manufacturing enterprise may assign inventory control to production if materials represent a very large proportion of its expenditures.

In other cases, inventory control may be set up as an independent unit reporting to the executive vice-president or even to the president. This is frequently the case with a chain of supermarkets where inventory is by far the outstanding expenditure. The chain may have large central stores reporting to the person in charge of operations. Since the importance of inventory control in such cases ranks after purchasing and sales, it is customarily independent of central stores from both supervisory and physical standpoints. In fact, the actual inventory records will probably be loacted in the concern's office building and locked whenever the inventory chief is absent. This type of setup is due not only to the large investment involved, but also to the frequency of loss through pilfering of the thousands of small items used in home consumption. Furthermore, one of the top executives always advises closely with the buyers in determining quantities, for which inventory control is a valuable guide.

Occasionally, inventory control is placed under supervision and control of central stores. There are also cases, as has been mentioned, where purchasing has charge of both central stores and inventory control.

Because the position of inventory control in the organization structure varies so much from company to company, no attempt will be made in this chapter to single out any one organizational arrangement as the most typical or the most desirable.

Conclusions

It has been frequently suggested that the factors involved in the various facets of inventory control might well be combined into a new activity that might be called "Materials Management." This idea would include: (1)

inventory management, which is responsible for policies controlling inventories at all stages of production; (2) inventory control, responsible for carrying out management's policies for control; (3) production control, responsible for routing, scheduling, and dispatching of the production processes;[6] (4) procurement, responsible for purchasing; and (5) traffic, responsible for both incoming and outgoing shipments. Space does not permit a discussion of the pros and cons of this proposal, but the advantage would be a closer coordination of the total concept of inventory control. Those opposed to the idea suggest that the five activities are specialties and should be kept separate. As an added argument against the proposal, they suggest its inherent threat of "empire building."

The management policy fixing the ratio between inventory investment and operating profits can be used for determining optimum inventory levels for all types of inventory. In all businesses carrying inventories, the investment involved may represent half the company's net worth. In spite of this fact, inventory control receives less attention than cash control in most concerns.

The situation with respect to inventory control is improving. It was not so many years ago that production stock rooms and tool cribs were left open and unattended, so that representatives of using departments could save time by taking care of their own withdrawals. Saving of time under such conditions does not necessarily reduce costs. It was the contrary conclusion that led to the locked tool crib accessible only to authorized persons. Subsequently, the "stockroom" received the same treatment. Later, both were put in charge of responsible attendants when the concern was large enough to warrant the expense.

As the supervised stock and tool rooms became more prevalent, plans for inventory control were developed. Management not only wanted company possessions to be safe from theft and damage, but it also wanted to know what was on hand and available at all times, not merely at stocktaking time.

The next step was for inventory control to keep records of the cost of all items so that charges to customer orders could be recorded at the level where the parts, materials, and supplies went into production. The relationship between inventory control and accounting developed slowly but steadily, with the result that they are now partners in control and costing.

QUESTIONS

1. What is the relation between inventory control and procurement?
2. What is the prime essential for successful inventory management?
3. How do Production and Sales often work against maintaining a reasonable number of inventory items in relation to the total investment level?

[6] See Chapter 10, "Production Controls."

4. How would you express the chief purpose of top management's control of inventories?

5. The text enumerates nine functions of the inventory control section. How many of them can you recall?

6. What are some of the pitfalls of the inventory problem which frequently lead to inventory losses?

7. Why is it reasonable to conclude that inventory policies should be more flexible than those of most other management activities?

8. Why do "sensitive" items rarely submit to standard quantity purchases, as do many other material classifications?

9. There are five elementary factors necessary for controlling inventories. What are they?

10. How does the perpetual inventory act as the control record for inventories?

11. Why is it that amount on hand, as it appears on the Balance of Stores record, is often greater than the amount of inventory "available"?

12. Why is it that the FIFO method of inventory valuation shows a higher inventory value than LIFO when prices are rising?

13. What is the relation between inventory classifications and symbols?

14. Why is the sales department often opposed to simplification and standardization of inventory varieties?

15. What do we mean when we speak of inventory control facilitating the interchange of materials among departments? What is the advantage of such interchange to the business as a whole?

16. Under what circumstances should stores-keeping be decentralized? Should control be centralized even if physical situation is not?

17. What is the advantage of maintaining a "float" on the production floor?

18. Under what circumstances is it advantageous to have materials go direct from vendors to production assembly lines?

19. To whom should inventory control report? Why?

20. How does the management policy of fixing the ratio between inventory investment and operating profits aid in establishing optimum levels of inventories?

CASE PROBLEM

MONARCH DISTRIBUTING COMPANY

The Monarch Distributing Company sells $250,000 worth of couplings annually. Although the normal trade discount given by the supplier on this item is 40 per cent of the list price at which Monarch sells to its customers, the annual investment for this one inventory item would be a considerable sum if the year's supply were bought on one order and stored awaiting customers' orders throughout the year. However, this lump-sum order of 10,000 couplings would entitle Monarch to an extra quantity discount of 10 per cent. This discount may be an advantage, since the sales experience of Monarch shows that its customer orders are received on an even basis during the twelve-month period.

Monarch's purchasing agent is trying to decide whether to buy from its supplier in one lump order, or to spread its requirements on a semiannual, quarterly, or monthly basis. He is advised by the vendor that the volume discount for these four different-sized orders will be 10 per cent, 6 per cent, 3 per cent and net, respectively. The P.A. figures that it will cost his company 25 per cent of the average gross-inventory value for annual carrying charges, and that the clerical cost of placing an order is $10.00.

PROBLEM: On what basis should Monarch buy its coupling requirements from this vendor?

Part Two • Suggestions For Further Reading

American Management Association, *Successful Production Planning and Control,* New York: Special Report No. 5, 1955.

Barnes, Ralph M., *Motion and Time Study, 4th Edition,* New York: John Wiley and Sons, 1958.

Brown, Robert G., *Statistical Forecasting for Inventory Control,* New York: McGraw-Hill Book Company, Inc., 1959.

Buffa, Elwood S., *Modern Production Management,* New York: John Wiley and Sons, Inc., Parts III and IV, 1961.

Crowningshield, Gerald R., *Cost Accounting: Principles and Managerial Applications,* Boston: Houghton Mifflin Company, 1962.

Dean, Joel, *Capital Budgeting,* New York: Columbia University Press, 1951.

Duncan, A. J., *Quality Control and Industrial Statistics,* Rev. Ed., Homewood, Illinois: Richard D. Irwin, Inc., 1959.

Fetter, R. B., and Dalleck, W. C., *Decision Models for Inventory Management,* Homewood, Illinois: Richard D. Irwin, Inc., 1961.

Gardner, Fred V., *Profit Management and Control,* New York: McGraw-Hill Book Company, Inc., 1955.

Gomberg, William, *A Trade Union Analysis of Time Study, 2nd Edition,* New York: Prentice-Hall, Inc., 1955.

Holden, Paul E., Fish, Loundsbury S. and Smith, Hubert L., *Top Management Organization and Control,* Stanford, California: Stanford University Press, 1941.

Ireson, W. Grant, and Grant Eugene L., *Handbook of Industrial Engineering and Management,* Englewood Cliffs, New Jersey: Prentice-Hall, Inc., Sections 5, 8, 14, and 16, 1955.

Koepke, Charles A., *Plant Production Control, 3rd Edition,* New York: John Wiley and Sons, Inc., 1961.

Krick, Edward V., *Methods Engineering,* New York: John Wiley and Sons, Inc., 1962.

Le Breton, Preston P. and Henning, Dale A., *Planning Theory,* Englewood Cliffs, New Jersey: Prentice-Hall, Inc., 1961.

Lewis, Ronello B., *Profit Planning for Management,* Englewood Cliffs, New Jersey: Prentice-Hall, Inc., 1961.

MacNiece, E. H., *Production Forecasting Planning and Control, 2nd Edition,* New York: John Wiley and Sons, Inc., 1951.

Magee, John F., *Production Planning and Inventory Control,* New York: McGraw-Hill Book Company, Inc., 1958.

Manne, Alan S., *Economic Analysis for Business Decisions,* New York: McGraw-Hill Book Company, Inc., 1961.

Mayer, Raymond R., *Production Management,* New York: McGraw-Hill Book Company, Inc., Parts 1, 2, 4, 5, 6, and 7, 1962.

Maynard, Harold B., Stegemerten, G. J., and Schwab, John L., *Methods-Time-Measurement,* New York: McGraw-Hill Book Company, Inc., 1948.

Metcalfe, Captain Henry, *The Cost of Manufactures and the Administration of Workshops, Public and Private,* New York: John Wiley & Son, Chapter II, 1885.

Moore, James M., *Plant Layout and Design,* New York: The Macmillan Company, 1962.

Mundell, Marvin E., *Motion and Time Study,* 3rd Ed., Englewood Cliffs, New Jersey: Prentice-Hall, Inc., 1960.

Muther, Richard, *Practical Plant Layout,* New York: McGraw-Hill Book Company, Inc., 1955.

Nadler, Gerald, *Motion and Time Study,* New York: McGraw-Hill Book Company, Inc., 1955.

Schewhart, Walter, *Economic Control of Quality of Manufactured Product,* New York: D. Van Nostrand Company, Company, Inc., 1931.

Seimer, Stanley J., *Cases in Industrial Management,* Homewood, Illinois: Richard D. Irwin, Inc., 1961.

Stedry, Andrew C., *Budgeting Control and Cost Behavior,* Englewood Cliffs, New Jersey: Prentice-Hall, Inc., 1960.

Welch, W. E., *Tested Scientific Inventory Control,* Greenwich, Connecticut: Management Publishing Corporation, 1956.

Whitin, T. M., *The Theory of Inventory Management,* Princeton, New Jersey: Princeton University Press, 1953.

Ziegler, Raymond J., *Casebook in Production Management,* New York: John Wiley & Sons, Inc., 1962.

•

The quotation at the beginning of Part Two is from: Captain Henry Metcalfe, *The Cost of Manufactures and the Administration of Workshops, Public and Private,* New York: John Wiley & Son, 1885, Chapter II.

Bookkeeping

Building an

Industrial Work Force

Justice and equity must be carried beyond the requirements of the letter. Problems arise when feelings are injured; people suffer injustices of a nature that cannot be covered by a written document or policy. Unless equity is done, constitutionalism loses its vitality. Although a business cannot be expected to function as a church or a family or a clinic, human values cannot be ignored without peril.

Indeed, a great corporation executive, as any great governor of men, is he who so conveys justice and equity in all his bearing that his people know that righteousness prevails within his realm.

BENJAMIN M. SELEKMAN

19

Personnel
Management

Personnel management and personnel relations are so closely related in practice that it is not always easy to say where one leaves off and the other begins. In many large organizations, both tend to be the responsibility of the personnel department; in a very small business, both are the concern of the boss. Nevertheless, if we are to understand the full complexity of the personnel function, it is important to make a distinction between the two approaches.

What differentiates the two is the *immediate goal* to which each approach is addressed. Personnel "management" aims to build an efficient organization for the accomplishment of company objectives through the judicious control of employees. The techniques of personnel "relations," on the other hand, are addressed most immediately to creating and maintaining a harmonious group of satisfied workers. That is to say, personnel management stresses the achievement of company objectives; personnel relations stress employee satisfaction.

Personnel management and personnel relations are frequently fused in practice because the same techniques will often satisfy both goals. Personnel management when considering the department's employment activities, lays emphasis on the first goal — attaining an efficient organization through proper techniques for matching personal qualifications with job specifications. In the effort to attain this goal, however, the second objective — that of satisfying the worker — is also served, for there can be no doubt that a worker is likely to be happier on a job for which he is best qualified. There is no contradiction, then, between the two approaches.

The difference, however, is real. Personnel's employment activities are clearly in the interest of the company, and not primarily in the interest of the individual. If the applicant for a job in a shoe factory is found to be highly skilled in making canoe paddles, the company does not add canoe paddles to its line merely to give the new applicant the satisfaction of working at his highest skill. The man must be fitted to the job, not the job to the man.

On the other hand, when the same company provides its workers with balls and bats and lays out a baseball diamond, it is equally clear that the expenditure does not directly aid in the manufacture of shoes. In the background of such activity lies the proposition that productivity is likely to be higher when the employees are happier. A harmonious group of workers rather than an immediate aid to the production processes is the immediate purpose of the company's expenditures for employee relations.

Foundations of Personnel Management

Good personnel management has three outstanding facets: (1) a cooperative and understanding chief, (2) a well-planned program, and (3) a group of written policies, principles, and objectives supported by management and practiced in all contacts with company employees.

Personnel management must be eternally conscious of the fact that the American worker is a citizen, a member of the organization where he works and often of a union group as well. These relationships require that Personnel deal with the worker as a member of at least two different organizations that seek his loyalty. Personnel also represents management to the worker and the worker to management. Such an assignment requires both scientific skill and human understanding. Another way to visualize the importance of personnel management is to consider that manufacturing industries now employ more than twenty million people.

Basic personnel problems

It is the job of personnel management to maximize productivity to assure the employer's profits as well as his ability to pay his workers a reasonable living wage. If the employer cannot attain his goal, his orders may decline until he goes out of business, or he may have the alternative of developing new labor-saving devices. If the worker cannot realize what he considers a fair deal, he has the doubtful privilege of finding other employment.

A second basic problem for Personnel arises from the natural psychological diversity of people with whom it must deal. Labor like management is made up of people with unique personalities, each with his own problems, desires, and sometimes baffling eccentricities. It is these intangible factors that make it unsafe for the personnel manager to put too much trust in guiding principles in situations where there is no real guide except the exigencies of the occasion.

The third problem is a general antagonism often directed against the personnel department. Even if he personally gives no grounds for resentment, the personnel manager find that his *role* itself is often frowned on by reason of its very nature. Personnel is a staff function set up to serve all departments by handling worker problems such as recruitment, interviewing, testing, hiring, placement, and training, to mention only the fundamentals. Since this staff department is a relative newcomer, it has taken over functions which not so long ago were exercised by other department heads. Even supervisors resent the intrusion. Hiring and firing was the double-edged sword often used by supervisors to maintain discipline and productivity. Most department heads question whether the new personnel function has learned to find employees more acceptable than those whom they formerly hired.

Organization

The personnel organization depends on the size of the company and the functional relationships within it, the importance of its personnel problems, and the capacity of its director. The structural design of the organization is affected by the following considerations:

1. Management's opinion of its importance
2. The influence of legislation and organized labor
3. Size of the company and the number of its plants
4. The nature of its production and labor problems
5. Training, experience, and personality of the director

When Personnel acts as a staff function, as it should, its organization is divided functionally and usually set up on a line basis. Figure 19.1 illustrates a functional setup on a line basis. This plan would be suitable for a large company with several thousand employees and complicated personnel problems. The question of multiple plants or businesses also affects the organization of the department. It may have direct representatives stationed in the various plants subject to its control, or each plant may have an independent personnel organization reporting to the plant superintendent. In the latter case, the department at the home office may exercise a general supervision for the purpose of suggesting improvements in operations and for controlling departmental policies.

Two other considerations affect the organization plan. One is the relationship of its activities to the chief of labor relations. Shall Personnel report to Labor Relations, or vice versa? Both plans are found in practice, and the decision seems to depend on the relative importance of the two in individual cases. We also find them combined in a single department called Personnel & Labor Relations, or sometimes Labor Relations takes precedence in the title.

Figure 19.1

Personnel Organization: Large Company, Single Operation

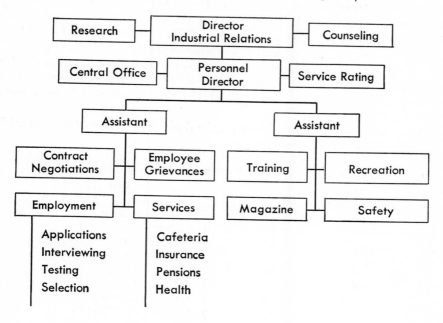

The other problem concerns the importance of Personnel and Labor Relations, considered together, in the total organization. Shall they report to some department such as Finance, or be set up as a major function reporting directly to the top executive? The answer depends on management's opinion of the importance of personnel and labor relations. It is often contended by trained personnel workers that the department should be headed by a vice-president, on the theory that organized labor will be more impressed and correspondingly amenable. Those who disagree feel that the department's director is in a better-protected position when he can tell organized labor that he must consult his chief (or the company's labor committee) before answering the important question they have just asked. This approach gives him time to consider various answers and their long-range effects.

Personnel Functions

In its widest sense, Personnel serves the interest of the company, the workers, and the community where the operations are located. In large concerns, the community service may have a broad social objective. Many employee safety programs, for example, have an indirect community benefit. A concern with which the writer was associated developed a national amateur championship baseball team. Its achievement was celebrated by a downtown parade and local band, led by the mayor. The company manufactured producer goods, so could scarcely benefit directly from the athletic achievement of its baseball team. The championship did, however, benefit the concern's recruiting program. Another manufacturer, through his personnel department, replaced a number of small frame houses with a modern playground for neighborhood children, none of whose parents worked for the concern.

The modern personnel program breaks down into nine major areas with sixty-nine distinct functions:

1. *Employment*
   Recruiting
   Interviewing
   References
   Tests
   Physicals
   Selection
   Placement
   Induction
   Counseling
   Transfers
   Promotions
   Exit interviews
   Records
   Reports
2. *Working Conditions*
   Sanitation
   Ventilation
   Lighting
   Heating
   Rest periods
   Food service
3. *Wages and Hours*
   Wage scales
   Incentives
   Bonuses
4. *Training — Education*
   On-the-job
   Apprenticeship
   Vestibule School
   Conferences
   Library
   Manuals
   Bulletins

5. *Health*
   Examinations
   First aid
   Home nursing
6. *Safety*
   Inspection
   Education
   Programs
   Hazards
   Compensation
7. *Welfare and Services*
   Unemployment insurance
   Accident insurance
   Health insurance
   Hospital insurance
   Life insurance
   Severance pay
   Retirement pensions
   Savings and loans
   Housing programs
   Social activities
   Athletic programs
   Employee periodicals
   Employee purchasing
   Transportation
   Legal aid program
8. *Research and Controls*
   Job analysis
   Labor turnover
   Accidents — records
   Absence statistics
   Worker morale
   Wages and living costs
   Community wage levels

Industry wage levels
Program planning
Labor legislation
9. *Employee Relations*
Grievance procedure

Female workers
Handicapped workers
Minority groups
Contract negotiations
Policy indoctrination

Principles and Policies

Principles are basic to the formulation of policies. Principles are statements of behavior which have proved to be successful guides in establishing harmony among workers and executives, and between the two groups. The best personnel principles are only special cases of group dynamics. The following are the most important:

1. *Establish reasonable hours, wages, and working conditions.* The meaning of "reasonable" is relative, but it can always be defined by the practice of the best-managed concerns.
2. *Treat employees as worthwhile individuals.* It is the antithesis of the older concept of viewing the worker as a commodity. He is a citizen, with the same complexities as the executive.
3. *Let the worker "in on the know."* Workers should be given news of general company interest before it reaches the public. Good communication of company and employee affairs minimizes suspicion and gossip based on ignorance of the facts. It builds confidence and creates the feeling of belonging.
4. *Substitute mutual dealing for paternalism.* Mutuality of employer and employee interests should lead to worker participation in decisions which affect those interests. It develops worker interest in company plans.
5. *Install new programs only after consultation with the workers.* In keeping with the spirit of trade unionism, workers want to bargain for changes affecting their personal interests.
6. *Give new programs time to work.* New ideas and procedures require time to take roots. Even when a new program is installed with the consent of the workers, it must meet the natural opposition of esablished customs.
7. *Practice established principles whole-heartedly.* If the workers have reason to feel that Personnel is giving only lip service to its stated principles, they will come to resent and oppose both the idea of the program and the way it is carried out.

Policies based on these principles should be written in clear and simple language, and communicated to all those affected. Policies are often set forth in an employee handbook, entitled "Rules and Regulations." An illustration of the subjects contained in such a handbook is taken from the index of the employees' manual of Sears, Roebuck & Company's *Let's Get Acquainted:*

Absences	Meal periods
Accidents	Moving
Appearance	Pay increases
Awards	Period calendar
Borrowing	Personal belongings
Bulletin boards	Profit sharing
Car insurance	Promises
Catalog selling	Promotions
Contingents	Rest periods
Correspondence	Safety
Courtesy	Selling ratio
Credit	Service awards
Deaths	Shoplifting
Delivery service	Split shifts
Employee accounts	Stockholders
Employee benefits	Store card
Employee classes	Store directory
Employee discounts	Suggestions
Group insurance	Telephoning
Health	Training
Hospitalization	Transfers
Illness	Vacations
Jury duty	Wages
Lending	Working hours
Lost and found	Wrappings

The Director

When companies are small, it is natural that the owner or chief should handle the personnel job. Prior to the present century, the personnel function was largely restricted to hiring and firing, plus whatever paternalism management cared to practice. During World War I, openings for personnel directors multiplied all over the country, especially with firms interested in war work. At that time, competent directors were in short supply. Their chief job was to draw workers from other companies and devise plans to minimize their further migration.

With the sharp recession following the First World War, personnel departments were dropped like frills in a panic. The demand for personnel services rose again as the boom of the twenties progressed, only to fall off sharply once more during the long depression of the thirties. Meanwhile, colleges were instituting courses in the various phases of personnel work so that a trained but relatively inexperienced supply was ready to serve business and industry during the war boom of the forties. With management's better understanding of the expanded personnel functions and the increased training and experience of the new professional group, the standards of service have steadily risen. From the early days when a friendly smile and a flair for back-slapping qualified a man to be personnel director, we have reached a point where the successful candidate must generally add formal training in human relations principles to a natural capacity for getting along with others.

What are some of the qualifications of a modern director?

1. *Ability to get along with others* is generally recognized as the prime requisite. If the director hopes to resolve social and psychological conflicts within the worker and management groups, and between them, he must first be able to secure acceptance for himself.

2. *Impartial service* must be the motivating force for success. The director must not only have such motivation, but he must convince the workers by concrete examples.

3. *Ability to use the scientific method* in reaching decisions is a tool for which the director has constant use. Decisions must be made promptly and without personal prejudice.

4. *Ability to listen* is important. Often the director will have heard the story of a complaint before the aggrieved worker recites it to him, and he may know further that the worker's version is not based on the facts. Nevertheless, he learns to listen attentively because he knows the therapeutic value to the worker of getting the story off his chest.

5. *Appreciation of the pride and efforts of others* is one of the main characteristics by which he gains the acceptance of the workers.

6. *Formal training in personnel techniques and methods* is, of course, a necessary part of the successful director's background.

Employment Activities

Earlier we listed the functions of the personnel department. The rest of this section will consider some of the activities dealing with "employment." The other activities will be considered in later chapters. It should be pointed out again that organization of the personnel function varies from company to company and that all sixty-nine of the activities previously listed are not necessarily found under the jurisdiction of Personnel.

The labor budget

To do a good recruiting job, Personnel must know well in advance how many employees will be needed in the various job classifications. When this information is scheduled, it is known as the labor budget. Most hiring is done on day-to-day requisitions from the using departments. This lack of system is popular because it requires little thought or planning. However, it can result in interruptions to production, poor worker selection, and loss of supervisory time.

Development of the labor budget received new attention during World War II when the federal government was exercising manpower controls. As the war progressed, labor budgets were used for making draft quotas.

In industry, the first step in a labor budget comes from estimated sales upon which production depends. Then the total production schedule is broken down into departments, with the numbers and classes of help required for each. The relation of these figures to current employment indicates preliminary estimates of numbers and types of workers who must be hired or dropped.

Job specifications

Lists of requirements for each job classification are necessary for matching candidates with job openings. The employment office must have both job and man specifications to perform its function satisfactorily. Job speci-

Figure 19.2

Analysis of Job Requirements

Job Title_____ Department_____

Sex_____ Age Range_____ Height_____ Weight_____

Strength Required_____ Visual_____

I. OCCUPATIONAL DETAILS	VI. PHYSICAL EFFORT REQUIRED
	1. Sitting bench or desk work?
	2. Light standing work?
	3. Operating light machines?
II. EXAMPLE OF TYPICAL WORK	4. Working with hand tools?
	5. Handling materials?
	6. Using heavy hand tools?
	7. Moving heavy materials?
III. TRAINING REQUIRED	8. Heavy and sustained physical
1. What actual schooling is needed?	work?
2. What training is necessary?	
3. What experience is necessary for acceptable proficiency?	VII. RESPONSIBILITY REQUIRED
	1. For the safety of others?
IV. SKILLS REQUIRED	2. For spoiled parts and materials?
1. What manual skills are required?	3. For machines and equipment?
2. What mental skills are required?	
V. MENTAL EFFORT REQUIRED	VIII. WORKING CONDITIONS
1. Degree of sustained mental effort?	1. Surroundings?
	2. Hazards?
2. Degree of initiative?	3. Connected expense?

Figure 19.3

Job Description

JOB TITLE. Typist I

LOCATION. Bureau of Business Research

MECHANICAL SKILLS. *20% of time*

5%   Cuts stencils for addressograph, types labels for leaflets, letters and manuscripts for publication. Types up form used in a statistical report.

15%   Operates calculator to compile and transpose figures. Uses adding machine and addressograph. Instructs temporary statistical employees in the use of the calculating machine.

CORRESPONDENCE, MAIL, FILE. *5% of time*

5%   Keeps file of addressograph plates and research publications. Card file of 2600 names on addressograph plates. Keeps file on all publications received from federal and state agencies, and economic and business concerns. Has contact with all departments seeking information on business subjects.

CLERICAL. *75% of time*

75%   Receives penciled rough draft layout of a table or series of tables, and sets up columnar sheets on which the units are classified by attributes. The classifications are frequently suggested by the incumbent. For example, from two arrays of statistics, she will take significant attributes from each, and subject them to testing to determine the most satisfactory grouping and size classification of these attributes for the purpose of combining and cross-classifying them in a new table. Also makes suggestions for the outline of summary or derivative tables by proposing the addition or deletion of items, or the choice of preferred items among several possibilities. Each of these procedures involves a considerably greater degree of judgment and comprehension of material dealt with than is required in compiling and computing. Following approval of the table outline in final form, she computes per capitas, per worker values, percentage distributions of total amounts, percentage relationships among categories, medians and other averages of a series of groups, ranges in a series of groups, percentage changes among years, and percentage changes and differences among areas.

MEETINGS. *0% of the time*

0%   No specific duties.

---

fications are obtained from job descriptions, which are compiled from job analyses. These are the three logical steps, in reverse order, for determining job requirements and the type of persons capable of meeting them. Figure 19.2 illustrates a job analysis and Figure 19.3 a job description form.

Recruitment

When Personnel receives a requisition for additional help from one of the departments, applications on file or new recruits must be used to fill the order. Among the various *sources* for recruiting new employees are newspapers, trade journals, employment agencies, colleges, present and former employees, and the "gate." This last source is a holdover term from the days when foremen did their own hiring at the plant entrance.

Good employees already on the payroll are often the best source for many kinds of recruitment. A letter addressed to the worker's home, stating that the company needs certain kinds of help and emphasizing that preferential treatment will be given to applicants suggested by employees, usually bring excellent results, in addition to making the recommending employees feel that management respects their opinions.

Interviewing

Personnel interviews are of three kinds: hiring, general or periodic, and exit. After recruiting applicants, Personnel must decide which candidates are acceptable. These selection tasks often require skilled judgments in a process which starts with the preliminary *hiring interview* to determine whether it is worthwhile to give the candidate further consideration. The second or more extended hiring interview comes after the recruit has passed the required tests and been given a satisfactory record by his references.

The *general interview* may have any one of a dozen purposes. One is for a discussion after the employee has been on the job for a short time to determine how he feels about the work and his boss. Other interviews may be for resolving worker conflicts, or discussing a contemplated promotion or transfer.

The *exit interview* can be very helpful for remedying shop conditions that frequently lead to grievances or "quits" by desirable workers.

One of the difficult problems of the interview is that there are so many types of interviewees, and so many different approaches that for the interviewer to match his approach to any one interviewee requires quick thinking. Two recognized approaches are the planned and the unplanned interviews. The first has all the questions planned in advance; the second allows the interviewer free reign. Obviously, the interview serves its purpose better when it can be conducted in undisturbed privacy.

Testing

Testing is probably the most controversial of personnel techniques. Opinions range from absolute reliance on test results to the conviction that many of them are merely whimsical inventions of psychologists. The truth lies somewhere between these extremes. The goal of testing is to find out quickly and economically whether an applicant will be successful on the job. The test score is merely a prediction of success or failure. Of the hundreds of tests available to personnel workers, the accuracy of prediction ranges from very high to very low.

There are two important measures of the accuracy of any test. The first is known as *validity*, which is a measure of the degree to which it accomplishes the purpose for which it was constructed. This can be measured best by comparing the test scores with subsequent performance on the job. The second measure of a test is its *reliability*. A common method for gauging reliability is to find out whether a test yields consistent scores when given to the same person at different times. A test may have almost perfect reliability and yet be totally invalid.

A distinction can be made among tests measuring proficiency, potentiality, and personality characteristics. *Proficiency* measures what the applicant can actually do at the time of testing. In this field, the "trade tests" are most dependable. They are applied to such fields as brick-laying and typing.

Often a candidate is not expected to have had any experience in the kind of job he is seeking, so his ability to learn is the primary question. Test of *potentiality*, or ability to learn, are used in such cases.

A third group of tests is used to measure *personality* characteristics thought to be relevant to the job being considered. These tests are relatively new and are not readily accepted by personnel departments.[1] One weakness of the personality tests is that many of them have been developed for use in the classroom and mental clinic, and have only limited usefulness in business.

In their present state of development, tests can be used only as an aid in selection and placement; they are rarely decisive. But as an auxiliary instrument, they are becoming increasingly valuable for personnel use.

References

The value of the opinion of a "reference" is another controversial matter. Communication with the reference is generally by mail, and the reply is likely to be a collection of rambling generalities. One way to avoid this result is to send a list of specific questions with a check-list of answers. Several observations can be drawn from experience about the dependability of references:

1. The applicant's references usually "puff" his abilities.
2. Occasionally the references are useless because it is obvious that someone is trying to get even for past grievances.
3. The applicant's ability may have improved or deteriorated since the reference's opinion was formed.

The author hired a number of satisfactory workers on the recommendation of parole officers. The officers reported in person and gave facts which amounted to the candidate's life history. The close relation between the candidate and his reference was cemented by the latter's authority to

[1] See "The Fallacies of Personality Testing," by William H. Whyte, Jr., in *Fortune*, September 1954.

return the client to his former residence for any infraction of company rules. Such references have proved to be reliable and cooperative. A foundry owner reported that fifty paroled convicts, housed in a dormitory on the plant site, were his most reliable workers.

Some of the best sources of information about an applicant are the personnel departments of other companies where the applicant has been employed. In industrial cities, the exchange of such information can be facilitated by local personnel officers' associations.

Selection

The selection decision depends largely on the application form, graded tests, and the interviewer's report. The chief of the requisitioning department customarily makes his selection on the basis of Personnel's recommendation. Test ratings lean heavily on battery scores to establish the applicant's adaptability to a specific job. In addition, training and experience are weighty considerations.

The psychological factor may be evaluated by appropriate tests. For executive positions, it is natural to assess the candidate's personality through interviewing. A few concerns, not satisfied with such an assessment alone, consider applicants' wives when hiring for managerial positions. The president of American Brake Shoe Company insists that "business doesn't hire men, it hires families."

The specification of *physical* job requirements is important in fitting the applicant to the nature of the work. The job requisition should indicate any characteristics helpful in making the selection. Figure 19.4 illustrates an employment requisition with job characteristics and corresponding checks from the physical examination. The supervisor fills out the requisition, and the plant physician decides whether the applicant's physical qualifications match the employment requirements.

Testing for *visual* qualifications is an important part of the physical examination. Upon visual skills may depend the quality and quantity of the worker's production, his accident record, his opportunities for promotion, his general morale, and occasionally his ability to retain a job. The necessity for visual competence in placement can be measured by the following advantages:

Increases production	Reduces labor turnover
Reduces accidents	Reduces absenteeism
Improves quality	Improves selection
Reduces waste	Improves morale
	Reduces training time.[2]

2 Training is the subject of Chapter 20.

Figure 19.4

Employment Requisition Form

HOURLY RATE

EMPLOYMENT REQUISITION

No._____

DEPARTMENT No._____ SHIFT_____ DATE_____

EMPLOYMENT DEPT. IS AUTHORIZED TO HIRE ONE
PERSON AS DESCRIBED BELOW

OCCUPATION	PART NO.	OPR. NO.	RATE	CHECK THESE ITEMS	
				MALE	
				FEMALE	
				INCREASE	

JOB CHARACTERISTICS—CHECK THOSE APPLYING

	REPLACEMENT	
	TEMPORARY	
	PERMANENT	
	EXPERIENCED	
	INEXPERIENCED	
	TOOLS	

STANDING	WALKING	CLIMBING	HEAVY	MEDIUM	LIGHT	FAST	OILY	DUSTY	NOISY	BENDING	TWISTING	PUSHING	PULLING	USES 1 HAND	USES 2 HANDS	USES BOTH HANDS & FEET	LIFTING TO WAIST	LIFTING ABOVE WAIST	REACHING OVER HEAD	SAFETY DEVICES REQUIRED	
1	2	3	4	5	6	7	8	9	10	11	12	13	14	15	16	17	18	19	20	21	HOURS _____ TO

REMARKS_____

FOREMAN_____ APPROVED_____ APPROVED_____

Transfer and promotion

In companies where transfer and promotion are carefully planned, the personnel department will probably provide a master chart classifying all jobs in the plant. Such a chart is divided into vertical columns representing the major divisions of the organization. Within each column, the jobs for that department are listed in descending order of importance. Thus, we might find in the top row of the column for Electrical Engineering the jobs of drafting supervisor and research director. The master chart of job classifications not only guides the personnel department in planned transfers and promotions, but at the same time it enables the employee to see the line of possible promotion within his own department, or his opportunities for transfer, at comparable pay, to other departments.

385

Records for controls

For personnel controls, the following records are pertinent:

1. Job evaluations	8. Merit ratings
2. Manpower inventory	9. Training records
3. Recruiting records	10. Employee discipline
4. Personnel requisitions	11. Absentee records
5. Interview records	12. Grievance records
6. Medical data	13. Accident records
7. Induction records	14. Labor turnover

Excessive absences suggests control by attacking the causes. Grievance records may point the finger to particular supervisors whose departments have more than a reasonable number of worker complaints. Accident records suggest machine-guard improvements, as well as worker-safety education and transfer or dismissal of accident-prone employees. Analysis of recruiting records indicates the best source of supply. Medical data reveal the relation between physical defects and unsafe operators.

Personnel forms

The number of personnel forms in any organization will depend on the number of functions that the various departments must perform. Serious thought must be given to reducing their variety, and those selected must be carefully drawn in order to minimize the possibilities of employee misunderstandings. Some excellent forms are available for specific purposes, such as separations, transfers and promotions, training, and accidents.[3]

The *application* form is often loaded with unnecessary details, some of which are objectionable to the applicant. Some state laws have forbidden questions about religion, race, and organizational memberships. Formidable-looking applications hinder recruitment, lose time, and confuse the main purpose. A *combination-purpose* form can often be prepared to take care of several personnel records. Figure 19.5 illustrates this type of form which was drafted and used successfully by the author.

Conclusions

This chapter has presented a skeleton discussion of the varied functions of the personnel department. Only those activities related to employment have been dealt with in anything like adequate detail. Subsequent chapters will deal with other facets of personnel work which have been touched upon briefly here — labor relations, health and safety, job classifications, as well as the less tangible psychological factors that can be grouped under the heading of personnel relations.

[3] The American Management Association has published a *Handbook of Personnel Forms and Records* (Research Report No. 16) containing forms for 137 different records.

Figure 19.5

Combination-Purpose Form

TO PERSONNEL				
CLOCK NO.	LAST NAME - FIRST - MIDDLE		BIRTH DATE	REQUEST DATE

MALE	FEMALE	MINOR	HANDICAPPED	VETERAN	RECEIVED BY PERSONNEL
REHIRE	NEW HIRE		RACE		

REQUISI-TION	JOB	DEPT.	OPER. NO.	RATE	HOURS	START

TRANSFER	FROM	TO
	DEPT. _____ SHIFT _____	DEPT. _____ SHIFT_____

SHIFT CHANGE	START HOUR _____	START HOUR _____
	QUIT HOUR _____	QUIT HOUR _____

JOB CHANGE	JOB _____	JOB _____
	DEPT._____ OP. NO. _____	DEPT. _____ OP. NO. ___

RATE CHANGE	BASE RATE _____	BASE RATE _____
	INCENTIVE NO. _____	INCENTIVE NO. _____

TERMINA-TION	JOB _____	DATE _____
	DEPT. _____ OP. NO. ___	

REASON:

_____ FOREMAN

EMPLOYMENT UNDERSTANDING

I HEREBY ACCEPT EMPLOYMENT AT ABOVE JOB RATE AND HOURS, UNDERSTANDING THAT ANY ADVANCE IN RATE DEPENDS ON MY BEING SATISFACTORY, AND CAN BE GRANTED ONLY BY MY DEPARTMENT HEAD '

_____ SIGNATURE

_____ FOR PERSONNEL DEPARTMENT

EMPLOYEE ACCEPTANCE

I HEREBY ACCEPT THE CHANGE IN MY STATUS AS NOTE ABOVE.

_____ SIGNATURE

Like all management activities, personnel is as good as its director is able to make it, with the cooperation of top management. Because the techniques involved are new and still lacking in scientific rigor, the personnel director himself must be a man of high competence, able to deal with others effectively and without friction, and to demonstrate to top management how his department plays an essential role in achieving company goals.

QUESTIONS

1. Under what circumstances should the management of personnel and personnel relations be separate assignments?
2. How would you set up requirements for the chief, program, and policies for a personnel department?
3. What is the basis of the essential conflict of interests between the employer and his employees?
4. Upon what circumstances is the organization of the personnel function dependent?
5. The text discusses nine general categories of the personnel functions. What are they?
6. What is meant by the statement that "the best personnel principles are only special cases of group dynamics"?
7. In view of the fact that the personnel activity does not get the sympathetic cooperation of the other departments, what attributes would you consider most important for the director of personnel?
8. How does the "labor budget" aid personnel in its recruiting?
9. What is often considered the best source for many kinds of job recruitment?
10. To what extent does the exit interview help Personnel in advising top management about improving job stability?
11. For what type of worker would you recommend the unplanned interview?
12. What reliance would you put on test scores? Would your opinion differ among job classifications? If so, for what classifications would you consider tests most reliable?
13. How would you go about appraising the validity of a particular test?
14. How would you rate the value of references in general? Which reference source would you consider most dependable?
15. Would you favor promotions within some job classifications on the basis of employment seniority to avoid personality conflicts?
16. The text lists fourteen records that can be used for control within the personnel function. If you were required to reduce the number to seven, which would you retain?
17. If you were compelled to select a single principle for guidance of the personnel function, what would it be?
18. What is the relation between job specifications and man specifications?
19. What would you consider the weakest aspect of most personnel interviews?
20. What are usually the chief factors in determining a selection decision?

CASE PROBLEM

OHIO PATTERN WORKS

The Ohio Pattern Works, located in Cincinnati, has been owned and operated by George Peterson for the past thirty years. Mr. Peterson learned his trade in the regular four year apprenticeship and served as a wood pattern-maker for a large concern before starting his own shop with three journeymen. Presently, the company employs 175 skilled mechanics making both wood and metal patterns for industry.

Mr. Peterson is unusually concerned about the selection of a new foreman for his wood pattern section. The previous foreman was with him nearly five years and was entirely satisfactory until six months before his separation from the company. Peterson discharged him because of the many complaints concerning his overbearing attitude from the journeymen whom he supervised. "One thing is certain," Peterson told his personnel director, "that man was the best mechanic on wood patterns in this state." The only explanation offered for his recent unsatisfactory supervision was the assumption that he had become so sure of his skills that he lost patience with his subordinates. Peterson wondered whether the change was due to the fact that the foreman had passed sixty years of age. He felt that possibly the new foreman should be a younger man, but he also feared that a young foreman might meet with prejudice from his subordinates.

A number of applicants were recruited from advertisements in trade journals and from among present employees, most of whom preferred that the new foreman should come from some other shop. Mr. Peterson had several conferences with his personnel director, impressing on him the necessity of getting as many facts as possible about the prospects' skill as wood pattern-makers. Eventually, the desirable applicants were reduced to two.

Artie Bein was thirty-five years old and a bachelor. During his seventeen work-years, he had been employed by five different shops in Cincinnati. On his present job, he had been president of his local union for nearly two years until he was promoted to foreman six months ago. Living in the same city, he was naturally acquainted with a number of the Ohio Company's pattern-makers, one of whom informed the personnel director that his union's executive committee was considering bringing charges against Bein for some unknown reason. Most of his references were satisfactory with the exception of the personnel director of his present employer who said "just so-so" in evaluating Bein's general qualifications as worker and especially as foreman.

Roger Saunders, the other prospect, was forty-five, married, and working in a neighboring state. He had had two jobs during his twenty-five working-years, having held the second job for twenty years. References from the personnel director of his present employer and from one of the vice-presidents of his national union reported that he was well liked by his fellow workers and apparently contented on his job. None of the Ohio Company's workers knew anything about Saunders.

The personnel director called in both Bein and Saunders and gave them written tests in which both appeared to be well qualified in their trade. He then interviewed each of them in minute detail and requested that they return the next day for a talk with Mr. Peterson.

Mr. Peterson was inclined to favor Artie Bein, because he was the younger man and already had had foreman experience. Peterson discounted as gossip Bein's possible trouble with the executive committee of his local union. Although Bein was still a member of the union, he had no voting rights as a member of management and was actually beyond the jurisdiction of the union as far as any action they might try to take. Furthermore, although most of the Ohio Company employees questioned on the subject said that they did not know Bein well enough to give an opinion, no one said anything against him except the individual who had dropped the hint to the personnel director asking him at the same time not to divulge his name to Mr. Peterson.

The personnel director was inclined to favor the Saunders application for several reasons. First, he was from another state and would presumably take the job without any pre-existing prejudices for or against him. Also he had been on his present job for twenty years and was married, indicating that he might be more conservative and make a more permanent foreman. The personnel director also preferred the general attitude that Saunders had shown during his interview.

PROBLEM: If it was your responsibility to choose between these two men, which would you select as foreman for Ohio's wood pattern division? Why?

20
Training and Development

Industry and business "train" their various classes of employees. Many of them also "develop" their managerial groups, including supervisors, middle-, and top-management. This is the major distinction suggested by our chapter title. "Training" involves instruction or drill in preparation for new or unfamiliar jobs. It has to do primarily but not exclusively with technical skills. "Development" is used in connection with the managerial levels and implies a broadening and improvement of skills already learned and used in practice. The distinction will be more fully exemplified as the chapter develops.

Every institution or organization trains its workers. Employees of all wage and salary levels are instructed by some person or activity responsible for their pay and the results of their labor. The housewife trains her maid through instructions, and the corporation president receives his instructions through management policies issued by the board of directors. The question, therefore, is not whether to train, but how to train. Experience has amply demonstrated that haphazard instructions are more expensive and less satisfactory than those which are formalized by scientifically planned training of workers and development of the management group.

Advantages of Worker Training

Training teaches employees in advance those things which they must know to understand their tasks and perform them satisfactorily. Formalized training also keeps records of worker performance in order to correct unsatisfactory work and to provide for the planned advancement of those doing superior jobs. The necessity for continuous training of employees is generally recognized among well-managed concerns. The skills demanded by modern business are developed as much by training as they are by experience. Good training, which is based on the successful experience of others, enables the trainee to reap greater benefits from his own experience. The profit motive requires the highest competence from every individual, and training is the best guarantee of competence on the job. Even with the best of mechanical equipment and materials, some companies experience decreasing productivity with increasing wages. The fundamental cause can usually be traced to the failure to utilize manpower potentials. Proper training reduces that intangible loss. Machines are made to perform standard tasks, but the human resources on all work levels must be trained to produce the most effective results.

Further objectives and advantages of proper training are:

1. Instructs the trainee in company history and products.
2. Improves motivation, which means satisfaction on the job.
3. Reduces accidents.
4. Reduces employee turnover.
5. Reduces production rejects.

Important Worker Training Factors

Need for training

Some of the obvious signs that indicate a need for training are:

1. The obvious lack of job techniques, poor worker methods, haphazard worker motions and planning, all due primarily to poor supervision
2. Failure to meet production standards or customer deliveries
3. A high ratio of production rejects, which indicates a lack of job training and results in poor worker morale
4. A poor safety record, which can also be traced to a lack of job training and poor morale
5. Generally poor worker morale, which is always evident when the other conditions exist

Management is to blame when morale is low because the worker does not know what he is doing or the correct way to do it. Good morale also depends on the worker's knowing what quality and quantity of production is expected of him. Most important, morale is usually a direct reflection of competence of supervisors or foremen, which depends primarily on their own training or lack of it.

Training objectives

Organized training is not a substitute for the experience that rank-and-file workers find in the line; rather, it is an equally important complement and spur to experience. Although training objectives differ with various companies, there are some fundamental goals, the chief of which is preparing qualified employees for the tasks to which they will be assigned. This preparation should not only cover the required skills, but should also develop in the worker the proper attitude toward his work. Worker attitudes may be guided into healthful channels by qualified trainers. The ultimate goal would be to so condition the worker that he finds real pleasure in his work. Such an attitude invariably maximizes productivity and this in turn is reflected in company profits.

Frequently the objective of training is to prepare the worker for advancement in his field or promotion to a higher skill. This objective is sometimes combined with the main purpose of preparing the trainee for his prospective job.

Training principles

The *job analysis* is necessary for indicating to the trainer the techniques to be considered in fitting the worker to the task for which he is preparing. It determines the nature and depth of the instructions and practices he is to receive. *Trainer realization of worker differences* is another essential guide for proper instruction. Unless trainee differences in mechanical adaptability, normal speed, and learning ability are considered in focusing instructions on the individual, results will be diffused by a sense of bewilderment. To secure maximum results, *worker motivation* must be stimulated to the point where he will welcome the training instruction and have confidence in his teacher. Motivation may be stimulated by occasional visits by some member of management, especially if the worker learns that the visitors took part in an earlier training group. The prime stimulant to motivation, however, is discerning and satisfying some of the individual's personal ambitions. The profitable use of these principles demands real leadership on the part of the trainer, who must be carefully selected in the first place, and then coached as to his proper attitudes and approaches.

Choosing trainees

One of the difficult preliminary tasks for the training director is to choose, in cooperation with other executives, trainees who possess sufficient ability, humility, receptivity, flexibility, and curiosity to take full advantage of a training course or program. If this part of the training task is properly performed, the supervisor selected for the program will be more inspired himself, because his trainees will have the motivation necessary for achieving good results.[1]

[1] Russell H. Ewing, "Management Training Objectives," (National Institute of Leadership, Los Angeles, 1958), p. 4.

Types of Training

Although training programs for workers are addressed to specific objectives, there are four general plans under which these objectives are realized: (1) *induction*, (2) *vestibule*, (3) *on-the-job*, and (4) *apprentice* training. Any worker-training plan should have in mind the general and basic desires of the trainees because irrespective of the subject matter or program approach, training plans will be more effective if personal incentives play a basic role. The average employee who wants to advance on merit is interested in assuming responsibility and working at full utilization of his ability. Encouragement gives him a feeling of importance no matter how menial his task. He wants his desires and accomplishments recognized and understood; he wants his supervisor to take a personal interest in him. All of these considerations should be implicit in planning and carrying out any training program for workers.

Induction Training. The aim of induction training is to make the new employee feel at home in his new environment. It tells him about his rights, privileges, and duties in his new group relationships. He is told about the history of the company and its products, and often taken on a tour of the plant with the other trainees. The location of the rest rooms and the cafeteria should be pointed out. Medical, financial, social, and recreational facilities for employees should be reviewed in detail. Company rules and regulations are explained, and finally the worker is told to whom he can talk when he has company or personal problems on which he wants advice.

On-the-job Training. The title of this plan explains its method. On-the-job trainees usually learn both the theory and practice of the job requirements at their benches from fellow workers who have already mastered the required skills. Usually the actual training under this plan is done by a journeyman at the next bench, or by the foreman. Only occasionally are regular teachers assigned to this type of training. Under most shop conditions, the foreman is too busy managing his group to do effective teaching, and the proficient journeyman at the next bench is not always willing or qualified to do a good training job.

On-the-job training is favored as a general practice by those who feel that the time spent in learning anywhere but on the job is largely wasted, or by those who feel that any of the other training methods are too expensive. This training plan cannot be of a general nature, but must be applied to the specific task for which the trainee has been selected. As with all types of worker training, the measure of training value against training costs is the real test of the plan.

Vestibule Training. This type of training is usually given in a room or section separated from the regular production or work area. Vestibule training is mostly concerned with production processes, but it can also be applied to various types of clerical or even industrial laboratory work. One purpose is to see that the worker receives instruction from someone who is adept at teaching under circumstances where the worker will not be embarrassed by the presence of other journeymen workers. Another idea involved in vestibule training is that it be directed specifically at some detail so that with the help of a skilled instructor, the worker can master the detail in a shorter time than would be possible when learning on the job.

There are several advantages to this type of training: (1) it is removed from the pressure of shop conditions with critical fellow-journeymen looking on, (2) it affords an opportunity to concentrate on the best methods of production, (3) operations are learned in a more pleasant environment, (4) machines and equipment are first-class and adjusted to learning operations, (5) competent instructors can be provided. Possible disadvantages are: (1) training may not represent actual shop conditions, (2) the time element in producing is given too little attention, (3) transfer from training to shop conditions may produce too much of a shock if not done properly.

We must balance these disadvantages against the decision of a training specialist who credits vestibule training with such achievements as a 75-per cent reduction in learning time, a 30-per cent reduction in labor turnover, and a 30-per cent increase in production.[2]

A. C. Rotheram, in charge of vestibule training for John Wright & Company of Birmingham, England, feels that one of the outstanding advantages of this type is that it provides "a training which, in addition to imparting the necessary job knowledge and skills, gives the trainee an appreciation of the purposes of his job and the nature of his own contribution to the work of the company as a whole."[3]

Apprentice Training. A long and interesting history lies behind this training method. All through the medieval period, regulations for apprentice training were detailed and strictly enforced. Apprentice training covers in a four-year period the principles and practices of the recognized skilled trades. On completion of apprentice instruction, the trainee becomes a journeyman, or worker qualified to practice his trade. For several centuries, apprentice training was regulated and controlled by the guilds, whose functions were later taken over by the unions. Of recent years, the federal and many state governments have been interested in establishing apprentice training on a higher level by suggesting programs and issuing certificates of proficiency. A number of states have inaugurated graduation exercises with speakers and state officers in attendance.

The essential difference between apprentice training and the other three

[2] Russell H. Ewing, "Vestibule Training for Tomorrow's Workers" (National Institute of Leadership, Los Angeles, Calif., 1958), p. 2.

[3] *Personnel* magazine, "Vestibule Training," May 1957, pp. 550–555.

forms is in its breadth and the fact that it covers both principles and practice. For example, the trade of foundry molder or core-maker is made up of a number of operations, for some of which a person may be trained under the vestibule plan in a short time. This plan is often adopted in war emergencies, when skills are diluted so that the work force may be expanded rapidly. The journeyman of the foundry trade not only can perform all phases of making cores and molds, but he also understands the relationships and sequence of operations, and the various methods and tools to be used for securing specific results.

Training Materials

Training materials consist chiefly of lectures, printed matter, case studies, and visual aids. The *lecture* may take many forms, and as an explanatory device, it is necessary in most training plans.

Printed materials are effective to the extent that the subject matter and presentation are appealing. Specially prepared printed or multigraphed material, useful for the following session, may be used to better advantage when it is distributed at the end of the current session. Explanatory outlines are often used to give trainees an over-all picture of a series of sessions, to afford an opportunity to see the beginning and the end, and the objectives as illustrated by all of the training materials. So-called "canned" materials, published by concerns specializing in this field, are often valuable aids when used as background or when directly related to the main subject matter.

Films, and the entire field of visual aids, have been growing in popularity. However, it must be understood that visual aids are only aids. Unless the instructor relates them directly to the principles and problems under discussion, they become merely entertainment or worse. The training value of visual aids depends on the subject, the quality of its presentation, the skill of the training instructor and the receptivity of the trainees. Visual aids are neither worthless gadgets nor the ultimate for training purposes. They will not take the place of an instructor nor change a poor program into a serviceable one.

The chief visual aids are motion pictures, slides, and opaque projections. The last two types may be used to show diagrams, photographs, charts, and drawings. The motion picture serves best where action is involved, as in office, sales, and production processes.

Slides are useful when arranged in sequence to show the steps of development in a process or situation, and to inject explanations of varying length for illustrations. Although they do not illustrate motion, they can be used to concentrate on individual situations for indefinite periods.

Opaque projections can be made from photographs, charts, or other materials from books or magazines. Multiplicity of available sources and ease of projecting are their chief virtues. Their limitations are the degrees of darkness required for good visibility, and the restricted distance over which they can be projected. Opaque projections are often made directly from original drawings in explaining assemblies. Figure 20.1 is an isometric drawing used for training by one of the large aircraft companies.

Visual aids are particularly serviceable for trainees when used to familiarize them with machines, methods, and materials. Figure 20.2 shows a worker engaged in a typical assembly operation, completing the job with the aid of a graphic chart. Visual aids add speed, vividness, and interest to the preliminary instruction period. It must be emphasized again, however, that they do not take the place of the instructor. Besides demonstrating how machines, methods, and materials are used, proper visual aids will show the *why* of these three phases of training — that is, they will show how the specific operation being demonstrated fits into the total pattern of production or office work. This aspect of training helps establish the importance of the worker's job. When visual aids are used, they help with the "presentation" of the subject, which is preceded by "preparation" and followed by "performance" and "follow-ups," for the purpose of checking on the degree of trainee comprehension and giving further explanations when necessary.

Figure 20.1

Isometric Drawing for Assembly Operations

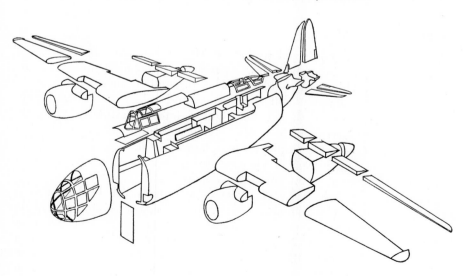

Figure 20.2

A Visual-Aural Training Aid

Courtesy: Raytheon Company

The promotion chart

A complete, well-publicized promotion chart stimulates the employees' use of company training facilities. It may even be a factor in the recruiting of desirable new workers. The promotion chart displays the types of jobs horizontally and their wage and salary ranges vertically. Horizontally, the chart should be divided into departments with the various jobs arranged in a descending scale according to wage or salary levels. The chart tells the employee at a glance how he can progress within his present job classification or by transferring to some other classification within his department or in some other department.

When the worker desires a change which he feels will lead to a more profitable future with his company, he is advised to consult his foreman or the personnel department to find out what additional preparation he will need to qualify for the change. If he follows the recommendations, he enrolls in some training program, within the company or on the outside, to prepare himself for the opportunity he seeks. In view of the results obtained from these charts, it is surprising how little attention is given to them by most concerns.

Supervisor Development[4]

The supervisor is a leader who needs development as comprehensive as that of his executive superior. It is at the management level of the supervisor that the struggle for production is lost or won. The supervisor is the person who must motivate the worker's performance by discussing his future goals and how to obtain them.

Several circumstances have led to the recent emphasis on supervisor training and development. The Wagner Act (1935) made management responsible for the acts of its supervisors, an obligation which suggested the necessity for instructing them in management policies. When the Taft-Hartley Act (1947) established the supervisor as definitely a part of management and denied him union negotiating rights, management was presented with an opportunity to do its part in solidifying the new relationship. Development programs in the art and practice of management grew apace. Supervisors began to be consulted in the making of management policies and decisions. In addition, pay boosts contributed to the establishment of their managerial status on a more realistic basis.

The purposes of supervisor development are primarily to improve production and labor-management relations, and to develop *leadership* qualities. While the technical phases of the supervisor's work are still emphasized, it has become recognized that the application of his technical skills is improved when supplemented with a knowledge of the fundamental techniques of human relations. The supervisor is also expected to minimize costs, wastes, and worker turnover. This is a job which opens many opportunities for continuous development.

The Supervisor's Development Needs. His primary needs are to improve his ability to plan, instruct, and lead. This is a broad order which requires the coordination of many phases of development. The thinking of mediocre supervisors is necessarily based on their experiences alone. They need to learn that decisions can be based on reasoned conclusions reached after adequate analysis. They should be taught that the same techniques of analysis can lead to better planning. They need to know how to manage themselves and their subordinates for maximum results. They must learn the principles which guide the practical application of their work. They must become familiar with the entire organization of which their activity is a necessary part.

There is another, more subjective, side to the supervisor's development. He must be made to feel that he has become a member of the management

[4] As discussed here, the term "supervisor" signifies all levels in charge of subordinates, including foremen.

team, sharing the goals and values of the other members of the team. He must be taught economic and industrial fundamentals in order to understand properly the relationships of these to his subjective needs.

There are also the technical details of his job, for which only continuous development on a planned basis will give him the progressive know-how necessary for attaining his shop ambitions. He must know his equipment, how it can be used to better advantage, how it is related to floor space and over-all productivity, and he must be familiar with the established system for handling materials. Record-keeping, power utilization, and safety are becoming more necessary. And finally, the principles involved in the successful handling of the work force are increasingly necessary as his subordinates develop group loyalties with their union.

Methods of Supervisor Development. The great bulk of supervisor development is done by conferences under the auspices of the training or personnel departments, or at meetings of the supervisor's club. Some companies send selected supervisors to special short college courses. Occasionally a large concern, or the local chapter of the Foreman's Club of America, establishes a series of weekly lectures, followed by discussion periods. When these series are set up by the clubs, their participants are drawn from a number of companies, a practice which greatly enlivens the discussions.

Important supplements to formal programs are the literature and magazines designed especially for supervisors. One of the useful services which these publications perform is that of supplying information on labor relations. Labor laws are explained and illustrated with case material, and suggestions are made about what should and should not be done in this difficult field.

Conferences are usually spoken of as "controlled" or "uncontrolled." The former is conducted with planned procedures and objectives; the latter has the advantages of spontaneity, but may also develop into a "glorified bull session." The chief advantage of the conference is its development of a critical or questioning attitude and the ability to analyze situations. The controlled conference analyzes problems, assembles and studies facts connected with them, both pro and con; it discusses the advantages and disadvantages of proposed solutions, and frequently tries to arrive at a group opinion.

The degree to which the conference stimulates thought and interest among the trainees depends largely on the caliber of the conference leader, and on his ability to plan the material and physical details of each session. The thinking through of typical problems, rather than memory work, should set the tone for these conferences. The foremen already know what kinds of problems arise on the job. They are seeking solutions. Because the solutions arrived at through the conference method are the product of group thinking, reflecting the attitude of all the participants, the individual supervisor automatically gets experience in listening to and weighing the opinions of others, and emerges from these sessions with a more rational, less opinionated approach to his managerial role.

The successful conference requires:

1. A qualified leader
2. A carefully selected group
3. A number limited to the purpose
4. Sessions of definite length
5. A regular schedule of meetings
6. Adequate conference-room facilities
7. Well-prepared outlines and materials
8. Problems of direct interest to the group

The *conference leader* must be just that — not a teacher or lecturer; the time for training has passed. The supervisors have plenty of problems; they are now interested in knowing how to think through to the answers. They need leadership, which means that someone must prepare the problems, materials, and meeting place, and then act as conference chairman, guiding the discussion, keeping it focused on the problem at hand, encouraging everyone to contribute, but keeping his own opinions in the background. To stimulate and control group discussion, the leader must prepare interesting problems (case studies), and assemble facts and plans of action to implement them. In many cases, demonstrations through the use of charts, graphs, diagrams, films, and blackboard work will highlight the problem and make it come to life.

A long list of subjects falls within the supervisor's field. The following is a selected example.[5]

Organization principles	Interpreting company policies
Planning and scheduling	Care of tools and equipment
Quality control	Worker morale
Safety practices	Work simplification
Merit rating	Time study
Company's future plans	Cost analysis
Department budgets	Techniques of instruction
Absentee problems	Inventory control
How to reprimand	Worker incentives
Job evaluation	Opportunities for promotion

The dissatisfied worker

Government Training Aids. The pressing need for improved productivity during World War II caused the federal government to sponsor plans for the

---

[5] Representative subject lists for supervisor conferences have been prepared by the American Rolling Mills, Middletown, Ohio, the Metropolitan Life Insurance Company's Service Bureau, *Factory Management and Maintenance* magazine, the University of Illinois' Business Management Service, the Department of Manufacturers of the U.S. Chamber of Commerce, and many others.

rapid training of the many new supervisors required and of those who never had the benefit of formal instruction in their field. Several top executives of large industries worked out the Training-Within-Industry (TWI) program which includes: Job-Instruction Training (JIT), Job-Methods Training (JMT), and Job-Relations Training (JRT). Prepared scientifically to produce speed and effectiveness in supervisor training, these three short courses were given to progressively larger groups until most of the supervisors engaged in any phase of war work were taught how to apply principles in supervising workers.

Executive Development

Programs for executive improvement include middle and top management. As a rule, until the past five years at least, plans for development of the executive group have left much to be desired as far as participation is concerned. Most executives are enthusiastic backers of programs for supervisors and operating employees, but many feel that the progress they have made to reach their present levels indicates that further development is unnecessary. Others convince themselves that they do not have the time — a reasonable proof of their need for management development.

Executive development may take the form of planned or unplanned conference groups at company headquarters or with some outside association, along with the executive members of other companies. The American Management Association and the Society for the Advancement of Management are two organizations offering special and over-all programs for executive development. Such sessions may take the form of annual meetings or periodic regional meetings covering specialized branches of management. The AMA divides its executive program into seven divisions: personnel, finance, office management, production, insurance, marketing, and packaging. Besides conferences in each of these fields, the Association supplies trainees with periodicals and publications specializing in the subjects covered. The SAM program operates largely through its scattered chapters which hold monthly dinner meetings, with talks on specific subjects followed by general discussions.

Within the past ten years, a number of universities in metropolitan centers have been offering "institutes," or programs of lectures and seminars on subjects relevant to management. These sessions last from two or three days to as many weeks. Their purpose is to develop a broader point of view on the part of their participants, as well as to introduce current material in government regulations and new techniques in the various fields of management. The institute sessions are usually opened by professors or other specialists who outline the subject under consideration, and this is followed by general discussion based on the experience of the participants. The underlying objective is to furnish facilities for training in "coordination, logical processes of thinking, and in human, social, political, and industrial values and vision."

Management development within the individual company invariably consists of discussion conferences on selected topics, frequently based on some current problem of the concern. These meetings are conducted by ranking members of management and are open to all levels above the rank of supervisor.

Many universities have adopted management curricula designed to train young men for future executive positions. Business executives are becoming increasingly interested in these groups, both as participants and as sponsors.[6] This type of sponsorship will doubtless hasten the development of cooperative plans, by which students of management will receive on-the-job experience with selected companies while they are still in college, probably extending their formal academic training beyond the conventional four years. Subjects for this type of executive development are either of a general nature, such as finance, personnel, costs, sales, productivity, and the like, or they may relate to specific problems of current operations, submitted by interested company executives.

There are a number of goals that may be set for the development of practicing executives, and this variety makes it rather difficult to generalize. It is reasonable to assume, however, that the fundamental objective is to encourage intellectual activity so that the executive will extend the breadth of his outlook. Such an accomplishment will give him a better insight into business problems in advance of their happening. To achieve this insight, he will have to develop a more rational, less opinionated approach to his managerial role. By and large, the goal is to broaden the specialist into a generalist. Too often chief executives reach their positions after many years' experience in finance, sales, or other compartmentalized activities. It is only natural, perhaps, that they should advance to the top with a fixed slant in the direction of their long and successful experiences, but that is not enough for the top jobs. The executive must overcome any personal resistance to learning and must demonstrate the capacity to direct his learning toward the goals of personal development, creative thinking, planning, and action. Part of his development must be demonstrated in his ability to solve management problems far enough in advance to prevent disastrous results. There has been a general feeling among the top-executive group that an executive is entitled to some satisfaction if he is right half the time in predicting and measuring future events that will affect his company. But how much salary is an executive worth who is wrong so often that his company loses money? Incompetent executives may temporize with that answer, but the owners (stockholders) of the company might justifiably muster a majority to say that such executives are worth "nothing."

In his position as leader the executive must not only be strongly motivated towards action and accomplishment himself, but he must, by his example,

[6] In 1952, Alfred P. Sloan, Jr., Chairman of General Motors, donated $6,250,000 to the Massachusetts Institute of Technology for a new management school, of which Edward P. Brooks, former vice-president of Sears, Roebuck, is Dean.

motivate his subordinates all down the managerial line. *"Motivation* is one of the manager's most vital functions, and yet one of the leading authorities on management states that 'less than 10 per cent of all assignments carry any motivation.' Motivation is largely a matter of getting people to want to do their best without the use of fear or force. To be successful in the long run, motivation should be directed toward achieving individual desires, group goals and company objectives."[7]

If an executive aims to be a leader of his subordinates, he must learn to communicate with them often, successfully, and painlessly. Though it is pleasant to circulate good news, sound internal relations would suggest that the executive communicate the bad news as well before it is learned through the grapevine. Motivation and communication might well receive the strongest stress in any program of managerial development. The stimulation of subordinates through an understanding of leadership, motivation, and communication should be the chief aims of executive development.

Conclusions

Probably more emphasis is placed on methods for instructing supervisors in human relations than on any other phase of training. Training literature continually expounds the basic values of good human relations and the approaches for stimulating them. Human relations emphasizes the art of dealing with people in such a way that they will want to do the things expected of them. It reaches its highest achievement in a successful combination of individuals engaged in a group effort.

All companies train their employees. The paramount question is whether to train according to an orderly plan, with tested techniques, recognized aids, and with capable instructors, or by haphazardly turning the new worker loose on his job location to find out for himself, trusting to the mercies and intelligence of those who found out the same way. To contend that the "hard way" is more effective and less expensive is simply to drive blind in unfamiliar territory. The successful training program must be based on these essentials which should generally be scheduled in the order listed:

1. Establish the need for training
2. Determine the objectives of the program
3. Sell management on the value of the program
4. Adopt sound training policies
5. Fix responsibility for the training program
6. Select and train competent instructors
7. Plan the program and announce its schedule
8. Sell the value of training to the employees

[7] Russell H. Ewing, "Management by Motivation" (National Institute of Leadership, Los Angeles, Calif., 1961), Preface.

9. Evaluate the results of the program
10. Report progress and final evaluation to management

Observations over the past fifty years, before competition became so keen and government regulations of business so prolific, point definitely to a smug satisfaction on the part of many members of top management. Although their protective coloring of position has been diluted by the numerous programs designed for their development, to a large extent executives have avoided these opportunities that would have made their tasks easier and their performances more satisfying to stockholders. Too many have used their authoritative positions to avoid mental development, while in other cases we cannot escape the conclusion that many have avoided development programs for fear they would expose their managerial weaknesses. In contrast to these attitudes, the strong executive avails himself of all opportunities to improve the effectiveness of his leadership.

QUESTIONS

1. What is the fundamental difference between training and development?
2. To what extent is the typical worker trained in various types of business?
3. What are some of the five indicators that suggest the need of worker training?
4. What is the relation between worker training and worker morale?
5. What are some of the objectives of adequate training programs?
6. Which of the four types or *phases* of training do you consider most valuable from the standpoint of management?
7. What are some of the disadvantages of on-the-job training?
8. What advantages does vestibule training have over the on-the-job plan?
9. What effect has the CIO had on apprentice training?
10. There are many types of training materials for use with workers. If you, as the trainer, were limited to two, which would you choose?
11. What is the chief value of the promotion chart to management and to workers?
12. Why does supervision development take a different approach from that used for subordinates?
13. How did the Taft-Hartley Act free the supervisor from some of the union restrictions found in the Wagner Act? What were those restrictions?
14. How do foremen development conferences differ essentially from those of upper management?
15. What are the essential requirements of a successful conference leader?
16. How do the federal and many state governments aid in training programs? What plan was adopted by the TWI program for hastening foreman development?
17. What is the chief weakness of the many programs for executive improvement? Who is responsible for that defect? Why?

18. To what extent have our universities contributed to upper management development? Do you have any way of knowing how successful the plans have been? Do executives with 20–30 years' experience listen to college professors? Why or why not?

19. What is the chief goal of development for practicing executives?

20. What subjects are usually considered in executive development?

CASE PROBLEM

PITTSBURGH STEEL CORPORATION

Pittsburgh Steel was founded in 1900. It produces cold and hot rolled and galvanized sheets, strips, and beams, and fabricates a full line of steel products and structures. It employs approximately 15,000 workers. Its training program was started in 1922, and a development plan was added ten years ago.

In 1961, the total program was analyzed by Allan Curlin, Director of Personnel, in collaboration with Lowell Watkins, his Training Director. It seemed perfectly reasonable to make a study of program results after forty years of operation. But another reason for the survey was the fact that the president of the company, Alfred Malphus, felt that some of the results, especially with respect to the development phases, were not commensurate with the increasing costs of the program. Among other things, Malphus was irritated to find that the average cost of developing college graduates for minor management positions was approximately $5,500 for the previous year, and that 20 per cent of the candidates were not making grades that assured their retention.

By 1960, the program had comprised four sections: (1) worker training, (2) foremen training and development, (3) student training and development, and (4) middle and upper management development.

It was easy to measure the effectiveness of the worker training program by comparing the productivity of those who finished the courses with the average of the regular employees. The results of this portion of the program appeared relatively satisfactory from management's standpoint, but some of the foremen who were responsible for on-the-job training complained about the time they were forced to take away from coordinating the work of their other subordinates. Several of the better foremen had made a point of reviewing this situation with the training director on two or three occasions without any promise of a change.

The company program provided for the training of new foremen through a series of lectures, which were concerned largely with instruction about company policies, a description of grievance settlement procedures, and explanations about the content of the labor-management agreement. The development conferences of the older foremen were devoted to the analysis of daily problems introduced by members of the group. This foreman section was more serious in that its members were apparently seeking suggestions from colleagues who had worked out the difficulties of similar problems. Both the lectures and the conferences were held after working hours on the foremen's own time. Some of the men felt that this practice was unfair since the objective of the program was to improve productivity and to reduce wasted worker and foreman time caused by prolonged settlement of grievances.

The student training and development program naturally divided itself into two parts. The total program lasted eighteen months with study of company operations consuming the first six. By and large, management methods as they applied to the steel business were the subject of the second period. The third or development period consisted of assigning students to department heads on a rotating basis through which they learned minor departmental duties by observation, instruction, and actual performance.

There was some evidence that the engineering and business groups of students were not always congenial. Also, a few student trainees offered too many suggestions for improvement to suit their temporary superiors in that part of the development program. Although such instances were exceptional, they appeared to make a decided impression on several members of middle management. Furthermore, too many students became weary of the eighteen months of tutelage and expressed displeasure with the delay of opportunities for showing their abilities.

The fourth phase of the general program sought to develop the managerial capacity of the members of middle and upper management. Two measures of the success of this section could be (1) the number of the members of middle management who advanced to upper management positions, and (2) the number of new members of upper management who had to be recruited from the outside when vacancies occurred. The survey report was not complimentary to this part of the program. President Malphus expressed his displeasure with the results, especially as upper management was concerned. It frequently happens that members of upper management feel that they have already "arrived" and that they get very little real benefit from outside suggestions even from their colleagues.

PROBLEM: Based on this sketchy survey of the results of the training and development program at Pittsburgh Steel, what suggestions would you make for its improvement?

21

Personnel Relations

As explained at some length in previous chapters, it is the special province of personnel relations to improve productivity through increasing the worker's interest in and satisfaction with his job.

Motivating productivity

Personnel departments have commonly tried to stimulate worker interest through such rewards as incentive pay, extended vacations, and various types of insurance. All of these have their effect while the worker is *off* the job. Even incentives stimulate interest in the pay check rather than in the job itself.

It is not our purpose here to try to isolate the secret of on-the-job motivation for productivity — whoever does so will be richly rewarded. But we have arrived at the point where we are confident that the stimulation of the individual's interest in his job is the only dependable path to maximum productivity. We know, further, that a worker's social relations on the job — his interactions with management and fellow workers — are immensely important in creating and maintaining that motivation, even if we can offer no precise formula for ideal personnel relations.

When workers were skilled artisans, they were naturally interested in their product because it was evidence of their personal skill. The Industrial Revolution undermined this worker interest by transferring his skills to the new machines. Because machine operators frequently matched the products of their skilled predecessors simply by pulling levers, a decline in job interest was a natural consequence. Motivation was maintained to some degree by the personal relationship of the worker with his supervisor. To the worker, the supervisor was the company, and in that sense, the worker still retained a personal interest in his shop associations if not in his product.

The next deadening effect on job interest was caused by large-scale production. Industrial functionalism relieved the supervisor of more and more of his activities until finally little was left except his responsibility for production. With hiring, firing, promotion, inspection, and other functions assigned to staff groups, the worker gradually began to look on his supervisor as a more or less helpless cog in the management machine.

Personnel is trying to find something to recapture the worker's interest in his job, an interest which has been slowly losing ground since machine production absorbed such a large part of his former skill. Our relatively feeble progress measures the difficulty of the task. The basic trouble probably lies in our applying piecemeal remedies without having made a fundamental diagnosis.

Building morale

For the purposes of personnel relations, morale may be defined as *the degree to which the worker finds satisfaction in doing the things that are expected of him.* This definition is not so simple as it may at first appear. The fact is that a worker may be the focus of more than one set of expectations. We shall be using morale to refer to the worker's state of satisfaction in performing the tasks assigned to him by *management.* But often the informal worker group will evolve a set of expectations quite different from management's. It is not an uncommon practice for a group of workers to agree among themselves on what constitutes a fair day's work. Then, if any individual exceeds the quota set by the group, he is liable to disapprobation from the other members. He will be labeled a "rate buster," or he may be ostracized from the social life of the group. Therefore, Personnel must consider the workers not only as individuals, but also as members of informal groups. The ultimate goal must be to make the many component groups want to do the things that will best serve company interests. This is more easily said than done, and there must be much more research in the area of group dynamics before management can expect any definitive answers.[1]

Components of Morale. The resident physician of a hospital does not ask the nurse, "What is the state of health in the ward tonight?" He inquires about the health of the individual patients. He has no cure for sickness in general, but only for specific illnesses. Similarly in business and industry, if Personnel is to do anything about morale, it must go beyond the statement that "morale is low" and find out in what particular respects morale is low. Each case of low morale must be seen as a particular illness requiring its own special treatment. An example of high morale which is not oriented to management's goals is the workers' wholehearted participation in a strike. Here the satisfaction is derived from fulfilling the expectations of the union leadership.

[1] Two brochures— *Training by Motivation* and *Management by Motivation* — published in 1961 by the National Institute of Leadership (Beverly Hills, California) contain excellent material on this elusive subject of motivation. They are highly recommended to those wishing to pursue this subject.

Experience has shown that within any group of employees, there are a number of specific morale builders, and sometimes an even larger group of morale destroyers. One of the fundamental purposes of personnel relations is to add impetus to the morale builders while minimizing the effect of the morale destroyers. What are some of the morale builders and destroyers over which the supervisor has at least partial control?

A Group of Experienced Supervisors Report[2]

Morale Destroyers	Morale Builders
Favoritism and nepotism	Square dealing with workers
Religious and fraternal preferences	Setting good example
Display of anger by supervisors	Recognizing ability — giving credit
Hasty and unwise decisions	Encouraging individuals
Wage discriminations	Planning department's work
Lack of punctuality	Keeping tools in condition
Untidiness in the shop	Encouraging suggestions
Agitation and rumors	Safe working conditions
Carelessness	Good housekeeping
Unfulfilled promises	Posted promotion programs
Jealousy	Encouraging loyalty
Dishonesty	Encouraging cooperative spirit
Hasty and unfair discharges	Equitable wage programs
Belittling management policies	Maintaining discipline
Paternalism	Giving clear instructions
Too many bosses	Keeping all promises
Too much display of authority	Avoiding mixed responsibilities
Poorly maintained equipment	Maintaining strong leadership

The Morale Survey. The morale survey attempts to measure employee thinking concerning company operations and management. It is used to discover those conditions, physical and human, which cause good or bad morale. It can be applied to management as well as to workers. Management attitudes are important because of their influence on worker actions. When a reasonable number of workers complain about a given situation, management has a definite problem for correction.

A poor survey will depress worker morale. It must be planned to fit the situation where it is applied. In general, these surveys may be made by questionnaires or interviews. While the former method is quicker and less expensive, the latter obtains more accurate and usable information on which to base analyses and conclusions. There are two types of interviews — the planned and the unplanned. The former asks definite questions and records

2 This information was contributed by a group of some seventy-five supervisors, selected from industries in Dayton, Ohio. They had an average service of about twenty years, and were members of the National Foremen's Association. The author conducted a series of weekly conferences with the group on "Management for Foremen."

the answers; the latter allows the interviewed employee to develop freely his own line of discussion.

There are a number of professional firms making morale surveys. Besides the many benefits derived from their experiences with different types of business concerns, they have the advantage of being relatively unbiased from the employee's point of view. This factor helps promote belief in the confidential nature of the replies given by the workers. Few employees will give opinions freely if they think that management will be able to identify them with their opinions. Properly conducted and professionally analyzed, surveys point out annoying situations, many of which are reasonable subjects for attention. To the extent that this is true, they also reduce employee grievances. In addition, they point the finger of responsibility at those supervisors and executives who cause poor worker morale.

Induction

An employee's first few days on the job can leave lasting impressions. Small concerns can accomplish satisfactory induction through the friendly attitudes of old-timers in their associations with the newcomer. In large companies, induction or indoctrination has a greater effect on employee morale than is generally believed. One source suggests seven ways to "handle with care" the new worker.[3]

1. *Greet him cordially,* make him feel that he is needed for the job.
2. *Show sincere interest* by discussing company policies.
3. *Explain the importance of his job* and its high work standards.
4. *Show him around,* pointing out the time clock, first aid, rest room and other facilities.
5. *Introduce him to fellow employees.*
6. *Help him to get instructions for the new job.*
7. *Visit him* during the first week on the job.

Besides welcoming the worker to the group, induction should provide information about the company, including its history and products. Explanation of the facilities and services as outlined in the handbook should be a part of the induction process. Working hours, rate, time and place of pay, rules for absences, rest periods, and vacation plans are examples of information desired by the newcomer.

In well-managed companies, special rooms equipped with charts and moving-picture equipment are in charge of trained instructors. These facilities may be used for job instruction and training as well as for induction.

One automobile manufacturer, with a four-hour instruction program,

[3] Condensed from *The ABC of Supervision* (Urbana, Ill.: University of Illinois, Business Management Service Bulletin No. 106, 1949).

devotes the first hour to introductory statements, answering questions and letting the newcomers know where they can find answers to the problems not discussed. The second hour is given over to a plant tour. The third is devoted to short talks by the nurse, the safty engineer, and the suggestion supervisor. The final session "touches on the more detailed and personal aspects of the employee's relationship with the company."

Communication

An American Management Association survey suggested that the most pressing industrial-relations problem is the need for better communications between employer and employee. Communication can and should operate both vertically and horizontally. Vertically, it carries information from management to workers, and vice versa. Horizontally, it means that individuals on the same levels of management or work force should communicate ideas of mutual or company interest. Communication on all levels and in all directions is absolutely necessary to good morale.

Management should have daily contacts with its subordinates all down the line. Foremen should keep workers informed of company plans and policies as they have been received from superiors. It is also the foreman's duty to see that messages about what the worker is thinking, questioning, and planning go up the line for management's consideration and action. Management "sharing" is a vital stimulation to employee "belonging."

How is adequate communication to be developed and practiced? There are literally dozens of ways. Top and middle management will seem less remote to the workers if they walk through the plant from time to time. Management discussions with employees about company affairs can be important, as the president of Jack & Heinz so ably demonstrated. His "us and we" talks to all plant employees over the intercommunication system developed such *esprit de corps* among the company's "associates" (employees) that they actually defended their management against public criticism. Letters from the president of the concern to the workers' homes about company matters or personal birthday and holiday messages are factual and social communications of high merit.

The extent to which top management communicates with all its levels, including foremen, often sets the pattern for the foreman's communication attitude toward his workers. Management dinners, forum discussions, speaker meetings, and periodic week-end conferences promote intraplant communication downward from the foreman level.

Suggestion system

There are two ideas behind the suggestion system. The apparent purpose is to increase productivity, reduce costs and accidents, and make the work environment more acceptable. The less apparent purpose is to stimulate personal participation in company affairs. Improved employee participation often has more valuable long-term results than the financial rewards for successful suggestions. The cash goes to the winner, but the spirit of the contest permeates the group.

The suggestion system has many boosters and critics. That it can be beneficial is attested by the number of large and successful concerns which have stayed with the plan. Early experiments with the idea proved that there are many paths leading to failure. In the first place, it must be conducted along technical lines and not as a side show. It requires selling to start with and good management for continued success. Merely installing suggestion boxes filled with blanks and providing for confidential depositories are not enough.

Suggestion systems are not so beneficial to small concerns whose workers have face-to-face access to top management. But in large companies, the impersonal approach is the only alternative. To operate a successful system in a large company, a full-time manager is required. There must be competent technical evaluation of the suggestions, and there must usually be group decisions about putting the suggestions into effect. The kind of awards and the way in which they are presented can make or break the idea. What to pay for acceptable suggestions should be a matter of announced policy; the awards usually range from 10 to 20 per cent of the first year's savings. When properly set up and managed, the suggestion system saves time and money, improves operations, keeps supervisors alert, and improves worker relations. It is the last of these which chiefly concerns us here. To be successful, the system must have top-management support, be properly organized with attractive rewards, have prompt action in accepting or rejecting ideas, and receive proper publicity.[4]

Stock ownership

In the early twenties, there was a decided spurt in the sale of company stock to employees. In some cases, the price was made attractive to hasten the process. Management figured that morale and productivity would be improved and employee dissension minimized if the workers participated in company ownership. This morale-boosting idea scarcely had an opportunity to prove its worth by the time the depression of the 1930's scored a knockout blow. Employee investors out of jobs fell back on their stock purchases to find that the market values were far below costs, even when there was a market. Workers felt that management had "taken them for a ride." The

[4] Successful ideas receive awards from $5 upward. In 1952, the Tennessee Coal & Iron Division of the U.S. Steel Company paid $10,000 to a section foreman for his drawing which showed how to achieve a continuous flow of broken coal from the miners to the mine car.

situation was so general that the stock-ownership plan for employees appeared to be definitely out for the future.

Recently, however, a steady rise in the stock market and national protective legislation have established a belief that the 1929 disaster cannot happen again. General economic education has convinced many workers that they, too, have a stake in our economic system. Finally, promotion of many executive stock-option plans have convinced the rank-and-file employees that they should participate in such deals. The Sears Roebuck profit-sharing employee trust owns about 30 per cent of the company's common stock. The employee-stockholders do not get their certificates, but they have received excellent profits on retirement. Many companies allow workers to withdraw investments before the stock is paid for, with or without interest, and a few companies agree to buy back employee-owned stock at the purchase price.

The present stock-purchase plans are still on trial, but with attractive features not found in the plans of the twenties. The Procter & Gamble plan has been in operation for sixty-five years. The American Telephone & Telegraph has found the idea profitable, selling two million shares to employees in five years. Early in 1950, the publisher of *The Milwaukee Journal* wrote in a letter to employees: "We of the *Journal* staff are convinced that no small share of this newspaper's continued growth, as well as its widely recognized excellent news coverage, is due to the extra effort of those who are its owners as well as its employees."

Conclusions

There are basic principles for the successful functioning of all human relations. In personnel relations they may be summarized as follows:

1. *Maintain fair wages, hours, and working conditions.* These are fundamental considerations not only from the standpoint of human relations, but for maximum productivity.

2. *Make the worker feel worthwhile.* Too often management relies entirely on the pay check, which many surveys show is not the primary worker consideration.

3. *Keep the worker informed.* The extent to which this principle should be carried depends on the circumstances, but it is evident that ignorance breeds suspicion, a poor foundation on which to build satisfaction and productivity.

4. *Eliminate paternalism.* The worker is not interested in management's "gifts." It should be realized that neither pay nor any other consideration earned by the employee is a gift from management or from the owners of the enterprise.

5. *Encourage participation in policy formulation.* When company policies are guided by basic principles, they cannot get out of hand. On the con-

trary, participation in policy-making begets participation in its effective application. Group particiation of employees in personnel policy-making and the formulation of rules and regulations for the operation of such policies is generally less "radical" than management suspects. The progress of employee participation in this field frequently demonstrates a higher level of worker intelligence than anticipated.

Personnel Services

Working conditions

The plant that is a good place to work attracts the best employees and builds team spirit. Team spirit increases productivity, and productivity makes profits. It is of paramount importance, therefore, that the plant should provide pleasant surroundings. What are some of the things that create such an atmosphere?

The *location of the plant* is important. It should be easily accessible by some inexpensive form of public transportation. Provision for loading and unloading workers under shelter from bad weather conditions is another desirable feature of a transportation plan. Adequate parking space on the plant grounds is a matter frequently dealt with by union committees.

Passenger tunnels leading to various departments within large plants are a convenience in saving time and the irritations of crowding. Tunnels within and between plants also serve company interests by minimizing production interferences caused by going through other departments.

Washrooms that are convenient, sanitary, and commodious are absolute necessities in modern business. The improved examples of the past few years have set a standard which companies must meet today if they wish to attract and hold good employees. Plenty of space in which to change clothes, adjacent to lockers with adequate ventilation, is also a necessity.

Good *color schemes* have both physical and psychological value and reduce accidents. *Lighting standards* minimize the fatigue that follows eye strain. Care of the eyes is emphasized in the Western Electric Company's new electronics plant, where lighting fixtures are recessed in an acoustic ceiling.

Individual *bench lamps* facilitate work on assembly jobs. *Magnifying glasses* are provided to ease the strain of close work. In the past few years, much headway has been made in the reduction of *dust, dirt,* and *fumes,* even in foundries. Finally, *noise control* is receiving scientific attention in the interests of both the workers and the company.

Economic security

There is an expanding group of economic services performed for employees by the personnel department. They include financial aid or subsidies to meet various personal contingencies. Aids in case of accidents, loss of health, old age, and death may also be classified as economic. In recent years, employers have been recognizing their financial responsibility for certain types of worker discharge, especially technological unemployment, where the worker himself is not to blame.

Group life insurance and hospital and surgical plans are often financed in whole or in part from company funds. The Social Security Act has assigned to the employer financial obligations which have added to the duties of the personnel department. Company pension plans have become expensive items. Because the NLRB decided (1945) that even voluntary plans requiring no employee contribution were "a condition of employment," they were made subject to union bargaining. Based on this finding and the Supreme Court decision (1948) in the Inland Steel case, large unions have demanded and secured pension plans.

Recreation and social programs

It is estimated that recreational programs cost business about four hundred million dollars a year. Such an expenditure should go a long way toward improving health and morale, although when carried to excess, the results may be just the opposite. Sponsorship of the recreation program often determines its morale and health values. The program which is sponsored and financed by management is not likely to receive enthusiastic support from the workers. The John Hancock Mutual Life Insurance Company has an employee recreation association which handles all sports, picnics, and social features for its four thousand members. A twelve-man board of directors conducts such an efficient organization that its income from dues and benefits makes it self-supporting.

The success of recreation and social programs depends largely on employee participation. People who work and play together will develop mutual respect and understanding. It may even be a morale booster to see a management team go down to defeat, especially when the play is sprinkled with humor. Social contacts among the employees and with management are helpful when they are properly conducted. There are instances, however, where late dances with poorly considered refreshments interfere with rather than boost the next day's production. Ill-advised social affairs are more likely to promote friction than harmonious employee relations. In a national survey, management ranked the promotion of sports at the top of its list of activities for improving employee social relations.

Food services

In the survey referred to above, both unions and management rated plant cafeterias in second place among activities useful in promoting employee morale. Unions and management are likewise convinced that food services should be the responsibility of management. Labor has definite ideas about cafeterias, but no desire to participate in their operation. Labor is equally sure that it wants company cafeterias to operate at cost, fearing that a company loss may be used as a bargaining point in contract negotiations. Both workers and management have agreed that it is a good idea for them to eat together — once in a while.

There is a definite trend toward professionally operated cafeterias, with management paying a fee for operation while maintaining control over menus. Cafeteria concessions to outsiders are rapidly becoming a thing of the past. With company control, it is understood that management absorbs any deficit resulting from cafeteria operations. Mid-morning and afternoon snack periods may be spent in the plant cafeterias, or be serviced from outside restaurants on wheels, from inside mobile food carts (see Figure 21.1),

Figure 21.1

A Modern Food Truck

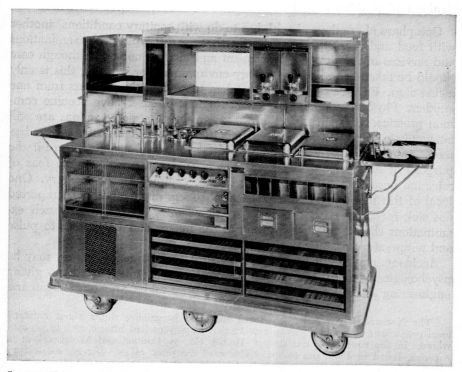

Courtesy: Shampaine Industries, Inc.

or from so-called coffee tote boxes. In some cases, vending machines serving sandwiches and hot and cold drinks are scattered throughout the plant or offices to save time. Professional food services offering these plans cater to office buildings and industrial plants.

Company cafeterias have become such a vital part of business that the NLRB has recognized the union's right to bargain about the price of meals.[5]

Some of the by-products claimed to result from cafeteria services are:

1. Higher productivity	5. Better worker morale
2. Reduced labor turnover	6. Healthier employees
3. Less absenteeism	7. Improved company loyalty
4. Fewer accidents	8. Better job applicants

With the idea of promoting these benefits, both the food and the dining rooms are receiving attention from specialists. Tables of varying sizes, appropriate decorations, and relaxing music are important elements of the cafeteria atmosphere. Departmental hot plates with their fire hazards are no longer necessary, and they are prohibited by some concerns.

Health and Accidents

One phase of employee health has to do with sanitary conditions, another with food and recreation, and finally there are the physical examinations and services of the first-aid department and visiting nurses. Although care should be taken to provide a sanitary environment for workers, this is only a first step. Further steps must be taken to protect the workers from one another. Physical examinations for contagious diseases have become common practice. It is surprising, however, to find that some unions are still antagonistic to certain medical examinations. Many locals of the foundrymen's union (AFL) forbid members to take physical examinations for the purpose of employment. This attitude is evidently based on the fear of rejection because of silicosis, a lung disease common to the industry. One local of this union opposed a physical check-up of members who reported out sick for three days or more. A compromise provided that such examinations should be made by one of the nurses and be limited to pulse and temperature examinations.

Accidents may result from faulty physical arrangements, or they may be psychologically motivated. For many years, management has been giving engineering attention to the elimination of physical hazards to the compara-

[5] The National Labor Relations Board approved bargaining rights about cafeteria meal prices when the plant was so remote that employees had little choice to go elsewhere. In the case of Weyerhaeuser Timber Co. vs International Woodworkers of America, heard in 1950, the company increased the price of its cafeteria meals from 55¢ to 85¢ in ten-cent jumps. The Board held that "conditions of employment encompass many noncompulsory aspects of the employer-employee relationship."

tive neglect of the human causes. The contributions of the personnel department to the reduction of accidents and the maintenance of health will be treated at length in Chapter 23 on Health and Safety.

Personal sales

Department stores started the practice of selling their goods to employees at a discount. The savings from purchases, sometimes paid for by deductions from weekly pay on an installment basis, were considered a part of the wage. Various retail and wholesale houses picked up the idea, restricted to sales from their own merchandise. Finally industry followed suit, buying the items sold to workers from vendors, on the company account.

Sales to employees at discounts present little difficulty when the employer has the merchandise in stock, but when this type of employee service must be performed by the company's purchasing department, it presents so many difficulties that it often causes more bad feeling than good. The typical purchase of the industrial employee has a value far above the average price of articles bought by employees from the stock of their retail or wholesale employer. Such a purchase is usually selected from a catalog. Because the employee does not have a chance to inspect this item before he buys it, he is frequently dissatisfied after he receives it. Furthermore, because of the relatively high purchase price, installment payments may be necessary, financed by the employer. As a result of these selection and payment problems, personal buying by industrial concerns for their employees is not generally popular.

Discipline

Disciplinary measures, or punishments for violations of the regulations, should be made an integral part of company rules. It is good practice to grade disciplinary actions not only with respect to individual rules, but also according to the number of violations. For many rules, the punishment has three grades, such as reprimand for the first offense, layoff without pay for the second offense, and discharge for the third offense. One company cites disciplinary measures as "one week to discharge" and "reprimand to discharge," leaving the degree of punishment more specific on the basis of the number of offenses. Another company numbers its rules from one to four, explaining that No. 1 means a "Pink warning in writing"; No. 2, a "Yellow warning in writing"; No. 3, "Lay-off not exceeding six days"; and No. 4, "Discharge." Offenses like theft of the company's or a fellow employee's property call for immediate discharge.

Rules and regulations

Occasionally, rules are divided into types, as "General Rules" and "Rules for Personal Conduct." It is the latter type that provides for disciplinary action. There may be as many as forty punishable offenses, of which the following are examples:

Falsification of records	Making unnecessary scrap
Ringing another's clock card	Horseplay of any kind
Using another's pass	Intimidating employees
Reporting late to work	Posting or removing notices
Leaving without permission	Loitering in washrooms
Possession of weapons	Sabotage
Refusal to obey orders	Restricting output
Throwing refuse on floors	Fighting on the premises
Violation of safety rules	Failure to wear badge

Frequently, the personnel director tries to have company rules and regulations made an integral part of the contract agreement. Unions are opposed to this plan on the grounds that rules are strictly a company affair, and unions do not want to be considered an official participant. From management's point of view, rules and regulations must be geared to situations which are subject to change, making flexibility a desirable factor. As a result of these two attitudes, the nearest the rules and regulations get to the labor contract is the appendix. In most cases, the rules for employee conduct are published in a separate pamphlet.

Absences

Absences interfere with work distribution in all departments, but are particularly hard on production. It is the personnel department's duty to keep absenteeism to a minimum, a job which starts with finding out the causes. The difficulty with analyzing absences arises from the proverbial unreliability of the reported causes. One personnel director summarizes the chief causes in four groups: illness, attending sports, oversleeping, and shopping tours. The best way to check faked illness is to dispatch one of the plant's visiting nurses to assist the unfortunate. Because the nurse occasionally learns from neighbors that the absentee is attending a movie, some union locals resist the use of these "veiled detectives."

The sportsman is an absentee problem only during certain seasons, while at other times he has an excellent record. In light of this fact, it has been suggested that a plant holiday be declared on some of the offending "opening days." The "Monday morning deep freeze" of the late sleeper is another difficult case. Some departments have enlisted the assistance of the wife or mother with fair success. The worker who takes off a day or two to spend accumulated earnings is an economic problem. It may be helpful to dole out an enforced vacation so that he will accumulate an economic deficit!

Women in Industry

Although it is sometimes contended that women in industry should be treated differently from men because they are unaccustomed to heavy and dirty work, the fact is that in many societies at different times women have done the difficult and monotonous jobs while the men hunted. Furthermore, modern industry is continually eliminating the drudgery of production so that women can fill many jobs with comparative ease. The U.S. Bureau of Labor Statistics estimated that the female labor force in July, 1961, amounted to about 24,500,000.[6]

Whatever differences exist between men and women in industry, they create problems primarily for personnel management and the supervisor. What are these claimed differences that frequently result in pay differentials for jobs that are assumed to be the same? One is physical strength. Women worked in foundries for the first time during World War II, and the International Foundry Workers Union demanded the same pay for men and women workers on the same jobs. Because many states have laws fixing the maximum weights that may be lifted by women, heavy moulds or casting were reserved for the men, who felt that such discrimination should demand pay differentials. In the new foundries, weight-lifting is being eliminated for both groups.

It has sometimes been argued that there are inherent differences in mental capacity and psychological reactions between men and women, and that these differences are all in the men's favor. There is some evidence that women have longer memories than men, but for the most part, psychological testing has demonstrated only that men are more likely than women to have acquired the types of knowledge and skill which are most immediately relevant to success in business and industry. The longer women remain in the business world, the more such differences will level out.

Marriage and maternity have brought new problems to business. Should women quit work when they marry or when they have children? On the whole, business and industry are progressively doing what they can to give a negative answer to both questions. Many companies follow the practice of the Swisher Cigar Company of Jacksonville, Florida, which has provided nurseries where mothers pay three dollars a week for the "twenty-four-hour children" and two dollars a week for the "day children." The fees are paid for food, supervised play, nursing attention, and the use of cribs. The company reports that the fees are not intended to cover the cost of the services. Figure 21.2 shows the rooftop playground, which is one of the nursery facilities supplied by the Swisher Company.

Irrespective of the claims and counterclaims, the personnel manager has a problem in any special treatment to be accorded women. It is an indi-

[6] Letter from Department of Labor, 8-18-61.

Figure 21.2

Roof Playground for Workers' Children

Courtesy: Swisher Cigar Company

vidual consideration for different businesses and in different parts of the country.

Women as executives

Year after year, women are filling an increasing number of executive positions both in merchandizing and industry with apparently satisfactory results. Their former disabilities, as well as the prejudices of the male, are evidently fading. If as is sometimes suggested, the female executive has any more emotional handicaps than her male counterpart, certainly she has no greater physical drawbacks. Her chief handicap would appear to be the difficulty of acquiring qualified training, but even that hurdle is lowering. Some concerns are allowing women to take company management-training courses, and there is at least one educational institution (the Harvard-Radcliffe Program in Business Administration) specifically set up to train women to be future executives.

Lack of permanence on the job does not appear to affect the executive woman so much as it does her sister in the office and factory. A study made at Columbia University showed that 90 per cent of women undergraduates intended to work after finishing college, at least until they had families. Twenty per cent of that group expected to work whether married or single, and another 30 per cent registered a desire to return to work after their children were grown.

It is fair to assume, however, from the many studies made in this field, that the majority of young women do not care to expend the time or the money for graduate work which they feel is necessary for success in the business field where prejudice still exists in spite of the exceptional cases of women holding high managerial positions.

Conclusions

Several recent studies have indicated that worker interest rather than worker rewards are responsible for motivating individual productivity. Industry has attained its present productivity by organizing itself with machinelike impersonality, a development to which the average individual does not react favorably. Depersonalizing foreman contacts by instituting staff agencies is decried, as is the present functioning of the suggestion system which seldom provides proper motives to the worker for presenting his ideas.

Individual prestige, a sense of achievement, and group approval must be Personnel's aim for cultivating happy workers and maintaining high productivity. There is no known formula for producing worker satisfaction with mechanized jobs; the problem must be approached from the human side. It is suggested that morale campaigns and suggestion systems "kill the mosquito, but fail to halt its breeding." Complete mechanization will minimize industry's human problems, but those workers who transfer to service and distribution fields will carry along their problems.

Personnel directors of the future will probably be groping for a way to infuse worker interest through some type of group dynamics. Such experimentation may require some fundamental changes in the general organization structure of business.

QUESTIONS

1. How does personnel relations aim to increase productivity?
2. What are some of the efforts put forth in the past twenty-five years by management to stimulate worker interest *on the job?* Why have they failed in large part?
3. How, in your opinion, should management proceed to improve worker motivation on the job?
4. What are some of the causes behind the decline in the motivation of workers in modern industry?

5. How would you define worker morale?

6. How many morale destroyers can you recall? (The text lists eighteen).

7. What are some of the criteria necessary for conducting a successful morale survey?

8. What is the relation between the induction of the employee and his subsequent interest on the job?

9. What problem did the American Management Association decide to be the most important in industrial relations?

10. How did Jack & Heinz develop such a high *esprit de corps* among its employees during World War II?

11. Why have so many suggestion systems failed to produce satisfactory results?

12. To what extent has employee ownership of the employer's common stock promoted better understanding of employer-employee relations? If you feel that most systems have been relative failures, to what do you contribute the causes? What remedies would you suggest?

13. What are some of the essentials for promoting good worker attitudes?

14. To what extent do plant working conditions promote recruitment?

15. What are some of the more desirable company recreation and athletic programs from the worker's point of view?

16. Should food be served in the company cafeteria at cost, or should the employer subsidize part of the costs? If neither plan meets with your approval, what do you suggest?

17. Do you believe that a worker who has been absent for three days or more because of illness should be compelled to take a physical examination before returning to the job?

18. What plan would you advise for making personal sales to employees in manufacturing concerns — or would you prohibit them entirely?

19. Do you feel that disciplinary measures for violation of company rules should be included in the union contract?

20. What effect do you think progressive automation will have on the employment of women in factory jobs? Do you believe they will be discriminated against to minimize male layoffs?

CASE PROBLEM

The Fireball

Joe Stahlman has been with the Portland Engineering Company for twenty years, starting as a pattern-maker at the age of eighteen, with a high-school education. Due to natural ability, study, and interest, he soon became one of the best pattern-makers in the area. He was worth a higher hourly pay than the union's journeyman rate, but the company was bound by its wage contract, so could not give him the hourly rate it felt his services were worth. Furthermore, World War II was in progress, and all wage increases had to be submitted to the NLRB for approval.

Joe was capable of long hours, and frequently worked as many as one hundred hours in a seven-day week. For such a workweek, he received about $200. He was temperamental above the average, and the company was frequently faced with the possibility of losing his services because of his continually asking for a higher wage rate, which had to be refused, and because he had difficulty getting along with fellow-workers, of whom there were about one hundred on the day shift and seventy-five on the night shift. Also, Joe knew that he was the best workman in the shop and that his repeated threats to quit disturbed the shop superintendent, as well as the president of the company, who was formerly a journeyman pattern-maker.

First the company tried to solve Joe's wage difficulty and retain his expert services by assigning him as part-time overseer of the fifteen apprentices, at a 10¢ an hour wage differential. His ability, speed and temperament made him a poor teacher. He had no patience with the learners, demonstrating the tricks of his trade with so much speed that they were loath to admit that they did not understand what he did or how he did it. The apprentices registered numerous complaints with the superintendent, and finally with the union committee.

Later the company assigned Joe to foremanship on the night shift, in another effort to retain his services. This job made him technically a part of management and paid 20¢ an hour differential over the journeyman rate. On this new job, Joe was exacting with the journeymen both in the quantity and quality of their work. As night foreman, he had to go on inactive status with the union, where he was formerly an influential member and at one time president of the city's seven locals.

Finally, the union brought Joe to trial for "working against his brothers." He was cleared of the charge by the examining committee, whose report was sustained by a membership vote of a bare majority.

PROBLEM. If you had over-all responsibility for the management of this shop, what course of action would you take with respect to Joe Stahlman, assuming that you wanted to retain his services?

22

Collective

Bargaining

Bargaining between organized labor and management might well be considered of prime importance if only because of the number and financial strength of the bargainers. The 1959 income of American business was $399,648,000,000.[1] The three largest of the approximately one hundred unions with memberships of 5,000 or more, as of June 30, 1960, were:

1. *Teamsters,* with 1,600,000 members
2. *Auto, Aircraft, &Agriculture,* with 1,089,000 members
3. *Carpenters,* with 731,000 members

The total organized labor group rose from 17.5 millions in 1955, to 18.4 millions in 1957, and their annual revenues rose from $458,000,000 to $620,000,000 during the same period.[2]

These measures of power need not be disturbing since experience suggests that financially powerful groups have no desire to weaken their positions by long drawn-out struggles. An even brighter light in future struggles between organized labor and management can be seen in the fact that the unions have millions invested in American industry, and the same is true of many of their members. Indeed, the pioneers of the American labor movement had nothing in common with the Karl Marx type who had "nothing to lose but their chains." Comparatively speaking, our labor pioneers were the aristocrats of the working group, and today's financial figures place them well up in the "propertied" class.

Development of collective bargaining

Bargaining collectively by employees is a natural consequence of the disadvantage of their dealing with employers as individuals. Individual

[1] Department of Commerce, Office of Business Economics.
[2] *Business Week,* December 21, 1957, p. 105.

negotiations become difficult as business units expand to the point where the workers lose personal contacts with the members of upper management. This was the situation when the workers decided that their interests would be better served when acting as an organized group. By 1791, the carpenters, shoemakers, and printers had formed local organizations in Philadelphia, New York, and Boston. They sought shorter hours, higher wages, apprenticeship regulations, and "exclusive union hiring" which came to be known as the "closed shop."

In the early 1800's, collective bargaining was frequently used in labor-management disputes. The first recorded bargaining conference took place in Philadelphia in 1779 to discuss demands of the shoemakers. Similar bargaining meetings soon followed in Philadelphia and New York with the printing crafts.[3]

The "trampling committees" of those early unions checked the employer's wage records to see that they complied with the bargaining agreements. These unpaid agents were replaced by paid "walking delegates" who, in turn, gave way to the full-time "business agent" with increased duties.

As labor organizations expanded their influence and demands, employers formed defense associations especially to combat wage demands. Bitterness on both sides led to the employment of professional "strikebreakers" by management and "goons" by the labor organizations. Both of these trouble-making groups were frequently armed, with results that attest to the disastrous effects of the failure to bargain collectively in good faith.

The Noble Order of the *Knights of Labor,* founded in 1869, was the first national union to attain any marked degree of success. It started with the Philadelphia local of garment workers and expanded slowly into other crafts. For about ten years this organization functioned as a secret society with an elaborate ritual. It operated secretly because of management's bitter antagonism toward unions, which led to the blacklisting of members.

The organization maintained centralized national control over its locals, in contrast to the large degree of local autonomy now practiced. Its chief purpose was to reconstruct society on a cooperative basis. This plan did not allow the Knights much time for collective bargaining. Rather, they attacked "the money power of the banks" through the establishment of producer and consumer cooperatives. They did, however, make certain demands of all employers, including the eight-hour day, equal pay for equal work by men and women, abolition of child and convict labor, and public ownership of utilities; but they used only educational and political methods to further their purposes.

Decline of the Knights came primarily through internal conflicts between those members who favored collective bargaining and those who were determined to change our economic society through political channels.

[3] *Brief History of the American Labor Movement* (U.S. Bureau of Labor Statistics, Bulletin 1000, 1951).

Another conflict developed between those who favored an industrial union of the skilled and unskilled, and those who sponsored separate craft organizations. The Knights started on the downgrade after the organization of the American Federation of Labor in 1886, but continued in existence until 1917.

In 1881, six fairly strong craft unions — the printers, iron and steel workers, molders, cigar makers, carpenters, and glassworkers — met at Pittsburgh to form the Federation of Organized Trades and Labor Unions, with the announced goals of higher wages and better working conditions. With about 45,000 members, it remained relatively weak as a national organization during its first five years of life. But when in 1886 the Knights of Labor, at their national convention, refused to recognize the jurisdiction of the large craft unions, a group of these unions joined with the FOTLU to form the *American Federation of Labor*. The AFL began with approximately 140,000 members. By the outbreak of World War I, its membership had increased to 2,000,000 and this figure had doubled by 1920.

In 1920, the AFL was the dominant union in this country, numbering about 75 per cent of all organized workers. The only important unaffiliated groups were the four railroad brotherhoods. The outstanding industrial union was the United Mine Workers, which was the largest AFL affiliate when it joined, in 1902. From this time until the beginning of World War I, union-management dissension increased measurably. The three outstanding reasons were the large increase in power of the unions, the number of bitter strikes in which persons were killed on both sides, and the rise of scientific management, which was strongly opposed by organized labor.

The next outstanding event in the field of organized labor came with the formation of the *Congress of Industrial Organizations* in 1938. Its establishment arose from a dispute within the AFL concerning the admission of industrial unions. Because the AFL was composed almost entirely of craft unions, there were thousands of semiskilled and unskilled workers in the mass production industries who were not eligible for craft union membership and consequently had no effective instrument for collective bargaining with their employers. At the 1934 convention of the AFL, it was recognized that some provision must be made for the admission of industrial unions, which would bring together all the workers in a single industry. During the following year, the AFL granted charters to industrial unions in the automobile and rubber industries, but craftsmen were excluded from them. This exception merely intensified the differences, so that the question again became prominent at the 1935 convention, where a defeated minority report demanded unrestricted charters for mass production industries.

Shortly after this convention, six AFL unions formed the Committee for Industrial Organization, to promote the unionization of the mass production industries, for inclusion within the AFL. After the group was joined by four additional AFL unions, the executive council of the AFL asked that it disband, which it refused to do. Its member unions were consequently expelled from the AFL at its 1936 convention. As a result of this action, the Committee was transformed into the Congress of Industrial Organizations and held its first convention in 1938. It was set up as a loose federation of autonomous national unions, governed by a central board composed of representatives from its affiliates.

In the intervening years since 1938, various attempts were made to amalgamate the AFL and CIO. The joint committee appointed for that purpose (1953) appeared on the surface to have opportunities for success. However, differences in fundamental organizing plans, the disputes about top jobs in the new union, jurisdictional differences, disputes concerning craft and industrial unionism, and union finances presented problems that made success appear anything but bright.

Nevertheless, both organizations approved unification at their 1955 conventions, and ratified the general contract terms which had been worked out previously by an executive committee representing both groups. Early in December 1955, the ten million members of the AFL and the five million members of the CIO formally merged as the AFL–CIO. President of the AFL became president of the new organization, and the president of the CIO became head of a new Industrial Union Department. The executive council was made up of the President, the Secretary-Treasurer, and 27 vice-presidents.

As predicted in the first edition of this text (1956), there has been plenty of trouble and confusion since the merger. The Teamsters, Baking and Confectioners, and Laundry Workers unions have been expelled for violations of the new union's Ethical Practices Code. The most spectacular of the three expulsions was that of the Teamsters under President James Hoffa. The Teamsters were accused of three offenses. One was harboring a large number of officers who had criminal records. Another was the so-called "Trusteeships" set up by Hoffa over local unions, giving him one-man power over their destinies. The third was alleged misuse of the union's Welfare Funds.

Most of the confusion during the past six years has resulted from jurisdictional disputes between the craft and industrial unions within the merged group. There have also been political differences, especially between several of the state federations. During the past six years, there has been an increase in strikes, the most notable of which was the steel strike which was prolonged and costly to both sides. It may also be noted that during this period, business has fairly well "held the line," probably because of the recession. The result of all this has been a decline, during the period, from 40 to 38 per cent of eligible memberships in the AFL–CIO.

Collective bargaining and the law

The attitude of the law toward collective bargaining may be divided roughly into four periods:

1. Before 1842   — Suppression
2. 1842–1935   — Toleration
3. 1935–1947   — Encouragement
4. 1947–Present — Promotion and regulation

The first labor law of record is the Statute of Laborers, passed by the English Parliament in 1351 to stabilize wages which were getting out of hand because of a short labor supply following the Black Death. Part of this statute, and many others that followed, declared that any combination of workers for collective bargaining was unlawful, and the courts held that any combination of workers for joint action was a criminal conspiracy. The records show that the principle was applied in this country prior to 1842, when the right of workers to combine for the improvement of wages, hours, and working conditions was generally recognized.

During the second period, the government neither encouraged nor discouraged unions, and the courts no longer held that union activities, including strikes, were criminal conspiracies. Because of the absence of specific legislation, the courts were often called on to decide whether picketing, boycotts, and blacklists were legal. Injunctions were frequently obtained against labor union actions, but here again it was the court, not the government, that was making the decisions.

Several Acts of Congress encouraged unions and collective bargaining between 1914 and 1932. In 1890, the Sherman Anti-Trust Act forbade combinations in restraint of trade. When the courts applied this prohibition to unions in the famous Danbury Hatters Case, the unions were strong enough to influence public opinion and Congress so that they were specifically excluded from the provisions of the Sherman Act by the Clayton Act of 1914.

The Railway Labor Act of 1926 expanded labor's rights by stating that railway workers could choose their own bargaining representatives. Another feature of the Act which promoted collective bargaining was outlawing of the "yellow dog" contract by which workers promised as a condition of their employment that they would not join unions.

The Norris-LaGuardia Act (1932) stated that "yellow dog" contracts could not be enforced in federal courts. In addition, it provided for limitations of the courts' power to issue injunctions in labor disputes. The Fair Labor Standards Act of 1938 fixed minimum wages and regular hours for persons employed in interstate commerce. The Public Contracts Acts (Walsh-Healey) and the Davis-Bacon Act applied provisions of the Fair Labor Standards Act to government contracts and construction work.

The National Labor Relations Act, known as the Wagner Act, was approved in 1935. It represents the high point of government encouragement of the unions. It prohibited employers from interfering with the organization of unions or from refusing to bargain collectively. It named five types of unfair labor practices forbidden to employers, against which "cease and desist" orders would be issued.

The pro-union policy of the national government continued until the passage of the Taft-Hartley Act (1947), the purpose of which was to re-establish a balance between the collective bargaining powers of employees and employers. A portion of the Act expresses this purpose: "To insure that the rights of the individual employee and of the public are protected against abuses on the part of either labor or management." Its chief feature for accomplishing this end is the enumeration of unfair practices for labor, to balance those already provided for management under the Wagner Act. The Taft-Hartley Act is a revision of the Wagner Act, which remains on the statute books.

Contract Negotiations

Collective bargaining is supposed to result in a labor-management contract. If not, its controversial features may have to be settled through arbitration, action by the NLRB or, as a last resort, by an economic contest — the strike. Collective bargaining finds its real and highest test in the arguments, diplomacy, and compromises which make up the contract negotiations. The contract purports to spell out a meeting of the minds on activities affecting both employers and employees. It represents the high point of collective bargaining, especially since its provisions spell out the rules that govern the relations between the two groups for at least a year.

The contract phase of collective bargaining is necessarily conducted by representatives of organized labor and management. Management's representatives are appointed by top management, headed by the director of personnel or labor relations, or a management consultant skilled in the labor field. Labor's representatives are often selected by vote of the membership. The leader of the union committee may be a professional representative of the international union. It is not unusual for both sides to be represented by legal counsel whose duty should be to inform his client in matters of law and procedure. It often happens, however, that attorneys take an active part in the negotions, frequently to the detriment of the management cause.

Anyone with extensive experience in labor contract negotiations often recognizes the relative disadvantage of the company's lawyer. He is usually a general practitioner, or corporation lawyer, on a fee basis. The union's attorney, on the other hand, specializes on labor law and negotiations on a full-time salary. He was probably a labor organizer before he studied law for the avowed purpose of representing unions in negotiations. He knows more about labor law and negotiations than the average company's attorney can hope to learn from his limited practice in this highly specialized field. The company that believes such a difference exists often engages a management consultant who specializes in collective bargaining.

When members of top management participate in contract negotiations, their superior authority can have a detrimental psychological effect on management's leader in the negotiations, as well as add to the distrust of the labor committee members. In addition, these top-management members of the negotiating team will occasionally make a suggestion that leads the negotiations in the direction desired by the labor group. When such a contingency arises, labor is quick to drive a wedge in the new opening.

The customary approach to contract bargaining is for the labor group to submit a list of its "demands" to management, either before or at the first meeting. Management is immediately put on the defensive in resisting demands, which is a purely negative approach. The advantage of the positive approach has been recognized by organized labor for a long time. Even "good faith" bargaining soon becomes a matter of compromises on both sides. But when management has no positive proposals, it has nothing with which to trade in compromise.

With the present development of collective bargaining, both sides have started to recognize the value of presenting "proposals" rather than "demands." Only psychology is involved, but it is good psychology. Since negotiations progress in inverse ratio to the amount of heat engendered, it is desirable to keep the meeting on a factual and amicable basis. A recess for coffee and sandwiches, or refreshments, served at the negotiating table with both sides present, often lowers the temperature of the discussions and allows for a fresh start.

Contract Provisions

Contract provisions have increased in number and content as the problems of mass production, big business, and distribution have multiplied. Typical contracts cover from fifteen to over one hundred pages, depending roughly on the size of the company. Examination of the contract of a typical large concern shows eighteen specific provisions with a nineteenth entitled "General Provisions," a sort of carry-all for minor considerations. The contract of a relatively small company has fifteen provisions, with a general final section. Twelve of the sections are common to both of these contracts. What are some of the contract provisions, and what disposition do they make of the problem involved?

Purpose. A General Motors agreement with one of its union illustrates the typical purpose clause.

The purpose of this Agreement is to provide orderly collective bargaining relations between the Corporation and the Union, to secure a prompt and equitable disposition of grievances, and to establish fair wages, hours, and working conditions for the employees covered by this Agreement.

Recognition. The recognition clause starts with some such statement as: "The Company recognizes the Union as the collective bargaining agent for all employees included in the . . . department (or classification) with the following exceptions: . . ." The list of exceptions is important.

Here the attempt is made to exclude everyone who may act in any managerial capacity for the company.

Discrimination. Here the company agrees that there shall be no discrimination against any employee because of his membership in the union or because of his acting as an officer, or in any other capacity, on behalf of the union. It is an affirmation of a section of the Wagner Act, and as such is obligatory on the company, irrespective of its inclusion in the contract.

Union Security. This provision recognizes two possible phases of company obligations. One has to do with the type of "shop" which is recognized, and the other states whether or not the company will deduct union dues from the pay of its workers for transmission to the union's representative.

Representation. This section deals with the number of union members who shall serve as its representatives throughout the concern. It often provides for the maximum amount of time these representatives shall use in serving union purposes on company time. It also arranges for meetings between company representatives and the union's grievance, shop, and other committees.

Recognition of Rights. While most contracts still spell out the "rights" of management and labor in the contract, it is coming to be recognized that because labor's rights are continually expanding as the result of administrative rulings and judicial decisions, management rights expressed in the contract may be relatively short-lived. In general, the union has the right of noninterference by management, and of appeal to the grievance procedure on practically any disputed question. One company has the following provision in its contract with its union:

It is recognized that the management of the Company, the control of its properties, and the maintenance of order on its premises are the sole responsibility of management. Other rights and responsibilities belonging solely to management are hereby recognized, among which, but by no means wholly inclusive, are the rights to decide the number and location of plants, the amount of supervision necessary, machinery and equipment, products manufactured, process of manufacturing, designing, engineering and the control of raw materials, and products which may be incorporated in production. It is further recognized that the responsibility of management for selection and direction of the work force, including the right to hire, suspend, or transfer, to relieve employees from duty because of lack of work, or for further legitimate reasons is vested exclusively in the Company.

There is some question among professionals whether such a listing of management's prerogatives actually restricts its rights to those enumerated in the contract. For this reason, some companies express management's rights in more general terms.

Grievance Procedure. Since the early settlement of grievances is extremely important in maintaining proper working relations between the employees and management, there should be no delay in following through with the various steps of the grievance procedure. The time allowed between steps varies from three to ten days. If a grievance may be defined as a "complaint of an employee which cannot be satisfied by his foreman," then many complaints will never reach the grievance stage. However, since union representatives like to have as many contacts as possible with union members, contract negotiators for the union will not ordinarily agree to this definition, however sound it may appear.

There are usually four steps in the grievance procedure: (1) contact between the worker (accompanied by his foreman) and his union representative; (2) contact between the union's grievance committee and some representative of the company, probably the personnel director; (3) contact between a representative of the international union and a representative of the company, customarily the director of labor relations or the company's labor committee, if such exists; and finally (4) arbitration. Figure 22.1 shows a typical form of a grievance report.

Arbitration. Arbitration sometimes provides that each side select a representative and that these two select a third, or chairman. If the representatives of labor and management cannot agree on the third arbitrator, which is often the case, they may appeal to the American Arbitration Association or the U.S. Department of Labor. Both agencies maintain panels of arbitrators. If the two original arbitrators cannot agree on anyone from the list, then it is the practice to ask either of the agencies for a directed selection of the the third member. Practice suggests that since the first two arbitrators are really advocates, the purpose of arbitration might be better and less expensively served by the selection of a single neutral arbitrator.

The arbitration section of the contract almost invariably limits the subjects eligible for arbitration. Some contracts list the exceptions, while others specifically designate the arbitrable questions. Interpretation of the contract provisions is universally allowed. Compulsory arbitration is seldom mentioned in the contract, except for the purpose of specifically excluding it. Both management and labor are customarily opposed to compulsory arbitration.

Seniority. Length of service, or seniority, is an important and sometimes determining factor in layoffs, promotions, and transfers. The difficulties arise in their applications. To settle the question of when seniority starts

Figure 22.1

Grievance Report Form

Dept. _____ Date _____ Time _____ A.M. / P.M.

Grievance _____

_____

_____

_____

_____

Employee's Name _____

Steward's Name _____

Report to _____ Foreman

Foreman's Reply _____

_____

_____

GRIEVANCE SETTLED ☐   NOT SETTLED ☐

NEXT STEP REFERRED TO _____

BY _____ DATE _____ TIME _____ A.M. / P.M.

REPLY _____

_____

_____

_____

GRIEVANCE SETTLED ☐   NOT SETTLED ☐

REFERRED TO TOP MANAGEMENT BY THE SHOP COMMITTEE _____

A.M. / P.M. _____ DAY OF _____ 19 ____.

MANAGEMENT'S REPLY _____

_____

_____

_____

_____

SETTLED SATISFACTORILY ☐   ARBITRATION ☐

for new workers, it is customary to provide that it shall apply after the worker has passed his probationary period and then date back to his original employment.

Seniority may be applied on a classification, departmental, or plant-wide basis. On the job-classification basis, distinction includes the qualifications and ability of the employee, as well as his length of service in the particular classification. Departmental and plant seniority may include both ability and length of service, but it is usual to fix it on length of service alone. Management often attempts to make seniority apply "when other factors are equal," but is ordinarily unsuccessful.

Application of seniority following transfer or promotion presents a problem. The usual rule is to designate the new job as "temporary" for a period of thirty to sixty days, after which the former seniority is picked up and reinstated on the new job. Application of the rule creates many heated arguments. If the transferred or promoted employee retains his former seniority, he may outrank in length of service many older workers in his new classification. If, on the other hand, his seniority must date from his promotion or transfer, then he is in a precarious position in case of layoffs and other decisions based on seniority.

There are several perplexing applications of seniority which cannot be discussed in this brief survey of the subject. It is, however, pertinent to list a few of the ordinary causes for loss of seniority.

1. Voluntary separation from employment
2. Discharge for cause
3. Failure to return after expiration of a leave
4. Remaining away for three days without cause or notification
5. Remaining away for seven days after notice to return to work
6. After layoff for a year or more

Production Standards. It is customary in many lines of business to determine standard times for performing operations, by stop watch or otherwise. Such standards frequently lead to disagreements. Because of this fact, it is good usage for the labor-management agreement to provide that standards shall be considered temporary until they have been tried out in operations under normal working conditions. Even after they have been definitely established, union representatives may secure the right to review them with technicians of their own choosing, preparatory to making the disputed standard a subject for the grievance procedure. It is also customary for the contract to provide that no satisfactory standard shall be altered unless some important change occurs in the materials, machines, or method of performing the work.

Working Hours. The hours of the regular working day are specified in all contracts for the purpose of figuring overtime and shift bonus payments.

Wage Rates and Plans. Wage rates are fixed for various classifications.

It is frequently provided that new employees shall start at some rate below the minimum of their classification, but advance to the classified rate within ninety days. It is also customary to provide that women shall receive equal pay with men for comparable quality and quantity of work on the same or comparable jobs. Usually, new jobs receive temporary classifications for a fixed period, after which they are made permanent by mutual agreement of management and the union. Various incentive and apprentice wage plans are spelled out in detail in the contract. The amount of extra pay for overtime and special work shifts, as well as any premium payments, are also fixed in the agreement.

Union Bulletin Boards. Provision for union bulletin boards may seem to be an unnecessary detail for the contract, but when it is not covered by the agreement, there is a tendency on the part of the union to have too many bulletin boards and to use them for purposes to which most managements would not agree. It is customary, therefore, to designate the number and locations of the boards and to provide that the postings must have prior agreement of some management representative.

Figure 22.2

Leave-of-Absence Form

LEAVE OF ABSENCE

Name _____ Clock No. _____ Date _____

Foreman _____ Job _____

Working Now? _____ How Long With Co.? _____ Absence Record _____

I request leave of absence, without pay, to start _____ and terminate _____

for the purpose of _____

I agree to the following regulations:

1. Before the expiration of a Leave of Absence, the employee shall apply for reinstatement, and if he is physically qualified, shall be eligible for reinstatement to any available opening suitable to his qualifications. A physical examination to determine such physical qualifications as may be required will be made at the expense of the Company.

2. If an employee on leave does not apply for reinstatement before the expiration of his leave, or if he accepts other employment during Leave of Absence without consent of the Company, or if he is physically unqualified to carry on his accustomed work, his employment with the Company shall terminate.

I do (do not) want Company Group Insurance continued in my name, and if continued I agree to pay my share of the premium cost.

Accepted for the Company   _____

                                                                            Employee

_____
Director Public and Industrial Relations

Leaves of Absence. This section occupies considerable space in contracts, indicating the difficulties it poses. Figure 22.2 illustrates a leave-of-absence form drawn up by the author for use in a plant employing about three thousand. Its provisions indicate some of the problems involved. Leaves for personal reasons up to about thirty days are customarily granted at the discretion of the foreman. Formal leaves are usually limited to about three months and must have management approval. In either case, seniority continues.

Sick leaves are granted automatically when supported by satisfactory evidence. Absence because of election to full-time union activity is also permissible without loss of seniority, usually with the provision that such absences be limited to one year. In all cases involving leaves, prevalent usage requires return of the employee at the end of the period, except by special permission, on penalty of being dropped from the rolls. A specific rule in most contracts provides that an employee will be discharged when the leave is obtained for the purpose of working for some other company. Absence for military service is prescribed by law, and does not affect the worker's seniority. Despite the law, "bumping"[4] by workers returned from military service has caused some nasty problems.

Vacations and Holidays. Vacation allowances are a customary provision in all contracts where they are granted with pay. The choice of time and the extent of vacations usually depend on seniority. The provision for holidays is easy to write after the agreement on how many there should be.

Strikes and Lockouts. The following represents a broad provision on this vital subject:

> The Union, its officers, agents, and members agree that as long as this agreement is in effect, or any extension that may be mutually agreed upon, there shall be no strikes, sit-downs, slow-downs, stoppages of work, or any other acts of any nature that tend to interfere with production, nor picketing of any nature, however peaceful, and it will not otherwise permit, countenance, or condone such acts.

In the same section, the company agrees not to hold the union responsible for wildcat or sit-down strikes which the union does not recognize. The company further agrees that there will be no lockouts as long as the contract is in force.

General. Duration of the agreement may be considered under this head-

---

4 "Bumping" refers to the displacement of a worker with low seniority by one with higher seniority within the same job classification unless the contract provides for plant-wide seniority. The "bumper" is the one who takes the job.

ing, including the conditions of operation between its termination date and the making of a new contract. Some contracts contain company rules and regulations following the official sections to which the company and union representatives have attached their signatures.

The Negotiating Job

The country's outstanding record of productivity over the years has been hampered by dissensions between labor and management. Handling labor-management negotiations from either side of the bargaining table is no job for amateurs. On labor's side, professionals are being developed constantly by intensive training and successful experience. Local unions are being serviced from central clearing houses of information and planned strategy. On management's side, too many companies are learning too slowly that they must match this professional skill of organized labor if they wish to maintain competitive labor costs.

Wise executive thinking has come to admit that labor relations with both organized and unorganized workers require staff counsel possessing special abilities and wide experience. Even when nature has been kind in developing the natural appeal of the executive in labor conferences, he must familiarize himself with the constant changes in state and federal regulations. He must study the shifting causes and effects reflected in the decisions of labor cases. These and other necessary preparations for the successful handling of employee relations cannot be acquired by inspiration. Daily production problems and employee relations are so absorbing that it is impossible for one person to give them both proper consideration.

Whether this subject is referred to as labor, industrial, or employee relations, it demands provision for that continuing process implied by the word "relations." In spite of this fact, many managements have treated the entire problem as though it were a once-a-year dusting off of the existing contract and a matching of wits to make a more favorable one next year. The objective should be real employee-management cooperation — the kind that produces satisfactory wages, working conditions, and profits. This is the true measure of successful employee relations.

The negotiators: labor vs. management

Common parlance often refers to the professional labor representative as a radical or agitator. Even when these appellations are true, the objective observer will appraise labor's actions merely as techniques to aid organizing or bargaining; they are not the substance on which conclusions are based nor plans mapped out. Management, on the other hand, must have professional counsel to counterbalance the confusion into which it falls when union tactics depart from the orthodox, as they often do.

We must remember that professional labor leaders have gained their union positions against stiff competition. Theirs is one field of endeavor where social standing does not lend a helping hand. Results alone determine their survival. No executive can afford to underestimate a labor opponent simply because he doesn't take the soft-glove approach. The labor leader may be tough, but he is not without brains and ability. He has listened to most of management's arguments so many times that he has the answer ready before the question is asked.

In addition to whatever individual capacity and confidence the labor leader has developed by standing on his own and having proved his mettle, the planned procedures and tested tactics of his organization are always squarely behind him. These tactics often result in moves which are disconcerting to managements who have not learned the defensive advantage of similar methods.

It is easy to predict that management's irritations and losses will increase, while productivity and profits decrease, in some proportion to the extent that they continue to maintain labor relations on a nonprofessional basis. This statment explains why progressive managements, with an eye to future benefits, are employing professional labor relations specialists under continuing contracts.

If we are not ready to call the making of labor agreements a profession, at least we can agree that it is difficult business requiring specialized know-how. An increasing number of attorneys are shifting their attentions to labor negotiations. Whether or not they are suited by training and practice to a field whose procedures are new and whose approaches are largely psychological is a moot question. Frequently, lawyers pursue the same "fight the case" attitude which they have used successfully in court. The results of such a victory in labor relations may mean a drop in employee satisfaction, less cooperation and productivity, and finally, lowered company profits — a Pyrrhic victory!

Management needs a recognized consultant in negotiations with organized labor. He must possess integrity, knowledge, skill, and courage. And, as one writer has aptly said, he must be able to recognize and cope with any curves thrown by labor's representatives and equally capable of resisting any desire to use similar tactics. Labor leaders are not slow to recognize the integrity of management's representatives, and labor deals more frankly after such confidence has been established. After all, intelligent laborites know that workers and management have more interests in common than otherwise.

The negotiations: labor vs. management

There is one outstanding difference between labor's and management's negotiating procedures. On labor's side, one man carries the ball at all times. The others join in only when invited by their leader, usually to back up his contentions. On management's side, there may be a chairman, but parliamentary discipline is either minimized or unrecognizable. The game is open, with labor making plenty of passes. The union's captain is also constantly alert for opportunities to make holes in his opponent's disorganized line by encouraging divergent opinion among management's representatives. This playing according to tight rules on labor's side with lack of unity on management's is an oft-repeated example of management's amateurish handling of organized employees relations.

Unions have learned their lessons in what was an uphill fight against superior odds. If it were to their advantage to have each local do its own bargaining, union strategy would have remained keyed to this level. The unions discovered, on the contrary, that a widened span of control through consolidation of locals under a centralized bargaining system is far more effective. As the span has increased, the union successes have multiplied. They simply pick out the weakest link in the chain of employers and exert pressure there to force through a new demand. When the "weak link" accedes to the demand, the union presents it to other employers. It is the ancient idea expressed in several languages as "divide and rule."

One manufacturer, commenting on the inability of many managements to get together for cooperative efforts in dealing with organized labor, suggested:

The Knights left the security of the Round Table to engage the Dragon individually. This reduced the Dragon's problems, both economic and gastronomic, and left him with a Round Table as a surplus property.

On the West Coast, management has made its path easier and its standing more secure through cooperating employer groups formed for the purpose of improving employee relations and bargaining methods from management's viewpoint. The growth of this simple but plausible idea must be a reflection of its success. In many areas, management has been able to present a united front to labor in contract negotiations.

The employer-group approach to labor relations has many positive advantages. It results in better knowledge of labor laws and practices, furnishes a fund of comparative contract provisions, and provides many uniform contract clauses. It promotes equal and fair treatment from the unions to all employer members. It enables union negotiators to bargain with employer specialists, a situation that promises to create more light and less heat. It promotes mutual union and management respect as the same group of opposing negotiators gradually learns to appraise the objectives that are common to both camps. It induces union representatives to deal with facts and realities in place of rumors. It improves labor-management harmony, which adds materially to productivity. Finally, it tends to put serious business on a business basis.

It cannot be emphasized too strongly that "labor relations" cannot be divorced from the more inclusive field of "employee relations." The first is affected in a very positive manner by the day-to-day operations of the latter. Solutions and programs that are effective in both areas have more to do with profit and loss than any other activity of management. These sketchy considerations should indicate that labor relations are one of management's most serious problems, both from the standpoint of the brains and skill required in handling them effectively, and from the standpoint of their direct effect on productivity and profits.

Conclusions

The contract that results from true collective bargaining is a long step in the direction of industrial peace, which is one of our foremost prescriptions for social progress. When the contract represents only the results of superior economic power on one side or the other, it provides merely for an armistice during which the weaker side prepares for a continuation of the struggle. History proves that where great struggles persist, one side eventually conquers to the detriment of both. In the industrial field in this country, a complete defeat by either side will vitally injure both sides, with the public suffering the consequences.

Neither management nor labor seems to recognize that the final alternative to industrial peace is some form of dictatorship. With our political system based on universal suffrage, and with labor solidarity increasing its influence in political decisions, numbers may well be the determining factor. This is the prospect that management must face. At the same time, labor runs even greater risks from continued industrial conflict. It has never won anything in our time from dictatorships. Labor victory may well lead in the same direction as management victory.

Only recently have we been making studies to find out what makes for industrial peace. There are many concerns in this country which deal with organized labor on a platform of mutual confidence. Our picture seems brighter when viewed from the perspective of industrial situations in other countries. Because our industrial relations, as evidenced in collective bargaining contracts, have such a tremendous influence on our general economic, political, and social systems, it is correspondingly important that the deep-seated emotional patterns on both sides be gradually exchanged for facts and the confidence to accept them. As this new pattern evolves, labor-management contracts will decrease in size and volume. Such a decrease is an indicator worth observing.

In 1951, the West German *Bundestag* gave trade unions the right to sit on the board of directors of coal and steel companies. These concerns were selected for the experiment because of their importance in the national economy. The formula, referred to as co-determination (*Mitbestimmungs-recht*), provides for a board of eleven members, five from labor and five from stockholders. The advocates of the idea insisted that the eleventh man be "neutral"; politicians urged that he come from the government group, and the stockholders insisted on his selection by their group. The final plan provides that the eleventh person be selected by the other ten, and if they cannot agree, then a mediation committee must present three names to the stockholders. Since this process must continue until the stockholders are presented with an acceptable choice, they actually hold the balance of power.

This return of "capital" to the dominant role, as opposed to the position which management has attained in this country through the invention of the proxy, is indeed interesting. Neither the virtues nor the deficiencies of co-determination can be weighed at this early date, but its possibilities for industrial peace are well worth watching.

QUESTIONS

1. Does the relatively comparable financial power of industry and organized labor lead to more or less stable relations between them?

2. What effect does the large union investment in American industry have on labor-management relations?

3. What difference in centralized control existed with the Knights of Labor as compared to the central control of AFL–CIO over its locals?

4. What disagreement caused six AFL unions to split from the AFL? How was the difference finally settled?

5. When was the "criminal conspiracy" label for joint action by a combination of workers abandoned in this country?

6. What was the purpose of the "yellow dog" contract, and how was it finally squashed?

7. The Wagner Act was frequently spoken of as Labor's Magna Charta. What was the purpose of the amendments to that act which were included in the later Taft-Hartley Act?

8. Can you name the four plans for settling labor-management controversies?

9. Why is it often contended that management's attorneys are at a disadvantage when dealing with organized labor's attorneys in labor-management disputes?

10. What is the real purpose of the so-called "Labor's Demands" as presented to management representatives at contract negotiation meetings?

11. How is "discrimination" interpreted as it appears in labor-management contracts?

12. Do you consider it advisable for management to enumerate its "rights" in contracts with organized labor? Give your reasons.

13. How would you define a labor "grievance"?

14. What is the final step in the grievance procedure?

15. Seniority may be applied on a classification, departmental, or plant-wide

basis. Which would you prefer if you were an employer of organized labor? Why?

16. Do you think that men and women should always receive equal pay for jobs in the same classification? Why or why not?

17. What preparation would you consider necessary before management could expect to deal successfully in labor-management negotiations?

18. What do you think of the industry-wide approach to labor-management negotiations on the part of management?

19. To what extent, in your opinion, is it advisable for management to employ a recognized consultant to aid or conduct its labor-management negotiations? Would you select an attorney for that purpose? Do you feel that such professional advice will shorten or protract the negotiations?

20. What is your opinion of the West German Government's plan for co-determination? Would you recommend its adoption in any phase of business in this country?

CASE PROBLEM

THE HORNER CASTINGS COMPANY

The Horner Castings Company is considering the advisability of eliminating its tool shop and having that portion of its work done by outside concerns specializing in toolmaking. The company has been led to consider this change after some twenty years' experience with its own tool shop partly because of the excessive number of grievances in the tool shop, many of which have been carried to arbitration, but chiefly because of the high costs in that department due to continued slowdowns by its workers.

The company's present contract with its industrial union provides for plant-wide seniority, so that it will be necessary to lay off a number of excellent employees in other departments in order to dismiss all of its toolmakers. The company naturally wants to avoid this undesirable situation. The change has been thoroughly discussed with the union officers and a special committee elected by the union members to negotiate the seniority dispute, about which there is a strong division of opinion among the union members. Those workers not included in the tool department, who have status falling within the range of seniority of the toolmakers, will lose their jobs if the contract provisions are complied with, and they are not sympathetic to an application of the plant-wide seniority rule in this case.

The company compiled figures to show the union that it can have its tool work done at lower costs by several outside concerns.

PROBLEM: It is admitted by all concerned that the contract provision of plant-wide seniority has produced a nasty situation for both management and many of the workers. How can the problem be resolved? What would you recommend as a basis for negotiating their differences without resorting to arbitration, where the company would probably be ordered to abide by its contract?

23

Health and Safety

Health and safety are closely linked in the career of every worker in industry and elsewhere. For one thing, the healthy worker is less likely to be a victim of accidents. Furthermore, the health of each worker is in some measure a guarantee of the health and safety of his fellow-workers. Finally, the health and safety of every individual are important elements in our national strength.

Today there is universal agreement — which has not always been so — that management should assume a leading role in the prevention of accidents. Management's role in maintaining worker health is perhaps not so obvious. There must be a continuous program of health research. The results of such an approach not only "pay off" in increased productivity and lower unit costs; they also improve our individual and collective ability to preserve our national existence through superior mental and physical well-being.

The health and safety program

Industrial medicine first comes in contact with the worker when he applies for a job. His physical examination has three special purposes: (a) to see that he is assigned a task that fits his general physical condition, (b) to protect other workers from the possibility of contagion, and (c) to protect the company against hiring workers whose physical condition may lead to accidents, or whose diseased condition may lead to later financial claims.

Added to these precautionary hiring measures, there should be a program of health education for those who are employed. The core of such education is the necessity for reporting health and accident cases while they are still considered trivial. First symptoms are the easiest to combat. Periodic physical examinations are becoming standard practice with well-managed companies. Safety education is combined with health education for two reasons. In the first place, workers in good health are less likely to have accidents. In the second place, the causes of many kinds of accidents are detectable in advance by the medical department, and hence avoidable through correction.

Because of industry's direct attack on the causes of accidents and poor health, its success in the reduction of occupational diseases has been outstanding. For example, lead poisoning in the paint industry and foundry-acquired silicosis are now the exception rather than the rule. Mechanical safeguards have been developed, chiefly through studies of industrial health departments. Air conditioning, forced ventilation and sterilization of air,[1] sanitation, and blood tests are suggestive of the means by which employers have reduced many occupational diseases close to the vanishing point. Enthusiastic about preventive programs to promote employees' health, executives are surprisingly uncooperative in participating in such programs. Conditioned by application to duty beyond the eight-hour day, they have been neglectful of their health, even with their family physicians. This executive avoidance of company health facilities has led, in some companies, to compulsory periodic health examinations.

As far back as 1951, the National Association of Manufacturers recommend the following essentials for a good health and safety program:

1. Adequate medical services, regardless of company size
2. Services of a qualified physician and nurse when needed
3. Preplacement and periodic physical examinations
4. Properly equipped and well-located dispensary
5. Trained first-aid attendant to deal with accidents
6. Vigilantly administered safety program
7. Special training for supervisors in accident prevention
8. Employee education in safety, hygiene, and nutrition
9. Control of sanitation, light, heat, and ventilation
10. Records of physical examinations, accidents, and absences

These precautions supply the controls over both health and safety. A partial program weakens the final results and sometimes reflects adversely on those elements which are practiced. Industrial health programs made a bad start because they were classed as "welfare," which is anathema to both unions and management. Industrial medicine had to undergo a complete change of front before it was acceptable. Since that transition, it has become one of the major considerations with progressive companies. A decade ago, the industrial physician was avoided by the workers as the hired agent of the company who would testify against them in compensation cases. Today the company physician is cheerfully accepted by most employees.

---

[1] The use of ultraviolet light for sterilizing the plant's atmosphere during the work day has almost as many opponents as it has proponents.

Industrial Health

Industry's interest

The Eastman Kodak Company has maintained an excellent employee health program for many years. Its handbook for workers explains in detail the services available at company expense. Progressive management has long since realized that worker health means better production at lower unit costs because it promotes the happiness of the individual. The Eastman program covers both general physical examinations and treatment; even optical, dental, and dietary disturbances are treated.

The former Jack & Heinz Company of Cleveland probably had the country's most complete program for employee health during World War II. Medical, dental, and eye treatments were provided on a twenty-four-hour basis in company dispensaries. Because of top management's belief in the importance of proper shoes for effective work, foot examinations and shoes were also provided. To assure a proper diet, company dining rooms served balanced meals without the aid of cash registers. Bowls of vitamin tablets were available on cafeteria tables. Special baths with steam rooms and professional rubdowns were another part of the company's health program. Finally, workers showing signs of general fatigue were sent on vacations to Honeymoon Island, off the coast of Florida, where the company maintained its own establishment. When asked how the company could afford such services, President William Jack explained that "it all comes from the fund which the employees create."

In 1947, the International Ladies' Garment Workers' Union and the Associated Garment Industries of St. Louis established a health center in that city. It is supported by the participating companies on the basis of 1 per cent of the employees' earnings. Several thousand workers are served in a specially designed and equipped building by a dozen specialists. Many other concerns have established extensive medical programs.

Industrial versus private medicine

The industrial phase of "socialized medicine" requires careful handling to keep in line with "professional ethics." To avoid criticism from the AMA (American Medical Association), it has been customary for employers to encourage workers to consult family physicians of their choice. Most industrial health departments maintain a panel of private physicians to whom workers can be referred on a rotation basis when they have no established medical connection. One authority explains that

at no time does the industrial physician attempt to urge the selection of any one physician, either a specialist or a general practitioner. Nor does he attempt to supplant the work of the private physician. This service is confined to examinations, tests, health programs, sanitation, and safety work, and to emergency treatments, plus occasional treatment which must be done while the employee is at work.[2]

Direct health services

The direct and indirect aids to workers, here discussed as contributions of the industrial health service, are usually considered as programs of the personnel department. (It is perhaps more common for the industrial safety program to be a separate department.) Included among personnel's direct health services are the following five subjects:

1. *First aid and hospitalization* are the fundamental remedial functions of industrial health. These services depend on a properly equipped dispensary, together with nurses and medical services fitted to the company's size and the nature of its product. Large organizations may maintain a complete medical service, while the smaller companies restrict themselves to a nurse on a full-time basis. In such cases, the physician is employed on a part-time schedule. Small adjacent concerns may pool their first-aid facilities to good advantage. Pooling of general health services among local companies in the same production field will become more general simply because it offers many advantages for an extended program at reasonable cost.

2. The *recreation* program is also related to the industrial health service. While some companies still believe that outstanding athletic teams are a contribution to the employees' health through the entertainment they afford, it is better practice to include the largest possible percentage of employees in the recreation program. Recreation on a professional basis should be charged to the sales department, since advertising appears to be its chief purpose.

Bowling is one of the all-employee sports which can finance itself. Golf is another industrial recreation that is gaining popularity on its own finances and momentum. Briggs Manufacturing Company is reported to have more than one hundred softball teams. Ford, Goodyear, General Electric, and many other large companies finance employee sports on a large and extensive scale.

It is psychologically obvious that employee-sponsored recreation builds a better spirit than the company-financed and managed kind. An extensive employee program also permits large groups of rotating members to take part in its management, offering a satisfying opportunity for many repetitive-job workers to use initiative.

3. *In-plant feeding* is no longer considered a social experiment. It is an accepted necessity for any concern, whether it is serviced by food-vending pushcarts, by the larger "meals-on-wheels," or by an elaborate cafeteria.

---

[2] John C. Aspley and Eugene Whitmore, *The Handbook of Industrial Relations*, 3rd ed. (Chicago: The Dartnell Corporation, 1952), pp. 994–995.

That in-plant feeding is beneficial and here to stay is one idea on which all levels of management and workers agree. It saves time and increases productivity through improvement of health and the morale which results from leisurely association. Many unions have voted company cafeterias second place among activities promoting morale. (Management's encouragement of unions took first place.)

After trying several plans for managing cafeterias, the accepted one clearly prefers operation by outside specialists under company policy and superivision. The outside operator receives a fee rather than profits. Many concerns are satisfied to lose money on cafeteria operations, believing that they are amply compensated on the production line.

One large concern summarizes the benefits of in-plan feeding as:

Better plant housekeeping	Higher morale and greater loyalty
Fewer accidents	Healthier workers
Reduced absenteeism	Better grade of applicants
Lower labor turnover	Better foreman-worker relations

4. *Drinking water and tablets* are not the simple health services that one might assume. Management must exercise important controls to prevent drinking fountains from becoming a menace to health. Observations made at more than thirteen hundred drinking fountains resulted in listing fourteen separate ways in which drinkers foul or contaminate the fountain bowl.[3] Some of these malpractices can be minimized by posted warnings; a new fountain design eliminates others.

The tablets distributed to workers include salt, cold, vitamin, and aspirin. Salt-tablet dispensers are frequently found throughout shops where the work induces heavy perspiration. Vitamin tablets are distributed chiefly in company cafeterias. Cold tablets have been handed out generally by many first-aid dispensaries.

Reports on the effectiveness of cold tablets vary. No conclusion would be worthwhile unless it results from accurate data on a number of variables, covering reasonably large groups of those who took the pills and those who did not. The same is true of group benefits from vitamin pills. Some years ago the DuPont Company's medical department made an extensive study of the results produced by vitamin pills with large groups of its employees. The physician responsible for the study stated that the conclusions were not definite enough to be scientifically helpful.

Aspirin is the favorite "Monday morning" remedy dispensed by the health department. That there are as many aspirin tablets given out on Monday as on all other days combined is a sad commentary on the week-end habits of a segment of American workers.

5. *Defective vision, hernia, and bad teeth* are accepted as the most common worker defects, in the order named. As one authority stated it, "many

[3] Aspley and Whitmore, *op. cit.*, pp. 1000–1001.

workers are one-eyed and don't know it." Defective vision affects the accident record and production efficiency, as well as general health. Some firms have solved the problem of poor inspectors by visual correction or elimination of the defectives. It is now generally conceded that enormous industrial losses have been caused by defective vision.

The Ortho-Rater, shown in Figure 23.1, is an instrument for measuring eye performance. It was used in an exhaustive series of experiments over a four-year period to determine the relation between vision and accidents. These experiments also determined the visual skills essential for different jobs. Based on the visual skills required, predictions were made about the relation between defective vision and accidents. In an 18-day test, the group with inadequate vision had 50 per cent more accidents than the standard vision group. In a 38-day test, the percentage was increased to 75.

A program of visual correction is a profitable investment for any concern — industrial, retail, or even banking. In one industrial program, it was found that 40 per cent of the employees could not meet liberal standards. Corrective glasses were ordered for all those who failed to meet the tests and corrective goggles for those who needed them in their work. Two years later, another over-all test was made. The employees with defective vision had been reduced to 10 per cent, including those who had been tested and employed in the interval. The company reported that the quality of its product was materially improved, its productivity increased, and its accident rate reduced by 27 per cent. Top management support ensured cooperation between the medical and safety departments, and between the foremen and the workers.

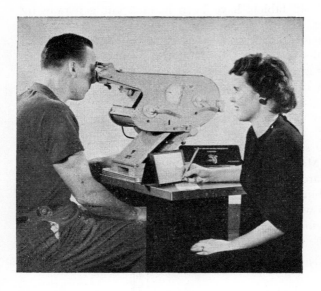

Figure 23.1

The Ortho-Rater

Courtesy: Bausch & Lomb Optical Company

Applicants should be examined for *hernias* and for bodily defects which would increase the probability of contracting a hernia. The employer should see that the condition is corrected or, if this is not possible, reject the applicant altogether. Otherwise, he may claim, at a later date, that the hernia was contracted on the job. It is equally obvious that no employee can be expected to do his best when he has *bad teeth*. Corrections here are not so difficult as with the other two defects, but employment should be based on the understanding that the necessary dental work will be done promptly.

Indirect health services

1. *"Plant-keeping"* or *sanitation* had its big boost during the twenty-five year interval between the two world wars. Ex-servicemen played some part in a new emphasis on plant sanitation. At the same time scientists advocated it, and well-managed concerns soon became famous for their cleanliness. Indeed they promoted public inspection tours to display their new pride. Most unprofitable companies have been slipshod in their housekeeping. Architects plan for factory cleanliness, and the makers of building materials develop some of their products with the same purpose in mind. Improved equipment and materials have produced high cleaning efficiency and better methods in use.

Industrial sanitation must attend to more than the plant and its equipment. Workers must be protected from one another. The proximity of workers in mass production makes personal cleanliness a necessity. To assure the good health which is essential for maintaning work schedules and increasing productivity, workers with colds and other contagious diseases must not be allowed to infect their fellow workers. It goes without saying that the utmost cleanliness is required of all cafeteria personnel; an infected scratch on a cook's finger can send a whole plant home sick.

It was the lack of sanitation that caused DeLessep's failure to build the Panama Canal, and it was the sanitation program of General Gorgas that made possible our success a few years later. Business has learned the value of personal sanitation chiefly from army experiences. Our army had more casualties in Cuba in 1898 from germs than from Spanish bullets. Napoleon's victory at Moscow was turned into defeat in large part by the typhus germ.

Plant sanitation expense is about 95 per cent labor and 5 per cent materials. A consistently followed program has been estimated to increase the work output from 10 to 20 per cent. Industry will improve plant and personal sanitation just as fast as it becomes clear that they produce direct savings.

2. *Vacations* with pay are directly beneficial to health and productivity. During World War II, it became common practice for employees to request and obtain the privilege of working through their vacation periods in order to obtain double pay. There is no doubt that both the company and the

workers lost by this arrangement. After the war, some workers insisted on continuance of the double-pay practice when the demand did not warrant it. Company officers who gladly went along with the no-vacation policy during the war had difficulty in convincing some employees that the real purpose of vacation was change from their daily tasks.

3. Much of the repetitive work of modern industry builds a nervous tension which results in a special kind of unhealthy fatigue. To what extent *rest periods* can bring relief has long been the subject of extensive experiments. The lesson of research in this area shows that for any kind of work — physical, mental, or a combination of both — over-all productivity is increased if the worker is allowed to rest before he tires himself out by working too long at one stretch. The practical problem for an industrial health program is to work out the optimum number, length, and spacing of rest periods.

It has been found that if workers are left entirely to themselves, they are quite likely not to apportion their rest periods wisely. Some workers who are highly motivated on the job will work very energetically and without pause for many hours and tire themselves so completely that they are practically useless toward the end of the day. A different sort of problem arises when no rest periods are provided, and workers sneak off the job in a self-defeating effort to relax.

Unfortunately there is no simple solution to the problem of rest periods. Some people need more rest than others; especially in assembly work it is not possible to adjust rest periods to the individual. The industrial health program must determine what is the best compromise plan for the situation. The important point is that some rest-period plan be officially installed and adhered to. The most common plan followed today is a fifteen-minute rest period in the middle of the morning, and another of the same length in the middle of the afternoon.

4. The *atmosphere* of the work place is also receiving more attention. The techniques of "controlled atmosphere" now extend to regulation of temperature and humidity, and the elimination of fumes and detrimental germs and dust particles from the air. Automatic control of temperature is not new, even in industrial plants, but humidifying and cleansing of the atmosphere are still somewhat novel. In most plants, the aim is to improve production and lower costs through the improved health and comfort of the workers. In some processes, such as lens grinding and artificial yarn "spinning," atmosphere control is also beneficial to the product.[4] Technical management magazines contain numerous advertisements of companies specializing in equipment for controlling the atmosphere. The growing effectiveness and

---

[4] The Gotham Hosiery Company claims that air-conditioning has made possible appreciable savings in nylon hosiery manufacture. It is claimed that abnormal temperatures and humidity cause the yarn to gum or kink when used on the finer-gauge machines.

declining cost of such equipment has led to windowless buildings where atmospheric controls can operate more accurately and at lower costs.[5]

5. *Noise, light,* and *color* are all factors to be considered in a health program. We have long recognized the bad effects of many industrial noises. The medical profession has now demonstrated that shrill notes make us nervous and low notes upset our digestive organs. And yet until recently, we have done little about the problem of noise except to send its victims to already congested hospitals. The English have been quicker than we to attack the problem closer to the source and give full-scale attention to taming industrial noise. One English writer, setting up the noise unit as a "phon," has decided that 130 of these phons constitute the limit of human endurance without discomfort. We use the decibel (db) as the unit of noise measurement.

After World War II, noise problems started to receive scientific attention at the Massachusetts Institute of Technology and the Armour Research Foundation. In 1955, the magazine *Noise Control* started publication under the auspices of the Acoustical Society of America. Similar publications now appear in several foreign countries, including Japan and the USSR. Permanent damage to hearing as a result of exposure to prolonged industrial noise has been recognized as a compensable injury by at least two state courts.[6]

Noise is being reduced in American industry, partly because management is coming to see the hidden costs of uncontrolled noise, and partly because unions are demanding correctives. The unnerving effects on the workers are indisputable. Noise increases absences, production costs, and labor turnover. There are two fundamental ways to combat these industrial noises: one is to eliminate them at the source, and the other is to absorb them with specially designed acoustical equipment. Finally, it is now realized that many factory noises result from unnecessary machine vibrations which can be remedied at far less expense than the physical and nervous damage to the workers.

The related factors of light and color may be made injurious or beneficial for the health of the employee. They are discussed in Chapter 19.

6. *Music* can be an indirect aid or a hindrance to worker health. Some of it might well be included under "noise." More and more plants are experimenting with music. Some are dropping the idea after a short unplanned program. To be healthful, music, like medicine, must be prescribed in kind for the purpose, and in doses suited to the patient. Industrial music fails

[5] The technical production advantages of controlled atmosphere are considered further in Chapter 13, page 252.

[6] Those interested in further information on this subject should consult Leo L. Beranck, *Noise Reduction* (McGraw-Hill Book Co., New York, 1960). Two other sources are the *Handbook of Noise Control,* also published by McGraw-Hill in 1957, and "Quiet Please" Albert E. Bachmann, *Harvard Business Review,* May–June, 1955, pp. 68–74.

unless it is planned. Screaming jazz in the cafeteria will cause more harm than good. A small, highly skilled group of Germans preferred opera to jazz, and waltzes to either. If music is to aid directly in the production and assembly processes, the rhythm of the music should bear a close relation to the natural rhythm of the work. Within the recent experience of the author, labor relations and productivity were observed at their optimum among a large group of skilled core-makers while they were mass-singing at their benches. The singing was purely spontaneous. If this natural inclination had been reinforced occasionally by music, these outbursts of rhythmic work would have been more frequent and more extended, with beneficial effects on production. The right tune, at the right time and in the right tempo, makes the most of the worker's latent propensity for music and rhythm.

7. *Records* which point to health troubles and their causes are absolutely necessary for maintaining a healthy group of industrial workers. Remedies for individuals and groups should be based on the known causes of their problems. Preventive programs must have a broad base of empirical data. Among the causes of industrial absenteeism, illness ranks first. It seems reasonable to predict that with the future development of direct and indirect health aids, business can cut absences in half, while increasing productivity at a fraction of the cost of our present remedial approach to the worker's health.

Industrial Safety

Modern industrial safety begins with plant design and layout. It is also concerned with machinery, equipment, tools, and material handling. Electrical, chemical, and fire hazards are all included in any scientific plan for protection of the workers. Hand and portable power tools are equipped with guards and automatic stops to protect employees from injury. In addition to all these precautions, numerous types of personal protective equipment are designed to minimize injuries resulting from contacts with the tools and dangerous working conditions of all kinds of general business and industrial hazards. In spite of all these precautions against accidents, the long record of injuries and deaths in this country furnish sufficient cause for continuous research and improvement against our mechanical hazards, unsafe living habits, and a too general personal proclivity to accident proneness.

From the handicraft era (through the Industrial Revolution) to the present development of mass production, industry has paid an ever-increasing toll in dollars and human suffering for preventable accidents. In recent years, due to scientific analysis and the resulting correctives, the accident curve has taken a reassuring dip.

"As early as 1867, Massachusetts had begun to use factory inspectors, and ten years later that state had a law requiring the guarding of dangerous machinery. From 1898, there were various efforts to make the employer financially liable for accidents, and in 1911 the first effective Workmen's Compensation Act was passed in Wisconsin, to be followed by a rash of similar laws in many other states."[7]

Three cycles of accident philosophy

The philosophy regarding industrial accidents appears to have gone through three broad historical cycles. The first was the *legal* phase, during which the employer cared little for his employees as a group, and defended his lack of interest behind legal barriers. The common law allowed, and the courts supported, the employer's escape from liability for injuries to his employees by any of three technicalities. *Contributory negligence* defeated the worker's claim by showing that the accident was caused, in part at least, by his own negligence. The *fellow-servant rule* exempted the employer from liability on the theory that some fellow worker's carelessness had contributed to the accident. And the *assumed risk doctrine* upheld the worker's assumption of risk by accepting the employment offered, and so relieved the employer from payment of damages caused by accidents.

The second phase might be referred to as the *social* or *humanitarian*. Public demand, union insistence, and increasing employer social interest did away with the legal hedges to liability for accident damages, and substituted statutory provisions for workmen's compensation irrespective of the cause of the accident. The first period blended into the second. Employers' liability laws were passed in Alabama and Massachusetts about 1885. These statutes made it more difficult for the employer to escape the payment of damages. Then came the workmen's compensation laws, the natural sequence of the growing sense of employer obligations. As the movement spread, its general implication was that the liability for accidents was with business, which should pay into state funds on a payroll basis so that all workers could be compensated if the injury resulted from their employment. The theory and practice of this second period was generally accepted by all concerned long before Mississippi fell in at the tail-end of the workmen's compensation parade in 1948.

The third phase might be called *scientific*. It ceases to emphasize liability, which it accepts without question, and gives attention to the preventive phases of accidents. Most large companies are already operating on this philosophy of safety on the assumption that it pays both socially and financially. The present attitude of progressive management toward safety is simply an adaptation of the methods of scientific management to the accident field.

[7] Quoting a March 31, 1961, letter to the author from the National Safety Council.

Accident measurements

Accidents are measured by frequency and severity rates. The *frequency rate* is the ratio of disabling injuries per million man-hours to the total number of man-hours worked. In this ratio the *disabling injury* is one which causes the worker to lose time beyond the day or shift in which the accident occurs.

The *severity rate* is measured by the lost days per million man-hours worked. These two measurements are used in appraising the effectiveness of accident-prevention programs. Figure 23.2 shows the industrial distribution of frequency and severity rates for 1959.

Accident costs

The two fundamental reasons for minimizing accidents are *humane* and *economic*. In spite of the universally accepted humane idea, it cannot be overlooked that since the main purpose of business is profits, it is only natural that management also gives serious consideration to the financial costs of accidents, and the savings which may be effected from safety programs. The possible savings undoubtedly have some bearing on a company's willingness to make financial outlays to minimize accidents. In other words, there may be a conscious comparison in some quarters of the cost of the program and its dollar savings. It is doubtful, however, that the dollar balance is given final consideration by modern management. One important factor is that concerns with low accident rates get the cream of the worker crop. That fact influences employee morale and hence productivity, which means a direct saving in unit costs.

There are two major costs resulting from accidents: (1) the direct or insured costs, and (2) the indirect and uninsured costs. The direct costs, including definite sums paid out for compensation and medical expenses, are fairly easy to calculate. The indirect, or uninsured, costs are more elusive, and are now estimated to equal the insured costs.[8] The causes of some of the wasted indirect or uninsured dollars are:

1. Idle time of the injured employee
2. Idle time of fellow-workers who help, watch, and talk
3. Idle time of foremen to assist injured, investigate and report, rearrange production, and train substitutes
4. Idle machines and tools
5. Upset production schedules
6. Welfare and benefit expenses
7. Full wages for low production of returned worker
8. Loss of possible profits.[9]

[8] These indirect costs were formerly estimated at three times the insured costs.
[9] A full discussion of most of these costs and several others may be studied in detail in Rollin H. Simonds and John V. Grimaldi, *Safety Management* (Richard D. Irwin, Inc., Homewood, Ill., 1956), Chapters 6, 7, and 8.

Figure 23.2

Injury Rates for 1962

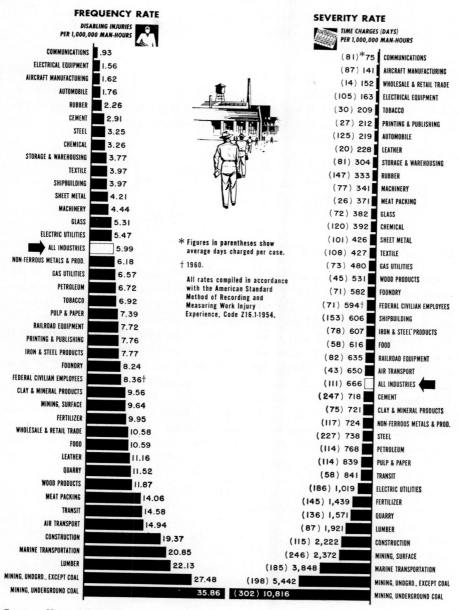

FREQUENCY RATE

DISABLING INJURIES
PER 1,000,000 MAN-HOURS

Industry	Rate
COMMUNICATIONS	.93
ELECTRICAL EQUIPMENT	1.56
AIRCRAFT MANUFACTURING	1.62
AUTOMOBILE	1.76
RUBBER	2.26
CEMENT	2.91
STEEL	3.25
CHEMICAL	3.26
STORAGE & WAREHOUSING	3.77
TEXTILE	3.97
SHIPBUILDING	3.97
SHEET METAL	4.21
MACHINERY	4.44
GLASS	5.31
ELECTRIC UTILITIES	5.47
ALL INDUSTRIES	5.99
NON-FERROUS METALS & PROD.	6.18
GAS UTILITIES	6.57
PETROLEUM	6.72
TOBACCO	6.92
PULP & PAPER	7.39
RAILROAD EQUIPMENT	7.72
PRINTING & PUBLISHING	7.76
IRON & STEEL PRODUCTS	7.77
FOUNDRY	8.24
FEDERAL CIVILIAN EMPLOYEES	8.36†
CLAY & MINERAL PRODUCTS	9.56
MINING, SURFACE	9.64
FERTILIZER	9.95
WHOLESALE & RETAIL TRADE	10.58
FOOD	10.59
LEATHER	11.16
QUARRY	11.52
WOOD PRODUCTS	11.87
MEAT PACKING	14.06
TRANSIT	14.58
AIR TRANSPORT	14.94
CONSTRUCTION	19.37
MARINE TRANSPORTATION	20.85
LUMBER	22.13
MINING, UNDGRD., EXCEPT COAL	27.48
MINING, UNDERGROUND COAL	35.86

* Figures in parentheses show
average days charged per case.

† 1960.

All rates compiled in accordance
with the American Standard
Method of Recording and
Measuring Work Injury
Experience, Code Z16.1-1954.

SEVERITY RATE

TIME CHARGES (DAYS)
PER 1,000,000 MAN-HOURS

	Industry
(81)*75	COMMUNICATIONS
(87) 141	AIRCRAFT MANUFACTURING
(14) 152	WHOLESALE & RETAIL TRADE
(105) 163	ELECTRICAL EQUIPMENT
(30) 209	TOBACCO
(27) 212	PRINTING & PUBLISHING
(125) 219	AUTOMOBILE
(20) 228	LEATHER
(81) 304	STORAGE & WAREHOUSING
(147) 333	RUBBER
(77) 341	MACHINERY
(26) 371	MEAT PACKING
(72) 382	GLASS
(120) 392	CHEMICAL
(101) 426	SHEET METAL
(108) 427	TEXTILE
(73) 480	GAS UTILITIES
(45) 531	WOOD PRODUCTS
(71) 582	FOUNDRY
(71) 594†	FEDERAL CIVILIAN EMPLOYEES
(153) 606	SHIPBUILDING
(78) 607	IRON & STEEL PRODUCTS
(58) 616	FOOD
(82) 635	RAILROAD EQUIPMENT
(43) 650	AIR TRANSPORT
(111) 666	ALL INDUSTRIES
(247) 718	CEMENT
(75) 721	CLAY & MINERAL PRODUCTS
(117) 724	NON-FERROUS METALS & PROD.
(227) 738	STEEL
(114) 768	PETROLEUM
(114) 839	PULP & PAPER
(58) 841	TRANSIT
(186) 1,019	ELECTRIC UTILITIES
(145) 1,439	FERTILIZER
(136) 1,571	QUARRY
(87) 1,921	LUMBER
(115) 2,222	CONSTRUCTION
(246) 2,372	MINING, SURFACE
(185) 3,848	MARINE TRANSPORTATION
(198) 5,442	MINING, UNDGRD., EXCEPT COAL
(302) 10,816	MINING, UNDERGROUND COAL

Courtesy: National Safety Council

This list gives no picture of the mental and physical suffering of the worker and his family or their money losses; nor does it account for the higher wage rates and inferior workers, both of which eventually become the necessary left-over choice of companies with high accident records. Concern over industrial accidents has become serious enough to support more than twenty organized safety services on a national scale.[10]

In its report of total accident costs for the year 1959, the National Safety Council divided the accident bill into visible costs and other costs. *Visible costs* include all medical costs and insurance, while *other costs* refer to the money value of damaged equipment and materials, production delays, and time lost by workers not involved in the accidents.[11]

TOTAL COST IN 1959	$4,200,000,000
Visible Costs	2,100,000,000
Other Costs	2,100,000,000
Cost per worker in industry	65

The worker as a hazard

Among the *personal* causes of industrial accidents in recent years was the rapid mass change to war production, which brought many new worker groups into most plants. They included the under- and over-age women, the previously unemployed, the long-time unemployed, and those who switched from clerical and other nonindustrial jobs. These groups often showed lack of ability, aptitude, attention, and interest. Not only was management guilty of hiring the emotionally and physically unfit; it was also responsible for their faulty instruction, poor discipline, and unsafe practices.

In some cases, insecurity of employment and general exhibitionism (horseplay) contribute confusion and accidents. Lack of proper selective techniques and scarcity of applicants cause many workers to be admitted with defective eyesight, organic weakness, bad teeth, and hernias. All of these personal factors have combined with a feverish industrial development to produce high-frequency and severity rates in many industries. Figure 23.3 shows the distribution of injuries to the human body.

People are the "unsafest" factor in business. They may be properly selected, adequately trained for their jobs, and taught to work and act safely, but with discouraging results because of the unpredictable psychological factor. Most unsafe acts of employees result from the following:

---

[10] *The Accident Prevention Manual,* published by the National Safety Council, and now in its fourth edition, presents the most complete survey of possibilities for accident prevention in industry.

[11] *Accident Facts,* National Safety Council, 1960 edition, p. 24.

3. Do you believe that management's safety programs have led to a situation where the individual has fewer accidents in the plant than he has at home?

4. What is the relationship among health, happiness, and productivity in industrial plants?

5. Would you class industry's programs for health and safety as socialized medicine? If so, do you accept the principle as it is applied in industry, even if you oppose "socialized medicine" as applied to any classification of the general population?

6. To what extent are companies' recreation programs related to their industrial health services?

7. How, in your opinion, should in-plant feeding be financed?

8. What is the purpose of the Ortho-Rater?

9. Do you believe that the usual lack of vacations (workers received time and a half or double time for staying on the job) during World War II resulted in impaired health of the working population?

10. To what extent has research found that rest periods are beneficial to worker health and industrial productivity? On what basis should the times and extent of rest periods be determined?

11. Would you be receptive to controlled atmosphere if it included exclusion of natural light, air, and noises? Would you feel different about a solid walled plant and a cave?

12. What is the effect of color schemes on productivity?

13. What legal evidence do we have of the deleterious effect of noises?

14. Where should the planning of modern safety begin?

15. Through what three cycles has the philosophy regarding industrial accidents evolved?

16. What is the relation between direct and indirect costs resulting from accidents?

17. What are the chief causes of unsafe acts on the part of employees that result in accidents?

18. How can accidents and injuries be reduced?

19. What was the probable per capita cost of adequate health and safety programs in 1962?

20. Which part of the worker's body suffers the greatest number of accidents?

CASE PROBLEM

The Custom Packing Company

The Custom Packing Company has an accident frequency rate of 10.20, which is 2.0 higher than the average for its industry, and 3.73 higher than the national industrial average, as both rates appear in Figure 23.2 of the National Safety Council. The company's severity rate has been determined, on the basis of 1959 figures, as about 420, which is only 16 higher than the rate for the meatpacking industry, and 334 lower than the national average severity rate.

Mr. Wilson, president of the company, has been concerned for some time about its "accidents" which he recognizes only by their number on a monthly basis, and their effect on the company's compensation rates. He has been discussing the accident situation with his engineering department each month as the figures are available. Although he is not conversant with the technical details of accident and safety programs, he has come to the conclusion that engineering is responsible for the upward trend in the frequency rate and the rising costs for all activities connected with the medical department and first aid.

In its defense, the engineering department has reported that all mechanical hazards have been cared for and all guards are in place. The chief of engineering confesses that he is not skilled in safety work, and suggests that Mr. Wilson have a survey made by some consultant conversant with the problems of safety and their correction, so that a scientific program for improvement may be worked out.

Mr. Wilson objects to the survey suggestion because he feels that it will interfere with production, and that any possible savings in the medical department's expense will not justify the cost of the survey and its results.

The Custom Packing Company has been in operation for twenty-five years, has a modern plant and about twenty-five hundred employees. Since most of its operations are performed by semiautomatic machines, its labor force is about 20 per cent semiskilled and 75 per cent unskilled. It is the latter group that has been accounting for most of the high frequency rate.

PROBLEM: If you called on Mr. Wilson to sell him on your safety survey plan, how would you answer his objections, explain the unreliability of his accident costs, and convince him, from the accident rates quoted, that his difficulty may stem from something other than mechanical causes? What do you think is the main reason for Custom's poor safety record, and how would you go about correcting it?

Part Three • Suggestions For Further Reading

Adams, Leonard P. and Aronson, Robert L., *Workers and Industrial Change,* New York: State School of Industrial and Labor Relations, Cornell University, 1957.

Cruden, Herbert J. and Sherman, Arthur W., Jr., *Readings in Personnel Management,* Cincinnati: South-Western Publishing Company, 1961.

Davis, Keith, *Human Relations at Work,* New York: McGraw-Hill Book Company, Inc., 1962.

Dunlop, John T., and Healy, James J., *Collective Bargaining,* Rev. Ed., Homewood, Illinois: Richard D. Irwin, Inc., 1953.

Fleishman, Edwin A., *Studies in Personnel and Psychology,* Homewood, Illinois: The Dorsey Press, Inc., 1961.

Flippo, Edwin B., *Principles of Personnel Management,* New York: McGraw-Hill Book Company, Inc., 1961.

Gardner, Burleigh B., and Moore, David G., *Human Relations in Industry*, 3rd Ed., Homewood, Illinois: Richard D. Irwin, Inc., 1955.

Glover, John D. and Hower, Ralph M., *The Administrator*, 3rd Edition, Homewood, Illinois: Richard D. Irwin, Inc., 1957.

Haire, Mason, *Psychology in Management*, New York: McGraw-Hill Book Company, Inc., 1956.

Harrell, Thomas W., *Industrial Psychology*, Rev. Ed., New York: Rinehart and Company, Inc., 1958.

Houser, Theodore V., *Big Business and Human Values*, New York: McGraw-Hill Book Company, Inc., 1960.

Johnson, Rossall J., *Personnel and Industrial Relations*, Homewood, Illinois: Richard D. Irwin, Inc., 1960.

Jucius, Michael J., *Personnel Management*, 4th Edition, Homewood, Illinois: Richard D. Irwin, Inc., 1959.

Karn, Harry W. and Gilmer, B. von Haller, *Readings in Industrial and Business Psychology*, 2nd Edition, New York: McGraw-Hill Book Company, Inc., 1962.

Kindall, Alva F., *Personnel Administration*, Homewood, Illinois: Richard D. Irwin, Inc., 1961.

Maier, Norman R. F., *Principles of Human Relations*, New York: John Wiley and Sons, Inc., 1952.

Pigors, Paul, and Myers, Charles A., *Personnel Administration*, 4th Edition, New York: McGraw-Hill Book Company, Inc., 1961.

Pigors, Paul, Myers, Charles A. and Malm, F. T., *Readings in Personnel Administration*, 2nd Edition, New York: McGraw-Hill Book Company, Inc., 1959.

Reynolds, Lloyd G., *Labor Economics and Labor Relations*, 3rd Ed., Englewood Cliffs, New Jersey: Printice-Hall, Inc., 1959.

Roethlisberger, F. J. and Dickson, William J., *Management and the Worker*, Cambridge, Massachusetts: Harvard University Press, 1950.

Saltonstall, Robert, *Human Relations in Administration*, New York: McGraw-Hill Book Company, Inc., 1959.

Scott, Walter Dill, Clothier, Robert and Spriegel, William R., *Personnel Management*, 6th Edition, New York: McGraw-Hill Book Company, Inc., 1961.

Selekman, Benjamin M., *A Moral Philosophy for Management*, New York: McGraw-Hill Book Company, Inc., 1959.

Strauss, George and Sayles, Leonard R., *Personnel: The Human Problems of Management*, Englewood Cliffs, New Jersey: Prentice-Hall, Inc., 1960.

Whisler, Thomas L. and Harper, Shirley F., *Performance Appraisal*, New York: Holt, Rhinehart and Winston, 1962.

Whyte, William Foote, *Industry and Society*, New York: McGraw-Hill Book Company, Inc., 1940.

Wolf, William B., *The Management of Personnel,* San Francisco, Wadsworth Publishing Company, Inc., 1961.

Yoder, Dale, *Personnel Management and Industrial Relations, 5th Edition,* Englewood Cliffs, New Jersey: Prentice-Hall, Inc., 1962.

————, *Personnel Principles and Policies,* 2nd Ed., Englewood Cliffs, New Jersey: Prentice-Hall, Inc., 1959.

•

The quotation at the beginning of Part Three is from: Benjamin M. Selekman, *A Moral Philosophy for Managent,* New York: McGraw-Hill Book Company, Inc., 1959, p. 219.

Compensating

Employees

In this field of wage and salary administration there is a strong emphasis on measurement because it is recognized that a systematic determination of economic rewards is more equitable than one based on arbitrary decisions, personal considerations, pressure ("the squeaky wheel"), and individual opinion. Arguments, friction, and counter-measures are reduced to the extent that economic rewards can be determined by impersonal and objective methods. Measure is, therefore, the key to equity in administering economic rewards.

Douglas McGregor

24

Wage Factors in
Labor Relations

However important working conditions and job security may be to the worker, it cannot be denied that the question of wages causes the chief controversial discussion in most labor-management contract negotiations. Wages are fundamental in the worker's mind when he considers his family's living standard. They also measure his personal importance in relation to his fellow workers. Money reward for personal achievement provides the normal motivation to productivity for the majority of workers. It was chiefly because the Industrial Revolution removed the worker's personal control over his wages that he joined organized labor groups to deal with his employer.

Wage principles

There are several fundamental wage principles which play an important role in fixing the general level of wages. What applications should be made of some of these principles is still a source of controversy both within and between labor and management camps.

Cost of Living. The reason most frequently given by labor for its demand for an increase in wages is a rise in the cost of living. During periods of rising prices, labor reminds management of this cost-of-living principle. On the other hand, when prices are falling, labor is equally vociferous in demanding that management hold the line in wages.

In actual practice, labor and management have agreed to tie wage changes to the cost of living only during periods of rising prices. Labor agrees for the simple reason that the plan promises higher pay during a foreseeable period. Management agrees because it is interested in some tangible stabilizing formula, and the cost-of-living index promises to relieve the pressure on wages in contract negotiations.

The Philadelphia Electric Company's "Market Basket" plan for wage determination worked successfully for several years, but was repudiated by labor during the depression of the thirties. The most widely used measure of the cost of living today is the "Consumer's Price Index for Moderate-Income Families in Large Cities." Issued by the U.S. Bureau of Labor Statistics, it measures changes in the average retail prices of food, clothing, rent, services, home furnishings, and miscellaneous items. If wages were geared to this measure permanently, living standards would tend to become frozen. It is for this reason that the cost-of-living principle is desirable for the long run only when it includes some fixed annual wage increase to provide for improving living standards, irrespective of changes in the Index. General Motors' five-year agreement with the United Auto Workers (CIO) was the first outstanding example of a cost-of-living contract with provision for a fixed annual wage increment.

Ability to Pay. Wages based on the company's ability to pay is advanced by both labor and management when it suits their individual interests. Sometimes the corporation's profit-and-loss statement provides labor with a basis for urging a wage increase; at other times, it gives management an argument in favor of decreasing wages or maintaining the status quo. As a principle, the idea seldom serves the purpose of the individual company. Union leaders occasionally suggest that a change in management might have a salutary effect on the complaining company's operating deficit. The conclusion is that periodic profits and losses of an individual company have little or no effect on general wage levels. If, however, general business conditions are pointing upward or downward, neither labor nor management can escape their consequences as reflected in the wage scale. Ability to pay has little effect on wage levels for the short run; but in the long run, its influence is inevitable.

Contribution to Production. The contribution to production by the worker is an almost unassailable principle for fixing wages, but it is impossible to apply in practice. The economic theory that land, labor, and capital are the factors of production is perfectly valid, but any practical method for separating the contributions of the three has not yet been discovered. Even if it were possible to segregate labor's contribution, endless controversy would arise over division of the "spoils" among the various labor groups and skills.

Productivity. Productivity would furnish an excellent criterion for the determination of the general wage level if it were possible to agree to an acceptable standard of production. Even in such an inconceivable situation, organized labor's objection would be based on its philosophy of the equal treatment of workers within given work classifications. However, production standards have led to the use of measures of productivity as partial wage determinants within a limited field. Such measures can be the basis of incentive plans and piecework rates, when organized labor accepts both the principle and the production standard.

Wage Fund. The wage-fund theory of the classical economists is akin to the belief that labor's contribution to the production process can be isolated. When it can, then labor's total share or wage fund has been established. The problem then arises of determining a fair split among the workers involved.

The Market Theory. The market theory of wage determination, based on the relation between the supply and demand of labor, is the most potent factor in fixing the general level of wages. The principle is also referred to as the commodity theory of wages. It likens wage determinations to the supply and demand forces that fix the market prices for commodities. It is particularly distasteful to organized labor for obvious reasons. Although the unions have done well in preserving their *official* wage rates during depressions, there usually develops an *unofficial* lower rate, often suggested by those union workers who are unable to find jobs at the official scale.

Wage policies

Every business organization should have definitely established and communicated wage policies. It is only through a declaration of policies that employees can have confidence in their employer. Company policies with respect to wages may be expressed generally, or they may be broken down into details. If the policy statements are kept general, personnel management is given greater flexibility; on the other hand, the more detailed announcements promote worker confidence and morale. The following descriptive titles emphasize the factors which should be included in an acceptable statement of wage policies:

1. Working periods that result in healthful fatigue
2. Extra wages for overtime and night shifts
3. Wage differentials for skill, responsibility, and working conditions
4. Recognition of individual merit
5. Fair standards of performance
6. Promotion from within
7. Payments for vacation and sick leave

It is sometimes suggested that announcements regarding wage practices and provision for prompt attention to wage complaints be included in wage policies.

Administrative Problems

Wage levels

Whenever there is a general rise in the wage level, management cries "inflation." As a matter of fact, rising prices are caused by either increasing production costs or increasing consumer demand. True, the cost of labor influences the cost of production, but it is not the only cost factor, as we shall observe. Furthermore, increased production costs do not necessarily follow increases in wages, either in the individual plant or in industry as a whole.

In the individual plant, wage increases may be offset by increased productivity (production per man-hour), by decreased costs of raw materials, or by increased production. Increase in man-hour production usually means that there has been a larger investment in machinery per worker. It may mean that methods have been improved. Increased productivity lowers unit overhead costs, and increased production leaves a wider margin for profits above the break-even point. Decreased material costs, other factors being equal, lower total production costs. If there is no change in any of the three factors mentioned above (productivity, material costs, and volume of production), then the cost of production is certainly raised by a wage increase, and the company will suffer diminution of profits or a loss unless buyer demand permits an increase in prices.

During the depression (1929–1933), worker productivity rose 25 per cent in many industries, and more in some. During World War II, productivity standards were mixed. While they rose generally in the war industries because of government pressure and incentive wages, they fell in civilian production. Between 1921 and 1938, average hourly earnings rose approximately 30 per cent, while productivity increased about 60 per cent. Under such conditions, wage costs per unit of output naturally fell. From 1933 to 1937, wages rose between 40 and 50 per cent in one large farm-implement concern. But because sales increased by more than 600 per cent during the same period, unit overhead and unit selling costs more than wiped out any increase in production costs due to wage increases.[1]

When there is a general wage increase of about the same percentage in all industry, costs of production will rise and so will prices unless there is a counteracting change in productivity, cost of raw materials, or production volume. The price rise will, in most cases, be the difference between the new wage increase and the resulting levels of these three factors. If a considerable portion of the working population is left out of the general wage increase, their lack of purchasing power will leave a larger pool of commodities for those groups which participated in the wage boost.

[1] Lloyd G. Reynolds, "Problems in the Administration of Wages," an address before the Pittsburgh Chapter of the Society for the Advancement of Management, December 13, 1945. Published in *Advanced Management,* Vol. 11 (March 1946), pp. 2–8.

Because of the controlling economic factors which determine the relations between wages and prices, it must be clear that the *purchasing power of the average worker is improved by general wage increases only when the resulting percentage of productivity increase tops the percentage of the wage boost.* For the erroneous ideas respecting the relations among wages, prices, and purchasing power, both labor and management are equally culpable. Labor preaches and advertises that national prosperity will surely follow wage increases due to the resulting rise in the purchasing power of the worker. Unless some compensating influence results, in the form of greater productivity, lower raw-material prices, or a larger volume of production, "prosperity" will flow only to that small segment of workers who participate in the wage increase. Other groups will pay the bills in the increased prices for the commodities made by those whose higher wages boosted their costs. Equally fallacious is the contention that wage increases cause higher prices while the purchasing power remains the same. Both labor and management oversimplify the situation and confuse the consumers.

"Fact-finding"

Early in 1946, the President asked Congress to grant him authority to appoint "fact-finding boards" to deal with important national labor disputes. The requested legislation empowered boards to find the facts and make recommendations based on them. Presumably the function of these boards was to recommend a wage change that would establish a proper relationship among wages, prices, and purchasing power. Without waiting for enabling legislation, the President appointed fact-finding boards to deal with wage disputes in the automobile and oil industries. During twenty years following the enactment of the Railway Labor Act of 1926, there were thirty-one presidentially appointed emergency boards to handle wage disputes in the railroad business. The pacifying results of these board studies are often cited as ample justification for "fact-finding" in wage disputes. What are the facts?

One fact not generally remembered is that the wage recommendations of two railway Emergency Boards were revised upward by the President. The first was in 1941, when the railway unions refused to accept the Board's wage recommendations and threatened to strike. The second came right after the government seized the railroads to prevent a national tie-up. Thus in at least two major cases in railroad fact-finding, the facts were pushed aside when they ran counter to the administration's labor policies. In the major steel and rail wage disputes of 1945–1946, fact-finding was abandoned in favor of negotiation by the Reconversion and Stabilization Board.

Fact-finding is the readily admitted scientific approach to any problem. However, when there is a lack of any principle to which the facts can be related for a solution, then their accumulation, even assuming that they are true and pertinent to the subject, is useless for the intended purpose. The situation is still worse when, in the absence of an objective principle, political policies are made the basis for applying or ignoring determined facts. These two factors — lack of accepted principles and the injection of political policies — create such a wide gap between the form and the substance of a solution to the problem that expediency steps in where objectivity fears to tread.

The guaranteed annual wage

Guaranteed wage plans provide the employee, with varied restrictions, take-home pay at a more or less constant rate. The purpose is to smooth out, from the wage standpoint, production peaks and valleys caused by irregularity of sales. There are several important matters that affect wage stabilization in any company. How long shall the guarantee period last? To whom shall the guarantees apply? What shall be the limit of the guarantee? What part of the possible financial loss resulting from the guarantee shall be absorbed by the company and by the workers?

Because of the ever-present danger of a downswing in the general business cycle, most companies restrict the guarantee period to one year, some to a shorter period. Otherwise, the possibility of financial ruin lurks in company commitments for guaranteed wage payments.

Another restriction relates to the selection of workers who shall be covered by the plan. Most companies start coverage after one year of employment; some use a shorter or longer period. Under some plans, the company sets up coverage limits for different job classifications after determining its total labor needs for the ensuing year. Within the classifications, guarantees are applied on a seniority basis, making it possible for the company to retain its more valuable employees during the periods of reduced production.

The amount of the guarantee is more of a problem than its duration or the extent of coverage. For this reason, guarantees differ widely in terms of company liability and the amounts of payment. The common practice is to establish a basic workweek and a basic pay check. If the workweek figures lower pay than the guarantee, the company pays the difference, which must be made up by the employee when longer hours or overtime permit. Another restriction is the financial limit to the company's guarantee, which may be fixed on the number of hours or dollars. The details of typical company wage-stabilization plans are discussed in the following chapter on Wage Plans.[2]

[2] For the employer's point of view, refer to "The Economics of the Guaranteed Wage," Report of the Committee on Economic Policy of the U.S. Chamber of Commerce, a twenty-five page pamphlet, published in 1948.

Title III of the federal Social Security Act, as amended in 1960, aids in stabilizing wages during the first thirty-nine weeks of unemployment. The compensation feature of the Act is carried out through those states which have approved legislation and the machinery for its operation. However, the restrictions are so numerous and the payments so small that the benefits can scarcely be referred to as wage stabilization.

Successful wage stabilization in industry, or any other type of business, must be predicated on leveling of sales, which in industry leads to leveling of production. Wage stabilization will not be effective on any large scale until the disruptive effects of business cycles can be brought under control.

Job stabilization

Unstabilized jobs, like unstabilized wages, result chiefly from seasonal and cyclical fluctuations. By and large, the two problems must be handled in the same way. Stabilization of jobs depends on accurate personnel-manning tables, which are impossible unless production can be based on sales which are accurately estimated and spread evenly through the year. Job stabilization is the basis of wage stabilization. Both are extremely important to workers and employers.

Individual companies can help themselves and their workers by scientific planning, operating, and controlling of sales and production and personnel procedures, in the order mentioned. But individual or spasmodic company success will not make a dent on the national problem of unstabilized production. Intercompany cooperation along the lines suggested will represent a forward step. Government assistance and regulation, in spite of their unwieldiness, will be necessary for any large improvement on a national scale. Only through that agency can we hope for the far-flung coordination of effort necessary to solve this problem.

Fringe benefits

Fringe benefits include such items as paid vacations, holidays, and sick leave, call-in and severance pay, night-shift differentials, health and life insurance, and welfare payments of various kinds, including the so-called royalties. The importance of fringe benefits stems from their rapid cost increase in the past twenty years. From 1947 to 1959, annual wages rose 83 per cent while fringe benefits were increasing by 206 per cent. A survey by the U.S. Chamber of Commerce of 1064 companies for the year 1959 shows that fringe costs amounted to 62.6¢ per hour for each employee. In that year, non-wage payments amounted to 52 billions, which was 19 per cent of the total payroll.[3] It is estimated that annual fringe benefits cost on

[3] *Nation's Business,* for August and October 1960, pp. 14 and 78.

an average of $773.99 per employee, in addition to the paycheck, and they are growing twice as fast on the average as wages.

There is considerable evidence suggesting that workers are well satisfied with the ratio of fringe benefits to wages. Some European countries have a much higher ratio of such benefits to wages than we do in this country, apparently to the European worker's satisfaction. Presumably, this satisfaction is based on the general growing desire for individual security.

Fringe benefits are often referred to as the *invisible pay envelope*, a fact of which management is not always conscious. The growing cost of fringe benefits attracted the interest of Congress by 1958, resulting in the Disclosure Act, effective April 1, 1959. It requires reports of all plans affecting more than twenty-five employees if the company's activities are involved in or "affect" interstate commerce. About 250,000 companies and the unions involved must file with the Labor Department, stating the types of plans as well as the benefits they provide. Only a few of the fringe benefits will be discussed because most of them are well-known.

Vacations are necessary for maintaining or improving health. Nonworking holidays may also be beneficial, depending on their use. Neither could be enjoyed by the average worker unless his wages were continued. Some observers contend that holidays have started to get out of hand as organized labor has succeeded in adding to them periodically.

The privilege of paid *sick leave* is frequently abused. Some workers appear to have a feeling that their efficiency might be questioned if they used less than their total sick-leave allowance. *Call-in* pay can scarcely be questioned, even though its designation is a misnomer. If a worker reports for duty in natural course, he should receive some reimbursement when no work is available. *Severence* pay usually refers to money due to the quitting worker who has made contributions to pension and other funds. However, there is another form of vested right which refers to the employee's privilege of working for a particular concern, a right which has a compensable value if he is forced to leave through no cause of his own, such as technological changes in production. If the employer is held liable for loss of jobs due to technological change, the burden may become so heavy during a period of fundamental machine improvements that the damages can scarcely be paid except from public revenues as a social obligation.

The *night-shift* differential is not so easy to justify. In the first place, it is a war baby; and in the second, there are many workers who prefer the "dog watch" to any other and complain strenuously when shifted to daylight hours. Experience suggests that if all workers were given their choice at the same hourly rate, management would have no trouble in manning the dark hours in most industries. Many foundry workers, for example, choose the cooler night shift during half the year, and prefer it for the other half because of established sleeping habits.

Little need be said about *health and life insurance.* Benefits paid or shared in by employers doubtless repay the investment through better work resulting from freer minds. The final fringe benefit is the so-called *welfare fund.* Its purpose is excellent; its results can be just as good as its management. The welfare fund is a comparatively ancient and honorable institution with many companies. It was fed in the past by contributions of workers to help distressed fellows financially. More recently, profits from various concessions, which are often considerable, have been assigned to the welfare fund. Then a well-known labor leader conceived the idea of creating a real welfare fund from "royalties" paid by the employers. Since royalties are usually paid for the use of others' ideas, the name given to this fringe benefit does not seem amiss. The Kaiser Company offered a $5.00 royalty on each car produced, hoping thereby to stimulate production. Many concerns are now paying royalties into employee welfare funds. Since the royalty idea has become more or less accepted, the problem has concerned the management of its funds. Labor claims it as an exclusive right; management insists on participating to protect its employees and because it feeds the fund. However that may be, co-management of the coal-mine fund by union and company representatives has been both quarrelsome and highly unsatisfactory from the standpoint of its beneficiaries.

Unclassified "fringe benefits"

A number of questionable fringe benefits might be discussed under this caption, but we shall refer briefly to only two which are attracting wide public interest. One is "featherbedding," a benefit defended by a number of labor unions. The other is the "conflict of interest," the name given to a practice which is indulged in by some members of management.

Featherbedding is sometimes spoken of as "made work." So defined, it refers to unnecessary jobs that accomplish nothing for anyone except the person who is paid for the job concerned. Railroad featherbedding has an ancient, if not honorable, lineage and has attracted the attention of several state legislatures. One application of this technique provides that firemen must serve on diesel locomotives whose fire are "stocked" automatically by a flow of fuel oil.[4]

Another example is the so-called "full crew" used to operate an engine and caboose. A third is payment on a trip basis for the train's crew, scheduled at a time when trains were making only a fraction of today's speed. A fourth example concerns absurdly high wages in certain cases, which are now (1962) attracting attention of the Congress. One wage item shows that whereas the Secretary of Defense is paid $480 a week, fourteen iron workers at Cape Canaveral, on national defense work, average between

[4] See "The Great Featherbed Fight," by Gilbert Burck, *Fortune,* March 1960, pp. 151 *et seq.*

$520 and $611 per week. Another cites an apprentice electrician's pay as $673 a week, equal to the salary of the Vice-President of the United States. It appears that an electrician at the Cape hits the top bracket at $748 per week.[5]

A fifth popular featherbedding plan, known as the "bogus," has been practiced in the publishing field since 1871 by the Typographical Union which prefers to call it "reproduction." This idea calls for a duplicate setting of type for that which has been received ready for use. "Boiler plate" advertising is a common example. One newspaper in Salt Lake City employs three typesetters on a full-time basis for setting up these boguses. Unused, the boguses are paid for and destroyed at the end of the day.

A lucrative fringe benefit enjoyed by management has recently received national publicity because of its practice by at least two of Chrysler Corporation's executives under the title of *conflict of interest.* A more explicit and understandable title would be "dishonest kickbacks from vendors." Under this plan, an executive with influence over his company's purchases, makes arrangements with a vendor company in which he has a stock interest to sell its products to the concern which he serves as a full-time executive. For his efforts on behalf of the vendor, the executive receives a kickback, or commission, on the negotiated sales in spite of the fact that his salaried interest is with the buyer. He plays both ends in favor of himself — in the middle. Judging from the widespread interest and general disapproval which has been aroused by these unclassified fringe benefits, we may predict that they will have difficult going in the near future.

Profit sharing

The purpose of profit sharing is to enlist the interest of the workers in the general progress and prosperity of their employer. Whether profit sharing accomplishes its purpose, and in what ways, is controversial. Its proponents and its adversaries are equally vociferous in their claims. One recognized writer in the field of personnel states that "profit sharing is no stimulant to production." Industrialists who have tried the plan, some for as many as twenty years, claim that it not only stimulates productivity, but that it also has many intangible values, not the least of which is improvement in labor-management relations. Most labor leaders are against profit sharing, contending that its purpose is to "pull the wool over the workers' eyes" by claiming partnership with management, thereby keeping down wages and undermining worker loyalty to unionism.[6]

Both sides cite statistics, often from the same source, to support their opinions of profit sharing. Actually, there has been neither progress nor

---

[5] From testimony before the "McClellan (Senator John L.) Committee," 87th Congress, 1961.

[6] Walter Reuther appears to be an exception, especially in his contract with American Motors Corporation.

decline in the recent history of profit sharing. There was a swing in its favor about 1918. The depression of the thirties put a damper on the idea, but it started to gain favor again after World War II. In 1948, the National Industrial Conference Board issued a report on the then-existing programs. One of its conclusions was that they were "more prevalent in small and medium-sized concerns where the worker may be in a better position to see the connection between his actions and the profitableness of his company."[7]

Management's favorable attitude toward profit sharing as a worker incentive is the limitation of its payments to those years when industry and business are making a profit. Another favorable factor is the fact that profit sharing increases the worker's purchasing power without affecting prices except as consumer demand is thereby increased. Finally, it does not add anything to the cost of production. It does not, therefore, contribute to the vicious wage-price spiral referred to by some economists.

Its adherents claim that profit-sharing reduces the cost of supervision because of stimulated interest by the workers. Marked improvement in labor-management relations is another advantage claimed by many businesses. This naturally leads to decreased costs because of fewer work stoppages. The adversaries' claim that profit-sharing leads to worker interference with management prerogatives is denied quite generally by those with experience.

Those opposed to profit sharing point out that large companies like General Electric abandoned the idea in 1947 after a fair trial. At that same time, there was an upward trend in the use of the plan. Opponents note further that profit sharing cannot be applied to industry generally, but usually only to those concerns with a long profit record,[8] and that the plan is vulnerable in any case because of the uncertainties of profits. Labor unions, they emphasize, are usually opposed to profit sharing, claiming that such funds belong in the pay envelope. Changes of management and mergers are two of the operating difficulties of the plan. It is contended that many of the plans are too involved for worker understanding. In any case, profit sharing should be introduced during a period of continuing profits.

There are various bases for distribution of profits to employees. Period of service is a favorite, percentage of wages is another, and there are still others. The existing wage structure should be maintained when a profit-sharing plan is installed so that the workers will have nothing to lose, also, profits should not be shared until after reserves and dividends have been provided for.

The National Tag Company's plant at Dayton, Ohio, worked out the formula shown in Figure 24.1, through its Junior Board, for distribution of

[7] National Industrial Conference Board, Inc., *Studies in Personnel Policy No. 97,* 1948, entitled "Profit Sharing for Workers."
[8] American Motors Corporation does not meet this profit criterion.

Figure 24.1

PRODUCTION BONUS PLAN

The amounts to be distributed to individual production workers under this Production Bonus Plan shall be based on the so-called *Point System,* in which point values be assigned to the various factors listed below, in accordance with the ranges as provided:

1. *Length of Service.* One (1) point for each year of continuous service.
    a. Continuous service shall not be interrupted by service in the Armed Forces of the United States.
    b. Continuous service shall not be interrupted by layoffs dictated by Company production necessities.

2. *Attendance.* Good (not over 3 days per year) ———— 20 points
   Fair (not over 10 days per year) ———— 10 points
   Poor (not over 15 days per year) ———— 5 points
    a. Attendance records shall not be affected adversely by absences caused by Company production policy.
    b. Attendance records shall not be affected adversely by absences caused by injuries received while on the job.

3. *Attitude.* Good ———— 20 points
   Fair ———— 10 points
   Poor ———— 0 points
   "Attitude" means general cooperation of the type that promotes good will among employees and with foremen, resulting in improved quantity and quality production.
   Ratings for this factor shall be made by Management.

4. *Tardiness.* More than 15 times ———— 5 points off the score
   Note: This allows for about one tardiness every three weeks.

5. *Rate of Pay.*
   The total of the points for Factors 1–4 inclusive shall be multiplied by the base pay rate in order to establish weighted averages.

Determination of Individual Production Bonus
1. The total of the weighted point values of all production workers shall be divided into the total amount of the production bonus to be distributed to production workers. This result determines the money value of the point.
2. Multiply the weighted point value for each individual production worker by the money value of the point as determined in the preceding paragraph. This result represents the money bonus to be paid to the employee concerned.

the production employees' share in the company's profits. It is not claimed that this case is typical. Rather, it was fitted to the local situation and contains several distributive factors.[9] So that the relation between production and profits would be emphasized, the idea was referred to as the "Production Bonus Plan."

Stock ownership

It was stated in the chapter on Financial Management that the sale of stock to employees has been used in a limited way as an aid in external financing. In the chapter on Personnel Relations, employee stock ownership was described as a plan for enlisting the loyalty of the workers, and the history of worker disillusionment with the plan was traced.

Whereas the profit-sharing worker participated in his company's good times, the stock-owning worker also shared its poor times. With the depression of the thirties, many employees offered their company stock for sale because they needed cash. Then they found out that the same situation which made them short of cash — part-time employment — turned company profits into losses. If the stock was "listed," the price offered was frequently less than half what the worker had paid for it. When there was no organized market, offers to buy were scarce at any price. For once, the worker looked at the economy from management's point of view, and he did not like what he saw. In most cases, he felt that he had been imposed on, and company loyalty was at a premium. Those who had left the company before the break in the market, and hence had part of their payments returned to them, were considered lucky.

It is rather easy to conclude that employee stock ownership, especially of common stocks, has not been universally successful. In most cases, companies now offer their common stocks to executives who, because of their broader experience, will blame the market rather than the company when the wrong phase of the cycle hits. Stock distribution to lower-paid employees has tended to be restricted for some time to preferred issues, where the dividend record is safer even if the market price is not. Some of the utilities have been aggressive in selling their preferred stock to both employees and customers, usually to create better public relations. Because of the favorable attitude of most state public service commissions toward the return on utility capitalization, such securities have represented a conservative investment.

Pensions

Pension plans of private concerns helped stimulate the public demand for social security, including its pension features. The establishment of federal

[9] The author was technical adviser to the Junior Board of Directors of the Company at the time this plan was drafted and later accepted by the Company, in 1947.

Social Security, in turn, reacted as an ever-greater stimulus to the general spread of private pensions, even among small and medium-size concerns.

Pensions pose several difficult administrative problems. One, and probably the greatest, arises from their comparative newness. Until a pension fund has attained financial strength, which can be tested only after maturity of its benefit payments, it is in the problematical category.

Evidence that pension systems have not been completely sold to workers appears in the negative pension vote of Ford employees to the company's rather generous offer of 1947. The question was whether the workers preferred an 11½¢ straight pay raise, plus about 3½¢ more for paid holidays, or a split of the same 15¢ which would allocate 8¢ to the pension fund and 7¢ to increased pay. High prices, union politics, and the provision for a 2-per cent employee contribution to the fund, all influenced the final vote. It is also probable that the vote was split by age groups. Workers past forty have a more pressing interest in pension plans.

Another difficulty of the employee pension plans of private business is the dispute about who shall make the contributions to the pension fund (or pay the premiums, if the risk is assumed by an insurance company). The employers often favor a 50-per cent contribution by the employees on the ground that it is the employees who get the full benefit of the fund. The employees, on the other hand, hold out for full payment by the company in most cases, arguing that pension costs are really an expense of doing business. Because the employees have won the decision in most cases, it is probably the consumer who bears the brunt of the expense in the end.

A new problem in pension plans is the resistance of the older workers to compulsory retirement. They argue that the psychological effect is bad if the employee is still fit and that pension payments force a reduction in living standards. They also point out that the company suffers in many cases where the employee between sixty and seventy is often better qualified and more dependable than many of his juniors. This problem was thrown into the courts when a group of prospective pensioners of the Firestone Tire & Rubber Company asked for an injunction against the pension plan negotiated by their union. The question for which they asked a legal opinion was whether it was permissible for a union to bargain away their right to work at any specified age. With increasing longevity, it is not unreasonable to expect oldsters to form a national association for the legal protection of their right to work. This is simply the industrial phase of the increasingly general problem of geriatrics.

Another pension problem is caused by loss of retirement payments by workers shifting employment. With the increasing mobility of labor, this problem will develop on a national scale. Its ultimate solution must be on some territorial basis. In the meantime, initial attacks against current handling of the problem are proceeding on an "area-wide" basis. Exchange of seniority among a group of small companies in the Toledo, Ohio, area failed because of internal union politics. In the latter part of 1950, the first of such agreements was made with seventy tool and die shops in the district area. Because of the prevalence of joint labor-management contract negotiations with groups of similar industries on an area basis, it is only reasonable to assume that area-wide pension-eligibility arrangements will be progressively added to many contracts.

Group annuity plans are favored by large companies. The Vick Chemical Company, for example, contributed 5 per cent of the first $3000 of the employee's base wage, plus 10 per cent of the base pay between $3,000 and $14,000. After three years, the plan is contributory for those workers who elect to participate to the extent of 2½ per cent of the wage up to $3,000 and 5 per cent between that amount and $15,000. The company contributes an equal amount. The fund buys group annuities from a regular life insurance company. Payments to employees depend on earnings, age, and sex.

The *trusteed system* is used by about one thousand companies. Some plans provide for worker participation, while others are paid for entirely by the company. Pension payments are made directly from the fund, the amount being related to years of service, age, and salary.

The *individual policy trust* provides for the purchase of individual employees annuity policies from insurance companies and is usually contributory. This is probably the most widely used plan and is particularly adaptable to small and medium-sized companies.

While retirement plans, either company financed or contributory, are not popular, they have some outstanding adherents. Probably the best-known fund plan is that of Sears, Roebuck & Company, started in 1916 and now (1962) in its 46th year of operation. Employees may contribute up to 5 per cent of their earnings, not to exceed $500 annually. The Company contributed 5 per cent of its profits until the past few years, when the amount was increased to 10 per cent. Sears' profit contributions are figured before federal taxes or dividends. As of December 31, 1960, the Fund amounts to $1,429,262,000. Prior to 1941, all receipts were invested in Sears' stock; since then, about 35 per cent has been used to buy outside securities.

Sears' trusteed stock is voted by a committee of three, none of whom is an officer or director of the Company. The record of member withdrawals of 1960, with member contributions and amounts withdrawn, were:[10]

Yrs. of Service	Avg. Value of Acct.	Avg. Employee Deposit	Avg. Profit
10–15	$ 11,283	$2,004	$ 9,279
15–20	22,950	2,609	20,341
20–25	51,825	3,939	47,886
25–30	84,643	4,804	79,838
30–35	133,710	6,038	127,672

[10] Information from a letter by W. G. Casterline, Assistant Treasurer Employees' Fund, dated May 16, 1961.

Conclusions

The cost of living and market theory as phenomena on which to base wage principles appear to be plausible in actual practice. Productivity, as exemplified in the several incentive-wage plans to be discussed in the next chapter, is also satisfactory in use. The employer's ability to pay is valid as a wage principle only in the long run. When the employer suffers a temporary loss, this principle will surely run into trouble with the workers; nor is it feasible for a short period during which the concern has an unusually high profit. To determine the worker's contribution to production is practically impossible under modern conditions, and the wage theory is also unworkable as a principle for fixing wages.

Wage policies as listed in the text, with the possible exception of the wage differential for the night shift, are a natural consequence of our growing social consciousness.

Production costs and customer demand are two important factors influencing wage levels. Large sections of organized labor and management either do not understand the relation of wages to total production costs or they are trying to fool the public in their own interest. Management often claims that any wage increase raises production costs, which is not true. On the other hand, labor claims that wage increases reduce unit production costs because of increased sales brought about by increased buying power, which can be equally fallacious. The problem of the relation of production costs and wages cannot be dealt with rationally without considering productivity, changing methods, improved tools and machines, and the changing cost of materials.

Wages cannot be guaranteed on a time basis without leveling sales, which is a difficult problem. Job and wage stabilization will eventually become a social problem which must be handled on a national basis.

Fringe benefits improve employee security in various fields. Some of these benefits, however, appear to be heading for a more rational approach in the not too distant future, while the "unclassified fringe benefits" may soon receive rough treatment due to an aroused public opinion.

Past events suggest that the worker's ownership of his corporate employer's common stock must be "hedged" by some sort of guarantee as to its resale value, if not for returns on the investment; otherwise, this idea may be expected to backfire and cause a decline in employee morale. The same is true, though to a lesser extent, of profit sharing and some of the bonus plans. Finally, we may note that pensions and annuities are gradually being considered a legitimate charge to production.

QUESTIONS

1. Which question causes the most controversial discussion in labor-management contract negotiations?

2. What experience did the Philadelphia Electric Company have with the cost-of-living principle as a determiner of wage levels?

3. How would you refute the ability-to-pay approach as a wage principle?

4. If contribution-to-production is a really scientific principle for fixing wage rates, why is it not used more frequently?

5. To what extent is the market-theory of wages prevalent in business? Why?

6. Under what circumstances is the purchasing power of the average worker improved by general wage increase?

7. What is the difficulty, in past practice, of wage determinations by fact-finding presidential boards?

8. Under what circumstances can a guaranteed annual wage be successfully administered?

9. What is the underlying essential for establishing job stabilization?

10. What is the relation of the "invisible pay envelope" to unit costs of production?

11. How would you argue about the justification for night-shift wage differentials?

12. What would you predict for the future of featherbedding in this country? Detail the reasons for your conclusions.

13. With what type of concerns has profit sharing been successful?

14. To what extent will company stock ownership by employees ease the disputes that arise in labor-management contract negotiations?

15. Do you believe that pension plans have any effect on worker productivity? Give the reasons for your opinion.

16. What effect, if any, will compulsory retirement have in the future in view of the continuous increase in longevity in this country?

17. How successful has the Sears trusteed stock plan been in securing the "cream of the crop" from the labor market?

18. What necessary condition must be established before productivity can be a reliable guide for determining the general wage level?

19. What is the difficulty with the classical economist's wage-fund theory for determining general wage levels?

20. Is it true, as the unions generally contend, that wage increases lead to increased purchasing power of workers, and hence to increased prosperity? Why or why not?

CASE PROBLEM

THE STANDARD SOAP CORPORATION

The Standard Soap Corporation has been notified by the union, which has the bargaining power for all of its production employees, that it will demand a guaranteed annual wage in its next contract. The present labor-management agreement expires in one month. The union did not include details in its demand, but did state that nothing less than a fifty-week guarantee on a forty-hour basis would be satisfactory.

Standard has been in business for ten years. During that period, it has expanded rapidly from 25 to about 300 employees. Its annual sales volume has increased from approximately $200.000 to nearly $3,000,000. The physical expansion required for this growth in the business was financed partly by mortgage and a preferred stock issue. About one-third of the new financing came from plowed-back profits to which there was no stockholder objection chiefly because the stock is closely held. All of the large stockholders are officers of the company, drawing rather small salaries because of their desire to build their equities in the business.

The small group of owner-operators are all practical soap-makers with little training in business methods. They have forged ahead by working long hours and watching production costs and customer credit risks. They learned from current business publications that there is a growing demand by organized labor for a guaranteed wage, but have given no special attention to the subject, probably because they felt that the lightning would not strike such a small business.

The concern's wages compare favorably with industry and community standards. It has also developed recreational and other employee programs, and operates a plant cafeteria where meals are sold below cost.

Profits have been fairly good ever since the business started, and have been higher than average for the past three years. The financial statement is excellent for the size of the company, but has never appeared in print except as a general summary in Dun & Bradstreet reports.

Although annual sales have been good and always on an upward curve, the nature of the business brings the heavy volume at housecleaning seasons, with usually a 50-per cent layoff of workers for two or three weeks during the summer and winter months.

PROBLEM: Standard has a real problem on its hands and is deeply concerned, to say the least. If you were engaged as its representative to deal with the union in settling this new demand, what information would you gather to present your case? What plan of approach would you develop, and what reasons would you include in your argument opposing the union's demand "at this time"? Would you employ any specialist to assist you, and if so, from what field? If you were forced as a result of the negotiations to offer some compromise plan, what would it include?

25

Wage Plans

All wage plans are based on one of two general ideas: (a) the amount of time worked, or (b) the amount of production turned out. The many variations developed from these two basic ideas represent attempts to satisfy divergent desires of the employer and the employee. The employer is always conscious of the cost of labor, whether he has a factory or a merchandising establishment. Labor costs frequently amount to half the total costs of the manufacturer's product, and it is his natural desire to keep wages down. On the other hand, the employee, once he has a sense of security in his job, is chiefly interested in his own and his family's living standard which is directly dependent on the purchasing power of his wage or salary. Naturally, the employee wants to keep wages up. Experimenting with various pay plans is promoted by the quest for a solution which will be mutually acceptable to these two opposite points of view.

We repeat that all systems of wage payments are variations or combinations of the two basic plans already mentioned. The problem of this chapter is to evaluate the strengths and weaknesses of the various plans, and to determine how a given wage plan can best serve a set of conditions by resolving the conflict between management's desire to keep down unit labor costs and the worker's desire to maximize his wages, irrespective of the cost to his employer.

The Day-Rate Plan

Wage payments based on time worked are customarily referred to as day work, although the actual wages may be figured by the hour, day, or week. Under modern conditions, wage payments are usually computed on an hourly basis. The employer furnishes the workplace, the required materials, and usually the tools needed for the job. The worker sells his time to his employer. In its elementary form, the day rate is simple for payroll accounting and equally easy for the worker to figure. This plan goes back to ancient times, and is still the more popular of the two systems.

In the early days of mass production, day work was the rule. It had the virtue of being easy to administer. Theoretically, workers paid by the hour will not feel pressed to sacrifice the quality of their product. Actually, it is still difficult to determine whether the day-rate plan assures higher quality than other forms of wage payments. Even if satisfactory quality can be assumed, however, it is still difficult for the employer to figure his unit labor costs in advance. When labor costs are an important element of total costs, this disadvantage may make pricing unrealistic. Furthermore, since the employer has no dependable way of knowing what his unit labor costs will be, he is often suspicious that they are unnecessarily high.

The problem is based primarily on the fact that people work at different rates of speed. When a straight hourly rate is paid for a particular type of work, the slowest worker receives the same pay as the fastest; but the employer is not getting as much for his money from the slow worker. If the differences in productivity were entirely attributable to the varying capacities of the workers, the employer might average his unit labor costs and so arrive at a reasonable hourly rate of pay. Experience proves, however, that all workers are not producing to the best of their ability. The reasons for slowdowns are many. There is no immediate financial gain for the worker who increases his effort under the straight hourly system of wage payment. Even though the extra effort may result eventually in promotion or a better chance of being retained when the working force is reduced, such rewards are in the future, and the worker's motivation is not immediate.

It is generally estimated that straight-time pay rates produce about 65 per cent of a reasonable standard production. Even at that rate, the employer also knows that day rates cost him more for supervision. When the Fair Labor Standards Act fixed the minimum hourly rate at a dollar, productivity assumed a new importance. This is even more crucial since the minimum has been increased to $1.15. The straight-time rate has another effect on the fast worker when modern industry sets up machine-paced jobs, where all concerned are on a dead level with respect to productivity. The general conclusion must be that there is no incentive for hourly rated employees to increase their output, except possibly for nonfinancial rewards.

Advantages of the Day Rate

1. The worker knows what his earning will be.
2. Emphasis is on quality of the work.
3. Payroll accounting is simple.
4. A satisfactory plan for machine-paced jobs is possible.
5. It permits workers to be shifted to various jobs.

Disadvantages of the Day Rate

1. Workers have no financial incentive to produce.
2. Unit labor costs are usually high.

3. Fast workers are often dissatisfied.
4. Costs of supervision are relatively high.
5. Earnings are usually lower than under other systems.

Variations of Day Work

Differential day rates

This is one of the plans that aim to overcome the dead level of worker wages by adding an incentive to the straight-time feature. It establishes a standard production rate and pays the slower worker on that basis. For those who can beat the standard rate of production, there is a higher hourly pay rate. The differential usually amounts to about 20 per cent, but it applies to only those time-periods when the fast worker is beating the standard rate of production. It is possible, therefore, for any worker to shift periodically from the higher rate to the lower, and vice versa. The purpose of this plan is to overcome management's objection to the low productivity characteristic of the original single-rate system of day work. Worker acceptance of the plan depends on the amount of the differential between the two rates, and the difficulty involved in meeting the upper rate.

Measured day work

Measured day work, which adds premium pay for desirable worker attributes to a scientifically determined base rate, attained prominence during the depression of the thirties. It is an anomaly, as its name implies. Its purpose is to inject incentives into day work without using the word "incentive." Like full-fledged incentive plans, it aims to overcome the workers' practice of gearing their output to the capacity or desire of the below-average worker. It offers an opportunity to the "fireball" to produce at his natural rate without being blackballed by his fellow workers. To the extent that it accomplishes these purposes, it is a good transition plan between the standard day rate and one of the numerous incentive plans.

Measured day work fixes the take-home pay within the rate range, of which the base rate is the minimum. The amount of pay above the base rate is influenced by such factors as productivity, quality, dependability, and versatility. Because the two main features of this plan are scientific determination of base rates and measurement of selected worker characteristics, the plan is actually a combination of job evaluation and merit rating, both of which will be discussed later.

Obviously, measurement of worker characteristics requires more paper work than the straight day-work plan, but it is simpler than most incentive plans. Also, the inducement factors are capable of fairly accurate measurement. *Productivity* is known from the worker's daily production record; *quality* is measured by the number of his rejects; *dependability* is determined by his attendance record; and *versatility* depends on the number of different jobs he is capable of performing.

The worker is rated periodically on the factors mentioned to determine his inducement pay, which is in addition to his base rate. New workers are usually rated monthly; others every three months. In no case does the worker receive less than his base rate, so measured day work offers the possibility only of increased take-home pay, never a decrease. The base rate may be raised or lowered by agreement between labor and management.

Because the base rate may be changed without affecting the inducements of the measured day rate, and because better performance can be obtained from the worker without the incentive "stigma," this plan is popular with management, especially where the union will not agree to any form of incentive pay. It is well liked by many workers, too, because it provides rewards for superior performance.

The disadvantages of the plan are the time lapse between performance and the time of fixing the rate of reward, and the possibility of disagreement over the weighting of the factors. Weighting necessarily involves some personal opinion. To the extent that supervisors determine the rewards, there is a tendency to take the easy way and rate the workers high to avoid their criticism.

Plans Based on Production

Wage plans based on production can be divided into two types depending on the basis for determining the wage: (1) the piece rate, based on *volume of production*, and (2) the premium rate, based on *time saved* in production. These are necessarily rated on established standards, determined either by experience or stop-watch timing. This section will deal with those plans which emphasize volume of production as the determining criterion, including:

1. Straight Piece Work
2. Taylor's Differential Piece-Rate
3. Gantt Task-and-Bonus
4. Merrick Multiple Piece-Rate
5. Emerson Efficiency-Bonus

Straight Piece Work. As the title implies, under this system the worker is paid according to the volume of his production. Before the Industrial Revolution, piece work was not primarily thought of as an incentive for greater productivity; its use was more likely a matter of convenience for the employer, who came to believe that he was paying out large amounts of pay for relatively unproductive labor. This was especially true when work was farmed out to be done at home where there was no check on the time required for a given volume of production. Piece rates were the logical answer to this problem.[1] With the rise of factories and the great increase in the number of people who depended on wages for their chief means of subsistence, the question of day work versus piece work took on a new significance. This wage question led, in the latter half of the nineteenth century, to a widespread movement among industrialists to substitute piece work for day work as a method of rewarding the worker directly for his output rather than for the amount of time he spent on the job.

The historical reasons for the deliberate slowdown of production were more than economic. The breakdown of the crafts into simple, repetitive operations, with each one performed by a different person, robbed the worker of that pride in craftsmanship that makes a man's work psychologically rewarding, whatever his pay. Various incentives followed this dilution of the craft skills. Among others were annual bonuses, rewards for time-saving ideas, employee stock-ownership plans and profit sharing, but none of them was geared directly to output in such a way that as the worker's productivity increased, his earning also increased.

In its pure form, straight piece-work was as easy to administer as day work. Every unit of product was paid for by the piece. A worker's wage was simply the number of pieces he turned out multiplied by the rate per piece. Management now had a way of figuring labor costs with precision. Any worker who put forth extra effort could take home a wage higher than he received under the day rate. It seemed that piece work was a solution to the perennial wage conflict between labor and management. But no sooner had the plan come into general use than problems began to arise. For a time it was the workers who suffered under the new system, but it was not long before employers, too, discovered that piece work was no panacea.

When plants began to change over from day work to piece work, it was found again and again that individual productivity would suddenly rise — that the day workers, as management had suspected all along, really *had* been restricting their output. The piece workers, spurred on by the promise of the new high wages, devised more efficient methods for turning out their pieces. Furthermore, this was a period of rapid acceleration in the tempo of technological innovation. New machines were forever shortening the time in which a piece could be produced.

This spurt in productivity, if piece rates remained constant, resulted in all the gains going to the worker. If the rise in output were entirely attributable to the increased effort of the workers, then it was just and reasonable that they should receive at least a large portion of the gain. On the other hand, the new high levels of production often represented not simply in-

---

[1] Even today, piece rates are almost universally paid in those European centers specializing in the making of such quality items as beaded bags. The patterns are beaded at the homes of workers, whose piece rates depend on the complexity of the designs. The same wage pattern exists in many other handwork processes.

creased worker effort, but also large investments by the employer in new labor-saving machinery. In such cases, it was unreasonable to expect the employer to go on paying the same piece rates and put himself in danger at times of suffering a real loss. But whether justified or not, the general reaction of management was to cut the piece rates as soon as individual productivity began to rise. Naturally labor protested. It soon became common practice for the workers to defeat the purpose of the incentive system by deliberately restricting output for fear of new rate cuts when the level of productivity rose appreciably. Furthermore, the argument that day workers often advanced for restricting output — that if they worked too fast there would soon be no work left for them to do — was every bit as pertinent for piece workers, and often more so.

A second source of hardship for the worker on piece rates was that his income stopped altogether whenever there was an interruption in the flow of work. When machines broke down or the supply of materials ran out, there was a temporary layoff for the worker.

Because of these very real disadvantages, piece work came to be feared and hated by a large proportion of the workers, and this distrust has persisted among important sections of the labor force down to the present day.

Many of the employers were undoubtedly taking advantage of their workers. But many others were seriously disturbed. They had sincerely tried to find a just formula for gearing wages to output, and they saw that the formula was not always working out in practice. Aside from the hostility of labor, the piece-work system was revealing serious flaws. In some establishments, as we have said, workers were tending to restrict their output to a point just below the level where they feared there would be a further cut in the piece rates. In other places, as rates were cut, workers tried ever harder to keep their earnings at the level of the previous, higher rates. But there was a limit to what they could produce, and in the effort to exceed that limit, the quality of the output often deteriorated, sometimes to such a degree that the employer was losing more money on production waste than he had lost through low productivity under the day wage.

It became clear, then, that if the idea of incentive wages was to work out in practice, several conditions had to be satisfied. (1) Some method had to be found for stabilizing piece rates. Because technological progress could be taken for granted, employers could not be expected to promise their workers that rates would remain fixed for all time. On the other hand, the vicious circle which found the industrious worker putting out ever more effort only to be met with a new cut in the rates was grossly unfair to labor and could not be permitted to continue. (2) If labor were ever going to give its wholehearted support to the incentive system, some form of remuneration during periods of downtime beyond the worker's control had to be guaranteed. (3) Because of the low repute in which workers had come to hold the very idea of incentive wages, management had the major problem on its hands of convincing the workers that piece work was not a method of "sweating" the workers simply to fill the company coffers, but was a genuine plan for rewarding extra effort with extra pay, to the mutual advantage of management and labor.

These outstanding difficulties with piece rates were gradually met. In the first place, the early plan of fixing the time standard for making a piece was based on experience, if records were available. When there were no records, guessing was the substitute. The standard was eventually determined by time study, so that part of the trouble bowed to at least a semblance of scientific determination.

The next problem — that of changes in the pieces rates — was settled by mutual agreement between management and labor. The new plan provided that there would be no change in the rates unless there was some substantial change in the methods, the machines, or the materials used in producing the item. This idea provided a rational basis for discussion between the workers and management.

Finally, the downtime problem was settled by providing for straight hourly pay rates during time lost through no fault of the worker. In spite of these corrections, the piece-rate system still lags behind the day-work plan in popularity.

Taylor Differential Piece-Rate Plan. This plan is based on standard times determined by time study. It provides for two piece rates for each job classification. The lower rate is paid when the worker's time falls below the standard. The higher rate is paid when the standard is met or bettered. For example, if the standard time is 30 pieces per hour and the differential rates are 20¢ and 30¢, the worker completing 30 pieces would be paid 30 × 30¢ or $9.00, while the worker completing only 25 pieces would earn 25 × 20¢ or $5.00

Taylor conceived this plan on the assumption that low wages do not necessarily mean low-cost production. In conformity with his basic concept of the contributions which management and labor should make to the productive processes, he contended that it was up to management to plan the elements of production so that the mediocre worker *could* attain standard production and thus reduce unit labor and overhead costs. Taylor felt that the high incentive given to fast workers would encourage most of the workers so that they *would* lower unit costs.

Taylor's plan has not gained wide adoption because of its several outstanding disadvantages under present social concepts of business:

1. Unless management performs its production planning, and job control in a highly skillful manner, the worker's chances for meeting the standard are poor.
2. Pay for the poor or inexperienced worker is so low as to discourage him from seeking employment where the plan is in operation.

3. There is no guaranteed base rate.
4. The average worker so extends himself in trying to meet the standard that unions charge "speed-up" with some justification.

The advantages of Taylor's piece-rate plan are pleasing to the fast worker and to management because the former receives higher pay and the latter, lower labor costs. There are other advantages such as attracting the "cream of the crop" of applicants and removal of the tendency to limit productivity. Taylor also claimed that his piece-rate plan made unions unnecessary, but that was merely his opinion. In conclusion, we must note that Taylor's plan has very few takers at the present time.

Gantt Task-and-Bonus Plan. This plan guarantees the day rate for working time, plus another guaranteed rate for downtime caused by machine breakdown, lack of materials, or any other factor beyond the control of the operator. The worker receives his base rate for standard time or any time less than standard with a sliding-scale percentage premium of the base rate determined by the nature of the work. The object in fixing the premium percentages is to arrive at figures which will encourage maximum productivity. The standard time is fixed either by time study or from production records.

Gantt also made a contribution with respect to the supervisor's pay. He suggested that supervisors receive premium pay based on the number of his men who earned wage premiums. His purpose was to stimulate supervisors not only to train their men in the best methods, but to make every effort to see that they were supplied with good machines, tools, workplaces, and the proper materials on time.

Merrick Multiple Piece-Rate Plan. This plan is similar to Taylor's except that it provides for two premium rates:

Up to 83% of standard . . . . Low piece rate × number of pieces
From 83% to standard . . . . Regular piece rate × number of pieces
Standard and above . . . . High piece rate × number of pieces

The virtue of this system as compared to Taylor's is in the added encouragement it gives to the mediocre worker.

Emerson Efficiency-Bonus Plan. This plan guarantees the day rate and provides for premiums on a graduated scale proportionate to productivity. Standard times are fixed by time study under existing working conditions. To encourage new workers, a premium is paid when 67 per cent of the standard time has been accomplished. From this starting point, where the premium is only one-fourth of 1 per cent, it increases gradually up to 20 per cent. If the worker beats the standard time, he receives an additional

wage equal to the time saved at the base rate. Premiums are figured for
pay periods rather than for each operation on the basis of the worker's
efficiency rating. This rating, which is calculated by dividing the total of
the standard times by the total of his actual times, reflects the worker's
actual efficiency percentage and reduces the amount of payroll work. The
disadvantage of this plan is its complicated calculations which are confusing to the worker.

Plans Based on Time Saved

This is the other of the two production-based wage plans. The purpose
of this category is to induce the worker to reduce the time allowed for
completing the job, and it is on this time-saving feature that his bonus or
premium is figured. The three outstanding plans using this method are:
Halsey Premium Plan, Rowan Premium Plan, and the Bedaux Plan. All
three plans guarantee the worker his base rate if he is not able to attain
premium status.

Halsey Premium Plan. This system of F. A. Halsey was the first
standard-time plan to be introduced into American industry. Its purpose
was to overcome the objections to piece work and profit sharing by providing the worker a bonus on the saving from time allotted for the job.
This and the other two plans considered in this section guarantee the
worker's base rate irrespective of the time required to do the job. The
standard-task is determined from past production records, which have
naturally been made on a straight-time basis and so tend to favor the worker
on this new incentive plan. This method of setting standards eliminates the
necessity for time study, which often makes the plan more acceptable to
the workers. From this standpoint, the Halsey plan offers a good transition
from hourly wages to incentives based on time study or standard data.

All the time saved is shared by the worker on some agreed division,
usually one-half. For this reason, the plan is sometimes referred to as the
50-50 plan. The other 50 per cent is shared in some predetermined ratio
with supervision, indirect workers, and the company. While workers appreciate the opportunity to earn a premium without the possibility of loss, they
naturally prefer an incentive plan which pays 100 per cent of the time saved.

The Halsey plan has several advantages. It is simple; fast workers
receive premium pay while others get the base rate; the base pay is subject
to negotiation; and the payroll work is not complicated. Its two disadvantages are that the premium is less than the time saved, and there is a
tendency to continue the same production standard.

Rowan Premium Plan. The Rowan plan also guarantees pay at the base
rate for all hours worked, and like the Halsey plan, its standard times are
set on the basis of past production records. It differs slightly in calculating

the premium in that it adds to the worker's actual time a percentage of that time. The percentage is the ratio of the time saved to the standard time. If the worker saves one-third of the standard time, his pay is figured as one and one-third of his actual time for the operation. His pay under this plan would be less than a 100-per cent premium. Compared to the Halsey plan, it pays larger premiums for small savings, but it pays smaller proportionate premiums as the time savings increase. The purpose of this refinement of the Halsey plan is to make workers conscious of their premium earnings as soon as they start to improve on the standard time.

Bedaux Plan. The underlying feature of this time-standard plan is the Bedaux unit of time, or "B." The "B" includes calculated time for operating and resting, the proportion of the two depending on the circumstances of the work. Accomplishment is measured by the number of "B" units per hour. Sixty B's make the standard hour. The original plan gave the operator 75 per cent of the premium, retaining 25 per cent for supervisory and indirect labor. Many variations of this split premium have developed; in some cases, the entire premium goes to the worker. The wage on a 100-per cent premium basis is obtained by multiplying one-sixtieth of the base rate by the number of B's obtained.

Standards are fixed after a careful analysis of all the factors in a given operation. The operator is given a credit of one B for each minute of down-time caused by circumstances beyond his control. Since the B is a standard unit of work measurement, production records can be used for comparative purposes among all types of workers in all departments. This feature is important as a primary tool in production control. Obviously, this plan involves considerable clerical work as well as professional expense in fixing the B standards. The question of its worth as a wage determinant and control feature for individual and group production must be determined on a factual basis for each industry.

Table 25.1 on page 498 shows the percentage of plant workers paid in accordance with various kinds of time plans and incentive plans. The workers represent seventeen major labor-market areas grouped under the four broad geographic divisions of the country.

Other Incentive Plans

Multiple-factor measurement

The incentive plans just described vary from one another in the way in which they measure standard times and reward extra productivity. Today there are as many as two hundred different plans available. Most of them are the result of combining features of two or more existing plans. For example, by adding time study to a plan which historically was based on standards derived from past production records, a "new" plan is born.

Table 25.1

Percentage of Plant Workers Paid by Various Wage Plans in Manufacturing Industries in 17 Major Labor-Market Areas, 1953–1954

| | TYPE OF WAGE PLAN | | | | | | |
| | TIME PLANS | | | | INCENTIVE PLANS | | |
AREA	Single Rate	Rate Range	No Formal Plan	Total Time Plans	Piece Work	Bonus	Total Incentive Plans
NORTHEAST							
Boston	24	37	4	65	18	17	35
Newark—							
Jersey City	35	29	3	67	15	18	33
New York City	29	22	19	70	22	8	30
Philadelphia	35	21	6	62	22	16	38
SOUTH							
Atlanta	34	36	7	77	19	4	23
Dallas	18	57	15	90	7	2	9
Memphis	36	29	12	77	20	3	23
New Orleans	58	13	9	80	16	3	19
MIDDLE WEST							
Chicago	24	37	7	68	15	17	32
Detroit	78	10	3	91	4	5	9
Milwaukee	27	29	3	59	19	22	41
Minneapolis—							
St. Paul	37	42	4	83	9	8	17
St. Louis	40	33	1	74	14	12	26
FAR WEST							
Denver	42	26	4	72	20	8	28
Los Angeles	32	52	2	86	8	6	14
Portland	82	5	2	89	7	3	10
San Francisco—							
Oakland	87	3	—	90	6	3	9

Source: U.S. Bureau of Labor Statistics, Bulletin No. 1173 (1955), Tables 8 and 10, pp. 31 and 33. Some of the rows do not add to 100 per cent because of rounding off in the original tables.

Multiple-factor measurement tries to go beyond these plans and add another dimension to the determination of incentive wages. The techniques of "MFM" can be combined with those of many of the traditional standard-time plans. One of DuPont's management engineers explains that "MFM takes into account *all* the important factors influenced or controlled by the operator, including tool life, scrap and product quality, as well as quantity produced." As a substitute for incentives which "emphasize the physical effort and the number of parts dropping off the end of the line," MFM shifts the incentive emphasis to reduction of losses. It is contended that this plan rewards the operator's mental as well as his physical effort.

This idea requires that incentive jobs be surveyed to locate those elements which are under the worker's control. They must then be measured and weighted to establish a total performance standard for work measurement. Five elements are considered:

1. Degree of control exercised over the factor
2. Accuracy with which the factor can be measured
3. Extent to which management can aid in performance
4. Degree to which records offer information on the standard
5. The factor's contribution to effectiveness of the operation

Examples of the factors that might be used in a processing operation, with their respective weighted average, are: physical effort, 30 per cent; steam consumption, 10 per cent; production yield, 20 per cent; quality, 25 per cent; and scrap reduction, 15 per cent. It has been claimed that although the expense is greater in applying such bases for an incentive system, the savings are two to three times as much as under any plan which emphasizes only quantity of production.

Group incentives

Some businesses and industries are adaptable to group incentives because of the nature of their work. For example, foundry floor molders usually work in groups when there is a long run of large pieces such as engine bases. These groups are served by indirect labor helpers. On an incentive basis, the two types of workers fit together very conveniently into a single group, because the effort of the helpers has a decided effect on the production of the journeymen. Electric motor and steel production are other examples of natural group effort.

Group incentive plans have varied degrees of success, depending largely on the natural cohesiveness of the work group. When the groups are more or less artificial, these plans are likely to fail. Even natural groups may occasionally find themselves in situations which reduce their effectiveness. For example, if the journeyman floor molders belong to one union while their unskilled helpers are affiliated with another, there might well be friction.

Premium pay is based on production above a set standard for the group. It is split among members on the basis of their respective total wage, their base wage rate, or the number of hours worked.

The purpose of this plan is to increase production through teamwork, but it is only natural that there should be some slow individual members of the team, especially if the group is large. Ordinarily, the group interest either spurs such individuals to carry their share of the load or makes them feel that transfer to another job would be advisable.

The advantages to be expected from group incentives are increasing productivity and worker pay, with decreased supervision and accounting costs. The disadvantages are lack of individual incentive and the impossibility of measuring individual efficiency. To some extent, disadvantages of the plan are due to unnatural groupings. Any good team must be relatively free of personality clashes, and this is especially true of group production effort.

Incentives for indirect workers

It is often believed that standard times cannot be applied to such indirect work as maintenance, material handling, inspection, and clerical work, or to groups of oilers, setup men, cleaners, and helpers. As we learn more about analyzing repetitive operations in these fields, they will yield slowly to standard-time measurement. When that time comes, the costs of indirect labor will no doubt be reduced through supervision based on established time factors. Until then, many of these workers will continue to be thought of as among the "blind spots" of business.

When the calculation of standard times is not feasible, other less scientific methods can be used for establishing premium wages for indirect workers. One is *to include these workers in a suitable group of direct workers,* where their incentive pay may be related to premiums paid to direct labor and figured on total base earnings, hours worked, or base rate of pay. Another plan relates the premiums to *quality of the product,* to which indirect workers are acknowledged contributors. Some companies relate indirect worker premiums to the accident rate or plant cleanliness when these are relevant, or the record for meeting delivery schedules.[2] It becomes increasingly evident as studies and experiments are made that piece-work or standard-time plans can be applied to a considerable portion of indirect labor. In many cases where this is not feasible, proper analysis can establish a workable ratio of indirect- to direct-labor standard hours as a basis for determining premium pay for indirect labor. In these cases, the number of indirect-labor standard hours produced divided by the number of indirect labor's actual hours will fix the efficiency percentage of the group. Earnings of each member would be determined by multiplying his actual hours by his base rate and then by the efficiency percentage of the group.

[2] The American Rolling Mills Company of Middletown, Ohio, and the E. I. Dupont Company of Wilmington, Delaware, have worked out excellent standards for application of incentive wages to indirect workers.

Supervisors should receive attention in any consideration of incentive-wage payments. The two general approaches to this problem are through the measurement of either productivity or savings. Both relate to the supervisor as a member of management. Because his position is so important in the general field of management, Chapter 36 has been devoted to the subject, and discussion here will be limited. Suffice it to say that all standards applied to supervisor incentives should represent factors over which he can exercise control, such as downtime, scrap, overtime, supplies, maintenance, and repairs. Before any savings can be put on an incentive basis, it is necessary to establish a carefully itemized budget for the supervisor's department. It is in terms of these budget items that incentive goals for the supervisor must be formulated.

Incentives for white-collar workers

While not so well developed nor so generally used as in the production processes, incentives for *office workers and clerks* may be developed successfully for either individual or group accomplishments, depending on the type of work involved and the size of the office organization. Although it is a generally accepted norm that personal incentives produce more effective results, the productivity of many office workers is often affected advantageously by the other members of the group, thus suggesting group incentives in such cases. On the other hand, many concerns have successfully geared some office incentives to the individual, especially to operators of complicated office machines.

For the worker in the small office, most incentive standards are based on the personal judgment of someone in the general management group, especially when the workers are not organized. However, the effectiveness of even the small office force can be measured against general standards established by methods and time study corrected to account for local conditions, or specific standards can be set up for individual offices by the same techniques when the expense appears justifiable. Infrequently, even in large offices, specific jobs may be paid a piece-work rate. However, the operator time allowances which must be accounted for are only one of the details which make it difficult to set up mutually agreeable piece-rate plans for any kind of office work.

The first step in recognition of superior performance under a general incentive plan is customarily an advance within the rate range for the classification affected.

While many *salesmen* are paid fixed salaries, incentives based on volume of sales or commissions are common practice. There are many refinements of detail in the various incentive plans for salesmen. For example, they may include a minimum salary, calculated to cover living expenses, with commissions starting after a fixed volume of sales. Again, the "guaranteed" salary may be charged against a commission account figured on total sales. The purpose of the guarantee is to relieve the salesman's anxiety about a minimum living standard, but it does not assure his continuance on the job.

Commissions may be figured directly on sales volume or on a graduated scale, either up or down, in proportion to volume. It appears reasonable that progressive units of sales beyond some standard would require increased effort and be entitled to an increasing percentage reward. However, any commission plan may occasionally yield the salesman a higher total income than the salaries paid to the concern's corporate officers, with corresponding psychological repercussions. For this reason, the salesman's total pay is sometimes limited, to circumvent jealousies in the upper pay brackets of management. Occasionally, therefore, the commission percentage is figured on a regressive scale to accomplish the same purpose — a plan which is clearly contrary to the basic idea of incentive payments.

The salesman's expense account may offer a legitimate opportunity for indirect compensation when it is based on a fixed daily allowance. This expense plan is often substituted for the older idea of an out-of-pocket expense account because of the questionable elasticity of the latter.

How to pay salesmen for the most productive results has been the subject of perennial debate at meetings of the National Sales Executive Clubs, which have never agreed on any acceptable general plan nor indeed on patterns most suited to particular types of business.

Causes of Incentive Failures

There are numerous reasons for failure of incentive plans. The following are suggestive:

1. The *personal characteristics* of the concern's management and labor leaders may suggest defeat from the beginning.

2. Failure to secure complete *understanding and cooperation* of all layers of management and union officials before the plan is installed leads to suspicion based on ignorance.

3. *Poor standards* spell disaster, irrespective of which way they lean. If they are loose, premium wages will be high, and productivity may be close to the day-work pace. If the standards are tight, worker dissatisfaction will lead to accusations that management is speeding up the worker, and the plan will be well on its way to failure even if provision is made for challenging the rates.

4. *Ceilings on earnings* will surely lead to pegged production. If financial rewards are the aim of incentive payments, there should be no limit within the rules.

5. *Failure to improve methods* of the worker or his tools, machines, workplace, or materials before determining standard times is a fatal mistake.

6. *The premium scale must be adequate from the start.* If the scale results in low premiums for improved application by fast workers, the plan will not be acceptable.

7. *Poor scheduling of jobs,* including machine setup time, delivery of materials, and an excessive number of short runs, affect the worker's opportunity to earn premium pay. No matter how good the plan is on paper, it must produce results in action.

8. *Maintenance* is another factor in the worker's ability to earn high wages under any incentive plan. Poor tools and equipment are evidences of poor maintenance. Either will kill any incentive plan.

9. If the incentive plan is *too complicated for worker understanding,* it cannot be effective. To simplify it after complaints often makes matters worse.

10. *The plan must be tailored to the circumstances.* In general, it should include only those factors over which the workers have control. Otherwise, they will tend to work the plan to their own interests after they discover its loopholes.

These reasons for failure suggest basic principles which must be made explicit to all incentive workers:[3]

1. Base hourly rate will be paid regardless of production.
2. Standard times will not be altered except for important changes in methods, machines, or materials.
3. Premium pay will be proportionate to production above the standard.
4. There will be no limit on incentive earnings.
5. Any standard will be subject to the grievance procedure.

Executive Salaries

Executives, like the prophets, may be divided into the major and the minor. There is a distinct difference in salary ranges for the two groups, and the techniques for evaluating members of the two groups also differ.

Minor executives may be in charge of production departments, sections of sales, purchasing, or some other activity where supervisory results can be measured with a fair amount of precision. They are paid on a salary basis, with or without bonuses or other forms of incentive pay. There is still much trial and error in working out bonus plans for this group. If the bonus is related to sales or profits, its computation is simple, even if the plan proves defective in being either too liberal or too parsimonious. When bonuses are based on meeting budget estimates, then savings in materials, indirect labor, and maintenance present many detailed problems. Standards must be set for each control factor, and then all of them must be weighted to establish their relative importance. This type of bonus payment is not uncommon on the supervisory level; it is less common but still prevalent among minor executives on the departmental level.

The major executive level presents an entirely different problem, because

---

[3] For an excellent source of further details on the subject of wage and salary incentives, consult *Wage Administration,* by Charles W. Brennan (Richard D. Irwin, Inc., Homewood, Ill., 1959), Part IV.

generally accepted standards are lacking. Some thoughtful opinion sets a top limit on the reasonable earnings of executives. Many executives have a similar perspective on what should be considered reasonable top earnings for those who work with their hands. Some others contend that any executive is "worth what he can get," which is a rather blunt way of expressing the idea even if the reasoning is sound. It is also contended that executives should be paid according to the number of employees over whom they have general supervision. This criterion would make some top military leaders almost priceless. Volume of sales is another criterion, and profits have considerable prestige as a standard, provided that operating losses do not exercise a reverse effect on the salary level. Stockholders often complain when top executives are paid large salaries while they are actually losing money for the company through mismanagement.

One irate stockholder asked the company president, during the profit heyday prior to the depression, how he justified his salary. The ready answer was: "It is based on our company's profits under my leadership." In 1932 when company losses were in high figures, the same question to the same company president brought an equally quick response: "It is based on my ability to keep company losses to the minimum." So it is that the stockholder's point of view and that of the company's chief executive may be poles apart.

Increase in income taxes and the declining value of the dollar left many executives in a worse position in 1955 than in 1945. In many companies, the salary of the top executive is much more than double his take-home pay, which sometimes makes one wonder why they are satisfied to become book-keepers for Uncle Sam. When large bonuses are paid in cash, the total income may place the executive's income in a higher tax bracket, where the graduated income-tax rate has the effect of washing out any absolute gain in income. In such cases, the bonus is not much of an incentive. Salaries above the $150,000 level are usually justified on the grounds that they stimulate the executive's desire to serve his company to the best of his ability. One often wonders why such service should not be expected, irrespective of the salary, from men of this caliber.

How can we appraise the worth of a member of management? Slowly the evaluation techniques of the smaller fry are being applied to the members of management, but with considerable difference in the factors used. One large concern uses a "point system" involving ten factors: policy, planning, methods, administration, personnel relations, executive contracts, outside contracts, original thinking, and profits. A stockholder might be forgiven for asking why "profits" does not rank higher on the evaluation list.

In the last analysis, competition would seem to dictate the executive's salary. If the seeking concern wishes to attract him from the "Jones Company," the questions are: How much is he getting, and how much will it take to induce him to leave his present employer?

To overcome the tax difficulty, many companies supplement their executives' base salary with some form of deferred compensation, profit sharing, stock options, and fringe benefits. The purpose of all these plans is to lighten the tax load. The first three plans must be satisfactory to the Internal Revenue Department. Deferred compensation often takes the form of future pensions or promise of a "consulting" position after compulsory retirement. Profit sharing is always a debatable question with the stockholders who feel that the concern's profits belong to them. Another consideration is what happens when there are no profits. However, it is only realistic to assume that an executive whose personal interests are closely identified with his company will do his best to make the concern prosper. One approach might be by reducing expenses.

Stock option plans are particularly popular at present, due in part to certain provisions of the 1950 Revenue Act. However, this plan for future income, possibly on a capital gains basis, is hedged in with many restrictive details which cannot be discussed here. Fringe benefits offer a wide range of possibilities for the executive to increase his income by having his company take care of many expenses which might otherwise be personal.

Conclusions

The history of the development of the formal wage plans used in business and industry today has been presented in terms of the conflict between day work, with its encouragement of mediocrity, and piece work, with its emphasis on the incentive to produce. The attempt has been made to demonstrate that neither system, in its original simplicity, is entirely satisfactory either for management or for labor. The twentieth century has witnessed a gradual convergence of what once seemed to be irreconcilable approaches to the problem of "a fair day's pay for a fair day's work." The scientific techniques of time and motion study as well as the new cooperation of management and labor in setting rates have virtually eliminated the arbitrary practices which quite justifiably made the nineteenth-century worker rebel against the idea of incentives. In spite of the corrections which have been made to the former malpractices of wage incentive plans, only 27 per cent of the million production workers of 1958 were paid on an incentive basis.[4] Large sections of organized labor may still continue in their opposition to incentive wages, but it cannot be said that management has not tried hard to correct the abuses to which labor originally objected. Finally, that the incentive principle is still flourishing and even extending itself beyond its original habitat of piece-work and standard-time plans can be seen from its recent embodiment in the merit-rating systems for determining promotion under rate-range plans.

[4] Monthly Labor Review, May 1960, Vol. 83, No. 5, p. 460.

QUESTIONS

1. What are the two fundamental bases for establishing wage plans?
2. Why was the day work plan the general rule for wage payments even in the early days of mass production? What is its outstanding disadvantage?
3. How does the productivity of straight time pay rates compare with a reasonable production standard?
4. What are the chief advantages of the day work wage plan?
5. How does "measured day work" offer a good transition from the straight hourly rate to the new incentive plans? On what factors is it based?
6. Why has the measured day work plan become fairly popular with management?
7. Why has straight piece work been relatively acceptable to both management and the workers?
8. What were some of the past reasons for the workers' deliberate slowdown of production?
9. What eventually became the chief dissatisfactions of both workers and management with straight piece work? How were these dissatisfactions overcome?
10. Why should substantial changes in production methods, machines, or materials affect piece rates?
11. Why was Taylor's differential piece-rate plan so universally condemned by organized labor?
12. How and why did Gantt's idea of the "Task-and-Bonus" plan affect worker satisfaction with standard production times?
13. What inference is contained in Emerson's "Gospel of Efficiency"?
14. The Halsey, Rowan, and Bedaux pay plans were all based on production time saved by the worker. How did this special application of time standards affect worker and management acceptance of premium pay rates?
15. How was the Bedaux plan made more scientific than the other standard time plans in effect at that time?
16. How does Multiple-Factor-Measurement (MFM) promote still further the scientific application of standard times to wage payments?
17. What is the chief disadvantage of the group incentive wage plan, and how is that disadvantage usually overcome?
18. How can incentives for indirect workers be established?
19. What are some of the prime causes for incentive failures?
20. What techniques are used for determining the salaries of the major and the minor executives?

CASE PROBLEM

POWDERED METAL PRODUCTS

Powdered Metal Products makes metal parts from powdered materials of various kinds, including most of the metals. The main processes are die-making, high-pressure press operations, sintering (heating to secure hardness), and subsequent cold pressing to meet the usual close tolerances required in the specifications.

It is customary to mix various powders or grains to obtain the characteristics required for the use to which the finished parts are applied. This phase of the manufacturing process demands unusual skill and experience. The basic mixtures are determined by metallurgists, but experienced supervisors also experiment with new mixtures or alloys, occasionally with marked success. The degree of success is determined by the performance of the finished parts in the customers' operations. These mixtures, or formulas, are recorded for possible future use if they are satisfactory. The formulas are company property, and it has not been customary to give specific credit of any kind to the person directly responsible for their composition.

The dies, which consist of a hollow cylinder enclosing top and bottom close-fitting pistons, must not only be extremely accurate, but their dimensions must make allowance for the expansion or contraction of the powder mixture used. This part of the work is made more difficult because of the different expansions or contractions of the powder mixtures used in most of the processes. A first-rate toolmaker must have special training and long experience to make a difficult die. The dies are expensive, and mistakes are costly.

The sintering process also offers many opportunities for failure in the final product. The degree of heat maintained in the furnaces and the heating period are both extremely important. Either factor can spoil the entire furnace load, which has no reclamation value.

Expensive waste can, therefore, happen with any one of the three important processes. The volume of production is fairly well determined by the speed of the presses and the capacity of the furnaces. However, maximum productivity can be obtained only by fast and careful workers who must be closely supervised. The press hoppers must be kept filled with the powdered grains and the pressed parts removed at set periods for transfer to the furnaces; otherwise, they may be broken in the transporting trays because they are relatively soft as they come from the presses before sintering. The interval between unloading and reloading the furnaces is also an important factor in the productivity of that process.

It is not unusual to have to rework new dies. This may be done by inserting a sleeve where the main bore has been made too large or some other of many correcting methods developed by the die-makers. As has been mentioned, die-making is expensive under the best of circumstances, but costs are often increased when corrections are necessary. These faults are not caused so much by poor workmanship as by failure to make proper expansion and contraction allowances for the powder mixtures used in the presses. The superintendents of the die department shoulder this exacting responsibility. Well-made dies can be used for long runs and for repeat orders, but eventually they become so worn that they must be retooled. This operation often demands a higher skill than the making of the original die.

Powdered Metal Products has been in operation for twenty-five years. Although the process of making powdered metal parts is not new, its commercial use is not much older than the company. This situation necessarily made progress slow from the standpoint of profits. It would have been difficult, if not impossible, to set up a supervisory bonus plan until recently because of losses due to several exacting processes already described.

The company installed an incentive plan for most of its production workers two years ago, and it has given general satisfaction. Its supervisory employees, of whom there are twenty-two, have been with the concern for an average of fifteen years, and it is felt that in fairness to them, their services should be geared to some kind of bonus plan. Top management also feels that the company will benefit, judging from the results obtained from its worker incentive plan.

PROBLEM: If you are called on to devise a bonus plan for Powdered Metal Products' supervisors, on what factor or factors would you base it? Would you favor savings of materials, product losses, or productivity? Would you consider a profit-sharing plan or the degree to which the foremen met or bettered their department's budget? Would you pay the bonus in cash or company stock? How would you determine the standards on which your bonus factors are based? On what time period would you figure the bonus? Would you penalize those foremen whose departments failed to meet the standards you set up? How would you reward the supervisor whose improvements of methods or processes have meant sizable savings to the company?

26

Job Evaluation

"Equal pay for equal work" is the declaration that heralded the modern refinements in evaluating jobs, or recognized groups of job activities. Essentially, the purpose of job evaluation is to determine the relative worth of a selected group of jobs in a given business or department. Evaluation is applied to manufacturing, wholesale and retail concerns, offices, banks, government agencies, and many other activities. It covers unskilled and skilled workers, supervisors, and occasionally reaches up to the level of middle management. Recently, its application even to top management is being discussed.

Job evaluation is not new. For centuries it has been the custom of chiefs to fix the pay of their subordinates on the basis of what the chiefs consider each worker or group of workers was contributing to the total endeavor. This approach was, of course, purely subjective, and favoritism was bound to play a substantial role in the results. Even before the Industrial Revolution, the guilds determined pay levels for apprentices and journeymen as distinctive levels of worth. This early system, or lack of system, was undermined by the shift to mass production, with its breakdown of skills. When the factory worker was expected to know only one, or at most a few, of the skills required to complete the final product, it was inevitable that workers with different kinds of ability should begin to question their rates of pay.

Other factors favored the development of a differential wage structure. When industry began to expand in size and in the nature of its work assignments, differences in working conditions became more prominent. Foundry and steel-mill operations, for example, were necessarily performed under poor and even dangerous working conditions. The problem of rewarding workers for various degrees of training and responsibility became ever more complicated until a single pattern for differential wages was no longer possible.

As industry stepped up its demand for higher quality and increased productivity, other differences developed among the workers. Some worked faster than others, and some made a higher quality product. In many cases, the new and improved machines were taking over the skills of the worker, causing innumerable pay problems. When management started to keep production and quality records of employees in the many new job classifications, the workers became conscious not only of the results of their own efforts, but also of the comparative records of their fellow workers.

Employees are naturally interested in the amount of their pay checks and what these checks will buy for their families, and they are understandably discontented when they learn that workers in other classifications requiring the same or inferior skills are receiving higher pay. Discontent and lowered morale is also engendered when a worker has reason to believe that another person in the same job classification is producing fewer items with more rejects, yet receiving the same or higher pay. This source of worker dissatisfaction is susceptible to correction by what are known as "service ratings," which attempt to evaluate the worker's ability and service to his employer. *Service* or *merit rating*, which will be discussed in the next chapter, supplements the rating of jobs, which is the purpose of job evaluation. The difference between these two techniques is perfectly clear, but they are often confused in practice.

Some accomplishments of job evaluation

The primary purpose of job evaluation is to eliminate wage-rate inequities. No fair-minded person contends that job evaluation can be performed on a purely scientific basis, but it is at least systematic, which is a considerable advance over the lack of system which preceded it. The inequities of the former practices resulted in high unit costs and defective production. Experience has definitely demonstrated that both of these undesirable effects have been distinctly improved after the installation of a proper form of job evaluation. The chief causes for wage inequities are:

1. Improper job classifications
2. Different wage rates for the same type of work
3. Favoritism by some representative of management
4. Improper appreciation of job content

Evaluation by any objective method tends to relieve the pressure created by these inequities. Even though job evaluation is not yet scientific, in the proper sense of that word, because it involves opinions, it has been standardized to a great extent. It serves an important phase of modern industrial relations by rationally and systematically estimating the relative value of jobs. It is definitely demanded by the evolution of the human relations approach to management. In addition to its primary purpose of minimizing or eliminating wage inequities, job evaluation accomplishes the following:

1. Lays the foundation for a balanced wage structure
2. Furnishes important information for the personnel department
3. Establishes controls for payroll costs
4. Defines classified functions
5. Establishes authority and responsibility
6. Determines labor costs
7. Provides wage facts for negotiation with unions
8. Decreases grievances
9. Increases productivity by improving morale.

Preparation for Job Evaluation

Because a job evaluation must be acceptable to the workers if it is to produce maximum results, the workers must be informed of its purposes and methods before the evaluation starts. This first step should combine both communication and participation — two very desirable approaches for ensuring cooperation — by means of a letter from the company president to the home of every employee concerned. Figure 26.1 is a copy of such a letter prepared by the author for an actual case. Some authorities prefer to get job facts from the employees through personal interviews, while others feel that this approach is more embarrasing or simply less comfortable to the workers than the questionnaire plan.

This letter in Figure 26.1 produced excellent results by way of employee interest and participation. The effect was due in part to a prior frank discussion with the local union officers about the methods that were to be used in the evaluation. The company president participated in the meeting where the evaluation specialist acted as chairman. The discussions were aided by many frank questions and answers. One thing that should always be made clear by the specialist is his belief that no job evaluation can be purely objective, but that the emphasis is distinctly in that direction, and that facts are always to be the basis for decisions.

Reproduction of the accompanying questionnaire will help clarify this subject. It shows the important matters used in determining job values. In the hands of the employees, it also makes clear the underlying facts on which a systematic evelution is based. It helps to allay the suspicions of those whose jobs will be subjects for discussion by the committee. Because any group of workers can assume the privilege of "evaluating the evaluation," it is important that their representatives participate in the actual deliberations which lead to the final results. The usual practice is for the completed job evaluation to be discussed at a special meeting of the local union. If the workers' elected representatives have taken part in the work, the presumption is that they will feel the job to be reasonably acceptable. This fact lends considerable weight to the acceptance of an evaluation at the union meeting. Figure 26.2 is a reproduction of the Questionnaire.

Figure 26.1

To: All employees

You have no doubt heard about the proposed Job Evaluation to be made for all departments. I feel that it is necessary for every employee to assist our Committee of Union and Management representatives in collecting information which can be used in the work of evaluating all jobs in the plant.

As a result of this Job Evaluation, we hope to determine how any particular job or type of work rates in relation to all other jobs in the plant. Many factors enter into these calculations, such as training, skill, experience, education, responsibility, mental and physical effort, and working conditions.

The Committee will confine its studies and findings strictly to evaluating the JOB, and *not the person* performing it.

Job evaluations are difficult, and must be done carefully. We hope you will fill out the attached questionnaire to the best of your ability, and return it to your supervisor promptly. To get at the facts, all answers must be clear. They must be your own description of your work, in your own words. We are deeply interested in having your help in this difficult job.

The questionnaire will help with your Job Description. The final job descriptions must be made by those who understand such procedures, but usually the person who does the work can describe it better than anyone else. Your cooperation will help to eliminate errors, omissions, and prejudices which often occur when job descriptions are written by one person.

It will be better if you fill out the questionnaire at home where you can give thought to the questions without the natural disturbances of the plant.

Sincerely,

President

After assembling and analyzing the replies to the questionnaires, the committee is ready to make *job analyses* which describe the content of the job in considerable detail. After analysis, all essential features of the job are set forth in a *job description*. Finally, the *job specifications* state the physical, mental, and other requirements that the workers must have to perform satisfactorily. Examples of a job analysis and the job description are shown in Figures 19.2 and 19.3 of Chapter 19. With these facts at hand, the committee is ready to evaluate the jobs in accordance with the evaluation plan as set forth in the manual.

The evaluation manual

The job evaluation manual's contents depend on the desires of management and the committee chosen to make the evaluation. If the purpose is full coverage, the manual will include statements of policy and procedures,

Figure 26.2

Questionnaire

1. What is your *regular* job? _____ Department _____
2. Describe your regular work in full — explain exactly what you do. _____

3. Years spent in grade school _____. Years spent in high school _____
4. Other education (Correspondence, Night, College, etc.) _____

5. How long have you worked on your present job? _____
6. How long with this or other companies on similar jobs? _____
7. How long did it take you to learn your job so that you could do it in a satisfactory manner? _____
8. Do you make any machine setups on your regular work? _____
9. If your regular job requires *precision work*, to what limits do you have to work? _____
10. What degree of accuracy does your job require?
    High _____ Medium _____ Low _____ None _____
11. Is it probable that you might injure fellow workers on your job? _____
12. What degree of spoilage of parts or materials happens on your job?
    High _____ Medium _____ Low _____ None _____
13. Do you have to read blueprints on your regular job? _____
14. What per cent of your job is spend in "getting ready" — by machine setup, getting tools, materials, etc.? _____
15. What is the weight of the average part or object which you lift or move by hand? _____
16. Check below all the conditions which apply to your job:

Inside	Dusty	Machine
Outside	Fumes	Standing
Inside & Outside	Acid	Stooping
Clean	Noise	Sitting
Dirty	Rough Work	Heavy
Greasy	Close Work	Medium
Hot	Exacting Work	Light
Cold	Glare	Quick
Wet	Floor	Dangerous
Dark	Bench	Monotonous

17. Do you have to buy tools for your job? _____ Estimate the value of the tools you own which are required for your job $_____
18. How much does it cost per year to buy work gloves, work shoes, work aprons, etc.? _____

Name _____ Clock No. _____

Date _____

all job descriptions, and detailed methods of rating the jobs. In any case, the manual should serve as a guide for the committee making the evaluation, as well as other interested groups. The policy section might include, for example, a statement to the effect that the evaluation will not downgrade, as far as pay is concerned, anyone on his present job. Also, if the evaluation recommends lower pay for a given job, it will be effective only for new employees in that classification. When job descriptions are set forth in the manual, they will be helpful to future evaluation committees in event of changes in job content, or for evaluating new jobs. For the same reason, details concerning the methods employed in reaching job-value decisions will serve as useful guides in future evaluations.

If one assumes that intelligent committee members were involved in the evaluation and that they were acquainted with the jobs involved in the ratings, the manual should set forth the following subjects:

1. An introduction explaining the purpose of the evaluation and the general method for carrying it out.
2. A recital of authorization for the evaluation, over the names of both union and management representatives.
3. The extent of coverage of the evaluation program, noting the jobs that are included.
4. A list of the job factors to be used, with their definitions, and an explanation of the basic point values, if these are included.
5. Weights given to the various job factors and their variables, with explanatory guides for applying them.
6. Evaluation scales for determining factor point values.

It is also important from a psychological standpoint to list any job classifications which are to be omitted from the evaluation, explaining the reasons. The manual should be written in language clear enough to avoid any suspicion of double or hidden meanings. A sample page from a manual will clarify this part of the procedure:

Factor	*Maximum Points*
I. EDUCATION	
A. ACTUAL SCHOOLING	130
B. EXPERIENCE AND TRAINING	100

A. *Actual Schooling*
    Definition. This factor measures the general intelligence required for the adequate performance of the job.
    Discussion. Formal education is not essential in developing intelligence. However, it is customary to measure it in terms of equivalent schooling. Levels of education are established by listing the abilities which indicate stages of intelligence. It is immaterial whether this intelligence, or measure of education, has been established by formal schooling.

Example. A first-class pattern maker requires more education than a janitor. Satisfactory pattern-makers are found among high school and apprentice graduates. Less education is expected of a janitor. For job evaluation purposes, we conclude that a first-class pattern-maker's job requires an education equivalent to both high school and apprenticeship courses, but something less than a grammar-school education is required for a janitor's job.

Job Evaluation Plans

Different approaches to the problem of wage inequities have produced different plans for its solution. An evolution in evaluating jobs was natural as various companies sought to correct their wage difficulties on an independent basis. As they continued to refine their techniques, they started to borrow from each other to a large extent. Then the professionals began to compare methods and results, and this led to further scientific experimenting in the field. Already many mixtures of accepted plans are recognizable. It is not unreasonable to assume that as the experimenting progresses, we may expect a more generally accepted single plan to evolve, combining the best techniques of all of them.

The four basic plans of job evaluation are known as Classification, Job Ranking, Factor Comparison, and the Point System. Each of these will be described and evaluated.

The Classification Plan

Classification was the first plan for eliminating wage and salary inequities. Irrespective of its comparatively simple procedure and early crude applications, the record shows that it helped keep down employee complaints concerning wage irregularities. This plan is still used by state and federal civil service commissions, where it was first adopted. Industry has never made general use of the plan and is giving decreasing attention to it as a method of job rating.

The procedure starts with a series of standard "classifications" or groups, which are based largely on experience. They often require refinements to take care of changes in job content. The classifications are differentiated by relatively simple work descriptions which are generally recognized as acceptable to both management and the workers. With these classifications or labor grades established, all jobs are assigned to one of the groups. Each classification or group has its fixed minimum and maximum wage rates within which there may be one or more rate steps. Figure 26.3 is an example of general descriptions of two cost-accounting jobs — cost clerk and cost estimator — with one lower-graded rank within each classification. General classifications frequently require distinguishing categories within the group. For example, the "Machinist" classification would include separate descriptions for "Group Leader," "Worker," and "Helper." The same approach would be true of practically all of the trades. Graded wage rates are ordinarily more numerous in office work.

One of the chief weaknesses of this plan is its dependence on past records for determining standard job groups and their wage rates. Such an approach is generally recognized as faulty, and was one of the factors which prompted the search for a more objective basis for determining job values. Furthermore, the classification descriptions are often expressed in such broad terms as to make it difficult to allocate jobs with detailed characteristics not found in the broad description. Working conditions and physical requirements, for example, are usually not considered. Differences of degree in such factors as worker responsibility and mental effort required are frequently lacking among the lower classes of jobs. Such deficiencies are not so important in many office jobs, but they are often very serious in industrial job rating.

The relative inflexibility of this plan is another defect for industrial use. Industrial jobs, subject to frequent changes in content and to annual bargaining for pay rates, cannot be so easily pigeonholed as the plan assumes. Speed and low cost are the chief virtues of the classification plan. Its relative simplicity also aids in obtaining employee acceptance. In spite of these

Figure 26.3

Job Descriptions

RELATED EXPER- IENCE	OCCU- PATION	DESCRIPTION	NO. EMP.		SALARY RATES			AVERAGE LENGTH SERVICE
			M.	W.	Max.	Min.	Avg.	
		ACCOUNTING—COST						
3 to 5 Years	Cost Clerk	Sr. Compile complete factory cost of assemblies or finished products, from specifications, bills of material, requisitions and time cards, without detailed supervision. Verify costs on new products. Compare standard cost with actual cost. May involve preparation of necessary cost data for control of operations. Requires practical knowledge of products, manufacturing processes and procedures.						
	E-4							
12 to 18 Months	C-3	Jr. Compile factory costs on parts and assemblies following definite prescribed instructions under close supervision. Other junior clerical work as may be assigned.						
5 Years and Over	Cost Estimator F-2	Sr. Compile estimates of cost on standard and special parts or products, as a basis for pricing purposes. Should have engineering knowledge and be able to interpret engineering layouts and data. Requires extensive knowledge of products, designs, manufacturing processes and procedures.						
1 to 3 Years	D-1	Jr. Compile cost estimates on standard parts and assemblies working from positive information.						

Reprinted with permission from the American Management Association, Office Management Series No. 84

advantages, the classification plan often omits some relatively important job characteristics and is particularly weak in classifying the job of an employee whose work cuts across two or more classifications.

Job Ranking

Job Ranking arranges all jobs in the order of their importance. Because job titles and brief job descriptions are written on separate cards for the purpose of sorting them into a series based on their importance, this plan is sometimes called the Card-Sorting System. It is also referred to as the Job-to-Job Comparison Plan.

Various methods are used for ranking the jobs. The original work may be done by a small committee whose members are supposed to know something about all the jobs in the plant. With all job descriptions reduced to uniform-sized cards, the committee may start by selecting the easiest and the most difficult jobs, by consensus. Then certain other well-recognized jobs are ranked in between as standard guides. This process is continued until all jobs have been ranked in the order of their importance. Since the committee decisions are long drawn out as a rule, individual members may be asked to do their own ranking, with the committee meeting afterwards to iron out differences in the individual ranking.

Another method aimed at making the ranking more objective is to ask individual committee members to rank all jobs a second time without reference to their first ranking. After the final ranking has been agreed to, the committee sometimes divides the total number of jobs into groups for the purpose of setting group-rate ranges.

Job Ranking, like the Classification Plan, has the advantage of speed and low cost. But since its decisions are reached by comparing each job with every other, it tends to create more dissatisfaction than the Classification Plan. In a small plant, Job Ranking may be satisfactory if the members of the ranking committee know the jobs and can rank them without too many differences in their subjective appraisals.

There are, however, serious objections to the use of this plan for any situation other than a small shop. In the first place, it is difficult to find committee members who know all the jobs sufficiently well to arrive at a final ranking without a lot of compromises. In the second place, the final ranking is based on the over-all impressions of the judges, usually without adequate substantiating data. This makes it very difficult to support the ranking when worker dissatisfaction arises, especially since no records are retained or reasons compiled. Finally, it is difficult to fit new jobs or jobs whose content has changed into a system which was built on personal opinions to begin with. Certainly nothing like general satisfaction could result in such cases unless the original committee members were available to make the adjustment.

Factor Comparison

Factor Comparison gets its name from the method it uses in making job evaluations. In other words, this plan compares a number of factors as they are related to each job. The factors usually considered are *mental effort, physical effort, skill, responsibility,* and *working conditions.* Each of these factors is appraised for all jobs. The recognized method is to make an appraisal of one factor for all jobs before considering any of the other factors. This approach gives more accurate final results in that it precludes attempts to arrive at predetermined values for any one job. Evaluation by this system is frequently aided by the selection of "key jobs" covering a wide rate range. These jobs act as weather vanes for the raters because of their recognized characteristics and their generally accepted "market" rate of pay.

The first requisite in this plan is a set of adequate definitions for the factors used. With these definitions in mind, those making the job evaluations record their group decisions about the value of each factor on a "Comparison Scale," which uses a comprehensive range of values in cents per hour. Figure 26.4 is a typical Factor-Comparison Scale. In this example, the molder's job receives a total rate of $1.09. The total cents-per-hour values for the five factors equal the rate for the job classification concerned. This figure expresses its factor value in cents per hour.

It is readily seen that evaluating five factors for every job is a much more laborious task than that encountered in using the Classification or Job-Ranking systems. There are objectionable features other than the time and cost of this Factor-Comparison Plan. One is that the raters leave no data to show how they arrived at the money values of the various factors. Fitting new jobs into the scale at a later time becomes relatively difficult because of this omission. Furthermore, there can be no assurance that subsequent ratings are "level" with the original job ratings. In other words, the weighting of factors is mostly subjective and largely based on faith in the judgment of the original raters. Another defect of this system is its lack of any adequate basis for dealing with objections raised by union representatives. And finally, it is relatively difficult to re-rate job factors into new money values when negotiations between labor and management provide for a general wage change.

The Point System

The Point System is generally recognized as superior to the other three and is in more general use. The chief defect of the other systems is the lack of sufficient differentiation among the factor values used. Factor definitions, when used, are often too general for systematic application to the various jobs. The Point System overcomes this objection in its more analytical approach to factor values, the basis of which is *degree point values* for the

Figure 26.4

Factor Comparison Scale

Cents	Mental Effort	Physical Effort	Skill	Responsibility	Working Conditions
40					
39					
38					
37					
36					
35					
34					
33					
32					
31		Molder			
30					
29					
28			Molder		
27					
26					
25	Molder				
24					
23					
22					
21					
20					
19					
18					
17					
16					
15					Molder
14					
13					
12					
11					
10				Molder	
9					
8					
7					
6					
5					
4					
3					
2					
1					

factors considered. Degree values recognize a series of valuations for each factor, thus making it possible to relate more accurately the value of each factor used to the specific job for which it is a characteristic.

The first step under the Point System is an adequate job analysis. The final evaluation will be, to a considerable extent, just as good as the job analysis on which it is based. With this as a prerequisite, the next step is the determination of the job factors to be used. Usable factors may range from three to about fifteen. Usually they are broken down into subfactors, so that a "five-factor plan" may contain as many as fifteen actual factor evaluations. The specialists are not agreed on the correct number of factors for the best results. One group of factors found useful in an industrial job evaluation, with their maximum point values, is shown in Table 26.1.

Every job to be evaluated involves a greater or lesser degree of each factor or subfactor shown in Table 26.2. Thus to assign a total score to any job, we must have some way of finding out *how much* of a given factor is

Table 26.1

Weighting of Job Factors*

Factors	Maximum Weights	
1. Education		
a. Actual schooling	130	
b. Experience and training	100	
TOTAL		230
2. Skill, Manual and Mental		280
3. Responsibility		
a. For the safety of others	60	
b. For spoilage of parts and materials	50	
c. For damage to machines and equipment	50	
TOTAL		160
4. Mental Effort		100
5. Physical Effort		100
6. Working Conditions		
a. Surroundings	50	
b. Hazards to self	40	
c. Connected expense	20	
d. Burnout involved†	20	
TOTAL		130
GRAND TOTAL		1000

* From the manual of Hodges & Associates, Dayton, Ohio.

† Burnout refers to premature inability to continue at a trade because of some industrial disease or debilitating condition contracted on the job.

needed to perform the job satisfactorily. Table 26.2 shows a range of values for the variable factor of "Actual Schooling." The low point on the range — ability to carry out verbal orders — is assigned a total value of 5 points and given the code "A." Thus if a job is coded "A," there is the presumption that none of the other abilities on the list is required for performing the job successfully. The range of schooling requirements in Table 26.2 is arranged from the lowest to the highest. It is assumed that any given requirement involves more ability than all of the preceding ones. Similar ranges must be established for the eleven other variables shown in Table 26.1 before the job can be assigned a total score.

In addition to the usual group of job factors, a so-called basic factor is occasionally added. It represents characteristics which are common to all jobs, including the attribute of honesty, regard for the safety rules, and willingness to cooperate. To recognize these attributes and to add psychological worker acceptance, some arbitrary value such as 300 or 400 points is frequently added to the total of the evaluated factors. The relative positions of the job scores are not affected by the addition of these basic points.

Table 26.2

Range of Point Values for the Subfactor "Actual Schooling"

Code	Requirements of the Job	Points
A	Ability to carry out verbal orders	5
B	Ability to make a written report	10
C	Ability to work as a helper to a trade	15
D	Ability to comprehend requirements for flow of materials, etc., and control movements	20
E	Ability to operate a machine tool on repetitive work	35
F	Ability to make a simple mathematical calculation OR operate materials-handling equipment	50
G	Ability to carry out routine jobs without close supervision — such as setting up automatic machines or operating a crane	65
H	Ability to figure in fractions, decimals and percentages OR make emergency adjustments and repairs	80
I	Ability to apply the fundamentals and principles of mechanics, electricity or chemistry	95
J	Ability to understand and operate from complicated blueprints	105
K	Ability to make analyses, subject to supervisory checking; to use shop mechanics, including algebra and geometry	115
L	Ability to analyze requirements from sketches or blueprints without close supervision	130

The Point System has several advantages over the other plans in spite of its higher cost and time-consuming details. In the first place, it results in an accumulation of records which can be referred to later if worker objections are raised. Also, it tends to promote uniformity in evaluating new or changed jobs by using the same criteria developed for the original evaluation. In the third place, since it is more detailed and technical than the other plans, it is likely to be more objective. Finally, its determinations are frequently arrived at by joint committees of labor and management representatives, which lays a healthy foundation for initial acceptance of the plan by labor and for continuing cooperation.

Other Considerations in Job Evaluation

Setting the wage rates

The base rates and rate ranges for the Classification and Job-Ranking systems are figured from the company's wage experience. These wage rates should be corrected by industry and community surveys, to be discussed shortly, but the relationship among the job groups should be established by the evaluation.

Wage rates for the Factor-Comparison system are fixed directly by adding the money values established for the job factors or characteristics considered. As noted, there are usually five factors.

The Point System fixes job values in terms of points. Determination of the actual wage rates is a mathematical process, based on the value of the point. The wage rates of the high and the low job classifications are customarily determined by labor-management negotiations. These rates are a reflection of market pressures tempered by the going rates in the community and the industry affected. The difference between the high and the low point values, divided into the difference between the high and the low wage rates, establishes the value of the point. This point value, multiplied by the number of points for each job classification, fixes the base monetary values for the classifications. After this group of base rates is determined, it is the duty of the evaluation committee to check each classification rate against community and industry rates. The final result may throw some job classifications out of line on the basis of point values, but the differences will be few and relatively small percentagewise. Furthermore, the finished evaluation will be more realistic, and hence more acceptable to the workers, should explanation or defense become necessary.

The rate range

Under the single-rate system of wage payment, job evaluation sets the base rates for each of the classifications. When the rate-range rather than the single-rate plan is used, these base rates customarily become the mid-points of the ranges for the several classifications. The rate range provides for a series of wage rates below and above the midpoint. The spread of this range averages from ten to twenty-five cents, usually with steps amounting to five or ten cents below and above the midpoint. It is customary for a worker to start at the bottom of the rate range unless he has been transferred from some other job in which he was at a point in the range higher than the bottom rate of his new classification. This is likely to happen even when the worker is being promoted, because the rate ranges for adjacent classifications frequently overlap. Table 26.3 shows a typical rate range, and the overlapping of rate ranges is represented graphically in Figure 26.5.

Advances within the rate range are made on the basis either of seniority or merit. Labor tends to prefer seniority and management to prefer merit as the criterion for progression through the range. However, management often goes along with labor in agreeing on simple length of service as the criterion, reasoning that this automatic time-interval plan eliminates subjective opinions about a worker's progress and thereby reduces grievances. Grievances are sometimes more costly to production than the occasional expense of raising the pay of workers whose output has not actually increased when the designated time for a higher rate arrives.

Labor-market survey

Wage rates must have both internal and external balance. Internal balance refers to the fair relationship among all job classifications within the company; external balance means that the wage scale for the various classifications must compare favorably with the rates paid like classifications in the industry or community involved.

The actual wage and salary rates are determined by quantitative value differentials as they are related to the top and the bottom pay rates. As has

Table 26.3

Sample of Rate Ranges in Money Paid

Point Values	Base Rate	$5.00 Range	15% Range
350–399	$35.00	$32.50–37.50	$32.35–37.65
400–449	40.00	37.50–42.50	37.00–43.00
450–499	45.00	42.50–47.50	41.60–48.40
500–549	50.00	47.50–52.50	46.25–53.75
550–599	55.00	52.50–57.50	50.85–59.15
600–649	60.00	57.50–62.50	55.50–64.50

Figure 26.5

Rate Ranges Expressed Graphically

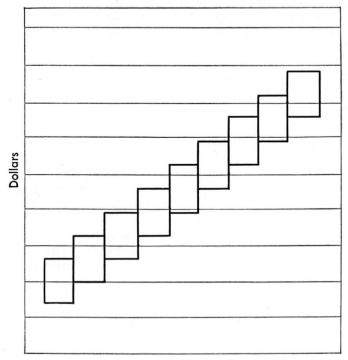

Points

been suggested, these top and bottom rates are often fixed by negotiation between management and the union. In many cases, however, the top and bottom wage and salary rates are influenced by a survey of the labor market. In recent years, the bottom rate has been fixed by state or federal legislation. However, these legal minimum rates are not always acceptable in labor-management negotiations, where the bottom rate is frequently set above the legal minimum by bargaining pressures or conditions of the labor market.

Evaluated rates lying between the top and bottom negotiated rates must be given serious attention in order to bring them reasonably into line with prevailing community and industry rates. It is against the results obtained from a labor-market survey of similar jobs within the community or industry that corrections are suggested for the corresponding evaluated jobs. The employer does not want any wage rate to be unnecessarily high, for obvious reasons. On the other hand, if any rated job is appreciably below the community or industry rate for that classification, the employer may be priced out of the labor market with respect to that classification. Organized labor demands that a rated job meet the community or industry standard, whichever one is higher, also for obvious reasons.

The results of the wage-market survey present a definite challenge to the rates determined by job analysis and evaluation. In the final round of negotiations, rated jobs must meet competition of the market. If one approaches the problem from another angle, the labor-market survey may be used as a corrective guide in fixing the top and bottom wage rates, thus furnishing the focal points for application of the classification differentials determined by the job evaluation. Any wage program put into effect without the benefit of a dependable wage-market survey is definitely headed for trouble.

The wage survey offers an opportunity to compare principles and practices in this important field. The inadequacy of those evaluations which have failed to use the survey technique have often contributed to the bitterness with which organized labor frequently condemns rated jobs and the plan which determined them. Therefore, the use of the labor-market survey for checking the wages of rated jobs cannot be urged too strongly. It not only adds reality to the final results of the job evaluation, but it hastens the day when job evaluation will become more generally accepted by employees.

Who should make the evaluation?

There is some difference of opinion as to whether the job evaluation should be made by company employees or management consulting firms specializing in this type of work. There are advantages and disadvantages both ways. The three simpler plans might well be worked out by company employees who know the jobs from the inside. Furthermore, the company representatives may be available for making desired changes in the rates when the content of specific jobs is changed or new jobs are added. Since the Classification, Job-Ranking, and Factor-Comparison methods are all highly subjective, it is almost necessary that the original rating group be available for changes.

With the Point System of job rating, the outside consultant appears preferable. It is true in this case, also, that inside or company employees will have a better initial idea of job content than the outside specialists; but the latter will have a more objective point of view and a much better understanding of the procedures used in this more specialized system. In addition, through training and practice, the specialist will probably make a better job analysis. The choice may be based on the question of whether it will be easier for employees to learn the system or for outsiders to analyze job content. There are several disadvantages in using employees to make ratings under the Point System:

1. They will be more subjective in their appraisals.
2. They will be less skilled in making job analyses because their long contact with the operations causes them to lose sight of the forest for the trees.
3. Employee appraisals may tend to lower worker morale.
4. Key men are often taken away from important jobs.
5. Actual costs are likely to be higher in the long run.
6. The advantage of job-rating experience is lacking, including ability to determine the proper number of job classifications.
7. The objective umpire is lacking.

The best method is probably found in a combination of the inside and outside approaches to the Point-System evaluation. Management consulting specialists would make the job analyses in cooperation with those who are constantly supervising the various jobs. The evaluation committee should include representatives of both management and the employees. It is in this part of the work that the outside specialist should be of great value. It is his job to harmonize conflicting points of view by objective application of the techniques involved. One common fallacy of the inside appraiser is his inclination to think in terms of the man on the job rather than of the job itself. This point of view always produces a prejudice in favor of the specific jobs held by committeemen, with consequent dissatisfaction among workers in other types of jobs.

Just as the inside participants will be invaluable aids to the outside specialist in making the job analyses, so the specialist will be able to lay the groundwork for training company and labor representatives in applying the principles and procedures of this technical form of job rating. With the knowledge gained in the actual evaluation process, company employees should be able to take over to a considerable extent in the later rating of new jobs, or rerating of jobs whose content has been changed. In any case, final decision about whether consulting service should be engaged depends on both company and worker attitudes. The size of the company and the nature of its work are other important considerations. Concerns employing a relatively large proportion of skilled or professional help will find it advantageous from the employees' point of view to engage specialists to do the evaluation. Unskilled or semiskilled workers are more inclined to be suspicious of technical approaches which they do not understand, whereas professional employees usually favor the professional approach to technical problems.

Conclusions

As is true of most management techniques, job evaluation is no panacea. All the plans have weak points and even real disadvantages, because personal judgment enters into all of them in varying degrees. To the extent that this is true, the evaluation procedure cannot be considered strictly scientific. Possibly it should be referred to as "systematic" rather than "scientific" until such time as its techniques permit more objective determination. However, it is a long step forward from the former lack of any formalized plan for fixing wage rates. Prior to the establishment of job-evaluation procedures, rates were determined by purely subjective considerations. Thus "squeaking wheels" obtained most of the wage increases. Individual and group pressures also played an important part in the rate changes for job classifications or indeed for individual workers within a classification.

Such haphazard methods result in lack of balance among job rates. It can be clearly demonstrated from experience that employees are more disturbed by the unfair relation between their rates of pay and those of fellow workers on the same or similar jobs than they are by the wage level itself. Under the rule-of-thumb plan of wage-fixing, the settlement of one wage grievance usually begets several more, with consequent wage turmoil. Irrespective of its present weaknesses, job evaluation was born of the necessity for improving such conditions.

Job evaluation does not, of course, guarantee sound labor relations. It is only part of a good personnel program. It can, and often does, bring labor and management together in mutual agreement on fair differentials in wage rates for various job classifications. Specifically, it reduces the number of wage grievances, especially when the established rates compare favorably with community and industry rates for the same or closely allied jobs.

After the job evaluation is finished, many managements make the mistake of concluding that the "ordeal" is over. They seem to be saying: "Thank God that's done!" Nothing could be further from the truth. To the extent that job content, community and industry rates, and other factors change, consideration must be given to new differentials among job classifications. "Dynamic" is a proper description for the relationship among job rates and, hence, for any job evaluation. New jobs must always be assigned a place in the job-rating scale.

In principle, job-evaluation techniques may be applied to all occupations. In practice, they are used for hourly rated jobs in production and all types of office work and, to a limited extent, in the salary field, with the top limit approximating $10,000. Beyond that figure, competition usually determines individual salaries.

QUESTIONS

1. What were the causes of the modern plans for job evaluations? What is the purpose of these plans?

2. How have modern job evaluations reduced the discontent of large segments of employees?

3. The text lists nine accomplishments of job evaluation. Which four are outstanding?

4. What background preparations are advisable prior to starting any job evaluation?

5. What is the relationship among the job analysis, job description, and job specifications as factors in a scientific job evaluation?

6. An acceptable job evaluation manual is a practical necessity for guidance of the evaluation committee. What other distribution would you recommend, and why?

7. Why have industry and other types of business made little use of the Classification Plan of job evaluation?

8. If it is true that the Job-Ranking plan of job evaluation is speedy and relatively inexpensive, why is its use more restricted than that of the other three plans?

9. What unique idea does the Factor Comparison plan of job evaluation use in expressing its factor values?

10. What technique peculiar to the Point System of job evaluations makes it more acceptable to both workers and management when changes are to be made in job content, or new job classifications are added?

11. What is the psychological value of the so-called "basic factor" often used in the Point System of job evaluations?

12. What guide line factors are used for determining the high and the low wage rates for the various classifications under the Point System?

13. How is the value of a point determined in cents under the Point System?

14. What is the value of the "wage-range" in job evaluation plans?

15. What is the purpose of the "Labor-market Survey" in externally balancing wage rates determined by the job evaluation?

16. Should the job evaluation be guided by some member or members of management or a management consulting firm? There are strong points to both plans. How would you reconcile them to best advantage for all concerned?

17. Why it is a good idea to have the job evaluation made by a committee of workers and management?

18. To what extent do the results of a good job evaluation minimize the difficulties in labor-management relations?

19. How far up the management line are job evaluations made in industry? Do you feel that they might be useful in still higher echelons?

20. Do you feel that it is better to fix wage rates directly in terms of money values of the various job factors, as is done under the Factor Comparison plan, or by job values in terms of points as used in the Point System?

CASE PROBLEM
GIBSON FITTINGS

Gibson Fittings, located in St. Louis, makes fire extinguisher systems and threaded parts for electrical contractors. It has been in operation for some twenty years and employs 270 workers, about half of whom are semi-skilled. Gibson management is really concerned about the many complaints it hears concerning its job evaluation plan. In fact, following a strike threat because of the inequities of the wage system, the director of personnel and union officers agreed to submit a list of unsettled grievances to arbitration. Arbitrators were selected by management and the union without difficulty, but the selection of the chairman or neutral member of the arbitration panel caused a lot of bickering. The federal Labor Department, in reply to a combined request of management and the union, sent a list of ten names. All of the suggestions were investigated by both parties to the dispute without results. The next step was for the Labor Department to name the chairman, which it did. As had often happened in the past, the professor of labor relations at Washington University was named for the job.

There were 15 separate grievances concerning the wage schedule then in effect. The situation was made more difficult because the present wage plan was the second adopted by the company in the past five years. For the first effort a committee of five foremen had used the Job-Ranking plan. The union served notice as soon as the committee started its labors that no plan adopted by any committee on which labor was not represented would be acceptable. As a result, after two years of continual disagreements, the company decided to try again.

For this second effort there was a joint committee of three foremen and three members selected by the union. The two sides were evenly divided and could not agree on a chairman, so they proceeded without one. The Factor Comparison plan was used this time. It resulted in a series of compromises in which labor and management tried to match "gives and takes." The labor representatives contended that one of the foremen, who had been with the company only three months, did not know the content of some of the job classifications that had to be considered. During the next two years, the content of several jobs were changed and four new jobs added. Since the committee left no usable records as to how it had arrived at some of the money values of the different job classifications, it was practically impossible to make satisfactory adjustments. After six months of turmoil for the personnel department, the decision was mutually reached to take the grievances to arbitration.

The arbitration panel decided ten of the grievances in favor of the company and the other five in favor of the union. Top management was so incensed that it refused to discuss the results with the chairman of the panel. The union membership nearly exploded when they heard about the attitude of the company's management. The final determination of the arbitrators was that a new job evaluation be made on the Point System so that future job changes would have some basis for at least semiscientific determination. The union was to pay half of the expense of the new deal, but they objected vehemently to this determination which was reached as the result of the chairman of the panel casting his vote with the management member.

The next step was to select the joint committee of management and employees to work out the wage plan. Due to their experience with the second try, it was mutually decided that there should be an outside management consultant who would act as chairman and cast a deciding vote when the two sides were in disagreement. Management proposed an outstanding man with an excellent background of training and long experience in the work. Labor, having no suggestion, simply replied that its attitude would be based on what happened during the first few days of the committee's deliberation.

PROBLEM: If you were the management consultant, how would you proceed to conduct the negotiations of the new job evaluation committee in order to assure a reasonable chance of its success and the subsequent adoption of its wage plan by the union membership?

27

Service Ratings

Job evaluation establishes the relative value of jobs; service ratings establish the relative value of employees. Although several other titles are used for employee ratings, such as merit, progress, efficiency, and performance ratings, "service rating" seems to receive a general preference. Job evaluation is expressed ultimately in money terms, while service ratings establish a set of standards for measuring the worth or value of an employee to his employer. Both procedures attempt to arrive at values in relation to some accepted standard measurement of the characteristics or factors involved.

Objectivity is the goal of all these measurements, and standards naturally help to achieve this goal. In both cases, however, since the standards are applied by human beings, full objectivity is impossible. Various devices are employed in both job evaluation and service rating to reduce the effect of the human or subjective element. Although the goal is difficult, satisfaction may be derived from the knowledge that we are working in the right direction.

There are several schools of thought relating to the best method for obtaining maximum objectivity in service ratings. One plan, known as the traitist theory, is based on the rater's judgment of certain selected traits of the employee. Traits include such criteria as ability to get along with people, emotional stability and motivation on the job.

Another idea opposes the rating of employee traits because, it is contended, they represent a subjective appraisal of intangibles. This plan proposes the use of performance records as the basis for rating. Its proponents feel that because the worker's performance records are based on facts, the subjective element is eliminated in the appraisal. One writer praises the rationale of this approach by asking: "Why, then, should we bother with mere inferences when we can make our judgments about the performance itself?"[1]

---

[1] A. C. MacKinney, "What Should the Ratings Rate?", *Personnel* magazine for May–June, 1960, p. 77.

A third school of thought about service ratings contends that both the trait and performance bases should be discarded in favor of a "goal" which should be set up as the criterion for satisfactory performance. Actually, this idea, which appears to be a corallary of the second or "performance" plan, is much questioned in practice.[2]

The discussion in this chapter is based on the assumption that the traits of the employee *and* his measurable work factors(referred to as "factors") should be considered in making his service ratings. It seems apparent that while performance factors emphasize accomplishments, personal traits, if correctly appraised, may be valuable in predicting future usefulness.[3]

History of service ratings

Service ratings, like job evaluations, have been in use for a long time, but the early methods of rating were purely rules of thumb. The British industrialist, Robert Owen, was the first employer to develop a system for evaluating his workers in the early 1800's. His appraisals were based on daily reports entered in his "character books." Dr. Walter D. Scott worked out a plan to rate newly trained officers during World War I. The Scott plan led to many technical improvements which did not, however, result in any substantial adoption of service ratings by industry. The National Industrial Conference Board survey of 1951 showed that fewer than 50 per cent of our industrial concerns had any plan for rating their employees.[4]

The idea of a scientific approach to service ratings was born of the necessity of getting away from personal decisions regarding transfers, promotions, pay increases, and disciplinary action. The larger the organization, the more harmful are arbitrary decisions in evaluating worker performance. One reason for the slow adoption of service ratings has been the insistence of some unions on using seniority as the basis for employee privileges, transfers, promotions, and wage increases, and have so provided in their contracts with management. The seniority basis for conferring worker privileges was often acceptable because the objective character of many of the rating forms was inadequate, and improvements did not develop fast enough. In other cases, service ratings fell into disrepute because of the failure of raters to do an acceptable job.

The purpose of rating

In Chapter 25, we spoke of service ratings exclusively as a criterion for promoting workers through a rate range, but employee evaluation schemes have many more uses than this. What are some of these uses?

[2] D. McGregor, "An Uneasy Look at Performance Appraisal" in the *Harvard Business Review*, May–June, 1957.

[3] "Traits" and "factors" are used synonymously by some writers. In this text, "factors" refer to performance records.

[4] Studies in Personnel Policy, Report No. 121, October 1951, p. 3.

1. *Morale.* An employee's desire to know where he stands with his employer is a human trait. A well planned and executed service-rating program helps satisfy that human desire, even when the ratee disagrees with the results. Because he knows what his boss thinks of his services, he has a working basis for acceptance or disagreement. If the rating is fair and the employee is receptive, there is a common ground on which to discuss his shortcomings with his superior. When service ratings can be handled in this way, they can be definite morale builders. When the ratings are unfair or the worker is belligerent, his loss of morale may have fairly widespread repercussions.

2. *Aid to Superiors.* With proper instructions about how to rate, the receptive supervisor becomes more conscious of the comparative values of his subordinates. This attitude helps him to improve the quality and quantity of work in his department. By substituting analysis for irritation, he aids and improves his own job of day-to-day supervision. With periodic appraisals, the supervisor recognizes the good and weak points of his workers. Although the rules occasionally provide that the supervisor is not obliged to discuss a worker's shortcomings except at rating times, he soon acquires the habit of talking over such weaknesses as they occur. Praise and criticism also become a daily working habit rather than a semiannual recorded valuation. When this changed relationship occurs, it improves supervisor-worker relations to their mutual advantage and their company's profit.

3. *Probationary Employees.* In personnel management, a probationary is a new worker who must serve satisfactorily for thirty to sixty days before his name is added to the "seniority list" with its many employment advantages. Unless his supervisor files some objection with the personnel department, the probationary worker's name is customarily added automatically to the permanent list of employees as of the date he started to work for the concern. For this reason, it is important that the personnel department be notified as to the status of the new employee before the expiration of his probationary period.

When the supervisor records items of the probationer's performance for the purpose of helping with his periodic service ratings, he is not only armed with data to aid in deciding whether to retain new workers past their probationary period, but he is also made conscious of the importance of probation. More often than not, supervisors allow the probationary period to pass unnoticed, sometimes to their regret. They find out after it is too late that they have a permanent employee who is unsatisfactory. This fault has become so common that the personnel department frequently maintains a tickler file on probationers for the purpose of warning supervisors that the probationary period will soon expire.

4. *Pay Adjustments.* Service ratings may well be used for pay adjustments, both upward and downward. This is especially true when the wage changes are within the rate range of the job classification and made on the

basis of merit rather than on some automatic progression plan, as discussed in Chapter 25.

5. *Transfer, Promotion, Layoff, and Dismissal.* All of these actions should be, in part, a reflection of the workers' service ratings, which are an important component of their personnel files.

6. *Recruiting.* The service rating is an aid in measuring the efficiency of the recruiting program and procedures, as well as the basis for improving both.

7. *Disciplinary Record.* The nature of disciplinary action may be tempered or intensified, within the limits prescribed by company rules, by the worker's service-rating record.

8. *Job Placement.* The relationship between the workers' prehiring records and their service ratings suggests that certain backgrounds indicate desirable traits for some types of jobs, while they are warning signals for other jobs. In this sense, the over-all analysis of service ratings by the personnel department produces valuable guides for screening applicants, irrespective of their test results.

9. *Training Plans.* Weaknesses disclosed by the worker's service ratings may serve as a guide to his supplementary training.

10. *Guide for Counseling.* Many concerns consider the service rating as a primary guide in counseling the employee regarding his strong as well as his weak points. Favorable factors may lead to suggestions for training in preparation for possible advancement.

11. *Handling Grievances.* The employee's service record can be an outstanding help in suggesting the proper approach for settling his grievances.

12. *Other Purposes.* There are several situations, such as requests for leave of absence, where the service ratings suggest the proper solution.

In conclusion, properly prepared and used service ratings are distinctly beneficial to employees, supervisors, and the employer, and they should be so considered for obtaining their maximum usefulness.

Rating procedures

The development of a rating system involves (1) selection of the traits and/or factors to be measured, (2) determination of the values or points to be assigned to each trait or factor, and (3) the specifications for determining the degrees into which the various traits or factors are to be divided.

1. *Trait and Factor Selection.* The selection of the traits and factors to be rated depends on what is to be evaluated. It may be that the ratee's worth to his employer will be the basis for determining these measurements. This would be true if the rating is to be used primarily for deciding on changes in his wage or salary. On the other hand, it may be desirable to measure those characteristics which will influence his future advancement. In the former case, such factors as production quality and quantity, super-

vision required, and cooperation would be of interest. They all affect the worker's present ability to contribute to the concern's welfare. In the latter case, measurement of personal characteristics or traits, such as dependability, initiative and loyalty, may be used for predicting the worker's potential usefulness over a future period.

These two groups of factors and traits measure different things and should not be combined indiscriminately. If used on separate rating sheets for the same class of workers, they may be useful in deciding whether or not individuals in the group are performing to the best of their ability. Separate ratings that produce confusing answers may indicate that the selection of factors and traits for the rating charts leaves something to be desired.

An excessive number of employee traits not only indicates lack of discrimination, but causes most of the outstanding complaints against service-rating systems in general. The usual number of traits on relatively successful charts varies from five to fifteen, depending on the nature of the company's business and the type of work of those being rated.

2. *Trait and Factor Grades.* Each trait or factor must be carefully defined and be mutually exclusive for satisfactory evaluations. Some are not only weighted or graded, but further measured by degree values within the grades. The relative weighting of the grades is difficult and presumably only approaches scientific accuracy. This is obvious when it is realized that the same trait or factor should be weighted differently when applied to different work groups. A factor that may be important in one group may be relatively unimportant in another. In other words, the weighting of the grades should relate to the situation where they are to be used. Whenever possible, examples of weighting distinctions should be given to illustrate and justify the rating instructions.

3. *Degree Values.* Various grade weights are frequently broken down into degrees of value. The range of these values is expressed in various ways, as indicated by some of the rating system illustrations in this chapter. For example, some systems show the degree values by a series of numbers arranged vertically; others indicate values within grades on a horizontal graduated scale.

To summarize, each trait or factor must be carefully defined. The grades into which they are divided must also be explained. Traits and their grades, including the range of degree values for each grade, should be tailor-made for the situations where they are to be used. General applications or dictionary definitions will not be generally useful in practice.

4. *Final Values.* The simplest range of values for individual factors or traits, and/or final rating scores, is "satisfactory" and "unsatisfactory," and there is some considered opinion favoring this elementary distinction. However, it is more usual to use finer variations, such as *unsatisfactory, below average, average, above average,* and *excellent* or *superior.*

A survey of a large federal agency by the author showed that the majority of employees favored a three-point range of *unsatisfactory, satisfactory,* and *superior.* It was further suggested that an unsatisfactory worker should be transferred by the personnel department on the assumption that his trouble might be the result of a personality conflict. It was also agreed that only two such transfers should be permitted; personality conflicts with three different chiefs were considered sufficient cause for permanent separation. The employees also suggested that the "superior" rating should not be given to more than one employee in fifty, and should be rewarded by a pay increase or job promotion. It was argued that this restriction of the "superior" classification would eliminate any tendency for supervisors to rate their subordinates too high.

The disadvantage of rating from "unsatisfactory" to "excellent" is that it allows too much leeway for basing decisions on the rater's personal opinions. What is a "very good" evaluation by one rater may be as low as "poor" with another rater evaluating a different group in the same department and using the same instructions. Furthermore, there are usually some raters who determine trait-rating scores on their general opinion of the ratee.

Good rating characteristics

1. There must be cooperation between the supervisors who do the rating and the agency responsible for planning and operating the system, usually the personnel department. Too often, the supervisor feels that he knows his subordinates without any scientific aids, which he considers time-consuming nuisances. On the other hand, compulsory cooperation in this field will never reach the desired goal.

A certain supervisor, opposed to the rating system in use which he did not understand, took considerable time to study its method of allotting plus and minus points for the various factors so that he could compel the system to yield the final score which tallied with his personal opinions. He actually rated himself in a sense by ignoring the plan and purpose of a system whose mechanics he attempted to master backwards.

2. The plan of service rating must be made as simple as possible, so that both workers and supervisors can understand it. It is not necessary that they comprehend the experimental techniques or the correlation analyses that underlie the final method of scoring debits and credits. Knowledge of these details is no more necessary to a favorable opinion of the system than is an understanding of the internal combustion engine to the pleasure of driving a car. Satisfaction in both cases derives from confidence in performance.

3. Those concerned must believe in the fairness of the system. This attitude can be produced at the start, if the rating system deserves it, by simple explanations of its operation. The receptive attitude can best be maintained by uniform application of the rating standards.

4. Maximum objectivity must be the goal. It is approached by emphasizing the simplicity of the criteria used in the rating scheme. It is fostered by the group training of supervisors in the use of the system, and by later spot checking to see that they comply.

5. The regularity with which a plan is used is an important factor in making the employees feel that it is worthwhile. The more confidence the employees have in the plan, the more they will try to correct their own shortcomings as revealed by the plan's ratings.

6. The employee should know his final rating and the reasons which contributed to it, thus giving him an opportunity to appeal if he feels that there has been an error or injustice. The right of appeal need not be burdensome or embarrassing to the rater since the burden of proof is on the employee.

7. Unusual services to the employer should have a place on the service-rating record. Since it is agreed that incentives may well take some form other than financial, every device should be used to develop them.

8. Service ratings should give credit for successful training sought by the employee while on the job. If in-service training is to become a major incentive to better work, it must receive recognition. Satisfactorily completed courses in line with the worker's duties, taken at recognized educational institutions, will ordinarily have a salutary effect on the quality of his work and should be noted on his service record. If the rating system is to "measure the man as a whole in relation to his worth to his employer," then additions to his knowledge in the field of his duties should receive consideration.

Rating Systems

There are two general plans for constructing a rating system. One has for its objective the comparative ranking of the employees being rated. It is used chiefly in making wage changes and promotions. The other plan compares the employee's performance with established standards. Its main purpose is to improve the ratee's performance. The former plan is referred to as "ranking," while the latter is known as "grading."

Most of the many rating systems are variations of the more generally accepted plans. Under the "ranking" system, three plans will be discussed: (1) *Man-to-Man*, (2) *Paired-Comparison*, and (3) *Forced-Choice*. Examples of the "grading" system will include: (1) *Graphic Scale*, and (2) *Check-List*.

Ranking methods

1. Under the *man-to-man* plan, the rater ranks a group of employees in the order of their value as he conceives it. It is customary to supply the rater with cards, each of which carries the name of a ratee. The cards are then sorted from the highest valued employee to the lowest. This form of

ranking does not show the differences in value of the ratees involved, which is a material defect for some purposes.

Man-to-man rating in its simplest form is speedy and inexpensive, but for best results, some refinements are needed. The plan is improved somewhat by dividing the ranked employees into various groups as highest, average, and poor, or a larger number of finer distinctions. Also, a few simple criteria can be used on a man-to-man basis, further improving the results. Some plans using this method describe the characteristics of representative workers of various grades.

It seems obvious that the man-to-man plan is as good as the experience of the rater with those concerned. A second rater might improve the validity of this plan if his knowledge of the group was adequate for the purpose. Too often, however, a second rater follows the lead of the supervisor's rating which makes his opinions purely perfunctory. Since the simple ranking of a group has very little scientific basis, its results are difficult to defend. Furthermore, additions to the work force pose problems of placement within the established rankings.

2. The *paired-comparison* method compares one employee with another. The plan is not new, but has recently been gaining in popularity. The rater is asked to state which of two employees is superior, either with respect to a given trait or factor, or on an over-all basis. The over-all rating is more popular. When the usual group of five workers are to be compared, there will be ten pairs for the rater to evaluate. The result of these comparisons is the basis for individual ratings. The theory supporting this plan holds that the average person can make a more reasonable decision when he is comparing two people than when he is rating one individual by comparison with some established standard.

The paired comparison plan apparently does reduce the error of judgment found in comparing a person to a standard, but not to the extent that many of its proponents claim. The further contention that the distribution of a large number of these paired ratings produces a normal curve has not been borne out in experience.

Paired comparisons are relatively easy for raters to understand, which makes their training periods short and consequently inexpensive. This plan is particularly effective when there are many ratees on the same or similar jobs. It is unsatisfactory when only a few are rated.

3. The *forced-choice* method is a form of check-list developed for the specific purpose of making service ratings more objective. Under some systems, the friendly superior of the ratee can practically "rate" his subordinate into a better job. The outstanding feature of the "forced-choice" rating is the supposed inability of the rater to predetermine the final score of the ratee.

One plan poses several groups of four categorical statements descriptive of the ratee's characteristics. From one or more of these lists, the rater is instructed to choose from each group the statement which has the most favorable descriptive value of the ratee, and the one that has his least favorable descriptive value. The following is an example of the type of statements submitted:

1. Reacts favorably in emergencies
2. Confused under new situations
3. Adopts worthwhile suggestions
4. Avoids new responsibilities

Only one of these characteristics is counted as favorable to the ratee, and only one has a negative value for the purpose of the scoring. The outstanding difficulty with the forced-choice system has two phases. The first is the problem of making valid discriminating statements, and the second is the decision as to which of the two favorable and unfavorable characteristics possesses the superior discriminating value. The first hurdle must be taken by those who are skilled in this type of work. The second phase is determined, usually, by a committee whose members are qualified to select the discriminative values of the prepared statements as they apply to the situation under consideration.

The Army developed this system during World War II, and it was adopted after the war for rating officers who were being considered for permanent commissions. Although the plan is not so widely used as other rating plans, it has had some adoptions by large industrial concerns, particularly when used in connection with some of the other rating plans. Its reliability coefficient has been rated above .70 by several studies, a rating which compares favorably with the reliability of other service ratings.

What are the advantages and disadvantages of this system of service ratings? In the first place, it is easy to figure final scores after the operating details have been decided. Secondly, it has been found effective in promoting objectivity. On the other hand, unless the paired statements are prepared with great care by professionals, they may not be distinguishing among the various levels of personnel being considered. Furthermore, it has been found in some cases that it is difficult to maintain secrecy of the code. Finally, the system does not furnish a basis for discussing his deficiencies with the ratee. This objection, however, may be overcome when the plan is used with some other rating system that does bring out the ratee's favorable and unfavorable characteristics.

Grading methods

1. The *graphic scale*, whatever special form it takes, is probably the most widely used rating system. In its simplest form, it is merely a series of graduated lines, each representing a trait or factor, with marks or spaces

indicating their relative value from the highest to the lowest. Figure 27.1 illustrates several types of graphic scales for recording the value of the "initiative" trait. To help the rater, the divisions on the scale are sometimes furnished with explanations of their values. The purpose of the several variations of scales is always the same — to assist the rater in making a correct and objective decision.

In some scales, point values are marked along the line. The sum of the values for the traits and/or factors, as determined by the rater, represents the employee's total score.

There has been considerable success with this rating system when the traits and factors and their values are properly weighted, and the raters do an acceptable job. The graphic scale is relatively easy to use because the principle behind it is generally understood. It becomes even more effective when it includes space for comments on each appraised item by the rater. The scores are reliable to the extent that the different raters have the same understanding of the instructions. When the raters do not agree in their interpretations of the value explanations, then the plan is open to "halo" and "constant error" effects. Also, it is often contended that the use of defined standards is something of a liability in scale evaluations. Another common criticism of the scale method of rating when traits are used is that they often overlap rather than being mutually exclusive.

2. The weighted *check-list* is a series of statements concerning traits or factors to be checked by the rater for each employee. Since the "list" should be made for each job group, a number of lists must be available to cover a large work force. Each statement has a numerical or scale value, indicating the ratee's performance. A total rating may be determined by adding the individual values.

Figure 27.1

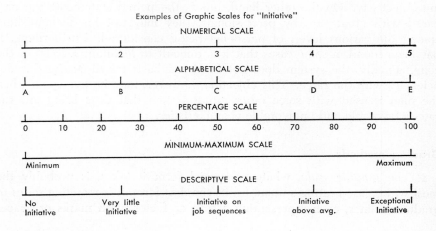

Examples of Graphic Scales for "Initiative"

NUMERICAL SCALE

1 2 3 4 5

ALPHABETICAL SCALE

A B C D E

PERCENTAGE SCALE

0 10 20 30 40 50 60 70 80 90 100

MINIMUM-MAXIMUM SCALE

Minimum Maximum

DESCRIPTIVE SCALE

No Initiative | Very little Initiative | Initiative on job sequences | Initiative above avg. | Exceptional Initiative

The development of good check-lists is difficult, as is also the establishment of fair weighted values for each statement. Trait values should be made by psychologists familiar with the type of work concerned. The accuracy of the list as a measure of the worker's worth depends on its pertinency to a homogeneous group. When one list is used for a wide range of jobs, the results have questionable value. It is also obvious that the weighted value for a given statement will be different for various job groups. One of the advantages of the weighted check-list derives from the leads it furnishes the supervisor in discussing the worker's strong and weak points with him.

Rating Problems

Rating procedures among various companies should depend on the purposes to be accomplished, the range of different jobs to be covered, the size of the various job groups involved, the ability of the raters, the time and expense funds available for the rating procedures, and the general level of acceptance accorded the system by the workers, management, and the union or other employee organization.

Who should be rated?

It is customary in introducing a rating scheme to evaluate only the hourly-paid workers. Unless the proposed system has been thoroughly explained to all employees and received reasonable acceptance by both workers and management, it might be advisable to start by installing the plan in a single department. Without attracting too much opposition the first year, the adopted system has a better chance to prove itself in operation. The experience can be used to good advantage in satisfying reasonable opposition by ironing out obvious errors.

If it is decided to rate all hourly employees from the beginning, the system should not be put into operation until a thorough educational program has been completed, with ample opportunity for all interested parties to be heard. One or two years' experience in rating this larger group will afford a still better opportunity for minimizing defects in the plan before attempting to introduce the rating of clerical, salaried, and management groups. Dfficult as it may be to rate the salaried and management groups, they should be included as experience and acceptance justifies. Among other advantages, inclusion of most management levels increases worker confidence in the general idea. It is understandable that rating managerial and clerical characteristics is more difficult than evaluating worker traits. However, if the system is satisfactory, it furnishes an excellent background for eliminating incompetent leaders.

Who should rate?

It is generally agreed that the employee's immediate supervisor should rate him in the first instance. The supervisor presumably knows most about the ratee. Intimate knowledge of the ratee's performance or traits does not, however, prevent the rater from registering a biased evaluation. It is more or less common practice to have one or two additional raters add evaluations to that of the immediate supervisor. Theoretically, this multiple rating is supposed to offset subjective opinions of the first rater. This theory would have considerable validity if the supplementary ratings were made independently, but this has not been the case in practice. Many rating forms provide for recording the so-called multiple ratings on the original rating sheet in parallel columns so that the two or three ratings for each factor or trait appear together when the record is complete.

Since the supervisor usually rates first, it is quite natural that the supplementary raters should be guided by the first rater's opinions. If the supplementary raters have had close association with the ratee, which is usually not the case, they may sometimes disagree with the first rater's evaluations, but this is not customary. In most cases, the first rater is a subordinate of one of the supplementary raters. If many of the latter's opinions conflict with the former's, the superior is, in a sense, losing confidence in his subordinate's judgment.

What actually happens in many cases is a discussion between the original rater and his chief. As a result, all the ratings are the same. One or more has certainly been determined by compromise. The less the supplementary rater knows about the ratee, the more inclined he is to accept the original rater's opinions. Under such circumstances, the "checking" process is largely illusory. When a third rater enters the picture, the results are often still less valid.

On the basis of these observations, it is an open question whether or not better ratings are obtained by a single rater who must carry the responsibility for the results. Some authorities believe that more than two raters split responsibility to the vanishing point. The assumed objectivity of multiple rating is more fictional than real, and for this reason often upsets the ratee who has good reason to believe that the second and third raters know very little about his job and still less about him.

A relatively few companies rate by committees. There may be a management committee or a joint committee representing management and the workers. While this joint evaluation may tend to minimize bias in some cases, it will surely increase the number of compromises and consequently split responsibility and make the approach less scientific. To the extent that economic pressures exert influence on either side, the scientific approach to service rating is largely perverted.

Size of rated group

There should be a limit to the number of employees evaluated by each rater. If the rater's load is too heavy, his main job suffers, and many of his ratings will not be dependable. The number of ratees who represent a fair rater's load depends on the number of traits or factors to be appraised and the degree values involved. In the long run, the question of the rater's ability to handle his allotment of ratees will be resolved by the appraisal of his ratings, assuming that the rating procedures make provision for this type of checkup.

Frequency of ratings

Most ratings are made on an annual or semiannual basis, although there is no generally accepted pattern. New employees should be rated more frequently the first year, particularly during the probationary period. Since wage adjustments and promotions may be dependent on service ratings, frequency of the ratings should coincide with the wage-adjustment periods. There is also the question of whether all employees should be rated at the same time. Although simultaneous rating is the rule, there are good reasons for staggered rating periods. When the ratings are staggered, the supervisor is able to give more attention to rating each case and to talking over the reasons for the final rating with each of his subordinates. It is also likely that staggered ratings cause less friction among employees, especially while the plan is not generally accepted.

Appraising the ratings

Poor ratings are worse than no ratings. They are worse than useless because they are morale destroyers. But it is not an easy matter to check the accuracy of ratings owing to the lack of standards. There are two criteria for evaluating ratings — validity and reliability. Service ratings must be examined on both of these counts.

Validity is the degree to which the rating actually measures the things it is intended to measure. It is best established by comparing rating results with the employee's performance on the job. If the record shows that one employee's performance is significantly better than another's, this same difference should be reflected in their respective service ratings. Because many rating forms include psychological traits, performance is not a completely satisfactory check, but it is probably the best measure we have at the present time.

Reliability is a measure of the internal consistency of a battery of rating items. One test of reliability is made by comparing the estimate of two or more independent raters of the same employee. In this case, independence means without consultation and on separate records.

Training the raters

Most raters' poor results come from not understanding the rating system used. That deficiency can be overcome by proper training, for which the conference method has been used most effectively. After the raters have studied their written instructions, they should meet in groups for discussing the over-all features of the system and its practical details. The final step is the question-and-answer period.

Effective rating is possible only after analysis of all the rating reports. Only then is it possible to observe differences in rater evaluations and plan for better common understanding. Possibly the most common weakness in rating is the phenomenon known as the "halo effect." This is the tendency of the rater to be influenced either by the rating that he has already given on some other attribute or his general impression of the ratee. It is very difficult to overcome this prevalent human tendency. Perhaps the best approach to its correction is in the training programs and the general group discussions following completion of the ratings. The danger of the halo effect should be emphasized at these conferences. The professional analyses of the ratings also furnish materials valuable in combating the halo danger.

Discussing results with ratees

One of the moot questions of service ratings is whether or not to discuss his rating with a given employee. This involves the further question of when such a discussion should take place, and the extent to which the results of the rating should be revealed. There is some sentiment favoring discussions between the rater and the ratee at the time the rating is being compiled. In a minority of cases, the employee is merely sent the result of his rating with a notification that he has the right of appeal if he feels that his rating is unfair. In most cases, the supervisor-rater discusses the rating in detail with the employee after he has received notification of his rating.

Which of these three approaches is most desirable? It depends to a large extent on the circumstances in individual cases. If there is general opposition to ratings *per se,* then prolonged discussions may merely feed the opposition. Higher salaried personnel are more prone to discuss their ratings with the idea of improving weaknesses. Discussions may be beneficial where the rating plan has been operating for only a short time. Frank talks with reasonably intelligent employees may bring out some helpful suggestions for changes in the rating plans themselves.

In addition to circumstances dependent on the reactions of the ratees, the questions of when and how far discussions should proceed may depend on the type of supervisor concerned and the value of his training in the area of service ratings. Management's attitudes, which are often well-known to the workers, also help determine this serious problem of mutual discussions. There is no patent answer to the question, but there may be serious results if the wrong approach is applied to a particular rating situation.

Conclusions

1. The halo pressure for subjective ratings is doubtless the chief defect of raters, and hence of ratings. Unconsciously pressured by this tendency, the rater places the worker in a fixed groove — high, low, or medium — and rates him accordingly.

2. Another common defect is to give too large a percentage of "excellent" ratings. This tendency is so pronounced in some organizations that the system requires the raters to write justifications for all "excellent" grades. There are two outstanding reasons for this exaggeration of "excellent" ratings. First, the supervisor is convinced that most of his workers are good because he trained them. Second, he has found out from experience that the worker who is rated high will not give him any trouble or register appeals.

3. Different raters naturally use different standards in spite of the detailed instructions for rating.

4. The difficulty of rating fairly the worker who performs different jobs for two or more supervisors is almost insurmountable.

5. Poorly drafted rating forms cause many rating failures. This defect usually arises when amateurs copy forms not suited to the conditions under which they are to be used.

These and other defects frequently cause the distribution of service ratings to be the signal for general employee complaints, for a period of lowered quality and quantity of work, and for a series of service-rating appeals. A high proportion of appeals from service ratings is not a measure of democracy in management, but rather an indication of poor administration of improperly constructed rating forms. The whole area of service ratings is one phase of management where we have a wide-open field for improvement.

QUESTIONS

1. If job evaluation establishes the relative value of jobs, what do service ratings establish?

2. As with job evaluation, the chief desirable characteristic of service ratings is objectivity. What is the *sine qua non* for promoting objectivity in both of these management techniques?

3. On what contention is the use of the "traitist" theory based? Is it likely to produce greater objectivity in service ratings?

4. Why have service ratings been slow to receive adoptions by industry?

5. The text discusses a dozen management uses for service ratings. How many of them can you recall?

6. Discuss the pros and cons of the effect of service ratings on employee morale.

7. How can service ratings be applied with success to probationary workers?

8. To what extent and in what ways can recruiting receive aid from service ratings?

9. What is the disadvantage of using too many factors and traits in service ratings?

10. What is the relation between degree values and the use of trait and factor grades?

11. If you were preparing a plan for a range of service rating values, how many would you include, and what would they be?

12. What are some of the essential characteristics of good service ratings?

13. Under the "ranking" systems for service rating, three plans are discussed in the text. Which plan do you favor, and why?

14. The "grading" system for establishing service ratings includes three different plans. Which of these plans do you favor, and why?

15. It is universally agreed that the workers' supervisor should rate his subordinates, but many plans provide for two or more raters for each employee. What do you think of multiple ratings?

16. How far up the management ladder, if at all, should the rating plan be applied to members of the management team?

17. To what extent does frequency of ratings affect employee morale?

18. How would you plan to test the validity and reliability of a rating plan?

19. Should service rating results be discussed with the workers? If so, by whom and how soon after the ratings are distributed?

20. How does the "halo" pressure affect service ratings?

CASE PROBLEM

THE CENTRAL REGISTER COMPANY

The Central Register Company is an old concern and a leader in its line of business. Because its management is progressive in its attitude toward new ideas, techniques, procedures, and machines, the company is considered a leader in espousing the principles of scientific management.

Central Register was one of the first companies in its field to install a merit-rating system for its office workers, of whom there are about three hundred. Of this number, about 80 per cent are women, scattered throughout the ten well-defined sections into which the general office is divided. Due to the company's well-planned employee policies, office-worker turnover has been well below the average. In fact, some thirty of the office workers belong to the company's Twenty-Five-Year Club.

The check-list rating system has been used for about five years. It was designed especially for the local situation, and in an effort to make it as comprehensive as possible, fifteen factors are used. The double-rating plan provides for evaluation of the ratees by their immediate superiors and by the general office manager. All employees are shown their ratings, which they are encouraged to discuss with their supervisors. The system provides for seven final grades, based on points assigned to the fifteen rating factors. The seven grades are: superior, excellent, very good, good, fair, below par, and unsatisfactory.

The plan provides for employee appeals from their rating grades, and a comprehensive form is provided for that purpose. The appeal board consists of three of the ten supervisors, with annual terms. Members of the board are appointed by the general office manager on a rotating basis.

About three years ago, the percentage of superior and excellent grades started climbing until they now comprise about 60 per cent of the office force. Several of the section supervisors are jealous of the other section ratings, which show a higher average than their own. In addition, the number of ratee appeals has increased by 300 per cent in the past two years. The appeal record shows that the original ratings have been upheld in over 90 per cent of the cases.

Ratings are made every six months. The past two ratings have resulted in a mild turmoil among the female workers. The accompanying office discussions and accusations include not only the disappointed ratees, but their friends as well, which tends to make the complaints appear objective. Within two weeks after the last rating, ten of the girls with "very good" ratings quit in a group because they were rated down from "excellent," a rating which they had maintained for two years. What downward ratings did occur were probably due to the general office manager's criticism about the poor distribution of the rating grades.

PROBLEM: The current rating situation in the general office has come to the attention of the executive vice-president, who has decided to do something about it. If you were engaged to study and correct this situation, what would you recommend, and why? What data would you accumulate to guide your decision?

Part Four • *Suggestions For Further Reading*

Belcher, David W., *Wage and Salary Administration*, New York: Prentice-Hall, Inc., 1962.

Bureau of National Affairs, *Pensions and Profit Sharing*, Washington, D.C.: 1953.

Gomberg, William, *A Labor Union Manual on Job Evaluation*, Chicago, Illinois: Labor Education Division, Roosevelt College, 1947.

Langsner, Adolph and Zollitsch, Herbert G., *Wage and Salary Administration*, Cincinnati: South-Western Publishing Company, 1961.

Lincoln, James F., *Incentive Management*, Cleveland 17, Ohio: The Lincoln Electric Company, 1951.

Louden, J. K., *Wage Incentives*, 2nd Ed., New York: John Wiley and Sons, Inc., 1959.

Otis, Jay L., and Leukart, Richard H., *Job Evaluation*, 2nd Ed., New York: Prentice-Hall, Inc., 1954.

Patchen, Martin, *The Choice of Wage Comparisons*, Englewood Cliffs, New Jersey: Prentice-Hall, Inc., 1961.

Patton, Arch, *Men, Money and Motivation*, New York: McGraw-Hill Book Company, Inc., 1961.

Patton, John A., and Littlefield, C. L., *Job Evaluation, Rev. Ed.*, Homewood, Illinois: Richard D. Irwin, Inc., 1957.

Taylor, George W., and Pierson, Frank C., *New Concepts in Wage Determination*, New York: McGraw-Hill Book Company, Inc., 1957.

Whyte, William Foote, *Money and Motivation*, New York: Harper and Brothers Publishers, 1955.

●

The quotation at the beginning of Part Four is from: Douglas McGregor, *The Human Side of Enterprise*, New York: McGraw-Hill Book Company, Inc., 1960, Chapter 7.

The Supporting

Industrial Functions

. . . . *it is important for the leader in many cases to know how to make use of technical experts. He should be able to select experts shrewdly, to stimulate them to their best work and to use their findings judiciously without being overborne by them. The expert, it has been wisely said, should be on tap and not on top. And the good leader can greatly extend his area of effective work if he learns how to draw on experts while still keeping technical opinions in subordination to his own more inclusive and therefore truer perspective of what he and his group are trying to do.*

ORDWAY TEAD

28
Procurement

Procurement has only recently become an important and correlated function of management. It was unusual indeed prior to World War I for purchasing to be ranked as an independent activity. During that period, it was usually a part of production. Because of emergency restrictions on many commodities, wars create special purchasing problems, and so it was that World War I focused management's attention on the buying function. But after the war, the situations where the purchasing agent continued to assume the importance that war had stimulated became again exceptional. However, the war so hastened the development of purchasing that the year 1915 marked the organization of the National Association of Purchasing Agents and the first university course on procurement.

The terms "procurement" and "purchasing" are still confused with each other in the field of management. Procurement is a more recent and more inclusive concept than purchasing. As the science of management developed, many important steps were added to purchasing, both before and after the issuance of an order to the supplier. This broadened scope was referred to at first as *serialized purchasing*. Today, with the systemization of these before-and-after steps, a new scientific procedure has emerged known as *procurement*. What has been added to the original purchasing activities can be summed up in the following scheme:

Procurement		
Preliminary Steps	Purchasing	*Subsequent Steps*
1. Requisition	1. Negotiations	1. Follow-up
2. Quality	2. Purchase	2. Receiving
3. Quantity	3. Payment	3. Inspection
4. Delivery		4. Storage
5. Vendors		5. Inventory
6. Routing		

Purchasing often controls the success of industrial and commercial operations as well as governmental activities. In medium-sized and large city governments, purchases amount to from 25 to 45 per cent of the total budget. In the typical business, the range is from 25 to 80 per cent of the company's expenditures, with an average of approximately 50 per cent.[1]

Opposition to procurement

The average ratio of purchases to total costs suggests the outstanding importance of procurement as a managerial function. However trite this observation, it is still frequently ignored. In the first place, many departmental users of various materials are naturally prone to feel that they can buy them to better advantage than can a purchasing agent who is not intimately acquainted with their use. Another reason for the frequent antagonism on the part of the individual department head is the fact that the procurement department ends his contacts with salesmen, whose stories and predelictions for entertaining customers are eliminated at a single stroke. And finally, there is the department buyer's commodity prejudices. He has always bought Triply sandpaper, found it satisfactory, and is positive that he can use no other.

Procurement Organization

Organization is an important tool of management on all levels, but it must be understood that it is merely a tool and not the job itself. For effective results, organization must be molded about a function or purpose; it is not an established pattern. Four phases of procurement organization merit discussion. The first is departmental purchasing. The second is concerned with the position of centralized procurement in the concern's total organizational hierarchy. The third applies to the internal structure of the department when it is set up on an independent functional basis. Finally, there is the problem of the large concern with scattered plants.

1. *Departmental Buying.* When individual departments of a company buy the commodities they use, the plan is spoken of as decentralized, a situation where procurement has no independent status in the general management hierarchy. Decentralized purchasing by using departments may well be referred to as "buying" because supporting research, standards, and control are conspicuously absent. When a department assigns one of its staff to buying on a part- or full-time basis, control rests with the department head, and buying may reach down to the supervisor level. The advantages already given for centralized purchasing suggest the disadvantages of allowing departments to do their own buying. Fundamentally,

---

[1] Because purchasing for resale is covered in many books on retailing and sales, it will not be considered in this text.

department heads and supervisors lack faith in specialized services or staff activities, unless it happens to be their own.

2. *The Position of Procurement in the Management Hierarchy.* Whether or not procurement is given one of the top-management positions depends largely on the relative importance of that function in the particular business. In some concerns, purchases loom large when compared to labor costs. In others, the opposite is true. Obviously, when purchases represent a large and varied volume, procurement ranks high in the organization. In such cases, it may be headed by a vice-president. When the procurement dollar is not so important percentagewise, the department is likely to be in charge of a director who may report to the vice-president in charge of production, the treasurer, or the plant manager. This is the customary plan in a medium-sized business where purchasing is centralized as a functional department.[2]

Relations to the general hierarchy may be split when a company buys a large volume of a special commodity, usually a raw material. For example, concerns manufacturing cigars or cigarettes frequently buy their tobacco through a special committee of top management or someone who is a specialist in that field. Large volume is only one of the reasons for committee or specialist purchasing. These special commodities are often "price sensitive," and usually quoted on commodity exchanges. As "sensitive," they may be subject to wide and rapid price fluctuations. Knowledge of market trends and seasonal factors are vital in this type of buying, and long experience is rightly considered necessary for good judgment in their purchase.

3. *Internal Organization of the Procurement Department.* Internally, buying is broken down into commodity classifications based on the amount and variety of items used. Each classification is ordinarily assigned to a single buyer if its volume and kind is considered important.[3]

In addition, there are clerical personnel assigned to one or more activities such as requisitions, publication, invitations to bid, computation of bids, purchase orders and contract awards, surplus and obsolete materials, purchase records, expediting, invoice-checking, record-keeping, and complaints.

[2] For classifying companies according to size, the N.A.P.A. *Handbook* considers businesses small when their volume of purchases is under $1 million, medium when purchases are between $1 and $10 million, and large when purchases are over $10 million.

[3] One commodity classification list is divided into twenty accounts covering general buying groups as follows:

1. Contractual services
2. Running contract services
3. Office supplies and equipment
4. Hospital supplies and equipment
5. Drugs and chemicals
6. Paints, supplies, oils
7. Cleaning supplies and equipment
8. Dry goods and clothing
9. Fuel and coal
10. Photo and engineering equipment
11. Petroleum products
12. Horticultural supplies
13. Hardware and cordage
14. Tools and appliances
15. Auto parts and supplies
16. Mechanical supplies
17. Electrical supplies
18. Building and road materials
19. Castings and forgings
20. Foodstuffs

All of the activities mentioned in connection with the internal organization of the department are usually arranged in some hierarchial sequence. At the top, there will be the manager, director, or vice-president in charge of procurement. In a large organization, there are one or two assistants to the chief. They will be largely concerned with direct management of the department with its activities divided between them on some functional basis. Their purpose is to ensure coordination within the organization, which is further secured by their reporting to the director. The individual buyers will be the chief supervisory interest of one of these assistants, unless the buyers are divided into two general groups with an assistant in charge of each. Both assistants will often conduct minor negotiations within their buying ranges with the advice of the director, and certify completed purchases to the treasurer for payment.

An office manager customarily has general supervision of all clerical help in order to give maximum service to the buyers, those in charge of stores, and any other activities of the department. Such services include assistance in connection with requisitions, deliveries, routing of purchases, keeping vendor lists up-to-date, follow-ups where they are necessary, checking of receiving and inspection reports, records of items in storage, and the general inventory of commodities on hand.

4. *The Company with Scattered Branches.* A business of two or more scattered plants or branches may use either a centralized or decentralized organization plan for its procurement department, or a combination of the two. The natural tendency would be to centralize purchasing for all branches at the home office. However, branch sizes and distances from the home office frequently require subordinate purchasing agents acting locally as auxiliary functions of procurement. Another factor is the occasional necessity for emergency buying, which can be done better at the branch. When price and quality are equal, the local market should be used in order to promote good public relations. Some publicity-minded businesses go even further in patronizing local markets.

When the central procurement department at the home office operates through its representatives in scattered branches, the question of their authority arises. If tight authority and control are retained in the central organization, the branch agent has no opportunity to exercise initiative, which may be an important factor in training men for promotions. The ordinary solution is to delegate considerable authority for spot, emergency, and local buying, with the home office exercising general control. Control may be maintained through policy manuals for general guidance and by requiring branch reports in a form that can be checked against prescribed policies, instructions, and operating standards.

Under branch operation with centralized control, the home office reserves buying responsibility for designated items. These are usually bought on long-term contracts, against which the branches may draw from vendors in accordance with their needs and against the original requisitions that they presented to the home office at the beginning of the buying year. Home-office purchases will include items commonly used by most of the branches. Raw materials are frequently reserved for home-office purchasing. It is clear that in such cases home-office procurement is both centralized and decentralized in operations, but that its control over all procurement must of necessity be highly centralized.

Procurement Procedures

There are two basic distinctions in the methods of procurement operations. One is the difference between centralized and decentralized procedures, and the other is the difference between institutional and negotiated buying.

Centralized versus decentralized buying

Centralized procurement means exactly what the word signifies — a plan for buying all materials, supplies, and equipment through a functional central office or department.

Decentralized (departmental) buying within a single large business often leads to fantastic results. Random examples include a dozen kinds of carbon paper, fifteen different lubricating oils, and as many varieties of soap and pencils. Purchasing agents report the use of several brands of cleaning powder, each department insisting that its choice is the *dernier cri*. One newly centralized department reported that the price range for the different brands was too wide and all the prices too high. It bought sodium phosphate ground fine as a single substitute at about one-quarter of the price of the brand-name items.

With decentralized purchasing, an unwarranted number of items accumulates in all departments. Absence of centralized procurement and the lack of standardization which invariably accompanies it, results in unnecessarily large investments in stock items — the sure road to creeping obsolescence. A legitimate form of decentralized procurement is that applied to scattered plants, as explained in the previous section. The combination of decentralized purchasing with centralized control is often advantageous under such circumstances.

The advantages of centralized procurement are so obvious and easily understood that its lack of wider application is difficult to understand, except on the basis of personal interest. Among its advantages, centralized procurement:

1. Reduces unit costs
2. Reduces overhead costs
3. Reduces accounting work

4. Increases cash discounts
5. Increases quantity discounts
6. Increases standardization
7. Improves specifications
8. Provides centralized inspection
9. Provides for central storage
10. Promotes interdepartmental exchanges
11. Centralizes sales of obsolete items
12. Reduces inventory investments
13. Aids services of suppliers
14. Reduces the area of petty theft
15. Checks refunds for "empties"

For private business, the financial advantages of centralization are probably greater than for public institutions because of the larger possibilities for negotiated buying. As the general principles of scientific management are more widely understood and accepted, the coordinative possibilities of centralized procurement will be so firmly accepted that it will cease to become a subject for serious debate.

Institutional versus negotiated buying

Institutional procurement has one great difference from that of private business. An institution must request sealed bids from prospective vendors for all purchases above a fixed amount. This method is known as *formal*, as distinct from the negotiated or *informal* plan. Negotiated purchases are those made between buyers and sellers who are dealing at arm's length. The formal method, on the other hand, provides that all bids shall be sealed when submitted, shall all be opened at the same time in the presence of the bidders, and the award given to the lowest responsible bidder. The maximum allowed for negotiated bidding by public institutions ranges from about $500 to $2,000. The lower the maximum fixed by law, the less opportunity there is for negotiation by the institution's procurement department.

There are several reasons for sealed bids. One is to prevent cheating by the purchasing agent. Another is to give equal opportunity to all taxpayers who may happen to be suppliers. Both features can be, and usually are, accomplished by negotiated purchasing. The sealed-bid approach is negative in that its chief object is to prevent something undesirable from being done. The positive approach aims at doing the desirable thing in the best possible manner. Experience shows clearly that the several varieties of cheating, through political pressure and otherwise, are just as possible — and perhaps just as prevalent — under the formal system of bidding.

Institutional bidding is based on the historical assumption that the management of public institutions is necessarily incompetent, with the result that prevention of dishonesty is emphasized. Methods of control have advanced considerably since sealed bids were made compulsory for most institutional buying. This lingering technique is a slur on the mental ability and personal honesty of buyers in the institutional field. Furthermore, it is often more expensive — a fact that most taxpayers do not realize.

Those opposed to negotiated buying for public institutions base their argument largely on the contention that "all taxpayers must have equal opportunity." In answer to this, one might well ask whether taxpayer-sellers have selling rights superior to the buying rights of the taxpayer-buyers.

Procurement Responsibilities

The responsibilities of procurement are divided, on an operational basis, into three general categories: (1) the basic duties of buying, (2) opportunities and decisions which procurement shares with other departments, and (3) controversial responsibilities which some procurement agencies have assumed.

Basic Duties

1. Select sources of supply
2. Interview suppliers' representatives
3. Visit plants of suppliers
4. Get quotations and conduct negotiations
5. Select the supplier and make award
6. Handle rejections and adjustments
7. Prepare schedules of requirements
8. Sell scrap, surplus, and obsolete items
9. Comply with governmental controls

Functions Shared with Other Departments

1. Decisions whether to make or buy certain items
2. Purchase of capital equipment and construction
3. Development of standards and specifications
4. Purchasing research
5. Inventory control

Controversial Responsibilities

1. Inspection
2. Stores
3. Salvage
4. Traffic

Since most of these activities are self-explanatory, only a few will be discussed. It is impossible in a treatment of this nature to go into details of procedure for all duties of the procurement department.[4]

Basic duties

Selecting the sources of supply is sometimes referred to as the most difficult job of the purchasing agent. For locating sources, he refers to trade journals and directories, industrial advertising catalogues, and salesmen. Salesmen are frequently the best source, even when they are not handling the particular item sought but are familiar with the field in general.

Interviewing salesmen, even those with whom there is no prospect of doing business, is part of the common sense of procurement. Very little that the purchasing agent reads is of equal quality or as timely as information gathered from salesmen. The same may be said of information which the salesman receives from the purchasing agent. The fact that they both know this accounts in large measure for their mutual helpfulness.

Visits to suppliers' plants are also mutually advantageous to both parties. Visits may serve to fix the purchasing agent's confidence in the supplier. They may also lead to helpful suggestions by the purchasing agent, acceptance of which will more firmly cement relations between vendor and buyer.

Preparing schedules of requirements necessarily involves dealing with the production and other departments, many of which are skeptical of their relations with procurement. The representative of procurement must not only have considerable knowledge of the specific fields of company interest, but he must be a diplomat in his dealings with other departments.

Sales of surplus and obsolete items involves the question of whether or not they really are surplus or obsolete. There may be an honest difference of opinion, which is not easy to resolve. Furthermore, many production men are not convinced that procurement knows enough about their requirements even to buy for them intelligently — much less sell their surplus obsolete items at the best prices.

Complying with government controls is listed by purchasing agents as their most trying duty when a long list of materials becomes critical in time of war or national emergency. However, this is a special situation and is not particularly disturbing to the procurement department in normal times.

Functions shared with other departments

Whether to buy or to make items used in production, or elsewhere, is a constant problem in many businesses. To buy on the outside fixes costs,

[4] For detailed discussions in the field of procurement, reference may be made to *Procurement* by Henry G. Hodges (Harper & Brothers, New York, 1961.)

whereas making involves direct and indirect materials and labor costs, as well as supplies and overhead. The cost uncertainties are eliminated by buying on the outside. Some concerns are so sure about the advantage of escaping both production headaches and the necessary investment that they buy most components on the outside and merely assemble them. On the other hand, how can the buying company assure itself that the price is fair, and will remain so? What about assurance of scheduled deliveries? Then, too, the question of revealing to an outsider some secret process may be involved.

Purchase of capital equipment and construction is a top-management decision, but procurement can help in obtaining answers to problems assigned to it. In these associations, procurement usually finds closer cooperation on the top level than from middle management.

Standards and specifications are bound together. In this field through research and negotiation, procurement probably has its greatest opportunity to demonstrate economic and social usefulness. Comparatively little was done to establish buying standards until the chief of procurement had worked his way to an established position on the top-management level. There are two areas in which buying standards must be developed — within a single company and among various concerns in similar fields. The latter is the more difficult task, but it offers almost unlimited opportunities for savings.

The National Bureau of Standards of the U.S. Department of Commerce offers the greatest assistance in commodity buying to both private and public institutions. The Bureau's experience with the purchase of vast quantities of supplies by the federal government, as well as its research work in support of that program, particularly fit it to help in the formulation of standards, in writing specifications, and in determining the best methods for testing. The Bureau issued its first edition of the *National Directory of Commodity Specifications* in 1925. Today it is the prime source of information on the subject. There is, however, one potential difficulty in connection with establishing standardized commodities and that is the tendency to rest on the oars after acceptance of trade standards. This tendency can delay, if not stifle, further improvements. Competition is probably our best guarantee against this easy attitude.

Research in the field of procurement has expanded rapidly in the past decade. This is particularly true of the problems of value analysis, "make or buy," in reducing costs, in buying equipment, finding substitutes and uses for new products. The department's outstanding contribution to research in the past decade has been in the field of "value analysis," which will be given separate consideration later in this chapter.

Inventory control is tied up with central stores. With proper cooperation, procurement may have a contribution to make in the effectiveness of this control activity. When procurement has jurisdiction over stores, as it frequently does, there is naturally no problem of cooperation between the two; however, such an arrangement often gives rise to new problems in cooperation between procurement and the production department.

Controversial responsibilities

Whether the procurement department should have responsibility for such functions as inspection, stores, salvage, and traffic is still a matter of controversy. Because these functions are so closely related to the purchasing process, the claims of procurement to organizational responsibility for them are not without merit. However, even if there is a probable need for some functional combinations for the purpose of better coordination within the span of control, it will be unfortunate if any one of the major activities is given the whip hand to work out a solution. The over-all, objective approach must be used when planning an improved organization. The final answer for the question as to whether to combine these four controversial activities or any of them under procurement must depend on the circumstances in individual situations.

Procurement Objectives

The objectives of procurement are: purchasing the proper quality, in the proper quantities, at the proper times, from the proper suppliers, with proper deliveries, and at the proper price. All of these are important; the omission of any one of them may result in an unsatisfactory transaction.

Quality

"Quality" has a special significance in procurement. It means such quality as is necessary for the intended use; no better, no worse. Presumably, the cost of a better-than-necessary quality will increase unit costs and may price the producer out of his market. If the commodity quality is inferior to that needed for its use, short-run unit costs will be lower, but the cost of defective products may soon increase unit costs, and — of serious consequence in the long run — result in loss of customers.

With a merchandising business, proper quality may mean that quality which the concern's customers want to buy, at prices they can afford to pay. Any other quality does nothing to help increase customer satisfaction or volume of sales. High-quality merchandise may have to be sold at no profit, or even at a loss. Low quality may result in dumping at a loss in some other market.

Quantity

The proper quantity refers to the volume necessary to maintain uninterrupted production or take care of continuing sales in a merchandising business. Interruptions to production caused by a shortage of raw materials can be costly. In continuous industries, such as blast furnaces, the loss is even greater. An oversupply, on the other hand, is costly because of such factors as storage and insurance charges, interest on the investment, and the possibility of deterioration and obsolescence.

Timing

The proper time is tied in with the proper quantity, but it may involve more specific considerations. Some large concerns, such as the automobile industry, may route their purchases to production centers on a time schedule. The purpose is to save time and the materials-handling expense that accrues when raw materials or components are delivered to central stores to be transferred later to production centers. When procurement issues an order to a supplier under such conditions, it specifies not only the day of delivery, but also the time of day and the number of the receiving gate. In this case, the timing of delivery is an essential prerequisite to satisfactory performance by the supplier. It is procurement's responsibility to see that such time schedules are met.

The supplier

The proper supplier is one on whom the buyer can depend for some of the various factors involved in his purchase. The supplier is responsible for delivering the quality and quantity ordered, at proper place and time, and at the agreed-upon price. Procurement departments invariably consider service ahead of price. *The chief considerations that procurement expects from suppliers in the order of their importance are: quality, service, and price.*

Delivery

The proper delivery refers to the destination requirements of the buyer. It may also include the routing given in the purchase order. The routing has a definite influence on the time of delivery and the cost of transportation. Proper delivery assumes an added significance when the buyer asks that portions of the order be sent to scattered branch plants.

Price

The proper price is one that bears a fair relation to the quality and service required by the buyer. It must also be a competitive price — no higher than the vendor charges other customers. Finally, it is a price which the buyer can afford to pay while continuing in a reasonably safe position in relation to his competitors.

Sensitive materials — those with frequent market-price changes — introduce another element into the proper price. This factor may be important enough to receive special attention in the purchase order. The order may call for a large quantity of a specified commodity, to be delivered in quantities as called for by the buyer, at the market price existing at the time of shipment by the vendor.

Value Analysis

Value analysis is a relatively new, scientifically organized method for reducing costs on manufactured items and for encouraging vendor cooperation in lowering costs of purchased items. The same objectives have been sought in the past through such procedures as purchasing analysis, cost analysis, and methods analysis. Value analysis, however, is different in that it sets up a planned organization, often forming a separate section of procurement. It deals largely with studies and analyses of product or component design, materials, methods, and costs. It is not a substitute for engineering and manufacturing cost-reduction work; rather, it is a more refined supplement. After design and manufacturing specialists have completed their work on a new project, value analysis can often reduce costs as much as 15 to 25 per cent.

Scope of value analysis

Value analysis has introduced two new features into procurement: one is the fact that its interests are company-wide; the other is its more intensive cooperation with vendors. This latter phase is often difficult to achieve. Since the vendor is normally not too receptive to inquiries about his methods, and especially his costs, naturally his reaction to this new value-analysis approach on the part of the buyer is often unpredictable. Financial analysis of the vendor's operations may extend to possibilities for reducing his overhead expenses, the substitution of lower-cost materials, savings in transportation and packaging, and possibly the elimination of unnecessary items in an assembly. Value analysis does not aim to "beat down" the vendor's price, but rather to lower it by reducing his costs.

How value analysis developed

Although the Ford Motor Company is credited with using the fundamentals of value analysis as early as 1947, it is generally agreed that the plan originated at the General Electric Company in 1948 when Larry B. Miles was instructed to aid its purchasing department by setting up a value-analysis service. His assignment was for pure analytic work without any authority over operations. The original purpose of reducing the cost of purchased components was approached by making design changes in the specifications.

The first product analyzed contained 115 parts, of which 35 were redesigned. Reduced cost to the buyer resulted from a different approach to the vendor. The request for a revised cost was based on an appeal to scientific facts rather than the prevalent method of negotiation. Developments followed to the point where Miles' value-analysis section was solicited by both General Electric's division managers and vendors for joint consideration of designs, plans, and specifications covering components bought in large quantities.

Techniques of value analysis

For the purpose of visualizing an assembly, its parts are laid out separately in juxtaposition, similar to an isometric drawing. The layout may be placed on a table or fastened to a wallboard. Such a plan enables the analysts to observe the relationships of the various parts. In general, the approach depends on the problem involved and the objective desired. For example, analysis of materials for surveying the possibilities of lower-cost substitutes would require a different setup from that of an analysis of an assembly study.

Organization for value analysis

It is generally agreed that there are three essentials to be met in making a successful value analysis: organization, a program, and qualified personnel. In a large or medium-sized concern, value analysis is usually a section of procurement. There are several reasons for this setup. First, procurement probably has more outside contacts than any other department except possibly sales. Second, procurement is essentially cost conscious. This should be true of most of the management group; but with procurement, discussion of costs is an everyday occurrence. Third, the new approach of procurement is away from "keeping down the expense of commodities" to "earning a profit for the company." Value analysis serves this approach by substituting cost and value facts in place of the old pure price negotiation with the vendor, and by striving to reduce the cost of assemblies by material substitutions, elimination of unnecessary parts, and improvement of production methods.[5]

Policy Decisions

Definitely established policies, in writing, must precede operations if the latter are to be coordinated. Policies are the guiding hand of coordinated management; they establish the working boundaries of supervision, and they prescribe the limitations of management control.

[5] The May 8, 1961 issue of *Purchasing* magazine is devoted entirely to Value Analysis in all of its most recent uses.

Source of supply

In fixing a policy for the source of supply, management must consider such intangibles as reliability, continuous supply, favorable price and quality combination, and service. In addition, the geographical location of the vendor is important.

As an example of *service*, an elevator buyer should give careful thought to the supplier who has a repair station close by. The same is true of production and office machines. High first costs are not necessarily determining factors in buying capital equipment. Continuous operation is more important. The value of service is measured in part by the time required for its availability. Traveling service men are not so valuable as on-the-spot repair stations.

Reliability is best measured by experience. That is the reason many concerns are loath to change vendors even when the new supplier offers distinct price and quality advantages. How long will the new source be available? Confidence is a valuable asset to any sales organization, and it is the spark of profitable trading. Is the offering price or quality a "loss leader," to be withdrawn after being used as an entering wedge? Does the new vendor have sufficient financial backing to continue in the market? Do his prices enable him to make a legitimate profit?

Continuous supply is vital to continuous production processes. Downtime is not only costly because of continuing overhead, but it can have serious effects in failures to meet promised deliveries. Customers are not interested in the reasons; they must depend on service.

Whether the sources of supply should be *single* or *multiple* is another policy matter. Is it better to deal exclusively with a single dependable vendor or to have at least two suppliers in the same field? Which plan assures better quality, service, and price? The answers may well be different for different commodities.

What *channel* should be used in buying? Should commodities be bought through wholesalers, distributors, manufacturers' agents, or direct from the producer? Careful procurement often demands different channels for various commodities, machines, and supplies.

The *geographical location of the vendor* affects freight and other carrying charges. Is the vendor located in a labor-trouble area? Weather is another factor that may affect deliveries if the vendor is located in territory subject to periodic floods or extremes of heat or cold.

Specifications

The purpose of specifications is to secure constructive application of scientific knowledge to service requirements. Specifications are exact requirements; tolerances are the allowances, plus or minus, as applied to the specifications. Tolerance allowances have an important effect on profits. They may apply to the size of a part, the warp-and-woof thread count, tensile strength, color, or any other quality for which the "specs" require a standard. If specifications are drawn loosely, they may defeat their purpose in production. If the tolerances are too "tight," the cost of production is increased and rejects multiply.

To do a good job from the management and production standpoint, engineers should know the use intended. Tolerances on bolts, for example, may be fairly loose without serious effect. On a microscope, the situation is different. The military has learned that engineers can make tolerances unnecessarily tight. The resulting higher costs may not be vital in a war emergency, but slowed-down production caused by unnecessary rejects can be serious.

Before the general use of specifications in buying, the customary procedure was to request a particular brand of the desired item. This practice led to all kinds of favoritism and graft. As specifications became prevalent, loose buyers satisfied public indignation if they represented a public institution — or their conscience, if they bought for private use — by requiring the brand article "or its equivalent," thus retarding the development of real specifications. Another step in less scientific purchasing is the "limited specification" which restricts competition to two or three bidders, or possibly only one. For example, in New York City some years ago, fire-engine specifications restricted the bidding to La France equipment. It is poor practice to draw specifications without consulting the "trade," but it is worse to allow the favored supplier to write them.

Although normal trade practice should prevail, occasionally a vendor is asked to bid on absurd specifications. The classic example is for "steer hides" for certain kinds of leather goods, in spite of the fact that it is impossible to determine the sex of the animal from its hide.

Good specifications reduce disputes between buyer and seller, where mutual confidence generates mutual benefits. Clear and honest specifications, free from limited-supplier or trade-mark clauses, promote competition. Anything which limits the number of competitive bidders, works to the disadvantage of the buyer in both price and quality. Good specifications are also an aid to good inspection.

Reciprocal buying

Reciprocal buying is illustrated by the well-known phrase, "You scratch my back and I'll scratch yours." It refers to an agreement by two or more concerns to buy one another's products. It is generally frowned on by purchasing associations. In most cases, reciprocal-buying instructions come to procurement from "above." In spite of the dubious nature of this business practice, it must not be assumed that it is illegal. Some reputable companies have a committee to consider when and where reciprocal buying is beneficial.

The chief advantage of reciprocal buying inures to the concern's sales department. From the buying standpoint, it tends to restrict the sources of supply. When reciprocal buying is practiced between two or more corporations, all of which are controlled by a parent company, the advantage-disadvantage score is probably a tie. The net advantage or disadvantage depends on the circumstances, each of which must be judged on its merits.

Collusion

Collusion among sellers can reduce honest buying to a hopeless task. In the electrical industry, in certain chemical compounds, and in fire hose, illicit combinations were proverbial in the past. For several years, six or seven chemical companies combined on the classical price of $1.00 for serum antitoxin. There are two plans for combating collusion rackets. One is to report them to the Federal Trade Commission and the other is to mobilize trade associations and state leagues of municipalities in a united frontal attack.

Prosecution of several large electric companies, by the federal Department of Justice, for collusive price fixing received wide publicity in 1961 because of the stature of the defendants and their devious methods. Seven top executives of five concerns, including General Electric and Westinghouse, were sentenced to 30 days, and 25 more received suspended sentences. Altogether, 44 defendants paid $137,500 in fines, while their companies were fined $1,787,000. The case centered around supposedly competitive bids involving billions, given to the federal government. The conspiracy consisted in fixing the bid prices by members of the group so that all members knew, in advance, what would be the successful bid price and who would be the successful bidder. The defendants were prosecuted under the Sherman Act of 1890.[6]

Forward buying

Forward buying may be focused on protecting the company's supply, or it may be speculative. The former is looked on as good practice if it is based on factual information. Speculative buying, however, is generally condemned in those cases where normal profits can be made by following the market, and large losses may result from wrong prognostications of future prices.

Writers on the subject of speculative buying usually condemn the practice for all producers. However, experience demonstrates that it may repre-

[6] For the interesting details of this case, see the article in *Life* magazine for February 24, 1961, pp. 30–31, by Robert F. Kennedy, Attorney General of the United States.

sent good business sense when restricted to sensitive-priced raw materials used in the productive processes. General price fluctuations are less pronounced with finished products than with sensitive raw materials. Under such conditions, and assuming that speculation in raw materials has resulted in an oversupply for production purposes, the speculating concern can sell its surplus for a profit if the market rises, and protect itself against heavy loss on a declining raw-material market by processing it into the finished product.

Personal purchases

Finally, the practice of buying commodities for employees so that they may secure more favorable prices requires a policy decision. We have already discussed the conditions under which personal purchases are ill-advised in the chapter on Personnel Relations. Some businesses view this practice as a commendable service which tends to improve worker morale. Others consider it a management headache which produces more bad than good feeling. Not only do personal purchases take up buyer and clerical time, but complicated problems of exchange and credit privileges are also likely to be involved. In general, this practice is declining.

Forms and Records

Forms and records contain the basic data from which reports are compiled, and the information contained in reports is management's guide for supervision and control. Such important uses establish the necessity for accurate information on forms and records, but too many forms or records are just as inexcusable as too few. Those competent in analyzing forms can often combine two or more existing items, producing generally favorable results. It is the unnecessary forms and records that lead to red tape.

The following list of forms for both private and public purchasing, though not complete, is suggestive:

1. The *requisition* form originates with the using department, and may be "regular," "emergency," "stores," or "interdepartmental." See Figure 28.1.

2. *Invitation-to-bid* form may be used for either negotiated buying or for sealed quotations. This category includes forms for legal advertisements and computation of bids. In either public or private procurement, bid and completion bonds as well as correction and cancellation forms may be used.

3. *Purchase-order* and *Contract-award* forms are fundamental in purchasing. Figure 28.2 is a copy of the standard purchase order adopted by the N.A.P.A. It is interesting to note that because most concerns prefer to use specially drafted purchase-order forms, the "Standard Form" has comparatively few adoptions.

4. *Record of test-analysis,* and all other types of inspection forms are important checks prior to payment of invoices.

5. *Claim vouchers* are occasionally presented by the buyer to the vendor to cover various expenses for which the vendor is liable.

6. *Coordinated purchasing* forms are used by companies having branches, or by public institutions which pool their requirements.

7. *Surplus* or *obsolete* items are reported on special forms, with space for before-and-after disposition records.

8. The *central stores record,* or perpetual inventory is an important form for keeping procurement posted as to the quantities of commodities in storage and available for production purposes. For similar purposes, a daily journal (or *purchase record*), a *vendor record* giving all pertinent details concerning suppliers, a *commodities record* listing the vendors in whom the buyers are interested, and a *price record* for past purchases are referred to daily by the department buyers.

Figure 28.1

Purchase Requisition Form

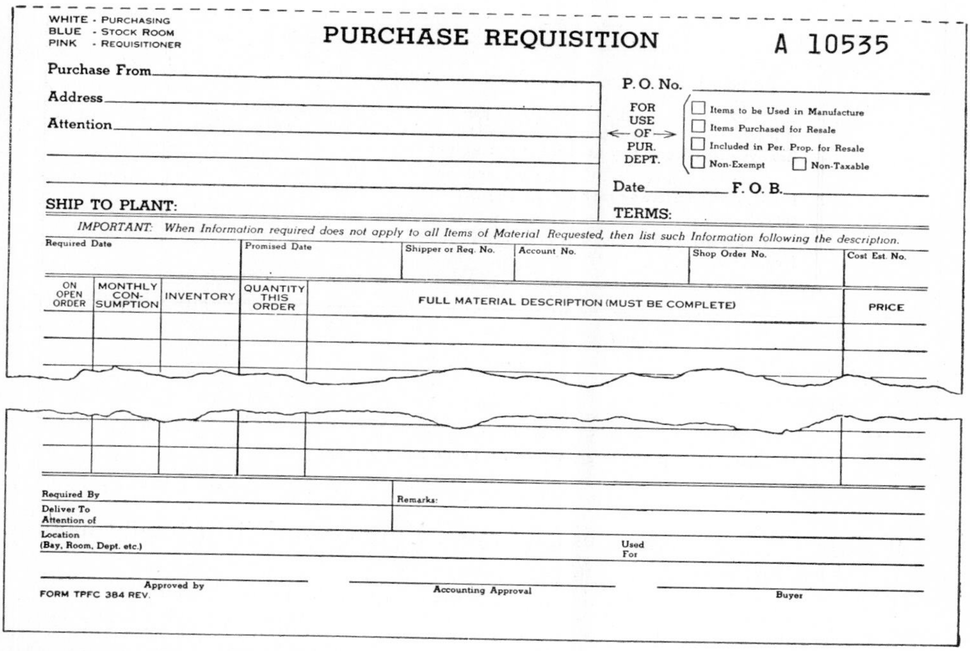
WHITE - PURCHASING
BLUE - STOCK ROOM
PINK - REQUISITIONER

PURCHASE REQUISITION A 10535

Purchase From
Address
Attention

P. O. No.
FOR USE OF PUR. DEPT.
☐ Items to be Used in Manufacture
☐ Items Purchased for Resale
☐ Included in Per. Prop. for Resale
☐ Non-Exempt ☐ Non-Taxable

Date F. O. B.

SHIP TO PLANT:

TERMS:

IMPORTANT: When Information required does not apply to all Items of Material Requested, then list such Information following the description.

Required Date	Promised Date	Shipper or Req. No.	Account No.	Shop Order No.	Cost Est. No.

ON OPEN ORDER	MONTHLY CON-SUMPTION	INVENTORY	QUANTITY THIS ORDER	FULL MATERIAL DESCRIPTION (MUST BE COMPLETE)	PRICE

Required By
Deliver To Attention of
Location (Bay, Room, Dept. etc.)
Remarks:
Used For

Approved by
Accounting Approval
Buyer

FORM TPFC 384 REV.

Courtesy: Thompson Products, Inc.

Figure 28.2

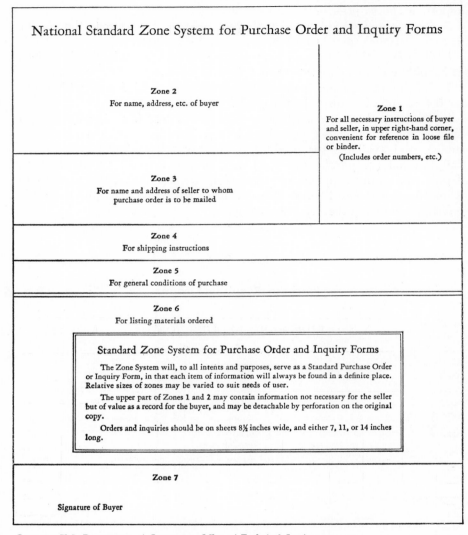

National Standard Zone System for Purchase Order and Inquiry Forms

Zone 2
For name, address, etc. of buyer

Zone 1
For all necessary instructions of buyer and seller, in upper right-hand corner, convenient for reference in loose file or binder.
(Includes order numbers, etc.)

Zone 3
For name and address of seller to whom purchase order is to be mailed

Zone 4
For shipping instructions

Zone 5
For general conditions of purchase

Zone 6
For listing materials ordered

Standard Zone System for Purchase Order and Inquiry Forms

The Zone System will, to all intents and purposes, serve as a Standard Purchase Order or Inquiry Form, in that each item of information will always be found in a definite place. Relative sizes of zones may be varied to suit needs of user.

The upper part of Zones 1 and 2 may contain information not necessary for the seller but of value as a record for the buyer, and may be detachable by perforation on the original copy.

Orders and inquiries should be on sheets 8½ inches wide, and either 7, 11, or 14 inches long.

Zone 7

Signature of Buyer

Courtesy: U.S. Department of Commerce, Office of Technical Services

9. *Expediting* procedure usually rates a form, which is naturally more detailed for institutional buying.

Large buyers of numerous commodities sometimes compile a *commodity index* for each major item to show price trends over a number of years as an aid to forward buying. A *composite commodity index* establishes a similar trend for a large group of commodities in which procurement is interested.

Measuring Department Operations

Organization and duties should have first consideration in an over-all survey. The former would include the accepted techniques for good management, and the latter should cover those things necessary to accomplish company procurement objectives. As with all surveys, the facts may be gathered from operating personnel, including the director, and then checked against actual operations.

A list of subjects for consideration should include:

Organization	Reports and records
Duties and policies	Dollar volume of purchases
Quality of personnel	Number of transactions
Aids to top management	Forward buying records
Department morale	Speculative gains and losses
Intraplant relations	Inventories and prices
Supplier relations	Backlog of requisitions
Community relations	Rush and overdue orders
Control devices	Surplus and obsolete records

The purpose of measuring all management activities is to check against existing methods and plan improvements. Departmental resistance to this procedure is a sign of laziness or of spectacular lack of appreciation for the fundamentals of scientific management. When the department members understand the principles of management, surveys are welcomed.[7]

Conclusions

Procurement has only recently emerged from supervision by the production department to take its place among the established group of management controls. Due to its new techniques used in value analysis, procurement is thinking of its contribution in terms of "profit making" rather than the simpler concept of purchasing. For too many years, it was considered an activity which anyone with common sense could handle and, preferably, the person using the commodities to be bought. Enlightened procurement personnel must receive the credit for the great strides made in its work. The application of scientific principles has now reached a point where top-management can be shown real values in dollars and smooth operations resulting from a well-planned and well-managed procurement program.

The recent exposure of conspiracy among the leading concerns in the electrical industry will be of material aid in procurement's future dealings

[7] *Cutting Costs by Analyzing Values* (New York: National Association of Purchasing Agents, Inc., 1952) presents a "practical purchasing program."

with that difficult situation. This surprising case will furnish a helpful precedent for bringing to justice those who have been shamefully successful in making a farce of the Sherman Act.[8]

QUESTIONS

1. What do we mean when we speak of procurement as "the modern science of purchasing"?
2. What is the difference between procurement and "serialized" purchasing?
3. The typical foreman has several objections to centralized purchasing. What are they?
4. Latin American countries pay their purchasing agents a percentage of the cost of materials and components they buy for the employer. What do you think of this plan of compensation?
5. Purchasing agents now frequently speak of their jobs as "profit making." This is a new idea of purchasing's function. How did it originate?
6. How is the organizational position of procurement determined in the management hierarchy?
7. How are the jobs of the individual buyers determined in a relatively large company?
8. Does the company with a number of scattered branches operate its buying activities on a centralized or a decentralized plan? If you believe the plan must be a kind of combination of some sort, explain how your plan would work.
9. How many of the fifteen advantages of centralized procurement mentioned in the text can you remember?
10. Which plan of purchasing — formal or informal — would you prefer if you were in charge of the department? Give your reasons.
11. What is the historical assumption behind the fact that most government buying is restricted to orders based on sealed bids?
12. Can you name ten activities of the procurement department?
13. About how many purchases should result from one interview with a vendor's salesman?
14. With what other departments should Procurement share the decision whether to buy or make a component?
15. What is the relation between standards and specifications?
16. How do we customarily express the fundamental objectives of modern procurement?
17. What is the special meaning or significance of "quality" in purchasing?

[8] Procurement can probably receive more aid from Quantitative Analysis than any other phase of management. The Learning Curve can be used in helping the vendor reduce his direct labor costs. Linear Programming applies to such procurement problems as economic ordering quantities, materials mix, inventory levels, make-buy decisions, and equipment investments. The Probability Theory is helpful in solving inventory control problems and the probable profits from expanding inventories. All of these techniques are discussed in Chapters 4 and 5.

18. How important is value analysis in modern procurement? Support your opinion.

19. What is your attitude toward reciprocal buying? Give your reasons.

20. What aspects would you consider in setting up a plan for evaluating a purchasing department's operations?

CASE PROBLEM

FULFORD DEPARTMENT STORES, INC.

Fulford Department Stores, Inc. mailed requests to bid on a list of bedding supplies for its twenty furniture departments to fifteen maunfacturers in its territory. The announcement stated that the bidding would be on a formal basis, that all bids must be sealed, and that they would be opened in the presence of the bidders on a specified date and time. The request further stated that price, specifications, quality, and opportunity for vendor service would all be considered in placing the contract which would amount to more than $100,000. It further requested that samples be submitted of materials to be used by the vendors for testing and inspection purposes, and that each bid should be accompanied by a certified check for $5000 to insure compliance in event of award — checks to be returned to unsuccessful bidders.

The items on the bid list included several grades of mattresses, with detailed specifications for each grade. Other items were pillows, woven wire springs, and studio couches, each with detailed specifications as to raw materials to be used, their patterns, strength, weight, etc. Packaging specifications were given and return of empties promised at the vendor's expense, when requested. Delivery by vendor's truck eliminated packaging requirements. All bids were requested f.o.b. Fulford's stores, a list of which were enclosed with the announcement as well as the quantities to each store.

The announcement stated that *separate bids were required on all four items.* Payment was promised the successful bidder within thirty days after receipt and acceptance of the merchandise. Fulford reserved the right to reject any and all bids.

Five bids were opened and tabulated as follows:

Bidder	Mattresses	Pillows	Springs	Couches
#1	$75,800	$8,320	$12,750	$22,000
#2	81,635	7,500	13,225	20,800
Alternate Specifications	70,500			17,225
		"All or none on specifications"		
	Lump-sum bid on all items $120,000			
#3				
#4	75,800	8,320	12,750	22,000
#5	(No bid)	6,275	(No bid)	18,800

PROBLEM: If you were the Director of Procurement for Fulford Department Stores, to whom would you award the contract?

29

Marketing

Definition

Just as one activity after another was added to the simple act of buying to form the new scientific procedure of procurement, so too has the addition of the many services related to selling been brought together and formalized into the department of marketing. Some of these formerly unorganized services were performed by the better salesmen who decided that it was good business to help their customers. As these informal services began to prove their worth, growing competition demanded that they be formalized as part of the marketing job. Gradually, as other ideas were tested in practice for sales promotion and control, they too were added to the activities of the new department.

In its simpler form, marketing was defined as a service to promote the distribution of goods to satisfy human desires. This type of service was forced on producers when they no longer had the time to devote a major portion of their attention to finding buyers for their products. Later, when the expanded marketing function required a broader base, it was defined as "the total of all activities involved in the progression of goods from the producer to the consumer, including warehousing, transportation, wholesale and retail marketing, advertising, and a substantial part of research, engineering, accounting, and financing."[1] Finally, the economist defines marketing as "the systematic, planned, and organized efforts needed to find, develop, and service the markets for the company's products and to identify and specify the products for the company's markets."[2]

The essence of marketing is to have a full appreciation of the potential customers' desires. It requires aligning a company's policies and objectives with customer requirements. Close coordination of a concern's production

[1] As defined by the American Society of Mechanical Engineers, which includes marketing within the broader function of distribution.

[2] From the Foreword by Peter F. Drucker in *Marketing Management* by Lazo and Corbin (McGraw-Hill Book Company, 1961), p. v.

and sales activities is of paramount importance for successful marketing. One of the basic differences between a sales department and a marketing department is the formalization of the responsibilities and duties assigned to each. A company with a sales department performs many marketing activities as a sideline in the normal course of selling; a company with a marketing department prescribes its activities and establishes the necessary management controls to insure their success.

Marketing activities

A fully developed marketing department usually deals with the following activities:

1. Field Sales
2. Sales Management
3. Selection and Training of Salesmen
4. Sales Analysis
5. Market Research
6. Customer Services
7. Advertising and Sales Promotion
8. Product Development
9. Packaging
10. Public Relations, Warehousing, and Shipping

Determination of which marketing activities should be included in the program of individual companies must be based on their needs and resources. In any case, the selected activities and the methods for their accomplishment should be included in a departmental manual. Regardless of the number of activities assigned to the department, marketing has secured a firm position in the top chain of command. It is usually considered of equal rank with production and finance. A brief explanation of the first nine of the activities previously listed will serve to emphasize their diversification.

1. *Field Sales.* This activity brings the company's salesmen in direct contact with its customers. Field sales might appear as a contact solely in the seller's interest, but actually it is just as often a direct benefit to the buyer. Most buyers readily admit that they learn more from salesmen than from any other source. In our discussion of procurement (Chapter 28), we pointed out that many companies require their purchasing agents to see all salesmen.

2. *Sales Management.* The management of field sales relieves the salesmen of most of their planning and paper work, thereby freeing more of their time for the main job. Conducted by the home office, sales management also serves as a centralized control of field sales activities. It is surprising to the student of management to learn that this aid to field selling is a comparatively new activity. No doubt it was difficult for some of the field

prima donnas to appreciate this derogation of their "freedom," but they have come to welcome it.

3. *Selection and Training.* In addition to certain general qualifications, successful salesmen must have special psychological characteristics which have been found necessary for their happiness on a difficult type of job. The scientific selection of salesmen has become a highly specialized skill which regularly helps those concerns which use it to avoid costly errors. Training misfits is very expensive, and a total loss.

Training may be on the job in the home office and plant, as well as in the field under the guidance of a successful salesman. If selling is an important factor in the concerns success, there may be a special training and refresher school. The National Cash Register Company has a self-contained and elaborate setup for this purpose, known as "Sugar Camp," in Dayton, Ohio. Some training schools even include instructions in competitors' products. The training period may run from two or three months to two years before the candidate receives his stamp of approval. The period of specialized training depends on the importance of selling in the company's operations. With well-managed companies, refresher training continues as long as the salesman is employed.

4. *Sales Analysis.* Progressive management wants detailed information about its sales operations. While unit production costs may be well-known, the real cost of selling is difficult to appraise. Paying a selling commission of 3 per cent does not mean that the cost of sales is 3 per cent. Consideration must be given to overhead, advertising, product research, and discounts. Few companies know which product, customer, salesman, or territory is most profitable. Selective selling cannot be programmed unless sales analysis is available.

The *sales quota* fixes the volume of sales expected from a given territory during some future period. Quotas are usually fixed on a product basis to aid production controls and to prevent salesmen from specializing on the sale of low-profit items. Fixing quotas depends on a number of factors. If it can be assumed that the territory is the same as it was during the previous budgetary period, the salesman's past record is important. Naturally, both the salesman and the company expect some quota increase from year to year, based on improved customer acceptance and good will. Company advertising and development work during the past year are considered in setting new quotas. New products and improvements in general business conditions in the given territory also affect the quota.

5. *Market Research.* All research proposes to lead to conclusions based on the analysis of relevant facts. Marketing research is being used to find out about customers, competitors, the relative merits of similar products, and a true picture of current and future market conditions. It also "includes the analysis and study of an organization's products and services, as well as the sales methods and policies which can be used effectively. The analysis

and study of proposed new products, sales forecasting, establishing sales potentials — all these fall within the area of marketing research."[3]

An American Marketing Association's survey of the marketing research studies made by 195 companies during 1957 shows that the four basic areas considered were: (1) products or services,[4] (2) markets, (3) sales methods and policies, and (4) advertising. The survey also indicates that the seven most important market-research activities were sales forecasting, analysis of market size, competitive position of company products, consumer acceptance of proposed new products, analysis of territorial potentials, estimating demand for new products, and comparative studies of competitive products.[5]

6. *Customer Services.* Customer services usually include assistance in merchandising, technical machine service, and sales information. When a textile fiber producer assists a mill in promoting sales of hosiery made from one of his fibers — that is merchandising assistance. When the mill cannot run the fiber satisfactorily and the fiber producer sends a technician to overcome the difficulty — that is technical assistance. When the mill asks its yarn suppliers about deliveries — that is customer sales information.

Many services performed for the consumer by both the producer and the retailer are so generally offered and casually accepted that they are considered an integral part of selling. In the case of producer goods — machine tools for example — installation and servicing frequently mean satisfactory operation for the buyer. The maker of machine tools often furnishes additional service by making periodic inspections and adjustments for a year as part of the purchasing price. This type of service aims to keep the customer pleased and to maintain periodic contacts for potential additional sales. Producer service to machines and equipment may be handled by traveling mechanics, by service branches in large cities, or by the salesmen for minor repairs and adjustments.

In the retail field, customer services are an entirely different problem. There is little general agreement about the amount or kinds of services, or indeed the advisability of any service beyond the bare minimum. Deliveries, credits, adjustments, returns, and guarantees have added a formidable cost in some lines. There is another and longer list of nonprofit services furnished to customers by many retailers, such as restaurants, child care, ticket agencies, travel bureaus, and organ recitals. All of these services, welcomed by the customer in the beginning, and maintained and extended by the retailer because of his desire to meet competition, are doubtless a part of good merchandising, but they add materially to the hidden costs of distribution.

7. *Advertising and Sales Promotion.* An effective program in this field

[3] Richard D. Crisp, *Marketing Research Organization and Operation* (American Management Association, Research Study No. 35, 1958), p. 8.

[4] For assistance in deciding whether to market a new product, see Market Research Series No. 6, of the Bureau of Foreign and Domestic Commerce of the Department of Commerve for a check-list on the "Introduction of New Industrial Products."

[5] *Ibid.*, pp. 48–50.

requires determination of company objectives, planning, direction, and control. The program must be an integral part of the total marketing plan. Even when the product under consideration may not achieve recognition or customer loyalty as compared to other consumer products, advertising and sales promotion represent an investment which can create sales and profits long after the program is over. It is the job of the advertising manager to coordinate the company's advertising program with its marketing plan.

8. *Product Development.* Most executives consider product development to be the life blood of business. There are wide differences, however, in the profits obtained under different circumstances. Few producers expect such a revolutionary development as has been taking place in the electronics field.

9. *Packaging.* Marketing research and product design have altered the box or barrel of our fathers until it is no longer "made"; it must be "engineered" for size, strength, and sanitation. Advertising has become such an essential feature of the customer's package that the advertising department boasts that it has transformed the old shipping box into a traveling billboard. But there are features other than advertising in the modern package. For example, it is considered good salesmanship so to design the container that the ultimate consumer can use it for other purposes after it has been emptied.

Modern packaging is also designed to protect as well as promote the product, and it is the job of the packaging engineers and advertising designers to balance these two features. From the engineering standpoint, it is important to design the container to save space and use the minimum of packaging materials. The satisfactory container is the one that can be packed easily and quickly, shipped safely, and displayed effectively. To the extent that the packaging materials keep down shipping weight, transportation costs are reduced. Modern packaging provides containers that are acceptable in the factory, in transit, in retail stores, and in the hands of the consumer.

Interdepartment Cooperation

Marketing cannot be considered in a vacuum. An example of the very real problems it must cope with is the friendly feud between sales and production. Salesmen want to offer the buyer every possible inducement in quality, price, and variety of product; the fulfillment of all buyer desires is a salesman's dream. On the other hand, production managers have an overwhelming desire to make as few varieties as possible; a single product is the production manager's dream. Because of this fundamental conflict of interests, the sales and the production department invariably clash, and both have excellent arguments to support their contentions. Sales explains that if the company fails to offer variety and special products, customers will drop off. In rebuttal, production contends that unit costs rise so rapidly with increases in variety of the products that the company would find it impossible to hold to competitive costs.

If it were not for top management coordination and control, the contest between the temperamental bosses of production and sales could "stop the works." Marketing management must offer a compromise that will satisfy both sides. The solution must be a compromise in which variety is maintained in nonessentials, while standardization of basic features permits mass production. With reasonable cooperation and the insistence of top management, marketing and production can usually find a satisfactory solution.

Good management requires good communication. This is particularly important in the area of credits and finance. Although credit control was formerly a definite annoyance for the average salesman, experience has demonstrated that he will accept reasonable credit controls rather than lose commissions or salary position because of excessive losses from sales to poor risks. Modern management requires an understanding of credits by sales personnel. Analysis and evaluation can determine the proper credit limit that a prospective customer should receive. Credit information should be sent to the market research manager, enabling him to advise salesmen as to the proper credit limits and terms of payment for individual customers. Close cooperation between the credit and marketing agencies is a must.

A special list of poor credit risks should warn salesmen that these buyers can be sold only on a cash basis. When salesmen are fully advised of such situations, they are able to avoid unnecessary calls. Without management assistance, it is obvious that salesmen would often be misled by the apparent sincerity of the poor-risk customer. On the other hand, some credit departments have a reputation for attaching too much importance to financial statements. Good management can sometimes turn a poor financial statement into a good credit risk, and by the same token, poor management can lead a good statement into bankruptcy. Sales and credit men must cooperate for the benefit of their common employer.

The director of marketing has much to offer in top-management councils where the basic decisions on product lines are made. Usually, a committee comprising the chiefs of production, finance, and marketing evaluates a product program that has been developed jointly by the research and development section of manufacturing and the product-planning section of marketing research. The production representative knows whether a proposed change is feasible with the existing or slightly modified machine and tool setup, the finance representative knows whether the company can pay for the modifications or necessary new machinery; engineering knows about the relationships among machinery, methods, controls, and the skills required for the contemplated change; and personnel knows whether workers can be hired for making the new product.

All of these activities must find a way to work together for achieving company goals, but marketing holds the key position in the decision. Unless it can sell the proposed products, their production will be ruled out or delayed. The purchasing budget is based on sales estimates, as is the personnel budget. Plant expansion or contraction, and the purchase of machines and equipment, depend primarily on future marketing reports. The pivotal position of marketing requires the other departments to cooperate with it as well as with each other. While these conclusions may seem obvious, the desirable conditions they bring about are often difficult to achieve in many concerns.

Marketing Strategy

Marketing strategy is the planning and direction of a company's operations so that it can secure the most advantageous market position that meets customer requirements. It is the bridge between long-range planning and short-term action. Marketing strategy helps company management define in more specific terms how it can achieve company objectives. In setting some of the framework for management decisions, it prevents short-term action from running counter to long-range goals. It acts as a guide to all management levels so that their individual decisions can take into account the needs of other departments. Good marketing strategy provides the most effective insurance for minimizing risks and maximizing profits.

When a company is operating within an over-all marketing strategy, it will have: (1) a clear picture of the domestic and foreign products now being sold in the U.S., (2) an estimate of future demand, (3) a projection of expected profit margins for various products, and (4) knowledge of the proper place of any particular item in the company's total product mix. All of this information enables top management to make the proper decisions regarding the type and quantity of machines required to satisfy the current and future needs of the company's customers.

When setting up a schedule for purchasing new equipment to replace obsolete or worn-out machines, management is primarily interested in lowering unit costs. Even in some large companies, it can happen that these decisions are made without the approval of marketing, in spite of the fact that they directly affect the company's marketing position. However, while a new machine may allow a reduction in unit production costs, the market for its product may actually be declining. The decision to purchase should involve consideration of the possibility of spending the same money on equipment which permits the production of more than one product line to open new markets immediately or in the near future.

As an illustration, let's consider a large firm with marketing offices in New York and manufacturing facilities in the South. Marketing plans to add a product in two or three years to supplement one now offered. The new product will require new equipment. At about the same time, production plans to replace obsolete equipment. Because of the distances involved, several meetings are scheduled between marketing and production personnel for the purpose of reviewing the company's short-term plans in light of its marketing strategy. As a result, production personnel is made aware of marketing's plans. So, in considering the various types of machine replacement, the final purchase is equipped with special attachments to make both the current and the planned product lines.

The saving in new equipment in this case was approximately $100,000, simply because one adaptable machine could make both products. In addition, the company had a better utilization of both equipment and manpower, offering substantial savings in production costs.

How is marketing strategy developed? The long-range plan, outlining company objectives and goals, provides the framework for specific planning on a day-to-day basis. In developing a marketing strategy, the first step is to subdivide the long-range plan into basic functional areas of production, marketing, and finance. The next step is to analyze the specific requirements in each area. This step would consider such factors as raw-material requirements, channels of distribution, and capital investments. The third step provides for effective scheduling, which entails a series of short-term coordinated plans to achieve the desired objectives. It is essential that these short-term plans be simple and workable so that they may be integrated into the day-to-day activities on all levels of management.

Marketing strategy must be tailor-made to meet specific needs. Experience proves that it provides the most effective insurance for minimizing risks and maximizing profits. It enables management to choose the best course of action; to adjust that course promptly when necessitated by changes in outside conditions; and to have an efficient and practical program which permits the company to make the most of its potentials.

Policy Decisions

Policies should represent standard decisions to meet recurring problems of management. They may affect over-all company operations, or be significant for only a single department. In any case, the purpose of policy statements is to save the time of executives and provide uniformity of action. Some of the major items of top-management marketing policy will now be discussed.

Pricing policies are generally established (1) to achieve a proposed return on investment, (2) to achieve stabilization of price and margin, (3) to maintain or improve a market position, (4) to meet or beat competition, and (5) as a reflection of product differentiation.[6] Pricing affects most marketing decisions, and most marketing decisions affect pricing policy. For example, the retail price that consumers would be willing to pay for a particular product might not allow a margin large enough to distribute that

[6] A. D. H. Kaplan, Joel B. Dirlan, and Robert F. Lanzillotti, "Pricing in Big Business," (The Brookings Institution, Washington, 1958), p. 128.

product through normal channels. If the company normally sells through distributors, pricing policies must give full consideration to the margins that will motivate distributors to market the product.

Channels of distribution policies are dependent upon the nature of the product, volume of sales, and trade practices. Some multi-product companies utilize a different channel for each product line. There is no set pattern other than that generally used for the product under consideration. Today, however, marketing is constantly changing the channels of distribution for a given product, thus offering the seller various alternatives depending on his financial ability. There is, for example, a considerable tendency to combine or skip channels. Experience has shown that many who have circumvented some agency of distribution have merely taken over its activities and are paying the costs associated with those sales functions. On the other hand, integration of channels leads to such advantages as (1) better control over product quality and customer service, (2) more effective distribution of the product, (3) reduction in the number of profits that must be paid before the product reaches the consumer, and (4) closer relations with the ultimate user.

Selective selling policies refer to the choice of those territories, customers, and products which will yield the maximum profit. It also means the elimination of those which do not yield a profit. It is an excellent plan for reducing the costs of distribution.

Sales activity may be intensive or extensive. The former realizes the most out of a given sales force to yield what appears to be maximum profit; the latter bases its hopes on future developments. Intensive selling is acceptable until it reaches the point of diminishing returns. This principle can be applied on a territory, customer, and/or product basis. It means the elimination of those factors which do not show a profit nor provide reasonable short-term prospects.

Sales analysis must be made for salesmen, sales territories, customers, and products to give an up-to-date picture of the relative profitability, and/or contribution to overhead of these four inter-related factors. Each must be correlated with the others. Top management must establish criteria for the elimination of unprofitable accounts, products, territories, or salesmen.[7]

Organization

The organizational structure of the sales or marketing department depends on a number of factors, the two most important of which are volume of sales and the nature of the product or products. Whether the department is confined to selling or embraces all the related activities which go to

[7] For a more detailed account of policy making areas for marketing, consult Hector Lazo and Arnold Corbin, *Management in Marketing* (McGraw-Hill Book Company, Inc., New York: 1961), pp. 45–46.

make up the broader function of "marketing," it is almost invariably on a high executive level, reporting to the president or executive vice-president. The general organization is determined by one of three basic considerations: *product, territory,* or *function.*

The *product* plan is used by concerns selling a variety of products. For example, an electrical equipment concern may make a full line of household appliances, pumps for the industrial trade, and motors for machine-tool builders. Obviously, each of the three lines has a distinctly different customer appeal, and may be sold through several different channels. In addition, these products are so different in operation and are put to such different uses that it would be difficult to train a group of salesmen as successful demonstrators of all three types of merchandise, not to mention the three different methods of customer approach necessary to do a good selling job. Figure 29.1 illustrates the product type of sales organization.

A well-known example of organization on a product basis is General Motors, which sells several trade-named passenger cars and trucks. Even within the passenger-car field, its sales organization is definitely split according to the name of the car, and competition among the various makes of this single commodity line is maintained at a high level.

The product basis of organization permits distinct sales approaches to different groups of customers. In addition, it makes possible pre-sale demonstrations and post-sale services of a rather special nature. With some products, neither demonstration nor service is necessary. In other cases, post-sale services have become so highly specialized that they invite criticism because of the unnecessary costs they contribute to the selling price.

The *territorial* plan for organization of sales is used to promote decentralized supervision and centralized control. This type places divisional managers in charge of assigned territories. The extent of their authority depends on the degree of centralization desired. In any case, a territorial organization makes for initiative on the part of the divisional manager and his subordinates. In addition, many territories have peculiar sectional customs and prejudices which can be catered to by the local sales groups. If warehousing is organized on a corresponding territorial basis, deliveries and services are substantially improved. Figure 29.2 illustrates the territorial form of sales organization.

Under real decentralization, the local manager will be circumscribed mainly by the headquarters policy manual. He also receives aid and suggestions which may or may not be applicable to his territory. Centralized control of many decentralized operations can be based on standardized reports from the divisional offices. Reports from each territory can be compared with one another in the home office and checked against established standards, thus furnishing a background for critical analyses and for suggestions sent out to the divisional managers.

Figure 29.1

Sales Organization by Product on Territorial Basis

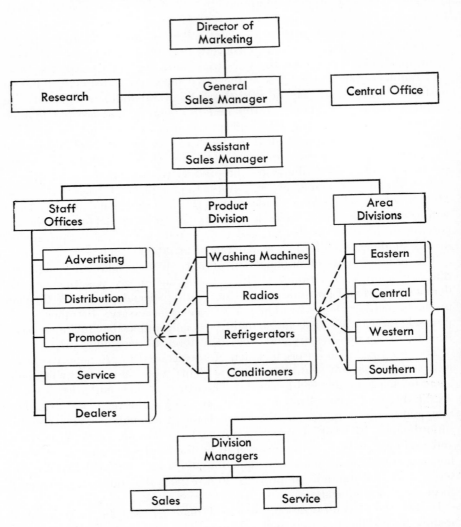

The *functional* plan of organization breaks down authority and responsibility on the basis of sales, services, advertising, sales promotion, research, and foreign trade. The functional organization may be applied to the home office, and if the territorial divisions operate as "marketing" units, it may also be applied to them. The chiefs of the various functional subdivisions at the home office report to the director of marketing. In a territorial setup, they report to the territorial director. The directors of the several functions at the home office perform staff services by giving information and advice to the function directors at each of the branch offices. Such contacts should not be in the nature of commands; often this information and advice are best transmitted through the general manager of the branch for the purpose of maintaining unity of command. Territorial branches may be organized on both a product and a functional basis at the same time if the nature and volume of the product sold warrant such a breakdown.

Figure 29.2

Territorial Sales Organization

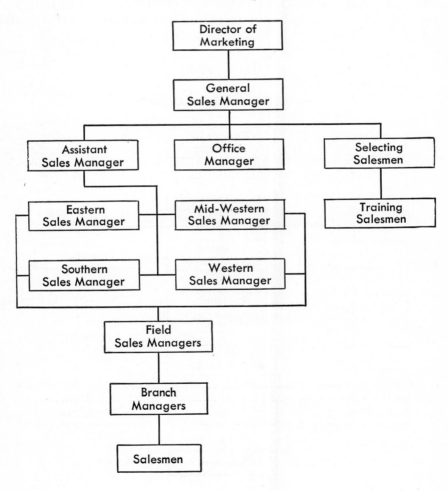

The number of functional divisions at the home office or territorial branches depends on the amount of work involved in performing any given function and on the importance of that function in over-all marketing operations. It may also be related, in part, to the personnel available for key jobs. Figure 29.3 illustrates the functional plan of sales organization.

Two other plans for sales organization are shown in Figures 29.4 and 29.5. The former illustrates the *committee type of organization,* and the latter shows how sales can be organized on the basis of *distribution channels.*

Director of Marketing

The main duties of the director of marketing are to supervise and coordinate the activities of his departments. If operations are organized on a functional basis in the home office and decentralized on a territorial basis, he will have two avenues of control and supervision. His control

Figure 29.3

Functional Plan of Sales Organization

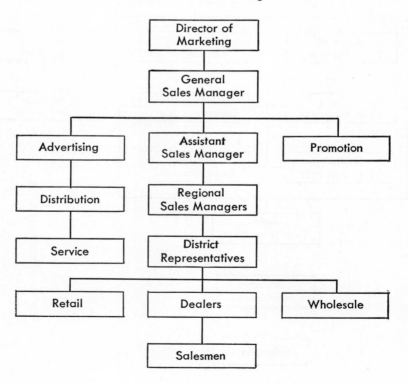

Figure 29.4

Committee Sales Organization

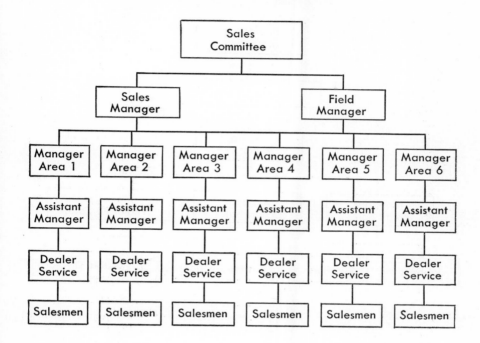

over home-office personnel will be exercised by direct contact and through study of reports. The same procedure will prevail with respect to the territorial branches, except that emphasis will be on reports rather than personal contact. At the same time, the director of marketing or his chief of sales, or their personal representatives should make periodic visits to branch offices for critical field observation.

The director consults with his chief of sales about general policies and strategy, including plans for coordinating sales efforts. He approves and aids in the determination of sales channels and the extent of sales territories. He consults with his chief of sales about the coordination of such functions as sales promotion, advertising, research, and service. He is directly interested in and responsible to top management for the cost of sales, which he watches closely in all of its ramifications — including warehousing, whenever it is allocated to marketing. Under the pressure of increasing public criticism, the cost of sales is being given increasing attention by the chiefs of marketing and sales.

Cooperation with other departments is another duty of the director of

Figure 29.5

Sales Organization by Channels

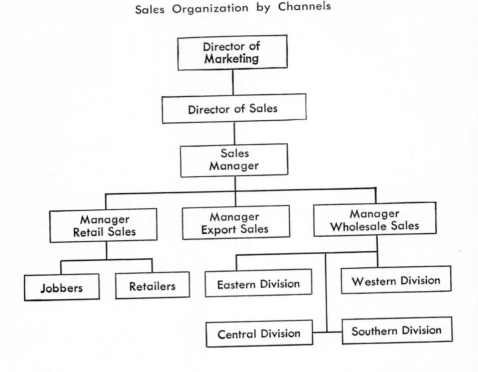

marketing. Coordination within his own bailiwick is promoted by cooperation with other departments. Both the production and credit departments
must coordinate many important decisions with those of the sales department, and this is true only to a lesser extent of engineering.

Customer and public good will are top strategy considerations for sales,
and they should be given the personal attention of the director. *Customer
good will* covers adjustment of complaints from large buyers, and discounts and credit terms for customers. Visits to customer plants and branch
offices often promote friendly contacts and sales. *Public good will* is maintained by participation in community affairs both at the home-office location and at the branch level. Membership in local civic organizations becomes a duty of important sales personnel in the field.

The Cost of Distribution

We have already suggested that marketing steps in to aid the producer
who no longer has the time — or sometimes even the know-how — to sell
his product. This specialized type of marketing must have been successful

in maintaining and increasing sales, otherwise it would not have survived. By expanding markets, it has increased the demands on production. Volume production leads to cost economies and lower prices which make possible larger sales to more people. This spiraling process has a distinctly beneficial effect on our standard of living. Everyone admits it, including sales organizations, which accept full credit for starting the process.

There has, however, been a widespread condemnation of the excessive costs of distribution, which include such items as packaging, servicing, warehousing, and transportation, in addition to selling. Although they admit that positive economic and social values result from "stimulation of demand," consumer and economic research groups have been asking for years whether all the costs incurred are necessary. Recent studies have pointed out that it takes two men to sell and distribute one man's production. A committee of the Twentieth Century Fund estimated that in 1929, only about 41¢ of the consumer's dollar represented production costs and the remaining 59¢ went to pay for distribution. Surveys made since that time have found that the costs of distribution have become even greater.[8]

The Distribution Committee of the American Society of Mechanical Engineers made a study of the same subject since 1929, but it did not arrive at any conclusion about what portion of the consumer's dollar was spent for distribution. It did find, however, that there have been a number of management economies effected in some sections of this field, but they have in large part been offset by increased expenditures for other phases of the distribution function.[9]

Marketing costs are a concern of the producer as well as the consumer since they often form a major part of his total costs, thus influencing the price of his product. In the past when management has tried to reduce costs, it has looked first to the possibilities of economizing in the production process. But with the steady increase in the cost of labor and raw materials since World War II, it is not surprising that more attention is being given to the long-neglected area of cutting selling and distributing costs. While production savings are, for the most part, under direct supervision of the manufacturer, such marketing factors as advertising and transportation are usually hired services, and hence more difficult to control. Pressure from consumer groups, however, is leading to searching analysis of distribution costs. Management's new engineering approach in this field should gradually lead to lower costs.

On the other hand, there is a school of thought, orginating chiefly in the advertising agencies, which holds that distribution costs, far from being too high, might well be increased in the public interest. This claim is sup-

---

[8] *Does Distribution Cost Too Much?* (New York: The Twentieth Century Fund, 1939), pp. 116–118.

[9] Published under the chairmanship of Stokes Tornlin, in the *Transactions* of the ASME in May 1953.

ported by the following argument. As distribution increases, the volume of production must increase to satisfy the ever-growing demand for the product. As volume of production increases, unit cost is correspondingly lowered. Thus, the argument concludes, the more money spent on increasing demand and facilitating distribution, the less the ultimate cost of the item to the consumer. A specific example will illustrate this reasoning.[10] Suppose that in 1870 it cost $250 to distribute a consumer item which cost $750 to produce. This would make the total cost of the item $1000. Now let us suppose that the same item can be produced today for $250 because of large-scale production made possible by large-scale sales. If we assume further that distribution costs have remained constant at $250, then the total cost of the item has been reduced to $500. Thus even though distribution makes up a larger part of the total cost today — 50 per cent, as against 25 per cent in 1870 — the increased distribution costs have had the effect of cutting the total cost in half.

There is some validity in this reasoning, but it is an over-statement of the case for distribution. Even if we accept the assumption that the demand for greater volume of production would not exist without the increased expenditures for promotion and distribution, it would nevertheless be true that the rate of savings effected by increasing the volume of production must eventually shrink to insignificance, for every manufacturing enterprise has a base of fixed costs which are practically irreducible. If, at the same time, the cost of distribution continues to rise, a point will eventually be reached at which the unit cost of the item will begin to increase. Clearly, then, management cannot accept this argument at face value. It must have ways of finding out, first, whether an increased expenditure for distribution will bring about increased demand for the item and, secondly, whether the resulting increased volume of production will bring about a commensurate decrease in the unit cost.

Let us admit that modern distribution techniques have contributed to the reduction of unit production costs. The question still remains: Why should not the application of scientific principles to large-scale marketing bring about reductions in the unit costs of distributing just as they have for production? Final decisions about distribution costs should not be based on the social and economic benefits which have resulted from modern marketing techniques, or on what the traffic will bear, or on the plea that their techniques have made a lot of jobs for a lot of people. The real question is whether or not the cost of current distribution methods can be reduced.

Establishment of more widespread and reliable standards in the various phases of marketing is a basic need. Proposals for points of attack come from both inside and outside the field. They include such suggestions as:

---

[10] Taken from *Does Distribution Cost Too Much? — It May Cost More*, a brochure published by the J. Walter Thompson advertising agency, at the request of the American Marketing Association.

1. Improved planning based on better cost accounting.
2. Application of engineering methods to market analysis.
3. Selection of accounts, territories, and products.
4. Simplification and standardization of styles and sizes.
5. Better methods of handling, shipping, and warehousing.
6. More realistic advertising and sales promotion.
7. Reappraisal of product design and expensive packaging.
8. Reduction of unnecessary and unwanted services.
9. Improved selection and training of sales personnel.
10. Better departmental organization.

In the final analysis, the buying public represents the chief pressure group for bringing about improved methods of distribution. That pressure will be effective only when consumers are educated to the realities of this over-organized field. The distribution agencies cannot be counted on to supply the leadership for training consumers in the art and science of buying; it must come from the consumers' organized groups.

Conclusions

The high cost of distribution is the outstanding subject for controversy in the field of marketing today. Although there is continuous complaining by consumer groups and organized opposition by cooperatives, the advertising fraternity has successfully spearheaded the defense. Improved standards in the various phases of marketing appear to offer the best means of reducing distribution costs at this time.

Organizational patterns better suited to their purposes offer another opportunity for the improved management of marketing. Better planning and more effective controls are always worth considering. Improved sales methods and "truth in advertising" are being promoted by national organizations interested in marketing.

Marketing research will probably work out some fundamental improvements which will benefit all parties concerned. The process will be slow, but it will be objective. Objectivity has been conspicuously lacking in too many of the discussions concerning distribution costs.[11]

QUESTIONS

1. What have been the main characteristics in the historical development of the marketing function? How have the changes affected the definition of marketing?

2. Of the ten activities of marketing listed in the text, what two or three would you criticise adversely from the standpoint of service or cost, or both? How would you correct the defects you mention?

[11] Several portions of this chapter were written in collaboration with Daniel L. Brier, Director of Marketing, Werner Management Consultants, New York City.

3. To what extent do you believe that the average concern knows which product, customer, salesman, or territory is most profitable? If you think the answer is "very slight," then how do you account for such loose management in this department? How can it develop proper controls?

4. Has excessive competition in marketing led to unnecessary customer services? If so, which customer services would you eliminate?

5. Do you believe that modern packaging is worth its costs in advertising and in reducing breakage and spoilage? What are the reasons for your conclusions?

6. What is the so-called "friendly feud" between sales and production? How can it be resolved, and who must do the job?

7. Why is close cooperation between the credit and the marketing agencies so essential?

8. What do we mean by "market strategy," and how is it used for minimizing risks and maximizing profits?

9. How are channels of distribution policies determined? What are the basic determinants involved?

10. To what extent are expenses reduced and profits increased by combining or skipping channels?

11. How is selective selling applied to territories, customers, and profits?

12. What are the three basic considerations on which the usual organization of marketing is determined?

13. What sales organization plan is used for promoting decentralized supervision and centralized control?

14. What is probably the most controversial question in connection with the marketing function?

15. Approximately what portion of the consumers' dollar is spent for distribution of goods?

16. What arguments do the advertising agencies use in urging higher expenditures for advertising and promotion?

17. What is the outstanding need, from a management standpoint, for improving marketing and its costs?

18. How is marketing strategy developed?

19. How many of the ten suggestions for improving marketing can you recall?

20. To what extent do you feel that objectivity has been used by specialists in the field of marketing in their efforts to improve its techniques and reduce its costs?

CASE PROBLEM

THE BRADLEY-EVANS COMPANY

The Bradley-Evans Company has been making industrial knives for about seventy-five years. Until the past decade, the concern's profits have been satisfactory. It has an established reputation for high quality, both in meeting customer specifications and in its own suggestions about design.

The transition from annual profits to losses has been due largely to job-shop methods. However, it is also true that the company has built its reputation and volume of sales on meeting all customer desires for quality knives. Because of its good reputation, the company does a large mail-order business. Salesman training requires at least six months in the plant for becoming acquainted with processes, kinds of steel, and the potential productivity of the various shops making the product. Because of the multiplicity of products, it takes considerable time for the salesmen to become familiar with the various shapes, sizes, and grades of knives and handles.

It is unusual for Bradley-Evans to receive an order for more than a dozen knives of the same specifications. Another problem is the habit of customers, even the large concerns, of placing frequent small orders, apparently in an effort to save themselves the expense of carrying excess inventory. It is not unusual, for example, to receive an order for five each of several different types of shingle or corn knives. This customer habit of buying on a hand-to-mouth basis obviously increases production costs.

The multiplicity and variety of small orders has made it difficult for the concern's semiskilled machine operators to become adept at their work. As a result, it has been necessary to requisition enough material from central stores to make about fifteen knives when the order calls for twelve to allow for possible spoilage of materials and defective workmanship. There has been no problem in getting the customers to accept overruns of from one to three knives, but on some of the more difficult items, the material allowance is often insufficient to fill the order. In such cases, a small supplementary order must be processed.

Bradley-Evans had a survey made of its operations. The report recommended establishing product standards for its line of knives as the basis for simplifying their variety. It was also learned that the continual adjustments for numerous small runs had shortened the useful life of many of the machines, which would soon have to be replaced. The survey showed further that the large number of small orders was causing some of them to be lost in the plant. When delayed delivery brought customer complaints, the order had to be duplicated at a direct loss. It was found that these lost orders were finding their way into the "surplus stock" room. (Management had been going on the assumption that this "surplus stock" was made up simply of overruns.)

As a result of the large number of small orders, the company is compelled to carry large inventories of strip steel in many sizes and qualities. The number of jigs, blue prints, and patterns give ample evidence of the complicated production situation which has been allowed to develop. The storage space for jigs and patterns was expanded recently because of the difficulty in locating items desired for repeat orders, many of which are marked "rush."

It is evident that Bradley-Evans needs more than product simplification, but the report of the consultants has convinced the company president that most of their trouble is coming from too much product diversification — a situation which has been growing gradually worse over the years.

Problem: What program would you work out for marketing the company's products to put it back on a profitable basis? Enumerate the steps you would take and the information you would need to reduce its product line to a reasonable and fairly acceptable basis. How would you get the company's old customers to accept your new sales policy?

30

Office Management

The office collects, stores, interprets, and reports information for use by the other activities of a business. When we speak of office management, we refer to a function rather than the space where its operations are carried out. Recent discoveries of ancient records attest to the fact that their making and storing is an old and important activity. Modern business record-keeping dates from the Industrial Revolution, when the growth of production and trade made it necessary for management decisions to be based on many kinds of stored information. So it is that the office function is often referred to as the paper-work activity. But the office does many things besides merely accumulating data.

Office activities must be so planned that the information in its files is quickly available for the use of management. It must analyze and condense many aspects of its information so that management can make correct decisions in time for their effective use. In this connection, today's office is sometimes referred to as the nerve center for management decisions and business operations. The correct analysis of office records provides for over-all controls by upper management, an outstanding necessity for the successful operation of any business.

Growth of the office function

The increasing importance of the office function is indicated by the relative growth of its employees as compared to the total working force. The U.S. Census Bureau's records from 1870 to 1950 show a percentage increase relative to the working force of from 2.5 to 12.3. Every decade notes a rising ratio of clerical workers as compared to the total working population. The record illustrates how the growing complexity of modern business is dependent on a multiplicity of data for its decision-making and for meeting growing competition. Some of this increase is doubtless due to the ever-increasing number of reports required by various governmental agencies.

Cost of office work

The expansion of office activities naturally leads to increased costs of general business operations. Whether part of this cost is unnecessary and what can be done about reducing it will be considered later in the chapter.

The average executive thinks of three factors when considering the effectiveness of his office. First is the cost of office work as related to sales volume. The other factors are productivity and quality of the work, both of which have an important effect on costs as related to sales. If an executive studies the history of office management costs, he will become interested in improving the efficiency of his own. In the early part of this century, the records show an average ratio of one office worker to ten in the plant. Now, due to the increased complexity of office work, the ratio is as low as one office worker to five production workers. Lack of progress in the scientific management of office work shares a large part of the responsibility for this poor showing. It is no wonder that the authorities in this subject feel that the office revolution is long overdue.

Extent of office work

In clarification of the general activities mentioned in the first sentence of this chapter, the office serves its employer in four important categories:

1. *Office records* cover a multitude of transactions such as financial reports, accounts receivable and payable, payrolls by classification and rates, and other company transactions which may be needed for reference by executives or service departments.

2. *Computations* are one of the main activities of the general office. Payrolls, discounts, and other financial transactions, bank accounts, reserve for dividends, statements, and statistical work of various kinds, including that for general management controls, are all representative of general office computations.

3. *Filing* is the orderly storing of papers and records so that they are immediately available when required. An effective filing system must be planned to make back records as easy to locate as current ones.

4. *Communications* are of numerous types for both internal and external exchange of ideas. Within the company there are conferences, activity memos, and instructions. Outside communications consist chiefly of letters, telegrams, transcribed telephone conversations, orders, and contracts.

The general office also acts in a purely service capacity for other activities of the company. It performs such facilitating services as duplication, mail, messenger, office supplies, reports, and often reception, in addition to the major services already mentioned. Office effectiveness is judged by its ability to render services adequately, correctly, and promptly. Not only the nature of the work, but its volume and scheduling must be geared to the departments which it serves. For example, its volume will fluctuate with the peaks and valleys of the workload in the production department or with such financial operations as collections, payrolls, and fiscal statements. This situation makes comprehensive scheduling difficult for many office services. Since one of the problems of office management is to devise methods for leveling its workload, the necessary changes must be worked out in cooperation with the departments served.

Office Problems

Office problems may be divided into four general categories: organization, planning, techniques, and control, and they will be considered in that order. Because office management is classified among the "nonproductive" activities, it has received relatively little attention until recent years. A growing recognition of the relation between office management and the work of the so-called productive activities, as well as its increasing relative costs, have led to serious attention to the possibilities of applying scientific principles to office operations.

Organization

As with other activities, the type and extent of office organization should be determined by the nature and number of its objectives. Obviously, the plans for obtaining these objectives must be aligned on a functional basis in the order of their importance and with due regard for their relationships with other departments.

Before discussing internal office organization, consideration should be given to its place in the company's general organizational scheme. The production, finance, and sales functions are usually considered of paramount importance in any business organization. Engineering, legal, personnel, and purchasing functions often rate second place, although their rank depends largely on the relative importance of their services to individual concerns. All of these activities serve production, finance, and sales. Office work is in the same category if it is centralized to serve the whole company, but of lesser importance organizationally if its activities are dispersed throughout the company's departments.

The rank of office services in the general organizational pattern depends on their importance. In an insurance, distributing, or financial organization, office work is of major importance, and the office manager assumes an important position in the organizational hierarchy. In an industrial concern, his importance is somewhat less. If office work within the concern is highly centralized, the office manager's position is more important than it is in a decentralized scheme, where the work is done within the several departments.

The Office Manager. The extent and effectiveness of office work is largely dependent on its manager, irrespective of his title, which may be office manager, controller, or chief clerk. In any case, the person who has charge of office work must have a thorough knowledge of his company's operations. If he has charge of a general office, his grasp of operations must extend to all departments of the business because he must cope with problems involving interdepartmental relations. He must have some research ability, be able to analyze situations for better planning and methods, be diplomatic, and know how to sell his services to the operating departments.

The manager of a large office should have executive ability along with a background of training and experience in the work. He must be patient and cooperative, critically creative, and possess facility of expression for gaining acceptance of his ideas and for making effective reports. The office manager who has these qualifications will find a real challenge in working out plans for his subordinates, his methods, layout, and general management problems.

The Office Manager's Boss. To whom should the office manager report? This is simply another way of asking about the relative importance of office activities. In a financial organization, the office manager will probably report directly to the president of the company. If, on the other hand, the office function is less important but highly centralized, he may report to an executive vice-president or to the vice-president in charge of finance. When the importance of office work, even though centralized, is considered minor, it will probably be placed under the control of the treasurer or controller. When the general office of small and medium-sized concerns acts as a purchasing and personnel department for the entire company, its enhanced importance may again bring it under control of the chief executive officer.

Office Personnel and Purchasing. Is it advisable for the general office or the departmental office to perform its own purchasing and personnel functions? In the large company where separate personnel and purchasing departments have been set up to serve the entire company, it often happens that the office management claims a special status for its activities. "Our personnel and purchasing problems are unique," the argument runs, "and therefore we should perform these two functions ourselves." This is the old argument, so often raised by line officers in every department, that service functions should be decentralized and placed in control of the departments directly concerned. The reasoning is no more valid for the general office than for any other department. The personnel and the purchasing departments can usually do a better job than the general office could do for itself.

Centralization or decentralization of office work refers to the method of handling its activities. When the office is centralized, it is subject to the control of one person.[1] Under an over-all centralized plan, correspondence and filing for the entire organization are done by sections of the general office. The decentralized form of office organization assigns office workers to the departments concerned. Both of these plans are pure types not often found in actual practice. If either type is adopted, experience dictates shifts one way or the other because of the disadvantages encountered or the suspected advantages of the other plan. Both schemes of organization have advantages and disadvantages, often leading to some sort of combination, in an effort to secure the advantages of both types. Before adopting any combination plan, it is well to consider the advantages of the two types.

Advantages of Centralization
1. Improves utilization of personnel and facilities
2. Enlarges opportunities for training and pay raises
3. Facilitates improvement and uniformity in methods
4. Increases specialization among the workers
5. Decreases costs of supervision

Advantages of Decentralization
1. Encourages specialization of departmental work
2. Improves supervision of those directly interested
3. Personalizes control over office employees
4. Minimizes delays in departmental routine

A combination plan customarily assigns the writing and filing of confidential correspondence and contracts to the operating departments, while correspondence and filing of a general nature, as well as messenger, mailing, duplicating, and communication services are centralized in the general office. The extent to which correspondence and contracts may be considered confidential depends on the nature and size of the concern, the repetitive nature of its office work, and the attitude of its executives. Trial and error usually determine the effectiveness of various combination plans, many of which represent shifts in emphasis due to reorganizations and executive caprice. The outstanding example of shifting control is in stenographic work, where the "pool" and individual service plans alternate as their relative advantages and disadvantages come to light.

A further refinement of the combination plan assigns stenographers and various types of clerks to individual departments, subject to general control of the central office. This method attempts to take advantage of better training methods and improved worker satisfaction resulting from company-wide clerical classifications with standard wage and salary scales.

[1] Centralization may also refer to the method of handling work within the office itself. Examples of this kind of centralization would be stenographic and filing pools.

Planning

The scientific approach, which includes plans based on analysis and synthesis of all the relevant facts, is just as important for effective office management as for production or any other function, and it is applied in the same manner. Any normal activity has problems which may be solved by the scientific approach, tempered by common sense. This approach simply breaks down the specific problem into its components for the purpose of study and analysis. The problem may be dynamic, but its isolated components can usually be reduced to static "pictures," an almost necessary plan for analysis. The scientific method is not difficult to understand, but its application often requires mental effort, which probably explains the resistance it often encounters.

When the objectives of the office operations have been clearly formulated — and this will always involve policy decisions on the part of top management — then plans can be devised for carrying out these policies in action. Planning involves procedures and systems which are essentially based on standards of some kind. Because business operations are decidedly dynamic, the planned systems which guide those operations must be kept in tune with the functions they serve. This means that they must be subject to periodic review so that they continue to be helpful in serving the control phase of management. A frozen system that no longer serves its purpose can be worse than no system at all. The lack of system at least permits flexibility, something which a frozen system prohibits.

Planning consists of determining what should be done, how, when, and where it should be done, and often includes who should do it. When unplanned work produces acceptable results, it is by pure accident; the natural result is confusion and uncoordinated effort. Peak workloads is a situation calling for careful planning. Rule-of-thumb decisions may provide for hiring extra help or working the regular staff overtime. Neither plan requires thought worthy of a manager. Excessive costs and wasted efforts are the customary result. Additional office machines or office service companies are more likely to be the proper solution to peak and valley workloads. Another feature that permits planning for unexpected workloads is increasing the versatility of competent employees, thereby permitting the shift of human factors from work valleys to its peaks. Most office work is repetitive in nature, lending itself to effective planning. Operating standards have been applied to many phases of office work.

Techniques

Simplification. The best way of performing any task is the simplest way. The prime tool for obtaining more and better office work with less effort is simplification. Another important result of simplification is reduced costs, in which management is always interested. Simplification may be applied to office organization, its machines, its methods, and its layout. In addition, simplified office procedures and methods should improve forms, records, and reports.

The application of the principles of scientific management to office principles and practices was first undertaken about 1925 by the late William H. Leffingwell. Much progress has been made since that time, but compared to the possibilities, it has been relatively insignificant. The two chief reasons for delayed progress are those usually encountered — general antagonism to change and the common belief of office managers that their job is different and apart from the usual run of management problems. Actually, office work is susceptible to the same kind of analysis as the production processes.

The specific reasons for the slow progress of scientific techniques in office management include the following beliefs of office managers:

1. Operation inefficiencies in the factory are observable immediately as unreasonable costs, which is not true in the office.
2. Standards are more easily set in the factory than they are in the office.
3. Factory errors are easily visible as scrap, while office errors are corrected without visible increase in costs.
4. Factory work is more repetitive than office work, which is therefore less susceptible to standardization.[2]

Simplification in office work results in a regular flow of work and effective management. Simplification of methods adds refinements to the flow of work. Paper work should flow from desk to desk, based on a suitable physical layout. Office work may be pictured on flow charts for major activities and on process charts for individual operations. It is only by the study of such charts that dependable improvements can be made with respect to movements, operations, interruptions, and inspections. Nonproductive time can be easily spotted and minimized. Combinations of individual activities will suggest themselves, as will changes in the sequence of operations. For example, a simple but too customary practice in office management is the assumption that all filing cabinets should be placed along the wall, whereas the frequency with which the filed materials are consulted is the only rational criterion for determining their location.

Standardization. Standardization formalizes simplified procedures. We have already spoken of the peaks and valleys in the office workload. There is an unfortunate tendency to hire office personnel on the basis of demand at the peak of the workload. Whereas most office managers complain that they are understaffed, the truth is that if they applied the methods which production has worked out, they would often find themselves overstaffed.

[2] W. C. Perry, "Why Work Simplification in the Office?" *The Journal of Industrial Engineering* (August 1952), Vol. 3, p. 7 *et seq.*

The scheduling of workloads and the timing for work standards should be set up only after a proper layout of desks and offices has been accomplished. Standard times for operations are absolutely necessary for proper scheduling and the best use of personnel and equipment. Most utility companies have learned that they can level their workloads by reading meters and sending bills on a geographical basis, spread over the days of the month. Office work can be subjected to the same principle on some different basis.

The need for standardization of office forms is obvious when one observes the numbers, sizes, colors, and composition of existing ones. Not only the different numbers on invoices, job orders, tickets of various kinds, requisitions, and routings, but the different locations of these numbers on the different forms is baffling and time-consuming. Without standardization, supervisory or top-management control is illusory, if not impossible.

Standardization establishes definiteness in operations as well as in duties and responsibilities. The duties of office workers, as well as the methods of their operations, should be worked out and reduced to writing in an operational manual. Standard workloads for various activities are important in work distribution, planning, and control. They are also a morale booster in that they make it clear to every employee just what is expected in quantity and quality of work to be performed. It takes the guessing out of the eternal question, "How am I doing?"

Office standards are important as they apply to methods, workloads, machines, and equipment. Workplace layouts should conform to the best operating standards, and office layout should conform to the most effective flow of work. The capacity of the general office is sometimes unnecessarily reduced by setting up private offices for supervisors. Private offices can interfere with as well as expedite the flow of work, and very few of them are conducive to supervision by observation. These comments do not apply to offices devoted to planning and controlling, two high-level occupations which cannot be combined satisfactorily with supervisory duties in a large concern.

Centralization. We have already discussed centralization in connection with organization, in comparing its advantages and disadvantages with those of decentralization. Here we are interested in centralization from the standpoint of managing the office work. The assembling of scattered office activities into a single department usually increases the opportunities for superior services at reduced costs by the use of modern machines and equipment. Most office work is more dependable when done on machines. In addition, machine operations invariably increase office productivity.

When office work is centralized, it is easier to train workers to acquire multiple skills in preparation for periodic shifting of personnel between peak and valley operations. Another contributor to improved office management is the improved working conditions of the past decade.

More attention should be given to grouping within the centralized department the so-called secondary office services, including typing, duplicating, and filing operations. These services are customarily improved by the specialization which results from centralizing them. In addition, peak and valley workloads can be still further leveled through the improved scheduling made possible within centralized groups.

The advantages and disadvantages of centralized service units must be weighed in reaching decisions. For example, it is often claimed that top and middle executives are hampered in their work by pool assignments of stenographers for secretarial work. The executive prefers the services of one secretary because she becomes acquainted with his problems and his vocabulary. The contention has considerable merit. The only solution seems to be full-time secretarial assignments for such executives. Their desires do not, however, vitiate the principle that the greater portion of stenographic work is better performed by assignments from a stenographic pool. The question of filing is another case in point. To what extent should filing be centralized, and when should files be maintained in the using departments? The answer depends on the amount of use required by those departments which insist on decentralized filing.

Control. Control is the checking of performance against plans. Standards are the prime necessity for exercising control in any phase of management. The virtue of setting up standard methods, procedures, and systems is, first, that they make many decisions automatic, freeing executive time for exceptional problems and, second, that when something does get out of control, the existence of standards makes it easy to locate the source of the trouble.

In Chapter 10, we saw how production-control systems are made up of routing, scheduling, and dispatching. All three of these procedures are based on planning and are used for controlling operations. Similiar procedures can be applied with equal effectiveness to the establishment of office routines. A single transaction can become very complex, involving operations in several different departments. For example, the purchase of an article is of primary concern to the purchasing department and to the department which will be using it, but the transaction may comprise operations in the receiving, inspection, and accounting departments, as well as in central stores. The records of all these operations are likely to be centered in the general office. If the transaction is to flow smoothly and economically, procedures must be standardized and systems must exist which will provide for the coordination and control of all these interlocking steps.

The control of office work includes the direction of its employees' activities so as to maximize productivity, quality, and service, and make them at least equal to accepted standards. But not all office controls depend on the application of scientific techniques. Some important controls are best maintained through direct contact between the superior and his workers. It is difficult, for example, to maintain standard productivity in the repetitious types of office work, except through inspirational supervision and direction. The control of costs is another difficult and important aspect of office management. It demands continuous supervision and frequent shifting of approach to prevent the lessening of its effectiveness.

Reports on office activities are one of the standard means of control. The conclusions and recommendations flowing from good reporting help office supervisors as well as those in other departments; but good reporting is impossible without adequate and timely records. In a very real sense, therefore, some office controls are dependent on records which have been adjusted to the purposes of control under a special set of circumstances. Thus the question of what constitutes good reporting is pertinent to the internal control of many office jobs.

Brevity, clarity, timeliness, and sequential presentation are the outstanding criteria of all reporting, but particularly of those reports issued by the central office. Visual presentations such as charts and graphs are particularly useful in forecasting and saving the time of executives and supervisors. In addition to the day-to-day control of office activities, an audit of general operations should be made periodically. To minimize the possibility of neglecting some phase of the work, a well-prepared audit check-list is a necessity. Such a list should be expanded from time to time as experience demonstrates the advisability of getting closer to the fundamental causes of difficulties in managing the office.

The measurement of values against the cost of office records and reports often results from adequate check-lists. Attempts are often made to establish the value of records and reports by the extent of their distribution. Obviously, use rather than distribution is the determining factor. Measurement and control of office personnel should follow, in part, from a considered application of the results shown on their service records.

Physical Facilities

Office location

Some businesses, such as insurance, real estate, and banking are fundamentally office operations. The location of their offices depends on the nature of their services and the type of customer they serve. However, because of the "office revolution," factors once considered paramount are giving way to new considerations in many offices. For example, large insurance companies have been moving from downtown buildings to the suburbs of large or medium-sized cities. The availability of parking facilities is one reason for the shift, but increased productivity resulting from a more appropriate environment is more important.

Industrial concerns occasionally have their office or administration building located at some distance from their plant, but the more prevalent custom is for factory offices to be located in the factory building. Within the plant, the top floor is occasionally chosen because of better natural lighting and reduced noise. The ground floor, on the other hand, offers easier access for outside business visitors and is more generally favored. Unit or specialized offices may be located adjacent to the department they serve. Similarly, large one-floor industries occasionally have office units of the personnel department located at strategic workplaces throughout the plant.

The purchasing office is frequently found to one side of the main entrance, probably to keep vendors' agents away from the production quarters, as well as to offer prompt service to the traveling fraternity whose time is limited by their own home-office scheduling. Availability, adaptability, light and ventilation, nearness to such employee facilities as washroom, proximity to industrial operations, and over-all costs all help determine the office location within the plant. Sometimes it is decided that these advantages can best be obtained by having a separate office building adjacent to manufacturing operations.

Office layout

Continuous flow of work and a pleasing appearance are two important factors in office layout. One text on office management lists nine major considerations in planning the office layout:[3]

1. Departmental Relationships
2. Flow of Work
3. Number of Private Offices
4. Use of Partitions
5. Personnel Space Requirements
6. Outer-Office Space Utilization
7. Elimination of Hazards
8. Flexibility and Expansion
9. Special Rooms

The importance of working relationships with other departments will naturally affect the layout of a general office. The flow chart will furnish the primary guide in applying simplification principles to the layout, including maximum utility in grouping of activities and the elimination of unproductive movements so as to accomplish a continuous work flow.

The trend in office layout is to reduce the number of private offices. The new idea of large office spaces is recommended by the psychologists for maximum productivity of routine activities. The new plan reserves private offices for those who hold conferences or do some type of research work.

[3] Charles B. Hicks and Irene Place, *Office Management* (Allyn & Bacon, Inc., New York, 1956), p. 250.

When the private-office demand is too strong among middle management, the so-called "modular" office is substituted. Figure 30.1 shows a small group of these DuPont functional unit offices which someone has referred to as "silly little tables with windshields." Modular offices are semi-private

Figure 30.1

Functional Unit Offices

Courtesy: E. I. Du Pont de Nemours & Co.

Figure 30.2

A Typical Office of 1895

Courtesy: Traveler's Insurance Company

and provide space for a larger number of minor executives and supervisors than does the "private" office grouping. Complete use of available space by DuPont-developed functional furniture is shown in the office illustration. The company reports that this arrangement provides a degree of quiet, privacy, and prestige not possible in open areas with conventional furniture.

Figure 30.2 illustrates the type of office from which the modular design is descended. It is evident that office space was not at a premium at San Antonio in 1895. It appears, also, that the female had already invaded the office precincts more than sixty-five years ago.

Movable partitions are not new. They represent an easy method for taking care of the desires for experimental changes. It is reported that the Navy used this idea to show its superior management efficiency over the Air Force; it put its partitions on casters. The other listed items conducive to good office layout are self-explanatory. It should be observed in passing that the production department is far superior to the average general office in its scientific planning for layouts.

Office appearances are important employee morale boosters and invariably lead to improved productivity; they also have an effect on customer relations. The application of color dynamics has become a technical aid to all kinds of work in the office and the shop. Lighting engineers have established beneficial standards. Regulation of the office temperature, ventilation, and cleanliness are all within the control of management.

Office equipment

Office equipment also has a distinctly beneficial effect on the total environment if it is properly chosen. But the pivotal relationship to equipment is in costs of operation. One answer to rising office costs is found in better equipment, better methods, and better surroundings. One large producer of metal office furniture summarized the situation in this way:

> It costs any company at least $3000 a year per employee — for salary, floor space and overhead — to operate its office. In an office of only ten employees, this means $300,000 over a ten-year period. For only 1 or 2 per cent of this fixed expense, the office could be outfitted with the finest, most modern, most economical and efficient metal furniture, plus the best in lighting and decorations.

The fact that offices in banking and insurance are almost invariably more attractive than those of industrial concerns is attributable in large part to the dominance of the production department in the typical industrial enterprise and the consequent neglect of the positive values to be gained from making offices more attractive.

Someone has rightly said that "office machines are the machine tools of management." The revolution in office machines during the past decade or two has been quite as fascinating as the progress of the textile machines during the first two decades of the Industrial Revolution. Office-machine progress of the next decade promises almost unbelievable results. Recent mechanical advances have expanded the range of management, thus making big business more amenable to the guidance of centralized control. Office machines are now available that make the increasing piles of paper work much smaller than they were at the beginning of the century. The compulsory needs of decreased costs and improved executive control will spur the progress of office-machine improvements.

The purpose of office machines is to save space, time, cost, and effort, and to improve the quality of the work. Microfilming has reduced to a small fraction the space formerly required for storing records. The electric typewriter has reduced the fatigue of the typist, increased her output, and saved the time and eyesight of those who must read carbon copies. Dictating machines have allowed time for secretaries to devote to other work. Bookkeeping machines have reduced errors, saved operator time and energy, and reduced the floor space required for that operation. The card-punching machine, card sorter, tabulator, and collator make it possible to process nearly a million accounts every day.

We have just about finished our first decade of experience with electronic controls for office work. Some of the results have demonstrated that with these new tools we will be able to use more refined techniques for managerial controls. An I.B.M. advertisement concerning the possible aids of its "305 RAMAC" machine to office work states that "instead of processing data in accumulated batches, each transaction is recorded in Disk Storage as it happens." It further claims that when the machine is used for inventory control and billing, it can from a single order:

Determine availability	Invoice the customer
Price each item	Prepare accounts receivable
Adjust stock balances	Accumulate data for sales analyses
	Credit salesman's commission account

This machine is only one of a number on the market for similar purposes. As a group, they pose the possibility of a high degree of automation in office activities; they represent the greatest step forward in the office revolution of the past decade. From this position, they pose two major problems: (1) How can the small operator afford to take advantage of this new equipment, and (2) What effect is it going to have on the employment of office personnel?

The most effective of these machines sells for as much as a million dollars and rents for approximately $25,000 a month. These figures put them beyond the reach of even the medium-sized companies. Ordinarily, management can be only amazed at the larger output of these complicated mechanisms with the same or fewer employees, and their economies in processing time, space, equipment, and greater accuracy.[4]

The answer to this problem is the establishment of "Service Centers" by several of the large producers of electronic equipment for office work. For example, the Univac Service Centers have made available to the smallest concerns all the advantages of machine accounting without the usual investment, rental, and staff problems. The service is used only when needed, and paid for as used. Peak loads can be rushed through this service at minimum cost to the user, especially if it has punched-card equipment. Under this plan, the Service Center can be used at nominal cost just as though it were a department of the using concern.

The second problem, that of the effect of these new machines on the employment of office personnel, has no easy answer. It may follow a course

[4] For more details, see the results of a survey of some twenty companies as set forth in the *Monthly Labor Review* of the U.S. Department of Labor for April, 1960, pp. 376–380. This article by Edgar Weinberg is entitled "Experiences with the Introduction of Office Automation."

something like that of employment shifts and unemployment during the first Industrial Revolution. If business in general continues to expand during this adjustment period, displaced office workers may be transferred to other jobs. There is no disputing the fact that office workers are already being affected by the new equipment. *Commonweal* magazine estimated that unions in the U.S. lost almost half a million members between 1956 and 1958, and the process is continuing.[5] Office employees of the United Steel Workers and the United Automobile Workers were chiefly affected. In April, 1960, the N.L.R.B. was asked to poll Local 889, a white collar union representing office workers at the Chrysler plants. The president of the local reported that in 1957 they had 5000 members, but only 4000 three years later, and "the loss is due mostly to inroads of automation in offices."[6] Chrysler had 200 payroll clerks when it turned over that work to a computer; after the change, the job required about 60 workers.

One saving grace for displaced workers caused by office automation is that it takes about three years for complete installation of an automatic system. In the meantime, the company affected has time to find reassignments for employees who have lost their original jobs. In the study of twenty new firms using electronic computers by the Bureau of Labor Statistics, it was found that about one-third of the original office employees were reassigned one year after the operation of the new computer. In conclusion, this is the type of problem that brings good fortune for those who have been trained for the new jobs, and at least temporary misfortune for those who have not. If handled wisely during the necessary waiting period, and if business prosperity continues, there appears to be no reason for union leaders to panic about the introduction of office automation.

Conclusions

Some of those conversant with the field of office management feel that the human antagonism to change will hold the techniques in that field to relatively slow, steady improvements. Others, and they are certainly in the majority in 1961, feel that the next few years will firmly establish the revolution of office equipment and management. The pressing needs for office management are better planning and controls. Improved organization and procedures are already being forced on office management by the advent of electronically controlled equipment. The typical office manager should seek the advice and assistance of specialists in organization and methods. Their analyses will lead to improvements patterned after some which have been installed successfully in the plant.

There is no doubt that electronic computing equipment will be increasingly used in some form by even the small companies. In the long

---

[5] Declining Union Membership," *Commonweal* (February 19, 1960), p. 562.
[6] Quoted from "Office Automation Hits the U.A.W.," *Business Week* (April 9, 1960), p. 58.

run, that change will bring about more office centralization. This shift to centralization will become more necessary as management must depend on information coming from the general office for the solution of its increasing competitive problems.

Finally, the effect of office automation on its personnel is still unknown. The answer will depend largely on how the managerial human element conducts itself in meeting this new challenge for social betterment.

QUESTIONS

1. Why is filing so important to office management?
2. What is the present ratio of office workers to the total working force?
3. What three factors does the modern executive consider in judging the effectiveness of office work?
4. In what general categories does the office serve its employer?
5. How is the peak-and-valley workload disturbing the efficient handling of office work? To what extent do you think the situation could be remedied by "pools" of different types of office workers?
6. Why is it advisable for the centralized office manager to have a clear understanding of the work of all the departments of his employer?
7. Is it advantageous for the general or departmental office to have charge of its own purchasing and personnel activities?
8. What are the advantages of centralized office work?
9. Do you feel that standards are more difficult to formulate for the office than they are in production? What are the reasons for your opinion?
10. To what extent could standardization be established in various phases of office work? How could standards be applied to methods, workloads, machines and equipment?
11. Do you believe that the accepted style of private offices could be improved to turn out greater quantity and quality of work at reduced cost? What changes would you suggest?
12. How can the control factors of routing, scheduling, and dispatching be applied to office work?
13. Where, in your opinion, should a centralized office be located in a manufacturing company?
14. What should be the determining characteristic of the plan for an effective office layout?
15. Do you feel that the production department has any responsibility for the uninviting appearance of many offices?
16. What are the prospects for a revolutionary improvement of office machines and equipment in the near future?
17. What effect, if any, will improved office equipment have on the ratio of clerical to production workers?

18. What two outstanding management techniques are needed for the more effective operation of office work?

19. How can the small office make use of the new electronic equipment?

20. Why was Procurement's interest in studying the advantages of the modern advances in office equipment practically nonexistent until about 1960?

CASE PROBLEM

UNITED DISTRIBUTORS, INC.

The general office manager of United Distributors, Inc., buyers for a chain of department stores in New England, has been severely criticized for some time by several of the buying departments of the company. The tenor of the complaints concerns his lack of cooperation in getting out the office work in proper shape and on time. It is also alleged that either his filing system is inadequate or he allows his staff to be dilatory in supplying requested correspondence, contracts, catalogues, specifications, and other papers to the buying departments.

United Distributors is owned and operated by a group of forty stores to serve as a centralized purchasing unit. Its operations are divided into thirty departments, each specializing in buying a classified group of merchandise. It is housed in a combination office building and warehouse for samples in a large industrial city. Its vendors are fairly well scattered throughout the country. Because there are definite buying seasons for most of the commodities on United's lists, "rush" periods follow one another in fairly rapid succession. The activity of these periods is intensified by the fact that the companies served by United, in their desire to keep inventory investment down, tend to place their orders at the last minute and then expect immediate delivery.

The office manager has called attention to this general rush atmosphere in defending himself before his critics. As a counter charge, he suggests that if the chiefs of United's thirty buying departments really wanted smoother operations, they would urge the department-store members of the buying syndicate to make up their requirements several months in advance, so that the general office could improve its service and not be put under constant pressure.

The general office has seventy-five employees, all engaged in typical office services. It maintains a stenographic pool and centralized filing for all buying departments. In assigning stenographers to buying executives, it makes an effort to send the same girl to each buyer whenever possible. The files are set up on a commodity basis, with a cross-reference index to help locate requested items.

The rush atmosphere has made for poor morale among the employees, most of whom are women. There is a more or less constant feeling among a complaining minority that they are given unfair workloads and that the manager favors those who appear to be doing a superior job because of less strenuous assignments. The turnover of office workers has been about 15 per cent, with most complaints coming from the newer employees.

The executive vice-president suggested a year ago that the manager should write an office manual to be used in training new employees who are now compelled to learn on the job by observation. Work assignments are made by four of the older women as requests reach the office. No attempt is made to group the types of assignments, nor have any work standards been established. The manager contends that the constant pressure of rush requests has made it impossible for him to find time to prepare a manual which, he agrees, might help the situation. His counter-proposal is that he be given two men to assist him in managing the office. He further contends that the girls are underpaid in comparison with other office workers in the city, and that management should install an incentive-pay plan so that he "can recommend selected jobs for higher salaries."

The office manager has been with the company ever since it started operations, about twenty-five years ago. He was first a clerk right out of high school, when there were five employees in the general office. Chiefly because he was the oldest of the five male employees in point of service, he was promoted to office manager two years ago, after serving in various clerical capacities for twenty-three years.

The general office is located in the center of the large second floor, with private buying offices lined around the outside walls. The personal facilities for the employees are excellent except for the lighting, which is admittedly below par. The office layout, which should be improved, is strictly conditioned by its center-of-the-floor location and supporting posts.

The office manager hires his own help, who are given the usual morning and afternoon rest periods, and two weeks' vacation with pay.

PROBLEM: If you were employed by United Distributors to survey their general office operations, how would you proceed in gathering the detailed information on which to base your recommendations? With the information already available from the statement of this case, what recommendations would you suggest to improve operations and morale in this central office?

31

Research and Development

Research is the scientific investigation of the known for the purpose of discovering the unknown. The late Charles F. Kettering, former vice-president of General Motors in charge of research, said that we need research to point out our present shortcomings and ways in order to overcome them and to add to our present store of fundamental knowledge for use in future developments.

Development is the improvement of existing things, ideas, and methods. It is frequently difficult to separate research and development. The latter is often referred to as research, probably because it sounds loftier. Both are important and each lends impetus to the other.[1]

There are two fundamental types of research — pure and applied. *Pure research,* also called basic and intensive, is the quest for new discoveries and new factual knowledge which it is hoped will lead to new principles or techniques. *Applied research,* also called extensive, is the application of established scientific principles and knowledge to the solution of specific problems. Here again the division is not clear-cut because applied research occasionally leads to discoveries which become part of the body of pure scientific knowledge. Pure research is pursued for its own sake, but often leads to discoveries not contemplated at the outset. DuPont's discovery of the nylon polymer is an example of pure research, whereas the development of the fiber from nylon is an example of applied research.

[1] Air Force Regulation No. 80–4 (March 1, 1949) refers to research as "studies and experimentation to insure timely improvements in concepts, techniques, and materiel for personnel utilization, training, management, planning, operations, intelligence, engineering development, production, supply, and maintenance, by application of the best scientific knowledge, personnel, and facilities to specific problems and promising fields." Although military verbiage seems to have lost its laconic quality in this instance, the definition appears to fit what we are here calling "development" rather than "research."

Fields of industrial research

Industrial and business research can be divided roughly into two fields
— technical and nontechnical. The technical field is largely devoted to
products, materials, mechanical equipment, and technical methods. The
nontechnical field covers the economic and social conditions affecting business and the many phases of management where research may lead to improved productivity, lower costs, increased sales, and the improvement of
labor-management relations. A brief list of research purposes, without
regard to their technical or nontechnical characteristics, would be to:

1. Reduce the cost of production, sales, and distribution
2. Develop new products, materials, methods, and machines
3. Improve materials and develop substitutes
4. Increase the use of existing products
5. Improve management techniques in all activities
6. Develop improved methods for coordination and control
7. Improve administration and public relations policies

In order to survive, individual businesses must make a profit in one or
more competitive fields. The pace is set by those concerns which keep in
the forefront with products and services at prices the public will pay. In
recent years, the pace-setters have been those firms which have realized
the value of research. What are some of the management phases of business and industry that can be corrected through research?

1. *Unsatisfactory products* put on the market while still in the experimental stage lead to expensive upkeep and unsatisfactory service for consumers. There are mechanical products so designed that they require
magicians to repair them. Products for which parts are difficult to obtain
are also unsatisfactory.

2. *Unsatisfactory service,* especially in the retail trade, leads to decreased
sales and profits. When a department store sells red porch chairs and
delivers green on Friday instead of Wednesday, as promised, with an error
in billing against the customer's interest, it needs quality control. The
nature of its failing can best be isolated by research.

3. *Selling prices too high* to meet competition or customer finances are
invariably found among the nonusers of research. Rising material and labor
costs can frequently be offset by improved management, machines, and
technical methods.

4. *Pre-recession planning* is often neglected or poorly done because the
economic facts are lacking or their significance is not appreciated. The
consequences of inability to plan for "suspected" recessions are obvious.
Worst of all is the "rule-of-thumb" plant expansion, with its increased
operation and management expenses. Unreasonable enlargement of physical facilities is one of the causes for the enforced transfer of ownership to

more competent management. Any contemplated expansion should be tempered by scientific research, which offers an opportunity to minimize shocks by analysis of social and economic factors.

5. *Waste of materials* can be reduced through research. The development and use of powdered metals for making small parts by pressure and heat (sintering) practically eliminates the waste that occurs from the machining method, besides doing a faster and cheaper job. This process was developed through research and is still being refined by it. Much avoidable waste results from the use of materials of unnecessarily high quality.

6. *Waste of manpower* by poorly scheduled production is often caused by the failure to study markets and to employ some of the tested means for better leveling of demand. Research can minimize a lot of the temporary employment and unemployment by companies which accept the "inevitable" as long as it produces a reasonable profit. The rational stabilization of industrial employment must develop on the company level through research. It cannot be accomplished by government fiat.

7. *New products that do not sell* could be avoided if large-scale production of them was begun only after receiving favorable findings from scientific market and product research, already a well-established technique. This procedure would prevent losses to the concern and to society. The Bureau of Foreign and Domestic Commerce of the Department of Commerce has issued a check-list on the "Introduction of New Industrial Products" containing the following items:[2]

1. The market
2. Buying habits of the market
3. Firm's relation to the market
4. Competition
5. Seller's price policy
6. Channels of distribution
7. Sales promotion
8. Management of sales force
9. Sources of ideas for new industrial products
10. Major purpose for which new industrial products will be made
11. Design and engineering factors
12. Production factors
13. Materials factors
14. Service factors
15. New capital investment factors
16. Relation of new products to existing plans

Questions are asked under each of these topics leading to answers that will help in formulating rational conclusions. In addition to the factors

[2] Market Research Series No. 6, 1937.

noted above, there are other pertinent queries listed in a category entitled "Other Questions." This bulletin is highly recommended to anyone desiring a scientific approach to the problem of determining whether or not to market a new product.

8. *Public relations can be improved* through appropriate research techniques such as the attitude survey. Questionnaires submitted to a sample of the general public invariably produce unanticipated criticisms of company methods, products, or services, some of which can easily be corrected. Research on the types and content of company advertising can determine the effectiveness of the program. The objectivity fostered by the use of research methods will help, more than any opinions of top management, to separate the company's false and uninteresting publicity from the true and pertinent.

It must not be forgotten that employees are a part of the public, and anything that builds the workers' loyalty to the company enhances the company's prestige in the community. When employees feel that they work for a good company, their attitude is bound to filter into the community and improve the personnel department's opportunities for recruitment. Also, a favorable employee reaction to company products or services is bound to be reflected in the attitudes of that part of the general public with whom the employees come in contact. Outsiders assume that the company's own workers know the value of its products.

Growth of research

Under the title "Research Booms," the editors of *Nation's Business* predicted that "big breakthroughs are coming in research in 1961." As examples, they cited new power sources, desalting of sea water, plastics for home building, and new and stronger metals. The use of satellites for expanding and hastening international TV communication is already in use. Industry's expenditures for research climbed from $3.6 billion in 1953 to $8.4 in 1958, to $9.4 in 1959, and over $10 billion in 1960. "Research work done by industry for itself and the government in 1962 could top $12 billion."[3] Specialists in the field predict that with accelerated spending for explorations in space, the research expenditures for 1970 may well top $20 billion.

The government's contribution to research of private firms amounts to 57 per cent of the total cost, due mainly to increased programs in defense, space, and atomic energy. The federal government is also financing a large share of the research work done by universities.

In 1954, the scientists and engineers on research payrolls numbered about 553,000; the number now so engaged is about 800,000 according to the latest government figures. The subject interests are shown by the training

[3] *Nation's Business* (June 3, 1961), p. 470.

of the bulk of these scientists. Engineers comprise 80 per cent of the total; the next highest is chemists, with about 20 per cent of the total.

Pure research is the weakest link of our research program, just as it has been for many years. In other words, most of our research is directed toward commercial objectives. Because pure research has an over-all social benefit, it seems proper that large research funds for that field should come from the public treasury. In addition, financial restrictions prevent even large concerns from some types of pure research. Whether or not it is a virtue, most of the government's research expenditures are for instruments of destruction. If the enormity of their power saves this nation from paralysis in the first instance and eventually raises our standard of living, the program will have been justified.

Industrial research

In spite of the government challenge, industrial research is not lagging. Figure 31.1 is the new research building of the Portland Cement Association which houses thirty separate laboratories. In 1950, some twenty industries contributed to a total investment of over seven million dollars for the establishment of quarters for three research institutes at the University of Chicago.

The arguments used to obtain these contributions are interesting. In the first place, it was easy to demonstrate that the success of many of our largest companies grew out of research, carried on in some cases while the companies were still very small. In the second place, it was pointed out that several European countries were far ahead of us in fundamental research. In fifty years, 20 Nobel prizes came to the United States in physics, chemistry, and medicine, while 119 went to Europe, of which 36 were for German scientists. It was also pointed out that during the last war, four of the outstanding research developments were "foreign born" — atomic fission in Germany, penicillin and radar in England, and blood banks in the Soviet Union.

General Motors, DuPont, Dow Chemical, General Electric, and Eastman Kodak are representative of our largest industrial researchers. At the same time, they are among the best of the stable profit earners.

University research has been growing steadily during the past twenty-five years. Originally small laboratories dealing mostly with pure research, they have been increasingly subsidized by business associations, such as the Leather Research Institute at the University of Cincinnati. Another factor contributing to the growth of university research is the practice of accepting contracts from industry and government agencies, with twofold benefits: the universities have been able to increase the knowledge of their scientists, while the purchasers of their wares have been assured the highest type of research ability at reasonable costs. In the neglected field of management research, the University of Pennsylvania has the Frederick Winslow Taylor Management Laboratory. In such a research center, business has an opportunity to cooperate in working out new management techniques which have been comparatively neglected for what is thought to be more profitable technical research.

There are numerous *private research* laboratories, usually nonprofit organizations with considerable funds at their disposal. Some operate nationally on a contractual basis, while others specialize on industry or regional problems. An example of the regional bureau is the Southern Research Institute, with headquarters in Birmingham, Alabama, sponsored by some of the country's largest industries.

The cost of research

Most research is expensive, but particularly pure research where profitable results are unpredictable. Business leaders who refuse to appropriate

Figure 31.1

New Research Laboratory

Courtesy: Portland Cement Association

Figure 31.2

General Motors Research Center

Courtesy: General Motors Corporation

large sums for research base their decision on its "gamble" nature. The question is: When do research appropriations cease to be reasonable? Many detailed questions must be answered before the decision makes any sense. Besides, the answer may well be different for various companies and fields of inquiry. The question of expense is a relative one, suggesting that the real question is: "Will it pay dividends"?

It must be remembered, too, that research failures do not always mean losses; negative results sometimes have value. As Charles F. Kettering has said, "Tell me the reason why something cannot be done and you have been helpful in narrowing my field of attack." That is to say, a research project may have to be abandoned because some one problem proves to be — for the time being at least — insurmountable. Nevertheless, the project is not a complete waste, for once the *cause* of failure has been isolated, future researchers in the area will know on what specific element they must concentrate their efforts.

Since it is not possible to eliminate uncertainty from research work, it should be kept under control. The costs should be kept consistent with the value of the solution sought. Even when the main purpose has not been achieved, the work already done occasionally accomplishes some unanticipated purpose of value. The first requisite of research control is the establishment of cost estimates by project. If the time and cost estimates are fair, then lack of results after the estimated time and money have been spent suggests frank discussion of the value of going further. The research record at the time of discussion, together with the opinions of the researchers, must be weighed by those with a subjective interest; to stop or go on is largely a management decision.

Some companies do not know the true cost of their research programs. Time and funds may be exhausted because operating departments are allowed to call on the research agency for answers to their production problems. The real cost of such research diversions is seldom known. Certainly no company should undertake a program beyond its current financial ability on the theory that it is a sure profit bet for the near future.

Research and taxes

The tax laws occasionally slow research progress because of the different tax treatment of capital expenditures and expense items. Expenses can be deducted during the tax year, while tax deductions for capital outlays must be spread over the life of the item concerned. Research projects are frequently considered capital outlays for tax purposes unless the taxpayer's research department has been long established. Because some research reaches no profitable conclusion and other types are intangible, it is often difficult if not impossible to calculate the various projects properly, even when they are not chargeable to expense.

These complications between taxes and research, and the uncertainty of the latter, occasionally lead business men to postpone the establishment of a laboratory or the pursuit of a contemplated research project. Business and industry want the cost of most research treated as an expense for tax purposes.

Research and patents

Who should own the patent rights to research projects financed by the government, and worked out to a large extent with government facilities? This new disturber of patent progress was brought before the Congress in 1961. The Long Bill, introduced by Senator Russell H. Long of Louisiana, provides for government ownership of patent rights under such circumstances. One or two government agencies have been following this practice for some time, but most of the departments allow the contractors to file for patent rights on results they work out under government auspicies. Under this plan, the government reserves the right to make use of such findings without the payment of royalties to the patenting contractors. The new approach for government ownership of patents on all of these discoveries has considerable support. Vice Admiral Hyman G. Rickover testified that "where the government bears all, or nearly all of the cost, where the facilities belong to the government and where the government bears all the risks, the people should own the patents." The main holdouts on this new plan are the Defense Department and the contractors.

The arguments against the Long Bill are that many of these research and development findings result from previous years of preparatory research, and the government is allowed to use the final results without paying royalties. The opponents also contend that the government is in no position to exploit inventions commercially, and if it did, such competition would be injurious to our competitive enterprise system.

In reply, the proponents of the Long Bill point to British practice where the government has set up the National Research Development Corporation, licensed to develop and produce new discoveries for use by the general public, with the government receiving the royalties. Maurice A. Crews, Assistant Commissioner of Patents, has contributed something to the controversy by citing a recent study which shows that 60 per cent of the patented discoveries come from individuals or small organizations. He also adds that the ratio of patent applications from individuals and small concerns has stood at about 40 per cent for the past two decades.

This attack on contractor rights to patents under such circumstances has a strong public flavor. It will be interesting to see the results and the effect it may have on private contracting of government research and development.

Research teamwork

The 1961 annual meeting of the American Association for the Advancement of Science emphasized the fact that scientific research has been so complex that future discoveries will have to be made by teams of scientists, representing various fields. This is the basic idea of Organization Research. More than one paper presented at the meeting emphasized the fact that when one individual finds an answer to a problem, it results largely from luck. This is especially true of pure research, a lagging field which will be boosted by more extended use of research teams. Dr. Frederick Dietz estimated that the U.S. Government devotes 1/10 of 1 per cent of its total expenditures for basic research, which is not nearly enough. He further contends that we can no longer depend on European sources which have supplied most of the basic research in the past. The field of astronautics is an outstanding example of the possibility of advancing a new frontier when it receives the combined attention of researchers from a number of branches of science.

The value of research

The evaluation of applied research may be based on several criteria, such as:

1. Its economical value as expressed by profits
2. Its social value as expressed by improved living standards
3. Its efficiency as expressed by its ability to meet budgeted time and costs
4. Its new products and improvements to existing products
5. Its improvement to existing processes
6. Its ability to discover or develop new raw material sources

The *economic value* as measured by profits was well expressed by a leading security analyst: "Study the names of the stocks known as market leaders and you'll have a list of corporations that engage in extensive research." In the long run, where large sums are required for a balanced research program, the records show that industrial research provides excellent returns. It is interesting to note that many large concerns have pursued their most profitable research work during periods of business recessions.

The *social values* of research stem from reducing the costs of existing products and the introduction of new products. Both help in improving living standards whose evaluation is difficult to measure.

The *efficiency of research methods* is one valid basis for measuring its value. The factor of effectiveness in the pursuit of goals would be expressed in the department's organization, program planning, and the coordination of its activities.

Cost reduction and product improvements should be credited to the social value of research, either directly or indirectly.

Improved processes reduce unit costs and possibly selling prices, and hence make another contribution to improved living standards. To the extent that research reduces processing costs, it offers opportunities for increased wages and dividends.

New raw material sources may have inestimable value as the old sources become depleted. They furnish immediate values to the extent that the substitute materials reduce the cost of production.

Any reasonable evaluation of pure research is extremely difficult except on a long-range basis. It must also be realized that research evaluations may be made on an over-all basis or on the results obtained from individual projects. One must be careful to differentiate these two approaches when attempting to evaluate research.

Management research

Research for improving the methods of management is relatively neglected, even by companies which hold research techniques in high esteem. Too many seemingly capable executives feel that they were born that way. This delusion often leads to undue self-satisfaction, especially when profits are showing reasonable vitality, in spite of the fact that selling prices may be unreasonably high. The prevalence of this attitude among corporate management, particularly just below the top level, has served to minimize management research on executive methods.

Good executive judgment, like good research, is reflected in decisions made after an objective analysis of all the facts. The high-salaried executive who makes intuitive decisions is often only high-priced, and caricatures of his type are not entirely without justification. Since he feels that there is no place for research in his private bailiwick, he is often in the position of denying to both investors and consumers the advantages that a research program could bring.

What is the cause of this defensive attitude? In part, it is due to a lack of training in the principles of management. Executives do not always appreciate the fact that current tested principles were once unknown theories, brought to light by analysis and trial, which means by research. Lack of familiarity with the causes of management problems is likely to forestall the best plans for solving them. Failure to consider all aspects of a management problem before making a decision is working by hunch rather than by that degree of scientific analysis which the problem deserves.

The development of controls and standards in managing is one fertile field for business research. Controls can neither be developed nor put into effect until known standards are available for use in exercising them. The development of control standards for the various phases of business and industrial management would furnish a much needed scientific foundation for dependable managing. If functional standards were available, many prospective concerns would remain in that category instead of being washed out later through legal process. The manager who justifies the size of his salary by reference to company profits during a boom and rejustifies it during a recession by pointing to the unexpectedly small size of his company's losses, should become interested in some of the answers which management research could supply.

Research and war

During World War II, articles in the Sunday supplements telling of the wonderful postwar offerings of scientific research helped to create the widely accepted myth that war was, in some way, justified by the stimulation it gave to research and the postwar rise in living standards. But even though it is a matter of historical fact that the by-products of war have subsequently contributed to the well-being of societies at peace, it is not therefore legitimate to contend that war is a good thing for research. The great technological advances of wartime were made possible only through large government expenditures to mobilize available research talent and to permit the concentration of many minds on a few all-important war problems. The same money and talent could be mobilized just as effectively in peacetime. One might reply that it has taken the stimulus of a major war to organize research on this vast scale. To the extent that this objection is valid, it is an unfortunate commentary on the arrangements which our society, at peace, makes for the organizing and financing of research. Had there not been a war, it is quite possible that nuclear fission would not have been developed as soon as it was. At the same time, if the government were freed from the threat of war, it is just as possible that funds which were used to pay for superbombs would have been available for large-scale research in such areas as the causes and prevention of cancer, polio, and heart disease — areas in which research today must be supported largely by voluntary contributions from the general public.

Far from being an intrinsic aid to research, war has the effect of stifling many kinds of research that might lead to higher living standards. The high tempo of applied research during a war is possible only because of the scientific theory that has been developed by basic research during the preceding period of peace. When rapid production of war materials becomes the outstanding demand, pure research is bound to suffer. War stifles research not only by dictating what problems will be investigated, but also by the blight it casts over scientific manpower. Trained scientists are diverted from their fields of greatest competence, and future scientists, if they are not killed on the battlefield, are at best losing valuable years of training in their chosen fields of specialization. Dr. Raymond B. Fosdick, former president of the Rockefeller Foundation, has said that war's interference with our scientific training "ground up the seed corn of scientific progress in the next generation to make a day's feed for the war machine." Successful war cannot proceed without exacting a high price from research.

Research organization

Research is frequently a function of the engineering division, but just as often it is organized as a separate activity with its director reporting to someone in top management. Another common characteristic of the research setup is an advisory committee consisting of such interested members of management as the heads of engineering, finance, production, and sales.

Besides lending its aid to the director of research in management procedures, the committee frequently fixes research policies, within the purview of general company policies. Research policies are concerned with the selection of projects, budget quotas, and criteria for determining whether a project should be abandoned. Such policies may set financial and other standards for research personnel and facilities.

The degree to which the committee guides policies depends on the circumstances in individual companies. Its power may be restricted or its approval may be required even before a research project is begun. In any case, its advice is probably welcomed on the question of whether to pursue a project past its original budget allowance. Committee decisions dilute the responsibility of the director of research in matters of high policy and low predictability. In addition, the committee system fosters the cooperative attitudes of other departments toward research.

It is customary in many organizations to break down research into its various fields. Some companies even allow research to be done by some of the operating departments concerned. For example, marketing research may be a function of marketing or sales, and production research may be assigned to engineering. As a general rule, there will be better cooperation among the various branches of research if they are centralized. Cooperation is important to the extent that it can lead to better studies and more

Figure 31.3

A Research Organization Chart

Organization for Research: The Procter & Gamble Company

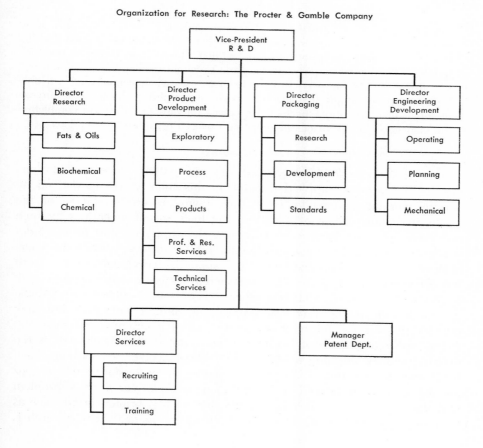

dependable conclusions. In some fields, the coordination of company research is necessary. In addition it offers opportunities to reduce costs. If the purpose of industrial research is to reduce operating costs, centralization of responsibility will produce better results. Figure 31.3 shows the research organization of a well-known company.

Research management

When research reaches the proportions it has in many of our industries and universities, the problem of its management becomes important. Scientists are not necessarily good managers, and good scientists, having a creative bent, do not care to be burdened with managing. New York University set up a course or curriculum in "Management of Research and Development," including twenty-eight subjects for which lecturers are drawn mostly from research departments of large industries. The University's prospectus states the need for and the purpose of the course as follows:

> The rapid growth of industrial research as an "industry," with its ever increasing roster of employees, makes it imperative that individuals be trained for the duties and responsibilities of its administration. There is an increased need for training subordinates and new personnel to carry out the continuing administration duties during the postwar period when research in connection with new processes, products and markets will present a complex problem. The purpose of this course is to train personnel to carry forward to successful completion the managerial problems of the industrial research organization.

Conclusions

Organized research has developed only since 1900. Prior to that time, most of the pure and applied research in this country was carried on by persons working independently in their own laboratories. Some of the results were outstanding — as witness the long line of inventions by such men as Edison and Steinmetz. However, the efforts of most of the independent researchers were undoubtedly lost to society because of unorganized and under-financed plans and sporadic individual efforts. Until the last decade, most of our notable research has been of the applied type. In the field of pure research, a number of European countries have led the procession for a long time. Several of our largest industries are now pledged to pure research on a large scale, with encouraging prospects.

The *research attitude* of letting the facts lead to the conclusions is the only foundation for dependable results. Preconceived conclusions have hurt scientific research, even in high places. A professor of one of our leading universities, called to Washington to do research on a problem with some political significance, reports that he was briefed in advance as to the conclusion desired. The correct attitude in management research is to judge objectively and recommend constructively. Fault-finding is not the proper attitude for industrial surveys and research. Besides immediate conclusions, management research contributes established criteria which can be fed back for use in subsequent problems of a similar nature.

Pure research is the feeder for subsequent applied research. Without the former, the latter will be largely sterile. There is a distinct opportunity for an enlargement of the basic research field in this country. It should not rest so predominantly in the hands of the federal government and a few of our giant industries.

Technical inquiry has been the major concern of industrial research. Its more tangible and profitable results have been one of the causes for the lag in management research.

Applied industrial research has two phases — the improvement of products, processes, and techniques, and the prevention, by warning against them, of futile management plans, products, and techniques.

Small-scale research has been giving way to the heavily endowed private and industrial laboratories, to the possible detriment of the total research purpose. Bigness in research cannot alone guarantee the greatest social benefits, especially with its opportunity to withhold, for financial reasons, some of the best fruits of its efforts. Some plan should be devised for the encouragement of small-scale research in fields fitted to its purposes and resources.

Wartime research should be appraised at its true value rather than be made the subject of human-interest magazine articles. When the situation is seen rationally by those on high government levels, including Congress, we shall avoid repeating the errors in the organization of research which occurred during the last war.

Management research must be established on an organized basis, similar to that of the technically applied variety. The application of organized research will increase the usefulness, reduce the costs, and aid in preventing some of the false starts of those concerns which already find managerial controls difficult.

Government aids to research should be accomplished by easing its taxes as well as by direct financial assistance.

Recorded research is imperative in all of its statistical and other details so that another scientist can take over if necessary; otherwise, some of its fruits are lost. Detailed progress records and findings are necessary even for projects which do not have a successful conclusion. Records save time and expense when they can be used in some later research by isolating the problem hurdle which could not be surmounted, and by pointing out which methods have not proved useful in attacking the problem.

The value of research, as measured both by profits and social benefits, has been so well established since 1940 that there is little doubt that research will continue to expand. A future danger for research could develop from its outstanding record of success, which might encourage large1 financial outlays than some firms could reasonably afford.

QUESTIONS

1. How would you define research? How would you define development?
2. Why is it that this country is behind several European countries in the pursuit of pure research? What can be done about it?
3. How does pure research aid applied research?
4. Why have most concerns done such a poor job in the field of pre-recession planning?
5. How would union philosophy influence management's research concerning the general subject of wasted manpower?
6. How would you plan a research project in the field of public relations?
7. What appears to be the relationship between the volume of research by industrial concerns and their profitability?
8. What arguments were used to induce some twenty industries to raise seven million dollars in 1950 for establishing three research institutes at the University of Chicago?
9. How has the recent development of research at a number of our universities benefitted their teaching programs?
10. Why is it desirable to save all the details of unsuccessful research projects?
11. To what extent can research be controlled — even pure research? On what two bases are attempts to control such research made?
12. How would you decide the delicate question of government right to patents resulting from the research of private concerns when all the bills are paid from government funds?
13. How has the teamwork of research developed the new quantitative analysis phase of Organization Research?
14. How can research be applied in the development of new raw material sources, especially in those fields where the old sources are becoming depleted? Can you give an example of this application?
15. What has been the chief cause of the comparative lack of research in the improvement of management techniques?
16. To what extent, in your opinion, has war research succeeded in raising the standard of living in this country?
17. To whom should the management of industrial research projects be delegated, and why?
18. Would you have research policies made by a committee of management, or would you leave it to the research director? Why?
19. How does New York University justify its curriculum for "Management of Research and Development"?
20. What danger is involved in industry's or government's management dictating the answer to research projects before the work is begun?

CASE PROBLEM

THE SEBRING ENGINEERING AND MACHINE COMPANY

The Sebring Engineering and Machine Company manufactures a diversified line of textile and special-purpose machines, and consumer hard goods. It has fifteen scattered plants, some of which specialize on particular products. The company employs about 15,000, of whom some 3,000 are skilled mechanics. Its products are distributed nationally, for which it employs an extensive and highly trained sales force.

Sebring's textile machines are sold to the hosiery, underwear, cloth, and neckwear trade. Competition is keen in this line because of almost continuous development in processes for styling and increasing machine productivity to cut costs. The concern's engineering department has carried the load for improving textile machines, besides designing special-purpose machines for its industrial customers, and its large line of equipment for the consumer and retailer trade.

To keep abreast or ahead of its competitors and to reduce the workload of its engineering department, the company has recently completed a million-dollar Research Center, to which it has attracted a group of about one hundred scientists, research engineers, and highly skilled technicians.

The program for the new Center has been compiled from suggestions made by various departments. These include the following:

1. Manufacturing asks that it study technical production processes for assuring uniform quality and reducing unit costs.
2. Sales wants the Research Center to develop new products, and improve the design and workability of current products.
3. Engineering has requested that certain of its more technical problems be assigned to the Center for suggestions which shall be referred back to engineering.
4. Finance submitted a request for the development of a five-year detailed program on income and expenditures, and plans for increasing sales through some device for financing customer purchases without disturbing company credit.
5. Purchasing is interested in an organizational study to determine the extent to which certain allied activities should be "serialized" under its control.
6. Personnel desires a scientific study of its training methods to evaluate their relative effectiveness and the possibilities of improving them. It is also interested in some new plans for improving labor-management relations, especially a new wage-incentive program that will increase worker earnings while reducing unit labor costs.
7. Management is interested in having the new Research Center develop standards for all company activities, so that controls can be made tighter and quicker. Its over-all suggestion is for a general organization survey to relieve what it considers laxities resulting from overorganization.

The Board of Control for the new Center is composed of its director, three of his top scientists, and three corporate officers of the company. The corporate officers are pleased with the proposed agenda, but the other four members of the Board of Control are not satisfied. They feel that the management leaders are trying to have all their activity problems solved at a high-speed tempo rather than on a scientific research basis. They are further concerned about the shifting to their shoulders of certain types of details for which the departments appear to be trying to escape thought, planning, and responsibility. Because 80 per cent of the research personnel were drawn from outside the company's ranks, the technical and majority members of the Board feel that although they should give weighty consideration to the suggestions submitted, they should first proceed with an over-all study of company organization, operations, and needs, and then submit a program to the Board based on their findings.

PROBLEM: Criticize the requests submitted by the departments. How would you set up the Center's program for improving the operations and management of Sebring? What divisions would you establish for operating the new Research Center? How would you determine and distribute its operating budget? Would you plan for any kind of pure research, and if so, what would be its nature?

32

Public Relations

When asked for a good working definition of public relations, Henry J. Kaiser, Jr., handed the inquirer a card: "Let your light so shine before men that they may see your good works" (Matthew 5:16). This not only points out the ancient lineage of PR, but it is an excellent hint as to its fundamental purpose. Between that Biblical date and today, PR has gone through many vicissitudes. Early in the century, one industrialist who was sure of himself and held public opinion in low esteem announced his public relations philosophy as, "Let the public be damned."

Shortly after the turn of the century, Ivy Lee, one of the pioneers of the PR fraternity, changed its guiding spirit to "Let the public be informed." Edward L. Bernays, who gained justified fame in this field, further advanced the shape of its goodwill philosophy. For some years during its development period, the chief purpose of PR was to explain away any prevailing beliefs about the "evils" that big business, its leaders, and the various industrial associations were practicing. The modern approach is to inform the various publics about what business is thinking and doing, and to let business know what its publics are thinking, so that its derelictions may be corrected. "Truth" appears to be the modern watchword of the large ethical section of the public relations group.

What made PR important?

Early professional attempts to develop acceptable public relations came mainly from specialists in the fields of journalism and advertising. Their job was to use the media they understood in order to combat the attitudes of the propaganda groups and organizations which believed that business was opposed to programs of social betterment. These early attempts to guide public opinion were far from successful, largely because their approach was both negative and narrow. They devoted too much time to proving that various allegations were not true. Their emphasis was on cleverly turned announcements and press releases aimed solely at advancing their employer's point of view. As this technique slowly spread a negative gospel, it eventually earned the label of "propaganda" from a large section of the general public.

The next development in the pursuit of good public relations had a double purpose. Management was still interested in having the public understand its objectives and methods, but it was also interested in learning what the public thought and wanted so that it would have a basis for altering some of its practices. It was this new interest in the public's opinions that caused the expansion of the concept "public" to include a number of groups, as we will presently explain.

The first big boost to the importance of public relations came with the depression of the 1930's. During the following twenty-five years, PR became firmly established as one of the prime needs of business. In the early part of that period, General Motors and U.S. Steel set up public relations departments. Then the aftermath of World War II gave another big push to the opportunities that PR appeared ready to utilize. Many concerns came to feel that there was a discernible relation between the financial balance sheet and a favorable public opinion. With recent years, the TV quiz programs and "payola" scandals prompted the television fraternity to spend $500,000 "for a program of constructive public relations."[1] Still more recently, the early results of Senator Kefauver's probe into some of the questionable drug prices led to the Pharmaceutical Manufacturers Association to employ a large PR firm to handle its public relations both during and after the hearings.

Such prompt reactions of big business to protect its public relations has been increasing the opportunities in the PR field at an ever faster tempo. The many examples of industry's reaching for a sustained public opinion in times of crisis has also had some reverse reactions. "The result has been an inflation of the legend that PR practitioners are a species of corporate medicine men whose black magic cures whatever ails the corporate psyche or balance sheet."[2]

How important is PR?

It is generally conceded that three out of four large concerns in this country now have fully organized public relations departments, whereas the ratio was one to fifty twenty-five years ago. And the number of counseling firms is increasing at an expanding rate. This situation would not be possible if there were any substantial truth in the "black magic" formula.

---

[1] "PR Today," *Business Week* (July 2, 1960), pp. 41–62. These pages present an excellent picture of what the title suggests, and they are recommended to anyone interested in a detailed background as well as the current situation.

[2] *Ibid.*, p. 41.

One recognized authority in the PR field defends its status: "There are crooks and double-dealers in public relations, just as there are perjurers in the profession of law . . . it seems, nevertheless, that only in this field do people overlook the overwhelming majority of honest men to make a judgment of the profession on the basis of the few mavericks who contaminate every sizeable group."[3]

It is estimated that U.S. business paid $2 billion for public relations service during 1960. General Motors has several hundred of these specialists covering a large part of the world. Public relations courses are given in over two hundred colleges. Not only do PR men rank on the top level of many large companies, but there is a feeling that their confidential relationship to the top spot often results in their landing there. A survey by the Public Relations Society of America of 125 companies with sales between $100 and $200 million shows that these companies' PR budgets range from $26,000 to over $500,000.

The two PR approaches

Public relations are carried on by inside departments or sections, or by outside counseling organizations, or by both. Small concerns usually hire outstanding consulting firms for special purposes on a fee basis. Medium-sized companies may have on the full-time payroll one or several PR specialists as a part of their regular organization. Large companies may have a PR department and employ additional outside consultants for special problems.

The *insiders* specialize in news releases, preparation of financial statements for stockholder or the public annual reports, and other forms of communication. Frequently they are also enlisted to aid in preparing data and releases for the marketing department. In all of these activities, and any others for which their help may be solicited, they invariably act as staff advisers rather than as line order-givers.

The *outside* phase of public relations is handled by firms which operate on a fee basis for special projects and/or on a retainer basis for general counseling. In these latter cases, the retainer is merely the base pay; specific assignments are billed usually on a time basis, the rate depending on the reputation of the PR firm and the standing of the "account executive" assigned to the client. The so-called basic fee has been explained as the charge made for "studying the client's affairs in a general way." As is usual for consulting work, the time-charge for an account executive is usually double the cost of his services to his employer.

The outside PR agencies may consist of a single counselor, or they may have as many as 250 employees. The outstanding firms make an annual charge of from $25,000 to $100,000 for services to a business association.

[3] Patrick J. Sullivan, "Madison Avenue Mafia," *America* (March 12, 1960), pp. 704–5.

In addition to the basic fee and separate charges for specific assignments, clients are billed for expenses.

In the past few years, the large PR firms have been adding specialists to their staffs. At present, the specialists are drawn mainly from the fields of psychology, finance, security analysis, engineering and other scientific fields, professional writers, and those skilled in working out legislative programs. Most PR consultants, however, will not engage in legislative lobbying.

Public Relations Contacts

The groups reached by public relations have come to include all of a concern's outside contacts and some of those that might be considered purely internal. It is practically impossible, however, to classify business contacts as outside or inside since many of them overlap to some extent. Actually, the ramifications and interrelations of any company's contacts suggest that the term "public relations" no longer describes the situation it purports to represent. It is desirable, therefore, to treat the various groups separately, discussing the nature of their influence and some of the successful methods for guiding opinions of the various publics.

Employees

Originally there was no idea of trying to influence the opinions of employees, on the theory that since they were paid an agreed wage for their services, there was nothing further to the relationship after the expressed or implied labor contract was fulfilled. If the worker was dissatisfied, he was free to sell his services elsewhere. Since his opinion of his erstwhile employer was not likely to have any public interest, nothing was gained by trying to influence it one way or the other.

Several realizations slowly reshaped management philosophy concerning the workers' opinions of the boss and his outfit. First, there was the realization that the employee was also a part of the consuming public. As his wages and standard of living rose, his potential spending made him even more important as a prospective customer. As a member of a consumer cooperative, his buying influence might be greatly increased. Second, there was the growing suspicion that the worker was paying more attention to the social and economic influences of business and industry.

Of more importance than these two was the increasing inquisitiveness and power of organized labor. It was recognized that some individual employee members of unions could have worthwhile influence within large organizations, a force for good or evil as far as the employer was concerned. When the employer and the union compete for divided loyalties on an emotional basis, the employer customarily receives the minority share. The employer's best plan for improving the worker's opinion is to earn his loyalty by word and deed rather than try to coax a favorable attitude by emotional appeals. We have already recounted the fate of the employee-stockholding plans. When the profits were only a fraction of what the employees had anticipated or failed to materialize altogether in the decade following 1930, the worker's attitude toward his employer was worse than before his stock purchase.

Most companies use more plans for creating favorable employee opinion than they use with any other contact. In a nationwide survey, the executives replying considered employee-management relations the most important phase of their public relations program.[4] It is not surprising, therefore, that there are so many plans for capturing employee good will. These plans include:

1. Employee attitude surveys
2. Open house for relatives and friends
3. The employee's handbook
4. Prompt handling of grievances
5. The employees' magazine
6. Circulars of business facts
7. Slide films and motion pictures
8. Question-and-answer meetings with officers
9. Nursery care of workers' children

The *attitude survey,* often made by some outside professional concern, determines the extent of worker satisfaction and dissatisfaction, and the causes for both. Harmful situations which can be remedied by management are frequently uncovered through questionnaires and interviews. The survey techniques have been improved to the point where progressive management uses them periodically to gauge changes in worker opinions. The survey method allows management to deal with justifiable complaints before they have a chance to grow into major grievances. When employees are convinced of the survey's anonymity and objectivity, their participation is surprisingly helpful to the interests of all parties concerned.

The *open house* is fast becoming a favorite means of swelling the pride of employees and their families in the workplace and its products. Before the open house, most wives knew little or nothing about what their husbands actually did at the plant. But when the workers' duties come to life during one of these plant exhibits, shop talk at home takes on more meaning, and the entire family enjoys a new association with the company. A frequent by-product of the open house is the family's realization of the difficulty and importance of the breadwinner's job. In a broad sense, the open house tends to stabilize industrial relations because of the wife's new interest in the work at the plant or office. The most critical questioning

---

[4] "Management Looks at Public Relations," National Industrial Conference Board, *Business Record* (December, 1953), Vol. 10, pp. 450–453.

about layoffs and strike votes often comes from the "old woman," to whom
the answer must make common sense.

One phase of the program which is often overlooked is the opportunity
to intersperse placard stories of company economics with the directional
open-house signs. As an experienced hand in public relations expresses it:

> Another important function of signs is to stress important economic aspects of
> management of the plant. The open house is probably the plant's most sig-
> nificant opportunity to give its neighbors factual statements counteracting some
> of the loose thinking that often leads people to look with disfavor on the
> private competitive system of enterprise. Signs can point out how much a
> machine costs; how many shares of stock it represents; the cost of operating a
> machine, including depreciation; how old the machine is; how much it has
> meant in the way of wages for its operators and dividends for its owners.[5]

The *employees' handbook* gives detailed information that a new employee
wants to know about company facilities, pay days, vacations, and other
matters. It should also be used to emphasize all company policies which
relate to the workers. Policies are important to new and old workers, and
they should be reduced to writing to inspire confidence in management.

The handling of *grievances* is always provided for in the labor-management contract and is discussed in the chapter on Collective Bargaining.
However, handling of grievances has a special significance in connection
with public relations in that they must be handled promptly in a spirit of
sincere interest, rather than because of the contract agreement. They must
be handled fairly and objectively even when the decision is against the
company. An acknowledged grievance handled quickly and fairly is a
boost for the company in the long run.

In most concerns, the *employee magazine* is usually the responsibility of
personnel. It can be an excellent medium for improving employee morale
and gaining acceptance for company policies. The magazine should deal
mainly with notes and stories about employees. When items are focused on
company activities in general, emphasis should be placed on the way in
which these activities are of direct concern to the worker. It has been
amply demonstrated that the outstanding features compelling reader
interest are photographs and stories of employees' children and grand-
children. The advantage of the employee magazine from the public relations standpoint is the opportunity it offers to create a family feeling among
a large group whose single common interest is working for the same company.

Circulars covering special topics refer particularly to matters important
enough to cause discussion throughout the plant, especially when erroneous

---

[5] From an excellent exposition of the open house by L. M. Stark, "How to Plan and
Run an Open House," *Factory Management and Maintenance* (February, 1949), Vol.
107, p. 97.

information is leading employees to false conclusions. It is better if these explanatory circulars are issued before gossip spreads. For example, it may be rumored that the company has just had a large contract cancelled, or that some improved automatic machinery will cause large layoffs. Both items may be true, but the conclusions derived from them may be absolutely false. Ignorance begets suspicion with almost everyone, and though belated facts allay suspicion, facts in advance create confidence.

Publicizing of business facts can be accomplished through circulars or through the kind of placards suggested for open-house exhibits. The economic facts of business in general, and of the worker's employer in particular, should be presented. They should be able to demonstrate the basic fairness of the distribution of the industry's income among the various factors of production.

Slide films and motion pictures can be used to arouse worker interest in the company by showing how the numerous components go into the finished products and of the importance of each department's contribution to the whole. They can also be used to show past social and athletic events, tending to enliven the company-family feeling.

Question-and-answer meetings with company officers will effectively dispel the worker's feelings about his ivory-tower bosses. A meeting presided over by the president is an excellent start in that direction, and when he can unhesitatingly answer questions, employee acceptance of company management is immeasurably furthered.

Customers

Customers and potential customers from the consuming public were voted the second most important contact in the survey referred to. Doubtless this opinion was influenced by the fact that established customers make up a large part of company good-will value. How is that value built and retained? Probably on the principle that the customer is always right — within reason. Many successful companies assume customer honesty. New customers are usually acquired by various kinds of advertising and publicity, some of which can be measured for results. But established customers are held and more new ones are obtained by fair treatment in daily contacts.

When the laundry returns a pair of high-priced sheets with frayed holes after the third washing and refuses the claim for damages by contending that the manufacturer is at fault — poor customer relations are demonstrated. The assumption that the laundry does not carry insurance for such purposes and desires to escape all such liability is fairly grounded. If the customer goes farther and writes his story to the manufacturer of the sheets, then his complaint is going directly to the source of a wide, unknown market. When the manufacturer asks to have the sheet sent back for inspection in his laboratory, the customer feels that there is a real interest, no matter what the outcome. When the manufacturer writes that his laboratory finds no fault with the sheet's construction, but does find evidence of dangerously strong cleansing materials, the customer is lined up still more closely with the producer of the sheets. But when the letter further states that the company is sending two new sheets along with the torn one, the customer will go out of his way to recommend that brand of sheets, and he will patronize another laundry. Similar examples are multiplied many times in the experience of the average consumer with similar reactions. They illustrate quite simply how to win and lose customers.

The community

The community has frequently been given third place in public relations importance, and has been the subject of most published material. Obviously, industrial relations are partly community relations. Many of the constructive programs in use today for improving public relations with the community arose originally as correctives for objectionable practices in the past. There was a time when the owners and managers of industrial concerns were indifferent to the slums in which their workers lived, when they gave little thought to the air and water pollution which the manufacturing processes created, and when they held themselves aloof from local institutions and community programs. This sort of indifference is rapidly disappearing as leaders of business and industry realize that in the long run what is good for the community is also good for business.

The community, small or medium-sized, is inherently afraid of the absentee power controlling local big business, but that fear can be dispelled by carefully planned programs for improving relations with the community. Action with respect to all of the following items should be considered:

1. Harmonious relations with employees
2. Participation in local government
3. Modern housing programs
4. Positive public health programs
5. Elimination of health problems
6. Street and traffic planning
7. Parks and playgrounds
8. Community educational projects
9. Local civic clubs
10. The community chest

Company executives should become community citizens with more than an average interest in its welfare. The company may hire professionals to guide the community program, but its executives must control it and stand out front in its execution. They must initiate the contacts with press and radio, schools, service clubs, and churches. The program should also include well-formulated plans for handling plant visitors and speech-making by company officials.

An example of community welfare was carried out by a rather small concern in the slum area of an eastern city, to the advantage of the neighborhood surrounding its plant and of the city as a whole, while at the same time the concern was furthering its own interests. The company owned a number of slum dwellings contiguous to the plant, bought for the purpose of possible future expansion. The neighborhood was well below par socially; several of its young men had criminal records. Because the company's policy was to spend nothing on improving its houses, the rent was made unusually low, thus attracting the dregs of the community. Gradually, the houses sank to a level where they became known as the "Bull Pens" by the bookkeeping department.

It was decided to make a drastic change to improve the neighborhood and reduce the vandalism that was causing destruction of company property. The board of directors decided to demolish the houses and build a modern playground on the property. Finished, it was a model recreation area for children in the age groups from five to eighteen.

As a result of this interest in community affairs, the company reduced its juvenile damages to the vanishing point, and obtained considerable favorable publicity for its product locally. Evidence of a new pride among surrounding property owners was seen in the fact that most of them put fresh coats of paint on their houses. Finally, several other enterprises in that factory and warehouse district were inspired to emulate this example.

Stockholders

In theory, corporate management is a model of economic democracy, but in practice it has long since degenerated into a form of economic totalitarianism. Because of the failure of stockholders to function as a group, owing in part to their geographical dispersion, directors and officers have been able to perpetuate their unquestioned rule almost indefinitely, especially if they maintain a reasonable dividend record. The corporate proxy makes it possible for stockholders to satisfy whatever responsibility they feel by simply signing their names once a year, making it possible for entrenched management to ignore the real owners between annual meetings.

Recent developments in public relations have been changing some of the substance of the stockholder relationship. Progressive management has been using every effort to have large stockholder representation in person at its annual meetings. Several large corporations have been scheduling regional annual meetings for the convenience of their stockholders. Luncheons have been served in an effort to make relations less perfunctory.

Question-and-answer periods have demonstrated that some stockholders know how to ask pertinent questions when they are given an opportunity.

Another innovation has been the readable annual report. In place of an unattractive brochure full of statistics and the annual financial statement, coupled with accounting and legal hocus-pocus, the company's owners are receiving readable and interesting annual reports, often illustrated. The past year's operations are reviewed and prospects for the future set forth. Such former "inside" secrets as officers' salaries and their stock interests are also listed.[6] With many other similar facts available, stockholder groups or individuals are frequently able to initiate changes in their own interests. With its 1960 Annual Report, General Electric issued a separate pamphlet entitled "Transition in Annual Reports" describing the changes that have taken place between its first annual report of 1893 and that of 1960. Its eight pages furnish useful source material for classroom discussion. It interprets the evolution of annual reporting in general, and describes General Electric's approach in particular.

The final opportunity for dissatisfied stockholders comes with the assignment of proxies to someone other than those proposed by the directors, for the purpose of bringing pressure or a change of administration at the annual meeting. Strangely enough, it is the public relations departments of the very companies where leadership has become intrenched through the long-standing disinterest of the stockholders which are now fostering this new stockholder activity and encouraging the real owners to use their primary instrument of control over company activities — the corporate ballot.

Vendors

Only within recent years has the value of good relations with suppliers been recognized. The older policy put the onus on the supplier, a burden which he might relieve unofficially, at least, by periodic presents, especially at Christmas, to the purchasing agent. With the establishment of a give-and-take relationship, it became the mutually accepted philosophy that the vendor was giving value received for payments made by the buyer's company, and that the company's interest was best served by having trusted vendors from whom it could expect value received, plus service.

In place of the rather arrogant habit of letting the salesman cool his heels in the waiting room, to obtain a lower price and a subservient attitude, good practice today recognizes that it pays not to keep the salesman waiting, but to treat him with the same courtesies which the company hopes are being extended to its own salesmen. Since some salesmen have behind them the publicity weight of press and radio combined, it is considered good business relations to be on the same side with such power.

[6] The Scott Paper Company has a specially designed and interpreted report for students.

Many concerns now go out of their way to supply vendors' representatives with buying manuals so that their time may be conserved and their activities properly directed in knowing whom to see and where he may be found. An excellent idea to improve vendor relations is to have on display in the waiting room the products, parts, and materials used by the purchaser. It prompts ideas in the salesman's mind, and may lead to profitable suggestions and contacts for the company's buyers.

Press and radio

Some public relations directors are too prone to appraise their value to the company by the amount of free time and space they obtain from the press and radio. This attitude can easily backfire in company relations with these publicity media. The purpose of the press and radio is to dispense news with a public interest, and they often pay to obtain such information. Because they are interested in carrying publicity items only when they have genuine news value, a company does not improve its relations with press and radio by fretting every time its promotional material fails to get a free play in the mass media.

When press and radio releases have a public interest, they are excellent sources for maintaining good public relations. Many times the press or radio is after details about something which it has learned from other than company sources. Occasionally, company officials are interested in killing the story altogether, or at least in omitting some of the details.

To get a fair share of what it wants from press and radio, the company must be prepared to give what the other side requires. When the relationship is established on a basis of mutual confidence, the public news agencies have a good record of sticking to their word.

Government

This phase of public relations is not so difficult as it is precarious. What law applies to a given situation, and what does it mean? What effect may one expect, in maintaining good governmental relations, from the turnover of administrative officers on all government levels?

It is impossible to choose the layer of government that can do the most harm or the most good. The various values of different contacts depend on the nature and size of the concern involved. A small concern with one plant may find close cooperation with the local government authorities most valuable. Without minimizing the importance of local government relations for large companies, it is obvious that most of their important governmental problems and relations exist on the state and national levels. Until administrative law has a more solid basis in this country, relations with governmental agencies must perforce depend to a considerable extent on the attitudes of those who administer the rules and regulations which give effect to laws. This situation makes the management of governmental relations a job requiring skill and experience.

Organization

The organizational setup for handling public relations depends on such factors as the size and nature of the company, whether it sells consumer or producer products, the nature and extent of territory it serves, the capacity of its executives, and the recognizable value of good public relations for long-term success. When profits are considered from the long-run standpoint, they include social as well as economic values.

In small concerns, one person can handle all phases of public relations, thus assuring coordination if not balance in the distribution of attention and fund allotments. Every company, no matter how small, exercises some form of public relations, be it for good or poor results. When one person performs this function on a part-time basis, the results will be commensurate with his general ability and his comprehension of the program as a whole. In either case, public relations is likely to report to the owner, president, or executive vice-president, unless it happens that one of these persons is handling the job. Since the aim of public relations is to influence the opinions of many different groups, the higher the function is placed in the management hierarchy, the more likely is a given amount of effort to achieve the desired results.

In larger concerns, the head of public relations may report to a top executive officer, or to the chief of advertising or industrial relations. In some cases, the function is responsible to a committee of two or more executives. When this is the procedure, the purpose is to program activities that have stood the test of distinctly different points of view. Figure 32.1 is an organization chart of the General Foods Corporation's public relations department.[7]

Conclusions

Since the "human touch" is always an important element in public relations, some executives feel that professional programs are too impersonal to get the desired results. In some instances, professionalization of this phase of management has gone so far that the specialists have not even met the company's operating chiefs. This impersonality can also develop within the company just as easily as when outside counsel is employed.

Since public relations contacts of all kinds should reflect the spirit and policy of management, any professionalized program should be controlled critically and carried on to a large degree by company executives. Only in this way can the spirit of the company be relayed to the public or an effective coordination and balance of company policies be publicized.

[7] *Public Relations Handbook* (Prentice-Hall, 1950), p. 796.

Figure 32.1

A Public Relations Organization Chart

General Foods Corporation Department of Public Relations

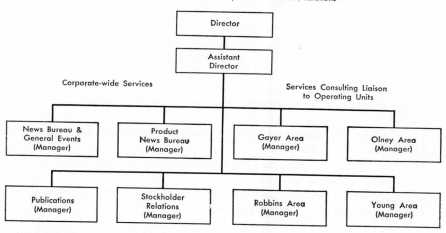

Note: This organizational plan provides for
both functional and territorial groups.

Business and industry have been one of the chief factors in molding and changing our economic and social concepts and daily living habits. There is no doubt that they will play just as important a part in that process in the future. Public relations, as it is dealt with in this chapter, has become an essential activity of business and industry. To the extent that public pressure is increased, management leaders must do an acceptable job in our complicated social and economic environments. They will be judged by their actions, and their actions must demonstrate their good judgment and the sincerity of their expressed social purposes. Their developing social practices of the past few decades give promise that they will fulfill their public obligations.

The effects of public opinion on business profits and the extent of this influence are aptly expressed by Paul Garret, vice-president of public relations of General Motors: "The continuing end responsibility of management is, and always must be, to sell its products *against competition at a net profit*. But who could have envisioned the winding chambers in the *labyrinth of public opinion* through which management must successfully pass today to reach a net profit? Public opinion is but the shadow cast by what the company does, and the executive's behavior is largely instrumental in casting that shadow."

QUESTIONS

1. How did Ivy Lee change "the public be damned" policy of public relations shortly after 1900?
2. What circumstances developed the importance of public relations on a national scale?
3. What are the twin fundamental purposes of good public relations today?
4. What are the relative advantages of having public relations conducted by an inside department or an outside counseling organization? Would you prefer some other plan? What would it be?
5. Many specialists have been added to the staffs of large public relations concerns. What are some of the fields from which these specialists are drawn — and why?
6. What are the chief inside and outside contacts which are now being influenced by public relations programs?
7. Why have company employees apparently become such an important factor in this public relations business?
8. What is the relationship among the so-called attitude survey, public relations, employee morale, and company profiitability?
Would you suggest some different plan?
9. Should the employee magazine be edited by union or company representatives?
10. What, in your opinion, is the best plan for improving customer public relations?
11. How did company executives get interested in community relations originally?
12. What are some of the community affairs in which executives can interest themselves to the benefit of their companies?
13. How have changing conditions and programs at annual stockholder meetings indicated the trend in public relations with the real company owners?
14. Why is it that many companies whose management leadership has been entrenched for years, are now urging stockholders to express themselves at the annual meetings or through their proxies?
15. Until recent years, the burden for good relations between buyer and seller was put on the seller. Why has the situation changed to a 50–50 basis, and what is the advantage to the buyer?
16. What is the chief weakness displayed by many concerns in their relations with the press and radio?
17. What is the outstanding difficulty in maintaining good relations with the various layers of government? Which layer causes most anxiety?
18. To whom does the chief of public relations report in fairly large companies? Would you suggest some other supervisory relationship?
19. What weakness tends to develop in public relations when an outside organization takes full charge without any apparent company contact?
20. How can the company "open house" exert an influence on stabilizing labor-management relations?

CASE PROBLEM

HENDERSON AND JOHNSON

This concern started business in Harrisburg, Pennsylvania, about twenty-five years ago as wood cabinet makers, with five employees. All their orders were on a custom basis, usually coming directly from the general public. By giving superior service and offering moderate prices, the partnership grew gradually until about 1950 when it started to specialize in complete kitchen installations under the trade name of "H&J." It was among the early concerns to swing into this new field, which soon became a "must" for contractor-built homes.

Both partners saw the handwriting on the wall and envisioned a rapidly growing production volume. Henderson felt that their many successful cabinet installations during the past fifteen years, always with the H&J trademark prominently displayed, would ensure their share of the custom-built kitchen business. Johnson, on the other hand, believed that although their past performance would be helpful with contractors, advertising was necessary to bring "H&J Custom Kitchens" to the attention of housewives. A two-page letter was sent to all building contractors within a radius of fifty miles. It suggested, among other things, that they visit H&J's modern plant to look over its variety of installations and modern machinery.

The letters and newspaper advertising did bring a considerable amount of new business and visits from a dozen contractors. The newspaper advertising was stepped up after three months. Next came a display advertisement in the classified section of several telephone books. The partners tried to keep a complete check on the sources of their new business by asking each new customer about the source of his interest. The newspaper advertising appeared to be most fruitful. The telephone directory display was helpful only when some subscriber was considering a new kitchen installation.

The newspaper display ad was run only on Sundays, in Harrisburg and in two other cities of about 100,000 population. The copy was put together by the two partners and was changed every week. It was clearly unprofessional but had plenty of personal appeal. Many of their ideas came from advertisements of other concerns, but it was easy to discern the personal touch of a skilled mechanic. When the publicity budget had been costing $150 a month for about six months, the business increased to the point where the partners were considering factory expansion. Their slow but steady growth had caused little necessity for bank loans, and even when these were used, they were always temporary. Expansion would require considerable additional investment, which they felt must come from mortgaging the plant or incorporating to secure outside capital. They were afraid they might lose control of their business if they incorporated. They even considered taking in another partner.

While these new visions were being considered by the partners, it was decided that Johnson would go to the builders' supply convention in Philadelphia to get a line on the latest developments in kitchen installations. In addition to displays of builders' equipment and all kinds of supplies, several advertising agencies were on hand, advising their participating customers and looking for new business.

Johnson met a Mr. Marcus Witt at the hotel convention headquarters. On the look-out for ideas, Johnson introduced himself to several men who were wearing convention badges. Marcus Witt was a member of Joel Kantner & Associates, public relations counselors of New York. He showed an unusual interest in the progress of the H&J concern and especially in its expansion. The two men went to Johnson's room to continue the conversation. During their get-together on the second night, Mr. Witt unfolded his idea of a safe plan for the H&J contemplated expansion. He explained how common stock was more attractive than preferred, but showed how the former could be divided into voting and nonvoting kinds, with the partners holding all the voting stock. Johnson knew little or nothing about corporate financing, but this idea had an instant appeal.

After the convention, Witt went back to Harrisburg with Johnson, where he unfolded the details of his plan to the two partners. To increase their interest, Witt suggested that his firm might be willing to handle sale of the new stock for 2 per cent of the sale price, which should be at par because of the excellent history of the company. The New York office was contacted by phone, and the plan approved. Within the next six months Kantner & Associates had sold the new $100,000 issue, and H&J were on the road to new heights.

It was only natural, after the stock deal transaction, that the new H&J Corporation should have professional counseling advice to ensure its expansion, so Kantner & Associates were hired on a year's contract at $500 a month. The contract called for the Kantner firm taking over all details, thus allowing the company to give full time to production. The first monthly bill included $725 for "expenses" in addition to the $500 service fee. The Kantner office explained, in reply to the H&J inquiry, that the monthly expense account would naturally be lower after the program had hit its stride.

As Kantner's publicity came to their attention, both partners were amazed at its content. Mr. Witt wrote that the purpose was to first create a "public image" of the company, and later an image of each of its new officers, until finally their products were "floated over on the general public in irrepressible impulse waves." This approach was as new to the former partners as the voting and non-voting stock had been. Even more astonishing was the fact that the first ten months showed nothing like the increase in sales predicted by Kantner & Associates.

PROBLEM. How would you explain the apparent unhappy reactions of Henderson and Johnson to the events that followed Johnson's meeting with Mr. Witt; and what recommendations, if any, would you make for future changes?

33

Appraising a

Department

The measurement and appraisal of most departments, however much they may differ in operating details, follow a general pattern. The purpose of a survey is to study the situation as it exists and make suggestions for improvements. Every survey must evaluate the internal organization and operations of a department almost as if it were an independently functioning unit; but at the same time, the department must be appraised in terms of how effectively it contributes to the functioning of the larger organization of which it is only a part. Furthermore, to be effective, the survey must give individual attention to the *personnel, organization,* and *operations.* It must answer two questions: How efficient are the individual operations and operators, and how suitable is the organization in which the operations are being performed?

Why survey?

1. *To Improve Operations.* The question might well be asked: Why attempt to measure a department if its chief is competent and making a serious effort to do a good job? The answer is that any diagnosis aims at making improvements in operations. Experience with departmental surveys has shown that competent operators usually welcome the opportunity to have their activities evaluated against objective standards.

The good manager or supervisor is always surveying his job, seeking for improvements. If he is a real leader, he knows that his function is to see that his subordinates accomplish, in the most efficient manner, the purposes for which his department was established. It makes little difference to him whether the suggestions for improvements are the result of his own observation or come from one of his subordinates or some outside observer. If the suggestion will improve operations, he welcomes it. The incompetent chief, on the other hand, feels that he alone is qualified to evaluate the effectiveness of operations under his jurisdiction, and he resents the assumption that an outsider can make any real contribution to his management. The competent manager is perpetually on the lookout; the incompetent is always on the defensive.

2. *For Executive Control.* In the second place, the departmental survey should establish standards for executive control. This phase aids top executives both to check and to measure the department and its chief. Under proper controls, department activities are measured realistically rather than by guess or rumor. Sneak suggestions by back-stabbing peers within and without the department are minimized to the extent that the top executive has accurate and inclusive controls. Controls serve both the department chief and his superior. They provide the latter with means of detection and appraisal, and they serve to assure the department chief that appraisals of his job as well as orders affecting his policies are based on established standards rather than the sudden inspiration of top executives.

3. *To Define Relations with other Departments.* In the third place, a good survey should expose the relations of the department under investigation to all the other activities of the concern. The observer should be on the lookout for certain recurrent sources of interdepartmental conflict. The following examples are typical:

Production and Sales. Production wants Sales to press for commodities that Production can make to best advantage.

Production and Purchasing. Production contends that it alone is the best judge of what commodities to buy for its own use.

Production and Personnel. Production is sure it can do a better job of hiring for its activities than Personnel is able to do.

Sales and Purchasing. Sales insists that the customers know more than Purchasing about the types of materials and components that should be used for making company products.

Sales and Personnel. Sales contends that it can do a better selection job among potential salesmen because of the special psychological factors involved.

Purchasing and Engineering. Purchasing insists that it is just as capable as Engineering in criticizing specifications and feels that Engineering is often too exacting to the detriment of costs.

Purchasing and most departments. Most departments feel that Purchasing makes preposterous claims about its buying ability, and they believe that those who use the commodities know better about quality, service, and price.

Finance and Research. Finance wants Research to set a financial limit to its expenditures for each research project which, Research contends, is impossible in most cases.

Research and Production. Research resents the minor problems which Production asks it to solve as an interference with its more important research programs.

Central Stores, Traffic, and Inventory Control. All three contend that Purchasing is trying to absorb them, if it has not already done so, for its own "empire-building," but to the disadvantage of the organization as a whole.

Before business activities became highly functionalized, management's problem was producing enough to satisfy the demand for its products. But fully automatic machines promise to evolve a situation, and that relatively soon, where distribution rather than production will be management's chronic headache. The new competitive demand for lower costs compels both a scientific operation of all management functions and a closer knit interrelation among them. Controls furnish the tools for improving these interrelationships, and departmental surveys supply most of the background for fashioning the improved tools.

Measuring the service activities

Some departments, such as personnel, purchasing, and accounting, perform *service functions* which are *relatively difficult operations to measure.* The two preliminary questions in measuring service activities are: What types of measurement are available, and which ones shall be used?

A survey shows what is happening at the time it is made, with respect to both organization and operation. It first depicts *things as they are.* Then, with analysis and synthesis, it should form the basis for setting up a plan for *things as they should be.* But until it is possible to determine how good activities can be, we have only a relative standard. Frankly, we are still at the stage of determining standards for service functions such as procurement and personnel on the basis of "before-and-after" operations of the better managed departments. Furthermore, such techniques as simplification, methods improvement, time studies, layout, and flow of work are not so easily applied for the betterment of service departments as they are to the more tangible nonservice activities. In procurement, for example, we have the problem of measuring the service of intangibles in a field of unsettled boundaries. This does not mean, however, that the capable purchasing agent cannot make improvements as a day-to-day proposition.

One measurement of a service department is the degree of acceptance it enjoys from the departments which it serves. Another measure is the degree of rising or falling expenditures of the service department being surveyed. Although indicative of general acceptance and cost trends, such findings are not so accurate as the measurement of the production department, for example.

At the same time, it is possible to recommend, as the result of survey observations, the contraction or expansion of a service department's activities. The relative lack of standards in such a situation makes it necessary to compare the cost and value of services after the suggested change has been made. In many of the more concrete situations, these cost and value factors can be determined with relative exactness prior to the suggested change. In other words, the measurement of service departments cannot be determined so scientifically as the nonservice activities.

Measuring the organization

Now let us consider the question of departmental organization. We do have general standards for organization and they apply to departments as well as to over-all management. To measure the probable effectiveness of a department's organization, we should find answers to the following questions:

1. *Is the type of organization fitted to the department's job?* Is it clear, for example, that the operating setup has specific applications for the type of work assigned to the department? It is obvious that scattered plants require a different organization from that of a single operation. Furthermore, the organizational structure must sometimes be planned for a situation where a single raw material such as tobacco, wood pulp, or cotton fiber represents a large portion of the total purchases. The relative importance of any function should be reflected in the general organizational pattern. It might report to the production manager or the controller. If it is recognized as more important, it might be managed directly by a vice-president.

2. *Is the functional division within the department on a sound basis?* This query not only includes assignments of specific jobs, but also an examination of the flow of work within and among such jobs. The flow of work should be first examined in the department's office, if it has one. There, an acceptable flow provides for a natural sequence of jobs arranged in desk-to-desk or office-to-office order. It avoids crisscrossing of assignments and paper work. The approach to the department's other activities starts with a floor plan and flow-chart analysis of the job as it is being done. Subsequent studies lead to suggestions for improvement. Actual practice in this part of a survey has produced some amazing results in savings of time and space, as well as reduction in errors.

3. *Is there a proper ratio of superiors to subordinates?* We often hear the situation humorously expressed as "too many Chiefs and not enough Indians." It is not only unnecessarily expensive to support a faulty ratio, but it is bad for employee morale. There is nothing more pathetic than a chief with an insufficient workload, unless it is a chief who is not conscious of his lack of work. If the chief's job includes planning, that is a different matter. There are situations where a man staring into a blank corner for hours is really producing in a big way, but such a man must be either planning or analyzing ideas or stiuations.

4. *Are company and departmental objectives clearly defined?* And have

responsibility and authority been plainly set forth and properly delegated? Company and departmental objectives, as well as the degree of delegated responsibility and authority should be made clear in the departmental manual. The manual should also provide for communication of company and departmental policies to all concerned. If the department is so small that it can be operated by two or three persons, the manual may not be necessary. But the larger departments cannot operate successfully unless the manual provides answers to the questions noted above. Without written guides to action, individuals of the group may often be working at cross purposes or in opposition to general company policies. With manual instructions, the chief's time is saved from attention to repetitive details of operation.

5. *Are decisions being made at the lowest competent level of supervision?* This has to do with the delegation of authority to subordinates. It is the chief operating technique of the "exception principle" which provides that the top manager in any group shall be free to consider only the unusual problems, leaving routine matters to be decided lower down the chain of command. The point emphasized here is that such matters should be delegated down the line just as far as competent decisions are likely to result.

6. *Are programs and schedules planned in relation to the budget?* Because of the importance of the budget as a guide to action for subordinates and a control device for chiefs, departmental programs and schedules should be planned with the budget estimates in mind. If the department's expense budget was correctly estimated, it should be adhered to within reason. That does not mean that the year's expenses should exactly meet the budget's estimates.

7. *Is the flow of work organized for maximum efficiency?* It is practically impossible to answer this question without making a flow chart for the department. The flow chart pictures in static form the department's dynamic activities. Study of the chart's "things-as-they-are" suggests possible improvements. The specialists look for savings in time and space. Savings may be accomplished by combining, eliminating, or changing sequences, to mention a few of the possibilities.

8. *Are workers employed at their highest skills?* It is not difficult to recognize the low worker morale which results from poor placement, either above or below acquired skills. Wise management puts the unusually dull on dull jobs, and there are such jobs in industry. For a worker to do his best, he must be relatively happy on the job. That means that his job must represent a challenge suitable to his ability.

9. *Are all available controls installed and working?* This is a difficult question to answer. In the first place, it assumes knowledge of available controls which will differ among departments by size, nature of the problems involved, and other factors. When controls are available and used, the manager knows what is happening and where he is headed. And what

is almost as important, when the worker knows that effective controls are installed and being used, the headaches of management are considerably reduced.

The measurement of activities

There are three primary problems which must be considered before starting to measure the department's activities. One is *the measures to be used,* another is *by whom should the measurements be determined,* and the third is *by whom should they be applied.*

The following items are subject to measurement, but with the warning that some of the answers, even when correct, are of doubtful value in appraising the department's over-all effectiveness.

Personnel. How is the morale of the workers? Their attitude toward their work is a reflection, to some degree, of the chief's competence. Most subordinates actually enjoy working for a good leader. He is accepted when they respect his knowledge of the job and his ability to lead them. He must be sure of himself and, at the same time, show that he is always eager for suggestions. He must know how to pick capable workers to start with and then be adept at coordinating their efforts on the job. In other words, he must know how to develop teamwork.

Are departmental employees competent? To what extent are the records of their experience on past jobs supported by their performance on the present job? Has provision been made for training them to do a better job, and to do a job requiring higher skills? Does the department have a merit-rating program so that employees know where they stand? Are the merit-rating reports shown to the workers, and their deficiencies discussed with supervisors? Does the department have a clearly defined compensaiton policy? Does the policy include incentives for superior performance?

Methods. Does the department have standard operating procedures? Are they clearly communicated to the workers? Are the methods kept up-to-date by such tests as necessity, simplification, and proper sequence? Are simplified forms used to make operations speedy, accurate, and effective?

Budget. How do the department's budgetary estimates compare with its expenditures? If the estimates are too high, has the department strained itself toward the end of the budgetary period to expend all the money allotted to it? If the estimates are too low, where does the fault lie? It is difficult to decide whether the underestimated expense budget or the comes-out-to-the-penny variety is worse. The first indicates inadequate budgetary planning, while the second suggests adherence to the letter but not the spirit of the budgetary principle.

Standard Costs. Standard costs are predetermined so that they may be compared to actual or current costs to see whether or not costs are "out of control." Cost standards are predetermined on the basis of facts, including experience and controlled experiment. The experiment must use direct and indirect materials that are best suited for the purpose they are serving, include motion and time studies to fix direct costs, and an analysis of machines and equipment so that the time may be geared to a reasonably high standard.

Establishment of a standard cost requires control over purchasing inventories and material handling during the entire operation. These controls must be maintained as planned in all experiments made to establish the standard cost under consideration.

Two other important factors are used in fixing standard costs. One is indirect labor, which is customarily figured as a percentage of direct labor costs. This percentage is fixed for various activities or operations on the basis of experience. Occasionally, the ratio is applied uniformly throughout the business. The other factor is the overhead ratio which may apply to a department, a production center, or to the entire business. The ratio may be a percentage of direct labor costs, direct labor and material costs, or the total cost of the operation. In any case, this factor of standard cost is added just before the desired profit item.

Occasionally, standard unit costs are dependent on so many variables as to be only relatively useful. In such cases, empirical costs must play an important role in determining standard costs. Actual costs are known from adequate records, and are not available until all details have been recorded. Only then can the total of actual costs be compared to the predetermined standard to decide whether or not the activity is "under control" from a cost standpoint.

Flow of Work. The measurement of this item is often a fruitful expenditure of time and money. There is a tendency by those on the inside to continue to accept the existing work flow. This attitude is based on the unconscious assumption that methods which have been used successfully in the past must be not only correct but the best possible. However, since operations are constantly changing, so too must the method of performing them change. Another factor which tends to retard the establishment of the best work flow within the department is the typical chief's understandable lack of training in the techniques of industrial engineering. Dynamic activities cannot be studied, except perhaps by a genius, until they have been reduced to static pictures. Process and flow charts accomplish this transformation. When departmental activities have been reduced to a static picture, they may be subjected to that type of study and analysis which leads to improvement. In Figures 33.1 and 33.2, which illustrate the present and proposed methods for an office procedure, the advantages of using a process chart speak for themselves.

Figure 33.1

Process Chart of the Present Method of an Office Operation

Present Method [x]	PROCESS CHART	
Proposed Method [ ]		

SUBJECT CHARTED __Requisition for small tools__   DATE __12-10-47__

Chart begins at supervisor's desk and ends at typist's desk in   CHART BY __J. C. H.__

purchasing department   CHART NO. __R 136__

DEPARTMENT __Research laboratory__   SHEET NO. __1__ OF __1__

DIST. IN FEET	TIME IN MINS.	CHART SYMBOLS	PROCESS DESCRIPTION
		●○▽□	Requisition written by supervisor (one copy)
		○○▽□	On supervisor's desk (awaiting messenger)
65		○○▽□	By messenger to superintendent's secretary
		○○▽□	On secretary's desk (awaiting typing)
		●○▽□	Requisition typed (original requisition copied)
15		○○▽□	By secretary to superintendent
		○○▽□	On superintendent's desk (awaiting approval)
		○○▽■	Examined and approved by superintendent
		○○▽□	On superintendent's desk (awaiting messenger)
20		○○▽□	To purchasing department
		○○▽□	On purchasing agent's desk (awaiting approval)
		○○▽■	Examined and approved
		○○▽□	On purchasing agent's desk (awaiting messenger)
5		○○▽□	To typist's desk
		○○▽□	On typist's desk (awaiting typing of purchase order)
		●○▽□	Purchase order typed
		○○▽□	On typist's desk (awaiting transfer to main office)
		○○▽□	
		○○▽□	
		○○▽□	
		○○▽□	
		○○▽□	
		○○▽□	
		○○▽□	
105		3 4 8 2	Total

Reprinted from Ralph M. Barnes, Motion and Time Study (New York: John Wiley & Sons, Inc., 1953) with permission of author and publisher

Figure 33.2

Process Chart of an Improved Method for the Same Office Operation

			PROCESS CHART
Present Method ☐			
Proposed Method ☒			

SUBJECT CHARTED___ Requisition for small tools _____ DATE ___ 12-12-47

Chart begins at supervisor's desk and ends at purchasing agent's desk _____ CHART BY ___ J. C. H.

CHART NO.___ R 149

DEPARTMENT___ Research laboratory _____ SHEET NO.___1___ OF___1___

DIST. IN FEET	TIME IN MINS.	CHART SYMBOLS	PROCESS DESCRIPTION
		●○▽☐	Purchase order written in triplicate by supervisor
		○°▽☐	On supervisor's desk (awaiting messenger)
75		○°▽☐	By messenger to purchasing agent
		○°▽☐	On purchasing agent's desk (awaiting approval)
		○°▽■	Examined and approved by purchasing agent
		○°▽☐	On purchasing agent's desk (awaiting transfer to main office)
		○°▽☐	
		○°▽☐	
		○°▽☐	
		○°▽☐	
		○°▽☐	
		○°▽☐	
		○°▽☐	
		○°▽☐	
		○°▽☐	
		○°▽☐	
		○°▽☐	

	SUMMARY	PRESENT METHOD	PROPOSED METHOD	DIFFER-ENCE
Operations	○	3	1	2
Transportations	○	4	1	3
Storages and Delays	▽	8	3	5
Inspections	☐	2	1	1
Distance Traveled in Feet		105	75	30

75 | | 1 1 3 1 | Total

Reprinted from Ralph M. Barnes, Motion and Time Study *(New York: John Wiley & Sons, Inc., 1953) with permission of author and publisher*

Savings and Losses. This criterion may be applied at a number of points. What, for example, has been the net gain or loss from changes in methods, procedures, records, and types of control? What have been the causes for changes in the cost ratio of direct to indirect workers? What recent machine substitutions have been made to replace hand work? What differences in operating costs have resulted from these changes? What other changes can be made to advantage? Some of these items can be accurately measured, and they naturally reflect the chief's managing ability. Trends can be forecast either by quasi-scientific methods or by hunch. Neither is infallible, but hunches have been found to be the less dependable.

What is the loss in dollars, as well as the intangible loss, due to errors and delays? To what extent does the lack of standard specifications in the production department contribute to such losses? How many discounts are lost because of lack of coordination among the operating departments? What about the savings from the sale of scrap and obsolete machines and materials?

Who should make the survey?

By whom should the evaluation be made? The departmental survey may be an outside or an inside job. The inside survey is made by the department's chief or some other officer of the company, such as the controller. The outside survey is made by some management consulting firm. What are the advantages and the disadvantages of the two plans?

Those on the inside naturally know more about the department's activities than anyone brought in from the outside. Outsiders cannot do a good survey job without cooperation from the insiders. But balanced against this superior knowledge of current operating details is the question of objectivity. It is often suggested that surveys should be made by outside consultants coming from a distance. This idea is based on the hope that distance will eliminate any warping of judgment by friends or enemies. Another objection to the inside survey is that those engaged in it, especially if they are chosen from the department, might better give their time and attention to the work for which they were hired, and for which they are presumably better fitted. Balanced against this are certain indirect advantages which favor the inside survey. It serves to stimulate departmental thinking along the lines of continuous analysis and improvement. However, if an outside survey discloses that a series of major improvements is in order, one might justifiably conclude that those in charge were not capable of making the survey in the first place. When subexecutives are assigned to the survey, they are inspired to make suggestions which they would not ordinarily make during the regular run of everyday business.

The two chief advantages from hiring outside consultants are their objectivity and specialized skills. From interviews and exhaustive check-lists of questions, the professional consultant can find out enough about the operating details of an activity to make it unnecessary for him to have had actual operating experience in the department being surveyed. In fact, it is often claimed that operating experience acts as a handicap in that it tends to develop preconceived opinions about what factors are desirable or undesirable.

How does the outside consultant go about surveying the department? First, he studies the over-all organization chart as well as the departmental chart. Then he interviews top management. Among other things, he seeks to find out where the official chart differs from the facts. He inquires about the scope of responsibility and authority of the department being surveyed. He finds out where policies are made, who makes them, and why. He tries to get a clear picture, if possible, about where the department chiefs fit into the company organization and councils. He wants to know who is the department chief's superior, and to how many persons he reports, if more than one, and why. In other words, he knows from experience that there is often a difference between facts and appearances, and he wants to learn both.

Then the consultant interviews the department head. Underlying the entire survey is the desire to make his department a better operating unit. Does the chief know his job, and what is his background of training and experience? The successful manager of one type of activity is usually successful in other lines. Learning the facts about an activity is not difficult for a trained mind, but the management of any activity is quite a different thing.

Does the chief know how to delegate jobs? Ability to delegate is an almost instinctive matter, and one that is difficult for some men to learn. It is important because it determines the time the chief will have for planning and organizing his work. Does he want to grow, or is he obviously waiting for his pension date? Is he a leader? Does he have the respect of his subordinates?

Making the survey

The prosecution of any kind of operation or study should be based on a plan. The following steps comprise a general plan for making either a departmental or an over-all management survey:

1. Determine the objective and purposes of the study.
2. Outline the scope of the survey, particularly with reference to its limitations. The degree of thoroughness to be applied is determined, in part, by the time allowed, the funds available, and other factors, including the purposes of the study.
3. Assign staff members to various details of the survey in such a manner as to assure a tie-in among the activities to be studied, and provide for that distribution of the examining personnel which will obtain maximum results.

4. Prepare a uniform plan for making memoranda, including those obtained from field notes and published sources, as well as those obtained from interviews with officials.
5. Set up instructions for contacts with outside individuals. This includes the types of information to be sought, from whom it is to be obtained, and the basis for such requests.
6. Make a general plan of working procedures so as to assure coordinated effort toward a common purpose. This plan saves time, minimizes working at cross purposes, and eliminates many nonessentials.
7. Coordinate and arrange the findings into a report.
8. Summarize the recommendations, which must be supported in the body of the report.

The operating manual

Every successful department, unless it is very small, has an operating manual. By spelling out what is to be done, and who is to do it, the department's work is more effective and employee morale is enhanced. Some of the old-timers contend that organization charts and operating manuals minimize flexibility. They are correct, but without these management tools, flexibility loses its meaning. Unbridled flexibility means that no one but the top executive knows the rules, and he can change them at his pleasure. Furthermore, the lack of manuals leaves a great void when the chief executive dies or quits. Absence of a manual or organization chart is usually a sure sign of a poorly managed department, but its presence does not necessarily indicate the reverse.

The next question, assuming that the manual exists, is how good is it? Does it tell what it should? Does it include enough of the required answers, and are they based on the best practices? Is it kept up-to-date? Is it communicated to everyone who should be guided by it?

Records, reports, controls

Records, reports, and controls are all indexes of how well or poorly the flow of work is proceeding. The department chief's superior cannot possibly keep his finger on the department pulse unless he receives regular reports based on adequate records. This statement is even more true for the head of the department himself. Reports furnish the basis for supervisory control. Then the question arises as to the adequacy of the department's records, as well as the sufficiency and the timing of its reports. Records should form the basis for comprehensive reporting, but at the same time they should not duplicate or overlap. These faults are just as often found in reports as they are in the system of records.

Controls should be so devised that they furnish the background for measuring departmental activities by both the department chief and his superior. They should be designed in the first place by the head of the department and subjected to real scrutiny and revision by his superior, who is finally responsible. Outside technical criticism can be of considerable help. Fashioning controls and adapting them to reports is no easy job. This part of the department's work requires the highest type of managerial skill.

What are some of the activities that can be subjected to control in the purchasing department, for example? In general, they include such items as the number of orders placed, the number of invoices passed, the total dollar value of invoices, and the average cost of issuing a purchase order, records of cash discounts, and the percentage of small orders. Records of the percentage of rush and overdue orders are important for control purposes because they measure how successfully operations are being timed. The number of changes in the time of issuing purchase orders and bid requests are some indication of the department's alertness to market conditions, and its ability to adjust to them.

Purchasing records should furnish other items for control purposes. Are they set up so that they show whether the proper prices were paid? Do they show the situation with respect to deliveries? Do they furnish information in proper form for exercising inventory control as it relates to forward buying and slow-moving stocks? Do they show administrative expenses, storage and warehouse costs, and the details of waste disposition?

Many departments make no reports at all, and many others compile reports that are unsatisfactory for control purposes. Department heads are often loath to make reports which they believe will not be read by their superiors. Unfortunately, many superiors do neglect reports coming up from below. But when this is the case, the very process of investigating the situation and formulating the reports furnishes valuable guidance for those who do the job.

Policies

Any good survey will measure the adequacy of department policies and find out how well they are integrated with over-all company policies. Conflicts between department and company policies should be eliminated. This observation may seem trite, but the fact is that conflicts are the rule rather than the exception. The cause is usually found in the making of department policies too far down the management line. Such policy formulation might be satisfactory if the results were later scrutinized carefully by top management for eliminations, corrections, and additions. It has been assumed too often that a department chief is capable of making his own policy manual and that it will automatically dovetail with company policies. This has not been true in practice.

Company policies guide the interrelations among management, employees, customers, and the public. Both over-all and operating policies are bound to touch each of these groups. The tenor of all policies should be to maximize the company's interests with all four groups. This is a difficult task because natural conflicts exist among the four categories. Here is one field where the objective specialist can make valid suggestions. He is more likely to see the forest as well as the trees.

It must also be emphasized that policies are not static. They should change with the conditions which they serve. Successful management is dynamic, and it must adjust to changed situations in all of its relationships. Policy changes are just as necessary as product changes if the profits are to be maintained.

Attitude appraisal

Finally, there is the attitude appraisal. No matter how well any particular job is being performed according to the accepted techniques and methods, it will be judged ultimately by the nonexperts. What do the other departments think of the one being surveyed? And what, for example, do vendors think of the department? Possibly some outside opinions may be unfair, but little can be done about correcting unfair opinions until the criticisms are known. With the facts at hand, there is a starting point for correcting errors and changing opinions, if they are based on misunderstandings.

Conclusions

In conclusion, no activity of any kind can be improved unless the facts are known. We are still more or less at sea until we can compare with accepted standards those generalizations which are obtained from the facts. The chief who seeks appraisal of his department always practices self-appraisal of his activities. When possible, he also seeks the objective appraisal of others, especially of those whose training and experience enable them to make their judgments on a scientific basis. When the department chief does not welcome an activity survey, it is not unfair to assume either that he fears such close scrutiny of his work or that he has become convinced that his management is a complete success. Both attitudes are dangerous. Fear feeds on itself and eventually leads to disaster. As someone has shrewdly observed, "The head turned by success is face to face with failure."

QUESTIONS

1. What is the purpose of a departmental survey?
2. Why is it that relatively incompetent department chiefs are the ones who are most likely to resent having their jobs appraised?

3. How can departmental surveys improve executive controls?

4. Give some illustrations of the possibilities of departmental surveys improving cooperation of their respective chiefs and improved coordination of their activities.

5. Why is it that service functions are more difficult to survey and appraise than line departments?

6. What questions must be answered in attempting to measure the effectiveness of the organization of a department?

7. How can we establish a relatively satisfactory ratio between the number of chiefs and subordinates in a department?

8. Where should departmental decisions be made within that section of the total organization?

9. How does the relation between scheduled department programs and their budget estimates affect the success of the department?

10. What are the three preliminary problems which must be considered before starting to measure the department's activities?

11. What is the relation between the effectiveness of the personnel department and worker morale?

12. How important are operating procedures to effective departmental management?

13. What is the necessary prerequisite in determining whether or not department costs are out of control?

14. How can a good survey improve the flow of work within a department? What management technique is used to determining the before-and-after effect of the suggested improvements?

15. Who should make the departmental survey, and why?

16. What are the sequential steps that a qualified appraiser takes in collecting information for the purpose of his survey report?

17. Propose a general plan (steps) that seems to you to promise a successful survey.

18. How does scrutiny of the departmental manual give rational clues as to its management? Do you think that a good manual minimizes flexibility in its management? How can flexibility be maintained?

19. How can records, reports, and controls be indicative of a proper flow of work within a department?

20. What part do established policies and worker attitude appraisals play in measuring a department?

CASE PROBLEM

STANDARD PUMPS

Standard Pumps grew steadily with the industrial West Coast over a period of sixty years. Lack of serious competition in its early days made for profits, a surplus, and a degree of management satisfaction that carried the concern with comparative ease until a decade ago. Its general line of pumps for the oil industry, mining, and farms was already well established with the trade when the third generation of the closely held corporation was starting to get hold of the business.

When volume and net profits began a downward trend, the board of directors decided to build a branch plant in the Middle West to specialize in the manufacture of pumps for gas stations. It was felt that the necessary labor for a small assembly operation would be readily available in that section of the country, where several aggressive gas pump concerns were located and metering components manufactured.

Because the new setup was largely on an assembly basis with few highly skilled mechanics, one of the "old school" and less cooperative executives was selected to operate the new plant. The home office did not expect operating results to be outstanding the first year, but by the middle of the second year both costs and volume were so far from the planned target that the directors decided to find out why.

A former operating friend of the branch plant manager was sent to make a general survey of the branch-plant situation, with its 150 employees. It was felt that the two old friends would cooperate in pooling their experience to find out the cause of the trouble and suggest the remedies. It was also believed that since the branch was almost entirely an assembly operation, relieved of major office and accounting problems, purchasing and sales, the survey job would not entail more time or knowledge than the two men could give it. The appraisal would be made easier because the branch manager had recently employed a second assistant.

The following are some of the facts that the "inside" unprofessional survey disclosed:

1. The two assistants to the plant manager were ranked as co-foremen with equal responsibility and authority.
2. There were two unions in the plant. The 25 skilled toolmakers belonged to a trade union, while the 125 semiskilled and unskilled workers were members of an industrial union. Because of this situation, many of the toolmakers often had chips on their shoulders. Their helpers and the assembly operators were constantly registering grievances through their union stewards.
3. The entire operation was housed in one large room, where the co-foremen directed the work force as a whole.
4. The employment record showed a labor turnover of 25 per cent for the first 18 months of operation.
5. Jealousy was already developing between the two co-foremen, who complained about each other to the general manager.
6. The more recently employed co-foreman appeared to have the confidence of the majority of the workers.
7. The general manager stated that he had not prepared an operating manual because he believed in maximum flexibility for superior results, and the appraiser from the home office agreed with him.
8. Although the home office dispatched a time-study engineer to the branch shortly after it was in operation, no time standards were in use. There

was no apparent conflict between the time-study engineer and the general manager on this point.

9. The manager continued operations on a straight-time wage basis, "to secure a quality product."

10. Reports to the home office by the plant manager were sporadic and omitted some of the information asked for on the prepared forms which were supplied to him.

11. The final report, signed by the joint appraisers, concluded that the operations were progressing as well as could be expected under the circumstances, and that the admitted weaknesses would be ironed out as operations continued.

PROBLEM: The home-office management is not satisfied with the report. In fact the general feeling is that the situation is worse than was suspected. It was finally decided to engage an outside consultant to go over the situation and report recommendations. If you were hired for that purpose, what recommendations would you suggest from the fact as described? What, in your opinion, are some of the undisclosed background reasons for the present situation at the branch plant?

Part Five • Suggestions For Further Reading

Anthony, Robert N., and Day, John S., *Management Controls in Industrial Research Organiaztions*, Boston: Harvard University, 1952.

Beckman, Theodore N., and Davidson, William R., *Marketing*, 7th Ed., New York: The Ronald Press Company, 1962.

Cutlip, Scott M., and Center, Allen H., *Effective Public Relations*, 2nd Ed., Englewood Cliffs, New Jersey: Prentice-Hall, Inc., 1958.

Hicks, Charles B., and Place, Irene, *Office Management*, New York: Allyn and Bacon, Inc., 1956.

Hinrichs, John R., *Creativity in Industrial Scientific Research*, New York: American Management Association, 1961.

Hodges, Henry G., *Procurement, The Modern Science of Purchasing*, New York: Harper and Brothers, Publishers, 1961.

——, *Abastecimiento, La Ciencia Moderna De Las Compras*, Mexico, D.F.: Herrero Hermanos, Sucesores, S.A., 1962.

Holland, Maurice, *Management's Stake in Research*, New York: Harper and Brothers, Publishers, 1958.

Howard, John A., *Marketing Management*, Homewood, Illinois: Richard D. Irwin, Inc., 1957.

Kelley, Eugene J., and Lazer, William, *Managerial Marketing: Perspectives and Viewpoints*, Homewood, Illinois: Richard D. Irwin, Inc., 1958.

Knox, Frank M., *Integrated Cost Control in the Office*, New York: McGraw-Hill Book Company, Inc., 1958.

Lewis, Howard T., *Procurement: Principles and Cases,* Rev. Ed., Homewood, Illinois: Richard D. Irwin, Inc., 1952.

McCarthy, E. Jerome, *Basic Marketing, A Managerial Approach,* Homewood, Illinois: Richard D. Irwin, Inc., 1960.

McNair, Malcom P., Brown, Milton P., Leighton, David S. R., and England, Wilbur B., *Problems in Marketing, 2nd Edition,* New York: McGraw-Hill Book Company, Inc., 1957.

Neuner, John J. W., *Office Management, Principles and Practices,* 4th Ed., Cincinnati: South-Western Publishing Company, 1959.

Philips, Charles F. and Duncan, Delbert J., *Marketing: Principles and Methods,* Homewood, Illinois: Richard D. Irwin, Inc., 1960. (4th Edition)

Quinn, James B., *Yardsticks for Industrial Research,* New York: the Ronald Press Company, 1959.

Steinberg, Charles S., *The Mass Communicators,* New York: Harper and Brothers, Publishers, 1958.

Terry, George R., *Office Management and Control,* 3rd Ed., Homewood, Illinois: Richard D. Irwin, Inc., 1958.

•

The quotation at the beginning of Part Five is from: Ordway Tead, *The Art of Leadership,* New York: Whittlesey House, 1935, Chapter VII.

The Management

Team

.... *generally speaking, responsibility is feared as* **much as** *authority is sought after, and fear of responsibility paralyzes much initiative and destroys many good qualities. A good leader should possess and infuse into those around him courage to accept responsibility.*

HENRI FAYOL

34

The Board of
Directors

In this chapter and the two that follow, we will take a closer look at the responsibilities and the ideal attributes of the men on the Management Team who function on the three primary organization levels discussed earlier in Chapter 6. The Supervisor and his important duties on the Operating Level are the subject of Chapter 36. In Chapter 35, we will discuss the executive and the various coordinating skills he must command on the Managerial Level. In the present chapter, our subject is the Board of Directors, the men on the Administrative Level who must provide the conceptual, policy-formulating leadership of the organization.

Responsibilities of the board

The prime responsibility of the Board of Directors is *to protect the interests of the stockholder-owners,* who theoretically select its members. Stockholders' interests include their investment in the company and their prospects for dividends resulting from reasonable operations. It is the board's duty so to supervise and control the activities of management that there shall be reasonable protection of stockholder investments. The board's liability for failing in its protective capacity is not clear, but it certainly extends to any act of malfeasance or misfeasance in its official capacity. Under certain circumstances, board members may be held jointly and severally liable for company losses due to their derelictions of duty.

The second duty of the board is *to act as the administrative or over-all policy-making body of the corporate organization.* The board is concerned with top policies which establish guides for subordinate policies made on the other levels of management. Policies made by lower management levels and departments must follow the line laid down by board policies whenever applicable. The purpose is to obtain integrated management which will prevent the various management levels and departments from working at cross purposes.

The administrative function requires conceptual skills. One authority in the field of administration defines conceptual skill as "the ability to see the enterprise as a whole; it includes recognizing how the various functions of the organization depend on one another, and how changes in one part affect all the others; and it extends to vitalizing the relationship of the individual business to the industry, the community, and the political, social, and economic forces of the nation as a whole."[1] It is this conceptual skill that enables the board to establish basic company policies.

It is occasionally stated that top managerial executives make over-all policies. This idea stems from the fact that one or more members of the managerial level who are serving on the board make suggestions concerning policy based on their experience as active members of management. No doubt many top policies result from such suggestions by members of management, especially by the president when he is both the chief executive and presiding officer of the board. But regardless of the source of any over-all policy statement, it does not became official until it is adopted by the board of directors.

The third duty of the board is *to exercise general supervision and control over management*. The chief purpose of this control is to coordinate such management activities as finance, production, and sales so that they tie in with the top policies of the organization. Without such supervision and control by the board, the functions of management might interfere with each other to the defeat of company objectives. Policies determined by the board should be clearly expressed and communicated to top management who are then responsible for formulating programs for their accomplishment. This board supervision of management programs does not always work out in practice. Such is the case when the chief executive officer, who is invariably a member of the board, outlines for board consideration a program which he has already put into effect. When this happens, an executive president, active on both the managerial and administrative levels, can embarrass the board. If such a practice is allowed to continue, the chief executive may gradually usurp the functions of the board.

The fourth function of the board is *to provide the top-level plans to further company objectives*. Most plans are of a subordinate nature and made on the managerial level, but their purpose is to implement the basic plans already laid down by the board. An example of administrative planning would be any decision to establish a manufacturing or sales branch. Such a plan should have consideration and action by the board. Taylor

[1] R. L. Katz, "Skills of an Effective Administrator," *Harvard Business Review*, Vol. 33 (January–February, 1955), pp. 35–36.

was very positive in his feeling that too much management planning was done too far down the line, even on the supervisor and worker levels. The reference was for the most part to production planning, but Taylor also contended that the board shirked its duty when it permitted the managerial level not only to devise basic plans, but to proceed with their execution without referral to the board for authorization. It should be re-emphasized that the problem of basic planning is to devise ways and means to accomplish company objectives, and that this is the board's responsibility.

The fifth and final responsibility of the board is *to provide continuing competent executive personnel for the concern.* The methods for carrying out this responsibility will be dealt with in Chapter 35 on "The Executive." It may be mentioned here, however, that many boards appear to select executive personnel on anything but a scientific basis. Such decisions are often based on the record made by the prospect while with some other company. There are other less reasonable methods.

Board types

Corporate boards fall into four broad classifications: inside, outside, professional, and mixed. These types have considerable influence on the way the boards conduct the corporation's affairs. The *inside board* is made up of members who are full-time employees of the company. The *outside board* is composed of individuals who are not on the company's payroll. The *professional board* members are specialists in various fields such as production, finance, or law. They often serve on a number of boards and make board fees their chief source of income. They give more time to company affairs and are paid higher fees than other directors. It is part of their job to keep themselves informed about details concerning company affairs in the field of their specialty. The *mixed board* is comprised of members from two or more of the other types.

When the president is the concern's chief executive officer, the inside board members are his subordinates in the management end of the business. For obvious reasons, it is not natural for these inside members to oppose the president's proposals. When the inside members make up a majority of the board — an arrangement which is not uncommon — it becomes evident that the president can practically control the board's decisions. On these boards, the minority may disagree as often as they wish, but it will be to no avail. It is not unusual for minority outside members to resign under such circumstances. With assured majority support, it is easy for the president to have his own way between annual meetings of the stockholders. Furthermore, he may continue indefinitely with single-handed control through the voting of stockholder proxies for what is known as the "management slate." This makes the board self-perpetuating, which is not only totalitarian, but affords the board opportunities to act officially for the benefit of its individual members. In passing, we should mention that there is a widely accepted reason for this self-perpetuating feature of the modern corporation. Its acceptance is based on the assumed virtue of the "continuity of policies and management," a virtue which may occasionally be only a mixed blessing.

In a recent example, the inside board of Company A, whose majority was controlled by its executive-president, was used in a perfectly legal manner for the personal benefit of the president. This gentleman was also president of Company B, in which he held stock control. Shortly after becoming president of Company A, he decided to sell Company B to Company A to relieve himself of its growing financial problems. As president of Company B, he sold his business to himself as president of Company A, giving stock in Company A to cover the purchase price. The deal was approved by the majority of the board of Company A. To make it more official, the attorney of Company A, who was also one of its board majority members, introduced at the next stockholders' meeting a resolution in which the stockholders stated that they approved all transactions of the board and management during the past year. The resolution passed. Irrespective of the purchase price involved, the deal shows how an inside board controlled by one man can be used for questionable purposes. The form of the resolution presented to the stockholders was ominously reminiscent of Nazi Germany's annual meeting of the Reichstag.

Outside board members are frequently merely "window dressing" to create confidence among the stockholders. Frequently they are well-known in the community and, occasionally, even nationally. It is proverbial that such members devote very little time to "home work" between board meetings. Usually, they are not sufficiently acquainted with company affairs to form reasonable judgments. It is worse when these outside members are taken on the board only because of their social connections with other board members. When the only incentive for "service" motivating a director is merely to boost his social prestige, he is not likely to be an effective or valuable board member.

Professional board members are probably freer from possible pressures exerted by management or powerful stockholders. Since they are professional, they are likely to resign if their advice receives scant attention from the majority. Their resignation from a board which later becomes involved in difficulties is an endorsement of their action. It may also bring them increased business.

Which type of board is best? That is indeed a difficult question; the answer depends to a large extent on the circumstances involved. Each type has its proponents and opponents. Majority opinion seems to favor the mixed or balanced board — if its members are able to carry out the director's duties as outlined at the beginning of this chapter. No one should be taken on a corporate board who is unable to further the purposes of the corporation.

There is usually little opposition to having two or even three members from the managerial level on the board. It is equally customary to believe that their number should not form a board majority for reasons already discussed. Yet in spite of the general belief favoring mixed boards, a number of successful concerns have all-inside boards, which they defend with enthusiasm. The Hercules Powder Company is an outstanding example. Its inside board started with the formation of the company in 1913, before it became a part of the DuPont Company. In 1959, all sixteen members were on the full-time payroll. The president and five vice-presidents have no active management duties. These six form the company's executive committee. The other ten members include six general managers, the treasurer, the secretary, and the heads of engineering and personnel.[2] Standard Oil of New Jersey is another outstanding example of the inside board. However, the 1959 survey made by the National Industrial Conference Board shows that only 4.5 per cent of the companies studied had wholly inside boards.

Hercules admits that there are objections to an inside board, but contends that their experience has shown that it best serves the company's purposes. They feel that an inside board is best for supervising the managerial level and for solving long-range problems. In addition, it is claimed that if promotion from within is an important incentive for management, then the inside board offers maximum opportunities for that incentive to operate. Hercules believes that its six inside non-managerial members are able to check on management more effectively than the same number of outside members who might not be so well acquainted with the facts involved. Furthermore, it is contended, the directors have been trained for their specific jobs. Finally, there is the element of convenience. Says Vice-President Paul Maysfield: "We can have a board meeting in five minutes if the elevators are running fast enough."

How the board is selected

The first board of directors in the history of most companies is composed of a group of men who are actively interested in ensuring the company's success through capable management. Usually, members of the group have known each other for some time, while others have become friendly through mutual participation in a common cause. It is also usual for the original board members to be relatively large holders of the new company's common stock. If the company starts as a small concern, the first board may collectively own stock control of it.

In most corporations, it is not many years before changes occur in the board's membership. The group gradually settles down to become a "fixture" in the life of the corporation. When old members drop out, the remaining board members fill the vacancies, in accordance with customary

2 "Making an Inside Board," *Business Week*, February 14, 1959, p. 153.

provisions in the by-laws. These new members are listed on the next "management slate" of director candidates to be voted on by the stockholders at the annual meeting, after which the new members are on their way to becoming "fixtures" also.

Theoretically, our corporations are described as democratic. Why not? Their owners vote for the directors who are custodians of the owners' interests between annual meetings. In turn, the directors who theoretically have been selected by the stockholders, supervise and control the company and its management, presumably in the primary interest of the company's owners.

In reality, the picture is quite different. As the concern grows, stockholders may be scattered all over this country and in some foreign countries. It is often expensive to attend a stockholders' meeting at some distant point. In addition, many small stockholders are not able to leave their jobs for the purpose. As a result, a scheme called voting by proxy was developed to cover such situations. According to this scheme, those who do not plan to attend the annual meeting send their "proxies" to the company's headquarters. The proxy reads:

KNOW ALL MEN BY THESE PRESENTS, that the undersigned hereby constitutes and appoints (A. B. Jones) and (A. B. Smith), and each of them, Attorneys and Agents with power of substitution to vote at the Annual Meeting of Stockholders of the (Acme Company, Inc.), to be held in the Ballroom of the (Lincoln Hotel) in Pittsburgh, Pennsylvania, on the 25th day of October, 1960, at 7:30 o'clock P.M., and at any adjournments thereof, according to the number of votes that the undersigned would be entitled to if then personally present, *hereby ratifying all which the said Attorney and Agent shall lawfully do in voting and acting as proxy of the undersigned upon the election of Directors for the ensuing year and upon all other matters or things that may properly come before the meeting.*

(Sign Here) _____

When all stockholders are "present" in person or by proxy, those actually attending the meeting will seldom be more than 10 per cent of the total. The proxy agents control the other 90 per cent of the vote. For what purpose? To vote for the management's choice of directors. To make the process simple and effective, the directors prepare a "slate" of proposed candidates for the consideration of the stockholders. There is practically no discussion about this slate. Whom do the directors propose for the ensuing year? They propose themselves. Since they control an overwhelming majority of the stockholders' proxy votes, they proceed to elect themselves. It is only in exceptional cases that the stockholders object to this simple and effective plan of "corporate democracy." As a further advantage, the slated directors find no hardship in conducting a campaign for re-election. Most boards spend stockholders' money to help ensure their own re-election. The following notice is from Chrysler's "Proxy Statement" of March 9, 1960:

> The Corporation will bear the expense of soliciting proxies in the accompanying form — (naming those who will vote the proxies). *The Corporation intends to use a few regular employees to solicit proxies*, either personally or by telephone, telegram, or special letter, and will make arrangements with brokers and other custodians, nominees, and fiduciaries to send this proxy material to their principals and may reimburse them for their expenses in doing so.

Could anything be more candid? The provisions of this statement are so universal that it seldom, if ever, occurs to corporate management that there is anything questionable about it.

Only when the company is losing money or when some large minority interest wants to be represented on the board is there any objection to these procedures on the part of stockholders. Actually, in many small concerns, very few (sometimes none) attend the stockholders' meetings except the incumbent board members who are interested in stockholder approval of their trust for the past year. The incumbents must also reorganize the board after their election. Reorganization consists chiefly of selecting officers — a foregone conclusion since in most cases they merely re-elect the old officers. Then the new-old board reappoints the same chief management officers. All this is done in the name of simplicity and continuity of policy.

If a minority group wants an opportunity to elect a representative of its own choosing to the new board, it, too, must try to gather sufficient proxies for the purpose. This recalcitrant group encounters two high hurdles. The first is to get a list of the company's stockholders, which is very difficult unless the minority has a confederate on the board or in a management position having access to the stock-record book. Even if it gets such a list, the minority must collect 51 per cent of the outstanding stock to succeed at the annual meeting. If they make both hurdles, the dissenters can elect an entirely new board.

Cumulative voting

Under democratic procedures, the majority rules. But it has been recognized for a long time that the minority should have some rights. In addition, "organization of rebuttal power through substantial minority stockholders can act as a valuable check on absolute power and ingrown management, and be a means of developing freedom of expression, which can lead to better decision-making."[3] In annual corporate elections of directors, the minority stockholders may obtain recognition proportionate

[3] Ernest Dale, "Some Foundations of Organization Theory" in the *California Management Review*, March 1960, p. 83.

to their voting strength by what is known as cumulative voting. Attorney Sol A. Dann of Detroit, owner of 5100 shares of Chrysler Corporation, introduced this resolution providing for cumulative voting at the April 19, 1960 annual meeting of the stockholders:

> RESOLVED THAT AT ALL elections of directors of this corporation, each shareholder shall be entitled to as many votes as shall equal the number of his shares multiplied by the number of directors to be elected, and that he may cast all of such votes for a single director or may distribute them among the number to be voted for, or any two or more of them as he may see fit, which right, when exercised, shall be termed cumulative voting.

Mr. Dann owned more shares of Chrysler stock than fifteen of its directors combined; and he owned more than twice as many shares as the company's president, but his voice was a cry in the wilderness. Chrysler management put his resolution on a memorandum sent to stockholders with their proxies, asking for a "yes or no" vote. Along with this ballot went the explanation that Chrysler management was opposed to the resolution for several reasons. *First*, it would create a "special interest group" if adopted. *Second,* a resolution for cumulative voting must be initiated by the board of directors, and the board must make a declaration that the amendment to the by-laws is advisable. *Third*, the Dann resolution would "create partisanship among the directors" to the detriment of the stockholders. *Fourth,* all Chrysler stockholders "have been protected" and "will be protected" by "the present system of voting." *Fifth*, the present system has elected a board that has "worked well" in behalf of the stockholders.

The opinions of the board are recited at some length to show the reasoning of a group which is evidently determined to perpetuate its position with the company by "block voting," a system whereby the majority elects the entire board. In fairness to the board members, it appears that some of the reasoning must be credited to strained legal logic. It is further interesting because Mr. Dann had accused some board members of acts detrimental to the stockholders. The resolution was defeated by something less than 90 per cent, and the management slate was re-elected. Shortly after the reorganization of the board, the president was promoted to chairman of the board and another director was named in his place. It is even more interesting to note that subsequently the UPI carried a story from Detroit on July 29, 1960, stating that the new president had been ousted after the company received his pledge "to return nearly half a million dollars in outside profits."[4] Mr. Dann had accused some members of

---

[4] *The American Institute of Management,* in a brochure issued as No. 19 of Vol. 3, in March 1954, entitled "The Great American Kickback," stated, "Every dollar that the kickback recipient does not pay tax upon makes the burden of government heavier for more honest taxpayers . . . The employee has no more right to pocket 'rebates' than he has to supplement his earnings by dipping into the company safe."

Chrysler management or board of receiving kickbacks from the company's suppliers, which is what happened in this case.[5]

Democracy in stockholder voting

The reasons generally given for proxy voting sound convincing under conditions where stockholders are too scattered to attend the annual meeting. Yet the results are simply not satisfactory, because they lead to totalitarian corporate management by self-perpetuating directors who can be called to account for their actions only once a year. Still worse, it is very difficult for the stockholders to take corrective action even then unless a cohesive group is able obtain a majority of the concern's proxy ballots. Professionals in the field of management have been trying for a long time to work out some plan for more representative voting by stockholders.

It occurs to the author that the plan used by most universities for electing alumni trustees might be practical for electing corporate directors. In the first place, anyone is free to make nominations. They are usually made by regional groups of alumni. Numbered ballots are mailed to everyone entitled to vote. Included with the ballot is a sheet displaying the pictures and backgrounds of all candidates. The alumnus marks his ballot and mails it back to the secretary of the university in a special envelope enclosed for the purpose. It is simple; its use has not been criticized; and it gives each voter a direct, clear-cut opportunity to express his choice. If the system were used for the election of corporate directors, one simple addition would be necessary on the ballot — the number of shares owned by each stockholder. *If it has been found satisfactory to have stockholders return proxies by mail, why not have them vote for directors by mail?* It will be argued by opponents that other questions will come up at the annual meeting. If so, they should be important enough to be known ahead of time, so let the stockholders vote on such questions at the same time, and return their choices by mail.

Since it appears to be the ultimate in conceit for the incumbent board members to nominate themselves, why not make the situation somewhat more democratic by having double the number of nominees for board membership placed on the ballot? If the board is at a loss as to whom they should nominate in addition to themselves, it might be reasonable to select the other nominees from among the larger stockholders. If the latter have been successful enough to accumulate so much stock, it may be presumed that they have some business judgment. Under this plan, the stockholders could also cast their votes directly by mail without surrendering their

---

[5] In May 1961, the $250,000 president of Chrysler, whom Mr. Dann opposed as incompetent because of large losses under his leadership, finally "resigned." It was the culmination of a long "fight" during which suits against Mr. Dann, by Chrysler, were financed with stockholder funds.

ownership rights to the present board. If it were considered helpful, the names of incumbent board members might be honored with stars. Another plan, though a feeble one, would provide blank spaces on the ballots where stockholders could write in their choices for directors.

Some citizen stockholders in our political democracy have been schooled to think that occasionally "it is time for a change." If the incumbent board has proved its competency, the distinguishing stars should assure their reward. After all, there is no reason to suppose that the owners of a corporation are less interested in its success than a self-perpetuating board, many of whom own only a negligible amount of the company's stock. To give the corporate voters the choice of "selecting" the one-and-only hand-picked slate resembles too closely the plan of political dictators.

The question of stock ownership naturally arises in selecting board members. How much company stock should be owned by inside and outside directors? It is difficult to make a decision in spite of the fact that the problem has been explored many times in national publications. One writer asks: "Is a director a good director if he won't even make a nominal investment in his company?" This question would not arise with a professional member of the board. On the other hand, there is a distinct possibility of danger when the president, for example, owns more than any stockholder.

In concluding this section, the following questions and suggestions are offered for consideration:

1. Why shouldn't minority stockholder interests be represented on a corporate board? They promote discussion by presenting different points of view. Continued board harmony can be dangerous for the stockholders.
2. Continuous holding of power occasionally becomes dangerous with groups as well as with individuals.
3. How can any corporate director possibly represent ALL stockholders with their diverse interests?
4. What is the purpose of trying to amend a corporate charter to permit cumulative voting if it is necessary for the board to make a declaration that the amendment is advisable?
5. Any company's statement that a system of voting under which management proxies elect a board "has worked well and should be continued" is questionable if earnings and dividends are decreasing.
6. Many cities have attempted to inject more democracy into their corporate affairs by providing for proportional representation in the election of their councilmen so as to give minority participation in their administrative group — the city council. Can it be that industrial board members are opposed to proportional representation?

The directors speak

Columbia Universitiy's Graduate School of Business and the McKinsey Foundation for Management held a symposium for corporate directors in

December 1957. Its thirteen members included presidents and vice-presidents of some of our largest corporations, such as the DuPont Company, Standard Oil of New Jersey, General Foods, H. J. Heinz, Roebling's Sons, A.T. & T., and General Electric. Here is a summary of their outstanding conclusions:[6]

> "1. The average does not give adequate direction to its company.
> 2. The attitudes of the average company's chief executive largely determine the effectiveness of its board.
> 3. Most executives would like a stronger board that would operate more effectively, and they are seriously concerned about how to get it.
> 4. Even if better boards could be obtained, the question as to their proper role remains unanswered. The relationships among the stockholders, the board, and executive management must be defined more precisely."

Dean Courtney C. Brown of Columbia's Business College suggests that "the real issue is the vital need for making the board an effective functioning instrument." Board weaknesses become clear only when the company's major problems are brought out in the financial statement. The far-reaching consequences of board weaknesses are seen when one realizes that the modern corporation is so much a part of American life that its directors are responsible to employees, customers, vendors, and the community, as well as to stockholders. Because of the relative inability of board members to become acquainted with the details of company operations, some members feel that it is up to management to formulate policies for *review and approval by the board.*

The use of board committees has been suggested for obtaining facts and making recommendations, but the delegation of board duties to small groups, many of whose members are a part of inside management, places the remaining board members even further from the exercise of personal responsibility.

Is the board boss?

The consensus is that every chief executive should have a boss — the board of directors. It is the board's function to attack and defend the executive's recommendations, policies, and actions. On the other hand, a minority of board members feel that the board and the executive president should not criticize each other. The two views offer a critical board on the one hand and a group of yes-men on the other. The former is after results, while the latter favors harmony.

It is not necessary for a board member to know the mechanics of a particular business if he is supplied with *all* the relevant facts. When difficulties arise, they have their roots in management's choice of the facts sub-

[6] See *Business Week,* December 21, 1957, p. 57.

mitted to the board. The outstanding defect of board supervision and control is that in most cases the guiding hand of power is management, who supplies the board with information that suits management's purpose. In other words, management's arguments lead the board in the direction management wants it to take.

It is invariably management, not the board, who reports to the stockholders. Only in exceptional cases does the board report on its trusteeship to the owners of the company. This sad situation may stem from the fact that many board members proposed by management are "big names" and nothing more, who have been elected by a block vote. One director of a large concern commented that "a good general, actor, politician, lawyer, or baseball player is not necessarily a good director."

It is only natural for the chief executive to swing his support to the election of directors who he feels will agree with him. The symposium referred to previously emphasized that irrespective of the type of board, it will be effective only to the extent that management desires it to be effective. This is particularly significant when one realizes that management is supposed to be the servant of the board. The crux of this anomaly is the fact that fewer than 10 per cent of board members even prepare for their meetings. In most cases, the board is not even presented with an agenda in advance of the meeting.

Conclusions

The evidence seems overwhelming that the majority of American corporate boards, as presently constituted, is not performing satisfactorily. There are several reasons for this situation. In the first place, board members are not customarily selected on the basis of the contribution they can make to successful management. Occasionally men accept board positions to further some outside affair in which they have a greater interest. In other cases, members are attracted to the board by what they consider social advantages, and to satisfy personal pride.

Furthermore, too many board members do not make it their business to learn enough about their company's affairs to arrive at considered judgments on really serious problems which arise in the fields of marketing, production, finance, and purchasing.

The remuneration constitutes the primary appeal to some board members. Many corporations pay from $3,500 to $15,000 annually to regular outside board members. While a considerable part of this income may be paid in federal taxes, that does not appear to diminish the prestige factor enjoyed by many executives whose salaries have already reached a high mark in six figures.

Another aspect of the present situation is that the average board member is very much like the general run of human beings — simply lazy. This is especially true if the company is making good profits. Many members of such boards relax and leave it up to management to produce a creditable balance sheet. Again, many years of continuous service on a particular board leads to ingrown ideas and lack of initiative. There are board members who seem to give their best energies, and some of the stockholders' money, only to perpetuating their positions on the board. Lastly, continued domination by the management group eventually leads to uncritical thinking on the part of many board members.

All in all, the present condition of the average board makes it seem fair to characterize it as the "dark continent" of American corporations. What to do about it is indeed a problem. At present, the best brains in the management field are not giving enough consideration to the functioning of the board and its relation to management. Not much help in solving the board problem may be expected from complacent board members. One certain way to encourage critical consideration of board actions is to allow minority representation: autocratic rule breeds satisfied lethargy. But most of our boards are opposed to any plan that will weaken their established positions under the old undemocratic rules. Cumulative voting is permissible in many states provided the company's by-laws do not prohibit it. Since so many corporation directors complain about the service they are "obliged to give" on boards, it seems strange that they will go to such lengths to oppose the cooperation of those who are interested in watching their investment from the inside.[7]

QUESTIONS

1. What is the prime responsibility of the board of directors?
2. What is the board's chief administrative duty?
3. Why are conceptual skills so important for directors?
4. What is the relation between the board and the managerial level?
5. To what extent does management make over-all corporate policies?
6. What are the four board types? Can you say which one is "best"? Why?
7. What are the advantages of a wholly inside board?
8. Which type of board member is relatively free of pressure from the management group?
9. What is the relation between the proxy and self-perpetuating boards?
10. What is meant by the company "slate" for electing directors?
11. Under what circumstances do stockholder objections to board supervision usually develop?
12. What are the five objections to cumulative voting that were presented to the stockholders of the Chrysler Corporation by its board of directors?

[7] For fear readers will feel that the author has some personal grudge against the American corporate board, he hastens to explain that before rising to the teaching profession, some ten years ago, he served on nine different boards in three states.

13. What was the nature of the kickback received by Chrysler's president?

14. How would you obviate the use of proxies in stockholder voting for members of the board of directors?

15. On what basis, if any, would you justify totalitarianism by corporate boards?

16. To what extent should directors hold stock in the companies they serve?

17. Why should minority stockholder interests be represented on corporate boards? If you think they should not, what are your reasons?

18. How can minority stockholder interests secure information from a corporation's stock-record books?

19. Which dominates company affairs as between the board and the management group? Why?

20. Who makes most of the reports of company affairs to the stockholders?

CASE PROBLEM

GREEN THUMB NURSERY COMPANY

The Green Thumb Nursery Company was started in Jackson, Mississippi, by George N. Burger in 1920. In 1925, Mr. Burger incorporated his business for $100,000. At that time, he was operating in about half the state. By 1950, three branches were established in central and southern Mississippi. The number of employees had increased to about 400, with some 200 working in the growing fields outside of Jackson. By this time, Mr. Burger was beginning to feel the strain of his expanded operations and felt that he should shift some of his business burdens. He became Chairman of the Board and picked one of his older employees to act as President.

From the beginning of the corporation in 1925 until 1950, three of the board members were Mr. Burger, his wife, and a nephew. The other two were James Mathias, who was elected President in 1950, and a young attorney who was a friend of the family. It was clear even after 1950 that the Green Thumb Nursery Company was a one-man concern in corporate form. The family held 75 per cent of the company stock, and the other 25 per cent was held by relatives with the exception of $10,000 which was bought by Mr. Mathias shortly before he became President of the Company in 1950.

After Mr. Burger's death in 1953, the chairmanship of the Board was left vacant. Mr. Mathias took over as General Manager as well as President. Although he had scarcely finished grade school before beginning to work (in a competing nursery) and had had no previous training or experience in management, Mathias had definite ideas about building a much larger company. The capital stock was increased to $200,000, and the board membership increased to eight, a move that created four vacancies. A broker who had been selected to sell the new stock was made a board member along with two other employees of the Company. The fourth vacancy was not filled immediately. Mrs. Burger placed $50,000 of her stock in the public offering. Mr. Mathias bought half of it by making a bank loan on all of his stock, which was well thought of because of its earnings record.

By 1957, Green Thumb's capital stock was again doubled, to $400,000. Its employees had increased to about 650. Because the stock had a par value of $1 and was sold for $3 during its dividend-paying period, there was a sizeable unearned surplus in addition to $75,000 profit surplus. Green Thumb paid its last dividend in the middle of 1957. During 1957 and 1958, the new president added eight branch sales offices and two growing fields, scattered throughout the state. He also bought out a medium-sized fertilizer company for $65,000, paying with Green Thumb's treasury stock. The former owner of the fertilizer company was elected to the Board vacancy.

To finance Company expansion, $300,000 in mortgage bonds were sold to an insurance company, payable $25,000 a year at 6½ per cent interest. A short time later, $150,000 was borrowed in a joint deal with three Jackson banks. The last borrowing was necessitated because of the growing amount of accounts receivable, which had grown to around $400,000, due chiefly to the landscaping of several large real estate developments whose prospects did not materialize.

Along with the establishment of the new branches, the new General Manager began to put his relatives on the payroll in key positions. Soon there were eight in salaried positions as branch managers and eight more employed in the wage group. When one director resigned, his place was filled by Mr. Mathias' brother. Rapidly the Board became largely a group of "yes-men" for the President. With personal control of the Board secured Mr. Mathias began to make fairly large expenditures without conferring with the Board until after the deals were completed. He was president of a small concern which he had started some years ago, and he now sold this business to himself as President of Green Thumb, taking stock for the purchase price. As a result of this deal, he became the largest of Green Thumb's 300 stockholders.

In 1959, the Company lost $75,000 in its operations, and in 1960, the loss was $140,000. By this time, the Company had depleted its earned surplus. Its stock sold for $2 in June 1959, and by the end of the year, some changed hands at $1 a share. By the middle of 1960, some of the stock sold for 85¢ a share. A well-trained executive who had been taken on the Board two years before resigned with an investment of 10,000 shares of Company stock. By this time, several of the larger stockholders were thoroughly discontented with Mr. Mathias' management and with what they considered the Board's delinquency in allowing the stockholders' investments to be jeopardized.

PROBLEM: If you were one of the stockholders who had paid $3 per share for your stock, what action would you take in attempting to save your investment?

35

The Executive

A strong management, assisted by well-trained personnel, is any company's most valuable asset. According to Dun & Bradstreet, more than 90 per cent of all business failures are caused by incompetent management. As we have seen, top and middle management, and supervisors — functioning on the managerial and operating levels respectively — make up the management ladder. At the bottom are the supervisors who are the subject of the following chapter. High quality on all rungs of the management ladder is necessary for business success. A mediocre executive with top-grade supervisors is more likely to obtain high productivity and achieve high quality in the company's products than a top-grade executive with mediocre supervisors. This observation is largely academic, however, because a top-grade executive *will have* good supervisors, either through proper selection or training, or both. Furthermore, top-grade supervisors will not serve mediocre executives for any extended period. All classes of management, including supervisors, want a leader who stimulates confidence and respect. If the subordinates are first-class, they can find jobs where they will be able to serve under leaders.

Executive Qualities

Leadership

All members of the management team should have one characteristic in common — they should be leaders. When other things are equal, the success of an enterprise hinges on the ability of the leader to influence all levels of the organization to work together as a team. There are, however, different types of leaders, many of whom appear to achieve success through entirely different approaches.

Leaders have been classified in a number of ways depending on their predominant traits. Alford and Beatty analyze leadership characteristics or traits as *intellectual* (gains followers through recognized ability in specialized fields), *institutional* (leads because of prestige of position), *democratic* (caters to majority desires of his group), *autocratic* (leads through domination and drive), *persuasive* (engenders cooperation through a likable personality), and *creative* (inspires others with ideas).[1] None of these traits will be found in its pure form in any one leader. Various combinations of them produce leadership qualities in different men.

Irrespective of the validity of leadership based on any of the traits mentioned above, it is becoming clear that the primary basis for successful leadership is the consent of those who are being led. The group spirit of the 1960's is distinctly self-determinative. This is a carry-over from the political aphorism that the safest foundation for the governor is the consent of the governed. Another important factor influencing the acceptance of the leader is the *objective of his subordinates* and the worker group. If the manager is considered capable of leading the group to the attainment of its objectives, they are likely to give wholehearted consent to his leadership. If the accepted leader fails to lead the group to its coveted goal, he is repudiated.[2]

Space does not permit a comprehensive follow-through of this factor of leadership, but it must be apparent that the *time and circumstances* also have a weighty influence on the acceptance of leadership. The idea is expressed in the phrase: "The times make the leader." It implies that a combination of circumstances make a certain person desired by a group which has a specific purpose in mind. Mass discontent in Germany based largely on a feeling of national inferiority brought forward Hitler, who declared that he would restore the country to its former position as a leading power among the nations. In England, completely different circumstances illustrating the same theory brought forth Churchill to oppose (and defeat) Hitler.

Whatever truth there may be in the theories we have been discussing, it has been demonstrated repeatedly that the qualities necessary for leadership can be learned and developed in practice. There is considerable truth in the contention that society is divided into leaders and followers, but that does not make it impossible for apparent followers to become real leaders under the right training. (Years ago it was contended that "policemen are not made but born, preferably in Ireland." The idea has been exploded long since.) Short courses in executive and leadership development are carried on by many universities and business associations in this country and in most of Europe. The idea was born here, based on the assumption that managerial leadership ability can be developed and improved by lectures and discussions among recognized leaders.[3]

[1] L. P. Alford and H. R. Beatty, *Principles of Industrial Management* (Rev. Ed.; New York: The Ronald Press Co. 1951) pp. 111–114.

[2] For an elaboration of this idea, see "The Dynamics of Leadership" by M. H. Mescon in the Journal of the *Academy of Management*, August 1958, pp. 13–18.

[3] "Developing Business Leadership in Europe" by Herbert B. Schmidt, in *Business Horizons* (Indiana University, December 1956, summarizes the activities of European leadership institutes.

In summary, it is worth repeating that however leaders may vary in their personalities and approaches, they are alike in their ability to achieve business objectives through the efforts of others whom the leaders have influenced in such a way that those who are led *want* to cooperate.[4]

Characteristics of Executives

In the general field of business, the management pattern is changing, making it necessary for the competent executive to adjust his actions and techniques accordingly. The executive of even twenty-five years ago would be unhappy and possibly unsuccessful in today's business environment. Organized labor is one outstanding reason for this change because of the encroachments it has made on the prerogatives of management. The ideal executive can be characterized as follows:

He is dynamic. He is competent. He is adaptable.
He has a strong sense of personal responsibility.
He earns the following of the people he leads.
He has a positive feeling toward people.
He has challenging standards of personal conduct and can keep business morale high.

Successful executives must have the following competencies:

1. The intellectual capacity to solve problems, and the health to support sustained mental effort
2. The ability to plan and organize on a broad basis and in a far-seeing manner
3. The vision to make correct decisions in most cases
4. The capacity and willingess to accept responsibilities
5. The knack of convincing and stimulating others

Executive selection

One of the problems encountered in hiring a new executive is that often those responsible for the selection are not able to enumerate the qualifications on which they should base their decision. Even if the required job specifications are agreed upon, it is extremely difficult to find out whether the candidate meets them. Candidates for executive positions usually have good personalities and are often better "salesmen" than the hiring committee members are "purchasers." When one realizes that the new executive may be on the company's payroll for twenty years at a salary well up in five figures, the purchase becomes important. However, the company com-

[4] *The National Institute of Leadership,* in Los Angeles, has probably given more thought to the fundamentals of leadership than any other organization in this country. "The New Leadership System" and "Fifty Tips for Successful Leadership" are two of its publications.

Figure 35.1

Check List for Selecting Executives

Does he know his job?
Can he make decisions?
Are his intellectual resources adequate?

Ability

Has his division or department forged ahead of competition since he was placed in charge?
Are his reports concise, accurate, and well organized?
Can he distinguish the relative importance of different tasks?
When quick decisions must be made, does he generally make the correct ones?
Is he tactful?
Does he anticipate needs, foresee and meet changing conditions?
Does he reserve adequate time for policy matters?
Is he a widely read and well informed individual? Does he retain facts and ideas?
Is he able to interpret financial statistics and business indices, understand accounting processes?
Does he delegate enough authority and responsibility?
Has he obtained loyal and capable assistants?
Can he judge accurately the capacities of those who work for him?
Does he keep his subordinates well informed concerning objectives, progress, and organizational changes?
Does he encourage participation by subordinates in solving problems?
Does he make adequate use of the services of specialists?

Integrity

Does he contribute independent thinking to discussions?
Has he respect for the leadership of his superiors?
Does he show confidence in his subordinates?
Can he give praise wholeheartedly when warranted?
Are his personal standards of accomplishment high?
Has he made himself an integral part of the organization?
Do his plans for the future include the company?
Is he respected and trusted in his community?
Does he devote adequate time to civic activities?
Has he a good credit record?
Does he permit constructive criticism by his friends and business associates?
Is he tolerant of persons of other religions, races, or customs?
Is he tolerant of opinions which oppose his own?
Can he admit mistakes readily?

Does he control his emotions?

Does he give credit when and to whom it is due?

Has he advanced subordinates without regard for friendship or family relationship?

Does he work as hard when not supervised or observed?

Industry

Is his work thorough, showing study of all possibilities?

Does he work steadily without growing discouraged?

Is he a "self-starter"?

Does he bring a specific job to completion? On schedule?

Is he observant?

Has he continued to study and learn in his present position?

Does he take an interest in company functions — sales, production, finance — not his immediate responsibility?

Has he educated himself for the position above his own?

Has he added to his responsibilities in his present position?

Has he developed a replacement for his own position?

Does he keep himself physically fit?

Does he maintain contacts with his field through trade publications and associations?

Does he have long range work goals?

Is he generally prepared with facts or figures to substantiate his ideas?

Does he avoid unnecessary work on comparatively unimportant details?

Is he willing to adopt new processes once they have proved effective?

Does he have a firm desire to succeed?

Does he approach new tasks with enthusiasm?

Courtesy, American Institute of Management
From *Corporate Director*, October 1956

mittee will buy a $20,000 machine on a more scientific basis than it will buy $500,000 worth of executive services — assuming a twenty-year company life span for both machine and man.

Since it has been found difficult for company executives to select an addition to their number on a scientific basis, various plans have been tried for "sizing up" prospects under normal social conditions. Large and medium-sized companies occasionally invite the prospect to an executive dinner for the purpose of allowing the participants to form whatever opinion is possible under such conditions. The author found it difficult to form a dependable conclusion after attending one of these probing dinners as the guest of a particular company's president. In this case, the president had a follow-up session in his office the next morning with each dinner guest of the night before. He asked: "Are you in favor of hiring this candidate?" He then went on to say that if the executive questioned answered, "Yes," he, the president, would not expect to hear about any future complaints or personality conflicts once the prospect had joined the company. This is a flimsy basis for successful executive selection.

A more grandiose plan is known as the "House Party Approach." It covers a week end, giving ample opportunity for all the "interviewers" to draw out the candidate from many angles. It has been used less frequently, but more successfully.[5]

Along more scientific lines, the American Institute of Management issued a four-page report on its proposed "Check List for Selecting Executives," in which it summarized the desired qualifications under three headings: Ability, Integrity, and Industry.[6] The report was accompanied by a checklist of detailed questions (see Figure 35.1) which were to form the basis of selection.

Executives are frequently hired purely on the basis of their outstanding performance with some other company. Under these conditions, the prospect is sought out; he is not necessarily looking for a change. Since there is, in his case, no competitor, the negotiations are limited to questions of salary and the opportunities offered by the new position. Most executives, however, are not sought after as well-known individuals. Rather they are factors on the executive market. Many times the important things which the buyer of executive services should know are either hidden behind, or colored by, the candidate's personality screen. In view of the large contemplated investment in a new executive, his hiring should be based on factual data covering a wide range. If the desirable exploratory methods are unknown or distasteful to the employer, he should employ a professional consultant in the field. Through training and experience, the consultant has learned how to get the information necessary to reach a valid conclusion.

[5] This plan is elaborated in an article in *Management Methods* magazine for August 1956, starting on page 17.

[6] October 1956 issue of Corporate Director, Vol. VI, No. 7.

One recognized commentator on this subject suggests that the candidate's experience and past behavior should be appraised according to the following criteria: attitudes, motivation, maturity, emotional stability, and aptitudes.[7]

A candidate's record for *ability to delegate authority* is an important consideration. If the successful executive is to schedule his daily tasks so that he will have sufficient time to plan and organize for present purposes and future prospects, he must delegate many problems to his subordinates. Indeed, the difficulty of the delegated duties should be increased from time to time if the subordinates have been successful in performing former assignments. Delegation not only relieves the executive's workload, but it promotes initiative all down the management line. *When to delegate* and *to whom to delegate* are two problems which must be handled wisely to assure success.

The *ability to communicate* is another important factor to consider in the selection of an executive. Without the desire and ability to communicate effectively with his management peers, his methods and plans are likely to be misunderstood, a hurdle that is difficult to overcome. Without good communications, executives fail to coordinate their programs, and subordinates often fail to carry them out. Executive orders are an important part of communication. When they are ambiguous, there is no clear meeting of the minds between the superior and his subordinate. Making an idea or order perfectly clear invites participation and provides the motivation necessary for accomplishment. The extent to which subordinates fail to accomplish what the superior intended, gives the latter an apportunity to gauge the effectiveness of his communication procedures and to make the necessary corrections.

The American Management Association states that "communication is the most important tool we have for getting things done. It is the basis for understanding, for cooperation, and for action."[8] When properly handled, communication promotes confidence and respect among subordinates and peers. It has been customary for a long time to speak of communication up and down and across the management group. It was explained that orders go down the line, and information comes up. Recent thinking on this subject holds that information should also go down, and plans and suggestions for actions should form a part of the upward flow. This interpretation of the older formula aids in creating and increasing mutual confidence, and indeed may have a pronounced effect on improving the quality of management decisions.[9]

[7] J. H. McQuaig, "Hiring Executives," *Advanced Management*, Vol. 14, December 1949, pp. 15–16.

[8] *Personnel* magazine, May 1955, Vol. 31, No. 6.

[9] An excellent summary for the study of successful communication is included in the "Ten Commandments of Good Communication," prepared by the American Manage-

Executive Functions

Executive decision making

At the beginning of our discussion of Quantitative Analysis in Chapter 4, we emphasized the fact that the managerial executive is constantly faced with the need to make decisions. The ability to meet this need is the prime quality that distinguishes the successful manager. His decisions must be sound, and he must be able to make them under pressure. He must also be right most of the time. The neophyte may be encouraged to learn that executive decision-making ability is not a mysterious, inborn trait. Nor is it inherited from successful ancestors. It can be improved by experience, and it can be strengthened by following the sound general principles espoused by professional managers. Decision making is further simplified when the manager learns to delegate recurring problems to subordinates, thereby saving his own time for exceptional problems which cannot be reduced to manual solutions. Staff advice and consultative management are also helpful, for the days of the executive who runs a one-man show are over.

Questionable Methods of Decision Making. There are a number of unsound approaches to decision making sometimes followed by unwise executives. One of these is the decision by *hunch* or *intuition*. The executive who follows his "feelings" about what action ought to be taken in problem situations may, with luck, be right 50 per cent of the time. But one of the distinguishing characteristics of successful managers is that they are consistently right more than half the time. Another shaky approach to decision making is the *conclusion based on experience*. The executive depending on this method considers his past success sufficient justification for relying on his experience. But his subjective mood may make it highly unlikely that he can compare all the conditions of his present problem with those of the past. Unless very close similarities exist, the chance for a useful solution of his current dilemma is highly unlikely. The older the experience, the less desirable its use as a precedent. It is not likely that the circumstances of a former problem can be used to analyze a present problem with any reasonable degree of dependability. A third unreliable approach to decision making is that of *experimentation*. The executive who commits his company to a course of action "for a while" to "see how it works out" will be shown the door before he has too many opportunities to expend company resources.

The Scientific Procedure for Decision Making. It will be no surprise to the student to find that the soundest decision-making procedure is simply a slightly different restatement of the scientific method already outlined in

ment Association (1955) and reprinted in *Readings in Management,* by Max D. Richards and William A. Nielander (South-Western Publishing Company: Cincinnati, 1958), pp. 141–143.

Chapter 4 as the quantitative analyst uses it. The managing executive often refers to it as "the engineering method of decision making." It follows several well-established steps.

Step 1: *Define the Problem.* This first step in rational scientific decision making is also the most crucial. A correct solution to the wrong problem is a pure waste of time, yet however elementary this first step may appear, it does not always receive sufficient attention in practice. It is important that the problem be defined precisely; and to avoid misunderstanding and loss of time, it should be expressed in writing. It is frequently difficult to decide on a clear and correct definition of the problem. Many business problems are so complicated that it is easy to confuse the real problem with some surface result or cause of it. Time devoted to a clear and correct statement is well spent. Without it, all subsequent effort is wasted. Executives who pride themselves on making a quick statement of a particular problem often fool no one more than themselves.

An interesting illustrative problem was brought to the author by the frustrated owner of a medium-sized hosiery mill. Briefly, the owner itemized all his costs, many of which were on a piece-work basis, from yarn to boxing, on the basis of a dozen pairs. Then he added what purported to be his overhead on a dozen pairs, which he figured on a percentage basis. His total was subtracted from his selling price obtained through a manufacturer's agent, leaving him a net profit of 22¢ per dozen. His problem: "How is it that I ship 75,000 dozen pairs at a profit of 22¢ per dozen, and have an overall loss of $850.00 when I should have a profit of $16,500?" A simple problem, but difficult to explain to one who had never heard of the break-even chart. In addition, it was necessary to point out to the owner that his overhead was out of line.

This example illustrates the importance of expressing the critical factor in the problem statement. This hosiery-mill-owner's production was not large enough to cover his costs and leave a net profit. His problem was to find his break-even point. The critical factor in any problem is the crux of the necessary solution.

Step 2: *Collect the Relevant Facts.* After defining the problem and isolating its critcal factor, as many relevant facts as possible must be assembled. If too many of the relevant facts have been omitted, some or all of the alternative solutions are likely to be comparatively useless. On the other hand, irrelevant facts may only cloud the central problem and delay the analysis, if indeed they do not affect the solutions adversely.

Step 3: *Analyze the Problem.* Analyzing the problem consists of studying critcially all the facts obtained in the second step both in themselves and in relation to each other. Peter Drucker suggests that "to make a sound decision, it is not necessary to have all the facts, but it is necessary to know what information is lacking in order to judge how much of a risk the decision involves, as well as the degree of precision and rigidity that the proposed course of action can afford."[10] One of the difficult parts of the analysis is the practical impossibility of eliminating the subjective element by the analyst. Herein lies the advantage of having more than one analyst working on this phase of the problem.

Step 4: *Develop Alternative Solutions.* Though most problems may have one best solution, they all have more than one possible solution. The development of the alternative solutions follows an analysis of the relevant facts. When too few solutions are offered for consideration, there is always the danger that the optimum solution is not included in the list. It is important, therefore, to search the subject until an inclusive list of alternatives is presented to the responsible manager for a decision. "The manager is too easily inclined to see only one alternative and to consider it the right one to follow. Nor is it enough for an executive, as some outsiders believe, to decide among the various alternatives which have been presented by his subordinates. . . . It is the manager's job to conceive of more and better alternatives."[11]

To help in this necessary job of uncovering as many alternative solutions as possible, a technique has been developed called "brainstorming." Its purpose is to enlist the assistance of a group with similar interests but with varied backgrounds who meet together and point up alternative solutions through discussions. Experiments made at the University of Buffalo show that ideas resulting are 65 to 90 per cent more numerous than those contributed by any individual. This plan is also referred to as the "uninhibited group approach to idea getting."[12]

Step 5: *Select the Best Solution and Act on it.* Selecting the most acceptable alternative and putting it into effect is the next step. This is often a difficult step to take, especially if no one alternative appears to be the outstanding solution. So it is that the manager is frequently forced to decide from a more or less negative standpoint. Which of the offered solutions requires the least financial outlay; which demands the least effort in making it effective; which appears to include the least undesirable repercussions or risk? And finally, when should the change be made?

It may happen that the manager is not satisfied with any of the alternative solutions because of foreseeable consequences of some kind. If his reasoning is sound and no further alternatives seem possible, it may be that his best decision is to maintain the *status quo* even if this course of action has some undesirable results. This is sometimes called "the decision not to decide."

Step 6: *Make Changes in Action if Needed.* Even if the solution acted upon proves to be a good one, it may be that certain minor "bugs" will be discovered and that the situation would be still further improved if these

[10] *The Practice of Management* (Harper & Brothers, 1954), p. 353.

[11] Theo Haimann, *Professional Management* (Houghton Mifflin Company, 1962), p. 114.

[12] Lester R. Bittel, *Factory* magazine, December, 1961, p. 87.

were removed. Such a dynamic approach is implicit in all phases of management and should always be a guiding factor in improving any solution that appeared to be the "best at the time."

Executive duties

From an over-all standpoint, the executive is responsible for coordination and profits. Under present competitive conditions, he cannot obtain profits for his company without rendering acceptable services, which result from coordination of the company's activities. An equally important objective of the executive is recognition of his concern's social responsibilities to the community, the general public, and the company's employees. Without adequate attention to all of these fundamental duties, no executive can hope to be successful in the modern world of business.

From a technical standpoint, the broad management duties are five: to plan, organize, direct, coordinate, and control. Properly executed, these duties will result in customer satisfaction and profits to the company. It is difficult to list the five technical duties in the order of their importance. Lack of attention to any one of them, even when the other four are expertly handled, can break down the effectiveness of leadership. Each of these functions can also be thought of as the focus of a set of managerial techniques. Around each of them, there has grown up a body of rules and procedures which guide management in the performance of these essential duties.

Planning. The superior executive will not only be constantly aware of the wisdom of planning all actions, but will also be familiar with the best techniques of planning. By management controls, he can measure the present situation; but only by proper planning procedures can he provide guidance for the future. Most plans are guides rather than inflexible courses of action. They should be flexible enough to be adjusted to any changes in the circumstances which originally gave rise to them. Because the specific techniques of planning under scientific management are described throughout the book, no attempt will be made here to outline their technical details.

Organizing. The next important focus of managerial techniques is building the organization structure. The whole of Chapters 6 and 7 are devoted to these techniques. Here we shall only point out that management's attention to the organizing function must extend beyond the formal structure as represented by the organization chart. The chart establishes functional relationships throughout the organization. Whether it is good or bad, there is always an implicit tendency toward managerial rigidity in the structure it sets up. Therefore, the smooth-running concern will often have an informal executive clique which operates chiefly through its social contacts.

This "kitchen cabinet" makes for harmonious operation of the formal organization. It can arrive at unofficial decisions in an atmosphere of mutual give-and-take.

Directing. The third focus of managerial techniques is the actual directing of operations after they have been planned and organized. Directing is based primarily on the positional authority of the executive group. That authority confers the right to command and to direct operations. The executive who does not exercise his official right to command is likely to lose that right to some natural leader who may take over unofficially with the consent of his followers. When authority is used laxly, it may be lost by default; at the other extreme, it may be lost through overuse because of a tendency to rebel by other members of the management team.

The right to command is best exercised by suggestion rather than by an order demanding compliance, although the right to command includes the *obligation* to secure obedience. It entails the further obligation of making orders understandable and of assuring that the person to whom they are directed is capable of carrying them out. Some orders are so detailed that they leave no opportunity for the exercise of initiative.

Coordinating. The fourth functional focus for the exercise of managerial techniques is coordination. This refers to drawing together in proper sequence and balance all activities and forces that go to make up the organization. Its formal basis is found in the right to command, and its informal or psychological basis derives from the necessity for group action. Coordination is apart from the other four functions of management in that it aims to make these others work together. For this reason, coordination may be thought of as the *primus inter pares* of managerial duties. Indeed, management is sometimes defined as the "intangible coordinator of activities."

Controlling. Finally come the techniques of control which measure results against planned objectives. There are numerous methods of control which must be adapted to the activities, objectives, or personnel to which the controls are applied. These methods and techniques are dealt with at length in Chapter 8 on Managerial Control and again in Chapter 9 on Managerial and Production Planning. Controls may be thought of as indicators of situations requiring management attention. They result from records which point out trouble spots. When a record shows that a situation is out of control, it does not necessarily mean that the person with responsibility for the unsatisfactory condition has himself caused it. The trouble may have been due to factors beyond his personal control and may include such things as inadequate machines or tools, improper materials, or insufficient skill of the worker. What it does mean is that the executive must act as trouble shooter until the situation is under control once again.

Two techniques of command and control which deserve comment are disciplining and discipline. "Disciplining," or disciplinary action, has to do with the sanctions or punishments for infractions of the establshed rules. "Discipline" refers to that attitude of a person or group which exhibits a desire to follow the rules established for guidance. It is inculcated through indoctrination. The aim of such indoctrination is to evoke the personal desire for team action through adherence to the rules of the game. In the military, discipline saves lives; in industry, it promotes productivity; in all types of organization, it is necessary for smooth-flowing operations.

Executive actions

In the course of translating his duties into action, the executive should be guided by the following general rules:

1. *Give attention to broad problems,* leaving the minor ones to subordinates.
2. *Delegate assignable duties,* thus adding to his own usefulness and accomplishments.
3. *Schedule his time* so that a balanced workday includes opportunities for consulting with subordinates, and for planning and organizing.
4. *Control the activities* of his company so he will know whether standards are being met, and if they are not, the reasons for failure.
5. *Visualize the results* of a course of action.
6. *Invite suggestions* to improve activities, methods, and plans to stimulate loyalty of participation.
7. *Discuss ideas* and future plans with associates.
8. *Consult with outside specialists* on technical matters in which none of his staff members specializes.
9. *Make decisions* on the basis of facts rather than hunches.
10. *Follow decisions with action.*
11. *Honor traditions* while remaining open to new ideas.
12. *Respect the value of principles* and the flexibility of methods.
13. *Communicate decisions* and future plans to subordinates.
14. *Praise liberally* and censure constructively.
15. *Confer with his peers* critically and his subordinates sympathetically.
16. *Train understudies,* and insist that his staff members do likewise.

Appraising executives

It has been customary in the past to apply service ratings only to those below the executive level. However, ratings are being developed and improved to apply to "key personnel," which includes the executive group. These ratings, like those for line workers, are used to determine first, how well the individual is doing his job, and second, what action should be taken on the basis of the findings. Figure 35.2 is an excellent executive-rating scale. Graphic-rating scales can also be used to advantage, regis-

tering the degree to which key personnel measure up to the desired qualifications. Here, as with most ratings, the big problem is to decide on the
factors to be rated.

Avoiding executive failure

An inflated feeling of authority is one of the major pitfalls of executives.
Kingston aptly expressed the idea when he wrote that "nothing more im-
pairs authority than a too frequent or indiscreet use of it. If thunder itself
were to be continual, it would excite no more terror than the noise of a
mill." Nothing entrenches an executive so thoroughly in an ivory tower,
beyond the reach of suggestions and the truth itself, as an exaggerated
opinion of the importance of his official position. Basic errors in judgment
and action are apparent when the executive:

1. Cuts across established channels and ignores accepted procedures because
   he does not understand organization.
2. Confuses flexibility with lack of procedures and policies because he wants
   others to believe he knows all the answers.
3. Keeps aloof from the rank and file, hoping to build an impervious wall of
   respect about himself.
4. Dislikes people, so does not get along with them.
5. Fails to visualize the future because he is enmeshed in details of the present,
   and hence is frequently amazed at the normal consequences of his actions.
6. Fails to coordinate activities because he cannot comprehend their relationships.
7. Creates the feeling among subordinates that he cannot be trusted; true or
   not, results are the same.
8. Resents suggestions out of established routine, causing him to make snap
   judgments or procrastinate.
9. Does not delegate responsibility because he enjoys having his subordinates
   come to him with their problems as if they were trying to "stump the
   expert."
10. Does not understand control procedures and so has only a haphazard check
    on accomplishments.
11. Hears only good news from subordinates because they know his mind is
    closed to the truth.
12. Makes improper decisions on incomplete data simply because there are
    some data missing.
13. Settles unfamiliar proposals by deciding that they cannot be done.
14. Appoints unqualified relatives to positions in the company.

There is a single word for number fourteen on the above list: it is *nepotism*.
This problem is becoming so prevalent in American business as to require
considered attention. There has always been an appreciable amount of
nepotism among the worker ranks, but in recent years it has been creeping
up into the management levels. One of the results of nepotism is feather-

Figure 35.2

Executive Rating Scale

EXECUTIVE RATING

Name _____   Date _____

Position _____   Time in present position _____

KNOWLEDGE OF JOB (Circle the square which best describes person being rated.)

RESPONSIBILITIES AND DUTIES	Thoroughly Understood	Generally Understood	Fairly Clear	Confused
COMPANY POLICY AND PROCEDURES AFFECTING WORK	Complete	Good	Sketchy	Insufficient
DETAILS	Complete	Good	Sketchy	Insufficient
NEW DEVELOPMENTS IN FIELD	Thoroughly Informed	Well Informed	Fairly Well Informed	Inadequate

PERFORMANCE ON JOB

ORGANIZATION AND PLANNING	Can Always Plan Work Independently and Expertly	Can Usually Plan Routine and New Work	Can Only Plan Routine Work	Cannot Plan Logically
JUDGMENT	Excellent—Can Trust with Major Decisions	Decisions Generally Show Clear Thinking	Can Be Trusted with Minor Decisions Only	All Decisions Have To Be Checked
IMAGINATION— CONSTRUCTIVE THINKING	Consistently Excellent Ideas	Good Practical Ideas	Some Original Ideas— Not Always Good	No Imagination
PRESENTATION OF IDEAS AND PLANS	Excels in Making Plans Effective	Generally Able To "Put Plans Across"	Average Ability in "Selling" Plans	Cannot Put Ideas Across
DELEGATION OF WORK	Successfully Delegates Responsibilities and Authority	Generally Assigns Duties Fairly and Intelligently	Has Trouble in Assigning Work	Tries To Do Everything Himself
EMOTIONAL STABILITY	Always Objective— Has Complete Self-control	Maintains Good Balance	Fair—"Blows Up" Occasionally	Over-sensitive— Cannot "Take" Criticism
ACCEPTANCE OF RESPONSIBILITY	Accepts Full Responsibility— Welcomes New Duties	Generally Stands His Ground—Accepts New Responsibilities	Tendency to "Pass the Buck" and Avoid New Responsibilities	Shies Away From Responsibility
RELIABILITY AND FRANKNESS	Wholly Reliable— Will Follow Plans, Admit Errors	Generally Reliable and Frank	Not Always Frank	Cannot Be Depended Upon
COOPERATIVENESS	Always Helpful and Cooperative	Will Generally Cooperate	Doesn't Always Try To See Other Point of View	Stubborn— Not Cooperative
EFFECT OF PERSONAL AND FAMILY LIFE	No Harmful Effects on Work	Rarely Interferes with Work	Occasional and Slightly Adverse Effect	Continually Bad— Serious Effect

What are his outstanding abilities? _____

_____

What are his principal points for improvement? _____

_____

Recommendations for improvement? _____

_____

Is his performance generally improving . . . remaining the same . . . or deteriorating? _____

Is he promotable? _____   To what? _____   When? _____

SUMMARY RATING—(Circle appropriate grade. Use above information in developing grade.)

1. EXCELLENT   + −
2. GOOD   + −
3. AVERAGE   + −
4. POOR   + −
5. FAILING   + −

Rater's Signature _____

Reviewer's Signature _____

bedding — employing a person who is not needed for the job. Some of our laws and labor-union pressure promote featherbedding to an extent that has attracted public attention. The railroads furnish a glaring example; even our civil service suffers from it to some extent. When featherbedding extends to the executive group, it disrupts harmony and coordination, and is very expensive.

In the October 1955 issue of the *Corporate Director* (American Institute of Management), it was pointed out that "of 23,000 companies studied, more than half revealed a threat of nepotism, and thus a threat of featherbedding. In less than 10 per cent of the companies is there complete freedom from featherbedding in management. In more than nine out of ten, at least one member of the management echelon should not be on the payroll." Management has a flimsy basis for complaining about labor featherbedding while it is guilty of the same practice. In the management group, the cost is greater and the example far more obvious. When banks merge, for example, the result is usually a plethora of vice-presidents who are free of obvious responsibilities. Mergers are a part of the featherbedding deal in many types of business. When executives are afraid to train capable subordinates, the hiring of relatives frees them from the threat of competition. It is assumed that relatives make secure "yes-men." In far away India, the Comprehensive Company Law of 1956 contained a provision that a stockholder's resolution must approve the employment of a director's relative.

The *Robot Executive* is one who worships the past. He does not fit into today's dynamic executive situation. Whether his desire is to "play safe" or to avoid mistakes by doing only what has been done successfully in the past makes little difference as far as managerial progress is concerned. In a word, this type of executive lacks the motivation of the pioneer, the group that put this country in the forefront industrially. There is a school of thought which feels that he is a "growing threat to American industry."[13] It is alleged by some psychologists that this pattern of conformity is due to the great size of such institutions as government, business, and organized labor, which tends to dwarf the individual and decrease self-confidence. The robot executive is another product of insecurity in a troubled world. Part of the danger lies in the fact that such robots should be participating in our modern industrial complex with its broad social responsibilities and implications. From another angle, any marked decrease in the number of our pioneering executives will slowly result in our yielding the industrial scepter which this country holds today. Mr. Greenewalt, president of Du Pont, emphasizes that this "cult of conformity" in which the individual subordinates himself to the organization and its established *mores* will surely eliminate executive identity and creativity if it is allowed to grow.

[13] "Robot Executives," an address by Louis E. Wolfson before the Louisville Sales Executive Council, November 10, 1958.

In the past, unoriginal conformist thinking would have strangled such innovations as installment sales, meat packaging, the assembly line, the supermarket, and prefabricated housing.

The creative executive, the self-starter, is needed today more than at any time in our history because of the rising tide of international competition. The institutional executive, with his numbing effect on initiative, should be replaced by idea men who promote initiative and are sensitive to the common cause. The best sign that the present holds for the future is the growing number of executive development seminars. Another source of hope lies in the business training programs of our colleges and universities. These programs can be stimulated and improved by more careful selection of candidates. We do not need the "Joe College" of the past who, though less numerous, is far from extinct, but able, ambitious young men who have shown signs of individuality rather than a tendency towards conformity.

The *kickback* is another expensive business practice for which the executive must assume responsibility. Government figures indicate that kickbacks are responsible for a 7-per cent increase in food prices. Kickbacks are forcing up the cost of clothing, automobiles, homes, and even factory buildings. They shrink our buying power and increase our taxes. In the recent Chrysler flareup, it was alleged that the company's president profited by nearly half a million dollars from rebates paid by suppliers in whose business he had a financial interest. The receipt of kickbacks is essentially dishonest in that it cheats the stockholder-owners. In addition, kickbacks are seldom, if ever, reported as income for federal taxes. One of the outstanding defenses of the recipient is that he did not ask for the rebate — it was simply given.

Executives frequently know about rebates being given to members of their staffs, and indeed they occasionally participate in the graft. One member of a management group, after leaving the employ of the concern where he had received kickbacks, testified that he was encouraged in the practice by "every officer of the corporation" to supplement his salary. The "round-robin" kickback is engineered within a group of executives who exchange merchandise gift certificates of equal value on alternate holidays, without embarrassment and with tax advantages.

More than one national concern is going out of its way to fight this dishonest practice. It is up to all executives to follow this example. Here are some suggestions for stopping the racket:

1. Place the most respected executives in charge of purchasing, inspection, and contracting — the vulnerable spots for kickbacks.
2. Let all employees understand that receiving kickbacks in any form is cause for immediate dismissal.
3. Inform all vendors that "gifts" to any employee in any form are forbidden, and that violation will stop purchasing from the offending company.

4. Eradicate nepotism. Relatives with unjustified earnings promote the receipt of kickbacks by those not so favored.
5. Expose publicly the attempts to extract rebates from suppliers.
6. Compel executives to set an example of honesty.[14]

Conclusions

The successful business leaders of today are professional executives. The addition of new departments in the industrial enterprise in the past decade demands professionals for their operation, coordination, and control. Some of the new functions on the top management level include directorships of the Budget, Management Development, Market Research, Organization Planning, Human Relations, and Systems and Procedures. Executives must know something about all of these new functions in order to coordinate them. In addition, they must have more than a speaking acquaintance with the New Techniques of Management discussed in Chapter 3, and with those of the Quantitative Analyst discussed in Chapters 4 and 5.

A few examples will testify to the new executive's progress in trying to familiarize himself with his new responsibilities. In 1946, the American Management Association had 9,000 members; in 1960, it had 30,000. In 1946, it had a budget of $350,000; in 1960 the budget was $800,000. Where 9000 members attended its meetings in 1946, the number attending its courses and seminars in 1960 was 70,000. At the end of World War II, only a few universities offered brief management-development courses for business executives. Today, the number has increased to 71.[15] Several large companies have made remarkable strides in furthering executive development. General Electric has a campus with dormitories, classrooms, and faculty. Westinghouse Electric conducts an extensive program. These and many others have developed since World War II. The super-executive has not arrived, but it is clear that promising groundwork has been laid, and the future promises better training and improved methods.

These beginnings concern the technical phases of the executive's development. There are other fields which will expand as management comes to understand more fully its social obligations. These will include relations with customers, the general public, and other countries. Profits must remain the chief purpose of management if it wishes to retain access to public funds for expansion, but its larger social and economic obligations will foster the expansion for which many less-favored nations are waiting.

On the less-bright side are the causes of executive failures and the reprehensible causes of unnnecessarily high costs, including nepotism, featherbedding and kickbacks. Unless these failings are corrected from the inside

---

[14] These suggestions are culled from the American Institute of Management's *Corporate Reporter* for March 1954, Vol. III, No. 19, entitled "The Great American Kickback."

[15] The number of development courses was obtained from "Intensive Courses and Seminars For Executives" (American Management Association, 1958) pp. 58–60.

within a reasonable time, legislation will be enacted as it has been in the past.

Finally, we may expect favorable results from the many new graduates of schools of business. Youth is temperamentally opposed to questionable practices in business and less conservative than age in its plans for correcting them. The function of undergraduate colleges should be to stimulate interest in the opportunities for both service and profits in business enterprises, with technical training and development left to graduate work or to the professional seminars of business associations.

The big step forward in management improvement will result from a recognized code of ethics based on an acceptable philosophy. These guides will develop slowly as the executive recognizes his social and economic responsibilities.[16]

QUESTIONS

1. What does Dun & Bradstreet cite as the underlying cause of 90 per cent of business failures?

2. What characteristic should all members of the management team have in common?

3. What is the primary basis for determining whether or not a given company has good leadership?

4. Why is the traitist theory — that certain characteristics naturally beget good leadership — largely illusory?

5. From an over-all standpoint, what are the two principal responsibilities of the executive? He is otfen judged by the number of his correct decisions, but what two factors indicate the measure of his judgment in solving problems?

6. What are the five broad duties of management as learned earlier in this text?

7. What are the necessary ingredients of good executive control?

8. What are the two principal situations which the executive of fifty years ago would find most distressing if he were operating today?

9. What chief personal qualities are necessary for today's executive?

10. The text mentions sixteen procedures which should guide the qualified executive in translating his capacities into successful action. Name some of them.

11. Since the solution of repetitive situations should be delegated to subordinates, the executive's skill and energy can be devoted to solving exceptional problems. What is the relation of the techniques discussed in Chapter 4 to the solution of both repetitive and exceptional tasks?

12. In solving any problem, it is advisable, if not necessary, to follow the five or

[16] A very enlightening article, "How Ethical are Businessmen?" by Raymond C. Baumhart, appears in the *Harvard Business Review* for July-August 1961, p. 7 *et sequi*.

steps in what is known as the research or engineering method. What are those steps?

13. One of the steps considered in the previous question is, "Gather the relevant facts." To what extent do irrelevant or incorrect facts lead to wrong solutions?

14. Why is the correct statement of any executive problem so important?

15. What is the outstanding problem in the selection of an executive?

16. What are some of the social obligations of the executive, and how should he go about meeting them?

17. What is meant by the "House Party Approach" to executive selection? How highly do you rate such an approach?

18. How would you draft a plan for appraising the work of the executive?

19. How important is the executive's ability to communicate with his peers and subordinates?

20. What are some of the causes of executive failure?

CASE PROBLEM

THE NATIONAL ROAD MACHINERY COMPANY

The National Road Machinery Company was founded in 1900 by Morgan Lewis after he had served a similar concern in various capacities for about twenty years. As a result of his last ten years' experience as general superintendent with his former employer, Mr. Lewis attracted such a wide following among road builders that National was a large concern by 1920 when its founder reached his sixtieth birthday. A general line of road machinery was being sold to city and state governments as well as to private contractors, but emphasis was gradually shifted to gasoline-driven scrapers and rollers. Specialization enabled the company to compete more easily and increased its business accordingly.

The "boss" mastered the principles of engineering and management by correspondence in his earlier days and practiced them constantly on the job. As a production man, he spent most of his time in the plants, even after the business became large. He knew all his key shop men and made it a practice to speak to everyone. When he saw a strange face, he made a special effort to make the worker feel at home and invariably asked him for suggestions to improve operations.

His courage in making radical mechanical improvements in the road equipment was recognized by the superintendents, and his energy was admired by most of his workers. The "boss" was distinctly the democratic and persuasive type. His search for ideas extended to members of the board, which encouraged them to accompany him on plant tours after their meetings. Above all, he seemed to be an inspirational leader by nature, and it was easy to see that he thoroughly enjoyed his job and its environment.

The shops were always equipped with modern machinery. Mr. Lewis had a philosophy that high-priced equipment and highly paid workers assured him the cream of the crop in both categories. He delighted in making it clear to all employees that they did not need to fear competition with such a combination.

He expounded similar ideas in the company magazine from time to time over his signature.

When his sixtieth birthday was celebrated by an all-day country picnic, his two sons had been part of the organization for about ten years. Their education was obtained on the day shift, but they were not spared the rigors of plant experience. Neither was mechanically inclined, nor was it necessary that they should be. A general business education would normally be as valuable to the concern as engineering training, especially since the enginering problems were improving rather than building from the bottom.

The "boys" were likable enough, but in a different way from their father. They didn't make many mistakes for the simple reason that they found it easier to go along. They also felt some resentment at what they considered was an unjustifiable attitude on the part of many supervisory employees. Their outside social interests had helped to keep their shop interests on an objective basis.

When Mr. Lewis was forced to retire and move to another part of the country because of his health, he selected a retired Army officer as president of the concern. He was influenced to this move chiefly because of the officer's wide experience with military procurment. It was Mr. Lewis' idea that sales would likely be the weak point of National's business and that his sons would be better fitted for looking after the production processes. This, he felt would be a perfect top-management combination. The general's thirty years' experience gave him easy entree to military buyers, while the boys had a thorough knowledge of production. The general should be president because of his age and the possibility of his stabilizing influence if friction developed between the two brothers.

As occasionally happens, a strong man makes his weakest decision toward the end of his business career. By the end of the first year under the new arrangement, the sons were agreed that the general's wings must be clipped, and the newly organized union felt the same way.

PROBLEM: From the consideration of executive qualities and the causes for its failures presented in this chapter, how would you explain National's loss of leadership in an industrial field? Two of the big questions are the new president's ability as an industrial leader and his relations with middle management. What characteristics do you feel that the new president must cultivate, and how could he go about it? If you were in the general's position, what would you do to secure the active cooperation of the two brothers? And if you were one of the brothers, what steps would you take to restore harmonious operations between top and middle management, with the idea of restoring National to its leadership in its field?

36

The Supervisor

Many executives who have come up through the ranks feel that the supervisor, or foreman, holds the key position for maintaining operations in smooth working order.[1] This appraisal holds for similarly placed subordinates in all lines of business. Whereas middle management has top management on one side and foremen on the other, the foreman is between his men and all the other layers of management. A further distinction between middle management and the supervisor, as members of the team, is the big difference in their status. In some cases even today, the supervisor is scarcely included on the management team, except through lip service.

Until the Taft-Hartley Act (1947) placed the foreman legally in the management group, the workers' opinion of their foreman ran something like this: "Some foremen are O.K., especially those who have been on the job for a long time, but most of them have swelled heads and don't know as much about their jobs as some of their men. They play favorites and throw themselves around like big shots, but they are afraid to tell the real big shots what's wrong with the place, and how the workers should be treated. They grab credit for good ideas and pass the buck to their men for the things that go wrong."

On the other hand, the supervisor's idea of his own status runs something like this: "He's the man who takes orders from everyone else in management about how to do things, and how to get the workers to produce. No matter how impossible the orders from above, the supervisor is supposed to carry on and report favorable results. At the same time, he is supposed to talk the workers out of all their gripes, and not let any complaints get to upper management. He never does enough, and gets the blame for everything that goes wrong below and above his job level. Government regulations are always making his job tougher. He works long hours for little

---

[1] The terms "foreman" and "supervisor" are used interchangeably in this text to refer to that level of management, in any kind of business, which has responsibility for direct supervision of the working force.

more pay than his men, and sometimes he gets less because the workers are paid for overtime."

Those two speeches have been made many times by typical supervisors and their men. They represent the extreme views, of course, but at the same time they do describe situations as they exist in some plants.

The foreman's self-apraisal has notable support from outside authorities. Professor F. J. Roethlisberger of the Harvard Business School, for example, gives this opinion:[2]

There is little question of the importance of the foreman to the smooth running operation of any industrial organization. Not only for practical, efficient operation, but also for healthy human relations his importance is universally acknowledged. . . . Here, *par excellence* is the "man in the middle." . . . Here is a man in the middle of the abstract and the concrete, in the middle of theory and practice, in the middle of good intentions and practical achievement, in the middle of the verbal and nonverbal worlds, and in the middle of changing technology and time-honored customs. Here in essence is the man of the hour.

Duties of the supervisor

What does the supervisor have to say about the things that are included in his daily task? The following answers were contributed by a group of some fifty foremen with average service records of more than fifteen years, from a dozen plants in Dayton, Ohio. They were participating in a series of discussions led by the author under the auspices of the Dayton Foremen's Club.

Responsibilities to Management
1. Watch after the quality and quantity of production
2. Keep worker morale at a high level
3. Cooperate with the upper layers of management
4. Keep management informed of all plant conditions
5. Keep the costs of direct and indirect labor, materials, and supplies within the budget allowances
6. Maintain safe working conditions in the shop
7. Be on the alert to suggest improved methods
8. Maintain good housekeeping in the department
9. Be loyal to management and its objectives
10. Maintain the necessary records and reports
11. Administer company policies correctly
12. Protect company property at all times
13. Guard the health of the workers

[2] From the Foreword to Abraham Zeleznik, *Foreman Training in a Growing Enterprise* (Boston: Division of Research, Graduate School of Business Administration, Harvard University, 1951), p. v.

14. Make his personal conduct a model for his men
15. See that rules and regulations are observed
16. Keep down the amount of waste and scrap
17. Use special care in inducting new employees

Responsibility to the Workers
1. Use the best methods for worker induction
2. Add a human touch to on-the-job training
3. Maintain safe working conditions
4. Promote cooperation and good will
5. See that workers are properly placed
6. Make honest merit ratings
7. Improve the efficiency of the workers
8. Maintain technical knowledge of the job
9. Keep the worker posted about his progress
10. Interpret company policies clearly and fairly
11. Set an example in his personal conduct
12. Keep workers informed on items other than policy
13. Treat the worker as an individual
14. Keep transfers and promotions on an objective basis
15. Maintain satisfactory working conditions
16. Encourage suggestions and give credit when due
17. Furnish inspiring leadership

These duties, as classified by experienced foremen, present a formidable task for any man who has been recently promoted from the bench.

Problems of supervisors

Chief of the supervisor's problems is the frustration which has resulted from "functionalizing" some of his past duties, and assigning them to service and staff departments. This loss of former responsibilities has weakened his authority at a time when he is being assigned new duties of a trying character. Prior to the general establishment of personnel departments, the foreman had the right to hire and fire. With the feeling on both sides that the worker owed his job to his foreman, who could fire him without interference, authority was relatively easy to maintain.

The personnel function, combined with the rising power of organized labor, wiped out this unquestioned authority. Personnel is now making hiring suggestions for the foreman's approval or disapproval. Since he is too busy to do recruiting, and because he knows nothing about the applicant except what the personnel department has told him, he approves. If he discharges a worker on "general principles," he has to defend his action before the union's grievance committee. The result is often a reversal of his decision by upper management, with consequent loss of face among his men. If, on the other hand, he appears to have good and definite reasons for his action, his decision may be reversed because of management's fear of union pressure or "for the good of the company." The shrewd foreman soon learns to ask the personnel department to transfer the objectionable worker, rather than discharge him.

The supervisor has been relieved of his former buying authority by the purchasing department. His ego, at least, was formerly boosted by his contacts with salesmen. Since it has now become customary to require passes issued by the personnel department for entrance of any outsider to a plant shop, salesman-foreman relations are restricted almost entirely to discussions in the offices of the purchasing department. Maintenance and repair work is done for the foreman by the maintenance department, which is sure that it knows more about his machines than he does. His materials, which the purchasing department buys on his requisition, but often without consulting him, are sent to his department by the material-handling section.

On the other hand, the supervisor must shoulder many new duties as a member of the management team. One group of new duties concerns legal regulations with which he must be familiar. The Business Management Service of the University of Illinois lists the following:

1. State employer's liability and compensation acts
2. Unemployment insurance acts
3. The Federal Security Act
4. State old-age assistance and pension acts
5. Fair Labor Standards Act and state wage acts
6. Acts governing the employment of females and minors
7. Factory inspection acts
8. Fair employment and nondiscrimination acts
9. Taft-Hartley and Wagner Acts
10. Walsh-Healy Act
11. The G.I. Bill of Rights

On his own level, the supervisor must plan, organize, direct, coordinate, and control just as the upper layers of management. In this connection, his chief job is to see that production goes on without interruption. But the details for his guidance are handed to him by the production-control department.

In dealing with his workers, he is often managing those who have divided loyalties. The share of loyalty they give their company and their union depends to a large extent on the personality of their supervisor and the activity of their union local. Top and middle management escape most of this direct contact with worker resistance by leaving the matter in the supervisor's hands.

Carrying out company policies is another problem of the supervisor. Without the privilege, in most cases, of participating in the drawing up of these policies, he must take them as they are handed to him and try to get his men to accept them as fair. Besides all these things, he may also be requested to contribute to flow-of-work programs, work simplification, morale building, and industrial and public relations.

How to choose supervisors

The best supervisor is the one who is able to get his men to *want* to do the things he wants them to do. The usual practice in filling foremanship vacancies is to pick the most skilled workman in the department or the one who has had the longest period of service. The thought behind this method is that he must know the technical phases of his department's operations. But though technical knowledge is certainly a great help, it is clear that the duties require management ability even more than technical skills. He must be able to lead his men. Leadership demands adaptability and the ability to learn as well as to be a sympathetic teacher. He must be able to evaluate facts for the purposes of settling grievances. He must be dependable, intelligent, and fair to both workers and the company if his men are to have confidence in his leadership. And finally, he must be able to proceed on his own initiative within the limits of the authority given to him.

The first general decision in supervisor selection is whether to promote from within or attract someone from another company. Many concerns have a fixed rule that promotions should come from within their own ranks. On the other hand, some production managers feel that a supervisor chosen from the outside has the advantage of starting on his new job without prejudices. Neither plan is good under all circumstances. The greatest need in supervisor selection is an objective method for determining the intangible qualification known as leadership. Tests are always inadequate in determining personality traits of this sort. References and data on family background are interesting, but scarcely informative about the candidate's future managerial ability.

Possibly foremanship could be measured by something like the kind of trade test which asks the candidate for a bricklayer's job to lay a reasonable stand of bricks. During World War II, the Assessment Staff of the Office of Strategic Services devised some ingenious methods of evaluating, among other characteristics, a man's leadership ability. For example, in the "Brook Test," a group of men with no designated leader would be taken to a stream where scattered around the bank were a number of boards (none long enough to span the stream), three lengths of rope, a pulley and a barrel with both ends knocked out, and a log. The group was told to imagine that the log was a delicate range-finder which had to be transported safely to the other side. To solve the problem, both planning and cooperative action were essential. Trained observers were on hand to evaluate the emerging ability of the group members. "The good leader was the one who commanded the respect and following of others, who had the ability to organize their ideas into a plan, and who was forceful enough to guide his colleagues to the completion of their task with a minimum of friction and a maximum of cooperation."[3]

How to improve supervisors

Top management is responsible for taking the initiative in improving company supervisors. Although comprehensive training is an important requisite, the program should not spend too much time on the psychology of getting workers to do what they are told to do. Many companies over-emphasize this phase of supervisor training. As they are a part of management, supervisors should be made acquainted with the principles of management. Knowledge of these principles can lead to the other desired objectives.

Knowing how to give orders is an important aid to the good supervisor. Broadly speaking, orders should be phrased as invitations to participate rather than as blunt commands. The way an order is given is just as important as what is said.

Keeping informed about company operations is a tool which a foreman can use to great advantage. However, he cannot use it unless he is kept informed by upper management, a procedure which is unfortunately lacking in many companies. Supervisors often learn about company matters from their men, who received their information from the union stewards. This inexcusable form of communication leaves the foreman chagrined in his dealing with his subordinates.

Supervisors should also be taught the fundamental economics of business. Instructions in methods improvement will enable them to cut costs. As an important part of their training, they should be supplied with manuals that answer the questions of daily routines and guide their planning.

If upper management wants supervisors to feel that they are a part of the management team, they must be treated as such. They should be given authority commensurate with their responsibilities. Their pay should provide a differential large enough to demonstrate clearly that their contribution is greater than that of the ordinary worker. A necessary adjunct of reasonable earnings is assurance of job security. Supervisors should also be encouraged to come forward with suggestions and be rewarded for acceptable ideas. Upper management should so act in their relations with foremen as to gain and keep their real confidence. Only then will they feel that they are a part of the management peerage. Finally, custom has established an office as the symbol of management. A place to make and keep records and reports, and to confer in private with workers is not only an outward sign of the supervisor's place in management, it *is* good management.

[3] The OSS Assessment Staff, *Assessment of Men* (New York: Rinehart & Company, Inc., 1948), p. 98.

Training supervisors

Successful supervisors are not born that way; they must be trained. Even if some are naturally adept at getting along with their peers and subordinates, there are many rules, regulations, and techniques in addition to the mechanical features of an operation which must be part of the stock-in-trade of any good supervisor. Many of these aids to acceptable supervision cannot be learned at the bench. Naturally, foremen must know how to deal with worker grievances, but parts of the answer to many grievances are found in company rules and regulations, and in state and national laws. Another important source is the labor-management contract. After all these things are learned, the supervisor's slant in management's interest is gained by indoctrination of company policies.

Several surveys made since 1958 show that worker grievances are increasing. Irrespective of the cause, and it may be due to poorly trained supervisors, the generally accepted remedy is broader and better training. Some of the favored subjects are labor laws, performance standards, the labor-management contract, and human relations. These relate to the supervisor's non-technical duties; he is usually well prepared in the technical phases of his department before he takes over as foreman.

There is an advisable follow-up to instructions in the company's contract with its union. After the supervisor has been instructed in the importance, meanings, and interpretations of the contract, and because he is in the first line of contact with the workers, he should participate in the next preliminary contract discussions. He will naturally have valid suggestions which can be used in the actual negotiations.

Management has many problems to be considered in training supervisors. How long will it take to get satisfactory results? How much will it cost? Should the training be done on company time? How long should a training session last? For these and many other problems, management does not have reliable answers, which proves that supervisory training is still in the experimental stage. The answer to "how long" runs all the way from two sessions a week for six months, to two or three years. How much does it cost? Most companies do not want to answer that question. In fact, they do not want to know the answer for fear of being disagreeably surprised. Inland Steel estimates that its training program costs from $2,500 to $4,000 for the average supervisor. There is general agreement that supervisors should be trained on company time.

Probably the approach to training that requires most attention at the present time is the selection of the human material to be trained. But even here there is no sure guide at present. The second problem is how to go about training. There are a number of ways. It is usually conceded that the training sessions should be generously sprinkled with discussions in which the trainees participate. Such sessions are often based on actual problems which the supervisory group is experiencing in its day-to-day work. Finally, there is the teaching materials and the teachers. Training of supervisors is still in the elementary stage, and a lot of trial-and-error will be necessary before acceptable standards are worked out. In the meantime, it is one of management's important problems because it is probably the best plan for keeping the supervisor on management's side of the labor-management fence.

Essentials of a Program for Improving Supervisors

1. Set clearly and honestly the company's policy with regard to supervisors; define their relationships with employees; and emphasize that the company will back them within these policies.

2. Admit, with reasons, the tough, in-the-middle position of the supervisor under today's labor conditions.

3. Establish in his mind a feeling of job security at least equal to that which organized labor tries to guarantee its members. Assure him that his job is not subject to the whims of some member of top-management. Urge him to think and plan ahead. Relief from fear-pressures will free his energies for constructive thinking.

4. Set forth clearly his status as a part of management, including his authority and responsibility, and see to it that these two principles of management are reasonably commensurate. Establish the line of authority above him, thus relieving him of the feeling that any one of two or three others have control of his destiny with the organization.

5. Help him to learn the art of supervision in handling his subordinates, how to satisfy complaints and grievances, how to improve relations with workers, how to get subordinates to want to cooperate, and how to grade performance and appraise workers. Such training should be made a continuous process based on conference and problem-solving methods.

6. Assure him that as a member of management, he has management's confidence. With this in mind, he should be told about decisions before they are put into practice, and before the "grapevine" or a union steward tells him about them. Only in this way can he be expected to develop a sense of "belonging." Also, sharing in minor policy determinations is an excellent developer.

7. Not only ask, but urge him to come forward with ideas and suggestions on labor policies, as well as with business and production plans for the future. Let him participate occasionally in the formulation of labor contracts.

8. Help him to advance the technical improvements of production, but always emphasize that it is the human element which dominates the mechanical for continued success.

9. Always keep in mind that to the employees the supervisor represents

the company. When he realizes this, he will want to play his part and play it adequately from a sense of pride.

Supervisor incentives

Most of the incentive-pay plans that have been applied to supervisors have been found wanting, and, as a consequence, most of them have been discontinued. Many failures have been caused by unsatisfactory selection of incentive criteria or standards. Some plans have not only been confusing, but they have retarded the progress toward finding workable incentive-pay arrangements applicable to the supervisor. A workable plan must obviously be based on factors over which he has control. One group of favored criteria includes volume of production, unit labor costs, total unit costs, and savings in scrap and supplies. These standards for measuring effectiveness frequently give cause for varying degrees of dissatisfaction.

In the first place, volume of production may be vitally affected by break-down of machines or the failure of raw materials or supplies in either kind or quantity. Machine breakdown may be the fault of maintenance, while the failure of raw materials or supplies may rest with the purchasing department or, possibly, with that section of engineering which made up the specifications. These and similar faults are attributable to management leaders above the supervisor level.

Unit-labor costs are often at least half the total unit costs, which also include materials, supplies, and production overhead. If production volume falls because of factors suggested in the preceding paragraph, labor and total unit costs invariably rise, a situation which the foreman cannot control.

Likewise, the amount of useless scrap made and the excessive volume of supplies used in processing may depend on the quality of materials, supplies, and tools furnished to each production department. There is a "one best quality" for all three. If the quality of materials and supplies is too high, total unit costs may price the finished product out of the market; if the quality is too low, the volume of scrap is bound to rise, again increasing total unit costs. To be held responsible for scrap losses, it seems reasonable that the foreman should be allowed to participate in the selection of materials, supplies, and tools used in the processes concerned.

Ability to meet his department's budget is another basis for establishing supervisor-incentive plans. But budgetary items are often subject to price fluctuations in materials, supplies, or labor, over which supervisor control is far from direct, if indeed it exists at all.

Departmental "efficiency" as an incentive index is relatively unsatisfactory because it may require definitions, explanations, and even a formula before it can be reduced to a usable standard of measurement. The efficiency index is frequently too complicated for the average supervisor. He is not sure that he knows how to influence the formula for his personal benefit, and is correspondingly dubious of what he does not fully understand.

When it is used, worker attendance is one of the incidentals comprising a group of incentive factors. The only apparent influence which the supervisor may have over good attendance by his workers is his ability to secure their cooperation. But because there are so many excusable causes for absence, his ability to decrease absences can have only a slight effect on the over-all attendance record of the workers.

Supervisor-incentive plans have been based on all of these factors individually at different times, or on combinations of two or more of them. For the most part, such plans are only partially, if at all, under control of the supervisor. Also, faulty standards are used to measure most of the factors. We are making the same mistakes in developing supervisor pay incentives that we made with wage incentives, where we were compelled to revise the piece-work plan because factors beyond control of the employees sometimes reacted to their financial disadvantage. In that plan, management was partially interested in releif from some of the task of managing, which was largely shifted to the worker. The same approach appears in large measure in the supervisor-incentive plans which have been discussed. As was the case with piece-work, many of the supervisor-incentive plans must be corrected to allow for lapses in management's planning and such items as machine breakdowns, shortage of usable materials and supplies, and poor tools.

In general, we are still groping about to find the correct basis for supervisor pay incentives. It seems rational to conclude that the reduction of those wastes which he can control to a reasonable extent is the best basis for establishing his bonuses. Four types of waste can be singled out:

1. Waste of worker time, due to his own fault
2. Waste of worker time, due to halting production
3. Waste of direct materials in making scrap
4. Waste of supplies

The following discussion of these four types of waste as factors for determining supervisor incentives emphasizes two advantages that make them preferable to those already discussed. In the first place, they represent factors over which the supervisor can exercise reasonable control. In addition, they offer a common method for measuring incentive bonuses based on ratios of actual performance for the various types of wastes to scientifically determined standards or targets.

To what extent can the supervisor control and minimize these four forms of waste? With respect to the first, we have already made some progress by establishing standard production times. When standards are available, to what extent can the supervisor induce the workers to meet or exceed them? It is a well-established fact that supervision has substantial influence in this field. Leadership, encouragement, capable training and instructions, and methods improvement, all applied constantly by the supervisor and his assistants, are necessary to the attainment of worker production goals set by time standards.

If the target level is reached, we may assume that the supervisor has done a satisfactory job, and some bonus payment is in order. The degree to which the target level is above past performance should be the basis for the bonus. This measure is represented by the ratio between past average performance and the target level, rather than by absolute quantities. Delay allowances which are beyond supervision's control must be taken into account in the final determination of the bonus. A large number of learners or significant changes in materials or processes are examples of those things which call for delay allowances.

The second waste — that of worker time due to halting production — can be under the supervisor's control to a large extent if he is permitted to participate in plans for avoiding it. Halts in production may be caused by lack of balance in machines, materials, or supplies. Machine breakdowns, defective tools and materials are other causes. In some instances, these delays are beyond the control of supervision, but in most cases, proper planning will eliminate them. In any event, it is apparent that pay incentives will encourage the supervisory group to adopt preventive measures.

The third and fourth items of waste — making scrap and wasting supplies — can be considered together. In some departments these factors may be relatively insignificant, but where the opposite is true, experience proves that great savings can be made by adequate supervision. Savings in these categories directly reflect the quality of supervision, and should be rewarded accordingly. Selection of tools and instruction in their proper use are waste-savers under the supervisor's control. Machine maintenance is another controllable factor that yields results in reduced scrap. The cost of supplies can be kept to a minimum by good housekeeping and careful supervision.

With these two types of wastes, as with the others, rewards should be based on the ratio of accomplishment to adequately determined standards of performance. To a large extent, the waste from scrap and the misuse of supplies varies directly with the volume of production. Bonuses based on the production of one item will be easy to determine because the standards are simple. When a variety of items is being produced, some common measure other than production is required. Possibly the ratio of the cost of scrap and supplies to the hours of measured work will give a satisfactory index for determining incentive bonuses under such circumstances. Experience shows that savings as high as 25 per cent can be accomplished by proper supervisory attention to the cost of scrap and supplies.

Foreman unions

The place of foremen in the management team must be considered in the light of its recent history. At the present time, their relations with the rest of management are fair to good. But during and immediately after World War II, the relationship was strained almost to the breaking point. It is important to understand the reasons for this strain in order to prevent its recurrence at some time in the future.

Foreman relations to management have gone through three well-recognized stages since the turn of the century. Prior to management's installation of staff services to relieve some of his supervisory burden, the foreman was definitely a part of the management team, with authority to hire, fire, promote, and transfer.

The second period ran roughly from the Wagner Act of 1935 to the Taft-Hartley Act of 1947. The Wagner Act, in its definitions of "employer" and "employee," left the foreman's status ambiguous. Sometimes the courts and the official labor agencies would classify him as an "employer," sometimes as an "employee." Furthermore, the gains achieved by the workers through the passage of the Wagner Act made for less differential between the supervisor and his subordinates. The supervisor could not count on top management for a clarification of his status and rights because top management was always afraid of being cited for "unfair labor practices."

The long period of strain was brought into focus in the summer of 1941, when four of Ford's foremen organized the Foreman's Association of America. In 1938, the CIO had made a strenuous effort to organize about nine hundred foremen in the automobile industry, only to abandon its effort a year later. However, the separate unionization of foremen caught hold like wildfire in the latter part of 1941. The FAA had almost 40,000 members by 1945, without paid organizers. Here was an organization to command respect, especially when it was realized that there were approximately a million foremen in industry.

The general feeling among supervisors that they were actually not a part of management was a grievance of long standing. That feeling was fanned into action by conditions which increased the hours and rates of many war workers until their take-home pay exceeded that of their foremen's salaries. Management believed that the chief promoters of the union were the large number of new foremen who had lately risen from the ranks, a contention which the FAA denied. There is no doubt that the younger supervisors were afraid they would lose their jobs when the war was over. On the other hand, many of the older group were afraid that the young men would take their jobs when production demands returned to normal. All of them felt that the pay differential between themselves and their workers was too small. Some felt that their authority was not in line with their increasing responsibilities, that the number of workers they supervised was excessive, and that since they had no grievance procedure, they could be fired without cause and without redress. In reply to this last objection, upper management assured foremen that its "doors were always open." But one cynic replied that the door was left open so that the foremen would not break the glass on their way out, a jest which really expressed the intensity of their feelings.

The new foremen's union was destined to a short and turbulent existence as a bargaining force. Prior to the National Labor Relations Act (Wagner Act) of July 1935, it was generally understood that foremen had a right to organize to protect their common interests. However, between 1943 and 1946, there were three important and conflicting decisions affecting foremen unionization.

The *Maryland Drydock Case* (May 11, 1943) was the first decision regarding the foreman's status under the Wagner Act. In this case, the National Labor Relations Board reversed its former stand and decided that supervisory groups were not entitled to collective-bargaining rights under the Wagner Act.

In the *Packard Case* (March 26, 1945) the NLRB reversed its decision in the Maryland Drydock Case, holding that employers were bound to bargain with supervisory unions if they were not affiliated with rank-and-file unions of production workers. This decision left open the right of affiliated foremen unions to demand bargaining rights with their employers.

Later the same year, the NLRB decided, in the *Jones and Laughlin Steel Company Case,* that the privileges and protection of the Wagner Act should be extended to foremen affiliated with a union of production workers. *Business Week* made the editorial comment that the decision came close to "creating a perfect or revolving mess, i.e., a mess when viewed from any angle."[4] Since the union in question was affiliated with the United Mine Workers, the decision was hailed as a John L. Lewis victory. The way was now open for the organization of foremen's unions on both exclusive and affiliated bases.

The cause of the conflicting decisions came from two definitions in the Wagner Act. It defines an *employer* as "any person acting in the interest of an employer," which certainly includes the foreman. At the same time, it states that "employees shall have the right . . . to bargain through representatives of their own choosing," and foremen are certainly employees. So the foremen were both employers and employees!

Industry was up in arms over the Jones and Laughlin case. General Motors made a public statement which was carried in newspapers and issued as a flyer. The question was: "Should management be unionized?" After explaining why the decision was bad for supervisors, for industry, for labor, and for America, General Motors stated its position as follows:

In General Motors, foremen are the MANAGERS of their departments. They participate in establishing management policies in both production and personnel matters. They have full authority to approve or disapprove the hiring,

4 No. 864 (March 23, 1946), p. 120.

to supervise the work, and to make work assignments of the employees under their supervision. They initiate wage increases, transfers and promotions. They are directly responsible for the efficiency and safety of their group. They have full authority when necessary to take immediate, appropriate disciplinary action for violation of shop rules, and other improper conduct of their employees. They are the first point of management contact and make the first management decisions on all matters relating to the employees under their direction.

The tide turned when the Taft-Hartley Act (1947) made foremen a legal part of the management team, and barred them from production unions. After a forty-seven-day strike against the Ford Motor Company, the FAA called off its pickets in July 1947. That event practically marked the end of the FAA as a bargaining force. Finally, the passage of the Taft-Hartley Act marked the beginning of a sustained and earnest effort on the part of upper management to make it more clear by act and deed that the supervisors were really members of the management team.

What foremen want

At least a month before the FAA called off its pickets and gave up the strike, the Ford Motor Company launched a new program to make supervisors a more effective part of management. It set up a new "Management Relations Department" with jurisdiction extending through the entire range of management, including foremen. The department took on new energy after the strike ended. Like most progressive managements, the Ford Company learned a good deal from the foremen's revolt. The strains in their ambiguous status had been present all along, demanding radical corrective action from top management. The strike served to bring matters to a head and to stir management into taking the prompt remedial action which it had long been clear would have to be taken sooner or later. Many companies started plans to give a new status to their foremen, and the situation has been continually improving. The Ford plan, like many others, provides more authority, more pay, more contacts with upper management, and greater job security for the entire supervisory group.

The Crosley Division of Avco Manufacturing Corporation has been able to measure the success of a new training plan for supervisors. Its program resulted from an obviously realistic approach — a survey to find out what supervisors wanted to learn. The training sessions are conducted by department heads on a discussion basis. The old method of lecturing to them was seen to be a bad psychological tactic in convincing supervisors that they were a part of management. The company believes that the new training approach is responsible for a 10-per cent increase in plantwide efficiency, reduction of the ratio between indirect and direct labor costs, and the development of team spirit among the supervisors.

What foremen needed most of all after 1948 was to find a new and safe landing place after the turmoil of war production expansion, rapid unionization, and the confusion of the NLRB decisions, all of which left them in an industrial no man's land. Management is now attempting a new setup based on the lessons learned during that period of confusion. Top management cannot accomplish its over-all purposes unless it is aided by a healthy relationship with its supervisory force. Only under such conditions can it re-establish the foreman as an effective means of two-way communication up and down the management ladder.

The supervisor is not only a representative of management to the workers, but also a representative of the workers to management. He is the direct contact with the company's employees. To his men, the supervisor *is* management. On that basis, the workers expect that some representative of management should have the authority to redress their grievances and stand up for their rights in dealing with upper management, who to them are a relatively nebulous group of men in an ivory tower.

The reasons why supervisors join unions express in part the things they want from management. In joining unions, they feel that their organization can accomplish more of the things they want than they are able to accomplish when acting as individuals. The Foreman's League for Education and Association reports fifteen reasons why foremen join unions. Most of the reasons for joining unions are short-range, and can be overcome by top-management with reasonable expedition.

The supervisor wants:

1. Job security
2. Closer contact with upper management
3. More authority in hiring, firing, and promotions
4. Salary commensurate with his responsibilities
5. Pay adjustment for prolonged overtime
6. Authority to carry out assigned responsibilities
7. An open path for the redress of grievances
8. An office of his own, with clerical help as required
9. Fringe benefits that are accorded management
10. Training geared to his job responsibilities
11. Necessary aid in training new workers
12. Recognition for usable suggestions
13. Management privileges based on foreman status
14. Participation in policies affecting foremen duties

Conclusions

Functionalized staff organizations, such as personnel, maintenance, production planning, and purchasing have sapped the supervisor's authority, while government regulations and increased activity of union locals representing production workers have increased his workload and his responsi-bilities. Periodic pay increases of his production subordinates have often decreased his pay differential, and in some cases where the worker re-ceives premium pay for overtime, holidays worked, and shifts other than the regular daytime period, workers' wages have actually exceeded his supervisor's take-home pay.

Professional staff offices tend to come between the foreman and the upper layers of management, as well as between him and his men. They also decrease the opportunities to make decisions directly affecting his work, decisions which he has long been accustomed to make without such assistance. Because these new departments have had the effect of lengthen-ing the chain of command between supervisors and top management, they have often turned out to be obstacles in the foreman's upward channel of communication.

Some way must be worked out to control the kind of bureaucratic man-agement which has tended to clutter the foreman's job with unnecessary and impractical duties. The bureaucracy of overspecialization in some management organizations is characterized by the same sort of vested interest delays, confusion, red tape, and lack of understanding which business so justly condemns in its relations with governmental agencies.

The supervisor is really in the middle as far as the management team is concerned. His situation is made more difficult because middle manage-ment often appoints him to his position on the basis of technical skills or seniority rather than for his supervisory ability, and then does not train him properly after he is on the job. In addition, on-the-job training of workers is frequently unsatisfactory because the supervisor has neither the teaching ability nor the time to do it properly. The production-plan-ning department instructs him about what to do, when to do it, and how to do it, thus curbing his initiative and increasing his frustration. His re-sponsibilities are not matched by his authority, and his rewards are meager in comparison with his responsibilities. Unionization and scarcity of labor often stymie his best efforts. Top management usually overestimates his abilities and underestimates his real worth. For the most part, the super-visor has plenty of grief without commensurate satisfaction.

With these factors in mind, it is understandable why the bench worker often turns down an opportunity to advance to the rank of supervision, while others ask to be put back at the bench after a short service as fore-men. In either case, their explanation is that the pay differential is not worth the headaches involved.

The blow-up in the foreman's job between 1941 and 1947 has served to attract the attention of top management to the point where many com-plaints have been given serious attention. From management's threats in 1945 to eliminate the title of foreman and substitute some other managerial arrangement, we have swung around to the decision that his place in the management hierarchy is here to stay, but must be made more important than it was for a decade prior to 1947. This is the situation at the present time. The foreman is beginning to feel the improvement and react favorably to it.

QUESTIONS

1. Is the supervisor really "the man in the middle," or does the person in the middle belong to middle management, as its members often claim?
2. The text lists seventeen responsibilities of foremen to management and an equal number to his workers; the total sounds like a formidable list. How do they compare with middle management's workload, in your opinion?
3. The supervisor's frustration due to shifting of some of his important duties to staff activities is very real. How would you alleviate his chagrin?
4. Taking away authority over his department's buying not only weakened the supervisor's feeling of importance, but it curtailed his social contacts with vendors' salesmen. What recommendation do you have for lessening the impact of this shifting of responsibility?
5. In what respect are the supervisor's over-all management responsibilities similar to those discussed in various places in the text?
6. In view of the supervisor's responsibility status, do you feel that he should participate in the formulation of policies affecting his work?
7. To what extent do the organized worker's divided loyalties — to his employer and to his union — make the supervisor's job more difficult?
8. What general considerations would you emphasize in the selection of supervisors? What weight would you give to their technical qualifications?
9. What plans would you propose for improving the managerial ability of supervisors? The text lists a considerable number, but would you include a reasonable degree of social mixing with the upper members of management?
10. Since many supervisors, due to substantial salary increases during the past decade, are probably owners of listed stocks, would you advise that their training include the fundamental economics of business?
11. How would you improve supervisor training in the field of labor relations, including the settlement of worker grievances?
12. To what extent do you believe it is in the company's interest that job security be assured to capable supervisors in some concrete manner? What plan would you devise for giving that assurance?
13. How would you prevent the supervisor's learning about future company plans from some of his subordinates who learned them from the union representatives?
14. A number of supervisor incentives have been tried, usually based on factors over which he has no control, and with only relative success. What do you propose?
15. What are the three stages through which supervisor relations with management have passed since the turn of the century?

16. What conflicting provisions of the Wagner Act affected the status of the foreman?

17. How did the vicissitudes of the FAA demonstrate the futility of organizing foremen as a labor group? How did the Taft-Hartley Act finally dispose of the matter?

18. What are some of the fourteen things that the supervisor wants from management?

19. To what extent do you feel that management has given supervisors authority commensurate with their responsibilities?

20. How would you implement the supervisor's desire to have "closer contact with upper management"?

CASE PROBLEM

THE ROBERTS EQUIPMENT COMPANY

The Roberts Equipment Company has been manufacturing pistons for automobile engines for over forty years. There were four foremen in the original firm, and these men exercised considerable power and authority over their departments. They hired and discharged their own workers. There was no plan for appealing their decisions if the employee felt that he had received unfair treatment.

Because of the autocratic rule of the supervisors, the workers formed a union in 1938, which was duly recognized by the National Labor Relations Board. The company found itself in difficulty with the Board almost immediately because of some of the practices of its foremen. The employees were threatened by the foremen with discharge if they joined the Union. Consequently, the company was found guilty of an unfair labor practice by the Board. Several other unfair practices were cited by the union because of actions of the foremen. In each case, the company was found guilty. To avoid further difficulty, the concern hired a personnel manager, giving him authority to hire and discharge employees.

During World War II, the firm expanded, adding ten more foremen and six assistant foremen to the supervisory rolls, making a total of twenty. The rank-and-file employees began to earn higher pay because of overtime. When the supervisors realized that their subordinates were receiving more pay than they were, they formed their own union. This organization was not too successful. With the passage of the Taft-Hartley Act in 1947, the company refused to bargain with its foreman union. Three of the foremen were retired, and their positions were not filled.

By 1948, the foremen had very little authority but considerably more responsibility. Among other things, they and the assistant supervisors were expected to train all of the employees hired by the personnel manager. In addition, the foremen were instructed to establish the production standards for the purpose of computing wage incentives. They were also called on to perform the maintenance and inspection functions in their departments. Grievances were handled by the union stewards through the personnel manager. Wage rates were set by the personnel department for all employees. Sometimes the foremen were consulted about individual wage rates, but usually they were not. Frequently, the union stewards knew more about what was going on about the plant than the supervisors did.

One foreman supervises 100 men on an assembly line, whereas the foreman of the foundry has 15 subordinates. All foremen are paid the same amount — $5200 a year. One old supervisor who is due to retire next year has been paid an additional bonus of $800 a year.

PROBLEM: Outline the steps you would take to make the supervisor a definite part of management.

Part Six • Suggestions For Further Reading

Albers, Henry H., *Organized Executive Action,* New York: John Wiley and Sons, Inc., 1961.

Argyris, Chris, *Personality and Organization,* New York: Harper and Brothers, 1957.

Cordiner, Ralph J., *New Frontiers for Professional Managers,* New York; McGraw-Hill Book Company, Inc., 1956.

Dalton, Melville, *Men Who Manage,* New York: John Wiley and Sons, Inc., 1959.

Davis, Ralph C., *The Fundamentals of Top Management,* New York: Harper and Brothers, Publishers, 1951.

Dimock, Marshall E., *A Philosophy of Administration Toward Creative Growth,* New York: Harper and Brothers, Publishers, 1958.

Folsom, Marion B., *Executive Decision-Making,* New York: McGraw-Hill Book Company, Inc., 1962.

Given, Walter B., Jr., *Bottom-Up Management,* New York: Harper and Brothers, 1949.

Greenwalt, Crawford, *The Uncommon Man,* New York: McGraw-Hill Book Company, Inc., 1962.

Guest, Robert H., *Organizational Change,* Homewood, Illinois: The Dorsey Press, Inc., 1962.

Haimann, Franklyn S., *Group Leadership and Democratic Action,* Boston: Houghton Mifflin Company, 1951.

Hardwick, C. T. and Landuyt, B. F., *Administrative Strategy,* New York: Simmons-Boardman, 1961.

Learned, Edmund P., Ulrich, David U. and Booz, Donald R., *Executive Action,* Boston: Graduate School of Business Administration, Harvard University, 1951.

Lawrence, Paul R. (and others), *Organizational Behavior and Administration,* Homewood, Illinois; The Dorsey Press, 1961.

McGregor, Douglas, *The Human Side of Enterprise,* New York: McGraw-Hill Book Company, Inc., 1959.

McNichols, Thomas J., *Policy Making and Executive Action*, New York: McGraw-Hill Book Company, Inc., 1959.

Smith, George Albert, Jr., and Christensen, C. Roland, *Policy Formulation and Administration*, Homewood, Illinois: Richard D. Irwin, Inc., 1962.

Tannenbaum, Robert, Weschler, Irving R., and Massarik, Fred, *Leadership and Organization*, New York: McGraw-Hill Book Company, Inc., New York, 1961.

Tead, Ordway, *The Art of Leadership*, New York: Whittlesey House, 1935.

————, *Administration: Its Purposes and Performance*, New York, Harper and Brothers, Publishers, 1959.

Whyte, William H., Jr., *The Organization Man*, New York: Simon and Schuster, Inc., 1956.

•

The quotation at the beginning of Part Six is from: Henri Fayol, *General and Industrial Management*, London: Sir Isaac Pitman & Sons, Ltd., 1949, Chapter IV.

Index